D1121996

The Birth of Development

NEW STUDIES IN U.S. FOREIGN RELATIONS

Mary Ann Heiss, editor

The Birth of Development

How the World Bank,

Food and Agriculture Organization,

and World Health Organization

Changed the World, 1945–1965

AMY L. S. STAPLES

The Kent State University Press
Kent, Ohio

Library of Congress Catalog Card Number 2005017208
ISBN 978-0-87338-849-8
Manufactured in the United States of America

10 09 08 07 06   5 4 3 2 1

LIBRARY OF CONGRESS CATALOGING-IN-PUBLICATION DATA
Staples, Amy L. S., 1969—
The birth of development : how the World Bank, Food and Agriculture Organization,
and World Health Organization changed the world, 1945–1965 / Amy L. S. Staples.
p.   cm. — (New studies in U.S. foreign relations)
Includes bibliographical references and index.
ISBN-13: 978-0-87338-849-8 (pbk. : alk. paper) ∞
ISBN-10: 0-87338-849-6 (pbk. : alk. paper) ∞
1. World Bank—History—20th century. 2. Food and Agriculture Organization of the
United Nations—History—20th century. 3. World Health Orgainzation—History—20th
century. 4. Economic assistance—History—20th century. 5. Food supply—International
cooperation—History—20th century. 6. Agricultural assistance—History—20th century.
7. Medical assistance—History—20th century. I. Title. II. Series.
HG3881.5.W57S73 2005
338.91'09172'409045—dc22   2005017208

British Library Cataloging-in-Publication data are available.

To My Grandmothers

GERALDINE SAYWARD AND MARJORIE ANGEVINE

*Whose love of God, family, teaching, and learning
serve as my constant inspiration*

Contents

Series Editor's Foreword

A spate of new studies has recently broadened the conceptual parameters of the field of U.S. foreign relations. Some scholars have explored the construction and projection of identity—both national and international. Others have shed light on the important role that international organizations have played in shaping U.S. foreign policy—and the role that Americans have played in shaping international organizations. Still others have helped to move our understanding of the Cold War from an exclusively East-West ideological conflict to a tendentious North-South struggle between the developed and developing worlds and to make plain the role of cultural assumptions in foreign policy formulation and implementation across those two worlds.

Amy L. S. Staples's innovative *The Birth of Development* makes a major contribution to the literature in all of these areas. Employing a wide variety of primary sources from repositories in six countries, it delineates postwar efforts to ameliorate the destructive role of the nation-state in world affairs by constructing truly international organizations with truly global agendas in the service to all of the world's peoples, not just a privileged few. Specifically, Staples brings to light the various developmentalist efforts undertaken by the World Bank, the Food and Agriculture Organization (FAO), and the World Health Organization (WHO). In illuminating the largely overlooked—and ultimately largely unsuccessful—early postwar efforts of these organizations, Staples argues effectively that their real significance lies in their goals, not their actual accomplishments. Yes, the World Bank, FAO, and WHO failed in the immediate postwar period to foster economic development, agricultural reform, and public health advances throughout the developing world. Far more important than their ultimate failure, however, are the nature and character of their developmentalist schemes.

The international civil servants who staffed the UN specialized agencies held a worldview that transcended national boundaries. Experts in economics, agriculture, and medicine/health, they sought to use their professional skills and specialized knowledge in a disinterested, dispassionate, and denationalized manner to improve economic conditions, food production, and health and living conditions for people throughout the developing world. Although a good many, but not all, of these experts were Americans, they subsumed their national identities to an

international one that privileged service to the world and had no place for individualized national loyalties. In their minds, their jobs as midwives to development throughout the nations of Asia, Africa, and the Middle East superseded any
loyalty or allegiance they may have held for their own homelands. Yet as Staples
makes clear, the international civil servants who staffed the UN specialized agencies often looked to one-size-fits-all solutions that failed to take account of local
customs, traditions, and realities. Unable to escape their Western-oriented mind-
sets, they accomplished little despite their deep knowledge, scientific expertise,
and good intentions. The role of cultural assumptions in derailing many of the
UN specialized agencies' developmentalist schemes is one of the most valuable
aspects of Staples's story, and it provides an important warning for similar present-
day development efforts.

Additionally, *The Birth of Development* places the UN specialized agencies in
their proper place as important post–World War II historical actors. As Staples
makes abundantly clear, nation-states in the developing world lacked the resources
to adequately address issues of development, food production, and health care.
The responsibility for addressing those problems therefore fell to international organizations, which alone seemed to possess the requisite professional expertise and
financial wherewithal. National rivalries, moreover, had been largely responsible
for the two world wars of the twentieth century and the scramble for foreign empire that had left much of Asia, Africa, and the Middle East underdeveloped. This
reality was not lost on those international civil servants who hoped to transcend
national boundaries in a wholesale effort to remake the world and eliminate the
glaring gap between the developed and developing worlds. For them, only real
international cooperation toward global economic, agricultural, and medical development could point the way toward a better tomorrow.

By bringing to light these early post–World War II international efforts to re-
shape and improve the world, Staples demonstrates that much more was under
way during that period than simply the solidification of the Cold War along East-
West ideological lines. These years, Staples establishes, were also marked by profound North-South tensions between the developed and developing worlds. The
cultural clashes that ultimately dashed many early developmentalist efforts reveal
the profound gap between these two worlds, as well as the difficulty of bridging it.
The end of the Cold War and the collapse of the Soviet Union have brought to the
forefront the North-South side of the postwar era, and *The Birth of Development*
is part of a much-needed and much-welcomed reconsideration within the U.S.
foreign relations literature.

Although the story told here is sobering and often depressing, it is also one
that must be told—and heeded—for it has much to tell us about that important
historical moment that Staples calls the birth of development. Given the current role of international peacekeepers and multinational aid agencies around

the world, this story is also extremely timely and makes clear that the issues that confronted—and confounded—early postwar planners and reformers remain in many ways unsolved even now. The unintended consequences of the early postwar international developmentalists also resonate in the present and shed light on current dilemmas concerning the ongoing challenges of globalization. Staples's book is international history at its best and a fitting inaugural volume for "New Studies in U.S. Foreign Relations."

MARY ANN HEISS

Preface and Acknowledgments

On the last day of a month's research at the World Health Organization (WHO) in Geneva, Switzerland, the archivist, Mr. P. L. Malaguti, bought me a cup of coffee and asked me about my project. I told him I believed that the folks who had led global development efforts in the generation after World War II had been animated by a progressive faith that the energetic application of expertise could change the world. Mr. Malaguti, an international civil servant with more than three decades of service to his credit, enthusiastically agreed with my thesis. But then he turned a bit nostalgic about the early days of his tenure, reflecting on what he saw as the apathy of current times, when news of epidemics and starvation did not seem to catalyze action. In the years that have passed between that 1995 conversation and this 2006 book, my studies and reflections have left me, as you will see in these pages, both less nostalgic about this aspect of the greatest generation's legacy and more optimistic about the future.

This book would not have been possible without the generosity and helpfulness of archivists like Mr. Malaguti at the WHO Archive, Mr. Charles Ziegler at the World Bank Group Archive, and Ms. A. M. P. Palazzani and Mr. Guiliano Fregoli at the Food and Agriculture Organization Archive, who treated me more like a guest than a researcher. Additionally, I was greatly assisted by countless people at the archives of the Public Record Office (PRO), the National Library of Scotland, the Franklin D. Roosevelt Presidential Library, the University of Georgia, the Columbia University Oral History Project, the U.S. National Archive at College Park, the Canadian National Archive, and the Hoover Institution on War, Revolution and Peace. The Interlibrary Loan staff at Ohio State University was also extraordinarily helpful in securing research materials for me from around the world for this project. On an ironic note, I would like to thank the International Monetary Fund for denying me access to its archive, an action that led me to move beyond international monetary policy and into a much broader study on development dynamics for my dissertation.

The funds needed to send a poor graduate student and assistant professor to all these archives were granted by a number of sources, all of which have the author's deepest gratitude. Ohio State's Graduate School Alumni Research Award funded a plane ticket to Europe, Ohio State's History Department funded my first research trip to the University of Georgia, the Society for Historians of American Foreign Relations (SHAFR) Stuart L. Bernath Research Grant funded my trip to the West Coast to explore the resources of the Hoover Institution, and Middle Tennessee State University's Faculty Research and Creative Activity Award allowed me to complete two weeks' research at the National Archives. As thankful as I am to these institutions, people, as usual, made the difference in my completing my research, degree, and manuscript. My parents, Leonard and Sally Sayward, as dubious as they were at times about this endeavor, gave me the financial wherewithal to spend three months in Europe, and my graduate advisor—Professor Michael J. Hogan—helped me secure funding for an "extra" year at Ohio State that helped me complete my dissertation as originally envisioned. Finally, the constant encouragement and thoughtful critiques of my colleagues in the Women's Work Group in the History Department at Middle Tennessee State University improved my work by sharing their various perspectives on this topic.

This manuscript benefited immeasurably from the incomparable team of Professor Hogan and Professor Peter L. Hahn, who were my mentors throughout my graduate program at Ohio State. Michael challenged me to think as broadly and theoretically as possible, while Peter ensured that my ideas were converted into clear, organized chapters. To this day, I keep in my top desk drawer a copy of the third draft of the second chapter of this manuscript. There is not a single sentence of that chapter that was not patiently and painstakingly rewritten as I sat next to Michael at his dining-room table for one entire afternoon as he taught me to be a better and more self-conscious writer. These two men, my advisers, helped me convert my ideas into this book and helped me grow from a graduate student into a professor. For all that went into these processes, I am profoundly thankful.

One key part of this process was being a member of one of the best diplomatic history programs in the country, full of bright, engaging graduate students who were more interested in helping than in competing with one another. Almost all of them read one or more parts of this manuscript, and I thank them all; but a couple need special thanks. Bruce Karhoff and Rowly Brucken not only have read this manuscript but helped me hone practically every idea in its pages, challenging me always to think more and more deeply about the issues. I am proud to count them still among my best friends. Ann Heiss and Carol Anderson served as my mentors in the program at Ohio State, encouraging me when I was most discouraged. Also, I had outstanding committees for my general exams and my dissertation at Ohio State. Professor Chad Alger in political science gave me wonderful insights into his field's literature on international organizations after serving as the external examiner for my "generals," and Leila Rupp's work on the international women's movement helped me to think about my own project more broadly. I was most grateful for her comments and insights on my dissertation.

This fine group of peers and mentors at Ohio State was leavened by outside scholars visiting our Graduate Workshop in Diplomatic History, which was sponsored by the Mershon Center for International Security Studies. I am extremely grateful for the interest in and suggestions for my project offered by such notable visiting scholars as Walter LaFeber, Emily Rosenberg, Walter Hixson, and Lisa Cobbs. Other historians have aided me over the years and have helped me immeasurably in the process of thinking about and writing this manuscript. Tom Zeiler has been my biggest supporter from the beginning; I could not have had a better mentor on the global dynamics of trade and development that are the core of the chapters on the World Bank. Richard Kirkendall was kind enough to read the chapters on the FAO on the strength of a minute-long conversation in an elevator at the annual meeting of the American Historical Association.

This book now seems to have gone full circle. Ann Heiss gave me expert feedback on my very first graduate writing-seminar paper, and I was absolutely delighted when she offered me the opportunity to contribute this volume to her series "New Studies in U.S. Foreign Relations" with Kent State University Press. During the long process of transforming my dissertation into this book, she provided encouragement through her words and example as an engaged scholar, and I am equally appreciative of her careful editorial eye, which has strengthened this manuscript in myriad ways. The staff at Kent State University Press has made the process of getting my first book published much less painful than I expected. I am also thankful to the anonymous readers who have helped me to improve this manuscript in whole or in part (as journal articles) over the past years. *Agricultural History, Diplomatic History,* and *Peace and Change* have my thanks for encouraging my work and allowing me to reprint substantially here my work that appeared in those publications. Finally, I would be remiss if I did not thank Derrick and Virginia Sherman, the whole Sherman family, and the University of North Carolina at Wilmington for the opportunity to present the Sherman Lecture in October 2003. That occasion inspired much of my conclusion.

Many others have personally supported and sustained me in this effort. Mr. Olick, my history teacher at Starpoint Central School, and Mrs. Kane, my first swim coach, made me believe in my potential. Tom Schaeper, Ed Eckert, and Joel Horowitz at St. Bonaventure University convinced me that I was grad school material. Rowly, Bruce, and Susan Mangus were wonderful friends and colleagues throughout my years at Ohio State. Susan Myers-Shirk has been the best friend and colleague during my years at MTSU, and my friend Farris Morris provided important encouragement during the final phase of my writing. Throughout this entire period, my husband, Tom, has always provided me with perspective and balance, studiously avoiding talk about the United Nations and economic development.

Though my grandmothers passed away between my entry into graduate school and the completion of my manuscript, these extraordinary women taught me much by their lives. After graduating from Cortland Normal School, my Grandma Angevine spent much of her life teaching school. She was the organist at the Peasleeville Methodist Church and loved holding Thanksgiving dinners for the entire family. In her spare time, she served as the unofficial historian of Peasleeville, New York. Not only did she record the early years of settlement and write a history of the Methodist Church in the area, but she maintained and extended the family genealogy. One of my enduring memories is of the complete set of *Encyclopedia Britannica* in the living room that served as a ready reference for any question that came up in conversation or her extensive reading. My Grandma Sayward was valedictorian of her college class at Plattsburgh Normal School in 1931. This achievement was all the more notable because she simultaneously bore the heavy responsibilities of maintaining a household after her mother's death halfway through her program of studies. She went on to teach school in Essex County, New York, for some four decades as she raised her three children. Grandma was a strong woman of faith who said the rosary daily and was an important part of the St. Philip of Jesus Catholic Church in Willsboro. Her greatest joys were reading, working crossword puzzles, and seeing her entire family together around the Christmas dinner table. I have been blessed by my family and their example, and it is in acknowledgment of this debt that I have dedicated this book to my grandmothers, Geraldine Sayward and Marjorie Angevine.

1

The Birth of Development

With the end of the Cold War, historians of international relations began to realize that the most significant conflict of the twentieth century was likely the North-South debate over economic development rather than the ideological East-West armed standoff. But few historians and even fewer Americans know much about the international efforts spearheaded by the World Bank, the Food and Agriculture Organization (FAO), and the World Health Organization (WHO) to promote economic development efforts that were at the heart of the North-South debate. This book, however, does more than simply provide a history of these three international entities in the postwar period. By putting these groups and their actions into historical context, it also illuminates a key moment in human history—what I have labeled "the birth of development"—when discrete groups of people with international stature, expertise, money, power, influence, and the best of intentions began working to better the lives of other human beings whom they had never met or known, for no reason other than the desire to improve the fate of the human race. Unlike imperial powers, these people did not seek to govern; unlike missionaries, they sought no religious conversion of program recipients; unlike multinational corporations, they derived no monetary profit from their work (other than their wages); unlike revolutionaries, they actively sought to avoid political questions; and unlike charitable organizations, they had access to broader influence and resources within the international community. Through their work, they helped to create a sense of an international community and an obligation among its members to promote the well-being of the whole.[1]

While it is clear that I see this as a majestic moment, it is certainly true that the push toward economic development described in these pages is far, far from an unalloyed success. Clearly the international civil servants studied here viewed economic development in the Third World as a process that would improve the lives and standard of living of peoples by rationalizing and modernizing economies and states. More often than not, however, their efforts tell a story of unfulfilled dreams, unintended consequences, bitter rivalries, and tragedies on a global scale. One reason for these failures was that the ideas of economic development studied here were based on an interpretation of European and American history in which investments of mostly foreign capital into a country's infrastructure and industrial capacity increased both national and personal wealth. But in focusing on the end product—development—these international civil servants often overlooked the human misery and social disruption caused by industrialization. The result of the application of this Western model to the Third World was disruption of extant social, economic, and cultural systems (often without providing workable alternatives) and a program of development generally characterized today as unsustainable, especially in terms of the high rate of consumption of natural resources. In other words, while motivated by the best of intentions, the UN specialized agencies did much harm. Yet these failures should not obscure the fundamental significance of people working on behalf of the human race as a whole instead of just one part of it. Indeed, I would echo the reminder that Brock Chisholm, the first director-general of the World Health Organization, gave his 1954 audience at the University of British Columbia: "The fact is that the peoples of the world are trying to do things now that they never had any idea of attempting to do before in the history of the human race, and because they are trying to do these things for the first time, it is not to be expected that their relatively primitive efforts should be successful on the first occasion or undertaken without difficulties."[2]

The story told in these pages is a story of beginnings—the beginning of the idea that development was an international obligation, the beginning of a broad international civil service, and the beginning of the continuing effort to find a way of promoting the well-being of the earth's people as a whole. Certainly the international civil servants described in these pages were not the first group of people to organize and work across international boundaries—far from it. They drew upon more than a century of international work and organization to take up an important position at the intersection of several realms of international activity: they formulated their own international ideas and plans, they consulted with nongovernmental organizations (NGOs) interested in their work, they often worked closely with other UN agencies, and they relied on national governments to approve their actions and budgets. Accordingly, their story offers important insights into the development of internationalism in the twentieth century. For it is clear that they actively and consciously constructed for themselves and their organizations an international identity that animated their revolutionary work around the globe. That international identity grew out of their faith in progressive ideals, their own professional ideology, and their commitment to building networks of cooperation that included a broad range of organizations.

These ideas had come to prominence in the generation before World War I, when the people of many countries attempted to adjust their economic, political, philosophical, and social structures to the jarring transformations caused by industrialization. That process had created national and international markets and systems of communication that integrated previously self-sufficient "island communities" into a national and world economy, with all the attendant implications for local cultural, political, and social institutions. Beginning in the 1870s, in response to these profound changes, a group of European and American philosophers discarded the platonic notion of pure forms and theorized that truth must be derived from experience, that politics should replace individual moral responsibility as the locus of reform, and that ethics could be derived only from a rational benevolence rather than an ideal notion of justice. From 1890 to 1920, these suppositions undergirded the Progressive and Social Democratic movements, which sought gradual, democratic, expert-guided change through reforms meant to remedy the worst ills and abuses of laissez-faire industrialization. Often starting with local reforms, people committed to Progressive and Social Democratic change usually came from the ranks of the new professional middle class—including educators, social workers, agribusinessmen, journalists, doctors, lawyers, business managers, and economists.[3]

These envoys of the new social, political, economic, and cultural order embraced the experiential and rational philosophy enunciated in the 1870s and 1880s, which complemented their own professional training. While each profession developed somewhat differently, these new professionals were more likely than their predecessors or contemporaries to have university degrees and, increasingly, state-bestowed certification to practice. Their educations were grounded in new scientific methods and in a determination to apply their studies to the betterment of the society and people around them. As part of this mission, these professionals often helped draft state and national legislation. The Pure Food and Drug Law of the United States is a prominent example of such Progressive-inspired legislation.[4] The international civil servants of the World Bank, FAO, and WHO inherited this faith in the ability of professionals to craft rational social policy, as did U.S. Secretary of Commerce Herbert Hoover, who believed that rational analysis and cooperation could replace conflict in negotiating between functional groups in the economy.

The First World War had stultified but did not stop the Progressive agenda. Professional businessmen in the United States, many of whom had constructed benevolent public images by contributing their talents to the war effort as dollar-a-year men, played a large role in remaking postwar America by cooperating with the government and even, to a limited degree, with workers in an attempt to rationalize economic and social issues at home and abroad. Under the leadership of Hoover, the Department of Commerce was at the center of this cooperation in the 1920s. Hoover was widely considered a model Progressive, an engineer whose personal fortune had been built on his professional expertise. As secretary of commerce, he sought, through rationalization of industry, agriculture, and labor, to cure many of the social ills that had been identified by the Progressives; he even promoted rationalization of contentious international economic issues, such as inter-Allied war debts. Hoover organized conferences, committees, business associations, and the expert analysis of economic statistics to show businessmen the advantages of rationalization not only for themselves but for American society as a whole. Like the Progressives, he believed that if he simply illuminated the facts of any issue, businessmen, as rational professionals, would take the necessary action to remedy the situation, making formal governmental regulation unnecessary.[5]

This voluntarist system of cooperation crumbled under the pressure of the Great Depression, however, and was replaced by a system that was far more formal and government-directed but that still sought to combine governmental expertise with cooperation between, and reform of, the various economic sectors (industry, agriculture, and labor). To carry out this task, the federal government employed many of the professionals who had been displaced by the economic downturn; the Agriculture and Treasury departments, for example, employed a legion of economists in an attempt to rationalize key sectors of the economy.[6] Interestingly, the history of internationalism followed a similar pattern, moving from individual and professional efforts at the turn of the century to more centralized, government-controlled initiatives by the eve of the Second World War.

Just as individuals and countries sought to adjust to the profound changes wrought by turn-of-the-century industrialization, people who believed that progress toward an international society, economy, and culture would be the primary characteristics of the twentieth century sought to facilitate this movement and to create appropriate institutions to foster this change. Legal internationalists strove to define and enforce a code of international law that would govern the conduct of countries in this new age, and at the Hague Conference of 1899 they succeeded in establishing the International Court of Justice. At the same time, economic internationalists, such as French author Gustave Hervé and British author H. G. Wells, argued that modern science and technology had contributed to an internationalization of capital and labor that made national boundaries obsolete, while socialists proclaimed their own particular brand of economic internationalism. Taking a different tack, cultural internationalists saw the world as a single community whose members, if they learned to communicate and cooperate with one another, could live together peacefully. During the period 1870–1914, some four hundred international organizations of all sorts came into being, prompting the 1910 creation of the Union des Associations Internationales in Brussels, Belgium. What the International Institute of Statistics, the Universal Postal Union, the International Council of Women, the Parliament of Religions, and the Esperanto movement all had in common was a belief that international meetings and cooperation would improve understanding, preserve peace, and promote the advancement of the human race. All of these forms of internationalism had their head-quarters in Europe or the United States, and they consisted almost exclusively of Europeans and North Americans (with an occasional Japanese representative), who were almost inevitably representatives of the upper classes of their respective nations. Like the rest of European and North American society, however, internationalism was changed by World War I, as internationalists of all stripes sacrificed the cause to the nationalistic frenzy of war.[7]

Four years of previously unimaginable slaughter led, however, to the rebirth of a cultural internationalism that was more broadly based, embracing people of all countries and extending beyond the elite levels of society. Ironically, the war itself was a cause, because it had emphasized the universality of human experience, something that was particularly evident in much of the war's writing. For example, the German main character in *All Quiet on the Western Front*, guarding Russian prisoners of war, reflects that

> any noncommissioned officer is more of an enemy to a recruit, any schoolmaster to a pupil, than they are to us. And yet we would shoot at them again and they at us if they were free. I am frightened: I dare to think this way no more. . . . But I will not lose these thoughts, I will keep them, shut them away until the war is ended.

Indeed, many combatants as well as noncombatants emerged from the war with a deep commitment to reviving internationalism and dampening the nationalism that had led to such brutal wartime excesses.[8]

The League of Nations was the most prominent example of this new internationalism. Its members hailed from around the world; it focused on intellectual, scientific, economic, and cultural matters as well as traditional diplomacy; and in these ways, it evidenced the increasing institutionalization of cultural internationalism, which had previously been more of a private effort. The postwar movement to spur intellectual cooperation and understanding across national boundaries led to the creation within the League of Nations of the International Institute for Intellectual Cooperation and of the International Educational Cinematographic Institute. These and other, similar efforts aimed at inculcating international relations and area-studies courses into college curricula, reforming school textbooks, promoting student exchange programs, and otherwise promoting internationalism among the young. A growing sense that the world was more knowable also came in an informal manner from the expanding number of tourists during the 1920s as well as from the increasingly global economy, which was marked by the spread of American goods and movies and their significant cultural implications.[9]

The Great Depression and the events leading to World War II led many countries to appropriate culture for nationalistic ends. Such nationalism might have been expected to quash cultural internationalism, but proponents of the movement clung to its tenets. Due to the fervor of 1920s internationalism, many of its institutions, such as the International Institute for Intellectual Cooperation, carried on into the 1930s. Both the League of Nations and the Comintern promoted cultural internationalism and condemned the Nazis' nationalistic assault on culture, symbolized as it was by book burnings, but the Americans, British, and Japanese also took steps to nationalize culture and to use it as an official tool of foreign policy. As war loomed larger on the horizon, cultural internationalists did not turn to nationalism as they had in 1914 but seemed to accept and even promote a definition of this new world war as an international crusade against the chauvinistic forces of fascism. In other words, culture and internationalism remained vital forces throughout the decade, even if their definitions were sometimes plastic.[10]

Postwar internationalism sprang from a loss of faith in the ability of the system of nation-states and traditional diplomacy to cope with modern problems, coupled with a search for solutions. Two world wars, a global depression, the advent of the atomic bomb, and the reality of biological weapons had convinced many people that the nation-state was obsolete "in a world where security and indeed life has become indivisible." Additionally, this common set of experiences served as a point of departure for a global discussion on how future international relations should be structured. The development of commercial airlines, telephones, radios, and newsreels also fostered a sense of belonging to a knowable, global community. Some commentators went so far as to declare that national sovereignty and loyalty were obsolete: "We shall survive as members of the human race or not at all."[11]

This potent mixture of disillusion and universality was the basis of the postwar international ideal, a new and expanded version of the internationalism of the 1920s. There was not only a United Nations organization, to which the United States belonged, but also an Economic and Social Council to oversee the varied work of the organization's specialized agencies, which included the World Bank, the Food and Agriculture Organization, and the World Health Organization. In other words, the internationalists had created new organizations that would, to an extent, shift the impetus in global cultural, social, and economic relations away from private groups and into these new international bodies as a counterweight to national strength. What was more, the people entrusted with running these new agencies largely maintained the Progressive and professional ideologies of their earlier training, which they saw as largely value neutral and objective. The UN agencies used the methods of public-private cooperation previously developed at the national level as models for their own work in the postwar years and specifically as ways to limit competitive nationalism, promote economic integration, and thereby establish a more stable and prosperous international system.

Moreover, they sought to apply scientific methods to their work and to promote cooperation among both public and private groups in order to eradicate outstanding problems and improve the quality of life for all groups and countries, whether measured in terms of income, employment, health, nutrition, infant mortality, or agricultural productivity.

This book explores this process and its implication in three parallel sections on the World Bank, the Food and Agriculture Organization, and the World Health Organization. In the introductory chapter to each section, I illustrate the development of a professional ideology and of international cooperation in economics, agriculture, and medicine respectively, and then proceed to detail the impetus behind the creation of each of these UN specialized agencies. The substantive chapters on each organization analyze the key elements in its development and its economic development work during the period stretching roughly from 1945 to 1965. Finally, in chapters 4, 7, and 10, I analyze a key part of the appropriate specialized agency's program, thereby providing a case study of how its international agenda worked in practice. This organizational framework, I hope, situates key developments in their proper historical context and thereby demonstrates how they fit together to form what I have termed "the birth of development."

In addition to illuminating this key moment in the past, this volume has much to tell us about today's world. The debates about globalization in all of its aspects is certainly not ended, but simply beginning. This book brings us back to some of the first and crucial days of that process, when people began seriously to consider how they might best live together on the planet they shared. While these days were characterized most often by failures caused by ignorance and inexperience, they also helped mark this as "the greatest generation." Today, the world continues to shrink due to jet travel, the Internet, and modern telecommunications, and globalization and international organizations have gained ever-larger places in our consciousness. The language we use and the ways in which we think about these phenomena today are deeply influenced by the thoughts and deeds of that first generation of international civil servants. By understanding these pioneers—the choices they made, the options they rejected, and the ideas they developed that did not come to fruition—we can better understand today the world around us as it is, as well as how it might be.

2

Constructing an International
Economic Worldview

During July 1944, the forty-four Allied and Associated states arrayed against the Axis powers met at the Mount Washington Hotel in Bretton Woods, New Hampshire, where they drafted the Articles of Agreement for the World Bank and the International Monetary Fund (IMF)—the most powerful international financial institutions ever created. The Bretton Woods Conference thereby launched a new era in international economic cooperation. As a discipline, economics itself was barely a half-century old, and cooperation across national boundaries to this point had been largely informal, tentative, and voluntaristic. The conference changed this; cooperation was now systematized and centered in these new UN agencies, which were run by economic professionals. The perceived lessons of the previous fifty years, notably the conviction that nationalistic and autarchic economic and financial policies had contributed to the Great Depression and the Second World War, were the impetus for the change. Peace and prosperity in the future, the delegates believed, required multilateral trade and convertible currencies, but the delegates held that in addition to these automatic economic stabilizers, new international regulatory, coordinating, and stabilizing institutions were needed. Professionals, much like themselves, would run these organizations, analyzing economic problems scientifically and dispassionately applying their expertise in order to coordinate national policies, promote development, and regulate the global economy. These were the lessons and goals that shaped policymaking at Bretton Woods and that guided the World Bank in the years ahead.

Also guiding the World Bankers in this new endeavor was a shared sense of professionalism, developed in the discipline over the previous half-century and clearly evident throughout the conference. U.S. treasury undersecretary Harry Dexter White and John Maynard Keynes of the British Treasury were central in drafting the Bretton Woods accords. White, the son of Jewish immigrants, and Keynes, the son of British aristocrats, were different in many ways, but they saw the world in similar terms—terms defined much more by profession and experience than by nationality or class. As part of this common professional ideology, they shared a progressive faith in the ability of experts to act objectively on behalf of the common good, which meant acting on the basis of "the facts" regardless of political considerations or national interests. This shared professionalism allowed the two men to write into the Bretton Woods accords a sense of international purpose and ultimately to lay the foundation for an international identity that characterized the individuals who later worked for the World Bank and the IMF.

Early Formative Experiences

This ideology and worldview were a direct outgrowth of the professionalization of economics, which combined an emphasis on the new social science methodologies with a continuing commitment to social improvement. Anglo-American economics evolved into an independent academic discipline by using new statistical and "scientific" methods to command authority and to differentiate itself from the humanities, but it did not entirely abandon its ethical and religious roots. Indeed, the most influential economist of the time, Alfred Marshall, who chaired the Economics Department at Cambridge University, embodied both the scientific and ethical dimensions of the new profession; he influenced an entire generation of economists, including John Maynard Keynes. Marshall convinced Cambridge to create an economics curriculum separate from history and moral science, because he believed that economists could and should meet the objective, apolitical, and impartial standards of the physical sciences. But he also pioneered the concept of welfare economics—the notion, in other words, that economic analysis must supply policymakers with the tools and information needed to improve the lot of humankind.[1]

The same sense of social purpose suffused the American economics profession, which also came into its own around the turn of the century, when such public issues as currency reform, the growth of trusts and railroads, and the rise of the labor movement encouraged a strong interest in the discipline and its ability to solve difficult economic and political problems. Influenced by this sense of purpose and confident of their own professional abilities, American academic economists rejected many of the ideas attached to laissez-faire and the neoclassical economic theory that supported it. In fact, the declaration of principles they drafted for the fledgling American Economic Association envisioned "the State as an agency whose positive assistance is one of the indispensable conditions of human progress." Although economists later abandoned this rhetoric as they strove to become more apolitical and dispassionate, the sense of social purpose it conveyed and the belief in government responsibility (which was emblematic of the Progressive Era) remained relatively constant in the American economics profession.[2]

On both sides of the Atlantic, economists and their professional cousins in banking sought to act on this sense of social purpose by translating their professional worldview and growing authority into prominent roles in national economic policymaking and international relations. On the national level, progressive American bankers and economists urged the creation of the Federal Reserve System, in response to the financial instability and attendant social problems that plagued the United States between 1873 and 1907. This system and similar reforms sought to remove questions of currency, banking, and money from the partisan political arena and instead to entrust them to nonelected economic experts, thereby enhancing the role of these experts in governmental policymaking and their self-constructed identity as apolitical professionals.[3]

American economists and bankers, together with their British counterparts, also tried to spread their newly acquired professionalism to other, usually less-developed, areas. Financial and governmental officials from both the United States and Great Britain energetically promoted the gold-exchange standard in the countries of eastern Europe and Latin America. They also urged these same countries to adopt a centralized banking system, tax and accounting reforms, and a formal system of revenue collection, all of which, they claimed, would lay the foundation for financial stability, increased trade, and more private investment. Montagu Norman, who headed the Bank of England, sent his employees across Europe, Latin America, and the British Dominions carrying this message. He also invited banking officials from these areas to visit London, where they could study the British system of centralized banking and learn firsthand how an institution like the Bank of England, which was supposedly run by disinterested professional experts, could contribute to financial stability and growth.[4]

All of these activities demonstrate the sense of mission that infused American and British economists and bankers in the early years of the century as well as their faith in experts, their belief that financial management offered solutions to far-ranging economic, social, and political problems, their conviction that fiscal restraint and responsibility were key to economic progress, and their tendency to equate economic progress with advancement toward "civilization." These financial experts believed that their prescribed reforms would replace revolution and anarchy with order and stability as well as integrate these less-developed nations into a mutually advantageous system of world trade. Economic regulation ensured the proper functioning of the mechanisms of credit and markets, which these Anglo-American officials believed were capable of instilling the "manly" virtues of discipline, regularity, and responsibility. In other words, these financial missionaries also saw themselves as advocates of moral and social as well as economic uplift.[5]

In the United States of the 1920s, these convictions seemed to be embodied in Herbert Hoover, who served first as secretary of commerce under Presidents Warren G. Harding and Calvin Coolidge and then as president himself. Although

Hoover believed that American prosperity rested in part on an expanding world economy, he did not believe that the government should be primarily responsible for promoting economic growth and stability, in large part because government involvement would actually politicize economic affairs and lead to inefficiency, waste, and war. Instead Hoover wanted the government to rely heavily on private, nonpolitical experts, who would supposedly act on a rational, scientific basis—not on the basis of political considerations. With these ideas as a guide, he encouraged Benjamin Strong, governor of the New York Federal Reserve Board, to cooperate informally with British and European central bankers to stabilize currencies and foster trade. Hoover also backed the formation of the Dawes Commission, a committee of business and banking experts appointed to reorganize German finances and determine that country's ability to pay reparations. He hoped to construct similar machinery to deal with the inter-Allied debts, which were a drag on the international economy, and he asked private banks to consult voluntarily with the Treasury, Commerce, and State departments to ensure that their loans did not conflict with national policy, were made only for "reproductive purposes," and would therefore contribute to global growth and stability.[6] Unfortunately, Hoover overestimated the ability of bankers, economists, and other professionals to solve the world's problems, just as he underestimated the negative effect that a high American tariff, war debt collections, and poor lending policies would have on the international economy.

The Great Depression convinced many that private bankers alone could not solve the world's economic problems, that more effective economic management was necessary, and that that management had to be more official and more international than Hoover had anticipated. Gradually, the locus of economic decision making began to shift from informal to formal mechanisms of cooperation and from the private banking community to national governments. To be sure, governments sometimes acted with little regard for the effects of their policies on other countries, as was the case with the London Economic Conference of July 1933, which collapsed when the conferees were unable to agree on a common approach to economic stabilization. But more typical was the realization that new international institutions and new forms of collaboration and government action were needed not only to deal with the Depression but also to guarantee growth and stability over the long term.[7]

Indeed, the Depression eventually precipitated new efforts at international economic collaboration. In 1934, for example, the United States established an exchange stabilization fund to sustain the dollar and then expanded the fund to support a number of other currencies and provide for consultation on common economic problems. In 1936, the Treasury Department formalized this arrangement in the Tripartite Declaration between the United States, France, and Great Britain, under which the three countries pledged to consult on ways to expand trade, end exchange controls, and avoid new international monetary disturbances. As it turned out, however, the signatories were unable to make progress toward their economic goals in the face of autarchic German trade and currency policies, and most came to believe that international monetary stability was only possible within a more broadly based international system.[8]

The Tripartite Declaration called for national treasuries to deal with each other directly rather than through central banks or private banking interests, a change that placed a new emphasis on government action. Reinforcing this new emphasis was the introduction of Keynesian economic theories, which stressed the paramount importance of government management of the economy, especially in spending and control of interest rates. These theories began to gain wide credence after 1936 among professional economists, who brought these ideas into government, where they began to shape public policy on a variety of issues, including those having to do with the international economy.[9]

Keynesian economists and government officials also moved toward more formal governmental efforts to alleviate the Depression when they focused on economic development. Traditional wisdom held that economic growth occurred as the result of large-scale private investment, but the New Deal seemed to demonstrate that the government itself could mobilize the resources necessary to promote development, at least in some areas. The Tennessee Valley Authority (TVA), begun in 1933, was the marquee example of this kind of government-funded economic development. It became the model for similar river-development schemes throughout the United States and the world, as well as for the Rural Electrification Administration, which brought electricity to rural areas across the country in order to encourage their economic development and modernization.[10]

By the beginning of World War II, therefore, the economics profession had become confident in its ability to improve both economies and societies. Not only had the profession distinguished itself within academia but governments had also begun to seek regularly the advice of economists. This had begun informally, as economists advised legislators on economic reforms and became more formalized as governments took increasing control of national economies. These governments also built upon the informal coordination of the international economy that had flourished in the Progressive and interwar periods. Now they were ready to build an international organization to formalize this economic work.

Bretton Woods: Constructing a Cooperative International Order

The movement toward formalized international economic cooperation seen in the Tripartite Declaration accelerated during the Second World War and culminated at the Bretton Woods Conference. Shortly after Pearl Harbor, U.S. treasury secretary Henry Morgenthau Jr. appointed Harry Dexter White to begin American postwar economic planning. White had fought in World War I, studied economics at Stanford and Harvard, and taught economics briefly before entering the Treasury in 1934, where he quickly became second in charge. Recognizing the close relationship between domestic and international economic issues, White was convinced that U.S. prosperity depended on the world's countries being wealthy enough to buy American goods and being willing to sell their raw materials. Because such an open trading system demanded a level of exchange-rate stability that could only be achieved through the cooperation of all countries, White considered establishing an international stabilization fund that would provide formal cooperative machinery as well as assets to support national currencies. At the heart of the plan was the New Deal concept of shifting responsibility for international economic policy from private and central bankers to national governments acting through international organizations.[11]

To create such a system, however, required some sacrifice of national sovereignty. In order to maintain stable exchange rates, each country would have to abandon high tariffs, export subsidies, foreign-exchange restrictions and controls, bilateral clearing arrangements, and domestic policies that promoted inflation or deflation. White knew that such sacrifices would be difficult for governments, but he believed that the benefits of doing so would be enormous. Keynes was not so certain. He and other British leaders who believed that the premature return to the gold standard in the 1920s was at the root of Britain's financial woes wanted to avoid any postwar system that would allow automatic stabilizers or powerful international institutions to deny national governments the flexibility they needed to determine their own economic policies. Therefore, Keynes and his colleagues sought to limit the power of the proposed International Monetary Fund while simultaneously seeking a well-endowed World Bank that would float large loans, build investors' confidence, and restore international capital flows to underwrite Britain's postwar reconstruction.[12] But whatever differences in emphasis existed between Keynes and White, they shared a professional ideology, a common view of the shortcomings of the interwar period, and similar visions of a postwar economic order based on formal international institutions staffed by experts. In the sometimes contentious three-year process of hammering out draft accords for these international institutions, the Allied economists came to think of themselves as "a group of friends working together for a common cause." This sense of common purpose and professionalism found its way into the *Joint Statement by Experts on the Establishment of an International Monetary Fund.*[13]

Central to the *Joint Statement*'s broad outline of the World Bank's operations was the clear desire for a bank with the necessary independence to pursue an international agenda. To establish sufficient financial strength, World Bank vaults would hold member contributions totaling $200 million in scarce gold and dollars, but to build its own economic resources and to attain a greater degree of independence, the bank would also charge borrowing nations a "fairly substantial flat rate commission." The bank's internationalism and professionalism, however, were as important as economic independence. To these ends, Keynes and the other Europeans believed that it should charge all borrowers the same rate of interest, that its lending should be based only on expert analysis of the desirability of a loan and the ability of the nation to repay it, and that its loans should be completely untied so that the proceeds could be spent in any country offering the needed goods and services at a competitive price. In other words, to Keynes and the other drafters of the statement, the World Bank was to be an international organization that so far as possible promoted the best interests of the international economy as a whole—a revolutionary idea that later became key to the identity of the World Bank and its staff as international public servants operating independently of national governments.[14]

A sense of optimistic possibility animated the Bretton Woods Conference, a spirit that grew out of a common sense of professionalism, the "lessons" of the interwar period, and the desire to construct a new global economy. Almost everyone at the Mount Washington Hotel seemed to view the world economy as a single organic unit that required international institutions to ensure its proper regulation. They also seemed to believe that the absence of effective international regulators, together with economically nationalistic policies, had been responsible for the Depression and world wars of the previous decades.[15]

At Bretton Woods, construction of the new international order required balancing different national interests without allowing any concession that could unbalance the multilateral system. There were a great many national issues to be balanced: the Mexicans wanted to move toward the monetarization of silver; the Indian delegation demanded the return of its blocked sterling balances in London; the Europeans were more concerned with the bank's role in the reconstruction of their economies, while the Latin Americans fought to advance the development function of the World Bank; the Soviets were suspicious of the Western powers and protective of their socialist system; and a large segment of the American people and Congress were only slowly abandoning their suspicion of international institutions. The task of reconciling these differences fell largely to the American delegation (aided by the conference's technical experts), but out of the process of reconciliation came the renewed conviction that it was possible to reconcile national interests with a new spirit of internationalism, that new international institutions could succeed where strictly national policies had failed, and that a new class of professional experts and international civil servants could avoid the problems that had marred the interwar era.

In negotiating with Great Britain and the Soviet Union, for example, the American delegation went as far as possible toward meeting those nations' reservations without compromising the core of the institutions' missions. In the case of the United Kingdom, the framework for cooperation had been laid during three years of preparatory talks, and this habit of cooperation, according to a British delegate, was the key to the conference's success. The U.S. delegates appreciated the willingness of Great Britain to contribute $1.2 billion to the lending pool of the World Bank, and they sought at every turn to consult with the British delegation, to work together on controversial issues, and to maintain good relations. Toward the end of the conference, Keynes went so far as to describe relations between the American and British delegations as "perfect."[16] More challenging was the task of cultivating the cooperation of the Soviet delegation and easing its suspicions, but Morgenthau was determined to secure full Soviet participation in the Bretton Woods institutions. Although Dean Acheson of the State Department thought that Morgenthau "coddled the Russians," and some of the Europeans also accused the U.S. delegation of caving in to Moscow, Morgenthau unabashedly emphasized his role in the Roosevelt administration's reestablishment of diplomatic relations with the USSR in 1933 and sought to portray himself as a friend, even a "grandfather," to the Soviet delegation. To garner the goodwill of the Soviet delegation, he and other Americans also acceded to the USSR's request for an IMF quota of slightly more than a billion dollars, an amount close to that of the British and one the Soviets thought emblematic of their standing as a major power. The Soviets appeared to be pleased with this concession, though they were less than happy when the U.S. delegation rejected their proposal that they and all war-devastated countries be allowed to reduce the amount of the capital they paid into the bank and the fund without a corresponding reduction in voting power. Fears that all nations would claim such an exemption and that the subsequent reduction in available capital would cripple the institutions had led the United States to issue this rare refusal.[17]

In addition to assuaging British and Soviet concerns, the American delegation at Bretton Woods also tried to meet the concerns of other countries in constructing the new international economy. Although these countries could not contribute as much to the resources of the fund or the bank, their participation was necessary if the international system was to function correctly. China and France, for example, were still important to the continuing war effort as well as to the stability of the postwar world, and because of this the U.S. delegation was willing to allot each a sizeable quota in the fund and bank, which gave them automatic seats on the executive boards of both institutions. The Third World nations represented at the conference, primarily India and the Latin American countries, also sought effective representation on these boards, primarily to promote their own interests, which lay largely in tapping international resources for their economic development. In these cases, too, the American delegation made concessions: India received a permanent seat on the boards of both organizations, while the Latin Americans received enough votes collectively to elect two executive directors.[18]

In spite of these national issues and the need to accommodate them, a spirit of internationalism continued to suffuse the conference, and many delegates hoped that it would also permeate the Bretton Woods institutions. They hoped the World Bank would become a community of countries that came together cooperatively to solve international problems in a rational manner, just as the conference had managed to deal effectively with national concerns at Bretton Woods. To be sure, the bank and the fund were not to be supranational institutions with the power to dictate national policies, but the charter of both institutions pledged member states to common policies and obliged each to uphold those policies. In addition, both organizations had the power to make recommendations to member countries and to refuse to underwrite their loan projects. They also had the ability to mobilize more capital than any single nation or private investor and to make this capital available without regard to political considerations. In these and other ways, they were empowered to act as truly international institutions of global cooperation and to do so, at least in theory, on the basis of professional, businesslike principles, not political or national considerations.[19]

Clearly, the Bretton Woods delegates hoped that their creations would bring a new day of international economic progress and cooperation. Hopes for the World Bank were particularly high, as the delegates believed that it would prevent a relapse into the horrible political and economic conditions that had characterized the interwar period and would usher in a new age of rising productivity, employment, and living standards through international cooperation. This hope for postwar cooperation and appreciation for the achievements of the conference was well expressed by Keynes, who had headed the commission responsible for drafting the bank's Articles of Agreement, when he moved to accept the final act at the closing plenary session of the conference:

> We have not been trying, each one to please himself, and to find the solution most acceptable in our own particular situation. That would have been easy. It has been our task to find a common measure, a common standard, a common rule applicable to each and not irksome to any. . . . We have shown that a concourse of 44 nations are actually able to work together at a constructive task in amity and unbroken concord. . . . We have been learning to work together. If we can so continue, this nightmare, in which most of us here present have spent too much of our lives, will be over. The brotherhood of man will have become more than a phrase.[20]

The cooperative nature of the new world order being constructed at Bretton Woods was not limited to cooperation between countries; on the contrary, the conferees also sought to foster a partnership between the bank and private enterprise to rejuvenate the international economy and to provide some regulation of private lending. To do so the bank would guarantee the bonds of nations undertaking reconstruction or development projects, in order to make those bonds attractive to private investors, and it would finance loans from its own resources when private investors were not available. Its relatively low interest rates and high standards would hopefully prevent both usurious rates in the private market and a relapse into the poor lending policies of the 1920s. In addition, the bank's lending to Third World countries was supposed to foster an environment conducive to private foreign investment while at the same time underwriting the kind of infrastructural projects—roads, railroads, communications, port facilities, and public utilities—that attracted few private investors. "If you build a public road you get no returns at all," explained Alvin Hansen, Keynesian Harvard economist and Bretton Woods adviser, "and yet it is extremely productive and induces private investment. It is that kind of loans this Bank has to make."[21]

The Bretton Woods delegates also realized that cooperation with private businessmen and bankers was a two-way street. If the World Bank was to be able to rely on Wall Street to buy its bonds and support its approach to international lending, the bank would have to win the New York financial community's confidence. For this reason the drafters of the bank's Articles of Agreement established a very conservative lending posture for the fledgling organization, under which it could not lend more than its $10 billion in subscriptions. Although most private banks could lend two or three times their reserve capital, the American delegation argued that Wall Street would not purchase the bank's bonds or recognize its guarantee of national bonds unless the World Bank adopted a very fastidious lending posture.[22]

As they left the Mount Washington Hotel, the Bretton Woods delegates could be justifiably proud of what they had achieved. The Articles of Agreement seemed to lay a sound foundation for international economic cooperation, and they had been provisionally approved by all the Allies, including the Soviet Union. But it remained to be seen whether they would pass muster with the U.S. Congress, which had been the bane of the League of Nations, and whether they would work in practice.

Passage of the Bretton Woods Legislation

If Wall Street's support was essential to the World Bank's success, congressional support was first needed to give it and the IMF life. To assuage concerns on Capitol Hill, Morgenthau and his colleagues had included congressional leaders from both political parties in the Bretton Woods delegation, and they also made sure that the United States would exercise a degree of influence over the World Bank and the IMF commensurate with its financial contribution to both institutions.[23] With the latter goal in mind, Congressman Brent Spence (D-KY), a Bretton Woods delegate and chair of the House Committee on Banking and Currency, was "unalterably opposed" to locating the headquarters of either the bank or the fund anywhere but in the United States. He believed that congressional ratification of the accords would be impossible under other circumstances and urged Morgenthau to express this to Keynes "as plainly as diplomacy will allow." Said Spence, "I don't know how plain that is, [but] profanity wouldn't hurt."[24] For similar reasons, he and other members of the American delegation also demanded a system of weighted voting that tied voting power to the size of a member's financial contribution. This system gave the United States something like a veto in both the bank and the fund and went a long way toward assuaging the concerns of conservatives like Republican senator Robert A. Taft of Ohio, who had proclaimed that Congress would never approve a "plan which places American money in a fund to be dispensed by an international board in which we have only a minority voice."[25]

Despite such conservative opposition, the U.S. delegation was confident that both Congress and the American people would ultimately approve the Bretton Woods accords, and not only because they secured the concessions that Spence and others had in mind. According to Edward E. "Ned" Brown, chairman of the First National Bank of Chicago and a conference delegate, the bank and fund were "clearly to the direct interest of American investors and the American public." Because the United States was certain to emerge from the war as the world's dominant financial, industrial, and agricultural power, it needed markets for its surplus capital and production if it hoped to avoid a recession, perhaps even another depression. The fund and bank promised to loan Europe and the Third World the dollars they needed to buy American goods and at the same time spread the risk of such loans across the international community rather than leaving it on the shoulders of U.S. taxpayers. Also, because the entire international community was, in effect, making the loans, the members of the U.S. delegation believed that "no country would dare default to an international organization of this kind."[26]

The hearings before the House and Senate Committees on Banking and Currency that followed the 1944 election vindicated the confidence and hard work of the Bretton Woods delegation and the Treasury Department. During the course of the hearings, the Treasury was able to reverse initially negative press coverage of the Bretton Woods accords and build something close to a consensus behind the notion that it was necessary to stabilize the entire international economy with fixed exchange rates and ample reconstruction loans. Over one hundred organizations adopted resolutions and statements recommending approval of the Bretton Woods legislation, and of these organizations none was more aggressive in its support than the Congress of Industrial Organizations (CIO).[27] In a pamphlet titled *Bretton Woods Is No Mystery,* which closely followed the Treasury's line of argument, the labor union asserted that currency instability disrupted international trade and hurt employment in the United States, that the total U.S. capitalization of both institutions would cost less than the country spent in a single week during World War II, and that the bank would create "a decent relationship between nations," "more exports and imports," and "more jobs." Indeed, the CIO claimed that foreign trade could create five million jobs in the United States, which was "the difference between prosperity and depression," and it lashed out at the private bankers who constituted the most persistent opposition to the Bretton Woods legislation. It accused the American Bankers' Association (ABA) and its chairman, Winthrop Aldrich, of seeking to monopolize the international economy in order to advance their own interests. According to the CIO, people knew that a banker-run international economy would again lead to world depression, fascism, and war and that far better results could be expected from the Bretton Woods agreements, which had been formulated over three years by economic experts who had "studied the problem not for personal gain but for the good of their own nations and for the good of the world."[28]

Nonetheless, opposition to the Bretton Woods accords came from a number of quarters. In addition to the ABA, organizations going on record as against the new institutions were the Association of Reserve City Bankers, the Bankers Association for Foreign Trade, the New York State Bankers Association, the Los Angeles Chamber of Commerce, the U.S. Chamber of Commerce, and the Guaranty Trust Company. Several individual economists also expressed reservations, particularly about the IMF. Together with the bankers, they supported international monetary stabilization but wanted it to begin with the British pound and other key currencies. They argued that the World Bank could provide the necessary currency stabilization loans, in addition to its reconstruction and development loans, without the extensive rules and regulations envisioned in the IMF accords. Congressmen Frederick C. Smith and Howard H. Buffett summed up this point of view in a minority report to the House Committee on Banking and Currency.[29]

But the committee report, some business and bankers' organizations, many Republicans, and, eventually, Congress as a whole concluded that large changes to the Articles of Agreement formulated at Bretton Woods would make it difficult for the legislatures of other signatories to ratify the articles. Any delay in doling out reconstruction loans or encouraging currency stabilization, they feared, would result in a repeat of post–World War I economic chaos. To those few critics who had argued for a return to the gold standard or individual and bilateral national currency stabilization, the committee responded that international monetary and financial cooperation was essential to a rebirth of global trade and investment. Two months of congressional testimony resulted in no substantial change to the agreements. The most substantive alteration in the enabling legislation was a new provision creating the National Advisory Committee on International Monetary and Financial Matters (NAC), which merely formalized consultation between

representatives from the Treasury and State departments and the American executive directors of the World Bank and IMF.[30] Now the sole remaining question
was how the Bretton Woods accords would work in practice.

Savannah: The First Meeting of the World Bank

Keynes's opening address at the inaugural meeting of the World Bank and IMF in
Savannah, Georgia, in March 1946 suggested appropriate christening gifts for the
newborn institutions. First on his list was "a many-coloured raiment to be worn
by these children as a perpetual reminder that they belong to the whole world and
that their sole allegiance is to the general good." He then suggested vitamins that
would instill in the bank and fund "energy and a fearless spirit, which does not
shelve and avoid difficult issues, but welcomes them and is determined to solve
them." Finally, as a complement to this fearless spirit, he urged "wisdom, patience
and grave discretion." For if the new institutions were to "win the full confidence
of the suspicious world," he said, they would have to act with a Solomon-like wisdom and "without prejudice or favour" in all their actions.[31] Keynes's words well
reflected the optimism of the Bretton Woods Conference, but these high hopes
were not to be realized, if the Savannah meeting was any indication. Compared to
the relative consensus and international goodwill achieved at Bretton Woods, the
proceedings in Savannah generated a surprising level of national bickering and
hard feelings. The divisiveness stemmed from the ebbing of the spirit of international cooperation that the U.S. delegation had tried to foster at Bretton Woods.
The new president, Harry S. Truman, and his treasury secretary, Fred Vinson,
seemed to pay little heed to the reservations and concerns of other countries and
opted instead for what the *Manchester Guardian* termed "steam-roller tactics."[32]
    France, India, and Great Britain had assumed that the headquarters of the Bret-
ton Woods institutions would be in New York City, close to the United Nations
and the world's financial capital and away from the political influences of the U.S.
capital. "These bodies could not be regarded as international institutions," warned
Keynes, if they "were being treated as an appanage of the American Administration,"
which would be the case if they were headquartered in the nation's capital. The
American delegation, however, believed that a Washington location was desirable,
because the bank and the fund would be close to foreign legations (which would
make consultation easier) and because it would symbolize the shift in responsibility
for international economic stabilization from private banking interests to national
governments. But rather than seeking the views of other national delegations or
even enunciating his own justification for the decision, Vinson had gone directly to
Truman, obtained authority to demand that Washington be the headquarters' site,
and curtly informed Keynes and the other delegates that the decision was final.[33]

A similar confrontation occurred over the role of the executive directors. The Americans saw full-time executive directors as key to making the World Bank an independent and professional authority. Keynes, on the other hand, wanted the directors to be "in close touch with their own central banks and Treasuries," which would be impossible if they were full-time, Washington-based employees. Similar differences led the British and Americans to disagree on bank officials' salaries. The Americans favored substantial salaries, seeing this as the way to attract talented individuals and thereby enhance the bank's stature and authority, whereas the British did not want to create a new class of international bureaucrats who had more prestige, authority, and money than national leaders. They eventually agreed on a compromise figure of thirty thousand dollars for the bank president and seventeen thousand for the executive directors, but the British, who were still disgusted that the head of the World Bank would be paid more than their prime minister, refused to go along and cast the only negative vote on the matter. Their thinking was accurately summed up in a *Manchester Guardian* editorial: "The American Treasury . . . seems to have made no secret of its belief that the United States, which pays the piper, has a right to call the tune. In fact, the worst fears of those who had always warned us that this was what the United States meant by international economic co-operation were borne out at Savannah."[34]

Keynes might have believed that Vinson had cursed the christening of his "twins," but the animosity at Savannah largely proved to be an aberration. In the next twenty years, the bank lived up to many of the hopes of the Bretton Woods planners and, to a large extent, recaptured the cooperative, international spirit of that conference. This reflected the professional heritage of the World Bankers (which combined equal parts of social responsibility, scientific expertise, and belief in the efficacy of cooperation) as well as the hard lessons of the Depression about the organic unity of the global economy. With this background, they constructed an identity for themselves and their bank that emphasized internationalism, professionalism, objectivity, and an apolitical nature, the very things that Keynes and the fathers of economics had stressed. Now the World Bankers were ready to undertake the new work of economic development on a global scale, a task they believed would change the world. They did ultimately do so, but often not in the ways they had anticipated.

3

The World Bank and

Development, 1945–1963

With the Articles of Agreement to guide them, the leadership and staff of the World Bank began their mission of crafting an international organization capable of promoting economic development and thereby transforming the global economy. Their view of this mission was influenced by strands of progressive thought and professional ideology; by the lessons they had learned from the past and their hopes for the future; and by their cultural and professional backgrounds. In their prewar roles in business, law, banking, and government service, many of the future World Bankers had already come to believe that the international system, and especially the global economy, was an organic whole and that autarchic economic policies were obsolete—a point clearly borne out, they believed, by the Great Depression. Furthermore, two world wars and the detonation of atomic bombs led the future World Bankers to the conclusion that another world war would mean the end of civilization and that new methods of international conciliation, or possibly some sort of world government, were therefore needed. They believed there had been an irreparable break with the past and consequently hoped to create a new world order. This belief, combined with the hopefulness and optimism of Bretton Woods, produced a new sense of themselves as international citizens and public servants who had the duty and power to rationalize and improve the global economy by promoting economic development throughout the Third World.

The spirit of optimism growing out of Bretton Woods, the successful wartime cooperation among the Allied powers, and the World Bankers' own faith in the ability of experts to analyze and solve a broad range of problems bolstered their conviction that they could act as managers of a new world economy. They envisioned an international economy that would operate as a unitary organism, limit competitive nationalism by integrating economies, and generate an economic growth in which all could share. Within this global framework, the World Bank would act as one of several institutional coordinators in the international economy. It would stimulate private investment, provide guidelines for international aid and lending, work closely with other global institutions, and build strong political economies throughout the Third World. In order to assume these responsibilities, however, the World Bankers had to cultivate a new international identity within the institution and themselves.

During the bank's first twenty years of operation, the World Bankers consistently defined themselves and their institution through a discourse of internationalism.[1] Internationalism, for them, carried connotations of peace, prosperity, and collaboration, whereas nationalism denoted unregulated economic competition, depression, and war, all of which had marked the years since 1914. In public speeches as well as in internal documents, in actions as well as in words, the bankers portrayed themselves as part of an international organization that was cooperatively owned by its members and run by an international staff. They contrasted this image with autarchic policies that could advance national goals only at the expense of the global economy as a whole.

The World Bankers believed that their institution was uniquely structured to act on behalf of the global economy, and they equated such actions with the common good. All member nations contributed to the bank's financial resources and decision making. Each country contributed 2 percent of its total capital subscription (based on its capacity to pay) to the bank in gold or dollars immediately, pledged 18 percent in its own currency, and maintained in its national reserves the remaining 80 percent, which was subject to call in case of emergency. Under the bank's system of weighted voting, these capital subscriptions determined the number of votes each nation had in the organization's decision making. In addition to its financial stake in the bank, each country was represented by one of the executive directors and by its own national delegation at the annual meetings of the board of governors. Each of the five largest capital subscribers (the United States, the United Kingdom, Nationalist China, France, and India in 1945) appointed an executive director, with the other seven executive directors being jointly elected by blocs of the remaining member states.[2]

By giving each nation a monetary stake as well as a voice in the bank, the World Bankers hoped to revolutionize international lending, which, to that point, had been largely determined by the financial and political interests of the government or private investor making the loan. By contrast, World Bank loans were to be based solely on economic considerations and were to be administered by denationalized experts who sought only the good of the international economy. With this as its credo, the World Bank staff believed that member countries would come "to consider their obligations towards the Bank as obligations towards themselves as a community and not as obligations towards a 'third party.'" They also believed that this sense of common cause would create an atmosphere of "mutual trust and respect" and would give the World Bank "an opportunity to establish a broader and more intimate kind of partnership" with member nations than was possible through commercial and bilateral lending.[3]

But the key to the World Bankers' internationalism was not the inclusion of all national voices in decision making but the creation of a denationalized professional staff that would run the organization under the oversight of these governments. This "strange new breed" of professionals would further the bank's mission by taking the global economy as their unit of analysis and excluding national views from decision making. Only "the international civil servant," according to the World Bankers, could make the bank truly objective and professional in its affairs. Eugene R. Black Jr., president of the World Bank from 1949 until 1963, put it this way: "We do not think of a man as a Dane, a Cuban or an Indian, but as an economist, a lawyer or an accountant. Our intramural differences are professional, not national." In theory, at least, this new mode of identity would allow the staff to approach its responsibilities as a team, "independent of national prejudices and emotions."[4]

The World Bank's structure also insulated it to some extent from many sources of national political pressure that the bankers believed would impair their independence and impartiality. The bank's president, for example, served a five-year term and was not subject to recall. Although World Bank capital reserves came from member states, the organization raised most of its lending capital on the world's bond markets, and it generated its own administrative funds through loan fees rather than annual appropriations from members. For these reasons, the World Bankers believed that they had greater freedom to act for the good of the world community than even the United Nations and its other specialized agencies, the budgets and leaders of which were often subjected to close scrutiny by member governments.[5]

Meyer and McCloy Define an International Identity

Although the first two presidents of the World Bank, Eugene Meyer and John J. McCloy, served only a total of two and one-half years, they helped ingrain internationalism into the discourse, operating procedures, and staff of the institution. To these men fell vital issues that largely determined the nature of the bank for the next quarter-century: the creation of an international staff, the raising of the bank's lending capital, the development of the institution's loan policies, and the determination of the proper balance of power between the executive directors, who were national representatives, and the president and his staff within the bank hierarchy.

Eugene Meyer accepted these challenges when he assumed the position of president of the World Bank on 4 June 1946. After heading a successful investment banking house prior to World War I, Meyer had served in various American governmental positions dealing with economic policy and had worked as editor and publisher of the *Washington Post* for six years before taking the top spot at the World Bank. John J. McCloy became World Bank president just nine months later, on 17 March 1947. A man admirably suited for the job, McCloy had moved frequently and easily between the public and private spheres. After receiving a law degree from Harvard, he had gained prominence as a Wall Street attorney and then as wartime assistant secretary of war before returning to private practice with the firm of Milbank, Tweed, Hadley & McCloy, lawyers to the Rockefeller family and its business interests, including Chase National Bank.[6]

Meyer's early personnel decisions laid the foundation for an international staff and institution. Without first consulting the executive directors, he appointed as vice president Harold D. Smith, an American who had previously served as director of the budget, thereby asserting the primacy of the president's office on personnel matters. Meyer saw this as essential to the success of the World Bank, because the executive directors were national representatives with agendas very different from the international agenda of the bank as a whole. The bank's retirement program also reflected a careful decision on his part to establish a permanent, international civil service within the institution. Some of the bank's executive directors and staff members had suggested a system of transferable individual retirement accounts, because they envisioned the staff as a rotating group of employees who would serve for no more than three to five years. But Meyer wanted a permanent, international staff that owed its loyalty solely to the bank, and with this goal in mind, he established an institutional pension fund for the benefit of retiring staff members. Salaries and paid leave for bank employees were also more like those on Wall Street than of the United Nations, and these policies too reflected Meyer's professional sensibility and experience as well as his desire to maximize the bank's autonomy.[7]

Meyer formulated his staff policies with an eye to winning the confidence of Wall Street, without which the World Bank could not achieve a measure of autonomy from national governments or fulfill its international mandate of funding reconstruction and development. Conversations between the U.S. National Advisory Council on International Monetary and Financial Matters (NAC) and New York banking and insurance firms had already made it clear that the World Bank would have to market its own bonds in order to raise lending capital; the earlier idea of a World Bank guarantee of foreign governments' bonds would not be sufficient to gain the confidence of American investors, at least not after the disastrous lending record of the 1920s and the loan defaults of the 1930s. The World Bank, as a completely new organization, faced an enormous task in restoring U.S. trust in overseas investments. But even more important to Meyer, and later to McCloy, was the independence that Wall Street investment promised the bank. If it could raise money independent of government subscriptions, the bank's decision making would be less affected by national influences and would be subject instead to the fiscal and economic considerations that professional financial experts, including those on Wall Street and in the World Bank, believed to be necessary. Meyer enjoyed a good reputation on Wall Street, but his own best efforts notwithstanding, in the end he was unable to inspire a similar faith in the institution he now headed. Many potential investors saw the World Bankers as idealists, more determined to save the world than to follow the sound business and banking principles that would safeguard stockholders' investments. Investors were suspicious of New Dealers and liberals like Henry Morgenthau Jr., Harry Dexter White, and John Maynard Keynes, all of whom had played fundamental roles in drafting the Bretton Woods accords, but what truly alarmed them was Truman's appointment of Emilio "Pete" Collado as the U.S. executive director. A liberal economist from the State Department, Collado exercised what amounted to a veto over the bank's lending policies, and he wanted to use this power to encourage large and liberal reconstruction loans to war-devastated Europe. Conservative investors interpreted such an attitude as a desire to transform the bank into a political organization, which would rapidly disburse its $10 billion in assets with little attention to economic considerations or the prospects for repayment.[8]

In order to placate Wall Street concerns and assert the authority of the president's office, Meyer sought to establish a cautious lending posture that was entirely contrary to Collado's aspirations. When the board of governors gathered for its first annual meeting, the bank had not made a single loan. In fact, it had received only three applications, one each from France, Chile, and Denmark. Despite extreme pressure from Collado to grant these loans immediately, Meyer insisted on a thorough examination of the overall credit standing of each country and the merits of each loan. Drawing on the lessons of the 1920s, he and his staff also instituted a careful system of end-use supervision in order to ensure that the disbursed funds were used in the manner outlined in the loan agreement. In these ways, Meyer set an important precedent in making economic criteria paramount in the bank's loan negotiations and agreements, but his successes in these areas angered Collado and were not sufficient to assuage Wall Street's concerns.[9]

Meyer's disagreements with Collado over loan policy were also part of a more fundamental dispute over the balance of power between the bank's president and its executive directors, a dispute that would determine to a large degree the bank's autonomy from national governments and therefore its ability to appeal to Wall Street. The Articles of Agreement gave the executive directors the vague mandate of conducting "the general operations of the Bank" and the president the equally ambiguous duty of "conduct[ing], under the direction of the Executive Directors, the ordinary business of the Bank." The discussions at Savannah had done nothing to clarify the precise working relationship between the two branches. Meyer tried to work out a solution, engaging Collado and the other executive directors in a constant battle over the issue, but he finally resigned in protest less than a year after taking the post. This abrupt resignation and the death of Vice President Smith of a heart attack shortly after Meyer's departure left the day-to-day business of the bank to the higher ranks of the staff, in whom Meyer had sought to instill an internationalist philosophy. These officials responded by creating an ad hoc structure to ensure that the business of the bank would proceed. They refused to allow Collado to sit in on these meetings, gave him instead periodic reports on pertinent issues, and thereby continued Meyer's policy of trying to enhance the authority of the president and his staff, their autonomy from the executive directors, and their independence from national governments.[10]

McCloy took the top job at the World Bank with a grim determination to centralize authority in the bank's executive and to limit the role of the executive directors—whose independence and power, he believed, had already had a detrimental effect on the bank's ability to borrow on Wall Street and attain a degree of autonomy from member governments. He accepted his appointment only on condition that Collado be replaced, which he was, and that the U.S. government support McCloy's efforts to consolidate power in his staff at the expense of the executive directors. Like Meyer, he believed that only a bank of truly independent and international stature had the ability to fulfill its mission and win support on Wall Street. The key to this independence, he assumed, was to be found in a strong executive and a staff of international public servants, not in the executive directors, whose national allegiances conflicted with the bank's international identity.[11]

The executive directors were ready to give McCloy a certain freedom of action in order to rejuvenate the bank's failing image, but they were not content with the subordinate position that the new president envisioned for them. As international financial experts, some of whom had helped to draft the Articles of Agreement, the executive directors believed they had the expertise and the responsibility to direct bank operations. Therefore, they were bound to clash with McCloy and his vision of internationalism within the bank. Indeed, the executive directors were soon complaining that the new president and his staff did not keep them abreast of the bank's activities, presented them with faits accomplis at the weekly board meetings, and generally treated them as "a sort of supervisory council with little more than formal duties." This resentment boiled to the surface when one of the executive directors, attending a group photo session with the new president, asked if the directors should pose with their rubber stamps in hand.[12]

The executive directors contested McCloy's definition of internationalism. Like the new president, they wanted the bank to be an international institution, but that goal, they argued, required the directors to take an active role in the bank's operations. Their board, they asserted, was more international than the staff of the bank, which was subordinated to a largely American leadership. According to the directors, if the bank was to be a truly "international institution in which the member countries remain interested and for the fate of which they feel a common responsibility," member states would have to see that their representatives played a major role in the bank's decision making. Roger Hoppenot, the French executive director, also pointed out that the bank would need "all the cooperation, energy, knowledge and work of all persons who belong to it, to achieve its aims."[13] But the executive directors failed in their attempt to redefine internationalism in the bank, not least because of the U.S. government's backing of McCloy. Internationalism within the bank was subsequently defined as denationalized professionalism in the service of the bank's president, as McCloy wished, rather than as a consensus among national opinions, as the executive directors had hoped. Ironically, the backing of the U.S. government had allowed McCloy to construct a Progressive-style strong executive staffed by professionals, a structure that gave the bank the autonomy it needed to gain Wall Street's confidence and to distance itself from the influence of national governments.

McCloy also took steps to ensure that his staff conformed to his ideal of professional internationalism. When he assumed leadership of the bank, he discovered that Leonard Rist, the head of the Economic Department and a French national, had excluded himself from staff discussions on a French reconstruction loan. McCloy reprimanded Rist. In the words of Robert L. Garner, who had become World Bank vice president upon the death of Smith, McCloy considered Rist's position to be "unsound," because the key to the bank's identity was an internationalism that superseded or even obviated national allegiances. That is, denationalized professionalism required staff members to perform their duties regardless of the country under consideration, because when one served the international community, there could be no conflict of interest.[14]

Once he had put his own house in order, McCloy had the credibility he needed to gain the confidence of Wall Street, in part by cultivating the World Bank's professional image. In a series of private meetings he assured Wall Street friends and acquaintances that the bank was not controlled by New Deal idealists but by bankers, businessmen, and economists who were ready to work in partnership with private enterprise to manage the global economy. The bank would not compete with the private sector, he said. Rather, it would aid private business by reinvigorating American and European faith in international investment and by making Third World economies more welcoming to multinational corporations and other foreign investors. In these and other ways, according to McCloy, the World Bank would cooperate with its private counterparts to restore the international flow of capital and investment, the apparent keys to prosperity.[15]

To give meaning to his words, McCloy filled important positions with men from the banking and business communities. Eugene Black, one of McCloy's colleagues from Chase National Bank and the son of a Federal Reserve banker, replaced Collado as the U.S. executive director. This change, one of McCloy's conditions for taking the top job at the World Bank, was also one of the keys to assuaging concerns on Wall Street. Robert L. Garner, the new vice president, had been a vice president of both the Guaranty Trust Company and General Foods. Other McCloy appointments included Chauncey G. Parker, a Washington investment banker, as director of administration and E. Fleetwood Dunstan, vice president of the Bankers Trust Company of New York, as director of marketing.[16]

McCloy, Black, and Garner spent most of their first months at the bank holed up in a Washington house loaned to them by the Rockefeller family, working day and night on a marketing scheme for the bank's bonds. In addition to McCloy's Wall Street contacts, the staff organized information sessions to promote the bank's image and credibility, and thereby its creditworthiness. Bankers and other potential investors from across the United States came to Washington to learn "the facts" about the bank and its operations. In addition, Black, McCloy, and other high-ranking staffers made a series of speeches across the United States in which they contrasted the World Bank's sound loan policies with the questionable lending practices of the 1920s and 1930s. Their hard work paid off when, less than four months after McCloy assumed office, the first issue of World Bank bonds was oversubscribed on Wall Street, raising $250 million.[17]

In line with the bank's professional ideology, McCloy maintained the primacy of economic criteria in the bank's early operations. In connection with its first loan, $250 million for French reconstruction, the bank staff discovered that the Crédit National had diverted to the French navy fuel oil that had been earmarked for reconstruction. France's required reimbursement for the misplaced fuel signaled to the world that the bank intended to enforce end-use supervision as part of its new international lending standards. McCloy, Black, and Garner also decided that the bank would make no loan to any country that was unwilling to work toward a settlement of its outstanding loan defaults. This stipulation became an issue during negotiations concerning the bank's first development loan, a $40 million request from Chile, when some Latin American nations accused the bank of acting as Wall Street's bill collector. The bank, however, retorted that its stipulation would do more than aid Wall Street or solidify its own standing in the bond market; it would also allow financially rehabilitated nations and Third World countries to enter the world bond market and therefore the global economy on their own in the future.[18] The World Bank's commitment to economic, rather than political, considerations was also clear from McCloy's support of a proposal for a $250 million loan to rehabilitate the Polish coal mining industry, with the understanding that a fixed proportion of the increased output would be sold to fuel-starved Western Europe in exchange for the dollars or gold needed to repay the loan. Such a loan promised to reestablish economic ties between Eastern and Western Europe and to aid reconstruction, but as the Cold War grew colder, it

became clear that the Truman administration had enough votes among the executive directors to reject any such loan. McCloy relented. Although he could set
an international economic agenda for the bank, he was still bound to respect the
final rulings of the executive directors.[19]

When McCloy left the bank after two years of service to become the Allied
high commissioner for Germany, he had attained his goal of establishing the international identity and professional ideology of the World Bank. He had also
established a close relationship between the private investment community and
the World Bank, a relationship that was strengthened by their shared professional
ideology. A key to that professional ideology was the central role of expertise and
a strong executive, both major elements in Progressive Era ideology. By declaring
its independence from national considerations, both through its private fund-
raising and through McCloy's ascendancy over the executive directors, the World
Bank had strengthened its image as an objective, expert organization, and this in
turn had enhanced its authority in the international realm.

With the bank's international and professional identity thereby established,
Eugene Black, McCloy's successor, could focus his energies on mending relations
with the bank's executive directors and on the bank's post–Marshall Plan mission—development lending.[20] Black reassured the executive directors that he valued their advice and input. But the terms of the reconciliation made it clear that
the staff would continue to be responsible for the preliminary stages of all loan
applications and would thereby frame the terms of debate for the executive directors. Black's charm and aura of professionalism also endeared him to a variety of
Third World nationals, a great asset for an institution with a mission that was now
limited to development financing in Latin America and the newly independent
countries of Asia and the Middle East.

Crusading for the International and Combating the National

The international identity, function, and purpose of the World Bank and its staff,
defined by Meyer and McCloy and perpetuated under Black's tenure (1949–63),
led it into frequent clashes with national governments, whose identities, functions, and purposes in the international community were necessarily different. Like his staff and predecessors, Black believed that the bank's international
structure and staff had inherent advantages over national loan programs. To the
World Bankers, the latter were intrinsically "political"—inefficient, unscientific,
and not geared to the needs of the larger global economic community—whereas
the bank's development loans were distinctly nonpolitical. The bank, Black said,
was not subject "to the many competing and conflicting pressures—political and
commercial—which must affect *national* financial institutions" and was therefore

able "to apply objective yardsticks to measure the financial and economic worth of loan applications"—an aspect of the bank's operations that the World Bank president valued "more than anything else." Additionally, its loans, unlike those of most national development agencies, were not "tied." Loaned funds could be spent in any country, and in fact all bank-funded projects required international competitive bidding. The World Bankers believed these provisions helped make the bank truly international, nonpolitical, and independent, which in turn helped it transcend issues of sovereignty and avoid charges of economic exploitation and political discrimination.[21]

Viewing their motives as professionally driven and "reasonably pure," the World Bankers had little hesitation when it came to demanding tax reform and other unpopular domestic measures as conditions for their assistance, since they saw these measures as essential to economic development. The suggested reforms (such as overhauling regressive tax systems, eliminating governmental waste and corruption, and avoiding inflation) were meant to ensure the benefits of economic development were shared with the working classes, in order to prevent discontent while also bolstering productivity and sociopolitical stability. Some countries seeking bank assistance might cringe from the potential political difficulties caused by such terms, but the World Bankers believed that their aid initiatives and conditions served the interests of both aid-giving countries that contributed to the bank and the recipients of such aid. International lending through the bank insulated both parties "from the frictions and tensions that inevitably attend a foreign lending program." Additionally, the World Bank was uniquely equipped to coordinate aid to meet the needs and capacities of borrowing and lending nations alike: it could lend in a variety of currencies; it had a vast collection of economic and statistical data to aid in formulating national development programs; and it brought together scarce international experts for technical consultation.[22]

As it turned out, however, the clash of antagonistic national ideologies in the Cold War imperiled the World Bankers' goal of constructing an international system of mutually beneficial trade, economic development, and prosperity. They feared that the "insidious arguments of communism" would lead some Third World countries to take a "short-cut" to economic development rather than the painful path the bank deemed necessary. The World Bankers also frowned on attempts by Third World nationalists to attain economic development outside the framework of a multilateral world economy. This was the case, for example, with Juan Perón's economic policies in Argentina, which, according to the World Bankers, represented a "classic example" of an "extreme economic nationalism" that fostered industrialization behind protective tariffs, promoted regional autarchy, and discouraged private foreign investment.[23]

Countries in the First World too were often guilty of putting their national concerns ahead of those of the global economy and were therefore also reprimanded

by the World Bankers. Throughout the 1950s the bank criticized European countries for their reluctance to make more of their currencies unconditionally available to underwrite the bank's loans. As a condition of membership, as we have
seen, each nation paid 2 percent of its capital subscription to the bank in dollars
or gold and promised an additional 18 percent in local currency as soon as it was
able to undertake this obligation. Only the United States and Canada had honored
this obligation, however, and the World Bankers were eager to obtain the compli-
ance of the Europeans as well, because their currencies would allow the bank to
finance development projects in Third World countries that were at or nearing
their limit of dollar creditworthiness. These "18 percent" funds would also ease
the bank's reliance on American resources, thereby allowing it to become more
international. But many European countries would only release these monies for
loans that would be used to purchase their own goods. To overcome these nationalistic obstacles as well as to diversify and strengthen its lending, the World Bank
applied verbal pressure but in addition was not averse to implied quid pro quos.
During a 1950 trip to Italy, for example, Black arranged for the release of the Italian
government's 18 percent contribution while at the same time discussing the bank's
participation in a development program for southern Italy.[24]

The most frequent clashes between internationalism and nationalism occurred
between the World Bank and the United States. As the leader of the West and of
the international economy, the United States had unique responsibilities in the
postwar world, obligations that the World Bankers often believed were honored
in the breach. True to their international and professional ideology, the World
Bankers criticized American policies and suggested alternatives that would benefit both the United States and the world economy. For example, many American aid programs paid little heed to the high lending standards that the World
Bankers had worked to establish. The U.S. government ignored the bank's insistence on economic stabilization when it granted aid unconditionally, as it did
with Brazil in 1951. The bankers were particularly annoyed by America's "fuzzy" or
"pseudo" development loans—in effect, dollar loans that carried a nominal interest rate and could take decades to mature. Although such loans might be more
palatable to Congress and the American people than outright grants, according to
the World Bankers they impaired "the integrity of all international obligations,"
in that they eroded developing countries' ability to undertake additional hard-
currency loans and were less likely to be repaid. Even U.S. loans that were conventional in terms of their period of maturity and rate of interest, however, were
flawed in the eyes of the World Bankers, because they were prompted by "political" motives, such as the desire to gain military or material advantage and other
"nonobjective" criteria that were very different from the conditions that applied
to loans by the World Bank. "A single country offering aid . . . wants to be loved,"
stated Black, "so it agrees to finance the plans which, justifiable or not, are dear

to the recipient government's heart. An international organization has no need to erect monuments to its generosity."[25]

Emblematic of the international-national conflict between the World Bank and the United States was the battle during the 1940s and 1950s over the Export-Import (Exim) Bank, which the World Bankers saw as the embodiment of American "political" lending. In the hopes of minimizing these conflicts, officials from the two banks began biweekly meetings in July 1947. The World Bank staff believed that the Exim Bank should limit itself to loans based on "exceptionally urgent political interests" and to export and commodity credits, which required the borrowers to make their purchases in the United States. It should, in other words, confine itself to "political" loans and should not impinge on World Bank responsibilities. In 1951 the bank and the Truman administration agreed in principle that "all requests for development loans from members of the International Bank should, except in special circumstances, be first considered by the International Bank." But the World Bankers also urged the administration to recognize its "responsibility to carry out [Exim loans] in a way which would not impair any development program the Bank was financing or the financial basis on which it rested." This request was the direct result of Exim Bank loans for development projects in Mexico, Iran, and Brazil, all of which the World Bank had refused to fund until internal economic reforms had been implemented. Unless the Exim Bank respected this standard, the World Bankers argued, it might well undercut the principle of international administration in development lending and the "nonpolitical" approach of the World Bank.[26]

To the World Bankers, another symbol of the U.S. tendency to put national considerations above those of the international economy were American trade barriers. The World Bankers attacked them as "archaic delusions," "a hangover from the . . . early 19th century," and the equivalent of "trying to ride through the age of the atom in a horse and buggy." For a country that depended on the health of the global economy for its economic security, American tariffs seemed entirely counterproductive. The Marshall Plan and military and development aid could not permanently restore the international economy's equilibrium. If the United States wished to close the dollar gap, Black and others asserted, it had to allow more countries to sell more products in America.[27]

Indeed, the World Bankers were frustrated by the nationalism that seemed to blind many American leaders to the realization that a healthy global economy was inextricably linked to world peace and that economic development would serve as the foundation for the construction of such an economy. Development would increase Third World living standards, decrease the possibility of desperation-fed revolutions, and ultimately provide the building blocks for the creation of liberal democracies. The World Bankers reiterated these points after the outbreak of the Korean War, when some American and European statesmen believed that development aid was expendable in a time of international military crisis. In an address to the Atlanta Chamber of Commerce, Black rebutted such short-sightedness with forceful poignancy: "Suppose that the processes of economic development . . . had been set vigorously underway in East Asia even a generation ago. Had that happened then it is not just hard to imagine, it is quite impossible to imagine, that China could have the government that it has today. Even more, it is absolutely inconceivable that Chinese troops should now be facing our soldier sons in Korea."[28] In this way, Black vented his frustration with nationalism and reiterated the importance of an internationalism that could aid the global economy and also the cause of world peace.

Managing a New Global Order

The World Bankers' belief in a perfectible, harmonious world derived from both their confidence in their own ability to serve as managers of the global economy and their conviction that they could harness other groups to pull together toward the bank's goal of economic development. The bankers believed that both free market forces as well as international facilitators like the bank itself could work together to catalyze private investment in the Third World. The bank's role in this partnership was to provide guidelines for international aid and lending, collect and disseminate information, and provide technical assistance to member governments engaged in development planning. Such a system would place limits on competitive economic nationalism and would allow both natural market forces and international coordinating mechanisms to integrate economies and thereby clear a path to both stable growth and international harmony.[29]

To establish the ground rules for international investment and development, the World Bankers lectured both Third World governments and multinational corporations on the need to work together in mutually advantageous ways. To their professional counterparts in the Third World, the bankers urged the creation of an environment that was conducive to private foreign investment, believing that only large-scale investment of this type could bring development and fully integrate their economies into the global capitalist system. The World Bank laundry list of suggested reforms included eliminating governmental corruption, creating a capable workforce through mass education, expunging discriminatory taxes on foreign investors, quelling fears of expropriation, and removing limitations on capital transfers. The World Bankers also urged Third World countries to discard their "outdated" image of foreign investors as dangerous imperialists and to realize that foreign investment was the key to economic development.[30] Simultaneously, the World Bankers exhorted their professional counterparts in the international business community to join them as allies in promoting capitalist economic development. When addressing gatherings of businessmen, the World Bankers often stressed professional responsibilities in overseas business dealings. Black, for example, entreated the National Association of Manufacturers "to look, not for temporary windfalls, but for sustained profits over the long run. All I am asking is that when you deal with foreigners and foreign markets you use the same business yardsticks you use at home. . . . The virtues which we prize in our economic system—competition, enterprise, steady growth—don't cease to be virtues at the edge of the oceans." By acting in such a manner, the World Bankers argued, smart foreign investors would be helping themselves. Responsible action abroad would undercut the appeal of communism and radical nationalism, minimize the risk of expropriation, stabilize Third World economies, and benefit foreign investors over the long term.[31]

As a corollary to the bank's efforts to reinvigorate international investment by fostering the proper environment, the World Bankers gathered economic data from around the globe to rationalize international aid programs, foreign investment, and the development plans of individual countries, a task that exemplified their identity as professionals who could objectively analyze and solve global problems. With such information, the World Bank could make better-informed decisions about development programs and remove the subjective element from its decision-making process. Additionally, other lending institutions as well as borrowing countries would be better able to judge national creditworthiness if they had precise figures, not only on foreign indebtedness but also on such hidden forms of debt as suppliers' credits and deferred payments.[32]

Like its data collection efforts, the World Bank's technical assistance programs exemplified the professional ideology of its staff members, who helped Third World countries define and prioritize development projects in rational, long-term national development plans. The bank devoted approximately 10 percent of its budget to technical assistance programs, which were "the very root" of its mission, according to Richard Demuth, director of the World Bank's Technical Assistance and Liaison Staff. The bank conducted nationwide economic surveys that were to serve as the basis for comprehensive development programs and dispatched technical advisors to aid governments with specific projects and economic sectors, such as electrical power and railroad management. The goal in both cases was to formulate development programs that the bank would then underwrite with its loans. It was this combination of technical advice and lending ability that formed the backbone of the bank's power.[33]

Recognizing its finite ability to carry out its ambitious global mission, the World Bankers forged ties with other functional groups in the international economy, including national aid and lending agencies, large philanthropic foundations, private research institutes, other UN and international organizations, central banks, national treasuries, universities, and professional associations. Working in concert achieved a number of advantages from the vantage point of the World Bank: it pooled scarce development resources and used them to the greatest possible effect; it allowed the bank to set minimum international standards; and it helped ensure that developing countries received the same advice from all sides. The bank promoted this approach by incorporating members of these groups into its survey and technical assistance missions, sponsoring both formal and informal forums for the exchange of information between the various groups, providing channels for their feedback on pertinent World Bank issues, and reinforcing these links through personal contacts. The World Bank, for example, fostered a good working relationship with the British in formulating and implementing the national components of the Colombo Plan (the Commonwealth counterpart to the Marshall Plan). In fact, because the British relied on the bank for capital and technical assistance, their development programs conformed more closely to bank standards than did most U.S. development efforts.[34]

Several aspects of the bank's cooperative outlook were evident in the creation of the International Finance Corporation (IFC). The member governments of the World Bank created and funded the IFC as an affiliate of the World Bank in 1956. It had its own funds and, until 1961, its own president—Robert L. Garner, the bank's vice president under both McCloy and Black—but it shared staff, facilities, and expertise with the World Bank. The IFC's mission was to underwrite private business ventures in the Third World, something the bank's Articles of Agreement precluded, because such investments lacked a government guarantee. Enterprises funded by the IFC were privately managed and drew more than half of their capitalization from private interests. Though it held stock in these enterprises, the IFC did not exercise its voting rights and sought to sell its stock to private investors whenever possible, thereby adding to the funds available for investment in similar enterprises.

Black had first suggested the idea of a bank-affiliated agency to promote private investment in 1948, when he was serving as U.S. executive director and feared congressional expansion of the role of the Exim Bank. Later, McCloy returned to the idea as a possible new avenue for bank activity when it seemed that Truman's Point IV program would displace the bank as worldwide provider of technical assistance and development funds. The idea of an international finance corporation languished for several years as the World Bank changed presidents and the world suffered through the economic and political trauma of the Korean War; the concept was resurrected by Truman's Advisory Board on International Development, which was headed by Nelson Rockefeller. The Rockefeller family, its business interests, and its philanthropic foundation had long exhibited an interest in accelerating the rate of economic development and private investment in the Third World. With these goals in mind, the Rockefeller Committee not only urged the creation of the IFC but also asserted that it was critical to the overall health of the world economy. Its report recommended an initial capitalization of $400 million;

when the Truman administration failed to act on these recommendations, the United Nations Economic and Social Council (ECOSOC) encouraged the World Bank to undertake a detailed study with a view to giving form to these ideas.[35]

The bank's subsequent report to the ECOSOC argued that the IFC would bring promising opportunities to the attention of private foreign investors and would bolster their confidence in the safety of overseas investments. The World Bankers were eager to do something to revive foreign investment in the Third World, which was still lagging behind pre-Depression levels. Many Third World countries were also supportive of the proposed IFC, as they were of other schemes that seemed to offer greater development resources. But the American government, which would provide the bulk of the IFC's capitalization, and some U.S. business interests remained unconvinced that such an agency was needed or that taxpayers' dollars should be invested in private industry abroad. American resistance finally collapsed under the combined pressure of Third World criticism and the possibility of more radical, alternative programs under the auspices of the United Nations. The Eisenhower administration announced on 11 November 1954 that it supported the creation of a World Bank–affiliated IFC. But the continuing leeriness of U.S. treasury secretary George Humphrey resulted in a ban on IFC equity investment as well as an initial capitalization of only $100 million—one-quarter of the amount recommended by the Rockefeller Commission.[36] Although these stipulations limited the IFC's utility and range of activities during its first decade of operations, the events surrounding its creation demonstrate the way in which the bank sought to revive private investment and to protect and promote its role as manager of the international economy.

Proselytizing around the World

The Economic Development Institute (EDI), the most elaborate of the bank's educational programs, clearly demonstrates the World Bank's efforts to expand its influence and promote its mission by educating others in its ideology and methods. Much like the Progressives, the staff of the World Bank believed that education was the key to personal, societal, and economic improvement. The bankers believed that they had uncovered a basic truth—the fundamental unity of the global, capitalist economy—and that they had an obligation to spread this truth to others, who would presumably recognize its value and embrace it. With this mission in mind, the World Bank created a variety of educational programs to inculcate these beliefs in a new generation of world citizens.[37]

The EDI's mission was to professionalize Third World bureaucrats. This approach not only addressed the shortage of administrative and technical expertise in the Third World, which was limiting the possibilities of economic development,

but also allowed the World Bankers to replicate their ideology and operating procedures in member countries. Ideally, the senior development bureaucrats from
the Third World who participated in the program would use their newfound expertise to educate those around them, elevate the quality of their countries' development planning and loan requests, and utilize national resources more efficiently. To this end, the EDI taught its twenty-odd students the lessons the World
Bank had gleaned from its activities around the globe. The Ford and Rockefeller
foundations, both of which were heavily involved in educational efforts throughout the Third World, provided funds to get the EDI off the ground in January
1956. The EDI curriculum reflected the professional and international aspects of
the World Bankers' faith in the possibility of economic development along capitalist lines, specifically following the model of the United States. It included an
introduction on the "past experience of economic development and on the general principles which may be drawn from it" before moving on to lessons on the
interdependence of national and international economies and ways to organize
and implement development plans in both the industrial and agricultural sectors
of an economy. Guest speakers and a series of field trips supplemented the formal curriculum. EDI students visited a Bethlehem Steel plant; the Tennessee Valley Authority's network of dams, power plants, irrigation systems, and fertilizer
plants; the Atomic Energy Commission's Oak Ridge, Tennessee, uranium-enrich-
ment facility; the Baltimore Railroad works; and the New York Port Authority.
The TVA was a particularly popular outing as many Third World countries, as
well as the World Bankers, saw it as a model of the type of large-scale economic
development that could be produced by large infusions of outside development
capital under close governmental supervision.[38]

To spread their message to an even broader audience, the World Bankers also
traveled the globe proselytizing about the benefits that would accrue from embracing an open, capitalistic, international economy. In the First World, they told
their audiences that economic development aid would create better markets for
their manufactures as well as more reliable sources of vital and strategic raw materials. The message, especially to American audiences, was that "the Bank means
. . . better business—better markets and better sources of supply."[39] The creation
of a truly international economy would also aid the ideological cause of the "free"
world, according to Eugene Black:

> Investment . . . in world development means nothing less than the illumination
> of the central idea of freedom. Freedom means opportunity for the individual
> person to act creatively so as to fulfill his aspirations—and to act with truth
> as his guide and with respect for the aspirations of others. This is the radical
> principle which has motivated all those who have fought for freedom. It is this
> principle that can give a great human meaning to economic development.[40]

To their Third World audiences the World Bankers promised that "sound" development programs would bring their populations out of grinding poverty and misery. The building of infrastructure would bring a new variety of goods to previously inaccessible areas and would facilitate exports to larger markets. Dams, power plants, and irrigation systems would provide freedom from the fear of floods, a longer growing season, and all the advantages of the modern electrical age. Such programs would provide employment and expanded economic opportunities. As countries and people enjoyed higher standards of living and improved lifestyles, they would come to appreciate the values of individualism, freedom, and democracy. This was the vision that the World Bankers held out to the Third World, if only it would embrace the potentialities of the liberal international economy.

For those who would take a different course, the World Bank staff warned of a dark future. If the industrialized nations did not provide enough aid to increase Third World living standards, underdeveloped countries would likely turn to communism or autarchy. As global markets and raw materials became inaccessible, the "free" countries of the world would be forced to retreat behind high trade barriers in a smaller and increasingly competitive international marketplace. National governments would centralize control over their economies, stifle entrepreneurship, and curtail individual rights, as had occurred in the 1930s in Italy, Japan, and Germany. If First World leaders did not fulfill their global obligations, a series of fortified and mutually hostile nation-states would replace the bank's dream of global peace and prosperity.

William F. Howell, World Bank director of administration, conjured up particularly strong images of war, death, and destruction in a speech to graduates of the University of Pittsburgh's Graduate School of Public and International Affairs. The international situation could not continue with "the world 'half skyscraper and half rubble,'" he stated, paraphrasing Lincoln's warning that "a house divided against itself cannot stand . . . this government cannot endure, permanently half slave and half free." Black filled out this dark picture and personalized it in his address to Oglethorpe University's class of 1955:

> If the turbulence of these [backward] countries continues, if the free nations of the world must remain constantly alert to assure that totalitarian forces do not emerge victorious from that turbulence, we will have to bear an ever increasing burden of armaments. More of our manpower, more of our production, will have to be devoted to defense; the upward movement of living standards may slow down and perhaps stop; the opportunities of young people like you to choose and make productive careers will become ever more limited. And fear for our own safety may lead to heavier and heavier pressure from society for conformity of thought and action, a deeper and deeper distrust of freedom of

expression, and narrower and narrower limits on our liberty as individuals to control our own destinies in accordance with our own desires.

But if the United States accepted its responsibilities, the rewards would be "the maintenance of a world in which Americans themselves can remain free, a world in which the members of this graduating class can live out their lives in peace, with their heads held high and with the smile of free men on their lips."[41] This was the Manichaean vision of the World Bank in its first decades of existence.

Deconstructing the World Bankers' International Identity

This ostensibly black-and-white worldview, however, contained far more shades of gray than the World Bank staff was willing to admit. Its identity and dichotomies (such as nationalism/internationalism) were carefully fashioned and regulated creations. John Maynard Keynes seemed particularly aware of the constructed nature of the World Bank's mission when he addressed the Bretton Woods delegates in his closing remarks: "We have to go out from here as missionaries, inspired by zeal and faith. We have sold all this to ourselves. But the world at large still needs to be persuaded."[42] For the next two decades the World Bankers took this directive to heart and preached that their international program of economic development would promote a prosperity that would be naturally followed by peace and well-being. The bank would do so by bringing experts from around the world together in a single international, technical organization that would then focus its attention on alleviating Third World poverty through economic development. Indeed, this was the new vision that had drawn them to the World Bank—an entirely new international creation that promised to play its role in keeping the world from destroying itself in another world war. But in this new endeavor of promoting economic development, the World Bankers were constrained by their constructed identity and their own cultural assumptions, which in many cases harmed their cause and did not allow them to consider alternative methods of promoting development.

The World Bankers hoped that integrating Third World countries into a relatively open, international market would promote global peace and prosperity, and it did indeed help sustain and revive the economies of the United States and Europe as well as enrich a number of Third World elites. But the dams, highways, and power plants built by the bank, which constituted the majority of its lending through 1965, entailed no fundamental change in the international division of labor. In economic parlance, any such radical change would violate the law of comparative advantage—the tenet that each country was uniquely suited by the location of natural resources and the education of its workforce to produce certain products more cost-effectively than others. In the 1940s, 1950s, and 1960s,

economic dogma held that the First World could more efficiently produce manufactured goods, due to its higher level of technology, educated workforce, available
credit, and extensive infrastructure, while the Third World should largely limit
itself to supplying raw materials and to limited processing of primary products.
World Bank lending for power, communications, transportation, and other infrastructural projects facilitated the extraction of raw materials and the transportation of exports and imports and therefore reinforced the position of Third World
countries as more efficient suppliers of raw materials and more avid consumers
of manufactured goods produced in the First World. This was the most "efficient"
arrangement in the eyes of the World Bank, the reason why it refused loans to
countries such as Perón's Argentina, which sought an independent path to development through the nationalization of foreign-owned corporations, import
substitution, and greater regional interdependence. In short, the bank's policies
had the effect of fostering dependent development in the Third World, resulting
in the exportation of both raw materials and profits to the First World.[43]

The World Bankers' belief that they must confine their activities to the "economic" realm also served to undercut its promise that economic development
would foster a respect for democracy and individual freedom. Their insistence
on evaluating only the economic merits of a loan and their refusal to consider its
political implications led the bank to make a number of development loans to
oppressive right-wing dictatorships as well as governments fighting to quash nationalist independence movements. The Netherlands received a World Bank loan
of $195 million less than a month after launching an internationally condemned
"police action" against the Indonesian nationalist republic governing the islands
of Java and Sumatra, in direct violation of the Linggadjati agreement signed earlier by the two parties. Because the World Bank deemed the reconstruction needs
of the Netherlands to be "of such a general nature," the loan terms were of "a
general and flexible character," which meant that there could be no effective end-
use supervision of the loan and that the Dutch now had the financial resources
they needed to wage war against the Indonesian nationalists. The bank also made
loans to dictators in Nicaragua and the Philippines, as well as to Portugal and
South Africa even after their flagrant human rights abuses led to UN resolutions
calling for an end to economic aid to both countries.[44] More generally, the World
Bank's concentration on the economic aspects of its loans, notwithstanding its
limited calls for Third World land reform and income redistribution, helped foster an increasing gap between the rich and poor in developing countries. In other
words, the World Bankers' differentiation between a "political" realm that was
outside of their purview and an "economic" realm with which they dealt allowed
them to ignore the political consequences of the economic policies they cham-
pioned and to avoid dealing with certain "political" issues, such as human rights
and economic justice, that clearly were tied to the economic structure.[45]

A second reality that was partially concealed beneath the bankers' differentiation between the "political" and the "economic" was the role that the World Bank played in the Cold War as it sought to spread a form of liberal capitalism. The World Bank, with initial resources of $10 billion, in many ways served as the West's counter to the Soviet Union's model of state-directed economic development in the bipolar battle for the loyalty of the developing countries after World War II. Development aid also seemed to promise the possibility of splitting the communist monolith, at least in the immediate postwar period. Although the Soviet Union never joined the World Bank after the Bretton Woods Conference, Czechoslovakia and Poland were members for several years. The bank staff began serious negotiations with both countries for reconstruction loans that might have fostered economic ties between Western and Eastern Europe had the United States, increasingly wedded to a Cold War policy of containment, not refused to back such loans. Indeed, World Bank criticism of U.S. foreign aid policies mainly flowed from a belief that they would harm the acceptance of liberal capitalist principles by Third World governments.[46]

The World Bankers' professional backgrounds, which separated economic and political factors, also led them to homogenize ideas and methods of economic development through their loan process and training programs. Indeed, upon reflection, it is not surprising that India, with its Oxbridge-educated corps of civil servants, received the lion's share of development aid during the period 1945–60, while the World Bank rejected other development loan proposals that lacked the statistical information and Western-style economic analysis it required. By establishing this type of analysis as a condition for funding, the bank provided an important incentive for Third World bureaucrats to adhere to its method of analysis and planning, even when such methods failed to contribute to an understanding of the critical development problems facing Third World economies. In addition to providing the incentive, the World Bankers provided the means, with some 1,300 Third World nationals passing through the doors of the EDI by 1971. For those governments lacking such a Westernized development bureaucracy, the bank dispatched technical missions that made a series of suggestions on constructing national economic plans.

According to some critics, such prescriptions were the wrong path to economic development, because they tended to create a literate, educated minority to manage, and in some cases impose, economic development rather than cultivate the enormous potential of the common people. Many who criticize the bank's efforts argue that a grassroots approach could have been executed more quickly and efficiently than a traditional, top-down development program and would have been more responsive to the needs of the people.[47] But the World Bankers under consideration here had no background or experience in such methods, which would have seemed experimental at the least when compared to what they saw as a large body of historical evidence dealing with the economic development of North America and Australia, as well as Europe's own process of industrialization.

The World Bankers' models of development also left out other crucial issues, such as the role of women in development and the effects of this process on indigenous people and the environment. The World Bankers, who were still 92.6 percent male as late as 1972, acted as if productive economic activity lay distinctly within the male sphere. The nonremunerative contributions of the world's women to the global economy were not recorded in the bankers' catalog of economic statistics and indices; they were thereby rendered invisible. It was the World Bankers' unspoken belief that economic development, urbanization, and modernization would naturally improve women's lot in life, but in fact the World Bankers' development strategies contributed to the erosion of women's status and economic well-being throughout the Third World during the fifties and sixties. New factories, which employed mostly men, supplanted many traditional craft industries that employed women. Even when women were not legally barred from new avenues of opportunity in the cities, societal traditions and taboos kept most of them in traditional or strictly sex-segregated roles. Development planners, far from recognizing the conundrum facing Third World women, branded them "backward," enamored with traditional ways, and unable to seize the increased opportunities offered to them. Therefore, the cumulative effect of economic development efforts during the first twenty years of the World Bank was catastrophic for women.[48]

Mid-century economic development programs also ignored environmental considerations as well as the impact of such programs on indigenous peoples. Modernization meant integrating the Third World into the global economy and urging it to export more goods in order to repay development loans and make the necessary purchases of First World technology. But this course increased pressure to exploit mineral resources as well as renewable natural resources, such as exotic hardwoods and animal pelts, often depleting them at a dangerous pace. Industrialization and urbanization in the Third World also wreaked the same havoc as they had in Western Europe and North America at the turn of the century: industrial pollution of the air and water, dangerous and overcrowded tenement housing, insufficient sanitary facilities, unplanned urban expansion, and a lack of social services. Other people were affected adversely as well. The huge dams that provided irrigation waters and electrical power also flooded thousands of acres that had previously been homesteads and fertile farms. The construction of roadways to previously remote or inaccessible areas, meant to facilitate access to raw materials and create national markets, sometimes caused the destruction of indigenous peoples and their lifestyles. These peoples were forced to conform to modern economic mores, which meant that they often faced extinction through the expropriation of their tribal lands, the introduction of new and deadly diseases, and the violence frequently associated with conflict between very different cultures. These conflicts were especially prevalent in Latin American rain forest and tropical areas, which received a sizeable proportion of the bank's development loans throughout the 1950s and early 1960s. Many of the same consequences had arisen from the economic development of North America—as American settlers moved West, they had decimated Native American peoples and expropriated their lands.[49]

It seems, therefore, that the World Bankers had adopted a flawed model from the beginning. But many of these limitations were not immediately evident in the 1950s and 1960s, and no other model seemed as viable in the years after World War II. By the middle to late 1960s, however, World Bank officials had begun to realize that their economic development plans were not having the intended effect. The optimism with which Eugene Black had once discussed ways to narrow the income gap between rich and poor nations had dissipated by 1969 to such a point that Mohamed Shoaib, World Bank vice president, admitted that closing the gap was no longer "a realistic consideration."[50] The snail's pace of economic development was utterly puzzling to some veteran members of the bank, including Harold Graves, director of administration. In 1969 he shared his consternation with an Italian audience: "The big investments in many cases have not been quickly followed by all the activities which they were supposed to stimulate and to support. The big rock has been thrown into the pool, but through some perverse kind of sorcery only a few ripples have been the result." Clearly, Graves was puzzled by the failure of the bank's carefully researched and thought-out infrastructural programs and loans; the only possible explanation was some sort of "sorcery" that befuddled the best-laid plans of the bank and its claims to scientific management of the economic development process.[51] The evidence, however, suggests that ultimately it was not otherworldly sorcery but very worldly, cultural, ideological, and professional constraints that were the undoing of the World Bank's model of economic development.

It is also important to compare this early model of development financing to some later versions. In its first two decades, the bankers promoted high-quality projects that were initiated by the governments of those countries and that did not overburden the recipients with debt, a trend that unfortunately was not to continue during Robert S. McNamara's tenure as World Bank president. In its first seventeen years, the bank disbursed $953 million, while in the thirteen years between 1968 and 1981 it loaned $12.4 billion, a sixfold increase in real terms. In addition to its traditional infrastructural projects, the World Bank under McNamara's leadership loaned for education, disease eradication programs, agricultural and rural development, poverty alleviation, and economic structural adjustment. While some of these programs, such as the campaign against African river blindness and the dissemination of hybrid cereal crops that heralded the second "green revolution," were notable successes in many ways, the bank's loans ultimately overburdened Third World countries with debt. With a project default rate approaching 40 percent by the 1980s and the simultaneous Third World debt crisis, Black's World Bankers, by comparison, seem prudent and their caution appropriate.[52]

Despite their shortcomings and failures, therefore, it is important to place the World Bankers within their historical context. Few people in the two decades that followed World War II accounted for the environment, women, or indigenous peoples in making economic calculations. But the World Bankers were among the few who concentrated on important international issues during a Cold War and decolonization process that heightened nationalism. The bank's international staff did important work in setting high standards for economic development projects and using its expertise for the common good of the world's people. Even though they fell regrettably short in attaining their goals, we can see the World Bankers' manifest intentions and occasional victories in their work during these two decades, which included economic diplomacy in Iran, India, Pakistan, and Egypt during the 1950s.

4

The International Economic Diplomacy
of the World Bank

The World Bankers made several ventures into the realm of economic diplomacy during President Eugene Black's term in office, and these ventures were a direct outgrowth of their international identity, global worldview, and Progressive faith. The bank's staff and leadership sought to foster their role as global managers who could use their expertise to resolve disputes between different international actors and to protect the overall health of the world's economy. To play this role effectively, they asserted their collective international identity and cultivated an image of themselves as impartial and objective referees who could be trusted by governmental and nongovernmental organizations alike. The World Bankers assumed that international crises were amenable to rational solutions formulated by dispassionate professionals; seeing themselves as just such professionals, they developed innovative approaches to these extremely difficult diplomatic issues.

Concerned about the health of the global economy and convinced of the problem-solving capacities of reason, capital, and technical expertise, the World Bankers sought constructive solutions to the Anglo-Iranian oil crisis, Aswan High Dam financing, and the development of the Indus Basin, shared by Pakistan and India. These incidents not only provide insight into the worldview of the World Bankers but illustrate the interplay between the international professionalism of the World Bankers, the anticommunist imperative of American foreign policy, Third World nationalism, and Britain's diplomacy, pointing to the relative strengths and weaknesses of each of these constructions. As we will see, the internationalist, economic worldview of the bankers allowed them to be more tolerant of Third World nationalism and less encumbered by the ideological conflict of the Cold War than others tended to be. But they were by no means ensured success in these tortuous diplomatic negotiations, especially since their own worldview had its flaws.

The World Bankers clearly framed their international diplomatic ventures with the artificial dichotomy between the "economic" and the "political." They sought to deal only with what they defined as the economic—the rational, the quantifiable, the solvable—in international affairs. They reiterated that theirs was an economic institution, not a political institution in the mold of the UN General Assembly. Indeed, the World Bankers on occasion even suggested that the UN's acrimonious political debates "might well be more temperate and illuminating, and solution to the problems made easier, if the initiative for analyzing the issues and recommending appropriate action was vested in a non-political and objective international secretariat." The world, in other words, might be a better, more peaceful place if international diplomacy were handled in the same way that the World Bank supposedly handled international finance.[1]

The World Bankers believed that their institution was well equipped to do what interwar economic experts had been unable to accomplish—solve international economic problems through the application of dispassionate and disinterested expertise. Additionally, the bank's legal staff ruled that the institution's diplomatic efforts served the bank's members, furthered its general objectives, and therefore did not violate its Articles of Agreement, which were mute on the question of the bank practicing economic diplomacy. Given the World Bankers' international, professional worldview, it is not surprising that they employed a "loose construction" of the articles so as to play a larger role in international affairs.[2]

The Anglo-Iranian Oil Crisis

No single raw material was as important to the global economy of the 1950s as oil, and so the World Bankers saw using the bank's international identity to seek an interim solution to the Anglo-Iranian oil crisis at the end of 1951 as a valuable opportunity to bolster the world economy. On the first of May of that year, the Iranian Majlis nationalized the Iranian assets of the Anglo-Iranian Oil Company (AIOC). In the subsequent months, the British enforced a blockade against Iranian oil products, while Iran, led by nationalist prime minister Dr. Muhammad Mossadegh, expelled British citizens, rejected proposals for a new agreement from the hated AIOC, ignored Great Britain's appeal to the International Court of Justice (ICJ), and laid the issue before the UN Security Council. With Anglo-Iranian negotiations deadlocked in November 1951, World Bank vice president Robert Garner took advantage of Mossadegh's visit to the General Assembly to offer the bank's good offices to break the stalemate.[3]

The bank was willing to act as mediator in this dispute because the crisis was having negative effects on the international economy as a whole and especially on the British and Iranian economies, which had been deprived of AIOC oil revenues and royalties, respectively. The World Bankers believed that if they could resolve the economic aspects of the dilemma and get Iranian oil operations going again, the political components of the crisis would seem less urgent, each side would become more flexible, and outstanding issues would finally be settled. If, however, the situation worsened, Iran would continue to suffer from the economic recession that resulted from the loss of royalties and of seventy thousand jobs in the oil fields. This, in turn, might undermine the government and provoke a civil war between contending Iranian political factions. At the same time, the British government would suffer the double blow of losing both AIOC tax revenues and an important source of the Royal Navy's fuel. More dangerous yet, the West as a whole might lose Iran to a communist coup or civil war. For these reasons, the bankers decided to act.[4]

The bank's preliminary plan of action aimed at easing the financial difficulties of both sides in the dispute, minimizing the damage to the global economy, and thereby creating an environment favorable to a long-term settlement. The World Bank, as Garner outlined the plan to Mossadegh, would arrange the funds necessary to resume operations in Iran and then act as trustee of the oil fields and the huge Abadan refinery, operating the properties and marketing the oil through established AIOC distribution channels. The proceeds from the sale of the oil, minus the World Bank's operating costs, would be held in trust pending a final compensation settlement between Iran and the AIOC.[5] Mossadegh encouraged Garner to make this same proposal to the British, who responded that the bank's scheme offered "good possibilities." In the resulting talks, the British insisted that AIOC employees should continue to run the Iranian oil industry and that the AIOC should continue to purchase and market both crude and refined oil products. The company and the British government were also anxious that any interim pricing schedule established by the bank not exceed a fifty-fifty profit split between the company and the country, as this had been the basis of the abortive final offer that the AIOC had made to Mossadegh's government.[6]

With a tentative go-ahead from both sides, the World Bank staff began drafting a formal proposal that it believed would salvage the Iranian oil industry and appease Iranian nationalism. The British, Iranians, and Americans all looked to the bank as the best chance for bringing an early and constructive end to the crisis. In order to restore the flow of oil and protect the legal rights of all parties, the World Bankers believed, it was essential that they themselves exercise exclusive managerial control, including full discretion to hire and fire personnel. They fully intended to rehire much of the former AIOC staff, including British nationals, because these individuals were most familiar with the Iranian operations and could speed their resumption. The bank's staff mistakenly believed the Iranians would accept the reintroduction of British workers, so long as they were responsible to the World Bank and therefore implicitly apolitical. To ease Iranian concerns about sovereignty, the bank created the position of full-time senior liaison between its interim management and the Iranian government and also agreed to provide complete information on the Iranian operations to both sides, concessions that the

AIOC had steadfastly refused to make. The bank, which above all wanted to avoid political disputes, gave the Iranian government responsibility for providing social and municipal services to the employees of the oil field and refinery.[7]

These hopes were soon dashed. When the World Bank's mission to Iran at the end of December formally presented this plan to the Iranian government, it learned how far apart the bankers' view of the crisis was from that of the Iranians. While the World Bankers hoped to avoid the thicket of political questions surrounding the crisis by approaching it as a strictly economic and technical matter, the Iranians clearly believed that any settlement, interim or final, was a matter of national interest and prestige and therefore could not be reduced to technicalities. Additionally, the bankers' focus on economic issues largely mirrored that of the AIOC, which also apparently failed to grasp the dimensions of Iranian nationalism.

Hector Prud'homme, the World Bank loan officer responsible for the Middle East region, and Captain Torkild Rieber, the bank's oil consultant and president of the independent Barber Oil Corporation of New York, began a fact-finding mission to Iran on New Year's Eve, 1951. They were to visit Abadan, evaluate the condition of the production and refining operations, and feel out the Iranian position on the dispute. Even before they left the United States, however, the United Press wire carried a statement by Mossadegh to the effect that talks with the World Bank had broken down because of British and bank insistence on a discount on oil sales to Great Britain. In addition, a member of the Majlis Oil Commission announced that Iran could alleviate its economic crisis by selling no more than five or six million tons of oil per year, an amount that it could produce without the reintroduction of foreign technicians. He further asserted that the publicly stated desire of the bank and the British to resume production and refining at 1950 levels was evidence of the West's desperate need for Iranian oil. Additionally, three days before the arrival of the bank mission, there was a riot in Tehran protesting the intervention of the World Bank in the crisis.[8]

These circumstances quickly convinced Rieber and Prud'homme that it would be difficult to contain their negotiations to the economic aspects of the case. Although the Iranians asserted that they "would be grateful" if the bank could arrange "a return to cordial relations" between their country and Great Britain, their reservations had been accurately reported by the press. Rieber, knowing that the bank's preliminary terms included rehiring British nationals, cautioned Mossadegh that obtaining the services of the large number of oil technicians needed to restart the Abadan refinery would be impossible if all British citizens were excluded. But the prime minister stood firm, and Prud'homme and Rieber began considering alternative marketing and personnel arrangements that might be more politically acceptable to the Iranians but still in line with economic realities. Prud'homme was concerned that if the British got "their backs up" about Iranian conditions, the bank would not be able to conclude an agreement and that without one the Iranians might pump, refine, and sell whatever oil they could at whatever price they could obtain. Such a scenario would lead the big oil companies to slash their prices in order to drive the Iranian industry into bankruptcy, and economic and political conditions in Iran would continue to deteriorate.[9]

The collision of Iran's nationalism with the World Bank's economic approach to the crisis came when Mossadegh received the bank's proposed interim agreement on 3 January 1952. Its assertion that the bank would engage personnel without respect to nationality and would market Iranian oil through established British channels angered the prime minister, as did the implication that the AIOC would receive one-third of Iran's oil proceeds under the proposed interim agreement. Mossadegh said the proposal "smacked of British high-handedness" and suggested that the bank "was merely a tool of the British." He made the same arguments in his written response to the World Bank, implying as well that Garner had violated the general principles agreed to in Washington. Since Iran was in full control of its oil industry, Mossadegh argued that any agreement to extract, refine, and market Iranian oil would have to acknowledge that the bank was acting solely on behalf of the Iranian government. Any implication that it was also acting on behalf of the AIOC, he said, would violate the spirit of Iran's nationalization decree.[10]

In response, the World Bankers tried to ease Iranian concerns by explaining the economic and business rationale behind the preliminary agreement. As an international organization, Garner restated, the bank could act only as a friendly, neutral facilitator working for the benefit of all parties involved. Furthermore, while only the Iranian government could authorize the bank to operate its oil properties, government micromanagement or hiring restrictions would impair the bank's ability to run the industry efficiently. Garner did back away from the bank's original language about a three-way distribution of profits, on the understanding that the AIOC would be compensated with Iranian oil products, but he stuck to the original position that the bulk of the oil exports would be sold through British channels. Such views led the U.S. ambassador to Iran, Loy Henderson, to conclude rather incredulously that the World Bankers seem to be "enveloped" in an "unrealistic atmosphere."[11]

The World Bank mission in Tehran grew increasingly frustrated as the political aspects of the negotiations seemed to overshadow what it saw as the more important economic realities. Prud'homme even suggested that the bank might leave the Iranians to "run their own show," believing that the travails of trying to restart their oil industry without extensive foreign technical aid would "teach the Iranians a lesson" and thereby improve the chance of reaching "a more desirable arrangement." Guided by this kind of thinking and convinced that there was nothing left for them to do in Iran, Prud'homme and Rieber ended their visit after two weeks, on 13 January 1952.[12]

The impasse continued when Garner traveled to Iran in February to make another attempt to reach an interim settlement. U.S. secretary of state Dean Acheson, British foreign minister Sir Anthony Eden, and Mossadegh all held out some hope that the bank's newest effort might break the deadlock, for none of them foresaw many other diplomatic options. Together with Rieber, Prud'homme, Samuel Lipkowitz of the bank's economic department, and Ellsworth Clark of the legal department, Garner hammered out a memorandum of agreement that Clark considered "a big step forward." The agreement, however, concealed "some very difficult problems, and in some cases [was] deliberately designed to do so." In the document the bank gave Iran veto power over all marketing arrangements, and the two sides agreed to a two-way split of oil profits, with the AIOC's share going into an escrow account on which the company could draw only after all aspects of the crisis had been settled. Two problems remained, though. One was the unresolved issue of British technicians and the other was that the bank, clinging to its international and apolitical identity, still refused to state that it was operating solely on behalf of Iran. This refusal kept Iran from signing the draft agreement.[13]

With this setback, the World Bankers realized that a solely economic solution was unlikely, but they still sought to arrange a solution to this global economic crisis. Recognizing the Iranians' "deep-rooted and pathological suspicion and fear of British political domination" and seeing no way to negotiate a workable interim agreement without British oil technicians, Garner asked the United Kingdom to make a concession. He asked it to withdraw its case from the World Court, where it was contesting the legality of the Iranian national decree, and instead enter into arbitration over compensation for the nationalized properties. Garner believed this de facto recognition of Iranian nationalization would be a political plum for the Mossadegh regime and might allow it to readmit British technicians, thereby making the bank plan workable without threatening Iran's fragile nationalist political coalition. The second prong of Garner's plan for gaining Iranian acceptance of the interim agreement involved Hossein Makki, Mossadegh's oil adviser and an opponent of the proposed agreement. Garner invited him to visit the United States and consult with U.S. oilmen, at the bank's expense. The World Bankers hoped that this would enlighten the Iranians about the "facts" of the situation and make them realize that technical, rather than political, criteria underlay the bank's insistence on readmitting British nationals.[14]

Rather than improving the situation, Garner's efforts provoked a public denunciation from the Iranians that obliged the bank to defend its international identity. Since the British had not been willing to go as far as recognizing Iran's nationalization and because the Iranians mistakenly believed that the invitation to Makki was a sign of the World Bank's willingness to meet Iran's original terms, the bank had little room for maneuvering in its March meetings in Iran. Less than two weeks after the negotiations started, an Iranian official told the press that the impasse between the two sides had occurred because the bank "acted against the prestige of Iran and gave unacceptable reasons for the return of the British experts." If the bank had truly wanted a settlement, he contended, American technicians, untainted by collaboration with the AIOC, could have been substituted for their British counterparts at the Abadan refinery. He asserted further that the bank's intransigence made its motives suspect. Prud'homme, annoyed by these statements, responded in the press that Iran had treated the bank with the same distrust as it would an interested national power, when in fact the bank had always conducted itself as a neutral international institution with the best interest of all its members in mind. The bank also felt impelled to issue a "factual summary" of the negotiations to date in order to counter the allegations of bad faith voiced by the Iranians. Although the U.S. State Department discouraged such disclosure because it might prevent any further negotiations between the bank and Iran, the World Bank felt compelled to defend its carefully cultivated reputation as an international, technical, and, therefore, apolitical institution.[15]

Despite strained relations, the World Bank continued to search for a combination of economic and political conditions that could solve the British-Iranian imbroglio. The World Bankers seriously considered suggestions that the bank agree to run, or hire a neutral international firm to run, the Iranian oil industry for an extended period of up to ten years. Such an extraordinary long-term commitment might dispel Iranian suspicions and thereby give the bank the freedom to hire whatever personnel it believed necessary and provide discounted oil to the AIOC in order to settle all outstanding British claims against Iran. But both sides in the conflict became more intransigent, each sensing that events were going its way: the British and AIOC saw the world oil industry expand to compensate for lost Iranian production and so became reluctant to make concessions; the Iranians were heartened by an ICJ ruling that Iran's nationalization decree was legal. As a result, the World Bankers ultimately found it impossible to disentangle the political and economic aspects of the situation. Seeing themselves as realistic businessmen and financial experts, they were frustrated by the Iranian negotiators, who seemed "bemused by hopes and theories, rather than guided by what is practical and possible in this very matter-of-fact, complicated industry."[16]

The Anglo-Iranian crisis came to an end in the summer of 1953, when a combination of popular and army discontent and Anglo-American covert operations led to Mossadegh's overthrow and left Muhammad Reza Shah as the absolute leader of Iran. After bitter negotiations involving an economically ravaged Iran, a largely powerless AIOC, and a frustrated yet powerful United States, the parties agreed to create a multinational Iranian oil consortium, a nominally nationalized group of Western firms with full rights to manage oil output and prices. Iran received formal title to all its oil and a fifty-fifty division of the net profits of production, but no share of the marketing or distribution operations. This was certainly less than the

Iranians had hoped for and in some ways less than the World Bank had offered in its proposed interim agreement. But given the British distaste for Mossadegh and the Foreign Office's stubborn refusal to make concessions, even after Mossadegh's overthrow and under intense American pressure, it seems unlikely that the World Bank could have negotiated an agreement acceptable to both sides.

Perhaps the World Bankers' belief that they could separate the economic and political aspects of the Anglo-Iranian oil crisis was unrealistic. Still, the bankers' plan did seem to offer a better solution than history provided. The World Bank's proposed interim settlement offered the Iranian government a way to ease its immediate financial problems, maintain its share of world oil output, and receive more effective control over its oil industry than it had under the AIOC. Additionally, if Iran had been able to reach an interim agreement with the World Bank at the beginning of 1952, the country and its people would have been spared much of the economic hardship of the oil crisis and the sociopolitical upheaval of Mossadegh's subsequent ouster. But in 1952, the World Bank's offer did not seem very tempting to either Iran or to Great Britain. The bank had only some managerial and engineering expertise and a short-term start-up loan to offer, at a time when the British hoped the International Court would nullify the AIOC expropriation and the Iranians expected an American loan that would solve their short-term economic problems.[17] In other words, both countries hoped to advance their national interests without having to compromise, and this zero-sum goal made them unreceptive to the World Bank's proposals, even though these proposals might have better served both countries' best interests over the long term.

The Ten-Year Journey toward the Indus Waters Treaty

The World Bank's combination of capital and technical expertise, which had not been enough to settle the Anglo-Iranian oil crisis, nonetheless proved key to the bank's most successful and arduous excursion into international economic diplomacy—the negotiations that culminated in the Indus Waters Treaty of 1960 between India and Pakistan. At the time of Indian independence, the Indus Valley supported the largest irrigation system in the world, serving approximately fifty million people. The partition of the subcontinent in 1947 divided the river system between the rival powers of India and Pakistan. Pakistan feared that India, which controlled the headwaters, might cut off Pakistan's water, turning its fields quite literally into a desert. The bank's ability to forge an amicable agreement for sharing and developing the resources of the Indus removed a source of great friction between the contentious neighbors, provided increased water resources for both countries, and established a more stable basis for further economic development.[18]

Negotiations between the two nascent nations prior to World Bank involvement demonstrated that suspicion, combined with a desperate need for water, would make a mutually beneficial settlement very difficult. India and Pakistan had reached in May 1948 a preliminary agreement on the management of these waters by which India would only gradually reduce the flow of water into Pakistan, with the understanding that during that time the latter would develop alternate irrigation sources. The Pakistani government later declared that it had signed the agreement only to prevent India from cutting off its waters from the Indus and that the accord, signed under duress, was invalid. This was the unsettled state of affairs when David Lilienthal, former director of the Tennessee Valley Authority (TVA), visited the subcontinent in 1951 and published an article in *Collier's* suggesting that the Indus be developed jointly for the benefit of both countries, just as the TVA had served the needs of several U.S. states. One month after the article appeared, the bank, following consultations with the American and British governments, offered its good offices and technical support for negotiations concerning further development of the Indus along the lines suggested by Lilienthal.[19]

The World Bank's call for technical and economic discussions about the Indus system was not universally appreciated. Pakistan enthusiastically accepted the bank's offer, as it had little to lose, but India declared that any negotiations would have to build upon the May 1948 agreement. The negotiations might well have been stillborn at that point had not Eugene Black, during a trip to South Asia the next month, convinced India to send engineers to Washington to work with Pakistani and World Bank engineers in formulating a plan for the Indus. In the meantime, both sides agreed to a standstill agreement under which neither would diminish the water available to the other for existing uses.

The incredibly complex nature of drafting a technical plan for the river system taxed the World Bank's technical expertise. The water flow of each of the six rivers that made up the Indus system varied from year to year and even month to month, and each river was subject to such variables as seepage and evaporation. Hoping to establish a reliable technical basis for the negotiations, Raymond A. Wheeler, a retired lieutenant general of the U.S. Army Corps of Engineers and the bank's engineering advisor, made a nine-thousand-mile fact-finding trip through the Indus system with Pakistani and Indian counterparts. Back in Washington, however, they were still unable to agree on a basis for joint planning, and each side began drafting its own plan for what it considered an equitable utilization of the Indus waters. The subsequent plans diverged substantially on important issues and threatened a new deadlock, so Wheeler formulated an independent bank proposal that he hoped would provide a technical solution and avoid political rancor. His straightforward plan would reserve the three western branches of the Indus for Pakistan, the eastern rivers for India, and leave each country free to construct storage facilities to avoid reliance upon waterworks on the other side of the border. To make up for the reduced flow to Pakistan, India would finance Pakistan's efforts to tap water sources other than the Indus. The bank believed that the plan was "simple, workable, and fair," but the Pakistani delegate was outraged that the bank was proposing to reduce the flow of water into his country by excluding the resources of the eastern rivers. The Pakistani prime minister backed up his position, and only World Bank threats to blame Pakistan publicly for a breakdown in negotiations kept that nation at the bargaining table.

With talks now two years old, the bank sought to appease the political sensibilities of both countries while maintaining its focus on the technical and economic aspects of the debate. As a concession to Pakistan, the bank appointed William A. B. Iliff, the bank's vice president, to succeed Wheeler as its ranking negotiator. The bank also hired its own consulting engineers to survey the situation and to draft two plans: a minimum plan to meet the historic uses of both countries and an optimal plan that would allow greater development and fuller utilization of the rivers' resources. The engineers' conclusions changed the complexion of the talks; additional storage works on both sides, they revealed, would be necessary even to maintain the status quo. In the meantime, a twelve-hour shoot-out between Pakistani border police and Indian troops dispatched to repair damage to one of the Indus irrigation canals reminded everyone of the potentially explosive nature of the problem. Increasing frictions and the high cost of the projected storage facilities brought negotiations to a standstill for another year.

The bank's ability to mobilize vast economic resources was the key to the next breakthrough in the talks. Technical talks brought the two sides no closer to agreement, but the bank's promise of aid to finance both Indian and Pakistani water storage schemes had the desired effect. Additionally, Black established a good relationship with Pakistani field marshal Ayub Khan, who now ruled the country and accepted a flow limited to the three western rivers. The World Bankers followed up on this tentative agreement with a series of bank-negotiated grants from Great Britain, the United States, members of the British Commonwealth, and West Germany to underwrite both countries' water storage facilities.[20] With an agreement in sight, Black and Iliff traveled to the subcontinent in May 1959, seven years after the talks had begun. There they received tentative approval from both sides, but disagreement over the schedule of water transfers during the transition period threatened to end the talks. Bank threats to withdraw its good offices and then two further rounds of concessions by India preceded the signing of the Indus Waters Treaty in the fall of 1960. The World Bank, with a great investment of time and resources, had performed a great service to the subcontinent.[21] The bank's international stature, technical expertise, and ability to grease the wheels of diplomacy with cash had been key to its success.

The World Bank's diplomatic efforts succeeded in the Indus Basin for a number of reasons. First of all, neither country in the dispute had a better alternative. Unlike the situation in the Anglo-Iranian oil crisis, India and Pakistan were unable to turn to covert operations, play the superpowers off one another, or negotiate construc- tively without mediation, so World Bank intervention was welcome. The World Bankers offered continuity, patience, technical expertise, and the ability to rally millions of dollars in development aid. Freed from superpower political intrigue, they were able to focus on the economic and technical aspects of the dispute, bring their expertise and professionalism to bear on the problem in a meaningful way, and therefore reinforce their own belief in their ability to improve the functioning of the international community. Their success should cause us to consider whether other international disputes would have been more easily resolved if they had been considered on their economic and technical merits rather than within the politi- cally charged, ideological context of the Cold War. It seems that the parties in the Anglo-Iranian crisis would have benefited from such an approach, and as we will see, the Suez crisis might also have been averted by an apolitical approach. The World Bank's economic diplomacy therefore casts a critical light on Anglo-Ameri- can diplomacy in the Cold War and on Third World countries' tendency to play superpowers off one another and thereby exacerbate international crises, making peaceful settlements unlikely.

The World Bank and the Aswan High Dam

The World Bank brought the same technical and financial skills to bear on its at- tempt to arrange financing for the Aswan High Dam, but this time its attempt to practice purely economic diplomacy ran head-on into superpower politics on the banks of the Nile River.[22] The bank first considered Egyptian development plans as early as 1950. After a July 1952 coup overthrew King Farouk and installed Gener- al Mohammed Neguib and Gamal Abdel Nasser, the bank was quick to work with the new regime, which it regarded as "the best Egypt has had for a very long time" in terms of its strength of leadership, its potential for stability, and its integrity. Such a strong and popular leadership, combined with Egypt's foreign exchange earnings from the Suez Canal, seemed to offer the necessary ingredients for an effective economic development program. Less than five months after the Egyp- tian revolution, Black personally invited the new minister of finance and economy, H. E. Abdel Galeel El-Emary, to visit the bank and discuss Nile development. The next month Black visited Egypt, where the new government presented him with plans for a high dam at Aswan that could hold all of the river's annual floodwaters. Such a dam would make year-round irrigation possible, prevent flood damage, guard against low flood years, and generate a sizable amount of electricity.[23] Nass- er considered the project "an urgent necessity for our life," for by allowing Egypt to increase substantially the amount of land under cultivation, the dam had the potential to raise the country's standard of living, meet the needs of a rapidly expanding population, and thereby fulfill Nasser's promise of two revolutions—not just a military revolution to depose a despised tyrant but also a social revolution that aimed for "a society built on justice, freedom, and equality."[24]

The bank's lending criteria soon dissipated the initial goodwill between the new Egyptian government and the World Bank, however. Nasser had already hired a West German firm to draw up specific plans for the project, formed an international commission to oversee the work, and applied for a $400 million World Bank loan to cover the estimated foreign exchange costs of constructing the dam. When the bank's loan offer was hedged with conditions and delivered to Cairo via the U.S. embassy, Nasser began to suspect that Black's initial enthusiasm for the project had been feigned and that the bank was in league with what he termed "the imperialist nations." He incorrectly believed that the bank, under Anglo-American orders, was dragging its feet in order to force Egypt into a compromise with Sudan, still under British suzerainty, over Nile water rights. The Aswan dam had the potential to expand Sudan's available water resources, but it would also flood an area that contained some thirty thousand Sudanese farms and homes. The British and Sudanese governments wanted to ensure an equitable division of the additional waters and proper compensation for the relocation of the displaced population before dam plans proceeded.[25]

Nasser's charge of bank collusion with Great Britain was a direct challenge to the bank's international self-image and threatened its ability to encourage economic development in the Middle East, an area with great potential for development but particularly sensitive to a revival of Western imperialism. Therefore, in January 1954 the bank sought to dispel Nasser's "erroneous impression" by dispatching to Egypt its Beirut-based representative, F. Dorsey Stephens, and Mohammed Shoaib, a Pakistani who represented the Middle East on the World Bank's executive board.[26] These bankers sought to allay Egyptian anxieties by explaining that the bank's reservations about the dam project were based on purely economic and technical concerns that were in no way connected to Anglo-American politics. The insistence on a pre-investment study of the resources of the Nile River, the bankers asserted, stemmed not from Anglo-American pressure but from the World Bank's duty as an international organization to consider the needs of all of its members who shared the resources of the Nile. As a conciliatory gesture, moreover, the bank promised a quick study of Nile resources and dispatched a technical mission to examine the work already undertaken on the dam to that point. These gestures apparently reassured Nasser. When Egyptian representatives visited bank headquarters in September 1954, they said that Egypt regarded the bank as "the only channel" for the foreign exchange loans needed to finance the dam and was gratified by the bank's interest in the project. In response, Black emphasized "that Egypt and the Bank have the same interests" in regard to the dam and that his institution was "ready to get busy" on the project.[27]

Though relations had been smoothed between Egypt and the World Bank, the bank's self-identification as an international economic institution continued to cause problems for the Egyptians. The bank still insisted that "because of its status as an international institution" it could not determine Egypt's creditworthiness or proceed with financing for the dam without an agreement between Egypt and Sudan on water rights and compensation for the relocated Sudanese.[28] Another obstacle arose early in 1955, when it became evident that Egypt, in order to speed the start of construction, wanted to award all the construction, engineering, and equipment contracts as a block to a single consortium of European firms organized by the West German company (the Hochtief and Dortmunder Union) that had drawn up the original plans for the high dam. The bank pointed out that competitive bidding was both a prerequisite for World Bank loans and in Egypt's best interest, because the bank's experience had shown that there was "no such thing as a 'standard price'" and that firms often put in bids "differing up to 30% and sometimes more."[29] These concerns mirrored, but preceded, similar concerns expressed by Great Britain and the United States, which began working with the World Bank in May 1955 on plans for financing the dam.

Nasser's announcement on 27 September 1955 that his country would purchase arms from Czechoslovakia provides a telling contrast between the World Bank's relationship with Nasser and that of the British and American governments. The latter considered the Czech arms deal a serious blow to their interests in the Middle East. State Department officials feared that it would endanger their Arab-Israeli peace initiative and their attempt to contain Soviet expansion along the Northern Tier. The Foreign Office worried about the security of the Suez Canal and about British prestige in the Middle East. In an effort to limit the damage and draw Nasser closer to the Western camp, the British and American governments agreed in December 1955 to underwrite approximately half of the foreign exchange costs of the dam.[30]

For his part, however, Black went out of his way in meetings with the Egyptian finance minister to state that the bank's attitude toward Aswan had not been swayed in the least by Nasser's arms purchase. The bank also took measures to ensure that in brokering an Anglo-American–World Bank financial package, it would not be seen as an agent of the British and U.S. governments but rather as an international institution that was simply offering its good offices. Black believed he was in a particularly difficult position as liaison between the bank and these three countries, because "I was with an international organization, and I had to keep my dealings free from politics." But as he had to admit, the bank "had as partners in [the Aswan project] men who were involved in politics," and it "had to have those partners to carry the deal through." Despite the bank's efforts to separate economic and political criteria, its "economic" reservations largely mirrored Anglo-American "political" reservations about Egypt. The bank's policy of close end-use supervision of loaned funds as well as its negative pledge commitment (which required a borrowing nation to make no commitments to other lenders that might impair its ability to repay the World Bank) seemed to preclude any further Egyptian purchases of Soviet-bloc arms.[31]

Showing its good faith, the World Bank worked to soften the impact of its loan requirements, iron out a final financial agreement with the American and British governments, and speed the beginning of construction. The bank had already worked with the U.S. Treasury to pressure Great Britain into gradually releasing Egypt's accumulated wartime pound-sterling reserves, which had been held in London to support the British currency. This significantly improved Egypt's ability to finance the foreign exchange costs of the dam. At the same time, the bank was willing to compromise on the Sudan issue, stating that it would not demand a ratified treaty but only a mutual agreement on outstanding issues. The World Bankers also opted to accept simultaneous negotiations with more than one consortium as meeting bank requirements for competitive bidding. Even when the U.S. government proved unwilling and legally unable to provide foreign aid funds for a project that would exclude American firms (which would be the case if all the contracts were awarded to the European consortium), the bank worked on a compromise that would exempt the first stage of the Aswan project from the bank's competitive bidding provision and use British contributions exclusively. As it turned out, however, this option was foreclosed by the Exchequer, which lacked the resources to finance any part of the project on its own, and by the State Department, which opposed American participation without competitive bidding.[32] Although the Egyptians chafed under the bank's loan conditions, these provisos were standard in international lending.

Despite the bank's efforts to address Egyptian concerns, it took some personal diplomacy on Black's part to dispel Nasser's contention that the bank's conditions violated his country's sovereign rights. When Black traveled to Egypt at the end of January 1956, he tried to convince the Egyptian leader that the bank's conditions were "perfectly reasonable" and, in fact, "just as much in the interest of Egypt as anybody else." After much hesitation, Nasser agreed to World Bank/U.S. competitive bidding requirements and postponed the start of construction until an agreement had been reached with Sudan. But he was unwilling to sign a final agreement until Britain and America guaranteed aid for the second as well as the first stage of the Aswan project. Black sought to assure the Egyptian leader that such aid would be forthcoming, but Nasser did not want Anglo-American aid to become a diplomatic lever that could be used against him. Indeed, when Nasser remained adamant about up-front financial promises and retained a strongly independent foreign policy, secretary of state John Foster Dulles and prime minister Anthony Eden considered harsher measures to bring the Egyptian leader into line with their own plans in the region.[33]

When Black returned from Cairo, he found himself entwined in just the sort of political conundrum that he had hoped to avoid: British and American states- men appeared ready to renege on their previous pledges to fund the dam. Dulles was facing bitter congressional opposition to aid for Aswan from the Israel lobby, from Southern senators who feared increased Egyptian competition in the inter- national cotton market, and from congressmen opposed to granting any aid to nonaligned countries. Nasser's recognition of the People's Republic of China fur- ther piqued congressional antipathy. On the British side, after Lieutenant-General Sir John Glubb, the head of the Arab Legion, and his senior British officers were ousted from Jordan at the alleged instigation of Nasser, Eden came to believe that Nasser was Britain's "Enemy No. 1 in the Middle East" and therefore had to go. Anglo-American attempts to foster anticommunism through the Baghdad Pact and to broker an Arab-Israeli settlement were also under attack by Nasser and his *Voice of the Arabs* radio broadcasts. Nevertheless, in another attempt to salvage the situation, Black visited Nasser in June 1956, with the disingenuous encourage- ment of the U.S. State Department and the British Foreign Office and succeeded in getting Egypt to accept the conditions of the Anglo-American–World Bank loan without amendment.[34]

Black returned to Washington after having cleared all remaining economic hur- dles, only to find the rug pulled out from under him by his Anglo-American part- ners. The United Kingdom and the United States had decided to abandon the "car- rot" of Aswan funding, in an attempt to discipline Nasser. When Black returned from Egypt, Dulles expressed concerns about the Egyptians' ability to finance the long-term dam project. Sensing that Dulles might be preparing to back out, Black assured the secretary of state that economic conditions in Egypt were unchanged and warned that all "hell might break loose" if the secretary withdrew his ear- lier offer. Black's worst fears were confirmed, however, when Dulles informed the Egyptian ambassador several days later that the Americans were withdrawing their aid offer because of U.S. and World Bank concerns about Egypt's economic ability to bring the project to fruition. Dulles's statement destroyed the prospects for an Aswan High Dam built with Western monies and also misrepresented the bank, which had remained willing to finance its part of the Aswan Dam because the World Bankers assessed its benefits independent of Egypt's fierce nationalism or its ideological position in the Cold War. In other words, the bank's offer had not been subject to the vagaries of international politics or questions of national prestige.[35]

In the subsequent Suez crisis, the British and Americans, as well as the World Bankers, reaped what they had sown. As is well known, Nasser responded to the loan cancellation by nationalizing the Suez Canal Company, as an alternate source of foreign exchange to fund the dam and as a symbolic act against the unrepentantly imperial attitude exemplified by the company. Because Dulles had also implicated the World Bank, Nasser believed that Black was in league with the British and Americans and even compared him to Ferdinand de Lesseps, the French builder of the Suez Canal, who was universally despised in Egypt for bringing the country under foreign control. After the nationalization, the British, French, and Israelis in turn invaded Egypt in October and November 1956, only to be met by opposition from both superpowers and many members of the United Nations. The Egyptians eventually built the dam, the initial domino in this chain of events, with aid from the Soviet Union. Reflecting back on the entire incident in 1964, Black noted that the entire foreign exchange cost of the dam would have totaled considerably less than the cost of the invasion and subsequent cleanup. Black was quite knowledgeable about these costs, because after clearing the bank's reputation with Nasser, the bank played a key role in reopening the canal and restoring economic relations between Egypt and the international community.[36]

To minimize the economic damage of the Suez crisis and to prove its good faith to Nasser, the World Bank undertook the work of clearing and reopening the canal. On 24 November 1956, at the suggestion of former World Bank president John J. McCloy, the bank loaned Egypt, under UN auspices, the services of Lieutenant-General Raymond Wheeler, U.S. Army (Ret.), its engineering adviser, to direct the clearing of thirty vessels that Nasser had sunk in the canal to impede the invaders. In undertaking this considerable task, the septuagenarian general displayed all the hallmarks of an international civil servant.[37] Wheeler cooperated closely with Egyptian authorities and, under the UN flag, oversaw his Danish, Dutch, Italian, Yugoslav, American, Mexican, Swedish, German, Norwegian, and Belgian crew. When a Yugoslav crane team arrived and announced that it would work alone, Wheeler assigned it a particularly difficult task and graciously agreed several days later to add some Dutch crewmen to the team, an act that helped to build "the mood, spirit and zeal" of "a real UN team," according to Wheeler. The British and French were initially adamant about joining in the salvage effort, and the Egyptians delayed the clearance group's work on several occasions in order to serve its own diplomatic agenda. Nonetheless, Wheeler walked this tightrope with grace, earning the respect of the Egyptians, the United Nations, the multinational crew under his command, and even some of the British. Wheeler's team, perhaps provoked by the vote of "no confidence" that their chief received in the British Parliament, not only cleared the channel but also refloated most of the ships and repaired the canal's dredging, communications, lighting, and workshop facilities—all thirty-eight days ahead of schedule (in three months and six days) and considerably under budget. Wheeler's speed and skill left the British and French little leverage or time to prevent the operation of an Egyptian-owned and -operated canal, especially when Wheeler publicly commended the work of the Egyptian Suez

Canal administration. The bank acted as the fiscal agent for this effort, collecting and channeling UN member contributions into the project, as well as helping to ensure proper dredging of the channel once it had been cleared.[38]

The alliance between the World Bank and Nasser's Egypt continued after the clearance of the canal. In July 1958, after several months of bank-led negotiations, Black was able to negotiate some $80 million dollars for Universal Suez Canal Company stockholders. Later that same year, Black flew to Egypt hoping to break an eighteen-month deadlock on the settlement of claims filed by British enterprises and citizens whose property had been seized during the crisis. As was his custom, Black carefully framed his mission in international and economic terms: "My business in Cairo is purely financial. I am not involved in any political questions at all. . . . All I'm trying to do [is to] help two countries which are members of my Bank." Black's settlement of this issue, along with the restoration of relations between Egypt and the French and British governments, cleared the way for subsequent bank loans and assistance that had been contemplated as early as December 1957. This aid eventually allowed Egypt's Suez Canal Authority to deepen and widen the canal, thereby allowing for passage of larger ships and two-way traffic.[39]

This case study shows how the World Bankers' identity as international economic experts allowed them to be more tolerant of Third World nationalism and to follow a far more constructive policy toward Egypt than Great Britain and the United States. Yet the bank was largely powerless to steer its own course in the midst of a conflict rife with Cold War tension. Nonetheless, the openness of these international civil servants to Egyptian development projects showed a real desire to improve the lot of the Egyptian people, a desire that eventually won the grudging respect of Nasser; Black was ultimately able to convert this into a tremendously productive role in Egypt, not only promoting development but easing strained relations between the Egyptians and British. This constructive relationship was in stark contrast to Egypt's contentious relationships with both the United States and Great Britain.

Conclusion

When compared to U.S. aid programs and the Anglo-American propensity to overthrow Third World nationalist leaders who were not to their liking, the World Bank's aid and diplomacy seem to have offered a constructive alternative. In the settlement of the Indus Basin dispute, the World Bankers' combination of technical know-how, financial resources, and international stature allowed them to negotiate a settlement that served the interests of both India and Pakistan as well as those of the wider international community. In both the Anglo-Iranian oil crisis and the furor surrounding the proposed construction of the Aswan High Dam, the bank negotiated in good faith and proposed solutions that seemed to promise more favorable outcomes than those actually obtained—economic turmoil and an absolutist monarchy in Iran and a war in Egypt. The World Bankers offered different and potentially constructive alternatives in these contentious events, pointing to the benefits that can accrue from incorporating more and different voices and perspectives into international conflict resolution.

In their forays into diplomacy, the World Bankers remained largely true to the identity they had constructed for their institution and for themselves as international technical experts. They strove always to be above national issues, even when clinging to the bank's role as an international facilitator sabotaged its negotiations in the Anglo-Iranian oil crisis. When approaching diplomatic problems, these bankers could muster substantial amounts of capital and impressive technical expertise, as was evident in the clearing of the Suez Canal and the negotiation of the Indus Waters Treaty. In offering this economic and technical assistance, the World Bankers, while constantly reiterating the divide between the "political" and the "economic," clearly understood that the two could not be divorced. This rhetoric, however, reflected a realization that their contribution to the international sphere would come through their economic work and that there were more than enough political actors already on the world stage. Nonetheless, if they abhorred the overtly political diplomacy that sabotaged their efforts in both Iran and Egypt, the World Bankers in fact played their own nuanced, supporting role in the ideological and economic Cold War, promoting development of capitalist economies in the Third World even when those regimes, like Nasser's in Egypt, were frowned upon by the leaders of the "free world."

5

Food and Agriculture in the
International Realm

A spirit of internationalism first animated farmers, agricultural researchers, and national governments in the 1870s, in response to increased global competition in agricultural commodity markets, new scientific advances in farming, and price instability in world markets. In response to these changes, agricultural researchers convened international congresses to share their findings, and countries joined together in the International Institute of Agriculture (IIA) to centralize the collection of agricultural market statistics and to disseminate information on agricultural legislation, scientific advances, and national agricultural policies around the world. Farmers were more leery of these changes but also banded together into local, national, and international cooperative organizations, in the hope of managing the laws of supply and demand to their own advantage. But while technical innovations, price instability, and global competition stimulated international efforts, the importance of agriculture to national economic health and to wartime success meant that international cooperation coexisted with sometimes fierce agricultural autarchy.

Despite the sometimes transient support for agricultural cooperation, however, the development of a body of agricultural professionals, the birth of nutritional science, and other technical advances contributed to a growing transnational consensus about the role of agriculture in international relations. The fundamental tenets of this consensus, which emerged in the interwar period, included the belief that science could give farmers the ability to grow enough food to feed the world's population on a nutritionally sound basis. Although flaws in global agricultural marketing and pricing structures prevented a new era of worldwide abundance and prosperity, an international body of agricultural experts—guided by the objective standards of science, economics, and nutrition—might be able to remedy these shortcomings, stabilize global commodity markets, and feed the world. These ideas, which began to emerge in the late 1800s, were more fully developed by the League of Nations, led to the creation of the Food and Agriculture Organization (FAO) at the end of the Second World War, and animated the staff of this new organization. In other words, the agricultural profession was influenced by the same process of professionalization and the same concepts of cooperation and rational regulation that had influenced economists at the turn of the century, and later the World Bankers.

The Growth of Scientific Agriculture

In the 1870s, the world's farmers faced problems arising from the globalization of commodity markets that came with the advent of transoceanic steamships, the invention of practical refrigeration, and the cultivation of the vast grain-producing areas of the American and Canadian prairies, the Argentine pampas, and southern Australia. The result was a worldwide agricultural surplus and depression that lasted until the turn of the century; it drove government officials and agricultural journalists in many countries to promote science as the best way for farmers to gain an edge in international competition. One promising avenue of scientific advance came in 1900 with the rediscovery of Gregor Mendel's laws of heredity, which offered farmers a method to obtain better livestock and crops. But due to the small-scale, decentralized nature of agriculture at the turn of the century as well as the indifference and even hostility of many farmers, national governments and farmers' organizations had to undertake much of this research as well as the development of new agricultural technology.[1]

In the 1890s, Denmark's government, in cooperation with the Royal Danish Agricultural Society and the Royal Agricultural College and Experimental Station, persuaded Danish farmers to use science to reorient fundamentally their agricultural production. Unable to compete with grain farmers in the Western Hemisphere, they largely abandoned that crop in favor of the production of cheese, bacon, dairy products, eggs, and fruit. This change was made possible by a state-funded system of farm advisers, technical assistance to agricultural cooperatives, practical education, centralized testing of farm machinery, intensified seed testing, and work in plant breeding, animal husbandry, soil analysis, and plant pathology on six experimental farms. Support for scientific farming also came from farmer-organized cooperatives that followed the tenets of scientific breeding, maintained strict standards for the cream content of milk, centralized production in butter and cheese factories that incorporated the newest manufacturing techniques, and thereby carved out a niche in European markets by providing consistently high-quality, specialty products.[2]

New World competition also hurt British grain farmers who received aid in their battle to remain solvent from new research centers that had been created by agricultural societies, private enterprise, universities, and governments. The first such center, the Edinburgh Laboratory, was founded in 1842 with the support of the Agricultural Chemistry Association of Scotland, and this effort was followed a year later by the creation of the Rothamsted Experimental Station. To get the work of these research centers to farmers in the field, scientists and politicians also created agricultural extension and education programs, which, together with a growing agricultural press and county-funded traveling lecturers, attempted to popularize the improved implements, fertilizers, and scientific information that had become available.[3]

Government-directed agricultural research and education were most widespread in the United States. In 1862 Congress laid the foundation for scientific agriculture by creating a federal department of agriculture and a national system of land-grant colleges that specialized in agricultural and mechanical instruction; the Hatch Act of 1887 supplemented these institutions with a federally funded system of experimental research stations. Then under the leadership of James "Tama Jim" Wilson (1897–1913), the U.S. Department of Agriculture (USDA) expanded its scientific work and strengthened its ties with these land-grant colleges and research stations. It also conducted fundamental research on such things as animal husbandry, insect control, nutrition, irrigation, seed quality, and plant breeding, and in 1902 it established its own graduate school to promote further research.[4]

Because agricultural research that did not reach the farmer could bear no fruit, the federal government created a parallel system of education to augment its national system of research institutions. In 1902 the USDA began conducting demonstrations on local farms to educate farmers. Two years later, Seaman A. Knapp of the USDA created a system of county agents to continue this work on a broader and more intensive basis. With passage of the Smith-Lever Act of 1914, the county agent system received federal funding and evolved into a national system of farm bureaus that drew together the considerable expertise of the land-grant colleges, their affiliated experiment stations, the Department of Agriculture, and farmers. These extension agents spread their technical knowledge through farm demonstrations, engaged in scientific field research, and encouraged the organization of 4-H clubs.[5] The development of this national system of education, which reached not only farmers but also their wives and children, demonstrated the Progressive Era faith in the ability of education to persuade common people of the benefits to be derived from scientific and technological innovations.

The ability of this system of land-grant colleges, county agents, farm bureaus, research stations, and USDA employees to bring scientific breakthroughs to the American farmer became clear with the widespread acceptance in the 1930s of hybrid corn and artificial fertilizers, which revolutionized U.S. farm productivity. Hybrid corn resulted from the interrelated efforts of researchers from the Carnegie Institution and the Connecticut and Michigan agricultural experiment stations. It was then adapted by local experiment stations to the specific conditions of each state, marketed through private industry, and spread to America's farmers through farm demonstrations and cooperative extensions. By 1950 more than 75 percent of U.S. farms planted hybrid corn. During the same period, the National Fertilizer Development Center of the Tennessee Valley Authority conducted research on the physical and chemical properties of the new phosphate fertilizers and on the interactions between different types of plants, soils, and fertilizers. The center, in collaboration with private industry, generated research that drove down the real price of the new fertilizers; this development, together with hybrid corn, greatly enhanced farm productivity and highlighted science's promise for helping farmers.[6]

This national system of agricultural research and education soon gave birth to a growing body of agricultural professionals whose ideology bore a strong resemblance to that of their contemporaries in economics. The new agricultural professionals wanted not only to bring the findings of science and economics to bear on farming but also to create cooperative structures that would bring government, farmers, scientists, private industry, and educators together for the benefit of American agriculture. Part of this professional ideology called for these experts to enlighten government leadership about the need for such structures and to lobby actively for their creation. One of the first of these agricultural professionals was Seaman A. Knapp, who began his career by teaching practical and experimental agriculture at Iowa State College, where he served as president from 1883 to 1885. His desire to bring scientific findings to farmers led him to undertake field demonstration work with a grant from the Rockefeller Foundation Educational Board and later to conduct USDA research on boll-weevil control and ways to adapt Japanese short-grained rice to cultivation in Texas and Louisiana. Convinced that agricultural professionals must bring their expertise to bear on national policymaking as well as technical work, he also helped draft the Hatch Act, which provided federal funding for agricultural research stations. These stations acted as sites for public-private cooperation, bringing the USDA, land-grant colleges, scientists, and farmers together to develop practical applications for new technical discoveries.[7]

Another group of agricultural professionals came from the new field of agricultural economics, founded by Henry C. Taylor and John D. Black, both of whom, like their counterparts in the larger field of economics, prompted agricultural economists to serve society at large by active participation in the policymaking process. Additionally, William J. Spillman, trained in agricultural science, worked within the USDA to make economics work for the farmer. In 1902 he began pioneering work in farm management, conducting surveys in order to determine what practices allowed the most successful farmers to flourish and then spreading such methods to other farmers through demonstration and extension work.[8]

This faith in the ability of social scientists to improve the lot of farmers continued to grow through the 1920s, when a second generation of agricultural economists, notably Milburn Lincoln Wilson and Howard R. Tolley, came to the fore. Wilson studied at the agricultural college in Ames, Iowa, worked at Montana State College, conducted experiments in dry-land farming, and became the state's first county agent before attending graduate school at the University of Wisconsin, where he came to believe that successful agriculture required better organized farmers and government activity on behalf of agriculture. He returned to Montana in 1924 and applied his economic and agricultural principles to the state's farming techniques in the hope of determining exactly what combination of acreage, labor, machinery, crops, methods, and livestock were needed for optimal operation. A contemporary described the experiment as "a scientific and carefully planned effort to transfer the industrial efficiency of modern factory methods to the farm." But Wilson, like his predecessors, recognized the need to spread the knowledge of such methods to everyday farmers, and with this goal in mind he organized the state into regions and appointed qualified men and women to spread information from the state college and research station to receptive gatherings of farmers.[9] Tolley came to agriculture via economics and the influence of Spillman, who convinced him that work in this new field would allow him to use his research and knowledge to help farmers maximize the economic return on their investment, much as business-men did. Tolley entered the USDA's Bureau of Agricultural Economics in 1922 and soon developed an ambitious "outlook program" that sought to apply the science of agricultural economics to the business of farming. This program attempted to determine the probable production, consumption, and price of farm products in order to aid farmers in adjusting their output to prevailing market conditions.[10]

Another branch of science that had a direct influence on agricultural policy in the interwar decades was the new field of nutrition. At the turn of the century, the discovery of vitamins, minerals, and deficiency diseases in both people and livestock caused scientists to reexamine the components of a healthy diet. Previously, most doctors and the general population had assumed that if people were not hungry, they had a healthy diet. But the creation of conscript armies during World War I provided governments with striking physical evidence that many people's diets were deficient. As a result, some governments began propagandiz-ing about the nutritive value of milk and green vegetables for civilian health.[11]

During the 1920s, nutritionists, like their contemporaries in agriculture and economics, began applying their laboratory findings to society at large. Carl Schiotz, professor of hygiene at Oslo University in Norway, developed a nutri-tionally balanced meal to feed children at school. The "Oslo breakfast" resulted in a significant increase in growth, health, vigor, and academic achievement among the students. In a parallel experiment, the Rowett Institution in Scotland, under the leadership of John Boyd Orr, provided 1,500 children in poor school districts of Scotland and Northern Ireland with a pint of whole milk each day for the 1926–

27 school year. The result was a marked improvement in the children's health, growth rate, and ability to learn, which in turn spurred a publicly subsidized program to provide free or cheap milk to schoolchildren throughout Scotland and later the entire United Kingdom.[12]

By the end of the 1920s, then, scientists as well as engineers, machinists, and businessmen were helping farmers increase agricultural productivity, nutritionists were celebrating these gains as the way to supply people with an adequate diet, and agricultural economists were providing farmers with the information they needed about market and production conditions to generate a good return on their investment. At the same time, moreover, similar goals were leading farmers, agricultural researchers, and governments to start organizing across national boundaries. This effort did not initially yield positive results, however, until the Great Depression of the 1930s, when national agricultural programs began to bog down and international action came to the fore.

Early Efforts to Organize Agriculture along International Lines

The agricultural crisis of the 1870s and 1880s that had initiated such a flurry of activity within a variety of countries also spurred action and organization across national boundaries. Specialized groups of agricultural scientists were the first to organize. Other, broader organizations, such as the International Commission of Agriculture and the International Co-operative Alliance, soon followed.[13] But the most ambitious attempt at transnational cooperation was the International Institute of Agriculture (IIA), which gathered commodity statistics worldwide and brought together governments from around the globe to discuss issues relating to agriculture.

The father of the IIA was David Lubin, a naturalized American citizen who during the depression of the 1890s sought to apply Progressive principles to the international realm and create an expert organization that could advise governments and farmers' groups and thereby rationalize global commodity markets. A successful California dry goods merchant-turned-farmer, Lubin had initially believed that farmers' cooperatives, government-funded research, and federal regulation of transportation and marketing monopolies could guarantee farmers an adequate return on their labors. By 1896, however, he had become convinced that while the laws of supply and demand determined food prices, farmers had no way of knowing what global supply conditions were. The lack of sufficient information contributed to wild fluctuations in commodity markets and led Lubin to the conclusion that only accurate statistics could improve market stability, rationalize production, and allow farmers to reap the just fruits of their labor.[14]

To this end the IIA would collect statistics, study economic and technical questions, and present its findings to member governments. The short treaty that created the institute eschewed more ambitious duties and explicitly guaranteed national sovereignty by excluding "all questions concerning the economic interests, legislation, [or] the administration of a particular nation." The final product's very innocuousness helped ensure its ratification on 7 June 1905, and the institute began regular operations on 25 May 1908. Those operations included an ambitious series of statistical publications about the world's supplies of agricultural commodities, price levels, and trade conditions; a system for tracking the spread of plant diseases; and monographs on agricultural cooperatives and credit.[15]

The International Institute of Agriculture performed valuable scientific and technical work. But this work was handicapped by the turmoil of World War I, an inadequate administrative structure, the growing monopolization of the organization by Italian nationals, a leadership that viewed other international agricultural bodies as rivals rather than allies, and a pervasive apathy on the part of member countries that resulted in the appointment of second-rate representatives and failure to provide data in a timely manner. Despite these difficulties and obstacles, however, the IIA doggedly continued to collect international statistics from its varied membership and to organize a series of valuable scientific conferences. In 1926 it hosted both the first World Wheat Conference and the first World Forestry Congress. With assistance from the IIA, the International Society of Soil Science, with 916 members from fifty-one countries, prepared a uniform nomenclature for soil classification and, in 1938, published the first installment of a world soil map. The institute also hosted diplomatic conferences, which resulted in a series of formal conventions that called for standard international action to control locusts (1922), protect plants from disease (1929), mark eggs for international trade (1931), and standardize methods for analyzing cheeses and wines (1934 and 1935, respectively) and for charting livestock heredity (1936).[16]

By the later 1920s, however, it had become clear that the world agricultural economy needed more than technical advice and that the IIA had lost the initiative in international agriculture to the League of Nations, whose 1927 World Economic Conference examined agriculture's role in the global economy. During World War I, agricultural production had soared to meet the vast needs of conscript armies, but the League conference observed that in the postwar period this additional food glutted global markets and resulted in a continuing worldwide agricultural recession. Despite a clear understanding of the problem, the only concrete action the conference took was the creation of an ongoing League Economic Consultative Committee, which included representatives from agriculture and was supplemented in May 1929 by a permanent subcommittee of agricultural experts. This first tentative work prefigured the important role that agriculture would play in subsequent international discussions held in the wake of the U.S. stock market crash and the deepening global depression.[17]

The Coming of the Great Depression

With the collapse of the stock market and the onset of depression, demand for agricultural products, many of which were already in surplus, hit bottom. Prices soon dipped so low that they did not cover the cost of raising and harvesting a crop, and many farmers became destitute. Governments were quick to act, at first through nationalistic agricultural policies, including import restrictions, production controls, direct relief, and price subsidization. Indeed, what emerged was an elaborate system of production controls and surplus storage schemes to regulate supply and stabilize prices. Using these and other devices, France guaranteed prices for wheat and wine; Denmark for butter; the Netherlands for fresh fruits, vegetables, butter, and flowers; Australia for fruit, butter, and sugar; Brazil for coffee; and Switzerland for milk, cheese, and meat. The most elaborate system of agricultural regulation was America's Agricultural Adjustment Administration (AAA), masterminded by Spillman, Black, Wilson, and Tolley and passed by Congress during the first "hundred days" of President Franklin D. Roosevelt's administration. The AAA oversaw a wide-ranging system of voluntary acreage restrictions, price supports, and marketing quotas, which in combination sought to restrict production and raise prices.[18]

Not everyone agreed that systems of production controls and price supports were the best solution, however. In 1934 Britain's modest system came under fire from John Boyd Orr, who said that such systems would save farmers at the expense of consumers, especially low-income groups, who spent up to 75 percent of their income on food. Instead, he urged a policy that would subsidize food consumption, which would thereby increase demand for agricultural commodities and raise prices. This approach of subsidizing consumption rather than constricting production later received theoretical undergirding from British economist John Maynard Keynes. Indeed, some countries did eventually seek to underwrite demand while regulating supply: Belgium instituted a national milk program for schoolchildren in 1939, the Dutch and Danish governments subsidized the sale of food to the needy, and in the United States the USDA instituted school lunch programs as well as a food stamp program for the poor and unemployed.[19]

But none of these national agricultural programs fundamentally improved the agricultural economy, and initially the League of Nations did no better. After consultations with the IIA and the International Co-operative Alliance in 1930 and 1931, the League published *The Agricultural Crisis,* which conveyed a universally bleak picture. The report concluded that a lack of purchasing power lay "at the very bottom of the world economic depression," but its recommendations, though presented with an urgency born of crisis, merely called upon national governments to protect farmers while they organized themselves into organizations that could control production and marketing. The recommendations of the World Monetary and Economic Conference two years later, when agricultural prices continued at a low level and the global depression worsened, evidenced greater desperation and less faith in the ability of farmers to redeem themselves through cooperative action. The length and severity of the Depression led some at the conference to conclude that the economy would continue at a low level for the foreseeable future, and the subsequent resolutions therefore put greater emphasis on restricting production and dividing world markets through intergovernmental commodity agreements. Such agreements were negotiated for tin in 1931, wheat and tea in 1933, rubber in 1934, sawn timber in 1935, sugar and beef in 1937, and coffee in 1940. A similar economic pessimism led to the formation of regional trade blocs. For example, the Ottawa agreements of October 1932 ended Great Britain's era of free trade by giving agricultural exports from the Dominions special access to the United Kingdom in exchange for reciprocal privileges for British manufactured goods. The Benelux countries followed with a customs union in 1932, and the Scandinavian nations cooperated on tariff policy under the Oslo Agreement. But these agreements, like domestic agricultural programs at the time, achieved few significant results.[20] Clearly, a change in thinking was desperately needed and would, in fact, eventually come from the League of Nations.

As the Depression dragged on despite remedial action at the national and international levels, a group of scientists, in tandem with the League, took a page from Keynes and radically challenged conventional thinking about the relation of food, agriculture, and nutrition to the world economy. Their landmark work laid the foundation for the FAO and was itself erected upon the "newer knowledge of nutrition" then emerging. Food production, according to their thinking, should be expanded, not reduced, in order to meet the nutritional needs of the world's people, elevate farmers' incomes, stimulate industrial production, and lift the global economy out of depression.

The basis of their ideas were several nutritional surveys of the 1930s that had uncovered a basic paradox: despite worldwide agricultural surpluses, malnutrition was pervasive in even the richest nations. In other words, the problem was not too much food but that the available food was not reaching the people who needed it because of flaws in the way it was marketed and priced. For example, *Food, Health and Income,* published by John Boyd Orr and the Rowett Institution staff in 1936, provided indisputable evidence that at least one-third of the population of the United Kingdom was malnourished. Orr's book described a vicious circle: poor people could not afford vitamin-rich "protective foods" (such as milk, eggs, and fresh fruits and vegetables), their subsequent poor nutrition had adverse effects on their health and stature, and their poor health often kept them from rising out of poverty. This scientific study provoked such popular outrage that it forced the British government to establish supplementary feeding programs across the country. On the international level, in June 1935 Drs. E. Burnet and Wallace R. Aykroyd of the League of Nations' Health Section published "Nutrition and Public Health," which boldly declared, "Deficiencies in important nutrients are a common feature of modern diets," especially deficiencies in the protective foods. Based on their findings, the authors called on governments to feed schoolchildren, take steps to prevent and cure food deficiency diseases, provide relief to the destitute, and train public health nurses and social workers in nutrition.[21]

The Burnet and Aykroyd report found its way onto the agenda of the sixteenth League Assembly on 11 September 1935, when Stanley Bruce, speaking on behalf of the British Commonwealth, proposed a "marriage of health and agriculture" and challenged the world's governments to invert their thinking. Rather than restricting agricultural production in order to raise food prices and save farmers from ruin, he called on countries to provide all of their people with a diet adequate for health. Doing so, he argued, would greatly expand effective demand for food, raise commodity prices, increase farmers' purchasing power, and thereby stimulate industry as well as agriculture. In other words, Bruce wanted to use nutrition as a lever to lift agriculture, and eventually the whole world economy, out of depression. Frank L. McDougall, Bruce's adviser in Geneva, elaborated on the way in which national nutritional policies could restart the general economy. If European countries, for example, reoriented their agriculture to the protective foods so needed to ensure proper nutrition and dropped their tariffs against grains and feedstuffs that could be more economically raised abroad, they would allow those agricultural nations to earn the foreign exchange needed to purchase Europe's manufactured goods. The originality of the Bruce proposal and the way it fit with the altered expectations of government brought on by the Depression caught the imagination of a weary world that had found other alternatives wanting. The League Assembly spent the next three days discussing this new approach.[22]

Bruce's proposals, and the new work on nutrition they catalyzed, rejuvenated the League of Nations, which found collecting, analyzing, and publishing nutritional information less contentious and more constructive than much of its diplomatic work. The League-appointed technical committee on nutrition, consisting of twelve physiologists and biochemists (including Orr), established a set of universally applicable minimum dietary standards, which were published in November 1936 as *The Physiological Bases of Nutrition*. The clarity of these standards made them an immediately useful tool for doctors, social workers, teachers, public health officials, and even homemakers. The committee of the whole—the League of Nations Mixed Committee on Nutrition—compared information on nutrition collected from a number of countries and international organizations with the yardstick established by the technical committee and published its final report, *The Relation of Nutrition to Health, Agriculture and Economic Policy,* in late August 1937. This report confirmed and amplified earlier findings of widespread malnutrition throughout the world and in its recommendations lent further credibility to Bruce's suggestions. Widespread malnutrition was due not to the "niggardliness of nature," it declared, but to "our failure to adapt our economic policies and distributive systems to the increased production of wealth which progress in the scientific field had made available." In other words, the report asserted, science had given farmers what they needed to feed all the world, and governments could, if they wanted, solve the paradox of poverty amid plenty.[23]

The League's technical work in agriculture and nutrition attracted worldwide attention, changed governmental policies, reaffirmed the value of international technical work, and thereby laid the foundation for a postwar international institution that would conduct scientific inquiries and issue expert reports in order to improve global agriculture and nutrition. *The Relation of Nutrition to Health, Agriculture and Economic Policy* was translated into a number of languages, summarized in various journals and newspapers, and celebrated as "the most important book published in the year." Suddenly, scientific knowledge became public information, and almost overnight the report's findings created an enlightened public opinion that pressured governments to put a new emphasis on providing proper nutrition for all of their citizens. Apparently the League's nutrition work convinced the Estonian government to reduce its tariff on fresh fruit and the Indian government to take similar action with regard to milk, because both did so, citing the nutritional benefits of the pertinent foods and expressing a desire to make them more available to the poorer segments of their populations. To encourage and coordinate governments' nutritional efforts, the League urged the creation of national nutrition committees that would coordinate and report annually on each country's efforts to improve nutrition. By mid-1938 some twenty governments had established such committees, comprising public administrators, scientists, agricultural experts, economists, teachers, and consumers. In February 1937, the leaders of these committees began meeting in Geneva to exchange ideas and experiences. Although the Second World War nipped this work in the bud, many of the same people came to Hot Springs, Virginia, and contributed to the creation of the Food and Agriculture Organization, which continued the work the League had begun.[24]

Agriculture and World War II

Governments put much of the League's nutritional work to the test during the Second World War as they sought optimal diets for their fighting forces and devised systems of civilian food rationing. National nutrition committees established under League guidance helped rationalize rationing systems around the world. Great Britain's comprehensive rationing system, for example, was based on the League's nutritional standards and Orr's advice. Pregnant and nursing women, infants, and children received free supplements of cod liver oil and orange juice, as well as first priority in purchasing milk, eggs, fresh fruit, and vegetables. As a result of these policies, Britain's infant mortality rate fell during each year of the war, the number of stillborn babies fell by 25 percent, and the death rate among children under ten and of pregnant women fell to record lows.[25]

The war showed not only the validity of the League's nutritional principles but also that science had given farmers all they needed to raise more food, as evidenced by the great wartime gains in agricultural productivity. The United Kingdom, as a large food importer vulnerable to submarine warfare, did everything it could to encourage home production, from promoting "victory gardens" to bringing new land under cultivation. Similarly, U.S. agriculture, even before Pearl Harbor, began to gear up to aid the Allies; once the United States entered the war, federal price guarantees, new tractors, artificial fertilizers, and hybrid corn contributed to a 20 percent increase in wartime food output with no significant increase in acreage and with 12 percent fewer workers.[26]

International experts in nutrition and agriculture, who had largely shifted from Geneva to Allied administrative councils, paid close attention to these vindications of their prewar theories and began to think about how they might be applied to the postwar world. The prospects for postwar cooperation on agricultural policy seemed particularly bright due to the close cooperation of the Combined Food Board, which brought together representatives from the United States, Great Britain, and Canada to ensure greater integration of their wartime agricultural production and more effective distribution of foodstuffs among the Allies. Some of the people influential in the League nutrition movement (especially McDougall, Orr, André Mayer of France, and Frank Boudreau of the United States) began considering a new international organization to deal with agriculture, food, and nutrition. Such an institution, they believed, would mesh with the ideals of the Atlantic Charter and with Roosevelt's statement that the war was being fought to secure "freedom from want." "It will be in the field of nutrition," Boudreau said in 1942, "that freedom from want will first find practical expression. For of all human needs our knowledge of man's need for food is by far the most advanced." Others made the same point in a variety of wartime speeches. Invited to the United States in 1942, Orr, for example, spoke to a variety of groups about his work in nutrition and his hopes for the postwar period. He and others received sympathetic hearings from IBM president J. T. Watson, Chase president Winthrop Aldrich, Vice President Henry Wallace, and the U.S. ambassador to Great Britain, John G. Winant.[27]

Creating the Food and Agriculture Organization

The active lobbying of this international body of experts for an institution that would bring the new information in agriculture, science, and economics together in order to provide the world's people with adequate nutrition led to the 1943 Hot Springs Conference, which created the Food and Agriculture Organization. McDougall, invited by Eleanor Roosevelt to a White House dinner, presented this hope to the president, who seemed interested but noncommittal. By 31 March 1943, however, perhaps driven by the idea that such a conference would provide war-weary peoples with hope or that the seemingly noncontroversial topics of food and agriculture would form a cordial lead-in to more problematic conferences on economics and a postwar international organization, Roosevelt issued invitations to an international conference on food and agriculture to be held at the resort town of Hot Springs, Virginia.[28] With minimal forewarning or preparation, delegates from the Allied nations met that summer to discuss a new vision for agriculture, food, and nutrition in the postwar world.

Hot Springs differed from most previous international conferences in that the focus was on technical questions handled by experts rather than on traditional topics of diplomacy. Governments appointed all the conference delegates, but most of them were technicians and experts in the areas of agriculture, nutrition, public administration, and economics. To a certain extent this made them more inclined to internationalism, due to the universal acceptance of biological and physiological laws and the multinational nature of science. This shared professionalism also meant that many of them were already familiar with the nutritional and economic work of the League of Nations as well as with one another. But there was a noticeable absence among this group of experts—Orr did not travel to Virginia, because the British Foreign Office thought his ideas (and likely his propensity for propounding them publicly) "unorthodox." Nonetheless, he did make an appearance of sorts. McDougall showed a film, *The World of Plenty*, to the delegates, in which Orr appeared and asked, "What are we fighting for?" When he answered his own question by arguing for a war against want, starting with the want of food, the delegates rose to their feet and cheered.[29]

Some of the work at Hot Springs seemed to have picked up where the League had left off at the war's beginning, by stressing the new knowledge of nutrition and the possibility of improving agricultural production to meet nutritional needs.

The conference also continued to record the state of the world's nutrition through statements made by national delegates about the situation in their countries and colonies. These statements revealed a pervasive malnutrition, especially in the colonial territories (a topic previously deemed a domestic matter not suitable for international discussion). But the most important legacy of the League's work for the Hot Springs delegates was its willingness to discard the dominant paradigm of the 1930s and to dream of a new era of expanded, rather than restricted, agricultural production—an era in which food might nourish the world's people rather than be destroyed after it had bankrupted its producers and drained the coffers of their governments. The optimism that flowed from this worldview blossomed into bold statements in the conference's final resolutions, such as, "Freedom from want of food, suitable and adequate for the health and strength of all peoples, can be achieved."[30] But such bold optimism did not ensure consensus on all issues.

The central dilemma of the conference was whether the new FAO would be an activist organization that would take vigorous steps to stimulate agricultural production and to stabilize prices, or whether it would be a reincarnation of the IIA and do little more than collect data and provide a forum for international discussion. Orr, McDougall, members of the U.S. delegation from the Department of Agriculture, the Latin American delegates, and several members of the British Food Mission in Washington supported the former approach,[31] while the British delegation and U.S. delegates from the State and Commerce departments vigorously espoused the latter. The final outcome was ambiguous, and the conflict between these two visions continued to shape FAO history for the next thirty years. In many ways, similar questions vexed the Bretton Woods Conference that created the World Bank: How much power and independence was the new international organization to have? How much sovereignty would member governments sacrifice to improve the global economy? To what ends would this UN agency put its new power?

The issues that brought this dilemma to the fore at Hot Springs had to do with whether the FAO would regulate the global supply of agricultural commodities in order to support world prices and whether it would distribute subsidized food to improve nutrition in the Third World. On these questions a potent combination of British delegates, U.S. undersecretary of state Dean Acheson, and U.S. assistant secretary of commerce Will Clayton usually cooperated to shunt discussion into less sensitive areas. Clayton and Acheson both believed that American prosperity and national security after the war would rely on an internationally managed system of free trade, and therefore both were wary of formulating a separate plan of action for agriculture. The British delegates, for their part, feared any rise in world food prices and therefore, by extension, feared a strong FAO with a membership dominated by agricultural producers whose economic well-being depended on relatively high agricultural prices.[32] But wartime uncertainties ensured that these concerns and much else about the future of the FAO were held in suspense.

The final resolution of the Hot Springs Conference created an interim commission that was to draft a constitution for the FAO and construct its organizational framework from the large, sometimes contradictory, and often ambiguous body of conference resolutions. The interim commission, which began its work on 15 July 1943, consisted of sixty-one representatives from fifteen countries divided into five technical committees and advised by two panels of experts, one on economic issues and the other on scientific matters. The end product of these committees' work reflected the continuing tension between the idea of the FAO as an advisory body and the belief that it should be an active regulatory agency. The strength of the FAO as envisioned by the interim commission lay in its strong, international staff and advisory structure. Like the World Bank, staff appointments would be based solely on technical expertise and would be made by a director-general of international repute; however, the FAO lacked the bank's financial independence. The FAO's national membership, meeting every two years as a conference, would direct the organization's program of work, decide upon the director-general's recommendations, and most importantly, determine the budget. The organization's proposed $5 million budget was a compromise between those who believed that $1.5 million was sufficient for an agricultural information clearinghouse and those who believed that $10 million would be necessary to finance an ambitious program to stimulate agricultural production and vanquish world hunger. The tentative constitution showed similar ambivalence: While it affirmed the organization's internationalism by stating that membership was to be universal (with no country being denied entrance due to diplomatic status or political system), the preamble to the constitution was not as forthright as the Hot Springs declarations had been. Instead of calling for freedom from hunger, it merely called on all signatories to better standards of living and nutrition in areas under their jurisdiction, improve systems of production and distribution of food, elevate rural standards of living, and contribute to an expanding world economy.[33]

On 16 October 1945, twenty governments having ratified this draft constitution, the signatories assembled at the Château Frontenac in Quebec for the organization's first regular conference. It included many men who had been championing the cause of an international food organization for years. One of them, Frank Boudreau, commented that he had waited "ten long years" for the birth of the infant FAO, ever since witnessing "the marriage of health and agriculture" at the League of Nations, "when Mr. Bruce officiated . . . and Mr. McDougall was the best man." The atmosphere at Quebec was indeed characterized by the type of anxious anticipation that comes with the birth of an infant. Meeting so soon after the conclusion of the war, conference participants were both optimistic and sober about the future. At the same time as they marveled at the awesome wartime achievements of Allied cooperation, they also confronted unprecedented destruction and disruption on a global scale, and they hoped that the new FAO could channel wartime cooperation into more constructive directions and thereby prevent a third world war.[34]

Exactly how this new organization could best carry out its mission, however, remained at issue. Some of the more advanced countries emphasized the FAO's role as a technical clearinghouse. They pointed to the new UN organization's absorption of the IIA's library, resources, and staff, which would give it a head start in its technical work, and to the newly unveiled plans for the International Trade Organization (ITO), which would deal with all commodities passing into international markets and preempt any FAO action in this area. To many it seemed a large enough task to collate bibliographies and abstracts of relevant technical information, summarize and disseminate information on national agricultural legislation and policies, and oversee global statistics on nutrition, food consumption, fisheries, rural welfare, forestry, agricultural production, and marketing. But other delegates and members of the Interim Commission placed more emphasis on actions that would bring immediate, positive results, such as feeding programs for vulnerable groups, an approach that had proven its effectiveness in various countries' wartime programs. "A mere fact-finding agency will not be sufficient," argued the New Zealand delegate, to fulfill the FAO's goal, clearly expressed at the Hot Springs Conference, of utilizing "the world's resources for the mutual benefit of all." To this end a number of delegates successfully argued that the FAO should have the power to dispatch technical missions to member countries requesting assistance.[35]

The advocates of an activist FAO gained further momentum with the election of the first director-general. To say that Sir John Boyd Orr, a strong-headed Scotsman renowned for his pioneering research in nutrition, was not the first choice to head the new Food and Agriculture Organization would be an understatement. The British government, still irked by his 1935 study revealing the extent of malnutrition in the United Kingdom and by his frequent public criticism of government policies, had not even sent him to the Hot Springs Conference, despite his international reputation as a pioneer in agricultural and nutritional research; only after the main body of the British delegation had been briefed and had departed for the Quebec Conference had the Foreign Office belatedly invited him as an unofficial observer. Orr spent much of his time in Quebec as a silent observer and tourist, because he could not bring himself to abide by the instructions given to the British delegation, which were to press for an advisory body with no executive authority. Orr only broke his silence near the end of the conference, when the chairman of the conference, Lester B. Pearson of Canada, asked him to speak. In a speech given with little preparation and no notes, Orr complained that the FAO was contrary to all his hopes, for "the hungry people of the world [want] bread, and they [are] to be given statistics." He believed that the FAO offered only empty promises—technical assistance without the means of purchasing needed equipment and supplies, and research when a series of studies had already revealed the great extent of malnutrition and had already indicated avenues for remedying this tragedy. In typically iconoclastic fashion, Orr called upon the conference delegates to scrap the work they had done to this point and seek the authority and funds necessary to allow the new FAO to rationalize agricultural production and distribution. This speech clearly did not endear him to his fellow British delegates. But British, American, and Commonwealth officials had already considered no less than seventeen candidates to run the new UN agency, and through "a devious process of elimination," as the British called it, they were ultimately left with Orr. The Anglo-American delegates sought to limit Orr's impact, however, by limiting the term of the first director-general to two years while promoting "indeterminate appointments and continuity of tenure" for subsequent FAO leaders.[36]

Though acclaimed by the conference and the scientific community, Orr was reluctant to take the helm, feeling hemmed in by the Hot Springs and Quebec resolutions, but at the urging of his wife, Mayer, McDougall, and Boudreau, he finally accepted the two-year term, expressing the same mixture of hope and anxiety that most of the delegates had already exhibited. While he stressed that the FAO's work could promote global health, prosperity, and cooperation, Orr also stated, "I am almost tempted to say that if this Organization succeeds it will perform a miracle." But given the stakes and his own optimism, Orr concluded by declaring that "we are living in a day of miracles. . . . The vision we have of a new world which FAO can begin to build must inspire us with the faith, confidence and hope which will enable us to overcome, one by one, the difficulties which we find." Key to overcoming such difficulties would be a staff of truly international civil servants who relinquished their nationalities, became "citizens of the world," realized "that the Hottentots of Africa and the Aborigines of Australia are as dear to them as the peoples to whom they belong," and were "prepared to give their lives to this great cause." Choosing to lead by example, Orr swore a declaration of loyalty at the conference's final plenary that eschewed national prerogatives and affirmed his single loyalty to the interests of the international organization he now headed.[37]

So the final outcome of Quebec was an organization with a conservative, circumscribed constitution led by a crusading and persistent nutritionist. Clearly the battle over the nature of the FAO was just beginning. Pearson seemed to see the battle lines forming as he addressed the conference for the last time: "FAO is, in the last analysis, people and governments. So it remains for us to make this Organization a success. I have no doubt of the competence and zeal of the Organization itself under its great Director-General," Pearson declared. "I have some fear, however, that the governments, because of apathy or ignorance, may not give FAO the support it should have; may not implement its recommendations or accept its advice." With the task to come in mind, the conference chairman closed by wishing the FAO "vigor, courage, and imagination" in carrying out its duties.[38]

In January 1946, Orr and his wife left their Scottish farm to take up residence in Washington, DC, at the provisional FAO headquarters. "It was in a gloomy and grim mood that I began work as the head of the new organisation," Orr recalled. Such pessimism might seem untoward given the great scientific and technical advances in agricultural productivity, the development and application of nutritional science, and the evolution of international cooperation in agricultural policy that had occurred during his lifetime. Indeed, Orr's ideology was that of the agricultural professionals who had conducted this earlier work. He believed, much like Howard Tolley, David Lubin, and Stanley Bruce, that science had given farmers the ability to produce enough food to feed the world properly but that flawed marketing and pricing systems thwarted this goal and left farmers with relatively low standards of living. But an international organization run by experts, Orr believed, had the potential to overcome these economic obstacles and feed the world's hungry. What gave him pause was his firm conviction that his goal of making the FAO just such a strong international organization would be opposed at every turn by national governments pursuing their own interests regardless of the good of the larger world community. He was right, and that conflict, which continued through the administrations of Orr's successors as well, is the subject of the next chapter.

6

The Limits of Internationalism

The Food and Agriculture Organization, 1946–1957

The work of the Food and Agriculture Organization in its first decade was truly unprecedented. For the first time an international organization was charged with ensuring that all the world's people had enough to eat—an enormous task, given that prewar surveys had estimated half of the globe's population was malnourished. Making the task even more daunting was the crisis that confronted the new organization when it formally began its work in 1946: the average European subsisted on 80 percent of his or her prewar diet, Asian rice production remained at one-third of prewar levels, and worldwide agricultural production was still down 10 percent over prewar levels, while global population had increased by 10 percent. As a result, some rations dipped below wartime levels, malnutrition was prevalent in Asia, and both national and international food authorities sincerely worried whether food supplies would last until the next crops could be harvested.[1]

The staff and leadership of the FAO faced these problems with a creed similar to that of their predecessors on the League of Nations Mixed Committee on Nutrition and with the same combination of confident professionalism and internationalism that the World Bankers employed in their economic problem solving. If the world's people could be properly fed, the FAO staff averred, the effort would greatly stimulate demand for agricultural products, raise and stabilize farmers' incomes and purchasing power, stimulate other sectors of the economy, and create a healthier and more productive world population. But while this seemed perfectly logical and not altogether impracticable from the international perspective of the FAO staff, implementing the concrete reforms needed to bring about such an upward spiral of prosperity would be difficult at best, if only because the issues involved impinged on the economic policies of sovereign countries.

Yet, despite the difficulties, the international identity constructed by the FAO's staff led that agency to pursue its mission relentlessly and confidently. The foundation of the FAO's mission, and of the ideology behind it, was a faith in the power of facts and science, the same faith that had inspired Progressive reform

movements and that had lent authority to the construction of professional ideologies at the turn of the century. Once the facts were known, these reformers
believed, the need for change would be self-evident to the public and to policymakers, and expert solutions could be formulated and implemented. The FAO
staff, based on its statistics pertaining to all aspects of agriculture, formulated
its international perspective on world food production and distribution, a perspective that echoed the themes of the Mixed Committee on Nutrition. While
the staff members despised the limitations on food production implemented by
North American countries for lack of regular markets, they realized that, because
these surpluses made up no more than 10 percent of the world's total food supply,
the key to overcoming global malnutrition was utilizing the newest technology
and scientific information to accelerate Third World agricultural development.
Because improved health and greater stability in this area was one of the keys to
global peace, or so they argued, agricultural development merited, even demanded, priority in any plan for general economic development. These were the components of the philosophy that animated the staffs and the first directors-general
of the FAO. But each leader pursued this common goal in his own manner, and
each had to seek popular support and government assistance, because the FAO, as
a specialized agency, could only advise, guide, and cajole—never demand.[2]

Sir John Boyd Orr, the first director-general of the FAO, offered the world an
international vision in which the food-deficit countries would receive low-priced
food, relatively high and stable prices for agricultural products, and flexible credit
to expand food production for internal and external consumption. His plan would
assure all farmers an adequate and stable standard of living so they would be willing and able to produce enough food to feed all the world, but it also envisioned
a more wide-ranging restructuring of global commodity markets than the United
States and the United Kingdom were willing to contemplate. As we will see, this
left the FAO to formulate a new strategy to attain its goals and to do so within the
budgetary and jurisdictional confines imposed on it by member governments.
Norris E. Dodd and P. V. Cardon, the two Americans who succeeded Orr, focused
primarily on technical assistance to Third World countries, on managing national
activities along international lines, and on limited programs to regulate the disposal of agricultural surpluses as the best available means of fighting hunger.

In the case of the FAO, as with the World Bank, these international civil servants
had embarked on a new international endeavor. At first they tried to ensure that
the global movement of food was determined by human needs and the scientific
principles of nutrition rather than by economic pressures and national prerogatives. Failing this, they embarked on an effort to revolutionize Third World agricultural production methods so that these countries could grow enough food to
feed their own people. Both goals were unprecedented, and both grew out of the
noblest of intentions; only the latter goal, however, was acceptable to a majority of

FAO member governments. Because the FAO did not have independent financial resources like the World Bank, the recalcitrance of member governments hampered its actions and agenda.

Orr's Activism

When Orr began his director-generalship, he believed that the keys to his dream of a strong FAO overseeing an enlightened international food and agricultural policy were a truly international staff and the global statistics necessary to make his case in the court of world opinion. Beginning with a number of people who had served on the Interim Commission, Orr recruited experts from as broad a geographical background as he could. He succeeded to such an extent that André Mayer, chair of the FAO Executive Committee, commented that after only one year "of seeking in turn advice from Chinese or Hindu, New Zealander or South African, South or North American, or from a European colleague" and realizing "that their hearts and minds are in agreement on problems which concern all of them and that they think only of solving them for the common welfare, one can look upon the future with hope." The problems that concerned them all in the first months were clearly established in the information and statistics they had collected and collated for the first *World Food Survey,* the findings of which were "alarming." Exacerbating the inadequate level of nutrition that had prevailed before the war was a growing world population and a severe European food shortage. Six years of warfare had overtaxed the continent's farm machinery and soil fertility; a particularly harsh winter in 1945, a poor harvest in 1946, and postwar shortages of machinery, fertilizer, transportation, and regular marketing mechanisms made a bad situation worse. In the United States, moreover, policymakers were unrealistically optimistic about the international food situation, and American farmers were not adequately mobilized to meet the postwar crisis. Realizing the potential calamity, the FAO responded to a call from the United Nations to assist governments in formulating appropriate long- and short-term policies.[3]

At the 20–28 May 1946 Special Meeting on Urgent Food Problems, Orr and his staff laid out the grim forecast and called on the assembled delegates to show "the same sense of urgency" as they had shown in the world war, for "this is a war against starvation and we must have the weapons to fight it." The main weapon was to be the International Emergency Food Committee (IEFC), a product of FAO consultations with the American and Canadian departments of agriculture. This committee was to study commodity shortages, set export prices, and allocate agricultural resources among all adhering countries. By abandoning the three-nation Combined Food Board and vesting operations in a broad, international organization that drew on the FAO's staff, facilities, and information, the IEFC could bring technical and scientific advice to bear on the facts of the case, thereby guaranteeing all countries of "the justice of its decisions."[4]

On 1 July 1946, a series of IEFC commodity committees, under the overall coordination of a central panel headed by D. A. FitzGerald, began its work. Thirty-five nations joined the IEFC, providing data on their food production and shipping capabilities and implementing the committee's recommendations. Only Canada, Argentina, and Australia refused to participate in this multilateral system for the allocation of scarce foodstuffs, which succeeded in preventing "an unrestricted scramble for foodstuffs, particularly cereals, the results of which might have been of the utmost seriousness." Orr, heartened by the constructive international response to his first call to arms in the war against hunger, began formulating the "proposals for permanent international machinery to deal with long-term problems concerning the production, distribution, and consumption of food" with which the Washington meeting had charged him.[5]

In an effort to move toward freedom from want, in July 1946 Orr unveiled his blueprint for a new world order to be achieved through a vast improvement in agricultural production and food distribution and consumption. As it turned out, however, Orr's worldview, grounded in science and internationalism, clashed with the postwar plans of British and American policymakers, whose national security policies were based on alliances, atomic weapons, unilateral international action, large peacetime militaries, and a system of managed free trade.[6] The Anglo-American definition of national security predominated in the early Cold War, but the FAO under Orr acted as a counterhegemonic force. As an international organization that included most of the world's countries, its suggestions and criticisms could not be ignored entirely, and it was therefore able to focus global attention on some of the shortcomings of the emerging world system.

Using the *World Food Survey*, the nutrition work of the League of Nations, and his own earlier studies as cornerstones, Orr's proposals asserted that the world's people had never been adequately fed and that to feed them in an age of rapidly expanding global population would require a gargantuan increase in agricultural production. Orr and others believed that the knowledge and resources existed to expand production vastly but that such a change in the absence of a profound transformation in established patterns of distribution would undermine prices and actually discourage production over the long term. The World Food Board (WFB) was therefore to serve as the midwife to twin revolutions in food production and distribution.[7]

Orr began by laying out a two-pronged attack on production difficulties. The key to increasing First World agricultural production was stabilizing commodity prices, because if global prices were high enough, farmers would have the incentive needed to maximize production. To this end the World Food Board would hold and finance buffer stocks of key commodities. It would fix a price for each staple and then array minimum and maximum prices within 10 to 15 percent of this initial price. When the world price approached the upper boundary, the board would release its stocks onto the global market, thereby depressing the price; when prices sank to the low mark, the WFB would purchase and store the surpluses, thereby buoying the world price by shrinking the supply. In this way, it would protect farmers from the effects of surpluses and consumers from the results of droughts and shortages. When particularly large surpluses arose, the World Food Board would finance additional holdings by borrowing against its agricultural assets. Once established, the board, by buying low and selling high, would presumably generate the income needed to offset the considerable costs of storage.[8] But this would not be enough to feed the world; Third World agricultural production would also have to be expanded quickly by providing the capital, equipment, supplies, and technical assistance needed to replace traditional methods of agricultural production with modern techniques. This task would require huge amounts of capital—money to buy imported machinery, hybrid seeds, pesticides, and fertilizers or to build indigenous factories to supply these items—as well as technical assistance to facilitate the adoption of new technologies. Concerned that existing credit facilities could not meet the unique needs of agricultural development in poor Third World countries, the World Food Board's credit facility, as envisioned by Orr, would provide long-term credits in recognition of the gradual nature of agricultural development and would gear its repayment schedule to indices of economic growth and equilibrium in the borrowing country. Orr called for unorthodox lending methods, but he argued that these international investments would "ultimately be profitable in the ordinary business sense," because they would increase Third World countries' productivity and purchasing power, facilitate global trade expansion, and raise health standards for the planet's population.[9]

The FAO director-general recognized, however, that global distribution, as well as international agricultural production, would have to be reorganized. Orr thought this latter need, especially in postwar conditions, was urgent enough to justify the short-term expedient of *giving* food to the world's poor to help them break the vicious cycle of poverty, malnutrition, disease, and shortened life. The World Food Board, he proposed, should therefore use some of its reserves, in the form of famine relief programs and concessionary sales (selling food well below the prevailing price), to feed those who could not afford the food necessary for health. This charitable function would also productively siphon off surpluses that might otherwise endanger the World Food Board's price stabilization operations. Finally, Orr asserted that concessionary sales would increase working efficiency in Third World countries. Although he saw the shortcomings of international charity and recognized that people's purchasing power had to be increased through a balanced combination of agricultural and industrial development, Orr emphasized feeding the hungry and putting the primary emphasis on agricultural development: "Food is more than a trade commodity; it is an essential of life."[10]

But Orr also argued, along the same lines as Stanley Bruce's earlier contention, that the World Food Board could act as the catalyst for global postwar economic prosperity. Feeding the world's people on a nutritional standard would require great increases in agricultural production, which, in turn, would provide the farmers of the world (two-thirds of the population) higher, more stable incomes. These agricultural producers would then use their increased purchasing power to buy more of the capital goods required to increase production further and to buy more consumer goods as well. In this way, industrial prosperity would follow agricultural prosperity in an upward spiral, preventing a postwar economic crisis.[11]

Not only would feeding the world's people buoy the global economy, Orr believed, but it would also serve as the first step toward a better world order. The WFB was a "definite and limited objective" with "profound human appeal" that would allow the countries of the world to "develop an atmosphere of mutual trust and good will which will make it easier for them to cooperate in solving other great and urgent world problems." In fact, "if we cannot agree on the basic human requirement, food," he warned, "there is no subject on which we can agree." Additionally, Orr believed, if all people received adequate nutrition, the idea that some classes and races were inherently inferior would vanish in the face of new realities.[12] As this rhetoric indicates, he sincerely believed that the world was a single community populated by people who were far more alike than different. While politicians obscured this commonality by emphasizing "such matters as boundaries, spheres of influence and different ideologies which tend to divide nations," the work of the FAO, providing the world's people with proper nutrition and raising the standard of living of all countries' farmers and agricultural workers, would be so eminently desirable to all nations and peoples as to be above politics.[13]

The World Food Board was not only apolitical but, Orr argued, not really anything new. Its objectives—rationalizing food production and consumption—were akin to national and international efforts undertaken during and immediately after the Second World War, including nutritionally based rationing programs and the work of the Combined Food Board and the IEFC. Indeed, to forestall criticism that his WFB plan would be too difficult to administer and far too expensive, Orr routinely pointed to the lessons of World War II. Certainly bringing countries together to feed their peoples would be no more difficult than bringing them together to fight the Axis forces, and it would be less expensive. More important to the director-general was the fact that "the end result, instead of being death and the destruction of real wealth, would be life ... and economic prosperity, which [are] the essentials of a permanent peace." Such a peace was the least the Allied countries owed the memories of the millions who had given their lives in World War II, including Orr's only son, who had been killed in action in

1942. In sum, Orr believed the world was at a crossroads: "Either cooperation for mutual benefit in a world policy, or a drift back to nationalistic policies leading to economic conflict which may well be the prelude to a third world war that will end our civilization."[14] Faced with such a clear-cut choice, he believed, a committed world population could overcome the organizational and financial difficulties inherent in launching the World Food Board.

Despite Orr's protestations to the contrary, the World Food Board proposals amounted to what one contemporary called "one of the most ambitious designs for international action ever put forward." The creation of essentially three new international organizations—a credit facility, a buffer-stock regulatory agency, and a distribution agency for concessionary food and famine relief—each with its own need for funds and high-caliber personnel, might have been too much to ask of governments struggling to overcome the disruptions of World War II and to restore their own economies. Orr also seemed to have underestimated his Anglo-American rivals, who had their own ideas for reshaping the postwar world.[15] But he had never thought small; he believed that the early postwar period was a unique moment in history when humanity's basic course could be altered or corrected, when people were still willing to make sacrifices for ideals, and when the unprecedented level of wartime planning could be continued with little difficulty. As the director-general of a United Nations organization who had enormous prestige in the global scientific community, his proposals demanded serious consideration and provoked a wide range of reactions.

The response of the British embassy in Washington and the U.S. State Department to a draft of Orr's World Food Board proposals in July 1946 demonstrated the ideological gulf between official Anglo-American opinion and the FAO director-general's ideas. The State Department found the proposals "disturbing," not only "impracticable" but "inimical to [America's] international trade policy." Just two days after receiving the draft, Will Clayton, U.S. assistant secretary of state for economic affairs, visited Orr and, speaking for the Truman administration, tried to dissuade him from presenting the proposals publicly. Clayton was a key force behind the proposed International Trade Organization (ITO), which, like the International Monetary Fund (IMF) and World Bank, was part of the postwar American attempt to construct a managed system of free trade. As the largest exporter of both agricultural and industrial products, the United States considered ensuring open markets for its goods paramount, not only because U.S. policymakers defined national security in terms of economic preeminence but also because the American way of life, based on consumption and the promise of expanding economic opportunities for its citizens, was presumably threatened by any form of autarchy. To support the World Food Board would be to diverge fundamentally from this policy direction. Also, to obey the dictates of such a board would limit the U.S. government's control over the country's agricultural production, its ability to use food aid to bring Third World nationalists into the U.S. fold, and its leverage in garnering international goodwill through food aid initiatives.[16]

Officials within the U.S. Department of Agriculture dissented from the State Department's view. They were more sympathetic to Orr's approach, because they had spent much of their energy and funds in the previous twenty years supporting American farm incomes and promoting record wartime agricultural productivity. From their perspective, the World Food Board potentially offered a way to maintain American farmers' high wartime incomes and large markets while obviating the need to support U.S. farm prices directly with taxpayer dollars. But the Department of Agriculture was out of step with prevailing postwar policy. Although the American delegation to the FAO's September conference in Copenhagen, Denmark, was instructed to recognize that international action was required to deal with questions of agricultural surpluses and nutrition, the cabinet was convinced that the ITO, not the World Food Board, was the appropriate instrument for dealing with these issues.[17]

The British embassy in Washington and members of the Foreign Office were as disconcerted as the State Department by "Sir John Boyd Orr's plan for an agricultural Paradise." The embassy staff was particularly annoyed by the "light-hearted manner verging on frivolity" with which the director-general dealt with the financial aspects of the World Food Board, for these were the most worrisome. The United Kingdom in 1946 was on the verge of bankruptcy yet was clinging to its role as a world power. In such a situation, high ideals and ambitious international schemes had to be reduced to their cost in dollars—the damage they would cause to Britain's balance-of-payments deficit. The creation of the World Food Board would mean not only an initial contribution of some £35 million (approximately $140 million) but a likely increase in world agricultural prices, which would especially hurt the United Kingdom as a large-scale food importer.[18] Orr's plan might increase demand for food exponentially, and the proposed concessionary sales might lead producers to raise prices for their regular customers, thereby constructing "a permanent form of relief to needy countries, financed by the less needy consuming countries." The British cabinet therefore saw a basic conflict of interest between food-exporting and food-importing nations, a view quite at odds with Orr's assertion of an identity of interests that would be served by the World Food Board.[19]

Nonetheless, the British Treasury and Ministry of Agriculture and Food recognized that some of its aspects could be turned to the United Kingdom's advantage, and they thereby lent a positive aspect to Britain's position on the WFB. For example, some members of the Agriculture and Food Ministry pointed to buffer stocks as a useful means of stabilizing grain prices, which could benefit Great Britain, and the Treasury opined that expanding agricultural production could result in more and cheaper food as well as larger markets for British industrial goods. But the cabinet in London, like its American counterpart, opposed the board, believing that the only solution to the problems raised by Orr was a high and stable degree of employment and purchasing power, not concessionary sales.[20]

Both pro– and anti–World Food Board partisans took heart from the report of the FAO Standing Advisory Committee on Economics and Marketing. The committee (an independent board of ten multinational experts appointed by the FAO on the strength of their professional reputations) endorsed the general idea of the board and made a series of recommendations aimed at making creation of such an organization practical. Instead of an independent agricultural credit facility, committee members suggested that the FAO offer expert advice to member countries that applied for World Bank or other development loans. The committee saw concessionary sales as a reasonable way to link the great productive potential of the developed nations to the desperate nutritional shortfalls of much of the Third World, but it also saw the dangers of having two or even three different prices for food commodities worldwide—one for regular international trade (Class I), one for concessionary sales (Class II), and one for indigenous production. Such a complex system would no doubt require extensive organization and regulation (e.g., to ensure that Class II commodities were not diverted into Class I trade) as well as considerable sums of money, all probably on a continuing basis. In light of such potential difficulties, the expert committee put forward an alternative proposition, that all or a good proportion of the food stocks be held nationally according to a common set of international management rules. This would greatly diminish start-up costs for the project, as the countries themselves would bear most of the costs of storage and the necessary capital could be raised domestically rather than having members make capital subscriptions to create the board. Other than that, the World Food Board would operate as laid out in Orr's proposals, buying and selling when global prices reached appointed low and high points and adjusting prices gradually to reflect changing market conditions. The committee also urged close cooperation with the ITO to reduce trade barriers that limited the free trade of food and agricultural machinery and so might interfere with World Food Board operations.[21]

A month later, amid this swirl of ideas about the proper way to organize global commodity markets, FAO members convened in Copenhagen to consider the World Food Board proposals. Orr prefaced the debate by reiterating many of his internationalist themes:

> I believe that the proposals we are making will take the nations a long way toward . . . freeing mankind from hunger and the fear of hunger, and ensuring that consumption shall keep pace with the increased production made possible by modern science, so that the produce of our farms, forests, and fisheries may find markets at prices fair to producers and consumers. By cooperating

to do these things, the nations will . . . be taking . . . the most fundamental step toward maintaining peace and bringing about world prosperity.[22]

Orr's ideas met with qualified approval from some quarters, acclaim from others, and caution from still others.

Countries suffering from food deficits, of course, strongly supported the proposals, which promised to raise the standard of living of their people and of their nations as primary-commodity producers. But no one was as enthusiastic as Fiorella La Guardia, former mayor of New York City and director-general of the United Nations Relief and Rehabilitation Administration (UNRRA), who urged the group to establish the World Food Board immediately, by acclamation, giving it full authority and funds to begin operations. Orr had presented the delegates with "the opportunity of the age," La Guardia argued, for if all countries could be assured of sufficient food there would be no more war. Some food exporters also endorsed the proposals, though less enthusiastically. Erik Eriksen, speaking on behalf of the host nation, exhorted his fellow conferees to "let the world see that we are strong-hearted, far-sighted and wise enough jointly to lay what may become one of the great cornerstones of a sounder, happier, and better world." But F. W. Bulcock, speaking for Australia, warned that "the ideals of FAO were easier to state than to translate into actual accomplishment."[23]

What Orr and the rest of the conference were waiting to hear, however, was the response of the United Kingdom and the United States, for these countries held the fate of the WFB in their hands. Britain's minister of food, John Strachey, cautioned the conference about the great difficulties that would attend World Food Board operations and asserted that even if such operations were called for, they properly fell under the jurisdiction of the ITO or United Nations Economic and Social Council rather than the FAO. But he did agree that buffer stocks held some hope of stabilizing world agricultural prices as well as alleviating current shortages. Strachey was followed by Norris E. Dodd, U.S. undersecretary of agriculture, who told the conference that his country was "strongly in favor of the general objectives laid down by Sir John Orr" and recommended the establishment of an FAO commission "to work out in detail an international program for the stabilization of agricultural prices at levels which will be fair to producers and consumers and which will bring about the improvement of nutrition throughout the world." In the end, the Copenhagen Conference unanimously approved the World Food Board proposals in principle and established an international commission, the World Food Board Preparatory Commission, to develop a concrete plan of action.[24]

Going into the commission's meetings, the British Cabinet sought a "severely practical but positive and constructive middle way," implementing those aspects of the proposals it thought beneficial and discarding Orr's "extravagant and vague" formulations. British policymakers hoped to do this by emphasizing full employment and agricultural development over concessionary sales. They also supported a scheme of national rather than international buffer stocks of agricultural commodities, along the lines suggested by the Standing Advisory Committee's report. For although the British cabinet was wary of the expense and of the possibility of buffer stocks "turning into a producers' racket," such stocks did hold the promise of stabilizing prices and smoothing out the world business cycle, both of which would aid the United Kingdom. Nonetheless, British distrust of an FAO dominated by agricultural exporters and Third World countries was evident in its insistence that control of even limited national buffer stocks be vested in the ITO's Interim Co-ordinating Committee for International Commodity Arrangements rather than the FAO. Cumulatively, these steps promised to minimize the United Kingdom's economic contribution while achieving greater stability in global agricultural prices.[25]

Concurrently, the American delegation received instructions that would effectively put an end to the WFB plans. Some State Department officials felt that Dodd's sympathetic public statement at Copenhagen had exceeded his instructions; they now made certain that there would be no confusion in the preparatory commission meetings. The United States would clearly oppose the World Food Board and promote instead the ITO as the sole body responsible for consideration of trade issues. Therefore the board was already effectively dead when the preparatory commission convened in Washington on 28 October 1946. Dodd, who had bestowed American favor on the proposals at Copenhagen, now asserted that his country would not support the World Food Board or any similar arrangement to meet the needs described so vividly in Orr's report. The apparent American about-face left the commission floundering, and the British memorandum, "A Positive Commodity Policy," became the focus of the commission's work.[26]

To the delight of the British, the preparatory commission, with strong U.S., Canadian, and Dutch support, now diligently went about turning the World Food Board proposals on their head. In place of Orr's assertion that everyone must be fed according to a health standard (through concessionary sales) in order to absorb available agricultural surpluses and catalyze industrial prosperity, the commission asserted that industrial prosperity (through First World full employment and Third World economic development) was needed to furnish the increased buying power necessary for the world's people to purchase the food they needed. The commission's committee structure reflected this reversal. Committee I dealt primarily with issues of development rather than food issues and organized a special joint committee on industrial development. This joint committee argued that industrial development was in greater need of international cooperation than was agriculture; it held further that while Third World agricultural development could act as a significant countercyclical measure in the world economy, extant institutions were sufficient for the funding of agricultural development—no independent credit facility under FAO auspices was needed. Only Committee II, which dealt with price stabilization and commodity policy, retained some of the original flavor of Orr's proposals, and even here British buffer-stock formulations dominated. While the committee agreed that buffer stocks should probably be held nationally for famine relief and price stabilization, specific stabilization measures for each commodity would be developed by intergovernmental councils rather than by an international food board.[27]

Remnants of the Orr plan also survived in the preparatory commission's consideration of limited concessionary sales schemes meant to protect or improve nutritional standards in the Third World. The American delegation had put forth these proposals, hoping that a limited program of concessionary sales would provide a safety valve to relieve the pressure on USDA price-support programs that accumulated agricultural surpluses. But this international aid would only be provided under two sets of circumstances: during times of acute food shortage and price increases, concessionary sales could be used to establish national programs to supplement the food supplies of vulnerable groups (e.g., pregnant women, children, adolescents); secondly, countries suffering from chronic malnutrition and recurrent famines could receive international food aid as a temporary component in programs pursuing a permanent solution to the underlying causes of the food shortage. But even in these cases, aid would only be available for the duration of the emergency, recipient governments would have to make substantial contributions to the programs, and the aid could not be used to replace what beneficiaries would otherwise purchase themselves. The British delegation insisted upon a further restriction: "The cost to the exporter of providing supplies at special prices must not be recovered by transferring any part of the burden to the price of commercial exports." Clearly, humanitarian and nutritional programs would not take precedence over economic issues.[28]

These very limited proposals came as a deep disappointment to the Indian delegation and others who had seen the World Food Board as a way to promote national health and development simultaneously. The Indians would not forsake their aspirations easily but rather put forward a proposal for "regional prices." Asserting that wheat surpluses in particular were imminent and would swamp any buffer stock arrangement, the Indians, in concert with the Chinese, would, for the benefit of both the wheat-producing and -consuming countries, accept the potentially disruptive surpluses at a price that was below prevailing world prices but, they argued, was better suited to the area's depressed purchasing power. India hoped that such low-priced grain would act "as a springboard" to raise the standard of its population's health, which would, in turn, foster improvements in working efficiency, purchasing power, and the pace of India's economic development. But the preparatory commission had decided that development must lead to health and not vice versa, so the Indians bitterly settled for the very limited concessionary sales arrangements put forth by the Americans and further watered down by the British.[29]

Authority for concessionary sales and for limited buffer stocks was to be vested in an eighteen-nation World Food Council that would also complete the work of the IEFC, exercise general supervision over FAO staff, review and approve its budget, coordinate national and international nutritional and agricultural programs aimed at increasing the production and consumption of food, and report to each FAO conference on the current state of agriculture and nutrition in the world. This new council replaced the extant FAO Executive Committee, which had been composed of individual experts who guided the organization's work between conferences. Executive Committee members opposed the change. They argued in a report to the preparatory commission that a board of eighteen national representatives could not be as international in outlook, because it would be "swayed by consideration of the special interests of the countries represented on it." They believed this constitutional change was hasty and entirely unjustified, and they speculated that it was calculated to reduce the power and authority of the director-general. But the Executive Committee report was largely ignored, and when the preparatory commission concluded its work on 24 January 1947, its final report recommended creation of the World Food Council and emphasized industrial development, full employment, and self-help.[30]

Ultimately, the World Food Council's title and job description were more impressive than its list of accomplishments. The council was formally established six months later by the subsequent FAO Conference in Geneva, Switzerland. However, it implemented none of the proposals to regulate supply or to increase demand, because the member countries, each of which had a veto, could not agree on the means to implement the preparatory commission's recommendations. This came as a great disappointment to farmers' groups and to Orr, as did the decision of FAO members to freeze the organization's budget at the five-million-dollar level and impose a strict budgetary and program review process that took some initiative from the director-general and his secretariat.[31]

With the defeat of the World Food Board proposals, Orr spent the rest of his term doing what he could with the limited authority available to him. He settled on the provision of technical assistance and the collection and publication of statistics as the most promising remaining avenues for promoting agricultural productivity, stabilizing commodity markets, and thereby helping to alleviate hunger. In 1946 the FAO began by dispatching technical missions to Greece, Poland, and Siam (present-day Thailand) to assess long-term agricultural needs and suggest practical ways of improving productivity. The director-general himself traveled extensively in Latin America and especially in the Middle East, where he discussed agricultural development with the Arab League. Pointing to the area's wealth, he urged the Arab countries to cooperate, particularly in large-scale irrigation projects; when pledges of such cooperation were forthcoming, the FAO responded by backing two projects of immediate, practical benefit to the countries involved—locust control and the elimination of rinderpest, a fatal disease that took a great toll on the region's livestock. Orr extended the latter program to Africa and Asia; in the latter area he also organized a rice study group in the summer of 1947 to address on a continuing basis the pressing nutritional needs of Asian populations. To further this regional work, the director-general also oversaw the creation of a number of FAO regional offices. But Orr clearly was not satisfied with this work. In proposing the FAO's program of work for 1949, the outgoing director-general described his organization as "an international extension agency"; after reiterating the ambitious mission originally entrusted to the organization, he bemoaned the fact that "the resources and powers entrusted to FAO are woefully limited in relation to these far-reaching objectives. It cannot order particular policies to be adopted; it can only advise, educate and persuade. It cannot embark on the executive functions of purchase and procurement in order to stimulate output and equalize distribution; it can only recommend, demonstrate, and discuss." It had indeed suggested wide-ranging and ambitious solutions to global food and agriculture problems, but member countries were more comfortable entrusting such issues to the working of the market, aided only by some limited international commodity agreements.[32]

Orr was happy to leave the FAO and the United States when his term as director-general expired. In fact, before boarding the ship that carried him back to Scotland, he wiped "the dust of America" from his shoes with a handkerchief, which he promptly threw into the harbor. The United States, he believed, "had missed a great opportunity for taking up the leadership of a prosperous and peaceful world." To Orr it seemed that the United States had learned nothing from the Wilsonian era and the failure to join the League of Nations, for it had again reneged on "its own great plan," this time of ensuring freedom from want.[33]

Certainly the WFB proposals had encountered a number of very real problems, such as national politics, balance-of-payments difficulties, and the means of financing a wide-ranging international organization. Additionally, it is difficult to imagine such an ambitious initiative succeeding in the early years of the Cold War, when the United Kingdom was retreating from a variety of international commitments (e.g., its military support of the Greek monarchy and its mandate in Palestine) and when the Republican Party in the United States was condemning the Truman administration for being "soft on communism" and attacking the UNRRA, which had provided food and equipment that ended up behind the Iron Curtain. Additionally, in all countries there was a desire to throw off wartime regulation and rationing and to return to "normalcy."

But Orr did not desire a return to a "normal" world marked by widespread malnutrition, poverty, and misery. He believed that feeding the planet's hungry was a scientifically attainable goal and an eminently desirable ideal in human terms. While Orr's proposals might have been idealistic, the FAO Standing Advisory Committee on Economics and Marketing, consisting of internationally recognized experts, did not find them impracticable. Much of the administrative machinery for the board already existed in the form of wartime food rationing organizations, and the impetus could have been drawn from the idealistic wartime rhetoric that had promised a world freed from want. This road was not taken, however. Instead the countries of the world slid into the Cold War, and food remained just another trade commodity, just another weapon in the superpowers' arsenal.

Dodd's Director-Generalship

In 1948 the assembled FAO membership elected as its second director-general Norris E. Dodd, a man who, as a former Oregon farmer and New Dealer in the Department of Agriculture, was, like Orr, sensitive to the need of the world's farmers for price stability and of its people generally for more and better food. But having attended the FAO Conference at Copenhagen as well as the meetings of the World Food Board Preparatory Commission, Dodd also recognized that the organization's members were largely unwilling to support a larger FAO budget or formal global regulation of agricultural commodities. Changing global circumstances also seemed to call for a shift in the FAO's mission. With the passing of the postwar food emergency and the implementation of the Marshall Plan, focus had shifted from Europe to the Third World, which increasingly demanded technical assistance rather than concessionary food. The relocation of FAO headquarters from Washington, DC, to Rome, Italy, symbolized this shift. Rome had earlier been home to the International Institute of Agriculture, but more important was the fact that the lion's share of member contributions to cover the organization's overhead could now be made in Italian lira rather than in U.S. dollars, which allowed Third World members to conserve their scarce dollar reserves. Also, in this European capital members of the FAO's staff and visiting officials of color would not be barred from the building's cafeteria, as they had been in the U.S. capital.[34]

Dodd, who oversaw the relocation, thereafter focused the FAO's activities on technical assistance to farmers, statistical intelligence to stabilize market conditions, and limited proposals for the constructive disposal of agricultural surpluses. Such steps, undertaken regionally, nationally, and internationally, formed parts of the "FAO's gradually developing World Food Program." In other words, under Dodd's leadership the organization (which had less than five million dollars to cover all overhead costs and to deal with a growing number of projects, ranging from forestry and fisheries to locust control and statistical collection) opted for small, practical steps toward increased agricultural production and freedom from hunger. The new director-general hoped that an increasing awareness of the need for international cooperation, in tandem with the FAO's success in these smaller projects, would eventually encourage members to think of the FAO as an international department of agriculture, overseeing a global agricultural revolution comparable to that in the United States overseen by the USDA.[35]

To aid him in this mission, Dodd inherited a staff already known for its ésprit de corps, great technical proficiency, and conscious eschewing of national and political attachments. The staff now grew even closer due to the shared hardships of relocating to Rome, and the director-general further welded the staff together with a sense of common purpose. His Policy and Planning Board, consisting of the heads of each FAO division and meeting each week, became the equivalent of an FAO cabinet, formulating a common organizational mission as well as forging close relationships within the leadership. The staff respected Dodd's down-to-earth quality. The director-general, who remained "a farmer at heart," believed that the best way to determine global conditions was to visit the world's farmers as well as its agricultural bureaucrats and researchers. In January 1949, Dodd undertook the first of many such fact-finding/goodwill trips, visiting fourteen countries in three months, opening the organization's Far East regional office, and attending meetings of the International Rice Commission and the Indo-Pacific Fisheries Council.[36]

Despite Dodd's emphasis on technical assistance, in 1949 the FAO tested the limits of what countries would allow the organization to do by recommending the creation of buffer stocks to stabilize and support commodity prices. When the U.S. Congress failed to ratify either the International Trade Organization or the International Wheat Agreement (which sought to stabilize wheat prices), Dodd decided that some global action had to be taken to address continuing agricultural trade difficulties. The problem, as recognized by the FAO Council, was that the dollar area produced much of the globe's food surpluses, farm machinery, artificial fertilizers, and hybrid seeds, while the rest of the world was largely dollar deficient and therefore unable to purchase these materials. Fearing that the United States and Canada would curtail agricultural production while much of the world was still hungry, Dodd, FAO assistant director-general Sir Herbert Broadley, and University of California professor John B. Condliffe formulated a plan for an International Commodity Clearing House (ICCH). Under the plan, FAO members would make contributions (based on their gross national product) to a five-million-dollar operating budget, which the ICCH would use to purchase food surpluses in the dollar area. It would then sell these surpluses for soft currencies (currencies not convertible into dollars or gold) or trade them for strategic raw materials; any foodstuffs remaining in its coffers would be channeled to needy countries at concessionary prices. In other words, ICCH planners hoped to provide a productive, international clearinghouse for the distribution of food surpluses without disrupting regular commercial markets, and once the crisis had passed it would use its accumulated currencies to finance a long-term system of buffer stocks that would stabilize key commodity prices.[37]

However logical such recommendations seemed to the FAO staff, member states—led by the United States, Canada, Australia, New Zealand, and France—rejected them outright, arguing that they overlapped with existing programs and would slow the movement toward general currency convertibility. As was the case with the World Food Board, they feared losing control over their food aid programs to a strong FAO that might override national policies, as well as developing a two-tiered system of food prices and having to compete with the FAO for strategic raw materials. Member governments did, however, recognize the danger posed by agricultural trade problems and so constructed a less threatening substitute, the Committee on Commodity Problems (CCP). This committee brought together representatives of key importing and exporting countries several times per year to deliberate upon pressing international commodity problems, coordinate "statements of need" from food-deficit countries with accounts of surpluses, and when necessary, recommend international action. Such action was tentative and limited, but it did establish a practical consensus on appropriate (i.e., free-market) methods for dealing with agricultural surpluses, which again became problematic in the wake of the Korean War. As was the case with the World Food Board proposals, this series of proposals and counterproposals again shifted the focus of decision making from a powerful international organization—the proposed ICCH—to a coordinating body of national representatives in the form of the CCP. Also as before, while member countries realized the need for programs to deal with hunger and agricultural surpluses, they were unwilling to vest an international organization with power over key resources.[38]

The United States, for example, opposed the FAO's proposal for an international system to deal with agricultural surpluses but established its own system to deal with them. To supplement and combine earlier disposal programs, Congress passed the Agricultural Trade Development and Assistance Act of 1954 (better known as PL [Public Law] 480) in response to the gargantuan agricultural surpluses that cost the federal government almost a million dollars per day to store and threatened to undermine USDA price supports. Although PL 480 resulted from domestic circumstances and was not initially intended as a foreign policy measure, it had wide-ranging international consequences. Besides leading to the quick accumulation of nonconvertible currencies in U.S. coffers, the new program could strain relations with fellow exporters and make deficit countries dependent on American foodstuffs. Nevertheless, the program met a real and continuing need to siphon off U.S. surpluses, was politically popular, and so received billion-dollar annual appropriations from Congress.[39] In other words, the United States was not so much opposed to the theory and operations behind the proposals for the World Food Board or ICCH as it was to moving the locus of decision making out of Washington.

With Dodd's efforts largely rebuffed, he returned his attention to technical assistance, which appealed to the director-general because it consisted of "the concrete and effective things that will produce more food and bring it to the world's hungry." FAO staff studies had created a consensus among the organization's members about what those "concrete and effective things" were, but initially at least the FAO did not have the money to undertake much of this type of work, especially when some members were in default on their payments and others sought ways to reduce their subscription to its five-million-dollar annual budget. As a result, before the Korean War FAO technical assistance was largely limited to one-time technical missions that were heavily subsidized by the requesting country.[40]

FAO's commitment to technical assistance received a boost from the UN's Expanded Program for Technical Assistance (EPTA), which was funded by voluntary donations from UN members and began to supplement the technical assistance programs of the UN specialized agencies in 1950. The underfunded FAO got the lion's share of the proceeds—29 percent of the total, or approximately another five million dollars—which Director-General Dodd termed "a godsend." Although the FAO was still limited in the type and extent of development aid it could undertake, it managed within two years to complete 163 technical assistance assignments in forty-nine nations using more than two hundred experts and to award almost five hundred fellowships for study in twenty-seven different countries. Like the World Bank, the FAO stretched its resources by paying for only part of each program, which helped ensure that the recipient country valued the project enough to commit its own resources and had a sense of full partnership in the enterprise. Dodd described the FAO system of technical assistance as "a world cooperative in which the members pool their technical and financial resources for mutual aid."[41]

This EPTA silver lining had a cloud attached to it, however. The FAO's technical assistance budget, and therefore its ability to help member countries, was not its own but depended on a multinational committee of donors (the Technical Assistance Board, or TAB), which proved less than reliable in subsequent years.[42] The obvious question was, why not increase the regular working budget of the FAO rather than make it dependent on EPTA to carry out its mission? The reasons were that, first of all, the latter method of funding gave the United States, as the primary contributor to EPTA and therefore the strongest force on the TAB, more control over the allocation of FAO resources. Also, the United States wanted the organization to focus on technical assistance rather than grand schemes for international commodity regulation. Not only did funding through EPTA help to ensure this, but the type of technical assistance programs funded channeled aid in a particular direction. Clearly, making real progress against world hunger was not a high priority in American foreign policy at this time.

The practical focus of EPTA was the transfer of expertise, usually by sending an expert to train a native counterpart while they cooperatively undertook a
specified project. The underlying assumption was that these agricultural and economic development projects would improve the lives of ordinary people in the
Third World, but all of these projects were to be planned and administered by national governments. This approach reveals the same emphasis on the replication
of experts in the Third World and on top-down development that characterized
much of the World Bank's educational and funding efforts, and it shared many of
the same shortcomings, including a lack of attention to the needs of women, who
were often important agricultural producers in Third World countries. A more
effective strategy might have focused on the human infrastructure needed to absorb development aid or on an overall food and agricultural development strategy rather than a set of independent, piecemeal projects. Such a goal could have
been advanced by placing a high priority on the improvement of governmental
administration, national research services, vocational training and education,
and rural improvement programs, but these avenues were effectively ignored so
long as the FAO funding structure remained largely dependent on EPTA funds.

Despite its shortcomings, Dodd was certain about the benefits of international
technical assistance. These programs, he declared, sent a strong message to the
world's farmers and peasants and ensured that "they feel they have been made
members of a great and glorious team fighting a fight for themselves, their neigh-
bours and the whole world,—a fight that will defeat no one and nothing except
starvation and malnutrition and social deterioration." That fight was, according
to Dodd and his staff, "a truly international and non-partisan effort, without regard to race or creed"; as early as 1952 the FAO drew technical experts from forty-
one Third World and First World countries. For example, the FAO employed an
Egyptian entomologist to work in Syria, an Iraqi expert on dates in Saudi Arabia,
a Korean veterinarian and a Peruvian cotton expert in Ethiopia, a Chinese silk
expert in Afghanistan, and an Argentine fisheries expert in Ecuador. Another advantage of FAO aid that often made it more desirable to Third World countries
was that, rather than being based on narrow, national, political objectives, the
FAO's apolitical program of technical assistance was "done in the name of a common humanity" and did not seek military alliances or economic concessions. But
the FAO's effort was tiny compared to Britain's Colombo Plan or the foreign aid
programs of the United States, and while Dodd publicly stated that these national
programs demonstrated a strong commitment to the goals for which the FAO
was established, he recognized that some countries "shopped around" for the best
aid terms, to the detriment of internationalism. Nonetheless, Dodd welcomed all
possible help in the race between population and food; there was less food per
capita in the mid-1950s than there had been before the Second World War, when
two-thirds of the world's people had been malnourished.[43]

Eventually, Dodd's ideal of the FAO as a global department of agriculture seemed to be coming to fruition. The international standing, technical expertise, and monetary resources of the FAO made it ideal for a variety of projects, especially those pursued on a regional level. In 1949 Dodd helped create the International Rice Commission, with seventeen member countries that pledged themselves to increasing rice production by sharing technical information and pooling resources. Similarly, in 1952, the FAO effectively coordinated the attack against desert locust in the Arabian Peninsula. The destructive power of locust and their refusal to recognize national boundaries stimulated international sharing of information, equipment, and chemical agents through the FAO, an effort that prevented any significant crop loss that year. Other regional projects that continued under the Dodd administration were the mass vaccination of livestock in the Middle East, Africa, and Asia against rinderpest and the introduction of hybrid corn to the Near East, as well as a whole variety of regional conferences on such topics as farming cooperatives and statistical techniques.[44]

Other international organizations also sought the expertise of the FAO. For example, UNICEF (the United Nations International Children's Emergency Fund) had large funds available not only for direct relief but also for projects that would result in long-term improvements in the health of mothers and children, who were particularly vulnerable to malnutrition. So when it wanted to increase the Third World's capacity for milk production, pasteurization, and processing, UNICEF looked to the FAO for technical assistance and fellowships to train indigenous technicians. Together with the nongovernmental International Dairy Federation and the World Health Organization, UNICEF and the FAO worked to increase the supply of sanitary, nutritious milk in countries such as India, Guatemala, and Colombia.[45]

As a complement to its technical assistance program, the FAO also expanded its information service. The FAO conducted a number of regional statistical workshops to enable its members to better provide complete, accurate, and uniform statistics for the FAO's 1950 *World Census of Agriculture,* its global inventory of forests, and its annual crop outlook reports. It also published a series of periodicals to inform and aid its diverse global clientele: the bimonthly *World Fisheries Abstracts,* the quarterly *Food and Agricultural Legislation, Unasylva* (on forestry developments), the *FAO Fisheries Bulletin,* and a monthly *FAO Plant Protection Bulletin.* By 1954 the FAO was spending approximately 14 percent of its annual budget, some $760,000 per year, on its publications, which were generally issued in the organization's three official languages (English, French, and Spanish). The FAO also maintained a substantial library, which not only served as a resource for the staff but provided materials to agricultural training centers, colleges, and universities; to national farmers' groups and nongovernmental organizations affiliated with the FAO; and to media outlets that solicited agricultural statistics and information. The emphasis on information sprang, in part, from Dodd's Progressive Era notion that if professionals understood the methods of alleviating world hunger, the problem would soon be overcome.[46]

Despite his natural optimism and faith in progress, Dodd recognized that technical assistance and information, in and of themselves, were inadequate to raise world nutrition and living standards. "Only the people who farm the land and fish the waters can produce more food," and to do so they needed secure land tenure, adequate credit, quality extension services, and improved tools, seeds, and fertilizers. If larger harvests brought a fall in prices and increases in rents and taxes, there would be no incentive for farmers to be more productive. But outside of making this knowledge available, the FAO could take no remedial action, for that remained the domain of national governments. This was the conundrum that Dodd and his successor, Philip V. Cardon, faced—the inadequacy of FAO actions in the absence of the power or funds to develop more adequate remedies for world hunger and poverty.[47]

The Food and Agriculture Organization under Norris E. Dodd accomplished a fair amount with rather limited resources. Like the USDA, it became known for its technical expertise and for the agricultural research and information it disseminated through its publications. It also organized important regional projects, coordinated activities with other international organizations, and garnered extra money for its technical assistance efforts from the United Nations. The countries that made up the FAO, however, while willing to accept its aid and to take actions to protect their own farmers, were unwilling to cede any control to the organization or give it the resources needed to undertake ambitious projects. As a result, the FAO had to rely on consensus to attain its objectives, and that was in short supply when it came to agriculture in the 1950s. As a result, the FAO's goal of global freedom from hunger remained distant.

Evaluating the First Decade

The years of Cardon's director-generalship were perhaps the most uninspired and discouraging in the FAO's early history. They began on a sour note, when the Republican administration of President Dwight D. Eisenhower denied another term to former New Dealer Dodd, who was beloved by the staff and much of the organization's membership. Cardon had been an agricultural researcher for much of his life, and although he had attended the Hot Springs Conference and other FAO meetings, he seemed to have developed little enthusiasm for the new organization and apparently came to office with little vision for the future of the FAO, as well as a history of heart problems. These deficiencies had a corrosive effect on staff morale, the low ebb of which was marked by the suicides of two staff members. Cardon did little that was innovative, carefully remaining within the boundaries established by his predecessors. Often with the assistance of other organizations (including UN specialized agencies, national and regional development bodies, and nongovernmental organizations), Cardon did continue a number of Dodd's regional initiatives, focusing on training in such diverse topics as farm broadcasting, irrigation and drainage practices, olive fly control, and wheat and barley breeding.[48]

But unlike his predecessor, Cardon seemed less adept at stretching the FAO's limited monies to pursue its global goals, and he was often on the defensive. He scaled back the FAO's participation in the UNICEF Milk Conservation Program, citing budgetary shortfalls even though the program provided a direct and relatively cost-efficient way to improve Third World nutrition and health. Relations with the International Labor Organization (ILO), another of the UN specialized agencies, also suffered under Cardon's administration. The FAO lacked the funds to provide technical assistance on ILO projects, yet it simultaneously insisted that the ILO "accept FAO's competence and responsibility in the agricultural field." Similarly, the FAO declined to provide studies for the UN Committee of Experts on Population Trends and Economic and Social Conditions, though the race between population and food had vitally concerned the organization since its founding. More importantly, in 1954, a destructive swarm of desert locust escaped the confines of the Arabian Peninsula and ravaged areas of northeast Africa; though many circumstances were beyond its control, much of the goodwill that the FAO had built up in the area evaporated.[49]

The shortcomings of Cardon's brief tenure, though problematic for the organization, serve to highlight the relative successes of his predecessors in navigating the often-treacherous waters of international affairs. While the FAO staff and leadership, like their counterparts in the World Bank, stressed the apolitical nature of their organization, it is clear that these international civil servants walked a difficult path between their own desires for global agriculture and those of national governments, other UN specialized agencies, farmers' groups, and nongovernmental organizations. While the FAO succeeded in organizing agricultural production and distribution under the auspices of the International Emergency Food Committee, it was not always as successful in mapping a productive course. John Boyd Orr's World Food Board proposals and Norris E. Dodd's International Commodity Clearing House aggravated member governments' fears about a powerful international organization. These fears led them to put tight controls on the FAO's finances, which, unlike the World Bank, were entirely dependent on annual appropriations.

Deprived of the opportunity to feed people directly, the FAO turned to the indirect methods of providing technical assistance and information through its publications. Under the leadership of Dodd, the FAO evolved into something akin to the U.S. Department of Agriculture, with its connections to land-grant colleges, experiment stations, and local farm bureaus. In the late 1940s and early 1950s, the FAO collected international data to aid farmers and rationalize commodity markets, gathered and disseminated the most up-to-date and expert information on technical issues, and aided farmers in a variety of countries in demonstration-type projects that were often part of its technical missions. It did all this with one-tenth of the USDA's annual budget. But by adopting the USDA model, the FAO was also adopting some of its shortcomings—its work did little to address the plight of tenant farmers and farm workers hovering on the brink of destitution, while it did much to help the larger farmers with greater capital resources. Indeed, in the United States, family farms are today quickly vanishing as agribusiness becomes dominant, raising questions about the safety of the food supply and the environmental impact of this trend. Although the model the FAO adopted had its shortcomings, the most powerful FAO member governments had closed off the more ambitious approaches that the staff had earlier formulated.

Despite the many errors in this trial period, the goal of the FAO, achieving freedom from want, remained foremost in the minds of its international staff. Orr, for example, remained keenly aware of the pioneering nature of the Food and Agriculture Organization as well as its fellow UN specialized agencies. Reflecting on the FAO's 1946 mission to Greece, the director-general mused that his international organization helped the Greeks draft their development plan, which would likely be funded by the World Bank and overseen by a variety of international experts. "This is something new in international affairs," he concluded. Developing countries also recognized the unique opportunity now offered. An Indian delegate pointed out that his country had never lacked human and natural resources, but that "under a Colonial economy, the central factor . . . [was] commerce and not the people's welfare." Now, with the help of the FAO the new government hoped to devote its resources to "the welfare of the people and . . . their standard of living."[50]

But the FAO had made little headway in helping member countries by 1956, when Cardon left office due to health problems. Rapid population growth meant that per capita food consumption was still lower in much of the Third World than it had been before World War II. The next director-general would face quite a challenge, meeting such enormous needs with a minimal budget and a membership that shied away from ambitious FAO programs. But this daunting task did not intimidate Binay Ranjan Sen, who had been a wartime food administrator in India and became the surprise favorite for the director-generalship over Dr. J. A. C. Davies of Harvard University and Sicco Mansholt of the Netherlands. Indeed, Sen pledged to launch "a frontal attack on the problems of widespread hunger and undernourishment," returning the FAO to its original mission with an innovative approach that brought more groups into the organization's work, helped overcome its budget difficulties, and eventually regained the confidence of its member governments.[51]

7

Redefining an International Role for the
Food and Agriculture Organization

The director-generalship of B. R. Sen (1956–1967) demonstrates the FAO's dogged dedication to the global fight against hunger, its faith in its expert abilities as an international technical agency, its ingenuity in creating an ambitious program within relatively strict budgetary confines, and its commitment to engaging a variety of organizations to work toward a common mission. Unfortunately, Sen's Freedom from Hunger Campaign (FFHC) also shows the great difficulty of successfully battling want and deprivation, especially when the world's largest food exporter and importer does not support that campaign. As the first director-general from the Third World, the Indian saw himself as an advocate for the poorer areas of the world, especially colonies that had just become associate members of the FAO under a 1955 constitutional change. Even though these new members could not vote and could not file independent applications for technical assistance, their very presence and their great need for international assistance served as a reminder of the high ideals for which the organization had been founded—to secure freedom from want for all the world's people. To this end, Sen launched the FFHC as "a frontal attack on the problems of widespread hunger and undernourishment." It was through this work that Sen revitalized the Food and Agriculture Organization.[1]

In this attack on hunger, Sen exploited the FAO's reputation as a body of international, apolitical experts in agricultural development; relying on his progressive worldview, he trusted that the dimensions of the problem would inspire the world's people to follow the FAO's lead in the fight to end world hunger. Starting with the organization's international scientific reputation, the director-general centered public interest and attention on "the known facts" of hunger and followed this initiative with a call to philanthropies, churches, national governments, ordinary citizens, industry, nongovernmental organizations (NGOs), and the UN specialized agencies to follow the FAO in a global campaign meant to remedy the problems it had exposed. The facts were indeed shocking: despite a fifteen-year effort, the FAO's *World Food Survey* revealed that per capita food consumption levels in Asia and Latin America were still below pre–World War II levels and were insufficient for health and energy. The 1959 FAO Conference responded by approving the ambitious Freedom from Hunger Campaign, designed to culminate with the 1963 World Food Congress, which would highlight the FFHC's achievements on the twentieth anniversary of the Hot Springs Conference.[2] In this way, the FAO attempted to recapture the activism present at the organization's founding by relying on NGOs rather than the organization's member countries, which had shown little interest in such ambitious global efforts as the World Food Board and International Commodity Clearinghouse. As a result, the Freedom from Hunger Campaign drew NGOs more closely into the work of the FAO, redirected the focus of agricultural development toward rural and human development activities, redefined the FAO's role in international affairs, and helped make world hunger a global issue and moral responsibility.

Although Sen sought the same goals as his predecessors—increased agricultural production and improved global nutrition—he took a new and innovative tack. In this activism he relied on the organization's staff, whose desire to revolutionize how the countries of the world looked at hunger and agricultural trade policy and to catalyze action on behalf of the globe's farmers and famished, had remained constant. He used this sense of mission to focus the attention of the world's population on global malnutrition and to prompt concrete remedial action through the Freedom from Hunger Campaign. In many ways, Sen's approach incorporated the best aspects of the programs of the previous directors-general, along with his own innovations. The Freedom from Hunger Campaign reflected, and Sen himself possessed, the same sort of crusading zeal to eliminate hunger that Orr had manifested in his World Food Board proposals. But, like Dodd and Cardon, Sen recognized that the FAO had limited resources and could not count on its membership to support ambitious global operations. Unlike the two American directors-general, however, Sen did not accept these limitations but pushed for and received higher budgetary levels, which he then supplemented with contributions from the NGOs that he actively integrated into the FAO's work. This cooperation, along with his own inclinations and the FAO's history of providing technical assistance, led Sen to concentrate on an approach to agricultural development that was more bottom-up in nature than any of his predecessors'. In other words, Sen's administration incorporated the best elements from the FAO's past with a bold new view of its future.

First Formulations

During a 1958 visit with President Dwight D. Eisenhower, Sen first enunciated his ideas about a campaign against hunger, and subsequently he brainstormed with the FAO Policy Planning Board about the main components of such a campaign. Even in these first discussions, it was clear that the FAO staff hoped that the stark facts of global hunger, when coupled with the FAO's knowledge of effective methods for advancing agricultural development, would "impel" the world to undertake "heroic efforts" against hunger under the leadership of the FAO, which loudly proclaimed its unique expertise for, and long history of, dealing with such problems. But from the beginning the FAO sought partners in its campaign. The UN specialized agencies cooperated on a series of basic studies touching on the intersection between their own functional specialties and the dilemma of hunger. On 10 July 1958, Sen officially proposed a campaign against hunger to the United Nations' Economic and Social Council (ECOSOC) in order to bring the program to the attention of all member countries as well as the ECOSOC's affiliated nongovernmental organizations, which FAO hoped would play a "vital part" in "stimulating and coordinating" the FAO's efforts.[3]

Information and education were to be the cornerstones of the Freedom from Hunger Campaign; the staff believed that "an enlightened and aroused public opinion [was] a sine qua non" for the campaign's success. This was true both of Third World nationals, who were to impress on their governments the need to make hunger a top priority, and of citizens in the First World, who would ideally urge their countries and charitable organizations to higher levels of international aid. They would participate in discussions, fund-raising, and even the realization of agricultural development projects through their churches, professional and business associations, and local community groups.[4]

To enlist the ordinary people of the globe in his campaign, Sen began his appeal to the NGOs in January 1959. His dramatic call to arms named hunger "the biggest human problem of the century, beside which other problems . . . are really trivial and of temporary significance." He declared that the conquest of hunger would increase humankind's "moral and intellectual stature" more than landing on the moon; he ended by calling on NGOs to stimulate public interest in the Freedom from Hunger Campaign.[5] These ideas quickly took root and bore fruit. Several NGOs passed early resolutions in support of the program (even before the FAO Conference approved the campaign in October 1959), while other NGOs contacted the FAO spontaneously to express their interest in the campaign. The appeal of the program was such that both Pope John XXIII and the Islamic Congress blessed the campaign and lent their prestige to its promotion. The NGOs saw the FAO as the ideal leader of such a wide-ranging campaign; not only did it have experience in agricultural development programs but its status as a technical agency lent it an aura of "disinterested international assistance." For this reason, many NGOs sought early and frequent consultations with the FAO in order to fit their own programs into its international crusade against hunger.[6]

With the assurance that NGOs would cooperate in the promotion and operation of the program, the FAO turned to the nations that governed the organization and found them intent on developing an extensive program of concrete activities to lend credence to the rhetoric of the FFHC. Sen had always recognized the need for extensive action to fight effectively against hunger, but initially at least budget constraints had forced him to confine the FAO's role to that of catalyst and manager of programs and monies coming through bilateral aid, increased levels of UN funding, NGO contributions, and increased levels of spending by Third World governments on agricultural development. But the American government, in particular, made an action component almost "a condition of U.S. support," and given such encouragement, the FAO staff quickly grasped the campaign's potential to make the organization a truly vital and important force in the drive for economic development (the thought of higher budget levels also likely danced in their heads).[7]

The action component of the FFHC, in tandem with strong NGO involvement, gave the FAO an opportunity to focus world attention on the possibilities of achieving agricultural development through human and rural development projects. These were quite different from U.S. programs that primarily sought to dispose of American agricultural surpluses in a manner that would develop future markets for U.S. agricultural commodities and build support for American foreign policy. Instead, rural development programs aimed to provide appropriate incentives and training to local populations so they could improve their own standards of nutrition and living. If these programs enabled a nation to produce most of its own food, that nation could conserve foreign-exchange resources, improve local nutrition, and insulate itself from the global commodity market's volatility. FAO rural development projects, for example, sought to interest farmers in fishing and small-scale poultry raising, thereby remedying protein deficiencies in local populations. In order to improve the quality of crops and decrease reliance on imported seeds, the FAO also promoted the creation of indigenous seed associations. Other, more traditional, proposals included fighting preventable animal diseases, expanding school feeding and home economics programs, improving poor grasslands that limited livestock and milk production, and using demonstration projects to encourage butter and cheese production that would raise the incomes of rural farm families.[8]

But these ideas would be for naught if funding for the FFHC could not be found. Although the FAO Council, the ECOSOC, and the Tenth Session of the FAO Conference all endorsed the Freedom from Hunger Campaign in 1959, the project received no operating funds, because the FAO budget for the next two years, which had already been determined, included none. Not to be deterred, the FAO secretariat shuffled existing budget and staff allocations to provide the resources needed to begin the campaign. To cover interim expenses, the FAO created the FFHC Special Fund to accept donations. The first contribution was $100,000 from the Catholic Bishops of West Germany, but further donations trickled into the fund too slowly to cover the expenses of the increasingly ambitious campaign. The staff, and especially Sen, did not lose heart but rather worked to reshape the FAO's mission along the lines of the FFHC. They were therefore heartened by the FAO Conference's decision to reelect Sen for a four-year term, breaking the tradition of two-year terms and giving him the power to carry the campaign through to fruition.[9]

The American Reaction

No contribution or support for the campaign was forthcoming from the Eisenhower administration. Indeed, the U.S. government had sought from the beginning to discourage or remold the Freedom from Hunger Campaign to fit the president's policy of promoting trade rather than providing higher levels of aid. In line with this policy, in April 1959 the U.S. representative to the FAO Council's ad hoc committee on the FFHC stressed the development of trade, surplus disposal programs, research efforts, and a global division of labor in regard to agricultural commodities. This was in sharp contrast to the FAO's objectives for the campaign, which included combating hunger and malnutrition, increasing indigenous food production, improving food distribution, and tackling hunger with the knowledge and resources already available. Additionally, the U.S. representative stressed how Third World countries might remedy "their problem" through extant avenues of aid and assistance, a view that was in stark contrast to the contention of the Indian government that the campaign should focus on "the obligation of the surplus countries" to aid "the deficit and poor ones." Another attempt to kill the newborn campaign came from the U.S. representative to the ECOSOC, who wanted to delete from the council's draft endorsement of the campaign any recommendation that member nations or NGOs support the FFHC.[10]

This attitude fit with Secretary of Agriculture Ezra Taft Benson's views on domestic agricultural policy, which were largely encapsulated in his first official statement at a 5 February 1953 press conference: "Freedom is a God-given, eternal principle vouchsafed to us under the Constitution. . . . It is doubtful if any man can be politically free who depends upon the state for sustenance. A completely planned and subsidized economy weakens initiative, discourages industry, destroys character, and demoralizes the people." While certainly fitting with the ideology of both the Republican Party and the Mormon church (in which Benson was a leader), this laissez-faire approach to agriculture rang hollow in the ears of many American farmers as well as agriculturalists throughout the Third World, who suffered from structural difficulties in making a decent living and who found

Benson's rhetoric insulting. Nonetheless, Eisenhower's domestic farm program stressed a gradual reduction in price supports, and Benson worked hard to rid the government of the stored commodities it had accrued as a result of past price support programs. Therefore, it is not surprising that the administration likewise resisted an international aid program to boost agricultural production through rural development schemes and instead sought to dispose of its own agricultural surpluses in a manner that would primarily develop future markets for American agricultural commodities and support its foreign policy.[11]

In the wake of Sen's initiative, however, and in response to Cold War confrontations in the Third World, Eisenhower began to lean away from the policy of "trade not aid" and toward a foreign policy of "trade *and* aid." The administration reconceptualized its foreign food aid program in the fall of 1958 and renamed it "Food for Peace," at approximately the same time Sen first approached the president with his Freedom from Hunger Campaign. But U.S. food aid, although rhetorically revamped and increasingly embraced by the State Department as a component of foreign policy, was still dominated by domestic economic concerns. Food for Peace was cut from the same cloth as the 1959 Department of Commerce export-promotion drive and the concurrent liberalization of Export-Import Bank terms, all of which had been developed in response to the worsening U.S. balance-of-payments situation.[12]

Sen chose to embrace the Food for Peace program as complementary to the work of the FAO and the FFHC, despite the cool reception of his ideas by the U.S. government and its construction of a parallel program. He defined it as one battle in the larger war against hunger. Perhaps Sen hoped that the American program would further emphasize the embarrassing agricultural wealth of the First World, the glaring hunger of the Third World, and the difficulties of bridging this gap on a bilateral basis; maybe the director-general was simply biding his time until the 1960 presidential election. Whatever his reasons, Sen's generous interpretation of Food for Peace avoided any invocation of American wrath, and he even garnered Eisenhower's imprimatur on the timely launching of the FFHC in the United States on 1 July 1960.[13]

Although the United States remained far more interested in surplus disposal than in rural development, by 1960 it was looking to obtain more from its food aid program. On 22 September 1960, Eisenhower suggested to the UN General Assembly the creation of a multilateral food aid agency. When President John F. Kennedy subsequently sent George S. McGovern, his Food for Peace director, to Rome in April 1961 to consider the feasibility of establishing such an international program, McGovern proposed a bold initiative. He suggested that any such agency not only disburse famine and disaster aid but also devote resources to school feeding programs and development projects—projects that were similar to the programs put forth in the FAO's Freedom from Hunger Campaign. McGovern suggested a three-year experimental period with a $100 million budget. The World Food Program (WFP), born of McGovern's proposal and parallel 1961 resolutions in the UN General Assembly and the FAO Conference, began its work on 1 January 1963 under the joint auspices of the UN and the FAO; by 1970 it had funded 550 economic development projects in eighty-eight different countries.[14]

But the operations of the WFP amply demonstrated the continuing conflict between national and international interests over the issue of food aid. The WFP's Intergovernmental Committee consisted of twenty members, equally divided between aid donors and recipients, and evaluated all requests for program assistance. It was free to disregard FAO advice on how the suggested projects would fit into national agricultural development programs and on ways to ensure that normal channels of trade would not be disrupted by the aid. Equally troubling, the WFP could provide only the types of food that had been donated to it, which were not always needed or desired; donating nations held all food stores until requested to ship them by the FAO, a stipulation that greatly slowed the shipment of emergency relief; and the WFP ceded all oversight once the food reached its port of call. While this provision safeguarded national sovereignty, it allowed wider latitude for the misdirection of aid and handicapped those countries lacking managerial expertise and the necessary infrastructure for effective distribution. But the program also had its advantages. Funneling more aid through multinational channels pleased many Third World countries that hoped to reduce their vulnerability to political pressure from donor nations, while donor countries appreciated that the WFP shared the international food aid burden, provided a mechanism for better coordination of food aid, allowed First World nations at least to appear responsive to Third World concerns about neo-imperialism, and at the same time provided a modicum of contributor control over aid disbursement. Now the FAO had, for the first time, the authority to initiate action and provide emergency food aid, rather than simply notifying member countries of the need for famine assistance.[15]

The World Food Program, although initiated under the previous administration, showed that Kennedy's food aid initiatives fit much more closely with the FAO's modus operandi than had Ike's. Just as the new president took Eisenhower's multilateral food aid initiative and made it his own, Kennedy revitalized and retooled Food for Peace, emphasizing Third World development over surplus disposal. To this end, he put a new emphasis on the use of food aid to promote social, economic, and agricultural development in ways that the FAO had earlier suggested. Such aid fed children in schools and clinics, induced local farmers to further their technical education, and paid wages for public works programs. Nonetheless, Food for Peace still maintained its strong trade emphasis and remained an instrument of American foreign policy. The Kennedy administration, for example, used food aid in an attempt to influence Algerian and Egyptian foreign policy as well as to prop up the U.S.-engineered regime and strategic-hamlet program in South Vietnam.[16] In other words, Kennedy, though moving toward the FAO in terms of methods, was still implementing them in search of primarily national objectives.

Getting the FFHC Off the Ground

The changes to the U.S. Food for Peace program and the institution of the World Food Program revealed the great influence that the FAO's new ideas about agricultural development were having on the world's leading agricultural producer, but these U.S. programs were pale imitations of the rural development ideology animating the FFHC. One of its cardinal principles was that local farmers and villagers must be actively involved, because unless "scientific knowledge, modern techniques and comprehensive agricultural development plans" were carried "to the farmers, herdsmen and fishermen, to the housewives, to the village merchants, to the local cooperative, the campaign is in danger of evaporating into bitter disappointment for the hungry and into pious hopes for the well-fed."[17]

Ironically, the FFHC's success in capturing the imagination of the world's people threatened to overwhelm the FAO in 1959, as requests for publicity material, speakers, suggestions on launching national campaigns, guidance for selection and refinement of action projects, and consultants for the production of the campaign's media coverage inundated the ad hoc FFHC structure and its twenty-five-thousand-dollar budget. FAO staff members did the best they could to maintain the campaign's momentum; because failure to do so, they believed, would "harm the cause of agriculture and encourage doubt in a normal and peaceable solution of one of the great problems of today and the future." But at the same time, a realistic assessment of budgetary sources led the FAO to declare that it would create only prototype materials in the organization's three languages, leaving national committees to undertake the costs of additional publications and translations. As 1960 dawned, campaign staffers had to admit to themselves that the campaign had "no money," but they hoped to overcome the budgetary shortfall by placing a surcharge on all action projects to cover FAO overhead costs and by accepting donations from NGOs for campaign administration. Despite fiscal problems, the action component of the campaign took shape with the 1960 publication of a catalog of potential action projects. The FAO staff hoped that the catalog, which encapsulated the FAO's fifteen years of field experience, would also "aid underdeveloped countries in thinking about agricultural action projects they might usefully adopt as parts of their development programs," but just as important was the fact that it provided concrete projects that countries, individuals, corporations, nongovernmental organizations, religious groups, and bilateral development agencies could underwrite.[18]

Such NGOs were the heart of the Freedom from Hunger Campaign. Not only did they share Sen's faith in rural development, but the director-general saw them as his best assets in spreading news of the campaign, conceiving of and financing action projects, and encouraging national governments to participate in the FFHC. To this end, Sen established an independent FFHC advisory committee that reported directly to his office and brought representatives of twenty-three NGOs together in January 1960 for a three-day discussion of the educational and fund-raising work that they might contribute to the Freedom from Hunger Campaign.[19] The FAO also recruited the world's youth, the same people who participated in volunteer programs like the Peace Corps, into its campaign. Sen was "most anxious" to integrate such volunteers into FFHC rural development programs. Additionally, youth organizations, such as the World Assembly of Youth (WAY) and the World Congress of Catholic Rural Youth, spread news of the campaign in their periodicals and contributed to its rural development focus through educational programs aimed at cultivating rural youth leaders in Latin America, Asia, and Africa. In recognition of the value of such initiatives, the FFHC Advisory Committee on Non-Governmental Organizations elected the WAY representative to be chairman of its second session.[20]

In addition to NGO support, the FAO sought help from industry for its Freedom from Hunger Campaign, and its earliest and most notable success was with the international fertilizer industry. The *FAO Fertilizer Survey* had established the great agricultural advances that might be made in the Third World through more extensive use of artificial fertilizers, especially in Asia, where only 3 to 5 percent of cultivators used fertilizer and almost none of it on subsistence food crops, despite the growing malnutrition in the area. In December 1959, fertilizer companies and associations from around the world gathered with FAO officials to formulate a plan to promote wider use of fertilizers and thereby "introduce the scientific method and modern technology into traditional agriculture." The FAO appealed to the industry to educate extension workers about the merits of fertilizer, improve distribution of their product in order to reduce its cost to the consumer, invest in fertilizer manufacturing in underdeveloped countries, and donate supplies for demonstrations and pilot projects. On 26 and 27 April 1960, forty-one representatives of the fertilizer industry met, agreeing to contribute $1 million over two years to the campaign's fertilizer initiatives. The FAO saw this endeavor as a "win-win" proposition: the recipient nation enjoyed a higher level of agricultural productivity, and the industry would have larger markets in the future.[21]

Other industries also contributed to the FFHC, hoping to garner similar advantages. CIBA, a Swiss pharmaceutical firm, published, in partnership with the FAO, studies on the detrimental effect of animal parasites on food production and underwrote the cost of a veterinarian to do fieldwork in Central America. The Dutch Bakers' and Millers' Association undertook a particularly innovative fund-raising effort for the FFHC. Realizing that most Dutch citizens remembered how they had suffered from hunger during the Nazi occupation, the bakers printed facsimiles of the last wartime ration cards and sold them to housewives for approximately 25 cents, with the proceeds used to underwrite a five-year program to expand wheat and barley production in the Near East. The project also involved contributions from the FAO, NOVIB (the Dutch organization for international assistance), the Rockefeller Foundation, and the Swedish FFHC national committee.[22]

In addition to providing a list of appropriate projects and a point of coordination among all participants, the FAO oversaw the program and ensured that its projects were carried out in a satisfactory manner. Specifically, all FFHC projects had to be approved by the FAO to ensure that they complemented development projects already undertaken in the area and would have a significant impact, and to do so it required periodic progress reports and a detailed accounting of all FFHC projects. Such precautions reassured potential donors that their money would reach its promised destination and provided the information that the organization used to publicize the campaign. The FFHC newsletter also fostered "a continuing sense of interest and devotion" as well as "a readiness to persevere in the activity through the long period of the campaign."[23]

It was at the national level, where the campaign "must be fought and won," that the FAO had the least control. While it urged each member country to create a broadly based FFHC National Committee to formulate and coordinate campaign efforts, some First World countries were unenthusiastic contributors to the campaign, and few Third World nations seemed ready to incorporate a multiplicity of voices in the decision-making process about development. The enthusiasm elicited by the campaign nonetheless led most nations to participate in the FFHC. President Kennedy, the prime minister of Finland, and French premier Charles de Gaulle became public boosters of the campaign, and eighty countries ultimately formed national committees. Among these, Poland provided training and advice to developing countries through its Institute of Human Nutrition, and Sweden matched every kroner raised from the public for the campaign.[24]

Perhaps the most active national FFHC committee was the one in the United Kingdom. Although British authorities had discouraged many previous FAO initiatives, this campaign did not require the Exchequer to make anything but voluntary contributions and instead relied for support primarily on the people of the British Isles. The United Nations Association of the United Kingdom spearheaded the campaign and on 20 January 1960 brought together more than thirty organizations for an informational meeting. The organizational representatives enthusiastically and earnestly listened to campaign plans, immediately sought FAO promotional literature and direction on the campaign, and drafted a proposal for establishing a national FFHC committee. The ready acceptance of the campaign came, in part, from a previous "war on want" movement in which colleges had raised money and awareness through "miss-a-meal" initiatives. In fact, the FAO had placed an exhibit at the "War on Want" national meeting, during which more than five thousand copies of one of Sen's speeches on the FFHC had been sold. The British people also seemed to see the campaign as a worthy effort for a former imperial power: "No country in the world has had greater experience than has our own working in underdeveloped countries. . . . It is up to us in the United Kingdom to see to it that we play a worthy part." When Prince Philip officially launched the campaign in June 1962, sixty-three British voluntary societies were already associated with the FFHC.[25]

The U.K. laid the groundwork for the FFHC with a broad educational campaign in 1961 that included the distribution of reading lists and discussion guides to adult organizations and a teaching guide to six thousand elementary and secondary schools. In many cases questions on world hunger became part of the regular curriculum and state examinations. With this educational groundwork in place, monies came from a broad variety of sources—for example, school children put together and sold a book of writings and illustrations; Peter Simper & Co. Ltd. provided free amusement equipment to group events that raised money for the FFHC; and the Oxford Committee for Famine Relief (OXFAM) and the Inter-Church Aid Appeal also raised funds. The British FFHC expert review committee approved more than two hundred projects worth more than £3 million, most of which, in keeping with the campaign's rural development focus, funded educational and training work "as a first step in making these countries independent of foreign advisors."[26]

To be effective, FFHC action projects had to be part of the recipient's overall economic development strategy. "Merely sending technicians to teach these countries know-how and scientific developments is not enough," Sen asserted in 1962. "We are telling governments that they cannot make any progress unless they take stock of their own resources, whether human resources or material resources. . . . It is on such bases that technical assistance can be effective." As an example, the FAO staff pointed to India, the first nation to establish an FFHC national committee, which evaluated FFHC projects and determined which would be most harmonious with India's own development plans. In some cases, the promise of additional resources through the FFHC provided the needed incentive for other countries to undertake such national planning. The FAO also warned Third World governments to recognize that the rewards of adopting progressive methods could be nullified by increased rents, interest rates, and taxes or by price-depressing surpluses unless they took steps to protect productive farmers through crop insurance, storage facilities, land-tenure reform, and national agricultural credit institutions.[27]

Despite the importance of campaign coordination at the national level, it was at the project level that the campaign could change lives for the better. To ensure that that happened, all action projects had an educational component. Only when target populations understood how the project might benefit them and contribute to overall national production goals would they cooperate to carry on the project long after the end of the campaign. For this reason, most FFHC projects included a demonstration component, such as school and community garden projects, that showed the local population the advantages of adopting new techniques. The FFHC also took a number of initiatives to expand the use of radio as a means of spreading agricultural information and news, especially in rural areas where illiteracy was a concern. At the beginning of 1963, the FAO and the United Arab Republic (UAR) jointly organized a month-long seminar on modern farm broadcasting techniques that was financed by the New Zealand Freedom from Hunger Committee and attended by experts from the UAR, New Zealand, Australia, Canada, and the United States.[28]

Another central tenet of the Freedom from Hunger Campaign was "Human investment is the most important investment of all." In line with this philosophy, some FFHC projects sought to increase the domestic production of protein-rich foods and thereby combat the prevalence of protein malnutrition throughout the Third World. The German Catholic and Evangelical churches sponsored projects in eastern and northern Nigeria that encouraged the growth of protein-rich legumes to improve nutrition as well as soil fertility; and in the province of Andhra Pradesh, India, where the majority of the population believed cows to be sacred, the Freedom from Hunger Council of Ireland sought to develop the pork industry by improving breeding techniques, training local veterinarians in swine care, and instituting a marketing campaign. One of the most ambitious and successful FFHC efforts to improve the protein level in local diets was the fishing boat mechanization project that the FAO launched in partnership with the Outboard Marine Corporation of the United States, which donated engines and spare parts to the West African nations of Togo and Dahomey (present-day Benin). In addition to introducing new technology, the FAO brought Senegalese fishermen to Dahomey to demonstrate new fishing techniques, and the African technicians who would repair the engines received internships at the U.S. plant. The FAO also called on the national governments to provide support services, such as tax-free gasoline depots, spare parts, and the salaries of two full-time mechanics.[29]

In tandem with the outboard motorization project, the FAO often included projects to improve the preservation, storage, and distribution of the greatly increased catches. For without ways to preserve food and get it to market, there was no incentive to produce more food and no way for the poorer classes to afford to augment their diets. Another FFHC project emphasized the potential for improving farmers' incomes and local nutrition by introducing elementary methods of cheese making. Cheese could be stored longer, transported more easily, and sold at higher prices than liquid milk. Taking a different tack, other FFHC projects called for farmers' cooperatives to build and maintain roads and to develop transportation cooperatives, while others encouraged the manufacture of simple wheeled carts for transportation.[30]

In order to build human infrastructure for the continuing war on hunger, some FFHC projects focused on educational efforts. The city of Bath, England, raised £65,000 to construct a farm institute and demonstration farm in Hombola, Tanganyika, which educated the local Wagogo people about improved methods of animal husbandry, soil conservation, food storage, and home economics. The British National Federation of Women's Institutes financed similar projects, including a farm institute in Karamoja, Uganda, and the University Research Farm in Trinidad. The Canadian Hunger Foundation likewise created the International Food Technology Training Center in Mysore City, India, in 1965. The center provided postgraduate education to qualified applicants throughout South and West Asia, Latin America, and Africa for more than ten years, and the utility of its work led other international development agencies from Canada, Denmark, Norway, Sweden, and the British Commonwealth to provide funds to expand and continue the curriculum. Other FFHC projects that supplemented Third World educational efforts included the expansion of the agricultural staff training institute in the British Solomon Islands and the opening of a nutrition center in Fiji to train dieticians.[31]

The rural development focus of the FFHC led to greater attention on women's roles in agricultural development. The FAO, prior to the campaign, had rarely spoken about the role of women in agricultural development and employed few women in decision-making positions. But the NGOs, especially the Women's International League for Peace and Freedom (WILPF) and the Associated Country Women of the World, demanded greater participation by women in FFHC decision making. At the 1959 FAO Conference, the WILPF delegate sarcastically commented that she "had looked forward to seeing at this Conference in the many delegations present here, a considerable number of women—women in key positions in their countries, experts in the various fields of economy, sociology, physiology, home economics, nutrition, rural housing, the many social services, vocational training, the eradication of illiteracy etc. Have we not always been told and are we not told even today that women ought to concentrate on just these activities?" Despite this justifiable show of indignation, many FFHC action programs included specific programs for women: the farm institute underwritten by the citizenry of Bath, England, provided Wagogo women with education in agriculture, home economics, hygiene, and child care; the FFHC radio seminars included informational programs specifically for women; and the British National Federation of Women's Institutes established in India and Rhodesia teams of trained home economists who did outreach work to rural women on literacy, health, hygiene, child care, and food preparation and storage. Through this work the Women's Institutes hoped to train local leaders, and the

Associated Country Women of the World used its Lady Aberdeen scholarships to
provide potential leaders with home economics education abroad.[32]

The World Food Congress, 1963

In 1963, to highlight the FAO's new approach to agricultural development, to
create further momentum for the campaign, to develop new leaders in the fight
against world hunger, and to give the organization's staff and leadership a chance
to showcase their expertise and ability, the Food and Agriculture Organization
convened a world food congress. Those who attended the congress were to assess
the progress of the FFHC, suggest what remained to be done to defeat hunger,
and lend a sense of urgency to the ongoing campaign. To set the tone for the
congress, on 14 March 1963 Sen convened a Special Assembly on Man's Right to
Freedom from Hunger that consisted of twenty-eight Nobel Prize winners and
other recognized leaders of "moral authority." Its manifesto declared, "We feel
that international action for abolishing hunger will reduce tension and improve
human relationships by bringing out the best instead of the worst in man." In
addition, during a World Freedom from Hunger Week, Kennedy and de Gaulle
issued special proclamations, the World Council of Churches sponsored a special
service in the Cathedral of St. Pierre in Geneva, the World Health Organization
made hunger the subject of its World Health Day, and nearly 150 countries issued
special FFHC stamps that raised money for and awareness of the campaign.[33]

When the World Food Congress (WFC) began in June 1963, more than 1,300
private citizens, academics, and NGO and government representatives from more
than one hundred different countries attended, many of whom had traveled from
the Third World, bearing witness to the importance of the FAO's efforts in those
areas of the world. Kennedy's keynote address echoed the rhetoric of the Hot
Springs Conference two decades earlier and of the more recent FFHC: "For the
first time in the history of the world we do know how to produce enough food
now to feed every man, woman and child in the world, enough to eliminate all
hunger completely. . . . We have the ability, as members of the human race. We
have the means, we have the capacity to eliminate hunger from the face of the
earth in our lifetime. We need only the will." He also took up one of Sen's themes
in pointing out that American surpluses could help hungry people but that they
were only a stop-gap measure. Indian president Sarvepalli Radhakrishnan also
spoke on the first day of the conference and reminded the congress of the great
moral purpose of the campaign: "The painful reality of the starving millions of
the world must rouse the conscience of those who are placed in better conditions," for all religions preached the need to "love thy neighbor" and the smallness
of the modern world made all people the neighbors of all others. These opening

addresses set the tone for subsequent discussions and panels that "were carried out in an atmosphere of high purpose and shared responsibility."[34]

A number of exhibits at the congress translated these abstract ideals into concrete terms by highlighting a number of rural development projects already begun under the Freedom from Hunger Campaign. But the main work of the congress was to bring together individuals as well as government officials from the global community to discuss the most important aspects of global agriculture and food issues. Each session was cochaired by one representative from a developed country and one from a developing country in order to lend the discussions balance and a broad perspective. In this way, the congress established international networks of individuals and organizations interested in issues of hunger and provided each delegate with a "rich harvest of ideas." The final resolutions of the congress affirmed the rural development focus of the FFHC and stressed the importance of national planning and international coordination through UN agencies. To this end, the congress recommended periodic food congresses at which the FAO director-general, aided by representatives from FFHC national committees, would apprise representatives of the global food situation and any new approaches for improving it.[35]

To close the congress, Sen placed a declaration before the assembly that summarized the tone of the congress and called for a global plan to feed the world's hungry. After asserting that "the persistence of hunger and malnutrition is unacceptable morally and socially, is incompatible with the dignity of human beings and the equality of opportunity to which they are entitled, and is a threat to social and international peace," the director-general called for a new ideology of development that would be based on the "fullest and most effective use of all human and natural resources." This declaration was approved by acclamation. The chairman of the World Food Congress, U.S. Secretary of Agriculture Orville Freeman, however, refused to preside over this session, because he believed the declaration was too radical. Although not bound by the resolutions of the congress, a number of governments and the FAO membership embraced many of its recommendations and conclusions. No doubt the acceptance of the FFHC and its plan of attack on hunger arose, at least in part, from the success of the World Food Congress in mobilizing public support and in illustrating the effectiveness of the FFHC's rural and human development projects.[36]

Aftermath of the World Food Congress

At the FAO Conference that followed on the heels of the World Food Congress, the member countries called for a continuation of the campaign through 1970. In the afterglow of the successful congress, Sen also proposed a substantially larger program of work and budget, arguing that the third *World Food Survey* and the World Food Congress had demonstrated the need for extensive and continuing FAO action; the FAO annual budget rose from less than $7 million in 1958 to $83.5 million by the end of Sen's tenure. The director-general used the organization's expanded resources and the momentum generated by the World Food Congress to continue the gains made by the FFHC. The new president of the World Bank, George Woods, responded to the call of the World Food Congress for an increased level of international financing to underwrite Third World agricultural develop-ment. Beginning in 1964, the bank used FAO personnel to evaluate and supervise agricultural development projects that the bank would finance, and this collab-orative arrangement was soon replicated in agreements with the Inter-American, African, and Asian development banks. By 1980 the FAO Investment Center had conducted feasibility studies for projects worth more than $13 billion. Particularly inspired by the World Food Congress were NGOs representing young people, which Sen called together for the first meeting of the Young World Assembly in October 1965. He hoped these young people would work together with the FAO in promoting bottom-up, people-to-people development, and to this end he estab-lished a division within the FFHC to promote youth activities.[37]

The Freedom from Hunger Campaign had also drawn a number of industrial concerns into the FAO's operations, and Sen continued to nurture these ties af-ter the congress. These relationships, he believed, promised to bring together the resources and knowledge necessary to increase the pace of agricultural develop-ment significantly. To this end, he participated in informal FFHC meetings with industrialists in Chicago, Rome, Paris, and New York City that showed that these businessmen also recognized the benefits that might accrue from a cooperative relationship. The 9 June 1965 meeting in New York led to a tentative understand-ing that the FAO and American industry should maintain liaisons on agricultural investment needs and prospects, pre-investment surveys, public information programs concerning world food problems, government-industry cooperation toward their alleviation, joint support for field demonstrations and research institutes, industry-sponsored training courses, and studies of food habits. But Third World countries were suspicious of this form of cooperation and feared the effects of large-scale investment by multinational corporations, and this suspi-cion effectively limited industry's role in the FAO's subsequent work.[38]

At the end of his FAO career, Sen reflected that the FFHC had been the "most rewarding" period of his life. Indeed, he could be proud that the campaign had led to a greater public realization of the extent of world hunger, that the World Food Program had developed methods of utilizing food surpluses for economic and so-cial development, and the FFHC had brought NGOs, UN agencies, national gov-ernments, and, to a more limited extent, industry together to launch a meaningful, coordinated, bottom-up development effort.[39] But that effort was soon cut short.

B. R. Sen left office in 1967, since he could not be reelected, due to a 1961, U.S.-sponsored amendment to the FAO Constitution (which was, by the way, reversed in 1977). The new FAO director-general, Addeke Henrik Boerma, was a citizen of the Netherlands who had come to office amid implied quid pro quos about higher levels of donations to FAO voluntary programs from the industrialized nations. His tenure ushered in a period in which the ideas of the Green Revolution—rather than the Freedom from Hunger Campaign—predominated, a period in which the FAO lost its leadership on the issue of agricultural development, a period in which the FAO's mandate fractured into several different organizations dealing with food and agriculture, and a period in which the FAO became increasingly politicized.[40] Ultimately, Sen did not achieve his most cherished goal—the end of world hunger. Indeed, many millions continue to suffer from malnutrition and hunger today, in part because the FAO could not bridge the gap between national sovereignty and international interests. While the FFHC influenced the United States' Food for Peace program, America's farmers and U.S. foreign policy imperatives, not the needs of the global community, played the largest role in determining American aid policies. Indeed, it is unlikely that Sen's vision will be achieved until food is no longer viewed as a national trade commodity or source of leverage in foreign policy but rather as a basic need and human right.

8

The Growth of International Cooperation
in Medicine

The World Health Organization (WHO) was the last of the wartime UN specialized agencies to be founded, despite a record of nearly one hundred years of formal international cooperation on health matters. The first International Sanitary Conference, convened in Paris on 23 July 1851, included both diplomats and physicians. The inclusion of doctors signaled their growing professional status, which was the result of medicine's grounding in the sciences of anatomy, physiology, and even mathematics. Later in the century, the discovery that identifiable microorganisms caused disease deepened the scientific basis of medical practice, prompted radical changes in medical education and licensure, and created public confidence in doctors that reinforced physicians' professional authority. This was an international phenomenon given the nature of medical study in the nineteenth century. The early superiority of French medical schools attracted students from around the world, and as the cutting edge in medical research and training shifted to Germany and eventually to the United States, a multinational student body followed. Not only students but also a growing number of international medical gatherings spread knowledge of the newest scientific findings. More important, however, was the formation of permanent international health organizations in the twentieth century.

The Pan American Sanitary Bureau (PASB) and the Office International d'Hygiène Publique (OIHP) were the first such organizations and were mainly concerned with the reporting and tracking of epidemic diseases in the Americas and Europe, respectively. Much broader in scope was the League of Nations Health Organization (LNHO), which not only undertook such epidemiological work but also established international standards for biological products, dispatched experts to advise member countries, took steps to advance medical education, convened international conferences for the exchange of health information, and established expert committees to advise the international community on the most effective means of fighting and preventing disease. The work of this health organization, however, was somewhat hindered by its subordination to the League of Nations, whose less than universal membership and declining influence before World War II detracted from the LNHO's influence.

The Second World War brought scientific advances in medical treatment as well as a determination to build a peaceful new world order. The key to that, the victors believed, was a system of international cooperation embodied in the United Nations and its specialized agencies. While the World Bank and the Food and Agriculture Organization had been planned during the war, ideas for the World Health Organization were developed only in the postwar period. In fact, the Economic and Social Council of the United Nations Organization—rather than the Allied powers—convened the International Health Conference that established the WHO's constitution, and the World Health Organization itself came into being only in 1948. The work of the OIHP, the PASB, and the League of Nations Health Organization served as models for the WHO, but its mission went beyond any of its predecessors, all of which were absorbed into the new organization. An internationalism based on professional ideology and the apolitical standards of science marked the work of the WHO and its staff; all of these elements had their roots in the nineteenth century.

Science, Professionalism, and Medicine in the Nineteenth and Early Twentieth Centuries

The practice of medicine underwent two scientific revolutions in the nineteenth century. The first, a clinical revolution, arose from the new natural sciences of anatomy, physiology, and chemistry and eventually replaced the earlier belief that disease arose from an imbalance in bodily humors with the demonstrable thesis that specific diseases attacked particular organs. The microscope and the subsequent development of bacteriology ushered in the second scientific revolution, which, in turn, established that disease arose from specific germs rather than from "miasmas"—supposedly disease-carrying exhalations from decaying organic material that spread through the atmosphere. Conjointly, these twin revolutions elevated medicine to the ranks of a scientific exercise, won the confidence of a rightfully skeptical public, and allowed physicians to gain the rank of professionals.

The clinical revolution of the first half of the nineteenth century brought to medicine the tenets of careful observation and scientific analysis that had flourished in other disciplines during the Enlightenment. Beginning in the great hospitals of Paris at the turn of the nineteenth century, medical practitioners, through careful observation and the recording of cases, first started to correlate clinical symptoms with the findings of postmortem examinations in order to determine which diseases attacked which organs. Their discoveries gave a great boost to the practice of medical surgery and simultaneously helped discredit homeopathy and other theories of medicine that traced illness to a single cause. The desire of these pioneering French physicians to hone their diagnoses also led them to develop more exact instruments and methods of examining patients and their symptoms, including the stethoscope, the clinical thermometer, and an elementary sphygmo-manometer (to measure blood pressure). Another attempt to make the practice of medicine more scientific was Pierre Louis's "numerical method," which he used to determine whether or not particular therapies could be correlated to recovery. In 1835, he used elementary statistical techniques to disprove the therapeutic value of bleeding and other such practices. Concurrently, medical chemists developed new, efficacious treatments using morphine, quinine, and ipecac. These advances helped transform medicine from a "conjectural art" into an "exact science," in the words of a Paris physician of the time.[1]

In response to this clinical revolution, curricula in medical schools in Great Britain, Germany, France, and the United States placed a new emphasis on the nat-ural sciences, and the demand for their newly trained graduates, who had extensive clinical or practical training, grew with the coming of industrialization. As the population and public health concerns of cities multiplied, recurring epidemics screamed for medical investigation and reform at the same time that the new and growing middle class demanded more and better doctors. The rising clamor for an improved caliber of physician also showed itself in the growing government regu-lation of and investment in medical education in Germany, France, Britain, and Canada as well as the formation of medical associations that played an increasing role in determining educational and licensing standards. But during this period, while science allowed doctors to identify and sometimes treat the onset of disease, its origins remained obscure and the subject of seemingly endless debate.[2]

By the mid-nineteenth century, however, careful epidemiological work was providing insights into the nature and control of communicable diseases. In 1847, Danish epidemiologist Peter Ludwig Panum decisively concluded that measles were transferred from one person to another, rather than arising from mias-mas. A further blow to the miasmatic theory came from British surgeon John Snow's studies of cholera, which demonstrated that the disease did not spread through the atmosphere but rather through contact with the infected excreta of the afflicted or water contaminated by the same. William Budd, a contemporary and compatriot of Snow, reached similar conclusions about the spread of typhoid fever that led him to suggest that boiling drinking water and disinfecting excreta and soiled linen with zinc or lime chloride would greatly hamper the spread of typhoid. While these scientific discoveries were often overlooked, fellow physi-cians and policymakers at the time who adhered to the miasmatic theory of dis-ease nonetheless initiated sanitary engineering projects to improve the quality of water and sewage disposal. Although based on bad science, such efforts had a salubrious effect on public health.[3]

It was the advent of powerful compound microscopes in the late 1830s that truly revolutionized the practice of medicine, by providing incontrovertible evidence that specific germs were responsible for each communicable disease. French scientist Louis Pasteur, British surgeon Joseph Lister, and German physician Robert Koch carried out the most famous early experiments in applying the new germ theory to the treatment and prevention of disease. Pasteur's work showed that air, water, or other media, if heated sufficiently to kill microorganisms, would not yield any type of life (such as mold). This scientific principle was applied not only to the "pasteurization" of milk but also to surgical methods by Lister. In 1865, in line with Pasteur's experiments, Lister reasoned that wounds could be similarly disinfected by using carbolic acid, and his subsequent experiments in Scottish hospitals showed a dramatic reduction in the rate of postsurgical infections. Koch was similarly intrigued by Pasteur's work and is generally credited with first discovering and analyzing the microorganisms responsible for anthrax, tuberculosis, and cholera. He also pioneered techniques for cultivating, dying, and photographing microorganisms, all of which greatly facilitated medical bacteriology in the laboratory and in the classroom. Pasteur, in turn, drew inspiration from Koch's work; beginning in the 1880s, he discovered the principle of acquired immunity and developed the first artificial vaccines for anthrax, rabies, and diphtheria.[4]

These experimental breakthroughs, coupled with the greater national wealth created by industrialization, transformed medical education and enhanced the professional standing of physicians. By 1860, German universities in particular had embraced this scientific revolution and constructed large, state-of-the-art university laboratories for medical research and education; the 1870s brought national educational standards and examinations for prospective physicians, with an emphasis on scientific study. In the same decade, Britain and France, which had clung to clinical education, also began to require all medical students to engage in some practical laboratory work. But it was the United States, where medical training had been the least advanced and regulated, that experienced the greatest transformation as a result of this scientific revolution in medical education.[5]

In the early 1890s, using its newfound wealth and blending the German and French models, the Rockefeller Foundation funded a state-of-the-art medical program at Baltimore's Johns Hopkins University, which had ample laboratory space for researchers and students as well as its own teaching hospital. Cornell, Harvard, Michigan, Yale, Wisconsin, and Chicago soon founded similar medical programs based on this model, all with financial backing from the Rockefeller Foundation. Indeed, by 1910, the university-based medical school with its own teaching hospital had become the goal and ideal both in North America and Europe, for it seemed the most effective way to combine scientific training and clinical experience. Increasingly, physicians' organizations and state and national governments made this model the standard for licensure, quashing homeopathic, eclectic, and botanical medical schools and largely displacing medical schools that had catered to African American and women students but lacked the resources mandated by this new model. Throughout America and Europe, medical schools raised admission standards and reduced enrollments throughout the twentieth century.[6] While no one can dispute the benefits of these advances in medical science and education, changes in training made medical treatment more expensive and therefore unattainable for some socioeconomic groups.

Early International Health Cooperation

Medicine throughout the nineteenth century was, like science generally, a particularly international endeavor. The medical centers of Vienna, Edinburgh, Paris, and Germany attracted a multinational student body. Doctors throughout the world also kept abreast of medical work being carried out internationally through the *Index Medicus*. Dr. John Shaw Billings, head of the U.S. surgeon-general's library, began publishing this monthly index of the world's new medical books and articles in 1879. He hoped that such a comprehensive listing, in tandem with vital and medical statistics, would give all doctors the benefit of years of experience and experimental findings, which would allow them to study disease in the aggregate and apply their findings to their own practices.[7]

Another means that physicians used to keep abreast of global developments in medicine was attendance at the variety of international scientific congresses that proliferated during the nineteenth and early twentieth centuries. One of the most significant of these was the International Congress of Medicine, which began meeting in 1867, met eleven more times before the turn of the century, and drew together physicians from all fields to share their research, insights, and experiences. At the International Statistical Congress (which began meeting in 1853), William Farr, the English registrar-general, shared the methods he had used to revolutionize vital and health statistics in the United Kingdom and also alerted others to the need for internationally comparable health statistics. In line with these recommendations, the congress formulated and revised an international list of diseases, which provided a common nomenclature for statistical purposes. The nongovernmental, scientific International Congress on Hygiene and Demography likewise brought together the leading authorities in the field and provided an international standard for sanitary practices that member countries sought to match. As medicine advanced and specialties began to proliferate, so did international medical societies, such as the

International Union against Tuberculosis.[8] Governments, as well as individuals, co-operated across national boundaries on medical matters during this period.

The International Sanitary Conferences, which brought countries together to prevent the spread of epidemic diseases, were some of the earliest functionalist meetings between governments. The European cholera pandemic of 1830 had led the Ottoman Empire, with aid from the European powers, to establish the Conseil Supérieur de Santé de Constantinople, which established a series of health offices (each with an Islamic director and a European-trained physician) along both land and sea travel routes to check and report on the health of European-bound voyagers. Another continental outbreak of cholera in 1847 inspired the states of Italy, Greece, Portugal, Russia, and Spain to impose quarantine regulations on all ships entering port from Asia and Africa. But these disparate and strict regulations, which had no scientific basis, endangered the profits of French and British seaborne commerce. Hoping to negotiate a system that would protect nations from epidemics without unduly hindering the flow of trade, the European countries met in Paris on 23 July 1851, each sending a diplomat and a physician to determine appropriate but limited quarantine precautions against the spread of cholera. Each delegate to this first International Sanitary Conference was to act in his individual capacity and was allotted one vote. Perhaps reflecting a growing professional consciousness, the physicians often voted with their fellow doctors rather than with the diplomat of their respective nation. When combined with ignorance about the nature of disease contagion, this tendency hampered the proceedings, and only France abided by the conference's final results. Nonetheless, the conference had established health and disease as appropriate topics for international discussion, a precedent that inspired nine more sanitary conferences before the turn of the century.[9]

The scientific findings of Snow and others had no impact on the second International Sanitary Conference (1859), not least because the diplomats had decided to exclude the physicians, who, the diplomats argued, did not sufficiently understand the significance of international sanitary regulations. But the physicians' absence did nothing to promote ratification of the conference's sanitary regulations, nor did their attendance at the third (1866), fourth (1876), fifth (1881), and sixth (1885) conferences, which continued to be marked by divisive discussion about the nature of epidemic disease, despite epidemiological advances. Although these conferences tended to fixate on the question of cholera, participants also discussed other issues, such as the mode of transmission of yellow fever and the epidemiological danger posed by the annual pilgrimage to Mecca and the opening of the Suez Canal.[10]

Significant progress in international health came only in the 1890s, when medical researchers began to understand the nature of epidemic diseases and when two cholera epidemics struck Europe in four years. All the participating European countries ratified the first International Sanitary Convention (1892), which defined quarantine regulations for all ships coming into the Mediterranean through the Suez Canal and reorganized Egypt's Sanitary, Maritime, and Quarantine Council. The second International Sanitary Convention (1893) required all signatory states to notify one another of any outbreak of cholera within their boundaries and reduced inland quarantine measures between states. The third (1894) and fourth (1897) conventions, respectively, dealt with the pilgrimages to Mecca and made plague subject to the same quarantine and notification regulations that already applied to cholera. In 1903, the eleventh International Sanitary Conference codified the results of the previous conventions into a single, 184-article international sanitary code and created the Office International d'Hygiène Publique (OIHP) to coordinate the enforcement and modernization of these conventions, but it only came into operation four years later.[11]

Just one year before, the countries in the Western Hemisphere had founded the Pan American Sanitary Bureau (PASB) to receive and disseminate information on the hemisphere's pestilential diseases, with a special emphasis on yellow fever. Although the organization was to have a permanent executive board of seven members, the U.S. surgeon-general and one or two of his staff essentially ran the entire organization on a shoestring budget. Despite its limited resources, in the years following the First World War the bureau provided technical assistance to port facilities throughout the Western Hemisphere, began publishing a monthly bulletin, and collected broad-ranging statistics for the OIHP from PASB members. But the most significant expansions in PASB activities came through collaboration with the Rockefeller Foundation and the U.S. government's Institute of Inter-American Affairs (IIAA), which oversaw bilateral aid to Latin America for health, education, and agriculture. The extra funds from these sources allowed the bureau to convene special regional conferences on hygiene, the treatment of leprosy, and sanitary education and engineering. This initiative continued throughout the 1920s and 1930s as the PASB traveling representative worked closely with the scientists of the Rockefeller Foundation, many of whom were then studying yellow fever and malaria in Latin America.[12]

Like the PASB, the initial work of the OIHP also concentrated on epidemiology. The first meeting of the OIHP, held in Paris in November 1908, consisted of nine national representatives and concentrated on cholera. But as the organization and its membership grew, so did its field of inquiry and staff. In addition to serving as the central collection agency for epidemiological information on pestilential diseases, the OIHP discussed measures for the prevention of leprosy, tuberculosis, typhoid, and venereal diseases as well as questions of water pollution and purification. After World War I, OIHP president Rocco Santoliquido proclaimed the need to reorient international health efforts from the almost exclusive focus on the quarantine of pestilential diseases to a new program that would build up national health services and thereby combat disease at its source. Lively applause greeted his announcement, although the new mission, as it turned out, fell to the new League of Nations Health Organization rather than the OIHP.[13]

The Interwar Health Organizations

The pandemics of influenza, typhus, and cholera that ravaged Europe after the First World War, much like the cholera epidemics of the 1890s, convinced governments to expand international cooperation in health, and they committed the League of Nations, in Article 23 of its charter, to promoting the international prevention and control of disease. The League of Nations Council, seeking guidance on how to best fulfill this directive, convened an April 1920 international conference of health experts, which called for a permanent health organization within the League of Nations framework that would not only monitor and report on the spread of disease, like the OIHP, but also fight it. The new health organization was to advise the League's membership on health matters, encourage international health cooperation, simplify and improve epidemiological information, and promote health matters in collaboration with the League of Red Cross Societies (LRCS) and the International Labour Office (ILO). But until such an organization could be created, the expert conference urged the creation of a temporary commission to fight epidemics in Eastern Europe and particularly in Poland, where typhus, relapsing fever, and cholera had spread from Russia in the disruptive postwar conditions.[14]

The epidemic commission's work, which embodied the new activist philosophy against disease enunciated by Santoliquido, was made possible by national contributions of staff and supplies and by the LRCS's earlier efforts in this area. Under the leadership of Ludwik W. Rajchman, commission officials worked with Eastern European health authorities to establish a chain of quarantine stations for disinfection and observation, a series of both fixed and mobile hospital facilities, and an epidemiological intelligence service to ensure prompt and full information about the outbreak and course of epidemic diseases in these nations. Collectively these measures helped stem the tide of infection and prevented its spread into Central Europe. Key to this success was that Rajchman, by stressing the commission's humanitarian and scientific goals, received cooperation from the new Soviet Union, which continued to participate in the League's epidemiological work. In the fall of 1922, the commission again went into action when Turkey expelled 750,000 ethnic Greeks, who arrived in Greece carrying smallpox, cholera, and typhoid fever. Aiding eighty native doctors and health inspectors, the commission vaccinated and treated 550,000 refugees. This work became the model for later international health emergencies.[15]

The successes of the epidemic commission led the League of Nations to entrust its permanent health organization to Rajchman as well. The League of Nations Health Organization (LNHO), established in September 1923, was part of the secretariat and initially consisted of fifteen specialists in public health, epidemiology, and statistics. Aiding it in its work was an advisory council from the OIHP and a directing committee of twenty international medical experts. The directing committee's members were chosen based on their technical qualifications, did not represent their countries, and came from a variety of European, Latin American, and Far Eastern nations, not all of which were members of the League. Thereby assured of a nonpolitical nature, the committee was charged with developing the LNHO's program of work and with providing expert advice to the League's council and assembly. The LNHO, under the committee's guidance, confined itself to practical, as opposed to theoretical, activities and to those either requested by a member government or those of a specifically international character.[16]

Rajchman's working philosophy was to promote the growing emphasis on preventative medicine through epidemiological work and by elevating the practice of public health and accelerating scientific advances through the organization's scientific and educational work. Rajchman shared these values with the International Health Division of the Rockefeller Foundation, which subsidized much of the LNHO's educational and epidemiological work. The LNHO similarly coordinated its work with other philanthropic organizations, private laboratories, and national health administrations, all of which helped to socialize health officials into a common system of international medical values and to spread modern practices throughout the world through a system of educational fellowships, international conferences, and expert technical committees. In other words, the LNHO helped to expand the medical internationalism of the nineteenth century beyond the circle of elite practitioners and researchers by embracing more mid-level administrators and up-and-coming officials and by cultivating a number of allies in philanthropy and industry to aid in this effort.[17]

The new health organization reported the OIHP's findings on plague, yellow fever, smallpox, typhus, and cholera as well as its own work on dysentery, malaria, scarlet fever, and diphtheria in its *Monthly Epidemiological Report*. Although the OIHP continued to exist and function during the interwar period, it clearly became subordinate to the new League health organization, in part because existing international sanitary conventions circumscribed its functions and philosophy. On the other hand, the LNHO, operating under a broader and more flexible mandate, even introduced new innovations in epidemiology. It worked toward standardized epidemiological reports as a step toward creating an international database on disease and, in 1925, incorporated the Far East into an international system of epidemiological surveillance for the first time with the creation of the Eastern Epidemiological Intelligence Bureau in Singapore. The bureau hosted yearly meetings of the area's health officials and became the locus of regional health initiatives as well. In this way, the Singapore bureau became a comprehensive health authority serving this part of the world and, in combination with LNHO health work in Latin America, helped these nations justify representation in the European-oriented League of Nations. In fact, Latin American, Asian, and even African representatives to the League consistently lobbied for expansion of the LNHO and its resources.[18]

In Europe, the work of the LNHO also extended beyond epidemiological work to a variety of educational initiatives. To promote international cooperation and an expanded view of public hygiene, the health organization, with funds from the Rockefeller Foundation's International Health Division, developed study tours in which national public health officials witnessed firsthand the methods other countries employed in pursuit of better public health. Between 1922 and 1930, some six hundred officials took advantage of this opportunity. Another educational initiative came with two international conferences in 1927 that considered technical difficulties in public hygiene programs. Lecturers came from all parts of the world, citizens from twenty different countries attended the conferences, and a practical demonstration accompanied each theoretical lecture. That same year the League's Commission on Education in Hygiene brought together the directors of key medical schools and health institutions as well as officials from the Rockefeller Foundation in order to establish an international curriculum for hygiene instruction that stressed prevention. Similarly, in 1926, the LNHO began a series of international malaria courses, and in 1931 it created an International Center for Research on Leprosy in Rio de Janeiro.[19]

To facilitate its mission as an international clearinghouse for medical information, the League of Nations Health Organization also created a number of technical committees to advise it on the most effective and up-to-date information on fighting disease. Such committees considered specific measures against malaria, sleeping sickness, diphtheria, tuberculosis, rabies, syphilis, cancer, and trachoma. These technical committees sometimes encouraged the LNHO to launch multinational research efforts meant to elucidate the nature and treatment of these diseases, and the results of this work often led national health administrations to implement the resultant technical suggestions. The LNHO also did pioneering work on nutrition, carried out experiments on the value of tuberculosis vaccinations, examined the public health aspects of the Great Depression, conducted a multinational statistical inquiry into the causes of infant mortality, and convened conferences on the various aspects of rural hygiene in Europe (1931), the Far East (1937), and Latin America (1938).[20]

Another aspect of the LNHO's work was its standardization efforts. It established a Permanent Standards Commission to set international standards for biological products used in the diagnosis, treatment, and prevention of disease. The

League's standardization work included determining common nomenclatures for medical research so that scientists and physicians in every land were, in effect, speaking the same language when it came to experiments, treatments, and pre-scriptions. The LNHO staff pursued similar standardization in health and vital statistics. To this end it convened meetings of European demographers in 1923, 1924, and 1925 in order to ensure that national statistics were internationally com-parable, because only in this way could it gain a more comprehensive picture of the global incidence of disease. At the last of these conferences, the participants agreed to a common set of rules for recording causes of death.[21]

Despite this valuable work, the influence and budget of the League of Nations, as well as its health organization, declined with the coming of the Second World War. A further blow to the work of the LNHO was the dismissal of Rajchman, its longtime medical director. Nevertheless, the organization's work continued throughout the war under the leadership of Raymond Gautier, a Swiss member of the LNHO who had founded the Singapore bureau. Any hope that the LNHO might continue its work after the war ended with plans to create the United Na-tions Organization to replace the discredited League of Nations. The LNHO's work would continue, but only in the work of the health division of the United Nations Relief and Rehabilitation Administration (UNRRA) and then in the World Health Organization (WHO), a specialized agency of the new United Nations. The latter was, in fact, the indirect result of the first. Szeming Sze and Geraldo da Paula Sou-za, both members of the UNRRA Health Division and participants in the 1945 San Francisco Conference for International Organization, drafted a declaration, which passed unanimously, that called for an international conference "for the purpose of establishing an international health organization."[22]

Planning for a Postwar Health Organization

The Economic and Social Council of the United Nations (ECOSOC) followed up on the San Francisco declaration by appointing sixteen health experts to a technical preparatory committee. This expert committee was to draft an agenda for the International Health Conference that was to be held no later than June 1946; the deadline was the result of the widespread belief that there was an urgent need for such an international health organization. In the preliminary discussions that began on 18 March 1946, several committee members urged the creation of a health organization that would be so broadly conceived that it could meet, and even anticipate, the postwar health needs of the entire world. "The goal could not be placed too high," according to Dr. Karl Evang of Norway. The Argentine delegate, Dr. Gregorio Bermann, concurred, arguing that wartime science had opened up almost endless possibilities for postwar medicine. While Dr. C. Mani of India weighed in with his opinion that it would be better "to start modestly" than to "fall short of realizing ideals set too high," Dr. Brock Chisholm of Canada, who would eventually become the first WHO director-general, expressed the general optimism and sense of possibility that animated the committee and the international medical community when he allied himself with the "visionaries." The draft preamble to the WHO constitution reflected the view of these visionaries. It proclaimed that good health was the fundamental right of "every human being" and defined health as "a state of physical fitness and mental and social well-being" and not simply "the absence of infirmity or disease."[23]

The basis of the committee's subsequent discussions was consideration of draft constitutions submitted by the delegates of the United States, Great Britain, France, and Yugoslavia. While each committee member was acting as a private individual, these drafts, with the exception of the Yugoslav version, represented formal government positions. There was a wide area of agreement in these drafts and in the initial committee discussions. The delegates conceived of a universal health organization in which all members would participate as equals for the benefit of all humankind. Its yearly assembly would bring together delegates (who would preferably be heads of national health administrations) from all member countries, each with one vote. A geographically balanced executive board of government-appointed public health experts would be elected by the assembly to supervise the work of the organization, and an international secretariat of exceptional technical expertise, headed by a director-general, would carry out the day-to-day work of the WHO. To facilitate its broad mandate, the new health organization would also cooperate with a number of official and nongovernmental bodies. But some questions, such as the exact number of members on the executive board and the location of the WHO headquarters, were left to the International Health Conference to determine.[24]

A more substantive question that the committee also left to the conference was the relationship between the WHO and the Pan American Sanitary Bureau. While all the delegates agreed that the OIHP, LNHO, and UNRRA Health Section should be absorbed into the World Health Organization, its relationship with the PASB was more problematic. The British delegate, Sir Wilson Jameson, supported "a strong headquarters" and wanted to postpone the creation of regional affiliates "until the central machinery was well established." On the other end of the spectrum was U.S. surgeon-general Thomas Parran, who argued that the PASB should be a "related autonomous" organization in "the orbit of the" WHO. Taking a middle position were the French, Norwegian, and Argentine delegates, who proposed "special transitional arrangements" whose aim was to utilize the facilities and services of the regional health organizations fully while simultaneously "developing them as quickly as practicable into regional offices of the Organization." Despite the chastisement of Chisholm, who urged the committee to "draw lines boldly across national boundaries . . . whatever the cost to personal or sectional interests," the delegates were unable to agree and simply forwarded two alternatives to the conference.[25]

The cooperative spirit of the Technical Preparatory Committee and most of its personnel carried over to the International Health Conference, which met in New York City from 19 June to 22 July 1946. These expert medical professionals, in seeking to establish a new international health authority, realized the significance and potential of their endeavor. Meeting "in the wake of the greatest disaster which has overtaken the human race since the Glacial Age," these medical scientists felt the keen need to turn away from "the science of destruction" and toward "our life-saving, our health-building sciences" to "help heal the wounds of war." But not only would the World Health Organization repair past damage and carry on the work of the previous international health bodies, it would also be a pioneering organization for the future, striking out into new areas of international health cooperation and exploring "new territory which the nations of the world can accept as added bases for lasting peace." Health would serve as an international "rallying point of unity," because, overseen by "professional people" who approached their work with "objectivity and scientific spirit," it would serve as a foundation for other areas of international teamwork. Additionally, failing to promote health around the globe could have disastrous consequences, for "sick and starving people do not make the peace or keep the peace."[26]

Mirroring this sense of common and urgent purpose, the conference proceedings, like those of the preparatory committee, demonstrated a wide area of agreement. After a short debate, the delegates agreed on the name "World Health Organization," reflecting the belief that the new organization should be universal (not confined to UN members) and have health, not simply the control of disease, as its goal. To this end, the conferees voted to admit future members with a simple majority, rather than a two-thirds vote by the assembly, but the leading powers at the conference did take steps to exclude Germany, Japan, and Spain from early admission to the organization. The overall emphasis on universality recognized that only a universal organization could effectively control the international spread of disease and promote health among all people through coordinated global action. To this same end, non-UN members participated in the conference, and non-self-governing territories, under Article 8 of the WHO constitution, received nonvoting associate membership in the organization and were, by virtue of a Liberian amendment, to be represented at the annual World Health Assembly and at regional meetings by a qualified representative of "the native population."[27]

The objective of this new universal organization, in the words of its constitution, was "the attainment by all peoples of the highest possible level of health," which the preamble defined in positive terms similar to those suggested by the Technical Preparatory Committee. In pursuit of this ideal, the constitution laid out five broad categories of WHO functions: field operations, educational activities, research and technical services, regulation of international sanitary conventions, and coordination of and cooperation with all organizations dealing with health. To carry out this work, the conference accepted without debate the organizational framework established by the preparatory committee. But perhaps the greatest advance in international health cooperation came with Article 21 of the WHO constitution, which gave the secretariat the power to consolidate and update the international sanitary conventions, and these revisions became automatically binding on all members, without the benefit of domestic enabling legislation, unless a government lodged a formal reservation within thirty days. This not only greatly accelerated the acceptance of changes in international sanitary regulations, created a unitary code for all countries, and prevented a return to the muddled series of conventions that had characterized the prewar period but also demonstrated countries' willingness to accede to the WHO's global medical authority. Part of the reason for this concession was the realization that no single nation could protect itself from the introduction of epidemic disease and that legislatures were ill equipped to decide on such technical issues.[28]

Despite this wide area of agreement, however, there were some contentious discussions at the conference, particularly when determining the proper relationship between the PASB and the WHO. The State Department had reconsidered its earlier position and in fact had instructed the U.S. delegation "to assure the supremacy of the [WHO] in all matters of world-wide concern." Complicating matters, however, was PASB director Hugh Cumming's spirited campaign against the new organization. He had urged Latin American governments to reject the WHO and campaign for an autonomous PASB, and at a dinner for mostly Latin American health conference delegates, Cumming described the WHO "as an entering wedge for Communism into Pan America." But the U.S. delegation worked hard to dispel Cumming's ideas, and after prolonged debate, the WHO constitution declared that the PASB "shall in due course be integrated" into the WHO, with this integration taking place "as soon as practicable through common action based on mutual consent of the competent authorities." Obviously, such a vague formulation was open to a number of interpretations, and it would, in fact, take several years for this integration to take place; but the principle of integration had been settled. By contrast, the conference had little trouble arranging for the absorption of the health functions of the OIHP, the League of Nations, and UNRRA.[29]

The conference, undecided on the issue of where WHO headquarters should be located, left this work to the World Health Organization Interim Commission. Established by the conference, this commission consisted of eighteen national representatives who would carry out the organization's work until the necessary ratifications of the constitution had been deposited with the United Nations. Its primary responsibility was to take over the epidemiological work of the OIHP,

League of Nations, and UNRRA. Additionally, the commission was to deal with any international health emergencies that might arise and to draft the agenda for the first meeting of the WHO's membership, called the World Health Assembly.[30] The WHO constitution, however, did not come into force until two years later. During this period, the interim commission became the de facto health organization of the world and undertook its work with all the confidence gained from a century of medical professionalism and international cooperation.

9

Constructing International Authority in the World Health Organization

The men and women who worked for the World Health Organization (WHO) were inextricably tied to their professional status as doctors and its attendant authority. That status had flourished during the Progressive Era, when physicians had successfully promoted the idea that their profession was grounded in science and able to improve society, especially in the new cities, where disease was rampant. As members of a scientifically based profession, WHO staff members had frequently crossed national boundaries: they studied in the world's medical schools and attended international congresses; their professional journals and publications nurtured these transnational relationships; and they often worked in more than one country during their careers and sometimes worked together in the Pan American Sanitary Bureau (PASB), the Office International de Hygiène Publique (OIHP), or the League of Nations Health Organization (LNHO) to contain and fight disease.[1] When these internationally minded doctors came together within the World Health Organization, they combined the scientifically based authority of their profession with a commitment to apolitical internationalism in order to garner a global authority that facilitated the often unquestioning acceptance of their recommendations and ensured that countries clamored for the organization's advice and assistance.

As the breadth and intensity of the international campaign against disease grew with the advent of the WHO, international health professionals, much like their cousins in the World Bank and the Food and Agriculture Organization (FAO), increasingly took the role of global managers, defining a common philosophy and health agenda in order to guide governments, charitable organizations, and professional societies toward the attainment of these common goals. This philosophy was most evident in its promotion of medical education and scientific research, the very activities that had lent the medical profession its authority in the previous century. The WHO awarded approximately two thousand fellowships in its first two decades and dispatched thousands of its experts to advise national

health authorities and to demonstrate the newest techniques in disease prevention and health promotion. Additionally, the organization played the role of international manager by coordinating and promoting medical research among national, international, and private organizations. An auxiliary to its research efforts
was the WHO's work in promoting the global standardization of health statistics
and pharmaceutical preparations, which facilitated the international exchange of
medical information. In these ways, the WHO built on the foundation laid by the
medical pioneers of the previous century.

The World Health Organization also used its international authority and impressive resources to pursue an offensive against a number of communicable and
environmental diseases. Rather than simply seeking to contain the spread of epidemic diseases or to treat the sick, the WHO took hold of a new philosophy of
fighting epidemic diseases (such as malaria, tuberculosis, and venereal diseases)
at their source and of promoting prevention through attention to maternal and
child health, environmental sanitation, and nutrition. By mobilizing its international reputation and authority, the WHO was able to pursue this two-pronged
strategy of education and disease fighting with some notable success over the
first two decades of its existence.[2] But the same ingredients that brought such
success—the WHO's offensive strategy of fighting disease and its international
authority based on the professional standing of physicians—also were the recipe
for its greatest failure, the Malaria Eradication Program (MEP), which will be
discussed in detail in the next chapter. This chapter will focus on the way in which
the WHO established itself as a professional, apolitical, international organization
and then set out to revolutionize not only how governments and the international
community dealt with medicine and disease but also what level of resources they
devoted to promoting global health.

The Interim Commission and the First World Health Assembly

The international and professional identity of the World Health Organization took
form first in the interim commission that met in the wake of the International
Health Conference. Consisting of health professionals who represented their governments, it was to establish the organizational framework and working relations
of the new UN specialized agency. But delays in obtaining the twenty-six ratifications of the WHO Constitution needed to obtain a quorum for the first meeting
of the organization meant that the commission's work continued for almost two
years and moved far beyond its original charge. Running on borrowed UN funds
and a secretariat and a staff who developed not only a "spirit of co-operation" but
also "a genuine friendliness" born of their mutual dedication to "the ideal of world
health," the interim commission carried out epidemiological work (reporting and

tracking the spread of epidemic disease), sent health missions to war-devastated countries, planned offensives against communicable diseases, provided fellowships to doctors in areas that had been occupied, fought a cholera epidemic in Egypt, and revised the International Sanitary Conventions. These activities laid the foundation for the WHO's mission and blended almost seamlessly with those of the permanent organization. The same philosophy and priorities guided both.[3]

To establish its authority as *the* global health organization, the interim commission not only assumed the duties of its predecessors (the League of Nations Health Organization with its Singapore Bureau, the OIHP, the PASB, the health section of the United Nations Relief and Rehabilitation Administration [UNRRA], and the Alexandria Bureau in Egypt) but improved these global health services. Although integration of the PASB proceeded at a snail's pace, just a few months after the establishment of the WHO Interim Commission (WHOIC), it took over the OIHP's epidemiological work, planned for the transfer of the office's library and archives, and agreed that the content of the OIHP's *Bulletin Mensuel* would be incorporated into the *Bulletin of the World Health Organization* and the WHO's *International Digest of Health Legislation*. It likewise took only a few months for the interim commission to assume the League of Nations's epidemiological work and to make arrangements to continue its important work in medical standardization and the regulation of habit-forming drugs. But the commission was not content to merely continue this work. Its innovations included using radio messages rather than telegrams to spread its daily epidemiological report across the globe, urging more widespread use of DDT to prevent the spread of insect-borne disease by aircraft, providing on-the-ground assistance to countries fighting epidemics, and revising the international sanitary conventions to reflect contemporary conditions.[4]

The WHOIC also played an active role in containing disease during the Egyptian cholera epidemic of October–November 1947. To combat the epidemic, the commission undertook the bulk ordering of cholera vaccine from thirteen countries, but the differing potencies of the vaccines complicated the operation and provided a concrete example of the need for international biological standardization. The imposition of overly strict quarantines by neighboring countries during the epidemic likewise added to the determination of the WHO's interim commission to reform the international sanitary conventions and make their application universal.[5]

The WHOIC's innovation and positive action in its epidemiological work was part of the staff's offensive philosophy when it came to disease. Indeed the staff believed that science had now provided doctors and sanitarians with the weapons needed to attack disease; they would no longer have to adopt the centuries-old defensive posture against sickness and death. Antibiotics, the insecticide DDT, and the Bacille Calmette-Guérin (BCG) vaccination, which arrested the development of tuberculosis, were the newest and most promising offensive weapons in the interim commission's arsenal, and together they helped determine the priorities of both the WHOIC and the WHO in its first years. Venereal diseases, now quickly and inexpensively treatable with penicillin, and malaria, the primary carrier of which—the mosquito—was being decimated by DDT, topped the list of WHO priorities, because both were devastating in their extent and cost and vulnerable to immediate, effective, international action. Tuberculosis likewise had been shown to be treatable with a form of penicillin (streptomycin) and preventable through mass inoculations with the BCG vaccine. The sense of urgency regarding these three diseases was such that the interim commission elected not to wait for formal establishment of the WHO before establishing expert committees to provide advice on the most effective plan of attack on these maladies. Additionally, the interim commission developed a campaign against tuberculosis in Europe that brought together UNICEF (the United Nations International Children's Emergency Fund), the Danish government, and Swedish health officials to inoculate some one million children per month against the disease.[6] This campaign against tuberculosis showed the WHOIC's early awareness of itself as an international manager of global health, bringing together the supplies and expertise of a number of different organizations in a coordinated attack against a common enemy.

A similar commitment to coordination was evident in the WHO's efforts to strengthen its most significant allies in the war against disease—national health services. To this end, the interim commission dispatched missions to war-devastated countries and began the rehabilitation of "the community of learning" in those nations that had been occupied during the war. Using approximately $700,000 from the now-defunct UNRRA, the WHOIC dispatched missions to Ethiopia, Greece, and China, their members hailing from Australia, Canada, Czechoslovakia, Denmark, Great Britain, Greece, India, New Zealand, Norway, Palestine, the United States, and Yugoslavia, thereby setting a pattern of using multinational teams of experts. In both China and Ethiopia, the WHO missions focused on training auxiliary health personnel and taking elementary precautions in environmental sanitation meant to prevent the spread of epidemic disease. Interestingly, the WHOIC mission in China was in communication with, and occasionally worked in, communist-controlled areas of the country, acting on the organization's stated disregard for the political orientation of any area requesting assistance. The mission to Greece focused on a single disease—tuberculosis. Devastated by Nazi occupation and civil war, Greece had nearly half a million cases of tuberculosis, few functioning sanitoria, and even fewer supplies. The WHO mission helped to create a tuberculosis department within the Greek Ministry of Health, rehabilitate sanitoria, restock dispensaries, and make more hospital beds available to tuberculosis patients. Rebuilding national health infrastructure also meant providing more than two hundred fellowships to specialists who had been closed off by the war, so they could familiarize themselves with the most recent medical and scientific advances by studying abroad. The WHOIC also sent international groups of renowned doctors to tour these countries and disseminate their expertise. For example, the commission organized, in collaboration with the American Unitarian Service Committee, study tours to Austria in 1947 and the Philippines in 1948.[7]

When the first World Health Assembly (WHA) convened on 24 June 1948, the WHOIC, which now employed a staff of 255, had through its actions laid out a bold vision for the World Health Organization. The WHO should not only contain epidemic disease but lead the war against communicable diseases and train the needed "soldiers" by strengthening national health services. The election of Dr. Andrija Stampar as WHA president symbolized the continuity between the interim commission and the permanent organization, a continuity that extended to the "spirit of harmony" that animated both groups' deliberations. Some attributed these harmonious relations to the fact that WHA members were primarily represented by public health experts who shared a professional identity with the organization's secretariat. That secretariat had established the assembly's agenda, suggested priorities in the WHO's program, and proposed a budget of $6,324,700 to undertake the work. The commission also suggested, and the assembly concurred, that the organization's headquarters be located in Geneva, with its reputation for both political neutrality and international collaboration (having been home to the League of Nations). Such a setting seemed particularly fitting for an organization that fashioned itself as an apolitical, technical group and that strove for universal membership.[8]

With an eye to achieving universal membership, the interim commission invited to the assembly all those countries that had earlier participated in the International Health Conference, although some had not yet ratified the WHO Constitution. As a result, fourteen such delegations engaged in the assembly's debates even though they could not vote. Additionally, the eleven countries that did not belong to the UN General Assembly participated on an equal basis in the World Health Assembly with UN members.[9] Another sign of the organization's desire for universality was evident in the work of the WHA Credentials Committee, which for all intents and purposes simply overlooked the reservations attached to the U.S. ratification of the WHO Constitution. Washington had deposited its conditional acceptance of the WHO Constitution with the United Nations just three days before the assembly began, stipulating that the United States could withdraw unilaterally from the organization with one year's notice, that Congress would not be committed to a specific legislative agenda by the WHO, and that a ceiling of $1,920,000 would be placed on the American contribution to the organization's annual budget. The United States was the only member to attach reservations to its ratification instrument, so the United Nations had decided that a vote of the World Health Assembly was necessary to admit the United States to full membership. Despite some private grumbling, the members of the Credentials Committee and then the assembly as a whole (by a unanimous vote) chose to ignore the legal implications and to accept the United States "in a spirit of cordial international collaboration" as a full member of the organization.[10]

But the U.S. budget ceiling had a detrimental effect on the WHO budget—$6.3 million was needed to fully fund its ambitious global assault on disease. Faced with the U.S. limit, the assembly reduced the budget by more than a million dollars (to an even five million dollars) without making any corresponding adjustments to its program of work. Karl Evang, the Norwegian delegate to the assembly and a member of the earlier Technical Preparatory Committee, was distressed by the assembly's vote to reduce the organization's budget below a level that he believed was sufficient to carry out the essential work of the WHO. He chastised his colleagues, who, after all, were "public-health people, not representatives of treasury departments," for their "lack of imagination and vision." But while Evang was undoubtedly focusing on the forty-two fields that the assembly had included in the WHO's program of work, other delegates were more cognizant of the fact that their assessments were to be paid either in U.S. dollars or Swiss francs, both of which were relatively scarce currencies in the immediate postwar period.[11]

In addition to setting the budget and program of work, the assembled nations of the World Health Assembly had to choose the leaders who would guide the WHO in its vital global mission—the director-general and an executive board. The director-general would handle the staff and day-to-day operations of the WHO under the oversight of the executive board, the eighteen members of which were to meet at least twice per year. Executive board members, though appointed by national delegations and receiving guidance (but not instructions) from governments, were to act as "trustees of the Health Assembly as a whole" rather than as representatives of a single country or area. In fact, in one case the Netherlands chose a Belgian national rather than a Dutch physician to fill its designated seat. At a later date, rather than lose the apolitical, expert character of the board through a proposed Australian amendment, the director-general at that time threatened to resign, because he correctly gauged that executive directors under national instruction would serve as financial watchdogs over the WHO's blossoming budget. Board members served three years, one-third of the board being replaced each year. At the first assembly, which members would serve one-, two-, or three-year terms was determined by lots, representing again the equal membership of all countries in the WHO. Along the same line, despite some disagreement among its closest allies, the United States, in order "to preserve the democratic procedures in the Organization," did not stand for reelection to the executive board in 1952 or 1956, allowing more countries to exercise leadership in the organization. The board's responsibilities included nominating the director-general, evaluating the work of the expert committees, providing authorization to the director-general for emergency activities, and submitting proposals, advice, and programs of work to the assembly.[12] For director-general, the first board nominated Dr. Brock Chisholm, who had been the Canadian deputy minister of health and welfare before serving as the executive secretary of the interim commission for two years. With its leadership, staff (mostly holdovers from the Interim Commission), budget, and program of work in place, the World Health Organization was now ready to develop its own brand of internationalism, an internationalism deeply embedded in the nature of the health profession and the experiences of the World War II generation.

Crafting a Staff of International Civil Servants

Chisholm, the man who led the World Health Organization in its first years, had in 1915, at the age of eighteen, gone to France with the 48th Highlanders, just five weeks after enlisting. He was twice decorated and rose to the rank of captain before returning to Canada. Chisholm received his MD, studied at Yale University's Institute of Human Relations, and practiced in London's Queen's Square and Maudsley hospitals before returning in 1934 to become Toronto's first practicing psychiatrist. He also resumed his role in the Canadian militia, believing that another war with Germany was coming. With the outbreak of World War II, Chisholm, as a physician, was ineligible for combat service, instead becoming the first psychiatrist to ever head any army's medical services. In that position, he developed the Pulhems Profile, which allowed the military to correlate mental and physical traits with appropriate assignments for soldiers. As a result, the Canadian military experienced fewer discipline problems from unauthorized absences, lapses in discipline, and drunkenness; the British military, suitably impressed, adopted the profile system as well. As the war wound down, Chisholm accepted a position as deputy health minister, where he showed many of the qualities that made him an apt international civil servant. Members of Parliament in Ottawa asked for his resignation in the wake of public criticism resulting from several public speeches in which he argued that parents should not lie to their children by telling them that Santa Claus actually existed. The deputy health minister responded to the parliamentary criticism by saying that he had simply expressed a valid professional opinion—that parents lying to children can have detrimental effects—and that while he would not resign, being fired for taking a principled stand seemed fine to him. (He kept his job.)[13]

Marcolino Gomez Candau, who hailed from Brazil, took the oath as the World Health Organization's second director-general on 15 May 1953. Candau, who had received his degree in public health from Johns Hopkins University, had served with the Institute for Inter-American Affairs in Brazil before moving into the World Health Organization, where he served as assistant director-general for advisory services and assistant director of the regional office for the Americas. In these positions he had shown an adeptness in dealing with governments and "had left a most favorable impression with the staff of the Secretariat." On the eve of Candau's election, the executive board was almost evenly divided about whom to nominate, and the British delegation strongly preferred someone in a high national position rather than a member of the international secretariat. Nonetheless, Candau received an overwhelming majority of votes cast during a private plenary session held during the 1953 World Health Assembly. Apparently, most countries saw Candau's international resumé as an asset rather than a liability, and he reinforced his international identity in his inaugural address, asserting that he was undertaking this challenge "with the strength based on the certitude that I am free from commitments to any national, racial or political group."[14]

Both directors-general of the World Health Organization demonstrated their commitment to professional competence rather than national or political ideology in their campaign of steadfast resistance to the McCarthyite regulations governing American citizens working for international organizations. Chisholm, even after months of discussions with U.S. diplomatic personnel, who became increasingly adamant, refused to distribute loyalty questionnaires, fingerprint, or send to Washington to serve as a congressional witness any American citizen working for the secretariat. Such actions, Chisholm repeatedly reiterated, fell outside of the secretariat's functions as laid out in its constitution and were wholly unrelated to the activities of the organization. If the United States insisted, these proposals would have to be submitted in writing to the World Health Assembly, which, he warned, might take the issue to the International Court of Justice. The director-general also refused to delay appointments to WHO positions until the "loyalty" of the nominees could be investigated by the United States or to take action against those employees who did not comply with American loyalty regulations. Additionally, the director-general consistently pressured the State Department (even after he had officially retired) either to exempt consultants to the WHO's expert committees from security investigations or greatly expedite the process, or else risk excluding U.S. citizens from these appointments. Candau maintained this pressure and was seconded by outraged medical researchers and physicians in the United States.[15]

Obviously, the leadership, staff, and consultants of the World Health Organization jealously guarded their identity as international health professionals, who not only hailed from a number of countries but went so far as obviating their national identities. Indeed, the very first article of the staff rules and regulations identified WHO staff members as "international civil servants" whose "responsibilities are not national but exclusively international." But by sacrificing their national identities, they gained a sense of international fellowship with others engaged in advancing the health of the world's people.[16] The sense of having a mission to improve the health of people throughout the world animated the staff and helped weld it into a group with an ésprit de corps that elicited favorable remarks. As the first WHO director-general, Chisholm laid the foundation for the staff's ésprit. A man characterized variously as a "genius" and "a true citizen of the world," the Canadian inspired "amazing loyalty" among his staff by combining remarkable efficiency and punctuality with a flair for consensus building. Employees and diplomats alike were initially startled by his taking regular lunches in the employee dining room and his drafting of dinner guests to form an informal orchestra of harmonicas for an evening's entertainment, but the unconventionality of this son of a coal dealer made him an excellent first leader for this pioneering organization. On the rare occasions that Chisholm believed that one of his staff members had betrayed this "objectivity as a scientist" (most often by adopting a rigid communist ideology), he responded by "taking [them] to task," "giv[ing them] a stiff talking to," and refusing to renew their contracts.[17]

Indeed, the construction of an "international civil service," with superior technical expertise and loyalty to the entire global membership of the organization rather than to any one country or region, was paramount to the WHO's members. Therefore not only did all incoming staffers swear an oath of allegiance to the collective membership of the WHO, but the organization also sought, as far as possible, to base appointments on competitive examination scores in order to ensure the highest possible level of technical expertise. At the same time, the WHO leadership recognized the need for the staff to reflect the organization's diverse membership without unduly weakening any country's national health services. After just six months nineteen different nationalities were represented in the top forty posts in the organization (although all but Egypt were European, American, or members of the British Commonwealth), and by the end of its first decade fifty-three of the organization's eighty-eight member countries had two or more nationals on the WHO's staff of 1,500, a higher proportion than either the World Bank or the FAO. But unlike their counterparts in these organizations, WHO staffers rarely stayed with the organization for more than three to five years. This was, in part, by conscious design of the organization's leadership, which required its staffers to be on the forefront of scientific knowledge in their field, something difficult to do if one remained in the organization and out of the research laboratory or the field.[18]

The staff's identity as apolitical professionals extended to the rest of the organization as well. Even as the Cold War heated up in late 1948, Dr. H. van Zile Hyde, the U.S. member of the WHO executive board, remarked with approbation that the Eastern European countries' approach to the organization had been "entirely professional" and conducive to a "real atmosphere of professional friendship." In contrast to the UN Security Council and General Assembly, the WHO was run on a "technical basis" by doctors from around the world who were "united on certain common objectives—the primary one being the application of preventative medicine on a mass basis." Similarly, the WHO's executive committee, whose members were to act as "disinterested citizens of the world," occasionally reversed their votes when they were acting under government instructions as delegates in the World Health Assembly—demonstrating, that is, the denationalization of those on the executive committee.[19]

Closely allied to this notion of solidarity within the medical profession was the conviction that this sense of international fellowship could extend to the rest of the people of the world, who could themselves "discover such common interest, the terrain of possible collaboration, the overlapping areas of curiosity and sympathy, of aspiration and mutual advantage, that bind the human race together regardless of ideologies or boundary lines." The issue of health, staff members were convinced, was an ideal place to begin discovering such "common interest," for it was truly international. It was "something that all men desire," and with the advent of intercontinental airline traffic it was increasingly difficult to maintain national health while epidemic diseases existed elsewhere in the world, for germs neither carried passports nor respected borders.[20] Additionally, many international health professionals saw health as a key to prosperity and peace and the physician as "the harbinger of peace." For these reasons, international health initiatives seemed the ideal place to begin building international cooperation, and medical professionals were to serve as its quiet missionaries, going about their work in the hope that they were building across national borders bridges that others would also traverse in time.[21] This faith was, however, tested in the course of the World Health Organization's campaign to unite national and regional interests into an unified global agenda for health, all the while warding off the corrosive influence of politics.

Reconciling National and Regional Interests with an International Agenda

The key to the WHO's international identity, on the concrete level of its organizational structure, was its nearly universal membership; the staff believed, in turn, that creating regional WHO offices was the key to maintaining that membership. For it was the mission of WHO's regional offices to ensure that the organization's operations met the concrete needs of its diverse members and so retained their loyalty and commitment. Another of the innovations of the WHO meant to facilitate universal membership was a provision for associate membership—that is, granting colonial areas independent representation at meetings of the World Health Assembly and the regional organizations. Representatives of associate members, who were to be chosen from the "native population," could suggest items for inclusion in the assembly's agenda, take part in all WHA proceedings, and submit proposals to the executive board, but they could not vote, hold office, or select members for the executive board. In recognition of these limitations, the WHO fixed the financial contribution of associate members at a low level. It was generally in the regional arena that associate members were most active in the World Health Organization. Chisholm also urged the regional organizations to break away from "old confusion" and adopt names "relevant to the real situation," which resulted in the "Western Pacific" region instead of the Far East and the "Eastern Mediterranean" rather than the Near East.[22]

But Chisholm recognized he was walking a tightrope. Though he deemed strong regional organizations essential to universal membership, he steadfastly believed that a single world health authority should act on behalf of the entire global community. While the director-general and his staff recognized the need for the organization to be close to the people it served, through the regional offices, they continually fought against too much decentralization. They feared that otherwise the effective power of the organization would be scattered among its six regions, making the Geneva headquarters little more than a statistics-collection agency. So while Chisholm began the constitutionally mandated process of establishing regional WHO offices, he reserved certain activities for the center: setting global priorities, coordinating regional activities, allocating financial resources, and serving as the central repository for technical aid, expertise, and the collection of statistics. To prevent the development of regional loyalties within the staff, the WHO also promoted a system of interchange between the regional and central offices so that no staff member would lose sight of the WHO's global mission. The director-general also, however, responded to the "felt needs" of the regional organizations, even when these needs did not reflect key priorities established by the global organization. In this way, the WHO sought to address the needs and problems of all its many members.[23]

In the development of the WHO's regional groupings, another aspect of its identity became vividly clear—its overt avoidance of and disdain for political issues. The WHO secretariat, which consciously cultivated an apolitical identity, basically allowed each country to choose the regional grouping to which it would belong. Confining itself to "the technical considerations involved," the executive board and then the assembly assigned the French North African colonies of Tunisia and Morocco to the European Regional Office, where the Paris government hoped they would be insulated from the Pan-Arabism of the members of the Eastern Mediterranean Regional Office (EMRO). On the other hand, Pakistan chose to join EMRO rather than belong to the Southeast Asian Regional Office (SEARO), which was headquartered in New Delhi, India. The first World Health Assembly decided that regional offices should be formed as soon as a majority of affected countries assented, and the nations of the Southeast Asian region took immediate action on this decision, convening just three months after the assembly closed and beginning operations on New Year's Day of 1949. The countries of the Eastern Mediterranean region likewise organized relatively early and established their headquarters by simply co-opting the staff and facilities of the Alexandria Bureau.[24]

One of the greatest political challenges to the WHO's regional organization arose in the Eastern Mediterranean region, but in it the WHO maintained a staunchly apolitical stand. Karl Evang, the president of the second World Health Assembly in 1949, exhorted his fellow delegates always to keep in mind that the "WHO is not a political body. It must never be. . . . We must all think and feel one for all, and all for one."[25] He might well have felt the reminder was needed, given the recent war in the Middle East, prompted by the creation of the state of Israel. Initially, it seemed that the WHO might be able to avoid the overtly political aspects in the region; the WHO provided health services to the Palestinian refugees, and even though domestic political unrest in Egypt had precluded holding the 1949 meeting at the regional headquarters in Alexandria, Israel and the Arab nations had met to conduct regional business in Geneva and the next year in Istanbul, Turkey. But after September 1950, Arab League countries refused to attend meetings with the Jewish state. The Arab nations suggested that Israel join the European region rather than the predominantly Arab Eastern Mediterranean region, much as Pakistan had chosen to join the Arab countries of this region rather than the Southeast Asian region. But Israel demurred, arguing that regional assignments should be based on health concerns rather than politics and asserting its right to choose membership in the Eastern Mediterranean area. The assembly, to a large degree, concurred, refusing to "determine questions of political character" or to allow the Arab nations simply to exclude Israel from the region. The work of the EMRO continued to be retarded by the refusal of its members to meet together, however; in response, the director-general tried to have each member submit a written report on health aspects in the region that would suggest a unified regional program, but Israel objected to such a regional "meeting by correspondence," saying it violated the spirit of the WHO constitution. It likewise rejected the 1953 division of the region's work into two subcommittees, since it appeared that Israel would form a subcommittee of one. Despite Israeli intransigence, the director-general refused to allow the Arab members to meet as a region without Israel. However, the Arab states began meeting anyway after 1954, and the EMRO director presented the resultant "opinion" to the WHA for action. It was not until 1984 that Israel finally asked to be transferred to the European region.[26]

While the initial furor in EMRO was at its height, the PASB was finally and rather quietly integrated fully into the WHO regional structure on 24 May 1949, after Uruguay ratified the WHO constitution and thereby made the membership of the two organizations congruent. The Pan American Sanitary Bureau maintained its name but also became the American Regional Office (AMRO) of the World Health Organization. It could undertake hemispheric programs independent of the WHO so long as the projects were independently financed and fit within the overall policy and programs of the parent organization. The work of the PASB, much like that of the WHO generally, became increasingly decentralized in order to meet the diverse needs of the region. In the 1940s the PASB had established zonal offices in Lima, Peru, and Guatemala City, Guatemala, to supplement the work of the Washington headquarters, and after 1952 additional offices sprang up in Mexico City, Mexico; Rio de Janeiro, Brazil; and Buenos Aires, Argentina. The PASB program, like that of its parent organization, focused on education and a direct attack on communicable diseases within the Western Hemisphere.[27]

If international health initiatives were relatively well developed in the American region, the opposite could be said for the African region, the problems of which were among the world's most severe and least documented. The WHO at first confined its activities to a survey of the area's health problems and an analysis of its sparse health and vital statistics in order to determine in what ways it might be of greatest service. Regional conferences on malaria and yaws (a form of venereal disease) followed, and these in turn prompted regional campaigns against these two diseases as well as an increased number of fellowships for the limited number of medical professionals in the region. The African Regional Office (AFRO) was among the last to organize, in part because of the time needed to clarify the rights and responsibilities of associate members within the regional organizations. Creation of the Western Pacific Regional Office was likewise delayed due to the civil war in China, the military occupation of Japan, and the initial reluctance of Australia and New Zealand to participate.[28]

But just as the WHO's regional organizations began to take shape, the Soviet Union and two of its Soviet Socialist Republics, Byelorussia and the Ukraine, notified Geneva on 21 February 1949 that they no longer considered themselves WHO members, in light of the organization's failure either to control disease "satisfactorily" or spread new medical information adequately. They likewise criticized the WHO's "swollen administrative machinery," the cost of which was "too heavy for Member States to bear." Albania, Bulgaria, Czechoslovakia, Hungary, Poland, and Romania followed suit over the next year and a half. Apparently, much of their disappointment stemmed from their belief that the WHO should provide members with vaccines, insecticides, antibiotics, and drugs, something that the assembly believed impracticable given the organization's limited resources. Chisholm, however, was unwilling to accept the withdrawals, stating that the constitution made no provision for such action and expressing his opinion that in any case it was "premature" to declare the organization ineffective. The director-general asked to visit the Soviet Union to dispel any misunderstandings about the WHO, but this request, as well as repeated appeals from successive World Health Assemblies thereafter, was ignored. The WHO nonetheless consistently refused to acknowledge the withdrawal of its "inactive" members, going so far as to suggest that the Soviet and

Byelorussian seats on the executive committee remain vacant. When the prodigal countries began to rejoin the organization in 1957, the WHO, in order to ease their return, assessed only a token payment of 5 percent of their dues during their "inactive" period, payable over ten years. This payment symbolized the WHO's contention that they had never truly left the organization, as well as its desire to encourage their resumption of active membership. Upon its return to the organization, the Soviet delegation repeatedly offered to put Soviet public health and medical expertise at the disposal of the organization's membership, regardless of political ideology, evidencing its understanding of the WHO's mission and identity.[29]

Nonetheless, it would be inaccurate to state that political considerations never came into play in determining WHO membership. Spain, under the leadership of Fascist dictator Francisco Franco, was not originally invited to become a member of the organization; later, East Germany, the People's Republic of China (PRC), North Korea, and North Vietnam were similarly excluded from the organization, not by a vote but by "tacit agreement." In the case of China, on 5 May 1950 the Republic of China telegraphed Geneva from Taiwan that it was withdrawing from the organization because it could no longer meet its financial obligations. Eight days later a telegram arrived from the PRC claiming to be "the only legal government representing the Chinese people," but the assembly ignored that message. Indeed, the WHO refused to recognize the legitimacy of Taiwan's withdrawal (as it had with the Eastern bloc withdrawals) and even continued its fieldwork and fellowship programs in that country. Three years later, the assembly overwhelmingly voted to welcome the return of (Nationalist) "China" to the organization, despite heated protests from India and Norway that the Taipei government represented only a small part of China's population. Nonetheless, its budget assessment was not revised downward (because no members were ready to take up the budgetary slack). The assembly, however, accepted a token annual payment of ten thousand dollars as meeting its financial obligations to the organization.[30]

In sum, the World Health Organization strove for universal membership, especially through its regional organizations. Given the realities of the Cold War and the Middle East conflict, however, the WHO's response to global political turmoil was by and large to avoid politics, whether that meant allowing countries to self-select their regions, ignoring the withdrawals of the Soviet bloc, or pretending that Taiwan was China.

Fighting for the Resources to Battle Disease

If the World Health Organization skirted political issues to further the cause of global health, it did not hesitate to push its members to make greater sacrifices for the WHO's mission. Nowhere was this more evident than in its budget battles.

Those battles were fought most consistently with the largest single donor, the United States (which paid 33–38 percent of the total budget). A congressionally imposed $1.92 million ceiling on the U.S. contribution had forced a reduction in the organization's first budget of more than one million dollars. When the first draft of the 1950 budget (which included an additional 219 staff positions) totaled $18 million, compared to five million in 1948, the United States and the United Kingdom asserted that they could not agree to such immediate and drastic increases and warned that so extravagant a proposal would derail efforts to eliminate the congressional ceiling. Nonetheless, seeing how the WHO's work fit with President Harry S. Truman's recent Point IV initiative (which was later institutionalized in part as the UN Expanded Program for Technical Assistance, or EPTA), the U.S. representative suggested that a "special project budget" be separated from the general budget, exempting it from congressional limitations. Accordingly, the WHO budget (after desultory cuts) was divided between an eight-million-dollar administrative/operating budget and a supplemental program of advisory and technical services that amounted to more than nine million. The latter "was taken into full account" in preparing the Point IV Program. The 1951 budget built on this model of expanded expenditures, and the 1952 regular expenditures rose 53 percent, while funds earmarked for supplemental projects rose more than 80 percent.[31]

The WHO staff was pleased with the expansion of its field programs that its EPTA allocations allowed, but the reliance on the bifurcated budget—an administrative budget to cover the organization's basic operations and a project budget for international projects—soon became a liability rather than an asset to the organization. Since member governments had to pledge each year the funds that went into the Expanded Program for Technical Assistance pool, the level of funds was unstable. In 1953 the World Health Organization found itself committed to $4.5 million in projects that were dependent on EPTA pledges that it feared would not materialize. Such uncertainty led some WHO members to declare they would prefer to forego such funding rather than have to cope with the uncertainty involved, but it was difficult to imagine where an additional $10 million per year might be found. By 1957 EPTA funding had somewhat stabilized, though at a slightly lower level; however, the WHO continued to be frustrated by various UN requirements, such as a quota on funds to be devoted to regional projects, that clashed with the WHO priority of promoting regional and global health initiatives.[32]

Not wanting to be too dependent on EPTA funds, Chisholm continued to press member governments to expand their contributions by presenting ever-larger budgets for approval by the executive board and World Health Assembly. The British and American delegations, however, did their best to put a brake on the growth of WHO budgets. In the 1952 budget hearings, the majority opted for a 53 percent increase over the previous year's high level and thereby brought the U.S.

contribution (which constituted one-third of the total budget) "perilously close" to the recently raised congressional ceiling of three million dollars. The American delegate believed that the growth in the WHO's program of work and budget was primarily the result of Chisholm's strong and dynamic leadership of the organization. By refusing to respect would-be American budget restrictions, he not only achieved significant growth in the WHO's capacity to carry out its ambitious global agenda but inspired, by the very scope of his vision, most contributors to make the additional contributions necessary to underwrite the WHO's work. The year 1953 witnessed a replay of the budget drama. The United States had hoped for some relief from the ambitious budgets consistently put forth by Director-General Chisholm, but his replacement, Marcolino Gomez Candau, followed in his predecessor's footsteps, proposing an increase of $82,107 in the 1954 budget, which put the U.S. assessment over the statutory limit. The British executive board member believed that a nine-million-dollar operating budget for 1954 was not justified, but the rest of his colleagues, having approved the organization's program of work, felt compelled to approve the corresponding funding. But the English-speaking countries were not done with their efforts to reduce the budget. During the May 1953 World Health Assembly, delegates from Australia, Britain, Canada, South Africa, and the United States suggested a figure slightly lower than the previous year's. This set off a firestorm of controversy (fomented primarily by the Indians, Liberians, and Norwegians) in the Program Committee, and although the reduction was approved, several delegations alerted the Americans that they would not support future U.S. budget-cutting efforts.[33]

The United States continued to be torn between a desire to play a more positive role in WHO affairs and the seemingly unending financial demands of promoting global health. Pushed by Candau's aggressive budgeting and the broad consensus in favor of the WHO's ambitious program, the State Department devised an accounting maneuver that gave it room under the congressional ceiling and allowed it, for the first time, to support a budget increase for 1956. With the United States spending some $40 million per year on bilateral health programs, it made sense for it to adopt a more positive approach. In fact, the State Department had long recognized the value of a prominent American role in the WHO's work and had worked consistently, though often unsuccessfully, to raise or preferably remove congressional limits on the U.S. contribution. But still the U.S. government found the WHO's appetite for new programs and monies almost insatiable. Candau suggested a 1958 budget that reflected a 27 percent increase over the previous budget, including a 44 percent increase in advisory services. Although most of the Soviet-bloc countries returned to active membership during this year, the United States found such increases "unrealistically high" and unacceptable. Instead, it sought some commitment to limiting annual budget growth to somewhere in the neighborhood of 5 percent in order to provide for "reasonable and orderly growth in the Organization" without unduly burdening the main contributors. But few other members wanted to dampen the enthusiasm and scope of the WHO's program. In 1958 America's compromise budget was rejected in favor of the director-general's original budget—an 8 percent increase over the previous budget. By 1959 the United States, frustrated with the ever-rising WHO budgets and its own inability to influence them, unsuccessfully proposed that budgets be determined by a two-thirds vote instead of a simple majority.[34]

The issue of budget assessments was also affected by institutional identity. The WHO's insistence that no member could withdraw meant all governments were assessed a share of the budget, even those that had withdrawn from the organization, though there was no expectation that they would pay. The WHO expected active members to pay their dues, but universal membership remained paramount. The number of countries in arrears on their payments had become significant enough by 1955 that the World Health Assembly revoked the voting rights of any member in arrears for more than two years; still, it chose not to enforce its constitutional right to suspend services to delinquent nations.[35] In this decision, as in its other financial calculations, the priority of the World Health Organization was attempting to further its global fight against disease by promoting universal membership and garnering the resources needed to wage its campaign against disease.

WHO Staffers as International Managers

The international identity and broad mission of the WHO also led the health organization to forge ties with a large number of UN specialized agencies, nongovernmental organizations, philanthropic associations, and medical groups. Additionally, the WHO used ties to these organizations to prevent duplication of effort and promote a single program of global health improvement. The WHO, in other words, often played the role of an international manager in health matters, much as the World Bank and the FAO did in their fields of expertise. In this way the WHO came to exercise greater influence in the global arena than it could have if it had relied merely on its own resources.

The WHO's internationalism, as defined by its staff, extended beyond its efforts at universal membership to embrace a number of national and international, governmental and nongovernmental organizations as well, all of which helped contribute to the achievement of the WHO's mission of promoting full health for all people. In particular, during the first two decades of the WHO's life its mission was linked almost inextricably to that of the United Nations International Children's Emergency Fund, which shared many of the same operational priorities as the World Health Organization. In fighting malaria, venereal diseases, and tuberculosis and in advancing nutrition and maternal and child health, UNICEF provided the supplies while the WHO supplied technical advice and medical personnel. The WHO Interim Commission, for example, had provided a pediatrician and a full-time medical adviser as well as technical and statistical advice to the UNICEF campaign against tuberculosis, which began in Europe with the aid of several Scandinavian Red Cross societies. The WHO also provided scientific advice, often in collaboration with the FAO, on UNICEF's nutritional work and its efforts to improve the health of mothers and children, and it reserved 10 percent of all its fellowships for the study of children's health issues. The two organizations also established a children's center in Paris for research and training in child welfare, nutrition, education, and health. In Liberia, the WHO and UNICEF cosponsored a pilot malaria-yaws project for Africa: UNICEF supplied $100,000 for equipment and supplies, WHO provided six international technical personnel as well as training for the Liberians working on the project, and the government committed more than $150,000 toward the effort.[36] Such joint WHO-UNICEF projects were the backbone of the WHO's field operations and of the later Malaria Eradication Program.

The WHO's work with the FAO was less prodigious than that with UNICEF but equally indicative of the WHO's philosophy. In addition to the joint FAO-WHO nutrition work, the World Health Organization also worked closely with the Food and Agriculture Organization in formulating policy on certain diseases (called zoonoses) that were spread from animals to humans; in an early initiative, the two specialized agencies undertook joint responsibility for a series of demonstration projects that extended over five years (1951–55) and ten million acres of malarial farmland. The goal was to increase food production in areas where poor health, particularly malaria, prevented cultivation of fertile land. As part of this project, the FAO and WHO established a demonstration area in the main rice-producing region of Taiwan, where the rice paddies created ideal circumstances for mosquito breeding, caused a high incidence of malaria, and hampered planting and harvesting. In a similar project, the two organizations sought to improve health and agriculture in the Zapotiaton Valley of El Salvador. The extremely malarial conditions in the valley forced much of the population to live some distance from their fields, which had an adverse effect on agricultural efficiency. Although the project was kicked off with some fanfare in 1951 and by 1953 served as a national training area for both nurses and social welfare workers, disputes between national and international officials about everything from personnel to project funds kept this operation from spawning successors.[37]

The World Health Organization obtained a great degree of cooperation with the other specialized agencies as well, including reciprocal representation at each other's meetings, the exchange of documents and publications, coordination of statistical services, and, where needed, formation of joint committees. The WHO

worked in coordination with the United Nations Educational, Scientific, and Cultural Organization (UNESCO) on a public education program on public sanitation. Other WHO-UNESCO projects were the Council of International Organizations of Medical Sciences, which coordinated international scientific congresses
in order to improve the efficiency of and participation in their work, and the
Interim Co-ordinating Committee on Medical and Biological Abstracting, which
sought to reduce overlapping between the two organizations. The WHO staff also
developed an informal, flexible working relationship with the International Civil
Aviation Organization (ICAO) in their joint work to prevent the spread of disease
by international flights.[38]

Despite its excellent relations with the other specialized agencies, perhaps the
WHO enjoyed its most productive relationship with the global medical community. The organization's expert committees and study groups not only gave the
WHO advice and spread word of the organization's work to the rest of the field
but provided an international forum in which differences of medical opinion
could be aired and consensus achieved. The WHO also reached out to physicians
through its liaison with a number of nongovernmental organizations. It drew on
the "enthusiasm, knowledge and experience" of these NGOs, the aims and purposes of which mirrored those of the WHO; the NGOs in turn received the right
to attend the World Health Assembly, participate in WHO meetings, receive organizational documentation, and submit memoranda to the director-general for
his consideration. Perhaps the best example of this cooperative work can be seen
in the technical discussions held in conjunction with each year's World Health
Assembly starting in 1956. These informal sessions, held concurrently with assembly sessions, brought together about two hundred WHO officials, national public
health workers, and NGO members, allowing for the rapid dissemination of the
newest ideas and knowledge on public health issues such as "The Role of the Nurse
in the Public Health Program" (1956), "The Role of the Hospital in the Public
Health Program" (1957), and "Health Education of the Public" (1959). By the end
of its first decade, the WHO had some forty NGOs involved in its work.[39]

But one of most important relationships between the WHO and the medical
community lay in the organization's work as the international manager of medical research. From the beginning, the WHO staff realized that the development
of its own, independent research facilities and program was beyond its means,
and that in any case marvelous laboratories already existed around the globe. Accordingly, the WHO recognized the superior work of certain facilities by naming
them "international reference laboratories." These labs had the proper facilities
to manufacture vaccines and other biological materials that met WHO standards
for purity and potency. In addition, the WHO supported a number of research
centers that undertook specialized work on diseases such as influenza, salmonella,
and tuberculosis. The World Influenza Center within the British National Institute

for Medical Research and the International Influenza Center for the Americas, for example, had the responsibility for determining the strain of influenza virus at work in any particular outbreak and for using its efficiencies of scale to produce enough relatively low-cost vaccine to ward off a recurrence of the 1918–19 influenza pandemic, which had killed more than fifteen million people worldwide. Such laboratories also served to train specialists from around the world. In exchange for these vital services, the WHO awarded annual grants, facilitated the exchange of personnel, and provided technical support and materials to the laboratories. By 1956 the organization had close relationships with some eighteen hundred institutions and laboratories worldwide.[40]

As the WHO's laboratory work suggests, one of the functions of the World Health Organization was to act as an international department of health, overseeing and supervising health activities around the world as well as undertaking work that could only be done internationally. For example, the WHO staff believed that making medicine a truly international enterprise required all the world's physicians, medical researchers, pharmaceutical companies, and national public health administrations to "speak the same language"—that is, employ the same nomenclature and terminology. To the WHO this meant the creation of a unified international pharmacopeia and biological standardization, work that the organization largely carried out through its expert committees. One of the major accomplishments of this committee work was the publication in 1949 and 1950 of the English, French, and Spanish versions of the WHO's *Pharmacopoea Internationalis,* which established a system of common names for all new pharmaceuticals sold internationally and listed the usual and maximum doses for commonly used drugs. This helped to eliminate confusion in international medical deliberations and protected international travelers from receiving incorrect prescriptions, for it was not unusual for the same drug to carry different names depending on the country or company of origin. There had been several regional pharmacopoeia, but no previous effort to unify them. The expert committee on biological standardization undertook a similar enterprise, setting standards of potency and purity for vaccines, antibiotics, vitamins, hormones, enzymes, and medicines (such as digitalis), as well as formulating tests to ensure proper identification of the type and Rh factor of blood. The biological standardization committee also formulated tests used in laboratories to diagnose tuberculosis, typhoid, and syphilis.[41]

Another WHO effort at international standardization and education focused on the importance of keeping and maintaining adequate statistics on the health of populations, the incidence of disease, and the causes of death, much as William Farr and Pierre Louis had advocated in the previous century. Without adequate statistics, the WHO argued, determining the most important public health problems and measuring the success of remedial programs was problematic at best. Fellowships, regional seminars, international conferences, WHO-subsidized

academic programs, and a number of WHO expert commissions devoted themselves to remedying this shortfall. Another step in this direction came with the 1948
publication of the WHO's *Sixth Decennial Revision of the International List of Diseases and Causes of Death,* intended to standardize the way in which causes of death
were reported and to clarify the extent of the world's most serious health problems.
To facilitate the correct use and general acceptance of this list, the WHO strongly
urged the creation of national committees on vital and health statistics to advise on
difficulties in applying the new classification. It also prepared a short, informative
booklet on the use of the list and set up a clearinghouse at the Geneva headquarters
to answer questions about application of these international standards.[42]

Another means of ensuring that the world's medical professionals spoke the
same language was through the WHO's educational initiatives, which included
the provision of formal educational opportunities for physicians and other health
workers as well as practical education through participation in the WHO's fieldwork, demonstrations, and advisory services in member countries. In its first year
of formal operations, the WHO budgeted $800,000 for advisory and demonstra-
tion work and $650,000 for fellowships and the provision of medical literature.
But it received requests for the former amounting to twice the budgeted amount
and requests for the latter exceeding four times the sum allocated. In order to
prioritize these claims, the executive board decided that each request should be
evaluated based on its importance to the requesting nation's overall health program, the ability of the country to provide these services without the WHO's
assistance, the chances for success of the program, and the degree to which the
program conformed to the recommendations of WHO expert committees.[43]

To accommodate changing international conditions, the program of fellowships
changed in nature over its first several years of existence. While most early fellowships went to European physicians from occupied countries, by 1950 there was a
growing emphasis on granting fellowships to Third World nationals and on creating international training centers in the Third World rather than simply sending
physicians to study in First World countries. With this switch in emphasis, there
was increasing interest in training auxiliary medical personnel rather than simply
doctors and nurses. Auxiliary personnel required less time and fewer resources to
train to an international standard and were equally needed in public health work.
Nonetheless, the WHO continued to award hundreds of fellowships each year to
physicians and sanitarians in advanced fields of specialized study.[44]

The World Health Organization, however, spent most of its time and resources
in the field rather than in the laboratory or the classroom. Going into the field and
demonstrating how to improve health—rather than simply sitting in an international headquarters, monitoring epidemiology, and issuing reports—seemed a
natural outcome of the WHO's ideology. WHO demonstration teams sought to
show the best ways in which modern medical techniques could be adapted to local

conditions, and it trained the indigenous personnel who would carry on the work begun by WHO teams. Much of the demonstration work in these first decades focused on diseases and methods of preventive medicine that promised to have a great effect on the area's standard of health. But all of the WHO's work—from promoting cooperative endeavors, medical education, and medical research to standardizing biological and statistical information—was aimed at one objective, the war against disease.[45]

The WHO's Fight against Disease

Given the breadth of its task, the WHO in the first decades devoted much of its attention and resources to the top priorities established earlier by the interim commission. Malaria, tuberculosis, and venereal disease were now easily treatable, and nutrition, environmental sanitation, and maternal and child health could prevent the onset of disease in many cases. If the World Health Organization could launch a dual program of offensive and preventative medicine, it had the potential to save millions of lives. Therefore, about a million dollars in the first WHO budgets was devoted to work in these areas, and beginning in 1950 the WHO, like the FAO, began receiving additional monies through the United Nations Expanded Program for Technical Assistance, which the WHO used specifically to underwrite operations in the field related to these priorities.[46]

In dealing with preventative medicine, there were no "wonder drugs" to fight the waste of human life and energy caused by the neglect of nutrition, sanitary engineering, and maternal and child health care. Also, the information about what needed to be done was generally well known. Therefore, the role of the WHO was to disseminate this information through fellowships, expert committees, and missions and field demonstrations.[47] Among its preventative efforts, the WHO program in maternal and child health (MCH) was the most thoroughly developed. It focused on demonstration teams and the central collection and dissemination of information on all aspects of the subject. To fulfill the latter end, the WHO called international conferences on children's health issues and established expert committees on maternal care, premature births, school health services, and midwife training. Supplemental activities consisted of fellowships, international training courses, traveling seminars, and regional conferences. In the field, WHO demonstration teams usually established MCH centers to treat mothers and children, provide prenatal care, and reduce infant mortality. There were normally two or three WHO nurses who supplemented the center's work by visiting homes in the surrounding towns and villages, providing advice, and referring cases to doctors at the center. Throughout the length of the demonstration period, WHO personnel also involved themselves in providing practical training to local doctors, nurses, midwives, and other health workers. These MCH teams often had, in addition, a complementary team of WHO nutritionists who taught the health personnel, as well as the center's visitors, the importance of nutrition, especially to infants, children, and expecting and lactating mothers.[48]

The other half of the WHO's priorities focused on attacking diseases of global significance that were especially treatable with new drugs or insecticides developed during the Second World War. One of these was tuberculosis. The WHO continued to cooperate through 1948 with the nine-nation anti-tuberculosis campaign of UNICEF and several Scandinavian Red Cross societies, which called for systematic chest x-rays to detect all infections within a selected population, streptomycin treatment of the ill, and BCG vaccinations for the others. In addition to providing its technical expertise, the WHO accepted responsibility for promoting research on the campaign, underwritten by a $100,000 UNRRA grant. As the postwar crisis in Europe ebbed, the WHO shifted to a long-term, worldwide campaign against tuberculosis, sending consultants to carry out surveys, advise countries on planning and undertaking antituberculosis campaigns, and provide international staff to set up treatment centers and train indigenous staff members. Such consultants were particularly sought to advise on the new forms of attacking tuberculosis (streptomycin therapy and BCG vaccination), and they also provided advice on ways of integrating tuberculosis activities within the overall public health program of a country or area. On the international level, the WHO expert committee sought to develop uniform procedures for the establishment of BCG vaccine laboratories, classification of tuberculosis, interpretation of x-rays, and laboratory diagnosis of tuberculosis, all of which undergirded its national efforts.[49]

Syphilis also flourished in wartime and postwar Europe, while treponematoses, regional variants of syphilis spread through nonvenereal contact, proliferated in the Third World. But the discovery of methods for mass-producing penicillin during World War II offered a fast-acting, relatively safe treatment of these diseases. The WHO Expert Committee on Venereal Diseases first concentrated its efforts on syphilis but then expanded its work to treponematoses, such as bejel, which was prevalent in the Middle East, and yaws, which afflicted most of the globe's tropical areas. The WHO used expert consultants to advise member governments on the establishment of demonstration schemes, training programs, venereal disease control efforts, prenatal antisyphilis programs, and the necessary laboratory facilities for proper diagnosis. The U.S. pharmaceutical industry underwrote some of these WHO demonstration efforts by donating significant quantities of the "wonder drug," and the WHO also established model treatment schedules for penicillin treatment.[50]

The WHO's campaign against malaria, which will be considered at length in the next chapter, followed a similar but more concentrated plan of attack as the efforts against tuberculosis and venereal diseases. In 1955 the World Health Assembly decided to attempt eradication of malaria from the world. With the additional funds that flowed into the antimalaria campaign, the WHO undertook, on a global scale, the demonstration work, training of indigenous personnel, and granting of fellowships for advanced study that characterized its other programs. But the MEP also had a large number of parallels to the general program of WHO work from 1946 to 1965. The MEP clearly fit within the professional ideology of the physicians and medical researchers of the WHO. Science had earlier provided physicians with the means to diagnose and prevent the spread of a number of diseases and therefore the means to attain professional status. By 1955 it seemed that modern science, with the invention of DDT, had once again given the international medical community a way to advance the field of medicine. Now, rather than simply treating and preventing diseases, DDT seemed to provide the means for eradicating a disease—malaria—that had stricken hundreds of millions each year around the globe.

In true progressive fashion, the members of the World Health Organization went about organizing a global campaign based on a standardized technique developed by the WHO through the cooperation of its expert committees, field demonstrations, and the laboratory research it sponsored. Additionally, the WHO believed that the eradication of malaria would uplift entire Third World populations. Where there had been sloth, hunger, and underdevelopment, the WHO believed that there could, with the eradication of malaria, be energy, increased agricultural production, and economic development. Also, of course, the international medical professionals of the WHO considered themselves the most qualified to lead such a global crusade. They had already established their reputation as apolitical, international experts with authority in the medical community and among the governments of the world. The WHO also applied its experience as international manager of several research efforts to its global eradication effort, which required a coordination of action on several levels. But, unfortunately, as we will see, the MEP's reliance on science, which had held so much promise in 1955, proved its undoing by 1969.

10

Exercising International Authority

The Malaria Eradication Program

In 1955 the World Health Organization (WHO) launched the most ambitious public health program ever attempted—the global eradication of malaria. The staff and leadership of the organization believed that science had provided the tools needed to accomplish the job and that they had created, in the WHO, an organization above politics and nationalism and therefore capable of succeeding in such a campaign. The Malaria Eradication Program (MEP) required the careful coordination of national and international aid agencies, the orchestration of diverse national programs, and the creation of a vast international infrastructure to generate and disseminate research, expertise, and education. In many ways, the MEP vividly demonstrated the strengths of the WHO's structure and of its international, professional identity. Nonetheless, its attempt to eradicate malaria failed, and this failure illuminated some of the significant weaknesses of the WHO and its worldview.

The Malaria Eradication Program rested on the WHO's foundational identity as a corporate body of scientifically based medical professionals housed in a universal, apolitical institution. When this identity intersected with the invention of new, long-lasting insecticides and an American willingness to devote foreign aid monies to a Third World health initiative, all the necessary ingredients for a malaria eradication program seemed to be present. While these factors made the MEP possible, what made it desirable was the fact that malaria killed more people than any other disease. Malaria is a parasitic infection of the blood that is spread from person to person by female mosquitoes. It is most prevalent in low-lying and tropical or subtropical areas of the world, where some 1.15 billion people resided in the 1950s. Before World War II, malaria annually struck some 750 million people with debilitating fever and chills for an average of six days per attack, caused approximately 7.5 million deaths per year, was responsible for 10 to 15 percent of all infant mortality, and contributed to the deaths of countless others by making them more vulnerable to opportunistic diseases like tuberculosis and pneumonia.[1]

The MEP attempted to advance efforts, begun at the beginning of the twentieth century, by doctors and engineers to control the mosquito, the vector or carrier of the disease, and thereby to reduce malaria's death toll. Their preferred methods of control were draining swamps, covering ditches, and otherwise eliminating mosquito breeding areas—techniques used at the turn of the century by Dr. William C. Gorgas of the U.S. Army to clear the isthmus of Panama of yellow fever and malaria, which had delayed construction of the Panama Canal. Larvicidal agents, such as Paris green and oil, were also used to control mosquito populations, and quinine (derived from the bark of the cinchona tree) helped prevent the onset of malaria in humans. In 1924 the League of Nations Health Section established a malaria commission to advise countries and public health workers on implementing such prophylactic measures. Beginning in the 1930s, malariologists began experimenting with weekly house-sprayings of an early insecticide, pyrethrum, to depress the rate of malaria in South Africa and India. Such control measures, while often successful, were costly and impractical for most tropical areas. With the outbreak of the Second World War, pyrethrum, which was mainly imported from Japan, became largely unavailable, while the need for an insecticide to fight the mosquitos that carried malaria, the lice that carried typhus, and the flies that carried dysentery and typhoid fever became more urgent than ever. In fact, to provide just one example, American fighting forces in New Guinea were reduced to 10 percent of their original strength due to malaria.[2]

Stepping into the breach and providing the key weapon for the later MEP was dichloro-diphenyl-trichloroethane (DDT). This long-lasting, highly effective insecticide killed flies, lice, and mosquitos (as well as many other insects) for months at a time with only a single application. The U.S. War Production Board encouraged its large-scale manufacture (some three million pounds per month) for use by the army and navy. Allied medical personnel used DDT powder to head off typhus epidemics in Algeria, Egypt, and Italy, where refugees were particularly susceptible to the disease because of the unsanitary and crowded conditions in many of the camps. American sailors and soldiers carried their own supplies to rid themselves of mosquitos, lice, and bedbugs; aerosol bombs of the new insecticide were used to protect the inside of tents, barracks, and mess halls from insects of all kinds. This chemical agent became one of the heroes of the war, heralded and praised in as many as twenty-one thousand newspaper articles by the end of the war, and soon thereafter it became available for general use. Commercial demand for DDT as an agricultural pesticide was extremely high, given the postwar food shortage; Greece, India, and Egypt used it to suppress malarious mosquitos, reportedly saving some five million lives by 1950. Such was its success that in 1948 the Nobel Institute awarded Swiss chemist Paul H. Müller, the inventor of DDT, its prize for medicine.[3]

The World Health Organization paid close attention to these advances and began to imagine even greater public health advances. The advent of DDT would allow a relatively small, mobile group of technicians spraying the interior of houses once or twice per year to achieve an unprecedented degree of mosquito control at a very low per capita cost. In fact, in early experiments the degree of control was so impressive that public health workers began to believe that DDT might kill enough mosquitos to end transmission of the malaria parasite from person to person. If this were to occur, people already infected could be cured without risk of re-infection and the malaria parasite would fade into extinction.[4]

The WHO staff, armed with this vision of malaria eradication, used its own carefully constructed identity as an international group of doctors serving the world community to make the global Malaria Eradication Program a viable possibility. By 1965 more than one hundred countries were participating in the global effort, employing WHO experts, carrying on a campaign based on World Health Organization specifications, and demonstrating the strength of that organization's vision. It is difficult, if not impossible, to imagine any one country or philanthropic organization being able to raise the necessary funds or to convince so many countries to consent to such a standardized, precisely timed, and invasive public health program.[5]

But with visions of malaria eradication dancing in their heads, the staff of the World Health Organization ignored scientific evidence that would have alerted them to the potential dangers of this elaborate program. Wartime experiments conducted by the Bureau of Entomology of the U.S. Department of Agriculture (USDA) had already raised questions about the safety of DDT. When applied at a heavy rate to a Pennsylvania oak forest, DDT killed not only all the gypsy moths (the intended target) but also four thousand birds within eight days and the ladybugs that had kept the aphid population under control. When applied less intensively, the pesticide did not seem to affect birds but still had disastrous effects on aquatic life, and in many cases the insects not killed by the DDT proliferated in the absence of their natural predators. The very attributes that made DDT so effective, its long-lasting nature and insolubility in water, also raised questions, especially when early experiments found that the pesticide built up in the fatty tissues of dogs exposed to it. The April 1945 USDA report, which was widely reported and based on these experiments, described DDT as a "two-edged sword"—equally promising and menacing.[6] But the WHO staff chose to focus on the promise of DDT rather than its potential dangers.

The Momentum toward Eradication

The discovery of DDT had far-reaching implications for medicine during the Second World War and in the years following. Absorbed through contact, DDT killed mosquitos, flies, lice, bedbugs, and other insects for as long as six months after application. The Allied forces used DDT extensively in the Mediterranean and Pacific theaters to suppress malaria, and wartime experiments in the malarious areas of Arkansas and Florida suggested that DDT would be most effective if sprayed on the interior walls and ceilings of buildings where mosquitos usually rested after biting humans. In the spring of 1944, the Allied Control Commission in Italy, working with a team of Rockefeller Foundation Health Commission scientists, carried out the first large field test of DDT house-spraying as a malaria deterrent in Castel Volturno, north of Naples. The success of this experiment led to an expansion of the test spraying area to the entire Tiber River delta.[7]

The World Health Organization and other countries seized upon these successes to promote similar campaigns of DDT house-spraying. In fact, in Argentina, British Guiana, and parts of South Africa malaria-carrying mosquitos soon disappeared entirely. The World Health Organization contributed to the prevailing optimism regarding DDT by sending expert malariologists to lecture at medical schools and conferences, encouraging the creation of centers for the study of malaria, and using its literature to spread news of the successes of DDT spraying. More importantly, in 1947 the WHO created an expert committee on malaria, which recommended further field trials of DDT as a malaria suppressant, and in 1948 it dispatched teams to conduct pilot house-spraying projects that demonstrated the utility of the new insecticide. These demonstration teams usually included an entomologist to study the biology and behavior of the local species of mosquitos, a malariologist to study the incidence and transmission of the disease, and a sanitary engineer to advise on the technical aspects of the spraying campaign. Each of these personnel was usually understudied by a local counterpart, who became eligible for further academic study under the program of WHO fellowships. While the WHO paid the salaries of the technical advisors, the United Nations International Children's Fund (UNICEF) provided most of the supplies, and host governments paid all local costs. These pilot projects enjoyed seemingly universal success in reducing infant mortality and the incidence of malaria. Even where the projects were not continued due to lack of funds, they highlighted the potential of a house-spraying program. In 1950 the Malaria Conference for Equatorial Africa and the Pan American Sanitary Conference both reflected this optimism in resolutions to use these modern methods in concert with the WHO.[8]

Although the early emphasis was primarily on malaria control, malariologists working on the WHO's expert committee began to guide the organization, and therefore the world, toward imagining the possibility of eradication. This school of thought was immeasurably strengthened when in 1951 a shortage of DDT affected the nationwide malaria control campaign in Greece that had begun in 1946 under the auspices of the Rockefeller Foundation. Lacking sufficient DDT to spray the entire malarious area, Greek authorities decided to discontinue spraying operations where malaria had been successfully controlled. In these areas of low malaria transmission, the Greek health department instituted a system of "epidemiological surveillance." In other words, it required doctors, clinics, and public health workers to report any suspected cases of malaria to state authorities and to provide the patient with antimalaria drugs immediately; public health authorities then investigated the source of infection, called for additional spraying if necessary, and followed up on any possible spread of the disease from the initial case. This system exceeded expectations in safeguarding the population from malaria outbreaks; the fifth report of the WHO Expert Committee on Malaria termed such discontinuance of spraying in tandem with epidemiological surveillance "both logical and feasible." Although it would require more funds and staff, greater efficiency in operations, and increased vigilance in surveillance, the prospect that spraying need not continue indefinitely promised to be less expensive in the long term than national malaria control programs.[9]

Eradication seemed to become more of a necessity than an ideal when the continued use of DDT resulted in the development of insecticide resistance among a growing number of the world's malaria-bearing mosquito species beginning in 1951. In other words, DDT became ineffective when mosquitos developed specific physiological characteristics, such as thicker tissue on the feet (inhibiting absorption of the insecticide) or a specific enzyme that neutralized it. While DDT-resistant mosquitos continued to be susceptible to the dieldrin family of insecticides (long-lasting insecticides of a different chemical composition) and dieldrin-resistant insects were vulnerable to DDT, the fear was that double resistance would develop in time and rob humankind of its most effective weapons against mosquitos and malaria. This grim prospect made interruption of spraying operations seem not only desirable but necessary. Global eradication, before double resistance could develop, now seemed imperative.[10]

Adding to the apparent imperative for malaria eradication, promoters of the idea argued that it would not only save hundreds of millions of lives but also money currently lost to medical costs, low labor efficiency, decreased learning capacity, high absentee rates, and low rates of capital investment. Officials in El Salvador, for example, estimated that the country lost $12.4 million per year in worker productivity and medical expenses, while the budget for its MEP was only $3.4 million, an expenditure that would end when the disease was eradicated. Malaria eradication also promised to spur agricultural development by allowing the cultivation of previously uninhabitable or underutilized areas. Just such a phenomenon had occurred in Ceylon (present-day Sri Lanka), where antimalarial operations opened some twelve thousand acres to settlement by ninety-one thousand landless people, and in Greece, where by 1957 rice cultivation had soared to ten times the pre-MEP level. Advocates of eradication also argued that it would promote tourism, make workers more efficient, and provide the nucleus for an efficient rural public health system. Additionally, malaria control cost approximately seventy-five cents per capita indefinitely, while eradication operations cost only twenty-five cents per capita—an expense that would end once malaria was eradicated. To countries not suffering from malaria, eradication proponents pointed out that inefficient use and cultivation of resources and lower worker productivity constituted an additional tax on imports of some 5 percent. Taken as a whole, advocates argued that malaria eradication promised to promote economic development throughout much of the Third World. In addition to appealing to economic theory, those calling for eradication also invoked history, arguing that malaria had been "an outstanding factor" in the decline of ancient civilizations, including the Mayan civilization of Yucatan, the Greek and Roman empires, and the Angkor Wat civilization of Cambodia. In this way, advocates posited malaria not only as a hazard to health but to civilization and its further development.[11]

The Pan American Sanitary Bureau, the American regional office of the WHO, became the first organization to act on these promises when it launched a coordinated campaign for hemispheric malaria eradication in 1954. In this effort it received supplies from UNICEF and pledges of aid from the U.S. International Cooperation Administration (ICA, later the Agency for International Development, or AID), which had already supported earlier control efforts as a means of promoting economic development. The PASB even established a special office in Mexico City to coordinate all malaria eradication efforts in the hemisphere. But the World Health Organization, prompted by high-ranking staff members who were malariologists and by its own expert committee on malaria, soon regained the initiative in malaria eradication.[12]

Organizing and Running a Global Campaign

In 1955 the ninety countries represented at the eighth World Health Assembly unanimously voted to devote the prestige and resources of the organization to eradicating malaria globally. The assembly urged the organization to take the initiative in the campaign, whereupon the WHO requested all countries to institute malaria eradication programs (MEPs) as soon as practicable. It also gave MEPs priority in requests for WHO technical assistance and created a special account to receive voluntary contributions to subsidize the effort. In 1956 the U.S. government pledged five million dollars, without which the campaign might have foundered for lack of funds, as well as raising and focusing ICA expenditures on malaria eradication. The Eisenhower administration hoped that such expenditures, if presented in an appropriately dramatic manner, could help to counter communist actions in Asia and the Middle East. These hopes were based on the fact that malaria eradication promised to provide low-cost proof in such politically critical nations as Iran, India, Thailand, the Philippines, Indonesia, and Vietnam that the United States was vitally interested in their populations. Also in 1956, the sixth report of the expert committee on malaria laid down the principles of malaria eradication and the specific methods to be used in attaining it.[13]

The World Health Organization then went about crafting a standardized program of eradication to be implemented globally, a plan that reflected the organization and staff's professional and international identity. A proper malaria eradication program, as spelled out by the WHO, consisted of four stages and lasted from three to ten years, depending on local circumstances. The preparatory stage, of about one year, laid the scientific background for the program with studies of local mosquitos and malaria incidence and saw to such practical needs as securing supplies, drafting enabling legislation, training local sprayers and staff, drawing maps of the area to be sprayed, and conducting a public education program to gain the cooperation of the populace. In the second or attack phase, which usually lasted three or four years, the interior of each domicile was to be sprayed twice per year with either DDT or dieldrin until malaria transmission had been stopped. In the consolidation phase, public health workers would search out, investigate, and treat any remaining cases of malaria and their causes. When no indigenous cases had been found for a period of three years, a period equivalent to the lifespan of the malaria parasite in the human bloodstream, the final, maintenance phase would begin in which public health officials were to guard carefully against any new introduction of the disease from infected areas.[14]

But the WHO's standardization began even before the launching of the program. In order to achieve success through such a rigorous and standardized program, the WHO, UNICEF, and the U.S. government created a list of twenty-two minimum prerequisites that a country had to meet before launching an eradication program. These provisions, together with the four-stage plan for malaria eradication, hint at the degree of precision and technical proficiency demanded by the MEP. In fact, WHO officials often used military terminology to describe how MEPs should be run, arguing that sprayer personnel needed "to be drilled" in their techniques. It also urged the creation of a specially trained malaria eradication service that would operate independently of extant public health services, like an elite military corps. Many Third World countries adopted similar analogies, envisaging MEPs as "military operations" whose "ammunition" was DDT and employing an elite corps of uniformed sprayers who looked like paramilitary forces.[15]

The first step toward obtaining such military precision in methods and effectiveness was a global standardization not only of the steps in an MEP but also of the methods, terminology, and statistical reporting, a trend that had been inaugurated in the international medical community more than a century before. The first step in this direction was the publication in English and French of a standard malaria terminology and a list of the names and properties of the new synthetic antimalarial drugs. The WHO encouraged similar standardization in the technique of evaluating MEPs and of making annual reports to the organization. Its journals, regional publications, and the *Malaria Yearbook* (first published in 1959) encouraged a similar standardization in nearly every other aspect of the campaign, from maintaining insecticide sprayers to methods of catching mosquitos in the field. The WHO even distributed standardized kits for field testing of insecticide resistance in mosquitos.[16]

To promote the level of scientific and professional standardization that it required, the WHO organized support services to undergird national MEPs and to provide them with necessary tools. In 1957 it created an independent Division of Malaria Eradication at the headquarters in Geneva, established malaria units at each regional office, and generally expanded its capacity to provide technical assistance to member governments pursuing eradication. The Malaria Eradication Division maintained a list of short-term consultants who were internationally recognized experts in malaria and whose advice would be respected in any country; they advised governments on drafting MEP plans of operations, pinpointed and remedied problems in national programs, and provided an expert assessment of whether a country was ready to move on to the consolidation or maintenance phase.[17]

To achieve success on a global scale, the World Health Organization recognized the need to train more health professionals. Integral to a successful MEP, WHO officials realized, was an extensive system of education for malariologists, national leaders of MEPs, laboratory workers, and midlevel supervisors. The lack of qualified malariologists to meet the demand created by the 1955 assembly resolution led the WHO to resort to "emergency measures," taking upon itself the education of medical graduates in malaria work. To create an educated corps of national workers for the MEP, the WHO provided funding, instructors, and student fellowships to malaria eradication training centers in Brazil, Ethiopia, India, Jamaica, Malaysia, Mexico, the Philippines, Sri Lanka, Sudan, Tanganyika (present-day Tanzania), Thailand, and Venezuela. Such centers used a combination of classroom work and extensive field training to educate malariologists, field supervisors of spraying operations, and medical officers in charge of epidemiological studies, as well as to provide refresher courses for senior officials. The WHO also provided fellowships to send malaria eradication officials to study other countries' MEPs. For example, a nation in the attack phase might send someone to study in a country already in the consolidation phase.[18]

By 1960 most affected nations had launched MEPs, and the World Health Organization undertook a number of strategies designed to see that these countries stayed the course. This WHO effort reflected the fear that national campaigns would lose momentum as they moved from the attack to the surveillance phase, with the lurking danger that shortcomings in these phases could lead to double insecticide resistance and make eradication all the more difficult. Therefore, the eleventh World Health Assembly urged member governments to ensure adequate support for their MEPs so that they would not stop short of eradication, and the Western Pacific regional office added a warning about "the dangers of the development of undue optimism and the underestimation of the administrative aspects" of the MEP. Sending a broad-based message, the WHO designated "The World Malaria Eradication Effort" as the theme for its 1960 World Health Day educational campaign. But to a certain extent the WHO's promotional campaign was also an effort to substitute encouraging words for money. For in 1959 the World Health Organization had moved away from its earlier policy of subsidizing the cost of local spraying personnel in Malaria Eradication Program countries, because contributions to the Malaria Eradication Special Account were no longer sufficient to meet this need among so many in the global MEP.[19]

The global MEP played into the WHO's strengths as an international organization experienced in managing relations among a variety of groups. The World Health Organization convened regional meetings of malaria eradication officials to facilitate mutual sharing of experiences. Between such gatherings, the WHO regional offices circulated newsletters and reports to provide updated information on national programs to other countries within the region. Such regional meetings and communications laid the necessary groundwork for regional eradication by leading the participants to the necessary conclusion that national plans had to be coordinated, especially in border regions.[20]

By bringing national representatives together to consult on such technical matters, the WHO promoted a functionalist brand of internationalism for which it was uniquely suited. In other words, the WHO, through the Malaria Eradication Program, created a habit of cooperation between countries by focusing on the highly technical issue of malaria eradication rather than on issues of traditional diplomacy or economics. Malaria eradication required international coordination, because, except for island nations like Taiwan and Cuba, all countries with MEPs had to contend with the possibility that new malaria cases could be imported from neighboring nations without MEPs or that mosquitos breeding on the other side of the border could spread malaria to its citizens. To minimize such eventualities, the WHO encouraged countries to coordinate their MEPs, particularly in border areas. More ambitiously, in 1958 it succeeded in bringing together the countries of southeastern Africa (Mozambique, Southern Rhodesia, Bechuanaland [present-day Botswana], Swaziland, and the Union of South Africa) into a single regional malaria eradication program that called for a coordinated spraying program established, supervised, and evaluated by a multinational coordination board. The WHO drew up similar programs to unite the MEPs of Peru, Bolivia, and Chile in 1948, of the colonies and nations of West Africa (Togo, Dahomey [present-day Benin], the Ivory Coast, Ghana, and Liberia) in 1958, and of the small countries of Central America in 1965. Such coordination of national

activities showed the World Health Organization's mission of promoting cooperation rather than competition in its regulation of global public health.[21]

The WHO's coordination of research endeavors showed a similar inclination,
with its blending of public and private resources to obtain mutually desirable
goals. The organization provided funds to a number of research facilities in the
Third World that served as reference laboratories, carrying on much of the work
for the regional MEPs. For more involved laboratory work, such as the determination of whether blood drawn from captured mosquitos came from humans
or animals, the WHO had made arrangements for testing at the Lister Institute
in London. Beginning in 1956 the WHO developed an international cooperative
program of research on the growing problem of insecticide resistance. To test
new insecticides and bring the most promising ones into the field, the WHO
additionally created a formal system of cooperation between industry, national
laboratories, and international aid agencies. The new formulations were tested for
toxicity and residual effectiveness on a variety of surfaces, then under field conditions. WHO officials also cooperated with private businesses, such as the Shell Oil
Company in Nigeria and the United Fruit Company in Guatemala, to promote
national malaria eradication programs, and the WHO often based its initial pilot
projects on information collected by such enterprises in malaria control projects
meant to protect their own workforces.[22]

Another cooperative component of the campaign was present from the beginning of the MEP, for while the WHO provided the overall coordination and technical assistance, it relied on UNICEF and hefty U.S. contributions (to the Malaria
Eradication Special Account [MESA] and the PAHO as well as through the ICA)
to provide the vehicles, insecticide, compression sprayers, and other equipment
needed for the campaign. Because malaria mortality was most pronounced among
infants and toddlers, UNICEF provided supplies as part of its global mandate to
safeguard the lives of children. From 1947 to 1957, it expended $26.4 million on
antimalarial projects in some fifty-six countries and colonies; with the launching
of the MEP it adopted a policy of providing supplies only to programs that explicitly worked toward eradication, as the most cost-effective way to protect the lives
and health of children in malarial areas. For the United States, foreign aid for malaria eradication was part of an overall aid strategy meant to solidify its alliances
and wage a successful cold war against the Soviet Union. In fact, Eisenhower used
the occasion of his 1958 State of the Union address to highlight the significant role
the United States was playing in this vital, life-saving campaign and to challenge
the Soviet Union to make similar contributions. Therefore, the International Cooperation Administration (ICA) expended $88.9 million to underwrite malaria
control projects in more than thirty countries before the advent of the WHO
Malaria Eradication Program, when Congress recommended a five-year commitment of some $519 million to be distributed through the WHO special account,

the Pan American Health Organization, and the ICA. This money was the key to the program, because it encouraged many Third World countries to make the domestic financial sacrifices necessary to undertake an MEP. The fear that such foreign aid might not be available in the future also added impetus to the "now or never" mentality of the campaign.[23]

But what ultimately made the Malaria Eradication Program most attractive to the personnel of the World Health Organization was the prospect of taking medicine to a higher stage of development. For centuries, doctors had confined themselves to trying to cure and contain the spread of disease, but in the late nineteenth and early twentieth centuries the practice of medicine had begun to focus on the *prevention* of disease. Now, it seemed to the WHO staff members that science had provided them with the tools and the opportunity to take medical practice one step further—the eradication of communicable diseases. Simply from a professional perspective, therefore, malaria eradication presented a tempting challenge. In addition, a successful MEP held the promise of saving millions of lives each year, eliminating sickness among hundreds of millions annually, saving billions of dollars in government expenditures on malaria control measures, and allowing the cultivation of once-malarious areas and thereby increasing agricultural production. To achieve these humanitarian ends the WHO gratefully accepted aid from UNICEF, with which it had worked closely on a number of other health projects, and from the United States, though the health organization did not share America's political and diplomatic motivations.

India: A Local Case Study

India offers a clear picture of both the potential benefits and the practical difficulties of eradicating malaria. One quarter of the 1.15 billion people in the world endangered by malaria in these years lived in India, where the disease killed 800,000 annually and temporarily debilitated another seventy-five million each year. The high malaria incidence retarded production in the Indian coalfields, beetle-nut plantations, and tea estates and impeded the development of irrigation canals, railways, and port facilities. The government estimated the annual economic loss to the country to be approximately ten trillion rupees (about $500 million) above and beyond individual expenditures on medicine and hospitalization. Because of the severity of the disease on the subcontinent, some of the earliest malaria control experiments had occurred there; the Malaria Institute of India had begun DDT spraying operations in Delhi in 1946 and conducted research on mosquito species in order to adapt spraying techniques to local conditions. Several Indian states and the WHO followed up on this work with pilot projects, which by 1952 had protected some thirty million people from malaria at a per capita cost of half a rupee.[24]

The economy and effectiveness of these efforts, as well as the WHO's active involvement, convinced the national government to extend the program to the rest of the country's 270 million citizens, beginning in April 1953. The National Malaria Institute, in collaboration with the WHO, UNICEF, the Rockefeller Foundation, and the U.S. Technical Co-operation Mission, drafted a plan that called for every wall and ceiling of every house and cattle shed to be sprayed twice per year with DDT. To carry out this ambitious program, India received funds from the American Point Four program (later ICA and then USAID) to finance the two hundred spray teams of 153 workers each, plus supervisory, laboratory, supply, and transportation support. The results were impressive. In 1957–58 there were forty-five million fewer cases of malaria than before the control program, and only eight of every thousand Indian children had any malaria parasites in their blood—a 79 percent reduction over the pre-control era. In the Punjab, the "breadbasket" of India, an additional 130,562 acres were brought into agricultural production.[25]

The success of the control program, the development of insecticide resistance among one species of Indian mosquito, and the World Health Assembly resolution for global eradication inspired the adoption of the world's largest MEP in April 1958, with the motto, "Malaria Eradication Is Now or Never." The MEP also appealed to the Indian government, because it promised long-term savings over malaria control and promised to create a large corps of public health workers. But the additional effort needed for eradication, rather than control, was significant. In order to spray each of the country's seventy-eight million roofed structures just once required some eighteen million tons of DDT and nearly sixty-one thousand sprayers; furthermore, structures in areas where malaria was particularly prevalent were to be sprayed twice. The MEP predictably suffered from supply and distribution difficulties in addition to personnel shortages in its first few years. The response of the Malaria Institute of India was an intensive training program and the construction of local insecticide plants.[26]

While malaria technocrats rather quickly addressed these concrete difficulties, the sprayers in the field encountered a number of cultural obstacles that the WHO had not initially addressed or anticipated in its campaign. A number of citizens refused to have their homes sprayed for a variety of reasons: concern over the caste of the sprayers, the belief that the DDT was too weak because it no longer killed bedbugs and other pests as it had initially, worry over the discoloration of walls, and the idea that such inconvenience was no longer tolerable given the great decline in malaria cases. But personal negotiation and a public health education campaign dramatically reduced the number of such refusals. Of course, not all people shared a negative opinion; some villages, in fact, fed all fifty members of the spraying team in appreciation for their work. Such cooperation allowed the campaign by 1960 to succeed in further reducing the number of infants and children infected with malaria parasites to one in a thousand.[27]

After three years of this intensified program of spraying, some areas switched to an intensive surveillance program, which included both passive and active means of finding cases of malaria. Passive surveillance came through the reporting of potential malaria patients from doctors, hospitals, clinics, and dispensaries, but it was the job of the country's thirty-nine thousand malaria surveillance workers, each visiting two thousand homes on a two-week cycle, to carry out most of the surveillance. During these home visits, the surveillance worker inquired about any cases of fever within the household, provided antimalarial medication to any potential cases, drew blood from all fever cases and infants, and forwarded all blood samples to MEP laboratory facilities. These labs examined a minimum of one hundred samples daily and determined which subjects were suffering from malaria. Malaria sufferers received follow-up visits from a surveillance worker, a five-day regimen of the antimalarial drug primaquine, and investigation into the possible source of the infection. This procedure, however, was sometimes hindered by India's rapid population growth, the influx of refugees from Bangladesh during its war of independence, the movement of nomadic populations, and a reluctance to allow infants' blood to be drawn.[28] Similar difficulties characterized MEPs around the globe. These obstacles notwithstanding, the MEPs succeeded in decreasing the incidence and mortality of malaria dramatically, although few managed the complete eradication of the disease within their boundaries.

Campaign Difficulties

Potential obstacles to malaria eradication had been evident even before the launching of the MEP in 1955, but the breadth of expert consensus about the feasibility of eradication, the presence of large sums of money to mount the campaign, and the urgency lent to it by spreading insecticide resistance had marginalized dissent. In addition, the WHO staff members had confidence that they could overcome technical difficulties, such as double resistance. But what the WHO had apparently not given sufficient thought to were national problems with MEP operations, administration, and finance, which were largely out of its control and which ultimately proved insuperable. A combination of technical and operational difficulties forced the WHO to abandon the MEP in 1969.[29]

From the very beginning, the WHO staff and other experts had recognized that malaria eradication in Africa presented the greatest challenge, because the disease was highly endemic there. But the fact that eradication in sub-Saharan Africa could "not be visualized in the immediate future" did not deter WHO officials from trumpeting global eradication as a possible and desirable goal. In Africa, transmission of malaria occurred without seasonal interruption and struck the entire population, because the two main malaria-carrying mosquitos (*Anopheles gambiae* and *A. funestus*) thrived at different times of the year and had relatively long lifespans. Additionally, the area's warm temperatures hastened maturation of the malaria parasite. Because of the unrelenting transmission of malaria in tropical Africa, children who survived to adulthood generally developed an immunity to the parasite that would be lost if the disease was suppressed but not eradicated. Together, immunity and endemicity meant that any program aimed at ending transmission of the malaria parasite would have to be carried out with a "degree of perfection" unnecessary in other areas, despite the fact that administrative, scientific, and transportation facilities in Africa were generally less developed than those in other areas launching MEPs. The lack of medical infrastructure also meant that there was very little reliable scientific data on malaria or mosquitos in much of Africa before the advent of the MEP, so WHO officials were starting from scratch in these areas, further hampering the eradication effort.[30]

African malaria resisted the WHO's standardized program in other, equally significant ways. The house-spraying methods used elsewhere might be ineffective in tropical Africa, where early pilot projects had demonstrated that some mosquitos did not rest indoors after drawing blood or were repelled from insecticide-sprayed walls before they absorbed a lethal dose. Another obstacle was the fact that the mud walls of some African huts absorbed insecticide, rendering it ineffective, sometimes in a matter of days. This combination of difficulties meant that many of the spraying programs in Africa succeeded in reducing the incidence and severity of malaria but could not stop transmission, which was key to eradication. In the 1960s, when MEPs in other regions were dramatically decreasing the incidence of malaria, almost half of all the world's people who continued to suffer from malaria were Africans.[31]

In Africa and other areas, the World Health Organization gamely sought solutions to a number of scientific and technical difficulties—obstacles the WHO staff confidently believed it could overcome, given adequate study. Beginning in 1960, double resistance became a reality in parts of Central America and in the Tigris-Euphrates Valley of Iraq and Iran, leading to the development and use of new insecticides, such as malathion and baygon, as well as larvicidal operations familiar from the days of malaria control. But many of the new insecticides were more toxic to humans, particularly the sprayers who were in constant contact with them, and this toxicity required often cumbersome and heavy protective clothing that was particularly problematic in tropical climates. Scientists also began to formulate new methods to control mosquito populations, including individual use of long-lasting mosquito repellents, genetic control of mosquitos, and the use of hormones to disrupt mosquito development and breeding.[32]

In addition to technical problems, the rational structure and tightly regulated schedule of the MEP also confronted the difficult realities of nomadic peoples, migratory workers, and natural population increase, factors that made full coverage and complete treatment almost an impossibility. Sometimes even efficient spraying operations failed to stop transmission, because new houses, additions, and roofs were constructed between sprayings and wall painting, or the buildup of soot from indoor fires, inhibited the action of the insecticide. The Brazilian MEP faced an almost insoluble problem in eradicating malaria among the Amerindians of the Amazon rain forest. If it could not eliminate this reservoir of malaria parasites, mosquitos would continue to carry the disease beyond the rainforest and would reinfect the rest of the Brazilian population in time. To combat some of these problems, the WHO conducted a number of experiments with mass chemoprophylaxis—the use of antimalarial drugs by an entire population in order to prevent infection and consequently transmission of the disease—to supplement or replace insecticide-spraying operations. Most of these programs, however, had unsatisfactory results. The need to take the drugs on a regular schedule and to attain complete coverage among the test population were the primary operational difficulties. One attempt to overcome these difficulties was the mixing of antimalarial salts into household salt, but antimalaria drugs promoted resistance in the malaria parasite itself. Despite these problems, however, antimalarials continued to serve a useful purpose in eliminating infection in incoming immigrants and nomads and thereby preventing a reintroduction of infection. Again, the WHO's ability to address a number of technical difficulties was evident.[33]

But other MEP difficulties were man-made and more difficult for the World Health Organization to address. Some countries seemed unable to end malaria transmission through insecticide spraying, not because of technical problems but due to human error in the spraying and supervision of sprayers. Also, the MEPs that successfully completed the attack phase faced other, no less daunting, administrative challenges in the consolidation and surveillance phases. For while WHO officials had argued that malaria eradication programs would provide a nucleus of rural public health officials, the frequent reliance on outside technicians and managers and the tendency to separate MEPs from other public health programs worked against such a development in many countries. In the rush to get an MEP started, it often seemed logical and expedient to bring in a WHO laboratory technician rather than to recruit or educate an indigenous technician, but the result was that rather than creating a domestic health system that could carry out the duties of the MEP's surveillance phase, the WHO often superimposed a well funded, internationally staffed program on a poorly funded, understaffed national structure that was unable to absorb additional duties.[34]

In other cases, countries simply were unwilling or unable to give the Malaria Eradication Program the same priority given other budgetary and national security needs. Budget difficulties in Latin American MEPs, which had led to suspension of operations in Paraguay in 1961 and reduced operations in both Argentina and Panama, triggered a near doubling in U.S. bilateral aid to the area through the Agency for International Development (AID) in 1963. Escalating tensions between India, home of the world's largest MEP, and Pakistan resulted in rising military expenditures that endangered the MEPs of both countries. Pakistan considered cutting its MEP altogether, while India in 1965 combined its malaria eradication program with other public health programs at a much lower level of funding. The resulting inadequacy of surveillance resulted in a dramatic upswing in the number of malaria cases springing from the few remaining areas where the disease had not been eradicated. One reason that national policymakers seemed so ready to sacrifice MEPs was the fact that their cost continued to be high even after the attack phase had been completed—proper epidemiological surveillance was necessary to eliminate remaining sources of infection and the chance of new outbreaks of malaria. However, it seemed counterintuitive to many officials that large expenditures were necessary when almost no one in their countries suffered from malaria any longer.[35]

Ironically, the success of the MEPs in dramatically decreasing the incidence of malaria played a part in the failure of national governments to provide adequate funding to ensure the complete eradication of the disease. For as the MEP decreased mortality and opened up new areas to agricultural development, it contributed to the Third World budget crunch as countries found themselves bombarded with calls to build new public education facilities for its growing population of children, expand public utilities and roads into newly developed areas, and allot more budgetary resources to family planning programs. Critics of malaria eradication argued that all it did was ensure that there would be more people who were unemployed, "ill-fed, ill-clothed, and almost literally with half a roof over their heads." A case in point, they argued, was the South American nation of British Guiana. Between 1945 and 1948, DDT spraying reduced the infant mortality rate in that country from 250 per thousand births to sixty-seven, with a simultaneous rise in the birth rate; the combination of the two overburdened the nation's socioeconomic system. Economists and national policymakers who set budgetary priorities seemed to take these arguments to heart and increasingly focused on the development of physical rather than human resources. They apparently believed that human development would naturally flow from economic development rather than vice versa. Faced with such skepticism, the WHO commissioned a series of economic studies to illustrate the concrete advantages, in dollars and cents, that malaria eradication yielded, in order to convince Third World politicians and bureaucrats to continue expending money for malaria eradication programs.[36]

The World Health Organization had never tried to hide the fact that malaria eradication would naturally result in population increases, but population issues were particularly volatile among the international organizations. Therefore, this aspect of the MEP had received little attention in the rush toward eradication—until it threatened to undo the whole program. The year before launching the global MEP, at the Second Asian Malaria Conference in 1954, the WHO and its membership had squarely faced the question of population increases in response to malaria eradication and had simply concluded that "no one knows or can accurately predict" how many people the earth could support if its resources were properly utilized, and that no one had "the necessary prescience or moral authority" to decide which areas would continue to be stricken with malaria and which would be freed from the scourge. Other commentators similarly shied away from a neo-Malthusian perspective, pointing out, quite rightly, that Malthus's predictions of a century before had not come to pass. Instead they highlighted the positive effects of the MEP on Third World development—while population was increasing, so was the efficiency of the workforce, now free from the debilitating effects of malaria attacks. Other social scientists showed that malaria eradication accounted for no more than 60 percent of total population growth, the rest being attributable to other factors. Additionally, these scholars argued that MEP-induced population growth could be expected to stabilize in time.[37]

The Malaria Eradication Program seemed to contain an insoluble paradox: as it began to succeed in saving hundreds of millions of people from the effects of malaria by overcoming significant technical and bureaucratic hurdles, national governments became more and more hesitant to fund the effort. The staff of the WHO found this to be a most frustrating turn of events. But its public statements that administrative and financial shortcomings, rather than its own technical efforts, were to blame for the failure of malaria eradication soon rang hollow.

Conclusion

The World Health Organization's Malaria Eradication Program collapsed when its keystone—DDT—crumbled. Although initial experiments had shown DDT to be nontoxic to humans and other warm-blooded animals, further scientific study pointed out the dangers of bioaccumulation (meaning that DDT collected in the fat of mammals until it reached toxic levels) and biomagnification (i.e., DDT absorbed by animals at the low end of the food chain meant that the carnivores at the high end absorbed more DDT than that with which they came into direct contact). Biomagnification was particularly a concern with birds that ate earthworms, which had a particularly high tolerance for the insecticide, leading to bioaccumulation among these birds, whose reproduction was impaired by thinning eggshells and high embryonic death rates. American naturalist Rachel Carson believed that the continued use of DDT would eventually lead to the extinction of a variety of bird species, and her best-selling book *Silent Spring* contributed to the popular outrage and environmental consciousness that led to outlawing the use of the pesticide in the United States. DDT was even more damaging to aquatic ecosystems, inhibiting the development and behavior of everything from green algae to fish. Additionally, the greatest advantage of DDT, its long-lasting effect, was also its greatest drawback: the insecticide continued to be absorbed into the food chain long after spraying ended, and it could travel, in water and in the food chain, far from the original location of the spraying. The insecticide turned up, for example, not only in Antarctic penguins but also in the breast milk of women around the world.[38]

The World Health Organization and the larger international medical community had overlooked early warnings about these potential environmental effects. As early as a 1949 International Technical Conference on the Protection of Nature, which was cosponsored by UNESCO, biologists had expressed reservations about the "miracle" of DDT, which was being hailed so unconditionally by much of the medical community. H. de Saeger, secretary-general of the Belgian Congo National Parks Institute, characterized the widespread use of "superinsecticides" such as DDT and dieldrin as "a crass error" committed "in complete ignorance of the environment." Dr. C. H. Curran of the American Museum of Natural History's Department of Insects and Spiders and Joseph P. Linduska, a biologist for the U.S. Fish and Wildlife Service, pointed to the damage that DDT wreaked on the food chains of aquatic animals, particularly fish and amphibians; warned that DDT killed beneficial insects as well as those that spread disease; and called for using DDT only in case of emergency.[39]

Throughout the MEP there had also been hints about the ability of DDT to unbalance local ecosystems; it killed some beneficial insects and worms, and certain pests, such as flies and bedbugs, developed insecticide resistance before mosquitos. These difficulties had also hampered the comprehensive spraying needed for a successful MEP, because they sparked an increasing tendency among homeowners to bar sprayers from their homes. In Taiwan, DDT killed the economically vital silkworm and led many to resist the national spraying campaign. A similar situation occurred in an African village where residents insisted that DDT spraying had resulted in their roofs collapsing. While on the surface this appeared to be a non sequitur, further investigation revealed that DDT had, in fact, eliminated a local species of spider that ate the worms that fed upon the roofing thatch; lacking a natural predator, the worms multiplied unchecked and feasted on the village's roofs, causing them to collapse. In other areas, home owners questioned the efficacy of DDT and the efficiency of sprayers when they noted an increase in the number of noxious pests such as houseflies, fleas, bedbugs, and lice. As these insects often developed resistance to DDT before the mosquito, their numbers did increase as spraying campaigns progressed, not because the sprayers were not doing their job but because insecticide application simply failed to kill as many as it had in the past. Such perceptions led some 10 percent of the citizens in Zanzibar (present-day Tanzania) to bar their houses to sprayers in 1960.[40]

But the World Health Organization staff chose to ignore early critics of DDT and to interpret evidence of the nondiscriminatorily lethal nature of DDT as individual technical difficulties requiring only a modification of technique rather than a rethinking of the very basis of the Malaria Eradication Program. Dazzled by the prospect of eradicating the world's most lethal and costly disease and frightened by the prospect that this opportunity might slip through its fingers, the World Health Organization led the charge in embracing DDT and in pushing for a global MEP. Whether driven by a desire for international acclaim or a humanitarian impulse, the program was premature. It began before all the scientific evidence on the new insecticides was in and in the face of evidence that it might be harmful to aquatic ecosystems; also, success relied on a level of public health infrastructure that simply did not exist in much of the Third World. But the mindset of the MEP was so fixed that despite the 1962 publication of *Silent Spring* and the subsequent banning of DDT use in the United States, it was not until 1969 that the WHO abandoned the MEP.

The price of this single-mindedness was staggering. While the damage to the environment is not measurable in dollars and cents, the cost of the MEP itself is. The WHO spent $57 million on the MEP between 1957 and 1964, UNICEF expended $54.4 million, the United States spent approximately $100 million in aid expenditures, and national governments invested something on the order of $5.6 billion during the same period. In return they received a temporary reprieve from malaria and a surge in population. An efficient public health service, economic development, and improved health remained unfulfilled promises in much of the world. In sum, the price was exorbitantly high. The Malaria Eradication Program consumed vast amounts of valuable and scarce national development resources, and it undermined some of the professional authority previously garnered by the World Health Organization. The WHO staff emerged chastened from the experience. It approached subsequent eradication campaigns against smallpox, polio, and leprosy with much more caution and far more thorough investigation beforehand. In the immediate aftermath of the MEP debacle, there was also a renewed emphasis within the organization on building national health systems that had adequate medical personnel, laboratory facilities, and technical support rather than on ambitious eradication schemes. In other words, the WHO sought to correct the shortcomings in its own organization and program that had fueled the MEP disaster. But this was poor consolation to countries whose plans for development had been hindered, rather than helped, by the WHO's almost glib assurances that malaria could be eradicated and would save countries many millions of dollars in the long run. The WHO, in this case, had used its medical professionalism and its position as the international health authority to foist upon the most needy countries of the world a plan flawed in both design and execution. In sum, the story of the MEP disaster should stand as a cautionary tale about good intentions as well as medical and international authority run amok.[41]

Conclusion

This book's introduction stressed the hope and optimism that surrounded the "birth of development," when the victors of World War II created a group of well-endowed international institutions staffed by professionals committed to improving the livelihoods, nutrition, and health of the world's people. At the end of this narrative, however, the reader might be feeling a bit pessimistic. After all, this book has recounted the superpower politics that trumped the World Bank's diplomatic efforts to settle the Anglo-Iranian oil crisis and to build the Aswan High Dam, several abortive attempts by the Food and Agriculture Organization to feed people better, and the World Health Organization's disastrous Malaria Eradication Program. Moving beyond the chronological framework of this narrative, moreover, would only increase the gathering gloom; the optimism of the "Development Decades" of the 1960s and 1970s dissolved in the debt crises and structural adjustments of the 1980s and 1990s. The end of the Cold War saw the foreign-aid coffers of the United States (already seriously depleted by the Vietnam War) practically close once the superpower competition for the Third World's loyalty had ceased. By the end of the twentieth century, much of the planet's population seemed to be living in and dying from levels of poverty, malnutrition, and disease little changed from the days after World War II when the specialized agencies of the United Nations committed themselves to improving the lot of humankind. In response, activists have focused their ire and frustration on the World Bank, the International Monetary Fund, and the World Trade Organization.

Yet we must not miss the overreaching story of progress told in these pages. Prior to the mid-twentieth century, there was no significant sense of obligation with respect to aiding people living in poverty and illness around the world. It was generally only at times of catastrophic natural disasters that people around the globe came to the aid of others, usually through the International Red Cross. The other significant exception were missionaries, who provided medical care, education, and material aid (as well as Western cultural habits and attire) to some in foreign countries, with the goal of religious conversion. Their impact on cultural and diplomatic relations, however, was more significant than their impact on the health and poverty of the people in these areas. When it came to national governments, even countries holding colonies did not invest much, if at all, in the human infrastructure of those areas. For example, the League of Nations' study of the world's nutrition in 1936 deduced that more than half of the people living in colonial regions were malnourished.[1]

But World War II witnessed a revolution in expectations that compelled the imperial and indigenous governments of most countries to contribute to the development of peoples throughout the Third World (a revolution funded in large part by the Cold War). The United Nations system and its specialized agencies played a key role in promoting this process. It gave colonial territories a voice in international affairs through its associate membership provisions and emphasis on indigenous representation. Additionally, it helped to hold imperial powers accountable, by requiring the submission of economic, nutrition, and health statistics from areas subordinated to colonial rule. Also, it is clear that these UN specialized organizations became the vehicles by which many colonial territories began to realize their dreams of independence and prosperity. Newly independent Third World countries, in turn, pushed the specialized agencies to fund more and more services and projects that might improve the lives of their people. But as we have seen in the previous narrative, most of those goals went unrealized during the two decades following World War II. The "Development Decade" of the 1960s did witness a growth in national GNP, but there was no correlating decline in malnutrition, infant mortality, illiteracy, unemployment, or the gap between the rich and poor countries. But the effort to address these shortfalls through more ambitious lending during the 1970s only laid the groundwork for the debt crisis and structural readjustment of the 1980s, which led many developing countries to abandon the social programs urged upon them in the previous decade. At the turn of the millennium, the world seemed to be posing the same questions that it had after World War II, but with seemingly less commitment to pursuing bold new strategies to improve lives.

The World Bank largely abandoned its conservative lending structure in the decades following Eugene Black's presidency; this might have been inevitable, given the growing demands of the new countries emerging from colonialism, but it contributed to the debt crisis of the 1980s, made the organization more vulnerable to political pressure from its executive directors, and undermined its reputation in much of the Third World. In search of new projects to fund and seeking to transform the institution from a bank to a development agency, the two World Bank presidents who succeeded Eugene Black oversaw an expansion of its lending in terms of dollars as well as the diversity of projects funded. Shifting from the earlier emphasis on traditional infrastructural projects, George D. Woods

(1963–68) and Robert S. McNamara (1968–81) expanded the bank's lending into agriculture, education, population planning, and disease eradication; increased development grants by funneling bank profits into the International Development Agency (IDA); and increased overall annual lending commitments from less than one billion dollars to $13 billion by fiscal year 1981. The richest countries, however, evinced a growing reluctance to finance the seemingly insatiable needs of the developing world; nonetheless, McNamara doggedly located new capital markets to fund the ever-higher levels of bank commitments, seemingly unaware that he was planting the seeds of an international economic crisis.[2]

Oil prices quadrupled in 1973 and doubled again in 1979, fueling both inflation and an economic recession throughout the developed world. The resulting rise in interest rates and fall in import levels meant that the poorer countries were, in effect, trying to run up an escalator that was going down—they accumulated more and more external debt and debt service as they fell farther and farther behind the First World economies. World Bank president Alden W. Clausen (1981–86), faced with the full brunt of an international debt crisis that started in 1982 as well as the conservative political ideologies of new leadership in the United States and much of Western Europe, responded with higher IBRD fees, variable interest rates on the bank's loans, and sectoral and structural adjustment loans that put a premium on private investment and free markets and that devalued government-provided social services, producer subsidies, and nationally owned enterprises. These practices led critics to accuse the World Bank of acting as the First World's collection agency—of putting stockholders' interests before those of the people who live in the countries that the bank is supposed to serve.[3] Clausen's successor, Barber B. Conable (1986–91), was a former Republican congressman from New York with no practical banking experience. He gained American support for IDA replenishment and a general capital increase for the bank only by bowing to Washington's demands to increase IDA lending to sub-Saharan Africa, limit credits to India and China, shorten the terms of IDA credits, and most controversially, reduce the U.S. share of the bank's funds without impairing its ability to shape the bank's decision-making process. As the bank worked more and more closely with the United States in response to the ongoing debt crisis, Conable found himself and his institution under increasing criticism for the effect of its lending on the environment and women. The former congressman, sensitive to these charges, admitted past errors, created a new environmental section to review prospective loans, and committed the bank to a number of highly visible environmental efforts, including preservation of rain forests and creation of the Global Environment Facility, but all this did little to assuage the bank's critics or to repair the bank's image throughout the developing world.[4] The FAO found itself with an even more serious image problem as it faced the new millennium.

The Food and Agriculture Organization floundered in the decades following

B. R. Sen's director-generalship, demonstrating little initiative and undermining much of the faith of the international community. This deterioration was evident fairly soon into the tenure of the organization's next leader, Addeke Hendrik Boerma of the Netherlands. Boerma focused his attention on funding the "Green Revolution," a tack that departed from Sen's earlier emphasis on small-scale, grassroots development, disenchanted much of the Third World, and left the organization unprepared to deal with the global financial and food crisis that began in 1972.[5] By 1974 the catastrophic dimensions of the world food crisis and a pervasive sense that the FAO could not handle the problem led U.S. secretary of state Henry Kissinger to call upon the UN General Assembly to convene the World Food Conference, which met from 5 to 16 November 1974 and catalyzed the creation of the International Fund for Agricultural Development (IFAD), the goal of which was to develop greater food production among the world's poorest farmers. IFAD seemed to attract both the optimistic hopes of the international community and its discretionary funds—to the detriment of the FAO. Viewed in a positive light, this fracturing of FAO's mission allows governments to pursue their policy goals through a variety of channels; viewed negatively, it allows those same governments to evade policies they dislike and weakens the ability of the staff in Rome to bring about needed changes in international agriculture.[6]

In November 1975 the organization's membership met and tried to regain the organization's place within international agricultural circles, but its directors-general have variously failed to develop a program that builds consensus and that feeds people. When the eighteenth FAO Conference met, the organization was clearly in crisis and in danger of eclipse by other development agencies. Edouard Saouma, a Lebanese national who had been with the FAO since 1962, was elected director-general amid promises that he would decentralize the organization, make it more cost-effective, and emphasize field, rather than theoretical, work, but within eight years his failures resulted in a no-growth budget as Scandinavian countries chose to channel their agricultural aid through different channels and as the United States began to withhold its contributions.[7] After eighteen years at the helm, Saouma was succeeded by Dr. Jacques Diouf, a native of Senegal, who promised he would streamline the organization and focus its work on making food-deficit countries self-sufficient. To this end, in 1994 he created the Special Program for Food Security, which gives monetary aid to poor countries to help them boost their food production (seemingly in direct competition with IFAD). But the lack of public criteria for receiving such aid and the preponderance of African recipients led some to charge that the director-general was primarily trying to cement reelection in 1999, by which time he was facing questions about whether the FAO should be involved in fieldwork at all.[8] Most recently, Diouf ignited a firestorm of protest when he publicly defended genetically modified foods and livestock as showing "clear promise" in the fight against hunger. More than

650 nongovernmental organizations and eight hundred individuals hailing from some eighty-three countries disagreed, calling the report "a declaration of war on the farmers it is pledged to support."[9] Today, much of the international community views the FAO as a bureaucracy in the worst sense of the word—a large, overstaffed organization that exists more for its own sake than for those it was meant to serve.

The World Health Organization has similarly struggled, if to a lesser degree, in its work over the past three decades. After the debacle of the Malaria Eradication Program (MEP), the World Health Organization was able to regain much of its lost prestige, but subsequent eradication efforts have seemingly replicated many of the same errors from the MEP. In 1967, on the heels of its malaria effort, the WHO embarked on a successful decade-long effort to eradicate smallpox. The WHO's focus on smallpox helped to catalyze the international crusade, its scientific expertise helped the campaign overcome a variety of technical obstacles, and its apolitical reputation allowed it to coordinate the global program. In 1974, building on the smallpox program, the WHO launched a childhood immunization effort focused on polio, diphtheria, pertussis (whooping cough), and tetanus that brought together the efforts of UN bodies, bilateral programs, and nongovernmental organizations. This effort increased the percentage of immunized children in the developing countries from 5 percent in 1974 to 50 percent in 1988 (with 75 percent of those children having access to immunization services). But immunization is a constant battle, and by 1996 structural adjustment programs mandated by the IMF and World Bank had undermined national support for public health programs and threatened much of the progress made. In addition to economic obstacles, the 1988 WHO target of "A World Without Polio" by 2000 has most recently been sidetracked by Nigerian Muslims' refusal to participate in immunization programs and by ongoing conflict in Sudan that has contributed to a doubling of African polio cases.[10] But not all difficulties are created outside of Geneva. The 1991 World Health Assembly's enthusiastic adoption of a proposal to "eliminate leprosy as a public health problem by the year 2000," based on the availability of an effective new three-drug "cocktail," overlooked gaps in knowledge on the disease's epidemiology (how it is spread) and led the organization to adopt a flawed model for judging progress against the disease and equally flawed approaches to eliminating it.[11] At the turn of the millennium the WHO's plans for disease eradication struck more and more people as rhetoric rather than realistic goals.

Like its fights against disease, the WHO's global work for health has also been hampered by a variety of obstacles, and its successes never seem quite able to match the needs and expectations it has helped to create. The environment in which the WHO promoted global health worsened significantly throughout the 1980s, 1990s, and 2000s. Declining aid levels, deteriorating debt situations throughout much of the Third World, and the diverging health agendas of the

First and Third worlds have limited areas of global consensus and hindered the WHO's work in building national health infrastructure, focusing on preventative measures, and setting international standards. Instead of making solid progress toward its stated goal of "health for all by 2000," the specialized agency seems increasingly engrossed in rear-guard actions to save significant portions of the world's people from the devastation of AIDS/HIV, tuberculosis, and malaria, as well as other disease outbreaks recently in the news—SARS and West Nile virus. These campaigns have produced criticism as well.[12] At the turn of the millennium, the World Health Organization was under fire from the global public health community for both its "sins" (what it had done) and its "sins of omission" (what it had failed to do). While reorganization and a certain defensiveness marked its response, it also rightfully pointed to its achievements, highlighting that it had "established health as a key factor in development."[13] But this achievement is dwarfed by the high ideals of the International Health Conference in 1946 and by the hopes and dreams of the millions who still struggle for survival and health throughout the world.

What are we to make of this mixed record of the UN specialized agencies and their development efforts? On the one hand, we see the best of intentions—the desire to improve the quality of people's lives regardless of nationality; on the other, we see dashed dreams, continuing poverty and disease, wasted resources, and organizational weakness. But even so, this is the story of human history at the best of times. Some of the best ideas in that history have been developed only after countless trials and errors and over decades, if not centuries. Americans are particularly proud of their history of democracy, and that history offers clear examples of the quantity of time, trials, and errors, not to mention international contributions, necessary to make that idea a reality. The Revolutionary War generation's ideas about democracy came from what they learned about Athenian democracy and the Roman republic, what they read of British thinkers' critiques of the monarchy, and what they personally experienced, which gave life to these ideas and histories. But the rhetoric of the Declaration of Independence had to be transformed into a blueprint for government, first in the Articles of Confederation and then in the Constitution, ratification of which occasioned rancorous debate throughout many of the thirteen states. Conflict between Thomas Jefferson and Alexander Hamilton (most famously), the development of rival political parties, and the hard work of constructing the infrastructure of the federal government characterized George Washington's administrations. But few Americans could vote during the early national period. By the time that Tennessean Andrew Jackson occupied the Oval Office, most states had removed property qualifications, but U.S. senators were still not directly elected until ratification of the Seventeenth Amendment in 1913. Women had to wait an additional six years for the ratification of the Nineteenth Amendment, which granted them the right to vote in all elections. African American males had been temporarily enfranchised during Reconstruction, but it was not until the passage of the 1965 Voting Rights Act that this constitutional right became a reality for most people of color in the United States. Eighteen-year-olds, who were deemed mature enough to fight and die for their country, only gained the franchise in 1971 with ratification of the Twenty-sixth Amendment.

Ironically, once practically all Americans had the right to vote, the level of voter turnout in elections dramatically declined. This seeming disengagement has sparked a number of efforts to "get out the vote" and reengage citizens in civic life, particularly young people. National campaigns, such as MTV's "Rock the Vote" campaign (founded in 1990) and the "American Democracy Project" of the American Association of State Colleges and Universities, have been supplemented by innumerable local efforts, such as the Find18 program of Nashville, Tennessee, which commits volunteers to finding and registering eighteen new voters, plus ensuring they get to the polls on election day. Other groups have focused on reenfranchising convicted felons, who in many states (particularly in the South) are permanently disenfranchised. The presidential election of 2000 also brought more Americans to a reconsideration of the role of the electoral college and the way in which it still mediates citizens' votes in determining who should hold the highest office in the United States.[14] In other words, U.S. citizens are still working at perfecting their version of democracy. So, if we were to hold up American-style democracy as one of the great successes of implementing and spreading a relatively new idea, we should perhaps have more patience for the founding fathers of development who staffed the World Bank, the Food and Agriculture Organization, and the World Health Organization. But patience does not mean accepting flawed models any more than American women or African Americans accepted being denied suffrage in a nation that loudly proclaimed its democratic principles.

During the twenty years that followed the Second World War, the Food and Agriculture Organization came the closest to developing a new model for development with its Freedom from Hunger Campaign (FFHC). The FFHC brought nongovernmental organizations into development work as full partners (a model driven as much by the lack of national funding as by ideals) and focused on smaller-scale, more "bottom-up" projects like building piggeries, equipping fishing boats with outboard motors, providing carts to facilitate the transfer of food crops to market, encouraging cheese production to save valuable and perishable milk supplies, and similar efforts. This experimental effort, however, was cut short by U.S. maneuvering within the FAO and overshadowed by the apparently dazzling prospects for agricultural development so loudly trumpeted by advocates of the Green Revolution.[15] The FFHC and the Green Revolution moved in opposite directions in terms of reliance on technology, but both still relied on expert analysis and the resulting "solutions." The failure of this type of development led to a large number of recriminations throughout the '70s, '80s, and '90s, and by the turn of the twentieth century a number of critics were calling for a new, "postde-velopment" ideology.[16] But such pronouncements seem a bit premature.

By the end of the twentieth century, a new model of development had emerged based on empowering and enabling the poor to act on their own decisions. Mov-ing away from the primarily expert-driven, "top-down" development models highlighted in the previous narrative on the World Bank, FAO, and WHO models of the 1940s, '50s, and '60s, these grassroots development organizations have, I be-lieve, pointed the way toward a new model of development worthy of the highest hopes and aspirations of those who created the specialized agencies of the United Nations. Two different examples of this philosophy in action demonstrate both where they depart from the activities detailed previously and where they conform to the ideals that underlay development after World War II.

In 1985 amazing things began to happen in forty rural villages in the Medak district of the province of Andhra Pradesh in India (about sixty miles outside of the regional capital of Hyderabad) when the nongovernmental Deccan Develop-ment Society (DDS) began working with a group of primarily *dalit* ("untouch-able") women. In other words, the DDS chose to work with those who occupy the bottom of the socioeconomic order in India. These rural women not only live in a patriarchal society but occupy the lowest caste. These dalit women are almost invariably poor and usually illiterate; their jobs are largely circumscribed by their caste to the most menial and labor-intensive work.[17] But the Deccan Development Society offered these women the power to change their world. The DDS board has defined its mission as empowering and facilitating the decisions reached by democratic consensus among groups of village women called *sang-hams* (usually comprising about sixty families), which usually meet well after dark, when their family and household duties are finally at an end. These sang-hams (which currently number seventy-five) create a solidarity that strengthens these vulnerable women. Sundaramma, a sangham leader, recalls, "We used to be very lonely. We would work all day and then we would be alone in our houses in the evening. Now we meet, work, talk and sing together. We share our burdens." The sanghams also provide the democratic arena in which they decide upon their collective priorities, those vital areas of their lives in which they need to develop and maintain autonomy.[18]

The women started with the most vital issue in their lives—food security. They wanted to have enough food for themselves and their families throughout the year. Discussion of this goal rather quickly led the women into a discussion of what crops were most suitable to the environment and eating habits of the villag-ers. What they came to realize was that while both the federal Indian government and the multinational agricultural corporations were doing all they could to en-courage the production of wheat and cotton, neither crop was well suited to the semiarid and drought-vulnerable conditions prevailing in the area and neither provided the nutrition and fodder of millet, a crop raised by previous generations in the area. The women of Andhra Pradesh reclaimed ten thousand acres of what had been marginal or abandoned land, providing jobs as well as new areas for the cultivation of millet. As a result, they were able to quintuple the amount of grain raised on this land. Using the same technique, they have brought thousands of acres of fallow or highly marginal land under sorghum cultivation, providing not only one thousand extra meals per year but fodder for over six thousand head of cattle, producing milk that provides needed protein in their diets.[19]

With such stunning successes to their credit, the DDS women shifted their goal from food security to food sovereignty—control over both their own agricultural production and the nutritional needs of their communities. As agricultural production thrived, the women, starting in 1996, provided an alternative to the governmental rations of wheat and rice doled out to the poor. Now through the Community Grain Fund, they provide the poor of their community with rations of millet that are produced, stored, and distributed locally, reversing the trend of dependency on the central government and returning the basic decisions about food and nutrition to the local community. They also created a seed bank that encompasses all the varieties of these local crops—which they have labeled "crops of truth" or "crops of the people." Seeds are held communally; rather than being sold, they are provided to any resident of the village, who then repays the community seed bank with twice the number of seeds borrowed.[20]

Having assured their children the food they needed to survive, the women turned to creating institutions that would allow them to thrive. They created *balwadis* for children aged two to six years old and Pachasaale—a "green school"—for elementary-school children. The balwadis provide early educational opportunities, adequate and nutritious food throughout the day (key to healthy development), and safe places for children while their mothers work in the field. The mothers of the villages provide the primary means of support for the balwadis; in addition, DDS has endowed land acreage to the balwadis to help them become self-sufficient in food, and in 1997 funding from the Dutch Bernard von Leer Foundation allowed for an expansion of balwadi activities. One such activity that the balwadi staff organized was a series of *jatras*, or children's fairs, that brought together some 750 children to play, dance, sing, paint, and eat together in "total freedom and total joy." When the Indian government began offering free child care in local facilities, the women chose to continue sacrificing their time and resources to maintain their balwadis rather than lose primary control over their children's care and nutrition. When the children of Medak district outgrow the balwadis, they move to the "green school" campus, which was constructed in 1993 with the central goal of creating "an empowered child" who will have the skills and talents to defend traditional society and culture in a modern age. To this end, the school teaches both a rigorous academic curriculum (which has allowed some village children to do well enough on national standardized exams to move on to higher levels of education) and a variety of vocational skills (such as pottery, carpentry, and ecological farming) as well as traditional songs and stories. This educational combination opens up the world to these largely dalit children while simultaneously instilling pride in their own community and culture.[21]

It soon became apparent that the work the women of Andhra Pradesh were doing provided not only better human care but also better earth care than had been the case before. As part of their land-reclamation process, they began planting trees through their Community Green Fund, which to date has put about one thousand hectares under cover of trees on a subcontinent that has witnessed an alarming rate of deforestation. Another planting program, begun in 1996, was the creation of medicinal commons (covering more than one hundred acres) in twenty-nine villages, where the local women raise and process medicinal plants and herbs, which form the backbone of traditional medical care for these villages.[22]

Another area in which the women of the Deccan Development Society are blending tradition with science and nongovernmental aid in a way that is environmentally sustainable is their move away from pesticides and toward a more environmentally sustainable method of protecting crops that at the same time helps develop the community and its inhabitants. Chickpeas are the most important cash and food crop currently grown in the area, but they are also the most susceptible to pests. Beginning with an inventory of traditional knowledge about outbreaks of pests and how best to handle them without pesticides, DDS instituted a crop insurance program, overseen by a group of twelve agricultural scientists assigned to measure the pest problem. In order to qualify for DDS crop insurance, the women have to plant a variety of crops in their fields (monocropping is not allowed), plant a variety of repellant and trap crops (such as marigolds and coriander), and physically pick the pests from the crops as they appear; only if necessary may they use a botanical pesticide, such as a distillation from the local neem tree or an extract of chili and garlic. The insurance program has given the participants the economic security needed to forego chemical pesticides, and only one year into the program, it shows a nearly perfect rate of pest control. Additionally, the physical picking of the insects from the crops, a practice that is spreading to other farms, provides much-needed employment to villagers as well. Again, earth care and human care have been shown to be mutually supporting.[23] After an initial period of introversion, those who have benefited from the DDS programs and philosophy have begun spreading this news. They have created elaborate displays and educational programs about biodiversity for regional festivals.[24] Now this message is being disseminated across the country and around the world, thanks to the sanghams' newest initiative—their move to develop media sovereignty.

The women of rural Andhra Pradesh noted that whatever radio and television programs they had heard and seen were fundamentally alien—neither representing their way of life and values nor presenting the values they do hold dear to a broader community. Rather than reject modern media outright, they are determined to shape those media and their respective technologies to meet their own needs and present their ideas to a larger community. Their radio station, while waiting for a broadcasting license, turned to a program of "narrow-casting"—taping in their studios programs that capture traditional songs, stories, and folk performances as well as educational programs and then distributing the tapes to the sanghams and communities. This work in media has also literally opened up the world to these dalit women. For example, one female videographer recounted with relish that a local landlord was so pleased that the annual festival he hosted was to be filmed that he invited the woman into his home—in clear violation of traditional caste customs—and moved the time of the festival in order to have better light for the filming. Another video producer, Edulapally Manjula, stressed the two aspects of her work that she most valued: "We can speak out our problems and express our thoughts in our own language. . . . When 'big' government officials come to our village we would like to record what they tell us."[25] This combination of empowerment and willingness to challenge existing authority has reached well beyond village boundaries.

The women empowered by the DDS have taken their message throughout the country and around the globe. They have been invited to speak about their programs in the national parliament in New Delhi, but these dalit women also helped challenge the central government's vision of the area's agricultural development future—called "Vision 2020," which was partially funded by the World Bank and the British Department for International Development. Participating in a *prajateerpu* (a citizens' jury), members of the communities served by the DDS listened to a variety of perspectives on the government's suggestions to reduce the number of people making their living from the land in the province from 70 to 40 percent, through a process of land consolidation, mechanization, and adoption of genetically modified crops. The resulting report, which refuted both the specific recommendations and their philosophical underpinning, was presented in both India and London, where it convinced the British Department for International Development to drop its support for Vision 2020 funding.[26] A similarly critical effort came from the DDS Community Media Trust, which produced a documentary on Bt cotton (a genetically modified crop) that both confirmed their own agricultural development strategy and educated others about the dangers of accepting the false promises of multinational agricultural corporations. These videographers have also become educators; recently, one member of the women's video team spent about two weeks in Peru training Andean women in the video techniques she and her counterparts had developed in India.[27]

The Deccan Development Society has been able to improve substantially the quality of life of thousands of rural dalit women in India by empowering a set of

autonomous democratic communities—the sanghams. The women of these sanghams have realized many of their aspirations not only by utilizing the best of their
traditional knowledge but also by embracing the best of the newest technology—
not genetically engineered seeds but the video cameras and radio broadcasting
equipment that will allow them to educate one another and the world. If, however,
the example of the DDS seems an insufficient, or perhaps a too geographically
limited, example to inspire a rethinking of development for the twenty-first century, the Grameen Bank has more than a quarter-century of experience under its
belt and has funded projects in a variety of Third and First World countries that
traditional banks and development agencies would not even consider.

Founded in 1976 in Bangladesh by Muhammad Yunus, the Grameen Bank
created and pioneered the idea of "microcredit"—making small loans to poor
people without collateral or formal training. His first microloan—the equivalent
of twenty-seven dollars—enabled forty-two people who lived outside of Bangladesh's Chittagong University (where Yunus was teaching economics) to purchase
their raw materials directly, rather than through middlemen who had previously
taken the majority of the profits and kept the laborers in poverty. This initial foray
into microlending and the refusal of conventional banking institutions to fund
his efforts led to the creation of the Grameen Bank, with the credo, "Discipline,
Unity, Courage, and Hard Work." In place of the traditional requirement for collateral, Yunus turned to what one commentator has called "reputation-based peer
pressure" to guarantee its loans. Potential borrowers at the same level are placed
into groups of five to ten. Initially, two of these people receive loans, and the ability of the others to borrow in the future is based on the repayment of this initial
pair of loans. All loans are paid back with interest within a single year by means
of small weekly payments. Six to eight borrowing groups meet weekly at a "center
house" (there are some sixty thousand in Bangladesh), which bank workers call the
organization's "heartbeat." There, borrowers make their loan installments, build
solidarity, and interface with bank personnel in a nonthreatening environment.
The Grameen Bank's work in Bangladesh has resulted in annual loans of $500 mil-
lion (most of which are received by women), 3.5 million depositors, a 95 percent
(or higher) repayment rate, the construction or improvement of 350,000 homes
(funded by three-hundred-dollar home loans), and six thousand scholarships per
year to the children of its clients. A World Bank study has found that one-third of
Grameen borrowers have used their newfound capital to rise above the poverty
line and that another third are on the verge of overcoming abject poverty.[28]

The Grameen model also reflects a variety of important social developments
that are not necessarily related to economics but are tied to the communities created by Grameen and its "Sixteen Decisions." The branch center leaders developed
the Sixteen Decisions during an annual meeting. This set of expectations, a list
of which hangs in each center house, includes a number of principles that would

have warmed the hearts of the founders of the UN specialized agencies: "We shall grow vegetables all the year round," "We shall look after our health," and "We shall always keep our children and the environment clean." This is not simply rhetoric. The sanitation and nutritional levels of Grameen borrowers are higher than those of their peers. One Grameen "decision" has garnered a great deal of international attention—"We shall plan to keep our families small." Yunus, like many current population commentators, argues that economic development is the most effective and least intrusive method of promoting population control. The statistics in Bangladesh seem to bear him out—Grameen women are twice as likely as other Bangladeshis to adopt family planning measures.[29]

In 1997 the Grameen Bank, like the Deccan Development Society, began promoting modern technology as a method of liberating the poor, but in this case with cellular phones rather than video cameras. The Village Phone Project has created sixty thousand "telephone ladies" in Bangladesh, who provide telephone service to 80 percent of all Bangladeshis. Not only do the telephone ladies provide service in the most remote and isolated villages, where there are no electrical or telephone lines (solar energy powers the system), but their charges are competitive with current landline rates. Like Yunus's original loan, this new Grameen initiative has allowed rural and poor Bangladeshis to eliminate middlemen and improve their income; it also seems to meet the goal of equity that several development commentators have identified as crucial in the introduction of new information and communication technologies in the Third World. The phones have also allowed Bangladeshis to expand their markets, gain information, and have a stronger voice beyond the borders of their home communities. They are no longer held hostage by those with information about market prices; they are no longer handicapped by their distance from the centers of education and political power.[30]

Starting in 2004, the Grameen Bank began a project to "explode the myth" that microcredit does not work for the poorest of the poor. Focusing on intergenerational beggars, Grameen is providing small loans (the equivalent of ten dollars) to help transform those who beg door to door in rural areas into peddlers. For beggars who lack limbs and beg in fixed positions, small loans allow them to supplement their entreaties with sales of soft drinks, fruit, and cookies. Such lending, which was expected to reach twenty-five thousand beggars within its first year in existence, is also part and parcel of the bank's argument that credit is such a foundational element in individual and national development that it should be regarded as a human right. More than a quarter-century of success has bolstered Yunus's contention that access to credit has the ability to unleash each person's creativity and energy and relegate poverty to museums. Of course, not everyone is a fan of Grameen, its methods, or their applicability to a variety of milieus, but no one disputes Yunus's creativity or his desire to see the elimination of poverty, which shines through in the concluding lines of his autobiography: "We have created a slavery-free world, a smallpox-free world, an apartheid-free world. Creating a poverty-free world would be greater than all these accomplishments while at the same time reinforcing them. This would be a world that we could all be proud to live in."[31]

It seems in the first years of the new millennium that some of the philosophy or theory of development has begun to catch up with these new models. A growing emphasis on the qualitative rather than the quantitative dimensions of development, though more difficult to measure, has begun to take root. Realizing that the quality of life "is not just about having, but also about being," some scholars have searched for a new model of development rather than accept the belief that development, by its nature, is irredeemably flawed. The most systematic enunciation of this new, qualitative development theory has been Amartya Sen's *Development as Freedom,* which argues that the expansion of individual freedom—which includes political freedoms, economic facilities, social opportunities, transparency guarantees, and protective security—is both the means of achieving development and its goal. To illustrate the interdependence of these freedoms, Sen points out that "what people can positively achieve is influenced by economic opportunities, political liberties, and social powers, and the enabling conditions of good health, basic education, and the encouragement and cultivation of initiatives." Additionally, "the institutional arrangements for these opportunities are also influenced by the exercise of people's freedoms, through the liberty to participate in social choice and in the making of public decisions that impel the progress of these opportunities." This Nobel Prize–winning economist recognizes the difficulties in measuring freedom and the virtual impossibility of unraveling each of these inputs, but he has nonetheless thrown the weight of his opinion behind rethinking, rather than abandoning, the practice of development—the practice of working toward improvement of people's quality of life.[32]

The determination of the Grameen Bank and the Deccan Development Society to think creatively and act decisively in order to improve the lives of those they serve makes them genuine heirs of the pioneering civil servants described in these pages. This does not, however, mean that these new development agencies agree with those created a half-century ago; indeed, they have disagreed loudly, repeatedly, and publicly. Nonetheless, the World Bank and the Grameen Bank have cooperated in a number of matters, and public forums on development policies, while occasionally contentious, have provided valuable vehicles for the communication and development of new strategies.[33] The World Health Organization has gone even farther toward this type of model in its most recent work on AIDS/HIV in the poorest and most isolated communities. Recognizing that successful treatment and prevention does not necessarily require expensive doctors and laboratories but does require a population that has meaningful "ownership, participation and a politicized civil society," the WHO is funding grassroots efforts in southern Africa and the Caribbean that have empowered people with HIV to change their lives through appropriate technology (in this case, medicine) and community-based support that grows out of their own traditions, needs, and hopes.[34]

One can only hope that perhaps this twenty-first century might see the institutions first created to develop the potential of all the world's peoples—the UN specialized agencies—infused with these new and creative ideas and thereby revitalized in their mission. For as Brock Chisholm, the WHO's first director-general, reminded us almost half a century ago, the United Nations and its agencies have no "brave new magic" that can solve the world's problems effortlessly. Instead, the human race must continuously learn from its trials and errors while keeping its eyes firmly fixed on the goal of universal human development.[35] Only such a mindset and such determination can accomplish all that those founding fathers of development had hoped for—and more.

Notes

1. The Birth of Development

1. This differs from views that "development" emerged either in the nineteenth century or as a result of President Harry S. Truman's 1949 inaugural address, which introduced the Point IV program. See, e.g., Gilbert Rist, *The History of Development: From Western Origins to Global Faith*, rev. ed., trans. Patrick Camiller (London: Zed, 2002), 71; Michael Cowen and Robert Shenton, "The Invention of Development," in *Power of Development*, ed. Jonathan Crush (London: Routledge, 1995), 27–43; and G. Esteva, "Development," in *The Development Dictionary: A Guide to Knowledge as Power*, ed. Wolfgang Sachs (London: Zed, 1992).

2. Brock Chisholm, *Nations Are Learning to Live Together* (Vancouver, Can.: Univ. of British Columbia, 1954), 5.

3. Robert H. Wiebe, *The Search for Order, 1877–1920* (New York: Hill and Wang, 1967), esp. 44–75.

For the philosophical underpinnings of Progressivism and social democracy see, e.g., James T. Kloppenberg, *Uncertain Victory: Social Democracy and Progressivism in European and American Thought, 1870–1920* (New York: Oxford Univ. Press, 1986), esp. 3–11; Gabriel Kolko, *The Triumph of Conservatism: A Reinterpretation of American History, 1900–1916* (New York: Free Press, 1963); Jean B. Quandt, *From the Small Town to the Great Community: The Social Thought of Progressive Intellectuals* (New Brunswick, N.J.: Rutgers Univ. Press, 1970); and R. Jackson Wilson, *In Quest of Community: Social Philosophy in the United States, 1860–1920* (New York: Wiley, 1968).

For the origins of Progressivism see, e.g., Samuel P. Hays, *The Response to Industrialism, 1885–1914*, 2d ed. (Chicago, Ill.: Univ. of Chicago Press, 1995); Richard L. McCormick, "The Discovery That Business Corrupts Politics: A Reappraisal of the Origins of Progressivism," *American Historical Review* 86 (Apr. 1981): 247–74; and David P. Thelen, "Social Tensions and the Origins of Progressivism," *Journal of American History* 56 (Sept. 1969): 323–41.

4. For the process of professionalization see Wiebe, *Search for Order*, 111–32; Allan R. Millett, *Military Professionalism and Officership in America*, Mershon Center Briefing Paper 2 (Columbus: Mershon Center of the Ohio State Univ., 1977); Alfred D. Chandler, *The Visible Hand: The Managerial Revolution in American Business* (Cambridge, Mass.: Belknap Press,

1977); A. M. Carr-Saunders and P. A. Wilson, *The Professions* (Oxford, UK: Clarendon, 1933); Mary O. Furner, *Advocacy and Objectivity: A Crisis in the Professionalization of American Social Science, 1865–1905* (Lexington: Univ. Press of Kentucky for the Organization of American Historians, 1975); and Michael J. Lacey and Mary O. Furner, eds., *The State and Social Investigation in Britain and the United States* (Washington, D.C.: Woodrow Wilson Center, 1993).

5. For Progressivism during the war see David M. Kennedy, *Over Here: The First World War and American Society* (Oxford, UK: Oxford Univ. Press, 1980), esp. 3–92.

For businessmen's contributions to the war effort see Robert D. Cuff, "Harry Garfield, the Fuel Administration, and the Search for a Cooperative Order during World War I," *American Quarterly* 30 (Spring 1978): 39–53, *The War Industries Board* (Baltimore, Md.: Johns Hopkins Univ. Press, 1973), and "Herbert Hoover, the Ideology of Voluntarism and War Organization during the Great War," *Journal of American History* 64 (Sept. 1977): 358–72; Paul A. C. Koistinen, "The 'Industrial-Military Complex' in Historical Perspective: World War I," *Business History Review* 41 (Winter 1967): 367–403; and Valerie Jean Conner, *The National War Labor Board* (Chapel Hill: Univ. of North Carolina Press, 1983).

For Hoover see Joan Hoff, *Herbert Hoover: Forgotten Progressive* (Boston, Mass.: Little, Brown, 1975); Barry D. Karl, "Presidential Planning and Social Science Research: Mr. Hoover's Experts," *Perspectives in American History* 3 (1969): 347–409; Ellis W. Hawley, ed., *Herbert Hoover as Secretary of Commerce, 1921–1928: Studies in New Era Thought and Practice* (Iowa City: Univ. of Iowa Press, 1981); "Herbert Hoover, the Commerce Secretariat, and the Vision of an 'Associative State,' 1921–1928," *Journal of American History* 61 (June 1974): 116–40, and "Three Facets of Hooverian Associationalism: Lumber, Aviation, and Movies, 1921–1930," in *Regulation in Perspective*, ed. Thomas K. McCraw (Cambridge, Mass.: Harvard Univ. Press, 1981), 95–123; Carolyn Grin, "The Unemployment Conference of 1921: An Experiment in National Cooperative Planning," *Mid-America* 55 (Apr. 1973): 83–107; Patrick D. Reagan, "From Depression to Depression: Hooverian National Planning, 1921–1933," *Mid-America* 70 (Jan. 1988): 35–60; Joan Hoff Wilson, "Hoover's Agricultural Policies, 1921–1928," Martin L. Fausold, "President Hoover's Farm Policies, 1929–1933," Gary H. Koerselman, "Secretary Hoover and National Farm Policy: Problems of Leadership," and James L. Guth, "The National Cooperative Council and Farm Relief, 1929–42," all *Agricultural History* 51 (Apr. 1977): 335–61, 362–77, 378–95, 441–58, resp.; American Engineering Council, Committee on Elimination of Waste in Industry, and Federated American Engineering Societies, *Waste in Industry* (New York: McGraw-Hill, 1921); Robert F. Himmelberg, *The Origins of the National Recovery Administration: Business, Government, and the Trade Association Issue, 1921–1933* (New York: Fordham Univ. Press, 1976); and Robert H. Zieger, "Herbert Hoover, the Wage-Earner, and the 'New Economic System,' 1919–1929," *Business History Review* 51 (Summer 1977): 161–89.

For 1920s associationalism generally see Ellis W. Hawley, *The Great War and the Search for a Modern Order: A History of the American People and Their Institutions, 1917–1933* (New York: St. Martin's, 1979); and Guy Alchon, *The Invisible Hand of Planning: Capitalism, Social Science, and the State in the 1920s* (Princeton, N.J.: Princeton Univ. Press, 1985).

6. For professionals employed by the federal government during the New Deal see Richard S. Kirkendall, *Social Scientists and Farm Politics in the Age of Roosevelt* (Columbia: Univ. of Missouri Press, 1966); Peter H. Irons, *The New Deal Lawyers* (Princeton, N.J.: Princeton Univ. Press, 1982); William J. Barber, *Designs within Disorder: Franklin D. Roosevelt, the Economists, and the Shaping of American Economic Policy, 1933–1945* (Cambridge, UK: Cambridge

Univ. Press, 1996); and Mary O. Furner and Barry Supple, eds., *The State and Economic Knowledge: The American and British Experience* (New York: Cambridge Univ. Press, 1990).

7. For prewar internationalism generally see Akira Iriye, *Cultural Internationalism and World Order* (Baltimore, Md.: Johns Hopkins Univ. Press, 1997), 13–14, 20–50; H. L. S. Lyons, *Internationalism in Europe, 1815–1914* (Leiden, Neth.: A.W. Sijthoff, 1963); and Kenten Druyvesteyn, "The World's Parliament of Religions" (Ph.D. diss., Univ. of Chicago, 1976).

For legal internationalism specifically see P. E. Corbett, *Law and Society in the Relations of States* (New York: Harcourt, Brace, 1951), 36; Henry Wheaton, *Elements of International Law*, 6th ed. (Boston, Mass.: Little, Brown, 1906); Gerrit W. Gong, *The Standard of "Civilization" in International Society* (Oxford, UK: Oxford Univ. Press, 1984); Hedley Bull and Adam Watson, eds., *The Expansion of International Society* (Oxford, UK: Clarendon, 1984); and Iriye, *Cultural Internationalism*, 20–21.

For socialist internationalism see Iriye, *Cultural Internationalism*, 33–35; and Gustave Hervé, *L'Internationalisme* (Paris: V. Giard and E. Brière, 1910), 89–172.

For liberal economic internationalism see Iriye, *Cultural Internationalism*, 23–26; Lyons, *Internationalism in Europe*, esp. 14, 125–26; Hervé, *L'Internationalisme*, 167–78; and H. G. Wells, *An Englishman Looks at the World: Being a Series of Unrestrained Remarks on Contemporary Matters* (London: Cassell, 1914).

8. Erich Maria Remarque, *All Quiet on the Western Front,* trans. A. W. Wheen (New York: Ballantine, 1987), 194. For similar wartime expressions of universal humanity see Ernst Johannsen, *Four Infantrymen on the Western Front* (London: Methuen, 1929).

9. For the cultural internationalism of the 1920s see Iriye, *Cultural Internationalism*, 56–90; Emily S. Rosenberg, *Spreading the American Dream: American Economic and Cultural Expansion, 1898–1945* (New York: Hill and Wang, 1982); Frank Costigliola, *Awkward Dominion: American Political, Economic, and Cultural Relations with Europe, 1919–1933* (Ithaca, N.Y.: Cornell Univ. Press, 1984); and Richard Kuisel, *Seducing the French: The Dilemma of Americanization* (Berkeley: Univ. of California Press, 1993).

For similar phenomena after WWII see Ralph Willett, *The Americanization of Germany, 1945–1949* (London: Routledge, 1989); and Reinhold Wagnleitner, *Coca-Colonization and the Cold War: The Cultural Mission of the United States in Austria after the Second World War,* trans. Diana M. Wolf (Chapel Hill: Univ. of North Carolina Press, 1994).

10. For cultural internationalism during the 1930s see Iriye, *Cultural Internationalism*, 91–130; Reinhold Niebuhr, *Christianity and Power Politics* (New York: Scribner's, 1940), esp. 16–17; and Thomas Ferguson, "From Normalcy to New Deal: Industrial Structure, Party Competition, and American Public Policy in the Great Depression," *International Organization* 38 (Winter 1984): 41–94.

11. Brock Chisholm, World Health Organization Director-General, "Responsibility for Health," address to the International Federation of Sanitarians Organization, 17 July 1957, George Brock Chisholm papers, vol. 2, folders 168–83, Canadian National Archives, Ottawa, Canada [hereafter CNA]; "Identity through Commitment and Involvement," Chisholm address to the Child Study Association of America, 2 Mar. 1965, Chisholm papers, vol. 5, folders 407–20, CNA.

For the construction of twentieth-century internationalism, I used the following works as guides: David Campbell, *Writing Security: United States Foreign Policy and the Politics of Identity* (Minneapolis: Univ. of Minnesota Press, 1992); J. Ann Tickner, *Gender in International Relations: Feminist Perspectives on Achieving Global Security* (New York: Columbia

Univ. Press, 1992), esp. 67–96; Leslie Sklair, *Sociology of the Global System,* 2d ed., rev. and updated (Baltimore, Md.: Johns Hopkins Univ. Press, 1995); and Benedict Anderson, *Imagined Communities: Reflections on the Origin and Spread of Nationalism,* rev. and extended ed. (London: Verso, 1991).

For references to the impact of the wars, depression, and atomic and biological weapons on their thought see, e.g., Karl Evang as quoted in "Seventeenth Meeting," in World Health Organization Interim Commission, *Minutes of the Technical Preparatory Committee for the International Health Conference, Held in Paris from 18 March to 5 April 1946,* Official Records of the WHO, no. 1 (New York and Geneva: WHOIC, Oct. 1947), 31; *Freedom from Hunger: Outline of a Campaign* (Rome: UN Food and Agriculture Organization [hereafter FAO], 1960), 1, 11; Karl Evang, *Norway's Food in Peace and War* (Washington, D.C.: 1942), 2; "Some Factors in the Psychology of War," Chisholm background memorandum for Preparatory Committee on Factors Influencing International Peace, 31 Aug. 1959, Chisholm papers, vol. 3, folders 231–41, CNA; and "Dangerous Complacency," Chisholm address to the American Humanist Association, 28 Feb. 1959, Chisholm papers, vol. 3, folders 184–200, CNA.

For references to modern transportation and communication making "one world" see, e.g., B. R. Sen, *The Basic Freedom: Freedom from Hunger* (Rome: FAO, 1960), 1–2, 7, as well as "Foreword," in James H. Steele, *Animal Disease and Human Health,* FFHC Basic Study 3 (Rome: FAO, 1962), 1; FAO Director-General Norris E. Dodd statement in Rome, Italy, 7 Aug. 1952, and "FAO: Prospects and Problems," restricted Dodd statement to the U.S. Inter-Agency Committee, 25 July 1950, both Norris E. Dodd papers, box 1, folder 5, Hoover Institution for War, Revolution and Peace, Stanford, California [hereafter HIWRP]; "Food, Farming and Peace," Dodd address at Bunker Hill, Indiana, 19 July 1948, Dodd papers, box 1, folder 7, HIWRP; and Jeannine Locke, "Brock Chisholm Speaks Out!" *Star Weekly Magazine* (26 Jan. 1963): 3.

For statements on the need for a broader loyalty see, e.g., "Health Challenges are Opportunities," Chisholm address to the Los Angeles Heart Association, 25 May 1960, Chisholm papers, vol. 4, folders 242–68, CNA; and "New Dimension of Responsibility," Chisholm address to the Temple Men's Club of Erie, Pennsylvania, 14 Feb. 1962, Chisholm papers, vol. 4, folders 306–19, CNA.

2. Constructing an International Economic Worldview

1. John Maynard Keynes, *Essays in Biography* (London: Macmillan, 1933), 165–79, 192–93, 207–14, 245–55, 273–77, 288–90; John Maloney, *Marshall, Orthodoxy and the Professionalisation of Economics* (Cambridge, UK: Cambridge Univ. Press, 1985), 2–4, 165–85; Alon Kadish, *Historians, Economists, and Economic History* (London: Routledge, 1989), 168–219; David Collard, "A. C. Pigou, 1877–1959," John Creedy, "F. Y. Edgeworth, 1845–1926," and Adrian Darnell, "A. L. Bowley, 1869–1957," all in *Pioneers of Modern Economics in Britain,* ed. D. P. O'Brien and John R. Presley (London: Macmillan, 1981), resp. 72–75, 106–109, 140–42, 168–69.

2. As quoted in A. W. Bob Coats, *British and American Economic Essays,* vol. 1: *On the History of Economic Thought* (London: Routledge, 1992), 351. See also ibid., 342–45, 350–57; William Breit and Roger L. Ransom, *The Academic Scribblers: American Economists in Collision* (New York: Holt, Rinehart and Winston, 1971), 39–42; and Allan G. Gruchy, *Modern Economic Thought: The American Contribution* (New York: Prentice Hall, 1947).

3. James Livingston, *Origins of the Federal Reserve System: Money, Class, and Corporate Capitalism, 1890–1913* (Ithaca, N.Y.: Cornell Univ. Press, 1986), 26–27, 215, 219–23, 226–30; Kolko, *Triumph of Conservatism*, 186–87, 218–25.

4. Emily S. Rosenberg, "Foundations of United States International Financial Power: Gold Standard Diplomacy, 1900–1905," *Business History Review* 59 (Summer 1985): 169–202; Diane B. Kunz, *The Battle for Britain's Gold Standard in 1931* (London: Croom Helm, 1987), 8–12; P. L. Cottrell, "The Bank of England in its International Setting, 1918–1972," in *The Bank of England: Money, Power and Influence, 1694–1994*, ed. Richard Roberts and David Kynaston (Oxford, UK: Clarendon, 1995), 87–90; and György Péteri, "Central Bank Diplomacy: Montagu Norman and Central Europe's Monetary Reconstruction after World War I," *Contemporary European History* 1 (Nov. 1992): 233–58.

5. Emily S. Rosenberg and Norman L. Rosenberg, "From Colonialism to Professionalism: The Public/Private Dynamic in United States Foreign Financial Advising, 1898–1929," *Journal of American History* 74 (June 1987): 59–82; Fredrick B. Pike, *The United States and Latin America: Myths and Stereotypes of Civilization and Nature* (Austin: Univ. of Texas Press, 1992), 169–71, 206–21; Emily S. Rosenberg, "Revisiting Dollar Diplomacy: Narratives of Money and Manliness," *Diplomatic History* 22 (Spring 1998): 160–75.

6. Hawley, *The Great War*; Melvyn P. Leffler, "Herbert Hoover, the 'New Era,' and American Foreign Policy," in *Herbert Hoover as Secretary of Commerce*, ed. Hawley, 149–71; Michael J. Hogan, *Informal Entente: The Private Structure of Cooperation in Anglo-American Economic Diplomacy, 1918–1929* (Columbia: Univ. of Missouri Press, 1977; rev. ed., Chicago, Ill.: Imprint, 1991); Lester V. Chandler, *Benjamin Strong, Central Banker* (Washington, D.C.: Brookings Institution, 1958); Stephen A. Schuker, *The End of French Predominance in Europe: The Financial Crisis of 1924 and the Adoption of the Dawes Plan* (Chapel Hill: Univ. of North Carolina Press, 1976), 10–11, 26–28; Georg Schild, *Bretton Woods and Dumbarton Oaks: American Economic and Political Postwar Planning in the Summer of 1944* (New York: St. Martin's, 1995), 77; U.S. Congress, House Committee on Banking and Currency, *Report to Accompany H.R. 3314: Participation of the United States in the International Monetary Fund and the International Bank for Reconstruction and Development*, 79th Cong., 1st sess. (Washington, D.C.: Government Printing Office [hereafter GPO], 1945), 13; Cottrell, "Bank of England," 86–90, 93–95.

7. For opinion shifts caused by the Depression see Kunz, *Battle for Britain's Gold Standard*, 2–6; House Committee on Banking and Currency, *Report to Accompany H.R. 3314*, 11–12; Robert Boyce, "World Depression, World War: Some Economic Origins of the Second World War," in *Paths to War: New Essays on the Origins of the Second World War*, ed. Robert Boyce and Esmonde Robertson (Basingstoke, UK: Macmillan, 1989), 55–95; and Cottrell, "Bank of England," 95–99.

For national efforts to deal with the Depression see John A. Garraty, *The Great Depression* (New York: Doubleday, 1987); Arthur M. Schlesinger Jr., *The Coming of the New Deal: The Age of Roosevelt* (Boston, Mass.: Houghton Mifflin, 1958); Paul K. Conkin, *The New Deal*, 2d ed. (Arlington Heights, Ill.: Harlan Davidson, 1975); Anthony J. Badger, *The New Deal: The Depression Years, 1933–1940* (New York: Hill and Wang, 1989); Réne Girault, "The Impact of the Economic Situation on the Foreign Policy of France, 1936–1939," in *The Fascist Challenge and the Policy of Appeasement*, ed. Wolfgang J. Mommsen and Lothar Kettenacker (London: Allen and Unwin, 1983), 214–23; and Max Beloff, *Dream of Commonwealth, 1921–42* (Dobbs Ferry, N.Y.: Sheridan, 1989), 185–98.

For international efforts see Lloyd C. Gardner, *Economic Aspects of New Deal Diplomacy* (Madison: Univ. of Wisconsin Press, 1964); Schild, *Bretton Woods and Dumbarton Oaks*, 77, 86, 94, 98; House Committee on Banking and Currency, *Report to Accompany H.R. 3314*, 12–14; Cottrell, "The Bank of England," 107–8; and Wallace McClure, *World Prosperity, as Sought through the Economic Work of the League of Nations* (New York: Macmillan, 1933), 233–44.

8. The Tripartite Declaration was later expanded to include Belgium, the Netherlands, and Switzerland. See House Committee on Banking and Currency, *Report to Accompany H.R. 3314*, 3, 14–15; Girault, "Impact of the Economic Situation on the Foreign Policy of France," 217–20; Cottrell, "Bank of England," 108–10; and Gardner, *Economic Aspects of New Deal Diplomacy*, 285.

9. For Keynesian ideas see John Maynard Keynes, *The General Theory of Employment, Interest and Money* (New York: Harcourt, Brace, 1936); and John W. McConnell, *Ideas of the Great Economists*, 2d ed. (New York: Harper and Row, 1980), 69–70, 76, 139–41, 182, 203–204.

For the broad acceptance of Keynesian ideas and practices see William J. Barber, "Government as a Laboratory for Economic Learning in the Years of the Democratic Roosevelt," in *The State and Economic Knowledge*, ed. Furner and Supple, 104–16; Roger J. Sandilands, *The Life and Political Economy of Lauchlin Currie: New Dealer, Presidential Adviser, and Development Economist* (Durham, N.C.: Duke Univ. Press, 1990), 54–95; Breit and Ransom, *Academic Scribblers*, 85–92; and G. John Ikenberry, "Creating Yesterday's New World Order: Keynesian 'New Thinking' and the Anglo-American Postwar Settlement," in *Ideas and Foreign Policy: Beliefs, Institutions, and Political Change*, ed. Judith Goldstein and Robert O. Keohane (Ithaca, N.Y.: Cornell Univ. Press, 1993), 76.

For new emphasis on formal government action in the international economy see Ikenberry, "Creating Yesterday's New World Order," 72; and Henry Morgenthau III, *Mostly Morgenthaus: A Family History* (New York: Ticknor and Fields, 1991), 336–37.

10. David E. Lilienthal, *The Journals of David E. Lilienthal*, vol. 1, *The TVA Years, 1938–1945* (New York: Harper and Row, 1964), and *TVA: Democracy on the March* (New York: Harper, 1944); McConnell, *Ideas of the Great Economists*, 225–26; Richard Lowitt, *The New Deal and the West* (Norman: Univ. of Oklahoma Press, 1993), xi; John A. Adams Jr., *Damming the Colorado: The Rise of the Lower Colorado River Authority, 1933–1939* (College Station: Texas A&M Univ. Press, 1990), 93–112.

11. Schild, *Bretton Woods and Dumbarton Oaks*, 84–85, 88–89; Morgenthau, *Mostly Morgenthaus*, 336; Gardner, *Economic Aspects of New Deal Diplomacy*, 284–88.

12. For White's views see Schild, *Bretton Woods and Dumbarton Oaks*, 89.

For Keynes's views see ibid., xi, 78–79, 81–82, 84, 90, 92, 95; Keynes address to the House of Lords, 23 May 1944, Keynes letter to White, 24 May 1944, and Keynes opening remarks at the first meeting of the second commission on the World Bank, 3 July 1944, all in Donald Moggridge, ed., *The Collected Writings of John Maynard Keynes*, vol. 26: *Activities, 1941–1946: Shaping the Post-War World, Bretton Woods and Reparations* (London: Macmillan, 1980), 16–19, 27, 74–75, 77; Ikenberry, "Creating Yesterday's New World Order," 58–59, 69–71; H. W. Singer, "An Historical Perspective," in *The U.N. and the Bretton Woods Institutions: New Challenges for the Twenty-first Century*, ed. Mahbub ul Haq, Richard Jolly, Paul Streeten, and Khadija Haq (New York: St. Martin's, 1995), 17; and Cottrell, "Bank of England," 110.

13. Roy Forbes Harrod, fellow of Nuffield College of Oxford University, as cited by David Rees, *Harry Dexter White: A Study in Paradox* (New York: Coward, McCann and Geoghegan, 1973), 230. See also ibid., 22–23, 229–32; *Joint Statement by Experts on the Establishment of an*

International Monetary Fund of the United and Associated States (Washington, D.C.: U.S. Treasury, 21 Apr. 1944); Keynes address to the House of Lords, 23 May 1944, in Moggridge, ed., *Collected Writings of Keynes,* 26:21; Ikenberry, "Creating Yesterday's New World Order," 57–59; undated draft of Morgenthau's acceptance speech for Bretton Woods, and undated speech welcoming delegates to International Monetary and Financial Conference, both Henry Morgenthau Jr. diaries, book 745, roll 214, Franklin D. Roosevelt Presidential Library, Hyde Park, New York [hereafter FDRL]; undated memorandum for Roosevelt, Morgenthau diaries, book 735, roll 211, FDRL; Susan Howson and Donald Moggridge, eds., *The Wartime Diaries of Lionel Robbins and James Meade, 1943–45* (London: Macmillan, 1990), 157–59, 163, 165; John Fforde, *The Bank of England and Public Policy, 1941–1958* (Cambridge, UK: Cambridge Univ. Press, 1992), 51, 54, 56; Morgenthau, *Mostly Morgenthaus,* 343–44; and House Committee on Banking and Currency, *Report to Accompany H.R. 3314,* 6–8.

14. Keynes letter to T. Padmore, private secretary to Chancellor of the Exchequer, with attached "Suggested Principles for the Bank," 9 June 1944, in Moggridge, ed., *Collected Writings of Keynes,* 26:51. See also ibid., 26:48–55, and Keynes's opening remarks at first meeting of the second commission on the World Bank, 2 July 1944, ibid., 26:76.

15. Minutes of American delegation meeting on bank quotas, 19 July 1944, Morgenthau diaries, book 756, roll 217, FDRL; "Bretton Woods, 1944," Columbia Broadcasting System (CBS) special program, 18 July 1944, Morgenthau diaries, book 755, roll 216, FDRL; letter to Bretton Woods delegations from Citizens Conference on International Economic Union, 13 July 1944, Morgenthau diaries, book 753, roll 216, FDRL; "Bridging the Gap," *London Times,* 8 July 1944; minutes of American delegation meeting on fund and bank, 2 July 1944, Morgenthau diaries, book 749, roll 215, FDRL; Roosevelt welcoming address for Bretton Woods conference, 29 June 1944, and Morgenthau acceptance speech, 29 June 1944, both Morgenthau diaries, book 748, roll 215, FDRL; letter to White from F. Phillips, British Supply Council in North America, 28 Aug. 1942, Morgenthau diaries, book 665, roll 166, FDRL; "Proposals for an International Clearing Union," secret memorandum by British Treasury, Aug. 1942, Morgenthau diaries, book 541, roll 157, FDRL.

16. Minutes of meeting between British and American delegations, 20 July 1944, Morgenthau diaries, book 756, roll 217, FDRL. See also minutes of American delegation meeting on Bank for Intenational Settlements (BIS) and bank quotas, 19 July 1944, minutes of American delegation meeting on bank quotas, 19 July 1944, and John G. Winant, U.S. ambassador to Britain, telegram to Secretaries of State and Treasury, 18 July 1944, all ibid.; minutes of American delegation meeting on Russian provisions, interest rates, and location, 7 July 1944, Morgenthau diaries, book 751, roll 215, FDRL; Winant telegram to Secretary of State, 13 July 1944, Morgenthau diaries, book 753, roll 216, FDRL; Howson and Moggridge, eds., *Wartime Diaries,* 171, 179–80, 182, 184, 188; Morgenthau, *Mostly Morgenthaus,* 343; and Keynes letters to Sir Richard Hopkins, Treasury Permanent Secretary, 25 and 30 June 1944, Keynes letter to Lord Catto, Governor of the Bank of England, 4 July 1944, Keynes letters to Sir John Anderson, Chancellor of the Exchequer, 14 and 21 July 1944, and Keynes letter to Morgenthau, 19 July 1944, all in Moggridge, ed., *Collected Writings of Keynes,* 26:64, 66–67, 78–81, 91, 96–97, 105–106.

17. Minutes of meeting of American delegation on BIS and bank quotas, 19 July 1944, Morgenthau diaries, book 756, roll 217, FDRL; minutes of meeting of American delegation on quotas of the fund, 3 July 1944, Morgenthau diaries, book 749, roll 215, FDRL. See also unattributed memorandum for Morgenthau on the questions at issue on the bank [prob. 24–28

June 1944], Morgenthau diaries, book 747, roll 214, FDRL; Howson and Moggridge, eds., *Wartime Diaries,* 185–86, 189, 192; and Schild, *Bretton Woods and Dumbarton Oaks,* 113, 122.

18. For concern with China and France see minutes of American delegation meeting on fund quotas, 14 July 1944, minutes of American delegation meeting on French participation in the bank, 15 July 1944, and minutes of meeting between French and American delegations, 15 July 1944, all Morgenthau diaries, book 754, roll 216, FDRL; minutes of American delegation meeting on fund, quotas, and publications, 10 July 1944, Morgenthau diaries, book 752, roll 216, FDRL; letters from Pierre Mendès-France, head of French delegation to Bretton Woods, to General Charles de Gaulle, 12, 15, 17, and 18 July 1944, in Pierre Mendès-France, *Oeuvres Complètes,* vol. 2: *Une Politique de l'Économie, 1945–1954* (Paris: Gallimard, 1985), 44–48; and Howson and Moggridge, eds., *Wartime Diaries,* 157, 171, 177, 186.

For concessions to Latin America and India see interview with A. D. Shroff, nongovernmental Indian delegate to Bretton Woods, as quoted in telegram from Merrell to American monetary conference delegation, 14 June 1944, Morgenthau diaries, book 743, roll 213, FDRL; minutes of American delegation meeting on fund, 1 July 1944, Morgenthau diaries, book 749, roll 215, FDRL; minutes of American delegation meeting on Latin and South American quotas, 10 July 1944, Morgenthau diaries, book 752, roll 216, FDRL; minutes of American delegation meeting on quotas, 9 July 1944, Morgenthau diaries, book 751, roll 216, FDRL; and Howson and Moggridge, eds., *Wartime Diaries,* 160, 165, 172, 175, 177, 180.

19. Minutes of American delegation meeting on bank instruction, 12 July 1944, Morgenthau diaries, book 753, roll 216, FDRL; Keynes letter to Padmore with appended "Suggested Principles for the Bank," 9 June 1944, in Moggridge, ed., *Collected Writings of Keynes,* 26:53; minutes of American delegation meeting on fund and bank, 2 July 1944, and minutes of American delegation meeting on quotas of the fund, 3 July 1944, both Morgenthau diaries, book 749, roll 215, FDRL; minutes of American delegation meeting on fund, quotas, and publication of monetary reports, 10 July 1944, Morgenthau diaries, book 752, roll 216, FDRL; minutes of meeting between American and Soviet delegations, 15 July 1944, Morgenthau diaries, book 754, roll 216, FDRL; minutes of American delegation meeting on quotas, 9 July 1944, Morgenthau diaries, book 751, roll 216, FDRL; Howson and Moggridge, eds., *Wartime Diaries,* 175–76, 193.

20. Keynes speech in moving to accept the final act at the closing plenary session, 22 July 1944, in Moggridge, ed., *Collected Writings of Keynes,* 26:101, 103. See also minutes of American delegation meeting on fund and bank, 2 July 1944, Morgenthau diaries, book 749, roll 215, FDRL.

21. Minutes of American delegation meeting on the bank, 11 July 1944, Morgenthau diaries, book 752, roll 216, FDRL. See also Arthur W. Crawford, *The Bretton Woods Proposals* (Washington, D.C.: Finance Department of the U.S. Chamber of Commerce, Feb. 1945), 43–44.

22. Rees, *Harry Dexter White,* 233; Howson and Moggridge, eds., *Wartime Diaries,* 170; Schild, *Bretton Woods and Dumbarton Oaks,* 127.

23. For bipartisan consensus among the U.S. delegation to Bretton Woods see Keynes letter to Catto, 4 July 1944, and Keynes letter to Anderson, 14 July 1944, both in Moggridge, ed., *Collected Writings of Keynes,* 26:81–82, 91; minutes of American delegation meeting on bank quotas, 19 July 1944, Morgenthau diaries, book 756, roll 217, FDRL; minutes of American delegation meeting on 25 percent clause, 12 July 1944, and minutes of American delegation meeting on bank, 12 July 1944, both Morgenthau diaries, book 753, roll 216, FDRL;

minutes of American delegation meeting on fund, quotas, and publication of monetary reports, 10 July 1944, Morgenthau diaries, book 752, roll 216, FDRL; minutes of American delegation meeting on fund exchange rates and quotas, 5 July 1944, Morgenthau diaries, book 750, roll 215, FDRL; minutes of American delegation meeting on fund and bank, 2 July 1944, and minutes of American delegation meeting on fund, 1 July 1944, both Morgenthau diaries, book 749, roll 215, FDRL; Howson and Moggridge, eds.,*Wartime Diaries*, 169, 188; and Morgenthau, *Mostly Morgenthaus*, 342.

24. Minutes of American delegation meeting on location of fund and bank, 14 July 1944, Morgenthau diaries, book 754, roll 216, FDRL. See also minutes of American delegation meeting on bank, 11 July 1944, and minutes of American delegation meeting on quotas, 10 July 1944, both Morgenthau diaries, book 752, roll 216, FDRL; "Bretton Woods, 1944," CBS special program script, 18 July 1944, and Morgenthau letter to Keynes, 18 July 1944, both Morgenthau diaries, book 755, roll 216, FDRL; minutes of American delegation meeting on location of the fund, 13 July 1944, Morgenthau diaries, book 753, roll 216, FDRL; minutes of American delegation meeting on Russian provisions, interest rates, and location, 7 July 1944, Morgenthau diaries, book 751, roll 215, FDRL; Howson and Moggridge, eds., *Wartime Diaries*, 184; Keynes letter to Morgenthau, 13 July 1944, and Keynes letter to Anderson, both in Moggridge, ed., *Collected Writings of Keynes*, 26:88–92.

25. As quoted in *New York Times*, 12 July 1944. See also Schild, *Bretton Woods and Dumbarton Oaks*, 115–16.

26. Minutes of American delegation meeting on bank quotas, 19 July 1944, Morgenthau diaries, book 756, roll 217, FDRL; minutes of American delegation meeting on fund and bank, 2 July 1944, Morgenthau diaries, book 749, roll 215, FDRL. See also minutes of American delegation meeting on bank, 12 July 1944, Morgenthau diaries, book 753, roll 216, FDRL; and Schild, *Bretton Woods and Dumbarton Oaks*, 107–8.

27. House Committee on Banking and Currency, *Report to Accompany H.R. 3314*, 1–2, 4; Keynes note on Bretton Woods, 14 June 1945, in Moggridge, ed., *Collected Writings of Keynes*, 26:196; *Charts Relating to the Bretton Woods Proposals: The Danger that Restrictive and Discriminatory Currency Practices Will Be Resumed and Intensified after the War Makes International Monetary Cooperation Essential* (Washington, D.C.: U.S. Treasury, 30 Apr. 1945).

Groups testifying in support of the Bretton Woods legislation included the American Association of University Women, American Farm Bureau Federation, American Federation of Labor (AFL), Americans United for World Organization, Catholic Association for International Peace, Citizen Conference on International Economic Union, Committee for Economic Development, Congregational Church's Council for Social Action, League of Women Voters, National Citizens Political Action Committee, National Farmers Union, National Foreign Trade Council, National Planning Association, Southern Conference for Human Welfare, Vermont Farm Labor Conference, and Women's Conference on International Affairs.

For initial press hostility to Bretton Woods system see Howson and Moggridge, eds., *Wartime Diaries*, 166; *Washington Post*, 1 July 1944; *New York Times*, 1 July 1944; *Wall Street Journal*, 1 July 1944; and Keynes letter to Hopkins, 25 June 1944, in Moggridge, ed., *Collected Writings of Keynes*, 26:63.

28. Joseph Gaer, *Bretton Woods Is No Mystery*, pamphlets of the Congress of Industrial Organizations' Political Action Committee, no. 1 (New York: Pamphlet Press, 1945). See also Crawford, *Bretton Woods Proposals*, 39–40, 45.

For similar arguments see Alvin H. Hansen, *After the War: Full Employment* (Washington, D.C.: National Resources Planning Board, Jan. 1942).

29. House Committee on Banking and Currency, *Report to Accompany H.R. 3314,* 4, 50–56, 111–13; V. Orval Watts, *The Bretton Woods Agreements* (Los Angeles, Calif.: LA Chamber of Commerce, 1945); *Testimony of Leon Fraser on the Bretton Woods Agreements Act* (New York: First National Bank of the City of New York, 1945). Montagu Norman, head of the Bank of England, also backed the key-currencies approach (Fforde, *Bank of England and Public Policy,* 39–42, 47–48, 51).

30. House Committee on Banking and Currency, *Report to Accompany H.R. 3314,* 1–5, 72; Schild, *Bretton Woods and Dumbarton Oaks,* 99–100. Bankers' associations approving the Bretton Woods system were the Board of Governors of the Federal Reserve System, Independent Banker's Association, and Pennsylvania Bankers Association.

31. Keynes speech at inaugural meeting of governors of the fund and bank, 9 Mar. 1946, in Moggridge, ed., *Collected Writings of Keynes,* 26:215–17.

32. *Manchester Guardian* as cited in Richard N. Gardner, *Sterling-Dollar Diplomacy: Anglo-American Collaboration in the Reconstruction of Multilateral Trade* (Oxford, UK: Clarendon, 1956), 267.

33. Keynes letter to the Treasury, 7 Mar. 1946, in Moggridge, ed., *Collected Writings of Keynes,* 26:211. See also Keynes letter to Hugh Dalton, President of the British Board of Trade, and attached "The Savannah Conference on the Bretton Woods Final Act," ibid., 221–22; Gardner, *Sterling-Dollar Diplomacy,* 258; Mendès-France letter to André Philip, French Minister of Finance, 16 Mar. 1946, in Mendès-France, *Oeuvres Complètes,* 2: 192–95; and Fred Vinson, "After the Savannah Conference," *Foreign Affairs* 24 (July 1946): 626.

34. Keynes letter to Robert Henry Brand, Chairman of the British Supply Council in North America, 8 Feb. 1946, in Moggridge, ed., *Collected Writings of Keynes,* 26:208; *Manchester Guardian* as cited in Gardner, *Sterling-Dollar Diplomacy,* 267. See also Keynes letter to Richard F. Kahn, British Ministry of Supply, 13 Mar. 1946, Keynes statement at Savannah, 16 Mar. 1946, and Keynes letter to Dalton with attached "The Savannah Conference on the Bretton Woods Final Act," all in Moggridge, ed., *Collected Writings of Keynes,* 26:217–19, 223–24, 227; Gardner, *Sterling-Dollar Diplomacy,* 260; Edward S. Mason and Robert E. Asher, *The World Bank since Bretton Woods: The Origins, Policies, Operations, and Impact of the International Bank for Reconstruction and Development and the Other Members of the World Bank Group* (Washington, D.C.: Brookings, 1973), 36–40; and Howson and Moggridge, eds., *Wartime Diaries,* 164.

3. The World Bank and Development

1. In this study discourse is defined as the language, practices, traditions, and operations utilized by the World Bankers to construct a coherent worldview in which they could act and to legitimate that construct. The power of their discourse was largely derived from their ability to mobilize economic resources and to influence educated public opinion to support the concerns they defined as legitimate while marginalizing others.

2. For the World Bankers' belief in a common good and their ability to act in its service see World Bank President Eugene R. Black Jr. address to the Los Angeles World Affairs Council, 16 Oct. 1956, Eugene R. Black Jr. papers, box 3, folder 8, University of Georgia

Archive, Athens, Ga. [hereafter UGA]; Black address to the Bankers' Club of Chicago, 10 Jan. 1951, Black papers, box 3, folder 3, UGA; Leonard Rist, World Bank Executive Director, address to the New York press, 8 June 1955, and "U.S. Foreign Economic Policy: An International Viewpoint," Rist address to the First World Trade Conference, 17 May 1954, both Article and Speeches file [hereafter ASF], box 21, folder 4, World Bank Group Archive, Washington, D.C. [hereafter WBGA]; Black address to the *New York Herald Tribune* forum, 19 Oct. 1952, Leonard Rist files, box 1, folder 2, WBGA; Rist preliminary memorandum to Black, 19 Dec. 1950, Rist files, box 1, folder 3, WBGA; Richard Demuth address to the UN Economic, Employment and Development Commission, 17 May 1951, Rist files, box 1, folder 5, WBGA; and confidential draft of Committee on Loan Policy report, 26 Feb. 1947, Rist files, box 2, folder 12, WBGA.

3. Beyen memorandum to executive directors and alternates, 22 Dec. 1948, Basyn files, box 11, folder 5, WBGA; Demuth statement to the Third Latin American Conference, 18 June 1951, ASF, box 8, folder 2, WBGA; "What Answer to the Challenge of International Poverty?" Black address to the Economic Club of Detroit, 20 Apr. 1959, Black papers, box 4, folder 1, UGA.

For other statements about the importance of the bank's status as an international institution see Demuth address to the University of Missouri School of Business and Public Administration, 14 Apr. 1950, ASF, box 8, folder 2, WBGA; Black address to the Board of Governors, *Summary Proceedings of the Annual Meeting of the Board of Governors of the International Bank for Reconstruction and Development* [hereafter *SP IBRD* and pertinent year] (Washington, D.C.: World Bank, 1950), 9, 12; *SP IBRD, 1954,* 8; *SP IBRD, 1956,* 9; Morton M. Mendels, World Bank Secretary, address to the Rotary Club of Chester, England, 25 Sept. 1950, and "The Role of the International Bank for Reconstruction and Development," Mendels address to the 52d Annual Convention of the Maryland Bankers' Association, 28 May 1948, both ASF, box 18, folder 2, WBGA; William A. B. Iliff, Assistant to the World Bank President, address to the Good Neighbor Commission of Texas, 3 Dec. 1950, and Iliff address to the UN Seminar Course, 26 July 1948, both ASF, box 14, folder 7, WBGA; selected tributes to Black on his impending retirement, *SP IBRD, 1960,* 24; and "The Work of the World Bank," J. Burke Knapp, Director of World Bank Operations for the Western Hemisphere, address to the Bonn [Germany] Parliamentary Society, 6 Mar. 1963, ASF, box 15, folder 10, WBGA.

4. "Ventures in World Order," Black address at Princeton, 1962, Black papers, box 4, folder 4, UGA; Black address to the Southern Industrial Editors Institute, 4 Nov. 1949, Black papers, box 3, folder 1, UGA; William F. Howell, World Bank Director of Administration, address to the University of Pittsburgh Graduate School of Public and International Affairs, 24 Jan. 1963, ASF, box 14, folder 5, WBGA. See also "Some Considerations Affecting Foreign Aid," Black address to the Economic Club of New York, 14 Jan. 1953, Black papers, box 3, folder 5, UGA; Rist statement at the information meeting with ambassadors, 25 Apr. 1949, Rist files, box 5, folder 29, WBGA; Demuth address to the University of Missouri School of Business and Public Administration, 14 Apr. 1950, ASF, box 8, folder 2, WBGA; Black address to the Investment Dealers' Association of Canada, 23 Feb. 1950, Black papers, box 3, folder 2, UGA; and "Savings and World Development," Black address to the National Conference on Savings, Inflation and Economic Progress, 15 May 1952, Black papers, box 3, folder 4, UGA.

5. Black address to Southern Industrial Editors Institute, 4 Nov. 1949, Black papers, box 3, folder 1, UGA.

6. Meyer led Eugene Meyer and Company on Wall Street before serving as the head

of the nonferrous metals division of the War Industries Board, special assistant to the secretary of war, and director of the War Finance Corporation during World War I. He went on to serve as a member of the Federal Reserve Board and as the first chairman of the Reconstruction Finance Corporation. During World War II, Meyer was a member of the National Defense Mediation Board. (Mason and Asher, *World Bank since Bretton Woods,* 40–42; Merlo J. Pusey, *Eugene Meyer* [New York: Knopf, 1974].)

7. Mason and Asher, *World Bank since Bretton Woods,* 42–45; Howell address to Dallas Civil Service Assembly, 19 Nov. 1947, ASF, box 14, folder 5, WBGA.

8. "World Bank Goes Wall Street," *Business Week,* 8 Mar. 1947, 17–18; "A Business Regime for World Fund," *U.S. News* 22 (18 Apr. 1947): 48–49; Mason and Asher, *World Bank since Bretton Woods,* 43–45; Kai Bird, *The Chairman, John J. McCloy: The Making of the American Establishment* (New York: Simon and Schuster, 1992), 282–85; Pusey, *Eugene Meyer.*

9. Mason and Asher, *World Bank since Bretton Woods,* 46–47.

10. For recollections about staff initiatives during the interregnum see Robert L. Garner, World Bank Vice President, 1961 interview transcript, Columbia Oral History Project, New York, N.Y. [hereafter COHP], World Bank Special Project [hereafter WBSP], 5.

11. Mason and Asher, *World Bank since Bretton Woods,* 95–97; Bird, *The Chairman,* 285–89; memorandum to the ad hoc committee of Board of Governors from Dr. Leon Baranski, Polish World Bank Executive Director, 21 Oct. 1948, Basyn files, box 11, folder 5, WBGA; Mendels, 1961 interview transcript, 1961, COHP, WBSP, 45–46.

12. Beyen memorandum to the executive directors and alternates, 22 Dec. 1948, Basyn files, box 11, folder 5, WBGA. Rubberstamp comment found in *Time,* 20 June 1949.

13. Beyen observations at the informal executive session, 10 Nov. 1948, and strictly confidential interview with Roger Hoppenot, French World Bank Executive Director, 24 Nov. 1948, both Basyn files, box 11, folder 5, WBGA.

14. Garner interview transcript, COHP, WBSP, 21.

15. Walter Isaacson and Evan Thomas, *The Wise Men: Six Friends and the World They Made: Acheson, Bohlen, Harriman, Kennan, Lovett, McCloy* (New York: Simon and Schuster, 1986), 23, 428–29; Mason and Asher, *World Bank since Bretton Woods,* 11–61; Bird, *The Chairman,* 284–307.

16. "A Business Regime for World Fund," *U.S. News* 22 (18 Apr. 1947): 48; "World Bank Goes Wall Street," *Business Week,* 8 Mar. 1947.

17. Undated confidential off-the-record remarks by Rist [late 1947], Rist files, box 1, folder 1, WBGA.

18. Mason and Asher, *World Bank since Bretton Woods,* 52–53, 153–58.

19. Ibid., 53.

20. Although Black had no formal training in economics and knew no foreign languages, he had the lineage and career experience that were vital to his new job. His maternal grandfather, Henry W. Grady, had been the orator of the "New South" during Reconstruction—one of the first and most outspoken advocates of Southern economic development in order to integrate the region with the rapidly industrializing northern United States. Eugene R. Black Sr. had served on the Atlanta Federal Reserve Board before being called to Washington by President Franklin D. Roosevelt to serve on the Washington board. The younger Black's career in finance had started soon after his graduation from the University of Georgia and World War I service in the U.S. Navy. He was released from the service in time to join a local firm in the final war-bond drive. Black's abilities in the area of bond sales led to his eventual elevation to vice president of the Chase National Bank.

21. "The Importance of Being International," Black address to the British Council of the International Chamber of Commerce, 5 Nov. 1957, Black papers, box 3, folder 9, UGA. See also Black as quoted in Demuth address to the UN Economic, Employment and Development Commission, 17 May 1951, Rist files, box 1, folder 5, WBGA.

22. "Ventures in World Order," Black address at Princeton University, 1962, Black papers, box 4, folder 4, UGA; memorandum from Black to Martin, 15 Jan. 1951, Rist files, box 1, folder 6, WBGA.

23. "International Lending: Then and Now," Black address to the National Association of Supervisors of State Banks, 10 Oct. 1956, Black papers, box 3, folder 8, UGA; Howell address to the University of Pittsburgh Graduate School of Public and International Affairs, 24 Jan. 1963, ASF, box 14, folder 5, WBGA.

For further bank worry about the lure of communism see Black address to the joint meeting of the Foreign Policy Association of New Orleans, 15 Jan. 1952, Black papers, box 3, folder 4, UGA; Black address to the Atlanta Chamber of Commerce homecoming luncheon, 7 Nov. 1951, Black papers, box 3, folder 3, UGA; "Common Sense and Economic Aid," Black address to the National Farm Institute at Des Moines, Iowa, 18 Feb. 1956, Black papers, box 3, folder 8, UGA; "The Importance of Being International," Black address to the British Council of the International Chamber of Commerce, 5 Nov. 1957, Black papers, box 3, folder 9, UGA; and Rist address to the Los Angeles, Portland, and Seattle Council on Foreign Relations, May 1953, ASF, box 21, folder 4, WBGA.

For other criticisms of Third World economic policies see Demuth statement to the Third Latin American Conference, 18 June 1951, ASF, box 8, folder 2, WBGA; Howell address to the University of Pittsburgh Graduate School of Public and International Affairs, 24 Jan. 1963, ASF, box 14, folder 5, WBGA; Black address to the Eastern District of the Investment Dealers' Association of Canada, 23 Feb. 1950, Black papers, box 3, folder 2, UGA; Black address to the Board of Governors, *SP IBRD, 1951*, 8; *SP IBRD, 1952*, 10; *SP IBRD, 1956*, 10; *SP IBRD, 1958*, 9; and memorandum to Garner from Sam Henderson, 25 Feb. 1949, Central Files, 1947–68: General Files, Organization [hereafter CF:GFO], box 6, folder 1, WBGA.

24. Black's schedule for Apr. 1950 European trip, undated, Black papers, box 5, folder 2, UGA. See also Harold N. Graves Jr., Director of World Bank Office of Information, speech, 17 Sept. 1951, ASF, box 12, folder 8, WBGA; Black address to the Board of Governors, *SP IBRD, 1951*, 8; *SP IBRD, 1953*, 10; *SP IBRD, 1954*, 10–11; "The World Bank as Lender and Borrower: A Ten-Year Report," Black address to Zurich Economic Society, 21 Mar. 1956, Black papers, box 3, folder 8, UGA; Rist memorandum to Black, Garner, Hoar, Ansel F. Luxford (World Bank Assistant General Counsel), Demuth, and Henry W. Riley (World Bank Treasurer), 17 Feb. 1951, and draft Rist letter to Hoppenot, 17 Mar. 1950, both Rist files, box 1, folder 1, WBGA; and confidential Iliff memorandum to staff loan committee, 21 Mar. 1950, Rist files, box 2, folder 10, WBGA.

25. Black address to the *New York Herald Tribune* forum, 19 Oct. 1952, Rist files, box 1, folder 2, WBGA; "Ventures in World Order," Black address at Princeton University, 1962, Black papers, box 4, folder 4, UGA.

For examples of the World Bankers' criticisms of American aid policies see also Black memorandum to Martin, 15 Jan. 1951, and "The International Bank as Management Agent for Administering a Program of Developmental Grants," Feb. 1951, both Rist files, box 1, folder 6, WBGA; "World Bank Chief's Warning on Aid: 'Wrong Handling Could Serve Communism,'" *London Times*, 4 Mar. 1960; "Some Considerations Affecting Foreign Aid," Black address to the Economic Club of New York, 14 Jan. 1953, Black papers, box 3, folder 5,

UGA; Black address to the Ninth Annual Cleveland World Trade Conference, 7 May 1954, Black papers, box 3, folder 6, UGA; Black address to the Board of Governors, *SP IBRD, 1951*, 8; *SP IBRD, 1952*, 10; *SP IBRD, 1954*, 10–11; Rist address to the Minneapolis Council on Foreign Relations (CFR), 12 Jan. 1953, ASF, box 21, folder 3, WBGA; and "Foreign Aid 'Oversold,' Black Says," *Washington News*, 5 Oct. 1961.

26. Unattributed memorandum on United States–International Bank relations, 24 Dec. 1952, Rist files, box 1, folder 2, WBGA. See also "Long Term Financing Institutions of the Western Hemisphere," Rist address to the Rutgers University International Banking Summer School, 10 July 1956, ASF, box 21, folder 4, WBGA; Black memorandum to McCloy, 25 July 1947, Black papers, box 1, folder 3, UGA; Black memorandum to Martin, 15 Jan. 1951, Rist files, box 1, folder 6, WBGA; "Problems of Bank Policy Arising from Recent Reports on Economic Development," confidential Rosenstein-Rodan memorandum, 16 Aug. 1951, Rist files, box 1, folder 5, WBGA; and Mason and Asher, *World Bank since Bretton Woods*, 159n, 160–61, 172–73, and 660–62.

27. Black address to the Ninth Annual Cleveland World Trade Conference, 7 May 1954, Black papers, box 3, folder 6, UGA. See also Black address to the *New York Herald Tribune* Forum, 19 Oct. 1952, Rist files, box 1, folder 2, WBGA; Rist address to the Minneapolis CFR, 12 Jan. 1953, ASF, box 21, folder 3, WBGA; "U.S. Foreign Economic Policy: An International Viewpoint," Rist address to the First World Trade Conference, 17 May 1954, ASF, box 21, folder 4, WBGA; and Black address to the New York Bond Club, 2 May 1952, Black papers, box 3, folder 4, UGA.

28. Black address to the Atlanta Chamber of Commerce, 7 Nov. 1951, Black papers, box 3, folder 3, UGA. For other bank references to economic development as a supplement to American defense see Black address to the Florida Bankers' Association, 3 Apr. 1951, and "World Bank Loans at Work," Black address to the National Foreign Trade Convention, 29 Oct. 1951, both ibid.; "World Bank Head Speaks at Alumni Day at University," *Waycross (Georgia) Journal-Herald*, 12 June 1957; Black memorandum to Martin, 15 Jan. 1951, Rist files, box 1, folder 6, WBGA; and preliminary Rist memorandum to Black, 19 Dec. 1950, Rist files, box 1, folder 3, WBGA.

For the World Bankers' equating development with peace see "A New Task for Science," Black commencement address at MIT, 4 June 1963, Black papers, box 4, folder 5, UGA; Black address to the New York Bond Club, 2 May 1952, Black papers, box 3, folder 4, UGA; "The World Bank as Lender and Borrower," Black address to the Economic Society of Zurich, 21 Mar. 1956, Black papers, box 3, folder 8, UGA; Black commencement address at Oglethorpe University, 5 June 1955, Black papers, box 3, folder 7, UGA; Rist address to the Los Angeles, Portland, and Seattle CFR, ASF, box 21, folder 4, WBGA; Black address to the *New York Herald Tribune* Forum, 19 Oct. 1952, Rist files, box 1, folder 2, WBGA; Black memorandum to Martin, 15 Jan. 1951, Rist files, box 1, folder 6, WBGA; Demuth statement to the UN Economic, Employment and Development Commission, 17 May 1951, Rist files, box 1, folder 5, WBGA; "Common Sense and Economic Aid," Black address to the National Farm Institute in Des Moines, 18 Feb. 1956, Black papers, box 3, folder 8, UGA; and "Honors for a Banker," *Buffalo (NY) Evening News*, 27 July 1960.

29. This section is derived from the corporatist theory of Michael J. Hogan, *The Marshall Plan: America, Britain, and the Reconstruction of Europe, 1947–1952* (New York: Cambridge Univ. Press, 1987), *Informal Entente*, and "Corporatism: A Positive Appraisal," *Diplomatic History* 10 (Fall 1986): 363–72. For other works informed by corporatism see Hawley, *The*

Great War; Charles S. Maier, *Recasting Bourgeois Europe: Stabilization in France, Germany, and Italy in the Decade after World War I* (Princeton, N.J.: Princeton Univ. Press, 1975), and "The Politics of Productivity: Foundations of American International Economic Policy after World War II," in *In Search of Stability: Explorations in Historical Political Economy,* ed. Maier (Cambridge, UK: Cambridge Univ. Press, 1987), 121–52; Robert Griffith, "Dwight D. Eisenhower and the Corporate Commonwealth," *American Historical Review* 87 (Feb. 1982): 87–122; Elizabeth A. Cobbs, *The Rich Neighbor Policy: Rockefeller and Kaiser in Brazil* (New Haven, Conn.: Yale Univ. Press, 1992); and Andrew P. N. Erdmann, "Mining for the Corporatist Synthesis: Gold in American Foreign Economic Policy, 1931–1936," *Diplomatic History* 17 (Spring 1993): 171–200.

30. Demuth address to Stanford University's Third Latin American Conference, 18 June 1951, and Demuth address to the Economic Commission for Latin America (ECLA), 31 May 1949, both ASF, box 8, folder 2, WBGA; letter from Per Jacobsson to W. Randolph Burgess, Vice Chairman of the Board of the National City Bank of New York, 12 Dec. 1946, Black papers, box 1, folder 2, UGA; *London Investor's Review,* 12 Mar. 1960; confidential Knapp memorandum on Black's visit to Brazil, 31 Mar. 1954, and Federico Consolo memoranda to Orvis A. Schmidt, Director of World Bank Operations for the Western Hemisphere, 7 and 8 Mar. 1954, both Black papers, box 5, folder 10, UGA; letter to Black from Leo N. Shaw, Senior Vice President and Manager of the Overseas Division of National City Bank of New York, 26 Aug. 1949, Rist files, box 1, folder 1, WBGA; Black letter to Symington, 24 Jan. 1952, Rist files, box 1, folder 2, WBGA; Rist paper on development, 30 Jan. 1948, Rist files, box 1, folder 4, WBGA; Black letter to Symington, 18 July 1951, Rist files, box 1, folder 6, WBGA; staff memorandum, 5 July 1951, Rist files, box 1, folder 5, WBGA; "A Fresh Look at Foreign Investment," Black address to the Trust Division of the American Bankers' Association (ABA), 10 Feb. 1954, Black papers, box 3, folder 6, UGA; Black address to the Texas Group of the Investment Bankers Association, 29 Apr. 1948, Black papers, box 3, folder 1, UGA; "Long Term Financing Institutions of the Western Hemisphere," Rist address to the Rutgers University International Banking Summer School, 10 July 1956, ASF, box 21, folder 4, WBGA; Beyen memorandum to the executive directors and alternates, 22 Dec. 1948, Basyn files, box 11, folder 5, WBGA; Black letter to Snyder, 3 Nov. 1952, Rist files, box 1, folder 7, WBGA; confidential memorandum on loan policy, 28 Jan. 1948, Rist files, box 3, folder 16, WBGA; confidential memoranda of meetings of bank financial policy committee, 1 and 2 Aug. 1963, Rist files, box 3, folder 18, WBGA; letter from Mohamed Shoaib, Pakistani World Bank Executive Director, to Syed Amjad Ali, Pakistani Minister of Finance, 16 Apr. 1957, Mohamed Shoaib files, box 2, folder 1, WBGA.

31. "Your Business and Your Country's Business Overseas," Black address to the National Association of Manufacturers (NAM), 5 Dec. 1956, Black papers, box 3, folder 8, UGA. See also letter to the chancellor of McGill University from Professor J. R. Mallory, Chair of McGill University's Department of Economics and Political Science, 29 May 1964, Black papers, box 1, folder 58, UGA; and Rist paper on development, 30 Jan. 1948, Rist files, box 1, folder 4, WBGA.

32. Demuth address to Stanford University's Third Latin American Conference, 18 June 1951, and Demuth address to ECLA, 31 May 1949, both ASF, box 8, folder 2, WBGA; confidential memorandum on IDA lending policy, 19 Sept. 1963, Rist files, box 3, folder 14, WBGA; "Africa: One Continent, Many Countries," Rist address to the Minneapolis CFR, 12 Mar. 1962, ASF, box 21, folder 5, WBGA; Rist statement at the information meeting with

ambassadors, 25 Apr. 1949, Rist files, box 5, folder 29, WBGA; Black address to the Eastern District of the Investment Dealers' Association of Canada, 23 Feb. 1950, Black papers, box 3, folder 2, WBGA; Shoaib letter to Mumtaz Hassan, Secretary of the Pakistani Ministry of Finance, 13 Dec. 1954, Shoaib files, box 1, folder 1, WBGA.

33. Demuth statement to Stanford University's Third Latin American Conference, 18 June 1951, ASF, box 8, folder 2, WBGA. See also Demuth address to the University of Missouri School of Business and Public Administration, 14 Apr. 1950, ibid.; Hoar letter to Shah, 14 Nov. 1951, Rist files, box 2, folder 11, WBGA; Graves address to the Economic Commission for Africa, 3 Jan. 1959, ASF, box 12, folder 8, WBGA; Mendels address to the Rotary Club of Chester, 25 Sept. 1950, ASF, box 18, folder 2, WBGA; Black address to the Board of Governors, *SP IBRD, 1960*, 18; letter to Iliff from Jeff Rucinski, Director of World Bank Operations for South Asia and the Middle East, 1 Mar. 1952, Black papers, box 5, folder 7, UGA; Black address to the LA World Affairs Council, 16 Oct. 1956, and "The World Bank as Lender and Borrower: A Ten-Year Report," Black address to the Economic Society of Zurich, 21 Mar. 1956, both Black papers, box 3, folder 8, UGA; "World Bank Loans at Work," Black address to the National Foreign Trade Convention, 29 Oct. 1951, Black papers, box 3, folder 3, UGA; "The International Bank for Reconstruction and Development and its Affiliates," Rist address to the SEANZA meeting, June 1962, and "International Assistance to Underdeveloped Countries," Rist address to the Conference of Business Economics, 21 Feb. 1964, both ASF, box 21, folder 5, WBGA; confidential draft of the report of the International Advisory Board, 2 Apr. 1951, Rist files, box 1, folder 6, WBGA; restricted economic staff report, 19 Sept. 1963, Rist files, box 3, folder 14, WBGA; confidential memorandum on loan policy, 28 Jan. 1948, Rist files, box 3, folder 16, WBGA; confidential memoranda of bank financial policy committee meetings, 2 and 6 Aug. 1963, Rist files, box 3, folder 18, WBGA; and Shoaib letter to S. M. Hasan, Director General of Pakistan Railways, 12 Apr. 1957, Shoaib files, box 2, folder 1, WBGA.

34. A sense of the bank's wide and varied connections is evident in the enormous number of people who sent their best wishes to Black following his operation at the Mayo Clinic. See Black papers, box 1, folders 50–55, UGA.

For bank cooperation with other UN specialized agencies and other international organizations see Demuth address to Stanford University's Third Latin American Conference, 18 June 1951, ASF, box 8, folder 2, WBGA; Mason and Asher, *World Bank since Bretton Woods*, 59–60; Rist memorandum to Black, 2 Feb. 1951, Rist files, box 1, folder 1, WBGA; confidential memorandum of bank financial policy committee meeting, 30 July 1963, and confidential memorandum of resumed bank financial policy committee meeting, 1 Aug. 1963, both Rist files, box 3, folder 18, WBGA; Black address to ECOSOC, Rist files, box 1, folder 2, WBGA; confidential staff committee report, 22 Mar. 1949, Rist files, box 2, folder 11, WBGA; "The Importance of Being International," Black address to the British Council of the International Chamber of Commerce, 5 Nov. 1957, Black papers, box 3, folder 9, UGA; and Rist memorandum to Eugene Meyer, World Bank President, 23 July 1946, Rist files, box 5, folder 28, WBGA.

For bank cooperation with Anglo-American development agencies see Black letter to Sir Sydney Caine, UK Treasury and Supply Delegation, 29 Jan. 1951, Rist files, box 1, folder 1, WBGA; Rucinski letter to Iliff, 1 Mar. 1952, Black papers, box 5, folder 7, UGA; and Demuth address to the University of Missouri School of Business and Public Administration, 14 Apr. 1950, ASF, box 8, folder 2, WBGA.

For bank cooperation with U.S. federal agencies see memorandum to Rist from Miss
Cathala de St. Sauveur, Rist's assistant, 20 Aug. 1946, Rist files, box 5, folder 28, WBGA;
Rist memorandum to Geoffrey Wilson, 3 Feb. 1964, Rist files, box 3, folder 18, WBGA; Rist
memorandum to Black, 4 Nov. 1952, Rist files, box 1, folder 2, WBGA; Rist memorandum
to Black, 27 Jan. 1950, and Black letter to Thomas B. McCabe, Chairman of the Board of
Governors of the Federal Reserve System, 1 Dec. 1949, Rist files, box 1, folder 1, WBGA; confidential Black letter to Gordon Gray, Special Assistant to the President, 27 Nov. 1950, and
confidential memorandum on the Gray Committee Report, 29 Nov. 1950, both Rist files,
box 1, folder 3, WBGA; and letter to Black from M. S. Szymczak, Federal Reserve Board of
Governors, with attached memorandum on the lending policies of the International Bank,
29 May 1950, Rist files, box 1, folder 4, WBGA.

For bank cooperation with other financial leaders see draft Rist letter to Hoppenot,
17 Mar. 1950, unattributed memorandum on people Mr. Black may care to see in Paris, 23
Mar. 1950, and Black letter to Svend Andersen, Danish National Bank, 25 Jan. 1950, all Rist
files, box 1, folder 1, WBGA; confidential Rist letter to Burgess, with attached confidential
memorandum, 25 Oct. 1947, Rist files, box 1, folder 4, WBGA; Black letter to Lord Trefgar-
ne, Colonial Development Corporation, 31 May 1950, Black papers, box 5, folder 2, UGA;
memorandum on arrangements, meeting, luncheons, etc. for BIS meeting, June 1950, Black
papers, box 5, folder 3, UGA; memorandum on invitations, arrangements, luncheons, etc.,
for European trip, May 1951, Black papers, box 5, folder 5, UGA; Black's itinerary in South
East Asia, Australia, and New Zealand, Feb. 1952, Black papers, box 5, folder 7, UGA; memorandum on luncheon plans during European trip, Feb. 1951, Black papers, box 5, folder 9,
UGA; memorandum on lunch dates during trip to London, Mar. 1955, Black papers, box 5,
folder 11, UGA; memorandum on appointments and schedule for trip to Europe, Iran, and
Egypt, June 1956, Black papers, box 5, folder 12, UGA; annex on people met during trip to
Africa, Apr. 1958, Black papers, box 5, folder 14, UGA; itinerary for European trip, May 1961,
Black papers, box 5, folder 21, UGA; Black's schedule for European trip, Apr. 1950, Black
papers, box 5, folder 2, UGA; and confidential Shoaib letter to Ato Menasse Lemma, Vice
Minister of Finance for Ethiopia, 16 Jan. 1957, Shoaib files, box 2, folder 1, WBGA.

35. For more detailed exposition of the Rockefeller plan see International Development
Advisory Board, *Partners in Progress: A Report to the President* (Washington, D.C.: GPO,
Mar. 1951), 89–90; and "Text of Summary of Report by Nelson Rockefeller Board on World-
Wide Aid Program," *New York Times*, 11 Mar. 1951. For more on Rockefeller's view of the
world economy and the role of private investment see Cobbs, *Rich Neighbor Policy,* esp.
1–20, 139, 235–53.

36. For bank's proposal before the ECOSOC and reactions presented before that body
see Black address on the international finance corporation proposal before the fourteenth
session of ECOSOC, 16 June 1952, statement by Isador Lubin, U.S. representative to the
ECOSOC, on the IBRD report, 17 June 1952, and ECOSOC press release, 17 June 1952, all
CF:GFO, box 7, folder 4, WBGA; and Walter Hill memorandum to Garner, 21 July 1953, CF:
GFO, box 6, folder 2, WBGA.

For American and other reservations regarding the creation of an international finance corporation see S. W. Anderson memorandum to Davidson Sommers, World Bank
General Counsel, 29 Oct. 1951, Sommers memorandum on meetings in New York, 31 Oct.
1951, and memorandum on the principal criticism of IFC proposal, 26 Dec. 1951, all CF:
GFO, box 6, folder 1, WBGA; letter to Crena de Iongh from A. J. L. Haskell, Deputy General

Manager of the Bank of Montreal, 19 May 1952, letter to Garner from Gilbert H. Cless, McKinsey and Company Management Consultants, 23 May 1952, and letter to Sommers from George A. Brownell of David Polk Wardwell Sunderland and Kiendl, 27 May 1952, all CF:GFO, box 8, folder 5, WBGA; letter to Black from James Muir, President of the Royal Bank of Canada, 2 Sept. 1952, CF:GFO, box 8, folder 6, WBGA; reports on the status of the proposal for an international finance corporation, May 1953 and June 1954, Gordon memorandum to Demuth, 17 June 1954, letter to Demuth from Dr. Enrique Lopez-Herrarte, 8 July 1954, Black letter to Burgess, 20 Oct. 1954, and Garner letter to Stacy May, Rockefeller Plaza, 29 Dec. 1954, all CF:GFO, box 6, folder 2, WBGA; and Burton I. Kaufman, *Trade and Aid: Eisenhower's Foreign Economic Policy, 1953–1961* (Baltimore, Md.: Johns Hopkins Univ. Press, 1982), 46–49.

For positive appraisals of the bank's ideas see E. Baring letter to Sommers, 19 Nov. 1951, letter to Crena de Iongh from L. Camu, Vice President of the Bank of Brussels, 21 May 1952, and letter to Crena de Iongh from A. Linder, Director-General of the Crédit Suisse Zurich, 24 May 1952, all CF:GFO, box 8, folder 5, WBGA; memorandum to Demuth from B. K. Nehru, Indian World Bank Executive Director, 18 May 1953, letter to Black from U.S. Representative Jacob K. Javits, Chair of the Subcommittee on Foreign Economic Policy, 30 Aug. 1954, and Black letters to Clarence B. Randall, Special Consultant to the U.S. President, 27 and 29 Oct. 1954, all CF:GFO, box 6, folder 2, WBGA; and speech by K. S. Hegde, Indian delegate to the UN General Assembly, 30 Nov. 1954, speech by Julian Saenz, alternate Mexican delegate to ECOSOC, 2 Dec. 1954, and bulletin from Brazilian delegation to the UN, 7 Dec. 1954, all CF:GFO, box 8, folder 2, WBGA.

For altered U.S. position see statement by Roger W. Straus, alternate U.S. Representative to the UN General Assembly, 30 Nov. 1954, CF:GFO, box 8, folder 2, WBGA; and Kaufman, *Trade and Aid,* 46–49. The Europeans and Canadians soon followed suit: "Aid for Overseas Development: British Readiness to Take Part," *London Times,* 3 Dec. 1954; and statement by W. F. de Gaay, Dutch delegate to the UN General Assembly, 4 Dec. 1954, statement by Charles B. Howard, Canadian delegate to the UN General Assembly, 4 Dec. 1954, and speech by Andre Armengaud, French delegate to the UN General Assembly, 6 Dec. 1954, all CF:GFO, box 8, folder 2, WBGA.

37. In addition to the EDI, the World Bank established the General Training Program in 1949 for junior development officials and two programs of individualized tutorials: the Special Training Program and the Public Finance Training Program. The General Training Program was the basis for the later, and more ambitious, EDI. Although smaller than EDI, by the end of 1959, the General Training Program had ninety-one graduates from fifty-two member countries.

38. Edward H. Berman, *The Ideology of Philanthropy: The Influence of the Carnegie, Ford, and Rockefeller Foundations on American Foreign Policy* (Albany: State Univ. of New York Press, 1983); Mason and Asher, *World Bank since Bretton Woods,* 324–34.

39. "World Bank Loans at Work," Black address to the National Foreign Trade Convention, 29 Oct. 1951, Black papers, box 3, folder 3, UGA. See also Black address to the Board of Governors, *SP IBRD, 1949,* 8; *SP IBRD, 1951,* 7; *SP IBRD, 1953,* 10; and "The World Bank: Retrospect and Prospect," Mendels address to the Canadian Institute of International Affairs, 9 Feb. 1955, ASF, box 18, folder 2, WBGA.

40. "Savings and World Development," Black address to the National Conference on Savings, Inflation and Economic Progress, 15 May 1952, Black papers, box 3, folder 4, UGA.

See also Rist memorandum to Black, 13 July 1953, Rist files, box 1, folder 2, WBGA; "World Bank Loans at Work," Black address to the National Foreign Trade Convention, 29 Oct. 1951, Black papers, box 3, folder 3, UGA; Black commencement address to Oglethorpe University, 5 June 1955, Black papers, box 3, folder 7, UGA; and Black address to the Board of Governors, *SP IBRD, 1950,* 9; *SP IBRD, 1951,* 10; *SP IBRD, 1959,* 11.

41. Howell address to the University of Pittsburgh Graduate School of Public and International Affairs, 24 Jan. 1963, ASF, box 14, folder 5, WBGA; Paul M. Angle, ed., *Created Equal? The Complete Lincoln-Douglas Debates of 1858* (Chicago, Ill.: Univ. of Chicago Press, 1958), 2; Black commencement address to Oglethorpe University, 5 June 1955, Black papers, box 3, folder 7, UGA.

42. John Maynard Keynes's address to the closing plenary session of the Bretton Woods Conference, in U.S. Department of State, *Proceedings and Documents of the United Nations Monetary and Financial Conference, Bretton Woods, New Hampshire, July 1–22, 1944,* 2 vols. (Washington, D.C.: GPO, 1945), 1:1110.

43. Black address to the Board of Governors, *SP IBRD, 1950,* 9; Jyrki Käkönen, *The World Bank: A Bridgehead of Imperialism* (Tampere, Fin.: Peace Research Institute, 1975); Mason and Asher, *World Bank since Bretton Woods,* tables 6–1, 7–3, E-1; Louis A. Peréz Jr., "Dependency," in *Explaining the History of American Foreign Relations,* ed. Michael J. Hogan and Thomas G. Paterson (Cambridge, UK: Cambridge Univ. Press, 1991), 99–110; Bharat Dogra, *In the Interests of Interest: Trade, Aid and Debt in an Unequal World* (Asthal Bohar, India: Disha, 1991).

44. McCloy recommendation to the executive directors, 6 Aug. 1947, as quoted in Mason and Asher, *World Bank since Bretton Woods,* 266. See also ibid., table E-6; Robert J. McMahon, *Colonialism and Cold War: The United States and the Struggle for Indonesian Independence, 1945–49* (Ithaca, N.Y.: Cornell Univ. Press, 1981), 168–78; and Bruce Rich, "World Bank/IMF: 50 Years Is Enough," in *50 Years Is Enough: The Case against the World Bank and the International Monetary Fund,* ed. Kevin Danaher (Boston, Mass.: South End, 1994), 6–13.

45. Joyce Kolko, *Restructuring the World Economy* (New York: Pantheon, 1988), esp. 3–14, 270–77, 346–51; Susan George and Fabrizio Sabelli, *Faith and Credit: The World Bank's Secular Empire* (Boulder, Colo.: Westview, 1994), esp. chap. 9; Bruce Rich, *Mortgaging the Earth: The World Bank, Environmental Impoverishment, and the Crisis of Development* (Boston, Mass.: Beacon, 1994).

46. Poland withdrew from the bank in 1950; Czechoslovakia's bank membership was terminated in 1954 (Mason and Asher, *World Bank since Bretton Woods,* 63–64).

47. Albert O. Hirschman, "A Dissenter's Confession: 'The Strategy of Economic Development' Revisited," in *Pioneers in Development,* ed. Gerald M. Meier and Dudley Seers (New York: Oxford Univ. Press, 1984), 90–91; Mason and Asher, *World Bank since Bretton Woods,* 161–66, 330–34; Frederick T. Moore, "The World Bank and Its Economic Missions," *Review of Economics and Statistics* 42 (Feb. 1960): 81–93; David E. Lilienthal, "The Road to Change: Development of People Must Be the Goal," *International Development Review* 6 (Dec. 1964): 9–14; Denis J. Sullivan, *Private Voluntary Organizations in Egypt: Islamic Development, Private Initiative, and State Control* (Gainesville: Univ. Press of Florida, 1994); George and Sabelli, *Faith and Credit,* esp. chap. 9; Michael Albert and Robin Hahnel, *Looking Forward: Participatory Economics for the Twenty-First Century* (Boston, Mass.: South End, 1991); Muhammad Yunus, "Redefining Development," in Danaher, ed., *50 Years Is Enough,* ix–xiii; Jeremy Brecher and Tim Costello, *Global Village or Global Pillage: Economic Reconstruction*

from the Bottom Up (Boston, Mass.: South End, 1994); and Sheldon Annis and Peter Hakim, eds., *Direct to the Poor: Grassroots Development in Latin America* (Boulder, Colo.: Lynne Rienner, 1988).

48. Ester Boserup, *Woman's Role in Economic Development* (London: Allen and Unwin, 1970) was the seminal work in the study of women and development. A good introduction to this and other feminist critiques of modernization and development theory is Jane S. Jaquette, "Women and Modernization Theory: A Decade of Feminist Critique," *World Politics* 34 (Jan. 1982): 267–84.

For other feminist critiques of development programs and theory see Tickner, *Gender in International Relations*, 67–96; Marianne A. Ferber and Julie A. Nelson, eds., *Beyond Economic Man: Feminist Theory and Economics* (Chicago, Ill.: Univ. of Chicago Press, 1993); Anne Marie Goetz, "Feminism and the Limits of the Claim to Know: Contradictions in the Feminist Approach to Women in Development," *Millennium: Journal of International Studies* 17 (1988): 477–96; Maria Mies, *Patriarchy and Accumulation on a World Scale: Women in the International Division of Labour* (London: Zed, 1986); Diana Pierce, "The Feminization of Poverty," *Journal for Peace and Justice Studies* 2 (1990): 1–20; Gita Sen and Caren Grown, *Development, Crises, and Alternative Visions: Third World Women's Perspectives* (New York: Monthly Review, 1987); Cynthia Enloe, *Bananas Beaches and Bases: Making Feminist Sense of International Politics* (Berkeley: Univ. of California Press, 1989); Roslyn Dauber and Melinda L. Cain, eds., *Women and Technological Change in Developing Countries*, American Association for the Advancement of Science Symposia Series (Boulder, Colo.: Westview, 1981); Sharon Stichter and Jane L. Parpart, eds., *Women, Employment and the Family in the International Division of Labour*, Women in the Political Economy Series, ed. Ronnie J. Steinberg (Philadelphia, Pa.: Temple Univ. Press, 1990); Mayra Buvinic, Margaret A. Lycette, and William Paul McGreevey, eds., *Women and Poverty in the Third World* (Baltimore, Md.: Johns Hopkins Univ. Press, 1983); UNESCO, *Women in the Villages, Men in the Towns* (Paris: UNESCO, 1984); Kathryn B. Ward, *Women in the World-System: Its Impact on Status and Fertility* (New York: Praeger, 1984); Kathleen Staudt, ed., *Women, International Development, and Politics: The Bureaucratic Mire* (Philadelphia, Pa.: Temple Univ. Press, 1990); United Nations Department of International Economic and Social Affairs, *World Survey on the Role of Women in Development* (New York: United Nations, 1986), esp. 12, 234–36; and Inge Khoury, "The World Bank and the Feminization of Poverty," in *50 Years Is Enough*, ed. Danaher, 121–23.

For women's roles within the World Bank see World Bank Group Staff Association's Status of Women Working Group, *Report on the Status of Women in the Bank* (Washington, D.C.: World Bank, 1981), esp. figures 1 and 2, and pp. 3, 18.

49. For World Bank efforts to deal with environmental concerns see World Bank, *The World Environment and the World Bank* (Washington, D.C.: World Bank, 1972); *Environment and Development in Latin America and the Caribbean: The Role of the World Bank* (Washington, D.C.: World Bank, 1992); Stephen D. Mink, *Poverty, Population, and the Environment*, World Bank Discussion Papers series (Washington, D.C.: World Bank, 1992); Barber Conable, "Development and the Environment: A Global Balance," Jeremy Warford and Zeinab Partow, "Evolution of the World Bank's Environmental Policy," Ernst Luz and Mohan Munasinghe, "Accounting for the Environment," Leif Christoffersen, "Environmental Action Plans in Africa," and "The Global Environmental Facility," all *Finance and Development* (Sept. 1991): 2–4, 5–8, 9–11, 17, and 29, resp; and Marshall Ingwerson, "World Bank Takes Steps to Help Environment," *Christian Science Monitor*, 22 Sept. 1989.

For critiques of these efforts and the effects of World Bank–led development on the environment and indigenous peoples see Rich, *Mortgaging the Earth;* Alain Lafontaine, "Environmental Aspects of Sustainable Development: The Role of the World Bank" (M.A. thesis, Carleton University, 1990); Vandana Shiva, "International Institutions Practicing Environmental Double Standards," Survival International, "The World Bank and Tribal Peoples," Pradeep S. Mehta, "Fury Over a River," and Cameron Duncan, "Reforming the Global Environment Facility," all in *50 Years Is Enough,* ed. Danaher, resp. 102–106, 112–16, 117–20, and 179–82; and George and Sabelli, *Faith and Credit,* esp. 162–89.

50. Black address to the Bankers' Club of Chicago, 10 Jan. 1951, Black papers, box 3, folder 3, UGA; "Development Assistance in Asia: Programs and Philosophy," Shoaib address to the Asian Regional Conference of the World Confederation of Organizations of the Teaching Profession, 21 Apr. 1969, ASF, box 24, folder 15, WBGA. See also "The Growing Gap between Developed and Developing Countries," Shoaib address to the U.S. State Department Foreign Service Institute's Center for Area and Country Studies, 8 Apr. 1968, ASF, box 24, folder 15, WBGA.

51. Graves remarks to Rome's Populorum Progressio Symposium, Oct. 1968, ASF, box 12, folder 8, WBGA. Part of the bank's unrealistic expectations for economic development in the Third World came from the examples that it had in mind of successful economic development projects: variously, the American South after Reconstruction, Canada, the Tennessee Valley under the TVA, and the state of Indiana.

52. Rich, *Mortgaging the Earth,* esp. chap. 4; Deborah Shapley, *Promise and Power: The Life and Times of Robert McNamara* (Boston, Mass.: Little, Brown, 1993), 464–580.

4. The International Economic Diplomacy of the World Bank

1. Demuth address to the University of Missouri School of Business and Public Administration, 14 Apr. 1950, ASF, box 8, folder 2, WBGA. See also Black address to the Southern Industrial Editors Institute, 4 Nov. 1949, Black papers, box 3, folder 1, UGA.

2. Letter to Black from Senator Alexander Wiley, Senate Committee on the Judiciary, 15 Feb. 1952, Garner letter to Wiley, 4 Mar. 1952, and Wiley letter to Garner, 8 Mar. 1952, all Central Files, 1946–1971: Operational Correspondence, Iran [hereafter CF:OCI], box 32, folder 1, WBGA; Clark file memorandum on Iranian oil, 5 Jan. 1954, CF:OCI, box 32, folder 7, WBGA; and Harold N. Graves Jr., "The Bank as International Mediator: Three Episodes," in Mason and Asher, *World Bank since Bretton Woods,* 600.

3. For fuller discussions of the events leading up to the nationalization of the AIOC see Mary Ann Heiss, *Empire and Nationhood: The United States, Great Britain, and Iranian Oil, 1950–1954* (New York: Columbia Univ. Press, 1997); Fakhreddin Azimi, *Iran: The Crisis of Democracy* (London: I. B. Tauris, 1989); Mostafa Elm, *Oil, Power, and Principle: Iran's Oil Nationalization and Its Aftermath* (Syracuse, N.Y.: Syracuse Univ. Press, 1992), 81–309; Homa Katouzian, *Musaddiq and the Struggle for Power in Iran* (London: I. B. Tauris, 1990), and *The Political Economy of Modern Iran: Despotism and Pseudo-Modernism, 1926–1979* (New York: New York Univ. Press, 1981); and Daniel Yergin, *The Prize: The Epic Quest for Oil, Money, and Power* (New York: Simon and Schuster, 1991).

4. Secret memorandum from Hector Prud'homme, World Bank Loan Department, to Sommers and Clark, 12 Dec. 1951, and Garner letter to Mossadegh, 28 Dec. 1951, both CF:OCI, box 31, folder 9, WBGA; undated secret draft memorandum to Prud'homme and Miss

Ruth Rieber, daughter/secretary of Torkild Rieber [approx. late Dec. 1951], CF:OCI, box 31, folder 2, WBGA; World Bank press release, 3 Apr. 1952, CF:OCI, box 32, folder 1, WBGA.

5. Unattributed memorandum on principal proposals, 22 Oct. 1952, CF:OCI, box 31, folder 7, WBGA; unattributed memorandum on the AIOC annual report and accounts, 27 Oct. 1951, CF:OCI, box 31, folder 1, WBGA; secret Hoar file memorandum on Anglo-Iranian oil, 10 Nov. 1951, unattributed secret memorandum on principal points discussed with both parties, 15 Nov. 1951, draft proposal to bank's board of directors, 16 Nov. 1951, and text of Mossadegh report to the Majlis, 25 Nov. 1951, all CF:OCI, box 31, folder 9, WBGA; background notes, Feb. 1952, CF:OCI, box 32, folder 1, WBGA; Graves, "Bank as International Mediator," 595–610.

6. Secret unattributed memorandum on the World Bank proposals, 29 Nov. 1951, CF:OCI, box 32, folder 4, WBGA. See also record of a meeting with representatives of World Bank and AIOC, 30 Nov. 1951, secret notes of meeting at House of Commons, 30 Nov. 1951, secret notes of meeting of 30 Nov. 1951 in Sir Roger Makins's office, secret notes on meeting in Garner's office, 4 Dec. 1951, and secret notes of meeting at AIOC main office, 1 Dec. 1951, all CF:OCI, box 31, folder 8, WBGA; and secret Prud'homme file memo, 6 Dec. 1951, CF:OCI, box 31, folder 9, WBGA.

7. Secret preliminary draft no. 3 of bank proposal, 18 Dec. 1951, CF:OCI, box 32, folder 4, WBGA; revised provisional draft, 28 Dec. 1951, CF:OCI, box 31, folder 1, WBGA; Garner letter to Mossadegh, 28 Dec. 1951, CF:OCI, box 31, folder 9, WBGA; Garner letter to British Ambassador Sir Oliver Franks, 2 Jan. 1952, CF:OCI, box 31, folder 10, WBGA.

8. Undated secret draft memorandum to Prud'homme and Miss Rieber [approx. late Dec. 1951], CF:OCI, box 31, folder 2, WBGA; confidential Graves wire to Garner, 28 Dec. 1951, CF:OCI, box 31, folder 9, WBGA; secretary's memorandum on Iran, 27 Dec. 1951, and translation of letter from Louis Goffin, Belgian Minister to Tehran, to Paul Van Zeeland, Belgian Minister of Foreign Affairs, for Basyn, 29 Dec. 1951, both CF:OCI, box 31, folder 9, WBGA.

9. Secret Prud'homme letter no. 3 to Garner, 2 Jan. 1952, CF:OCI, box 31, folder 10, WBGA. See also secret Prud'homme letter no. 2 to Garner, 1 Jan. 1952, and Prud'homme telegram to Garner, 2 Jan. 1952, both ibid.

10. Secret Prud'homme letter no. 4 to Garner, 3 Jan. 1952, CF:OCI, box 31, folder 10, WBGA. See also confidential Garner letter to Mossadegh, 28 Dec. 1951, Mossadegh letter to Garner, 3 Jan. 1952, and Prud'homme telegrams to Garner, 3 and 4 Jan. 1952, all ibid.; and secret unattributed observations on prime minister's letter, 6 Feb. 1952, CF:OCI, box 32, folder 1, WBGA.

11. Prud'homme telegram to Garner, 4 Jan. 1952, CF:OCI, box 31, folder 10, WBGA; AIOC memorandum, 6 Feb. 1952, CF:OCI, box 32, folder 1, WBGA; secret Prud'homme file memorandum on meeting with British, 1 Feb. 1952, unattributed notes for negotiating, 6 Feb. 1952, and AIOC's aide-mémoire, 6 Feb. 1952, all CF:OCI, box 31, folder 1, WBGA; Prud'homme telegram to Garner [Jan. 1952], and draft Garner letter to Mossadegh, 5 Jan. 1952, both CF:OCI, box 32, folder 4, WBGA; secret preliminary draft no. 4 bank proposal, 7 Jan. 1952, CF:OCI, box 31, folder 10, WBGA; secret unattributed observations on prime minister's letter to Garner, 6 Feb. 1952, CF:OCI, box 32, folder 1, WBGA.

12. Secret Prud'homme letter to Loy Henderson, American Ambassador to Iran, 14 Jan. 1952, and secret Prud'homme memorandum to Garner, 31 Jan. 1952, both CF:OCI, box 31, folder 10, WBGA. See also notes of meeting between Prud'homme and Majlis oil commission, 8 Mar. 1952, CF:OCI, box 32, folder 1, WBGA.

13. Confidential Clark letter to Sommers, 19 Feb. 1952, CF:OCI, box 32, folder 1, WBGA. See also unattributed background notes, Feb. 1952, and acting secretary's memorandum to executive directors and alternates, 8 Feb. 1952, both ibid.; and bank aide-mémoire for Iran, 19 Feb. 1952, CF:OCI, box 32, folder 4, WBGA.

14. Unattributed memorandum on Persia, 28 Feb. 1952, CF:OCI, box 32, folder 1, WBGA. See also Prud'homme secret comments on aide-mémoire, 26 Feb. 1952, Garner letter to Black, 6 Mar. 1952, Prud'homme telegrams to Garner, 9 and 12 Mar. 1952, Garner cable to Prud'homme, 14 Mar. 1952, Prud'homme letter to Mossadegh, 17 Mar. 1952, and confidential Prud'homme memorandum to Garner, 25 Apr. 1952, all ibid.; secret memorandum on meeting with World Bank representatives held in the Foreign Secretary's room, 22 Feb. 1952, and secret record of a meeting held in the Foreign Office, 21 Feb. 1952, both CF:OCI, box 31, folder 8, WBGA; and confidential Prud'homme file memorandum on Makki's trip, 30 July 1952, CF:OCI, box 32, folder 2, WBGA.

15. Summary of developments, 20 Mar. 1952, CF:OCI, box 31, folder 2, WBGA. See also translation of engineer Hassibi's press interview, 16 Mar. 1952, CF:OCI, box 31, folder 2, WBGA; and Prud'homme telegrams to Garner, 7, 9, 12, 13, and 16 Mar. 1952, notes on meeting between Prud'homme and Majlis oil commission, 8 Mar. 1952, confidential aide-mémoire, 10 Mar. 1952, Garner telegrams to Prud'homme, 12 and 14 Mar. 1952, Prud'homme letter to Dr. Shayegan, 13 Mar. 1952, contents of Hassibi interview, 16 Mar. 1952, Prud'homme letter to Mossadegh, 17 Mar. 1952, Mossadegh letter to Prud'homme, 27 Mar. 1952, draft cable to Mossadegh, 28 Mar. 1952, Garner wire to British prime minister Sir Anthony Eden, 1 Apr. 1952, World Bank press release, 3 Apr. 1952, Garner letter to Mossadegh, 4 Apr. 1952, Henderson letter to Prud'homme, 18 Apr. 1952, and Prud'homme memorandum to Garner, 8 May 1952, all CF:OCI, box 32, folder 1, WBGA.

16. Garner draft letter to Nasser, 24 Nov. 1952, CF:OCI, box 32, folder 2, WBGA. See also secret Prud'homme file memorandum on meeting in Garner's office, 24 Sept. 1952, secret Prud'homme file memorandum on meeting between Makki and Black, 26 Sept. 1952, Prud'homme file memorandum on the visit of Makki, Parssa, and Mahloudji, 14 Oct. 1952, and secret Prud'homme file memorandum on the meeting in Garner's office, 14 Oct. 1952, all CF:OCI, box 31, folder 7, WBGA; F. G. Bochenski memorandum on Iran's finances, 6 June 1952, Sommers memorandum to Garner, 30 Sept. 1952, and confidential summary report on the financial situation of Iran, 1953, all CF:OCI, box 32, folder 2, WBGA; and secret Henderson telegram to State Department, forwarded to Prud'homme, 7 Apr. 1952, Prud'homme memorandum to Garner, 7 Apr. 1952, Henderson telegram to Garner, 23 Apr. 1952, confidential Prud'homme file memorandum on meeting between World Bank and the British, with attached draft memorandum, 30 Apr. 1952, and secret Prud'homme file memorandum on Djahangir Bousheri's trip, 9 May 1952, all CF:OCI, box 32, folder 1, WBGA.

17. Mary Ann Heiss, "The United States, Great Britain, and the Creation of the Iranian Oil Consortium, 1953–1954," *International History Review* 16 (Aug. 1994): 511–35; Gabriel Kolko, *Confronting the Third World: United States Foreign Policy, 1945–1980* (New York: Pantheon, 1988), 72–77; Elm, *Oil, Power, and Principle,* 310–31.

18. This episode is described in Graves, "Bank as International Mediator," 610–27. World Bank archival records on this episode are not yet open to researchers.

19. Ibid.; David E. Lilienthal, "Another 'Korea' in the Making?" *Collier's* 128 (4 Aug. 1951): 22–23, 56–58, and *The Journals of David E. Lilienthal,* vol. 3: *Venturesome Years, 1950–1955* (New York: Harper and Row, 1966), chap. 2.

20. Dennis Kux, *India and the United States: Estranged Democracies, 1941–1991* (Washington, D.C.: National Defense Univ. Press, 1992), 150, 152.

21. Ibid., 152.

22. For bank's efforts in connection with the High Dam see Graves, "Bank as International Mediator," 627–43.

There are numerous accounts of the events surrounding the construction of the dam and the subsequent Suez Crisis. Representative historical works include Peter L. Hahn, *The United States, Great Britain, and Egypt, 1945–1956: Strategy and Diplomacy in the Early Cold War* (Chapel Hill: Univ. of North Carolina Press, 1991); Diane B. Kunz, *The Economic Diplomacy of the Suez Crisis* (Chapel Hill: Univ. of North Carolina Press, 1991); Keith Kyle, *Suez* (New York: St. Martin's, 1991); W. Scott Lucas, *Divided We Stand: Britain, the US and the Suez Crisis* (London: Hodder and Stoughton, 1991); David Carlton, *Britain and the Suez Crisis,* Making Contemporary Britain series, ed. Anthony Selden (London: Blackwell, 1988); Wm. Roger Louis and Roger Owen, eds., *Suez 1956: The Crisis and Its Consequences* (Oxford, UK: Clarendon, 1989); Selwyn Ilan Troen and Moshe Shemesh, eds., *The Suez-Sinai Crisis, 1956: Retrospective and Reappraisal* (New York: Columbia Univ. Press, 1990); Robert A. Divine, *Eisenhower and the Cold War* (Oxford, UK: Oxford Univ. Press, 1981), 71–104; and Wm. Roger Louis, "Dulles, Suez, and the British," in *John Foster Dulles and the Diplomacy of the Cold War,* ed. Richard Immerman (Princeton, N.J.: Princeton Univ. Press, 1990), 133–58.

Accounts by participants include Jacques Georges-Picot, *The Real Suez Crisis: The End of a Great Nineteenth Century Work,* trans. W. G. Rogers (New York: Harcourt Brace Jovanovich, 1975); Selwyn Lloyd, *Suez 1956: A Personal Account* (London: Jonathan Cape, 1978); Russell Braddon, *Suez: Splitting of a Nation* (London: Collins, 1973); Hugh Thomas, *Suez* (New York: Harper and Row, 1966); Dwight D. Eisenhower, *The White House Years,* vol. 2: *Waging Peace, 1956–1961* (Garden City, N.Y.: Doubleday, 1965), 20–57, 177–204; Anthony Eden, *The Memoirs of Anthony Eden, Earl of Avon,* vol. 4: *Full Circle* (London: Cassell, 1960); and Anthony Nutting, *No End of a Lesson: The Story of Suez* (New York: Clarkson N. Potter, 1967).

23. Bochenski memorandum to Didier Gregh, 22 Jan. 1954, Central Files, 1946–71: Operational Correspondence, Egypt [hereafter CF:OCE], box 8, folder 4, WBGA. For early relations between the bank and the Neguib-Nasser regime see also Black letter to H. E. Abdel Galeel El-Emary, Egyptian Minister of Finance and Economy, 11 Dec. 1952, and El-Emary letter to Black, Jan. 1953, both ibid.; and Black, 1964 interview transcript, John Foster Dulles Oral History Project, Princeton University Library [hereafter Dulles Oral History], 2–3 as found in Black papers, UGA.

24. President Gamal Abdel Nasser address on the Seventh Anniversary of the July 23 Revolution, 22 July 1959, and Nasser's address at the Land Distribution Ceremony at Edfina, 28 July 1959, both in *President Gamal Abdel-Nasser's Speeches and Press Interviews, 1959,* vol. 2 (Cairo: United Arab Republic Information Department, n.d.), 273, 322. See also Nasser, *The Philosophy of Revolution,* trans. Dar Al-Maaref (Buffalo, N.Y.: Economica Books, 1959), and "The Egyptian Revolution," *Foreign Affairs* 33 (Jan. 1955): 199–211.

25. For the Aswan international commission and its work see Bochenski memorandum to Gregh, 2 June 1953, and F. Dorsey Stephens, World Bank Middle Eastern representative, memorandum to Gregh, 9 Jan. 1954, both CF:OCE, box 8, folder 4, WBGA; and John Waterbury, *Hydropolitics in the Nile Valley* (Syracuse, N.Y.: Syracuse Univ. Press, 1979), 98–105.

26. Stephens letter to Rucinski, 9 Jan. 1954, CF:OCE, box 8, folder 4, WBGA. For further bank efforts to improve its relations with Egypt see confidential Bochenski memorandum,

1 Feb. 1954, and Stephens letter to Gregh, 16 Feb. 1954, both ibid.; John Exter letter to Stephens, 25 June 1954, CF:OCE, box 8, folder 5, WBGA; and "Common Sense and Economic
Aid," Black address to the National Farm Institute of Des Moines, 18 Feb. 1956, Black papers, box 3, folder 8, UGA.

For the bank's concern for its reputation in the Middle East see John C. de Wilde letter
to Gregh, 1 Feb. 1955, Cornelius Van H. Engert letter to Iliff, 16 June 1950, and Gregh letter
to de Wilde, 16 Feb. 1955, all CF:OCE, box 8, folder 5, WBGA.

27. Confidential Bochenski file memorandum on conversations with Egyptian representatives, 25 Sept. 1954, CF:OCE, box 8, folder 5, WBGA. See also letter to Black from Hussein Fahmy, Egyptian Permanent Council for the Development of National Production, 2
Nov. 1954, ibid.

28. Black letter to Ahmed Hussein, Egyptian Ambassador to the United States, 4 Apr.
1955, CF:OCE, box 8, folder 5, WBGA. See also letters to Hathaway from H. A. Morrice, Sudanese Irrigation Adviser, 3 and 27 Dec. 1954, confidential de Wilde file memorandum on
conversations with Dr. Mohammed Selim of the Egyptian National Production Council,
6 Mar. 1955, Stephens letter to Moffatt, 11 Apr. 1955, Stephens letter to Gregh, 14 Apr. 1955,
unattributed "Notes on the Nile Waters Controversy," 27 Apr. 1955, undated unattributed
"Nile Waters" memorandum [approx. Aug. 1955], de Wilde memorandum to Rucinski, 19
Aug. 1955, and confidential Moffatt file memorandum on conversation with State Department officials, 22 Aug. 1955, all CF:OCE, box 8, folder 5, WBGA; and confidential Stephens
letter to Rucinski, 1 Nov. 1955, and confidential Rucinski file memorandum, 26 Nov. 1955,
both CF:OCE, box 9, folder 1, WBGA.

29. Alfred E. Matter memorandum to Dr. E. Wayne Rembert, 7 Nov. 1955, CF:OCE, box
9, folder 1, WBGA. See also Black letter to Hussein, 4 Apr. 1955, CF:OCE, box 8, folder 5,
WBGA; and confidential Stephens letter to Rucinski, 1 Nov. 1955, and letter to Rucinski
from IBRD Paris Office, 16 Jan. 1956, both CF:OCE, box 9, folder 1, WBGA.

30. Hahn, *United States, Great Britain, and Egypt,* 186–94.

31. Black interview, Dulles Oral History, 28. For bank concern about being viewed as an
Anglo-American agent see confidential Sommers file memorandum, 19 Jan. 1956, CF:OCE,
box 9, folder 1, WBGA.

Interestingly, the bank had earlier dissuaded American State Department officials from
offering aid to the Egyptians for preliminary work on the dam. Confidential Moffat file
memorandum on conversation with State Department officials, 22 Aug. 1955, CF:OCE, box
8, folder 5, WBGA; and Moffat file memoranda, 7 and 20 Sept. 1955, CF:OCE, box 9, folder
1, WBGA.

32. For bank efforts to speed the drafting of the loan agreement see Moffat memorandum to Rucinski, 6 Dec. 1955, CF:OCE, box 9, folder 1, WBGA.

33. Black interview, Dulles Oral History, 28; confidential note for record of Black meeting, 3–4 Feb. 1956, CF:OCE, box 9, folder 1, WBGA.

For the principal aspects of the Anglo-American–World Bank offers to fund the Aswan
High Dam and Nasser's reservations about them see Kunz, *Economic Diplomacy,* 59–60,
202–203.

For results of Black's trip to Egypt see Black cable to IBRD, 1 Feb. 1956, confidential note
for record of Black meeting, 3–4 Feb. 1956, and secretary's memorandum to the executive
directors, 14 Feb. 1956, all CF:OCE, box 9, folder 1, WBGA; and Kyle, *Suez,* 123–24.

34. Nutting, *No End of a Lesson,* 27. For growing Anglo-American reservations about

their ability and desire to work with Nasser on Aswan see Hahn, *United States, Great Britain, and Egypt,* 194–210; Kunz, *Economic Diplomacy,* 60–72; Lucas, *Divided We Stand,* 78, 111–15, 126–37; Kyle, *Suez,* 94–113, 124–26; Robert R. Bowie, "Eisenhower, Dulles, and the Suez Canal," in *Suez, 1956,* ed. Louis and Owen, 189–96; Carlton, *Britain and the Suez Crisis,* 28–33; Thomas, *Suez,* 18–23; and Lloyd, *Suez, 1956,* 59–72.

35. Black interview, Dulles Oral History, 14. See also Graves, "Bank as International Mediator," 639–43.

36. For fuller accounts of the course and consequences of the Suez Crisis see the works cited in note 22 above.

For Nasser's sense of insult see Nasser's speech at the Huckstep Barracks, 30 Mar. 1959, in *Nasser's Speeches and Press Interviews, 1959,* 198; Lucas, *Divided We Stand,* 139; and Kyle, *Suez,* 131, 133.

For the bank's efforts in clearing the Suez Canal see Kyle, *Suez,* 502, 507, 519, 521, 544–45; and Kunz, *Economic Diplomacy,* 179.

37. Wheeler syllabus of report on the U.N. Suez Canal Clearance Operation to Dag Hammarskjold, UN Secretary-General, 25 June 1957, Raymond A. Wheeler papers, box 22, folder 3, HIWRP; Theo Jean Kenyon, "Gen. Wheeler Praises United Nations as World's Greatest Force for Peace," *Peoria (IL) Journal Star,* 5 Oct. 1957; "A UN Team Clears the Suez Canal: 32 Ships of Seven Nations Write 'New Salvage History,'" undated UN Information Centre for the Middle East press feature, Wheeler papers, box 23, folder 22, HIWRP.

38. "A U.N. Team Clears the Suez Canal: 32 Ships of Seven Nations Write 'New Salvage History.'"

For some of the complicated diplomatic and political problems facing Wheeler see Wheeler letter to Col. Mahmoud Younis, Egyptian Canal Authority Chairman, 5 Jan. 1957, Wheeler letter to McCloy, 28 Jan. 1957, and Wheeler syllabus to Hammarskjold, 25 June 1957, all Wheeler papers, box 21, folder 12, HIWRP; Leonard Leddington for AP wire, 15 Dec. 1956, unattributed AP wire, 14 Dec. 1956, and unattributed translation from "La Bourse Egyptienne," 15 Dec. 1956, all Wheeler papers, box 23, folder 11, HIWRP; "Points Made by Col. Younis in His Speech at Farewell Dinner for General Wheeler," undated, Wheeler papers, box 24, folder 2, HIWRP; and "Clearance of the Suez Canal: Report of the Secretary General," 1 Nov. 1957, Wheeler papers, box 25, folder 1, HIWRP.

For widespread respect of Wheeler's efforts see memorandum for Zouheir Kuzbari, UN International Clearance Information Officer, to Aly Zhalil, UN International Clearance Deputy Director, 14 June 1957, Wheeler papers, box 21, folder 5, HIWRP; letter from G. Martinez-Cabanas, UN Suez Canal Clearance Group, to Dr. H. L. Keenleyside, UN Director-General of Technical Assistance Administration, 20 Dec. 1956, Wheeler papers, box 21, folder 11; letter to Wheeler from Theodore Podger, UK Salvage Unit at Port Said, 23 Jan. 1957, and letter to Wheeler from Lord Mountbatten, First Sea Lord of Great Britain, 25 Jan. 1957, both Wheeler papers, box 21, folder 12, HIWRP; Wheeler letter to Mr. Leontic, Veli Joze salvage firm, 11 Apr. 1957, Wheeler papers, box 22, folder 1, HIWRP; Wheeler letter to Nasser, 1 July 1957, Wheeler papers, box 22, folder 4, HIWRP; Col. Mahmoud Younis, "The Future of Suez," *World Petroleum* (Apr. 1958); and "Points made by Col. Younis in his speech at farewell dinner for General Wheeler," undated, Wheeler papers, box 24, folder 2, HIWRP.

For Wheeler's separation from politics see personal and confidential Wheeler letter to Black, Wheeler papers, box 21, folder 13, HIWRP; "Egyptians Termed Able to Operate Suez Canal," *Norfolk Virginian-Pilot,* 28 Sept. 1957; Kenyon, "Gen. Wheeler," *Peoria (IL) Journal*

Star, 5 Oct. 1957; "Wheeler's Confidence," *Egyptian Gazette,* 14 June 1957; and Wheeler letter to Raymond A. Hare, American Ambassador to Cairo, 6 Oct. 1959, Wheeler papers, box 22, folder 13, HIWRP.

For Wheeler's commendation of the Egyptian operation of the canal see "Gen. Wheeler's Words Backed by 4,000 Ships," *Egyptian Gazette,* 6 Sept. 1957; "Egyptians Termed Able to Operate Suez Canal"; "Wheeler Praises Egyptians," *New York Times,* 5 Sept. 1957; "Wheeler's Confidence"; and translated Egyptian newspaper reports from United Nations Information Centre for the Middle East, Aug. 1959, Wheeler papers, box 23, folder 24, HIWRP.

For the bank's role as fiscal agent and its work in obtaining dredging see Wheeler letter to Hare, 6 Oct. 1959, Wheeler papers, box 22, folder 13, HIWRP; and "Clearance of the Suez Canal: Report of the Secretary General," 1 Nov. 1957, Wheeler papers, box 25, folder 1, HIWRP.

39. "Black Says Cairo Mission is Purely Financial," *Egyptian Gazette,* 1 Jan. 1959. See also Graves, "The Bank as International Mediator," 641–42; *New York Times,* 30 Apr. 1958 and 1 Mar. 1959; and *London Times,* 28 Feb. 1958.

For canal company negotiations see "Suez Discussions," World Bank press release, 23 Jan. 1958, Wheeler papers, box 23, folder 23, HIWRP; Arnaldo Cortesi, "Prospects Held Good for a Pact on Suez Monetary Settlement," *New York Times,* 10 Apr. 1958; "New Nasser Move on Suez Reported," *New York Times,* 17 Apr. 1958; and "Compensation Set for the Suez Canal," *New York Times,* 14 July 1958.

For Anglo-French negotiations with Egypt see "Britain to Resume Talks with Egypt on Claims," *Washington Post,* 29 Aug. 1958.

For bank loans and assistance for Suez Canal see file memorandum by David L. Gordon, World Bank, 9 Dec. 1957, Wheeler papers, box 23, folder 9, HIWRP; UN Information Centre for the Middle East press release, 7 Apr. 1958, Wheeler papers, box 23, folder 23, HIWRP; "United Arab Republic: Appraisal of the Suez Canal Development Project," restricted World Bank Department of Technical Operations report, 8 Dec. 1959, Wheeler papers, box 25, folder 2, HIWRP; World Bank press release no. 615, 22 Dec. 1959, Wheeler papers, box 23, folder 24, HIWRP; Caruthers, "Nasser Hopeful on Suez Parley"; "Big Job at Suez," editorial, *Engineering News-Record,* 14 July 1960; Jay Walz, "Accord Held Near on Loan for Suez," *New York Times,* 27 Aug. 1959; and Wheeler letter to Younis, 1 May 1958, Wheeler papers, box 22, folder 13, HIWRP.

5. Food and Agriculture in the International Realm

1. For the development and transportation of large-scale grain production in the New World see John T. Schlebecker, *Whereby We Thrive: A History of American Farming, 1607 to 1972* (Ames: Iowa State Univ. Press, 1975), esp. 151–73; Edwin G. Nourse, *Government in Relation to Agriculture* (Washington, D.C.: Brookings, 1940), 865–66; Edwin A. Pratt, *Agricultural Organisation: Its Rise, Principles and Practice Abroad and at Home* (London: P. S. King, 1912), 9; Gary W. Wynia, *Argentina: Illusions and Realities* (New York: Holmes and Meier, 1986), 31–34; Samuel Wadham, *Australian Farming, 1788–1965* (Melbourne: F. W. Cheshire, 1967), 18, 22–24, 37, 39; Louis Bernard Schmidt, "The Agricultural Revolution in the Prairies and the Great Plains of the United States," *Agricultural History* 8 (Oct. 1934): 169–95; and V. D. Wickizer, "Shipping and Freight Rates in the Overseas Grain Trade," *Wheat Studies* 15 (Oct. 1938): 69, 118.

For subsequent agricultural depression see Helen C. Farnsworth, "Decline and Recovery of Wheat Prices in the 'Nineties," *Wheat Studies* 10 (June–July 1934): 289–341; Christabel S. Orwin and Edith H. Whetham, *History of British Agriculture, 1846–1914* (Newton Abbot, UK: David and Charles, 1971), 179, 240–41, 249–61, 265, 268, 276–77, 285–86, 343–44, 356–57, 385; Pratt, *Agricultural Organisation,* 10; O. V. Wells, "The Depression of 1873–79," *Agricultural History* 11 (July 1937): 237–49; and T. W. Fletcher, "The Great Depression of English Agriculture, 1873–1896," in *Essays in Agrarian History,* vol. 2, ed. W. E. Minchinton (New York: Augustus M. Kelley, 1968), 241–55.

2. P. Lamartine Yates, *Food Production in Western Europe: An Economic Survey of Agriculture in Six Countries* (London: Longmans, Green, 1940), 85–86; Einar Jensen, *Danish Agriculture, Its Economic Development: A Description and Economic Analysis Centering on the Free Trade Epoch, 1870–1930* (Copenhagen: J. H. Schultz Forlag, 1937), esp. 178–81.

3. Orwin and Whetham, *British Agriculture,* 194–95, 197–99, 202, 278–81, 374–78; Yujiro Hayami and Vernon W. Ruttan, *Agricultural Development: An International Perspective* (Baltimore, Md.: Johns Hopkins Univ. Press, 1971), 137; G. E. Fussell, "The Collection of Agricultural Statistics in Great Britain: Its Origin and Evolution," *Agricultural History* 18 (Oct. 1944): 163–67; Sir E. John Russell, "Rothamsted and Its Experiment Station," *Agricultural History* 16 (Oct. 1942): 161–83; Raymond Phineas Stearns, "Agricultural Adaptation in England, 1875–1900: Part I," *Agricultural History* 6 (Apr. 1932): 84–101.

4. Hayami and Ruttan, *Agricultural Development,* 142–43; H. C. Knoblauch et al., *State Agricultural Experiment Stations: A History of Research Policy and Procedure,* USDA Miscellaneous Publication no. 904 (Washington, D.C.: USDA, May 1962), 14, 29–52; Gladys L. Baker, Wayne D. Rasmussen, Vivian Wiser, and Jane M. Porter, *Century of Service: The First 100 Years of the United States Department of Agriculture* (Washington, D.C.: GPO for the USDA Centennial Committee, 1963), 24–25, 41–48, 50–51, 451; Alfred Charles True, *A History of Agricultural Experimentation and Research in the United States, 1607–1925, including a History of the United States Department of Agriculture,* USDA Miscellaneous Publication, no. 251 (Washington, D.C.: USDA, 1937); Earle D. Ross, "The Land-Grant College: A Democratic Adaptation," *Agricultural History* 15 (Jan. 1941): 26–36, and "The 'Father' of the Land-Grant College," *Agricultural History* 12 (Apr. 1938): 151–86; Charles E. Rosenberg, *No Other Gods: On Science and American Social Thought,* rev. and exp. ed. (Baltimore, Md.: Johns Hopkins Univ. Press, 1997), 153–99.

5. Pratt, *Agricultural Organisation,* 26; Nourse, *Government in Relation to Agriculture,* 872–76; Baker et al., *Century of Service,* 43–44; Grant McConnell, *The Decline of Agrarian Democracy* (Berkeley: Univ. of California Press, 1953); Hayami and Ruttan, *Agricultural Development,* 143; A. Hunter Dupree, *Science in the Federal Government: A History of Policies and Activities to 1940* (Cambridge, Mass.: Harvard Univ. Press, 1957), 181–82; A. B. Graham "Boys' and Girls' Agricultural Clubs," and J. Phil Campbell, "Action Programs in Education," *Agricultural History* 15 (Apr. 1941): 65–68, 68–71; Knowles A. Ryerson, "History and Significance of the Foreign Plant Introduction Work of the United States Department of Agriculture," *Agricultural History* 7 (July 1933): 121–28; B. T. Galloway, "Plant Pathology: A Review of the Development of the Science in the United States," *Agricultural History* 2 (Apr. 1928): 49–60.

6. Hayami and Ruttan, *Agricultural Development,* 147–48, 150; Paul C. Mangelsdorf, "Hybrid Corn," *Scientific American* 185 (Aug. 1951): 39–47; George F. Sprague, ed., *Corn and Corn Improvement* (New York: Academic, 1955); Herbert Kendall Hayes, *A Professor's*

Study of Hybrid Corn Makers: Prophets of Plenty (New Brunswick, N.J.: Rutgers Univ. Press, 1947); C. L. MacDowell, *Two Ears of Corn, by Way of the Chemical Kettle: The Life Story of Charles L. MacDowell* (Stonington, Conn.: Pequot, 1954); Tennessee Valley Authority, *The TVA Fertilizer Program* (Knoxville, Tenn.: TVA, Sept. 1965); Jesse W. Markham, *The Fertilizer Industry* (Nashville, Tenn.: Vanderbilt Univ. Press, 1958); Vernon W. Ruttan, "Positive Policy in the Fertilizer Industry," *Journal of Political Economy* 68 (Dec. 1960): 634; H. H. Whetzel, "The History of Industrial Fellowships in the Department of Plant Pathology at Cornell University," *Agricultural History* 19 (Apr. 1945): 99–104.

7. Joseph C. Bailey, *Seaman A. Knapp: Schoolmaster of American Agriculture* (New York: Columbia Univ. Press, 1945); Rodney Cline, *The Life and Work of Seaman A. Knapp* (Nashville, Tenn.: George Peabody College for Teachers, 1936); Oscar B. Martin, *The Demonstration Work: Dr. Seaman A. Knapp's Contribution to Civilization* (San Antonio, Tex.: Naylor, 1941); Baker et al., *Century of Service*, 43–44.

8. John D. Black, *Agricultural Reform in the United States* (New York: McGraw-Hill, 1929), and *Federal-State-Local Relations in Agriculture* (Washington, D.C.: National Planning Association, 1950), and Black, ed., *Research in Farm Management: Scope and Method* (New York: Social Science Research Council, 1932); John R. Commons, *Labor and Administration* (New York: Macmillan, 1913), and *Myself* (New York: Macmillan, 1934); Baker et al., *Century of Service*, 48; Glenn L. Johnson, "Philosophic Foundation of Agricultural Economic Thought from World War II to the mid-1970s," in *A Survey of Agricultural Economics Literature*, vol. 4: *Agriculture in Economic Development, 1940s to 1990s*, ed. Lee R. Martin (Minneapolis: Univ. of Minnesota Press for the American Agricultural Economics Association, 1992), 976–81; Jensen, *Danish Agriculture*, ix; Mark Blaug, *Great Economists before Keynes* (New York: Cambridge Univ. Press, 1986), 56–57; James C. Malin, "The Background of the First Bill to Establish a Bureau of Markets, 1911–12," *Agricultural History* 6 (July 1932): 107–29.

9. As quoted in Kirkendall, *Social Scientists and Farm Politics*, 13. See also ibid., 1–7, 11–29; and Baker et al., *Century of Service*, 451.

10. Kirkendall, *Social Scientists and Farm Politics*, 1–7, 11–29; Baker et al., *Century of Service*, 43–45; Henry C. Taylor and Anne Dewees Taylor, *The Story of Agricultural Economics in the United States, 1840–1932: Men, Services, Ideas* (Ames: Iowa State Univ. Press, 1952).

11. For changing views of nutrition see David Lubbock, *The Boyd Orr View: From the Old World to the New, with Proposal for Action to Banish Hunger: The Late Lord Boyd Orr's Testament* (privately published, 1992), 23–24; and Baker et al., *Century of Service*, 36–37, 55, 83.

For WWI work on nutrition see Jay Cooke, "The Work of the Federal Food Administration," *Annals of the American Academy of Political and Social Science* 78 (July 1918): 181, 183–84; E. V. McCollum, "Some Essentials to a Safe Diet," *Annals of the American Academy of Political and Social Science* 74 (Nov. 1917): 95–108; J. F. Booth, "Our Hungry World," *Behind the Headlines* 8 (Feb. 1948): 4; Maxcy R. Dickson, "The Food Administration: Educator," *Agricultural History* 16 (Apr. 1942): 91–96; and Baker et al., *Century of Service*, 83.

12. Inger Johanne Lyngel, "The Oslo Breakfast–An Optimal Diet in One Meal: On the Scientification of Everyday Life as Exemplified by Food," trans. Alan Crozier, *Ethnologia Scandinavica* 28 (1998): 62–78, available at www.etn.lu.se/ethscand/text/1998/1998_62–76.PDF [accessed 5 Jan. 2004]; Warren C. Waite and John D. Black, "Nutrition and Agricultural Policy," *Annals of the American Academy of Political and Social Science* 188 (Nov. 1936): 221; Lord Boyd Orr, *As I Recall* (London: MacGibbon and Kee, 1966), 118.

13. For the early international scientific conferences see Frederick W. Kohlmeyer, "The

Movement toward International Cooperation in Food and Agriculture: Background of the FAO of the UN" (Ph.D. diss., Univ. of Minnesota, 1954), 26–27.

For the International Commission of Agriculture see Sergio Marchisio and Antonietta di Blase, *The Food and Agriculture Organization (FAO),* International Organization and the Evolution of World Society Series (Dordrecht, Neth.: M. Nijhoff, 1991), 4–5; Yates, *Food Production,* 26–27; Kohlmeyer, "Movement toward International Cooperation," 20–22; and Lyman Cromwell, *The Structure of Private International Organizations* (Philadelphia, Pa.: George S. Ferguson, 1933), 313–18.

14. Kohlmeyer, "Movement toward International Cooperation," 90–92, 95; Yates, *Food Production,* 27; Marchisio and di Blase, *Food and Agriculture Organization,* 5–6; Olivia Rossetti Agresti, *David Lubin: A Study in Practical Idealism* (Berkeley: Univ. of California Press, 1941); Willard Thompson, *David Lubin: Sacramento's Pioneer Merchant-Philosopher* (Sacramento, Calif.: Sacramento County Historical Society, 1986); Azriel Louis Eisenberg, *Feeding the World: A Biography of David Lubin* (London: Abelard-Schuman, 1965).

15. As quoted in Kohlmeyer, "Movement toward International Cooperation," 97. See also ibid., 103–104; Marchisio and di Blase, *Food and Agriculture Organization,* 5–6; David Lubin, *The International Institute of Agriculture and Its Influence on Economic Welfare: Reply to Some Comments Made by the Minister of Agriculture of France* (Rome: IIA, 2 Mar. 1911); U.S. Congress, House Committee on Agriculture, *Report of the Delegation of the United States to the General Assembly of the International Institute of Agriculture, 1911,* 62d Cong., 2d sess. (Washington, D.C.: GPO, 1911); Asher Hobson, *The International Institute of Agriculture: An Historical and Critical Analysis of Its Organization, Activities, and Policies of Administration* (Berkeley: Univ. of California Press, 1931); Luciano Tosi, *Alle Origini della FAO: Le relazioni tra l'Instituto Internazionale di Agricoltura e la Società delle Nazioni* [The Origins of the FAO: The Relations between the International Institute of Agriculture and the League of Nations] (Milan: Franco Angeli, 1989); and Louis J. Dop, *Le Présent et l'Avenir de l'Institut International d'Agriculture* [The Present and the Future of the International Institute of Agriculture] (Rome: IIA, 1912).

16. Yates, *Food Production,* 27–30; Kohlmeyer, "Movement toward International Cooperation," 28, 100–102, 104, 108–11, 118, 121; Tosi, *Alle Origini della FAO;* Hobson, *International Institute of Agriculture;* Cesare Longobardi, *International Collaboration in Agriculture* (Rome: Villa Umberto I, 1946); A. G. McCall, "The Development of Soil Science," *Agricultural History* 5 (Apr. 1931): 43–56.

17. For agriculture in World War I see Gifford Pinchot, "An Agricultural Policy for the United States in War Time," *Annals of the American Academy of Political and Social Science* 74 (Nov. 1917): 185; Wadham, *Australian Farming,* 42; Schlebecker, *Whereby We Thrive,* 209–12; Francois Monod, "Food for France and Its Public Control," *Annals of the American Academy of Political and Social Science* 74 (Nov. 1917): 86; G. E. Britnell and V. C. Fowke, *Canadian Agriculture in War and Peace, 1935–50* (Stanford, Calif.: Stanford Univ. Press, 1962), 23–62; and Almon R. Wright, "Food Purchases of the Allies, 1917–1918," *Agricultural History* 16 (Apr. 1942): 97–102.

For postwar recession see L. D. H. Weld, "The After-War Fall in Meat Prices," *Annals of the American Academy of Political and Social Science* 89 (May 1920): 51–54; James H. Shideler, *Farm Crisis, 1919–1923* (Berkeley: Univ. of California Press, 1957); Britnell and Fowke, *Canadian Agriculture,* 52–61; Joseph S. Davis, *On Agricultural Policy, 1926–1938* (Stanford, Calif.: Food Research Institute, 1939), 80–82, 174–75; and Wadham, *Australian Farming,* 45, 47.

18. P. Lamartine Yates, *So Bold an Aim: Ten Years of International Co-operation toward Freedom from Want* (Rome: FAO, 1955), 33, and *Food Production*, 85, 88–94, 99–100, 159–63, 313–17, 397–99, 405–7; Kohlmeyer, "Movement toward International Cooperation," 127; Garraty, *Great Depression*, 1–84; Davis, *On Agricultural Policy*, 173–76; Bruce R. Davidson, *European Farming in Australia: An Economic History of Australian Farming* (Amsterdam: Elsevier Scientific, 1981), 299, 301; "The Problem of Chronic Surpluses," undated, unattributed memorandum, Record Group (RG) 3, box 2, file 219, folder 2, Food and Agriculture Organization Archive, Rome, Italy [hereafter FAOA]; Chester C. Davis, "The Agricultural Adjustment Act and National Recovery," *Journal of Farm Economics* 18 (1936): 229–43; Edwin G. Nourse, Joseph S. Davis, and John D. Black, *Three Years of the Agricultural Adjustment Administration* (Washington, D.C.: Brookings, 1937); Kirkendall, *Social Scientists and Farm Politics*, 63–192; V. D. Wickizer, *The World Coffee Economy with Special Reference to Control Schemes* (Stanford, Calif.: Food Research Institute, 1943), 136–65.

19. For British system and its criticism see Rainer Schickele, *Agricultural Policy: Farm Programs and National Welfare* (New York: McGraw-Hill, 1954); I. D. Blair, "Wartime Problems of English Agriculture," *Agricultural History* 15 (Jan. 1941): 12–19; and Orr, *As I Recall*, 112, 115.

For other countries' efforts see Gordon W. Gunderson, "History of the National School Lunch Program," excerpted from *National School Lunch Program: Background and Development* (Washington, D.C.: USDA Food and Nutrition Service, n.d.), available at www.cde.state.co.us/cdenutritran/download/pdf/SEC26.pdf [accessed 5 Jan. 2004].

20. For the counterproductive results of some national agricultural support policies see Sally H. Clarke, *Regulation and the Revolution in United States Farm Productivity* (Cambridge, UK: Cambridge Univ. Press, 1994), esp. 3–6, 13–17; and John K. Galbraith and John D. Black, "The Maintenance of Agricultural Production during Depression: The Explanations Reviewed," *Journal of Political Economy* 46 (June 1938): 305–23.

For League work see Kohlmeyer, "Movement toward International Cooperation," 139, 141, 143–47; League Economic Committee, *The Agricultural Crisis*, vol. 1 (Geneva: League of Nations, 1931); and International Labour Office, *Intergovernmental Commodity Control Agreements* (Montreal, Can.: ILO, 1943), xiii.

For international commodity agreements see ILO, *Intergovernmental Commodity Control Agreements;* Joseph S. Davis, "New International Wheat Agreements," *Wheat Studies* 19 (Nov. 1942): 25–79; Alonzo E. Taylor, "The International Wheat Conferences during 1930–31," *Wheat Studies* 7 (Aug. 1931): 439–66; and Wickizer, *World Coffee Economy*, 166–239.

21. As quoted in Waite and Black, "Nutrition," 220. See also ibid., 219–21; Yates, *So Bold an Aim*, 36; Kohlmeyer, "Movement toward International Cooperation," 197–98; John Boyd Orr, *Food, Health and Income: Report on a Survey of Adequacy of Diet in Relation to Income* (London: Macmillan, 1936); Lubbock, *Boyd Orr View*, 25; and F. L. McDougall, "Food and Welfare," *Geneva Studies* 9 (Nov. 1938): 12, 27–28.

22. Orr, *As I Recall*, 119; Waite and Black, "Nutrition," 219, 222–27; McDougall, "Food and Welfare," 9–10, 49, 52, 54–56; Kohlmeyer, "Movement toward International Cooperation," 196, 199; Marchisio and di Blase, *Food and Agriculture Organization*, 8.

Bruce graduated from Cambridge University, was decorated during World War I, served as a delegate to the League of Nations assemblies on five different occasions, was a member of the League Council, served as Australian prime minister, represented Australia at several imperial and economic conferences in the 1920s and early 1930s, and was later the first chairman of the World Food Council, an organ of the FAO (Kohlmeyer, "Movement toward International Cooperation," 199–200).

23. McDougall, "Food and Welfare," 14–15. See also ibid., 26–27, 35, 41, 45–48, 50; Kohlmeyer, "Movement toward International Cooperation," 126–27, 142, 148–49, 194–95, 201, 204–205, 207, 211, 213–14; Waite and Black, "Nutrition," 219; Marchisio and di Blase, *Food and Agriculture Organization,* 9; and Yates, *So Bold an Aim,* 38–42.

24. *New York Times* as quoted in McDougall, "Food and Welfare," 14. See also ibid., 31, 44; Kohlmeyer, "Movement toward International Cooperation," 206–11; Marchisio and di Blase, *Food and Agriculture Organization,* 9; undated statement by the delegation of Great Britain to Section I, RG 3, box 5, folder 2, FAOA; and Booth, "Our Hungry World," 4–5.

25. Yates, *So Bold an Aim,* 44; Bela Gold, *Wartime Economic Planning in Agriculture: A Study in the Allocation of Resources* (New York: Columbia Univ. Press, 1949), 327–45, 373; Jules Backman, *Rationing and Price Control in Great Britain* (Washington, D.C.: Brookings, 1943), 25; Lubbock, *Boyd Orr View,* 26; Sir John Orr and David Lubbock, *Feeding the People in War-time* (London: Macmillan, 1940); Britnell and Fowke, *Canadian Agriculture,* 145–66; comments of Dr. Frank G. Boudreau, FAO Interim Committee Technical Committee on Nutrition and Food Management, proceedings of fourth plenary meeting, 18 Oct. 1945, RG 59, Decimal File 1945–49, 501.SA, box 2292, U.S. National Archives, College Park, Md. [hereafter NACP].

26. C. Addison Hickman, *Our Farm Program and Foreign Trade: A Conflict of National Policies* (New York: Council on Foreign Relations, 1949), 13–15; Yates, *So Bold an Aim,* 45.

27. As quoted in Evang, *Norway's Food in Peace and War,* 4. For postwar hopes see also Marchisio and di Blase, *Food and Agriculture Organization,* 9; Orr, *As I Recall,* 157–59, 161; Ritchie Calder, "The Man and His Message," *Survey Graphic* 37 (Mar. 1948): 99–103; and President Roosevelt's message to the delegates of the conference, 17 May 1943, as cited in "The Future for Which We Fight: Freedom from Want," 1944 discussion guide on the UN Conference on Food and Agriculture by the General Federation of Women's Clubs, RG 3, box 4, file 408, FAOA.

28. Marchisio and di Blase, *Food and Agriculture Organization,* 3; Howson and Moggridge, *Wartime Diaries,* 9; Irvin M. May Jr., *Marvin Jones: The Public Life of an Agrarian Advocate* (College Station: Texas A&M Univ. Press, 1980), 199–200, 203; Orr, *As I Recall,* 158.

29. As quoted in Calder, "Man and His Message," 101. See also *Life* (3 May 1943): 22; *Fortune* (Aug. 1943): 134; Yates, *So Bold an Aim,* 108; Orr, *As I Recall,* 160–61; and "The Future for Which We Fight," RG3, box 4, file 408, FAOA.

30. As quoted in Booth, "Our Hungry World," 6. See also Yates, *So Bold an Aim,* 49–50; Howson and Moggridge, *Wartime Diaries,* 13, 16–18, 34–36; undated statement by the delegation of Great Britain to Section I, RG 3, box 5, folder 2, FAOA; and Gunnar Myrdal's 1965 McDougall Memorial Lecture, 24 Nov. 1965, Dodd papers, box 2, folder 2, HIWRP.

31. For USDA position see Howson and Moggridge, *Wartime Diaries,* 13, 16, 27–29, 40–43. For Latin American support see ibid., 30, 43, 48; and Orr, *As I Recall,* 185–88.

32. For the British position on these issues see Howson and Moggridge, *Wartime Diaries,* 10, 24–25, 27–34, 37–44; undated statement by the delegation of Great Britain to Section I, RG 3, box 5, folder 2, FAOA; and *Time* (5 Nov. 1945): 28–29.

For State Department and Clayton's views see Howson and Moggridge, *Wartime Diaries,* 16, 30, 34, 40–41, 43–44, 47.

33. For a brief summary of the Hot Springs resolutions see "The Future for Which We Fight," RG3, box 4, file 408, FAOA.

34. Boudreau comments, proceedings of the fourth plenary meeting, 18 Oct. 1945, RG 59, Decimal File 1945–49, 501.SA, box 2292, NACP.

35. Comments of D. Wilson, New Zealand delegate, proceedings of the fifth plenary session, 20 Oct. 1945, RG 59, Decimal File 1945–49, 501.SA, box 2292, NACP. For emphasis on immediate action see also comments of E. Perez Cisneros, Cuban delegate, proceedings of the seventh plenary meeting, 22 Oct. 1945, and comments of McDougall, Boudreau, Dr. L. A. H. Peters (Chairman of Interim Commission's Committee on Agricultural Production), Dr. D. B. Finn (Chairman of the Interim Commission's Technical Committee on Fisheries), and Nicholas G. Lely (Greek delegate), proceedings of the fourth plenary meeting, 18 Oct. 1945, all RG 59, Decimal Files 1945–49, 501.SA, box 2292, NACP; and Report of Commission "A," 23 Oct. 1945, and Report of Nutrition and Food Management Committee, 28 Oct. 1945, both RG 59, Decimal File 1945–49, 501.SA, box 2293, NACP.

For emphasis on FAO's technical and statistical work see Rosenberger, "The FAO," RG 1.0, series K9, FAOA; Marchisio and di Blase, *Food and Agriculture Organization,* 11; Yates, *So Bold an Aim,* 56; comments of Dr. Becker, Chairman of the Interim Commission's Statistics Committee, proceedings of the fourth plenary meeting, 18 Oct. 1945, comments of R. J. Noble, Australian delegate, proceedings of the sixth plenary meeting, 20 Oct. 1945, and Tolley comments, proceedings of fifth plenary meeting, 20 Oct. 1945, all RG 59, Decimal File 1945–49, 501.SA, box 2292, NACP; and Report of Commission "A," 23 Oct. 1945, RG 59, Decimal File 1945–49, 501.SA, box 2293, NACP.

36. Orr, *As I Recall,* 161; confidential telegram from UK delegation in Quebec to Foreign Office, 28 Oct. 1945, Foreign Office Records [hereafter FO with appropriate lot and file numbers] 371/45647, British Public Record Office, Kew, England [hereafter PRO]; third report of the General Committee to the Conference, proceedings of the eighth plenary meeting, 27 Oct. 1945, RG 59, Decimal File 1945–49, 501.SA, box 2293, NACP.

For Orr see Orr, *As I Recall,* 13–164; Calder, "Man and His Message," 99, 100; and Lubbock, *Boyd Orr View,* i–vi, 25.

37. Orr comments, proceedings of the eighth plenary meeting, 27 Oct. 1945, RG 59, Decimal File 1945–49, 501.SA, box 2293, NACP. See also Orr comments, proceedings of the tenth plenary meeting, 1 Nov. 1945, ibid.; Orr, *As I Recall,* 164; and Rosenberger, "The FAO," RG 1.0, series K9, FAOA.

38. Pearson comments, proceedings of tenth plenary meeting, 1 Nov. 1945, RG 59, Decimal Files 1945–49, 501.SA, box 2293, NACP.

6. The Limits of Internationalism

1. For the postwar food crisis see J. W. Evans, "The Facts in the Case," *Survey Graphic* 37 (Mar. 1948): 105, 107, 179; FAO, *The State of Food and Agriculture: 1947* (Geneva: FAO, Aug. 1947), 5–8; and FAO press statement on the 20 May meeting on urgent food problems, 9 May 1947, RG 59, Decimal File 1945–49, 501.SA, box 2307, NACP.

2. For emphasis on facts see report of Professor André Mayer, Chairman of FAO Executive Committee, to FAO Conference's fourth plenary meeting, 3 Sept. 1946, RG 59, Decimal File 1945–49, 501.SA, box 2296, NACP.

3. Ibid. For international staff see also FAO Information Service Bulletin, 2 Apr. 1946, RG 59, Decimal File 1945–49, 501.SA, box 2295, NACP; and Orr, *As I Recall,* 167–68.

4. Proceedings of the first plenary session of the Special Meeting on Urgent Food Problems, 20 May 1946, and proceedings of the sixth plenary session of the Special Meeting on Urgent Food Problems, 27 May 1946, both RG 59, Decimal File 1945–49, 501.SA, box 2307, NACP.

5. *Report of the Second Session of the FAO Council* as quoted in Yates, *So Bold an Aim,* 78–79; "Mobilizing against Hunger," FAO Information Service Bulletin, 6 June 1946, RG 59, Decimal Files 1945–49, 501.SA, box 2307, NACP.

For IEFC operations see Sir John Boyd Orr, "FAO: The Year Past, the Year Ahead," *United Nations Weekly Bulletin* 4 (1 Jan. 1948): 17–19; *Functions of a World Food Reserve: Scope and Limitations,* FAO Commodity Policy Studies, no. 10 (Rome: FAO, 1956), 45; Orr, *As I Recall,* 168–71; Marchisio and di Blase, *Food and Agriculture Organization,* 15–16; Evans, "Facts in the Case," 179, 181; Yates, *So Bold an Aim,* 57; and telegram to U.S. Secretary of State from John L. Stewart, U.S. Agricultural Attaché in Paris, 23 July 1947, RG 59, Decimal File 1945–49, 501.SA, box 2308, NACP.

6. Michael J. Hogan, *A Cross of Iron: Harry S. Truman and the Origins of the National Security State, 1945–1954* (New York: Cambridge Univ. Press, 1998); Tickner, *Gender in International Relations;* Campbell, *Writing Security;* Melvyn P. Leffler, *A Preponderance of Power: National Security, the Truman Administration, and the Cold War* (Stanford, Calif.: Stanford Univ. Press, 1992); Chester J. Pach Jr., *Arming the Free World: The Origins of the United States Military Assistance Program, 1945–1950* (Chapel Hill: Univ. of North Carolina Press, 1991); Walter LaFeber, *America, Russia, and the Cold War, 1945–1992,* 7th ed. (New York: McGraw-Hill, 1993); Joan Hoff, "The American Century: From Sarajevo to Sarajevo," in *The Ambiguous Legacy: U.S. Foreign Relations in the "American Century,"* ed. Michael J. Hogan (New York: Cambridge Univ. Press, 1999), 183–231.

7. "Proposals for a World Food Board," FAO memorandum to member nations for submission to the Second FAO Session in Copenhagen, 2 Sept. 1946, Treasury Files [hereafter T with appropriate lot file and folder number] 236/92, PRO; *Functions of a World Food Reserve,* 4, 47; Marchisio and di Blase, *Food and Agriculture Organization,* 16–17; Yates, *So Bold an Aim,* 80–81.

8. "Proposals for a World Food Board," FAO memorandum to member nations, 2 Sept. 1946, T 236/92, PRO; "FAO and World Food Policy," Orr address to Farm and Home Week in Ames, Iowa, 14 Feb. 1946, "The New World Food Proposals," Orr address to the Canadian Federation of Agriculture (CFA), 29 Jan. 1947, Orr BBC broadcast, 5 Nov. 1945, and Orr statement to UNRRA Policy Committee, 20 Mar. 1946, all RG 1.1, series H1, FAOA; "Task for FAO," *London Times,* 5 Apr. 1946; "The Choice Ahead: One World or None," Orr address, 14 Dec. 1946, RG 1.1, series D1, FAOA; "The Effects of War on Agriculture," Orr article for Highland Agricultural Society, 1940, and "Food and the Ordinary Man," Orr article for *Chambers's Journal,* 1940, both Lord John Boyd Orr papers, box 1, folder 2, National Library of Scotland, Edinburgh [hereafter NLS]; "Better Neighbors in a Changing World," Orr address to National Farm Institute of Des Moines, Orr papers, box 3, folder 2, NLS; "Agriculture and National Health," unidentified Orr article, 1939, Orr papers, box 1, folder 1, NLS; and "The Role of Food in Postwar Reconstruction," Orr address in New York, 1942, summary of Orr speech to Association of Scientific Workers conference, 10 Jan. 1942, and Orr article for *Farmer's Weekly,* 1942, all Orr papers, box 1, folder 3, NLS.

9. "Proposals for a World Food Board," FAO memorandum to member nations, 2 Sept. 1946, T 236/92, PRO.

10. Ibid. See also "American Farmers Are Important to Peace," Orr article, Mar. 1948, RG 1.1, series D1, FAOA; "FAO and World Food Policy," Orr address at Farm and Home Week in Ames, Iowa, 14 Feb. 1946, and "The New World Food Proposals," Orr address to CFA, 29 Jan. 1947, both RG 1.1, series H1, FAOA; and "The Role of Food in Postwar Reconstruction," Orr address in New York, 1942, Orr papers, box 1, folder 3, NLS.

11. FAO press release, "Summary of Remarks of Sir John Boyd Orr," 30 Aug. 1946, and Orr speech presenting proposals for a world food board, 4 Sept. 1946, both RG 59, Decimal File 1945–49, 501.SA, box 2296, NACP; memorandum of conversation between Orr and Alger Hiss, U.S. State Department, 27 June 1946, RG 59, Decimal File 1945–49, 501.SA, box 2295, NACP; summary of Orr speech to Association of Scientific Workers conference, 10 Jan. 1942, Orr papers, box 1, folder 3, NLS; "Better Neighbors in a Changing World," Orr address to National Farm Institute of Des Moines, Orr papers, box 3, folder 2, NLS.

12. "American Farmers Are Important to Peace," Orr article, Mar. 1948, RG 1.1, series D1, FAOA; Orr BBC broadcast, 5 Nov. 1945, RG 1.1, series H1, FAOA. See also "Nutrition and the New World: Difficulty of Planning for the New World," Orr paper for joint conference, May 1943, "Revolution by Food," Orr article for *Sunday Chronicle*, 28 July 1943, and "Food in Relation to Post War Reconstruction: Food, the Starting Point for Post-War Planning," Orr article for International Chamber of Commerce, 22 June 1943, all Orr papers, box 1, folder 3, NLS; Orr speech presenting world food board proposals, 4 Sept. 1946, RG 59, Decimal File 1945–49, 501.SA, box 2296, NACP; and "Food and the World Crisis," Orr speech to Princeton Bicentennial Conference, 11 Oct. 1946, RG 59, Decimal File 1945–49, 501.SA, box 2298, NACP.

13. John Boyd Orr, "Foreword," to Czechoslovakian edition of Wendell Wilkie, *One World*, 6 Dec. 1946, RG 1.1, series D1, FAOA. See also "The Choice Ahead: One World or None," Orr address, 14 Dec. 1946, ibid.; Orr statement to Emergency Conference on European Cereals Supplies, 3 Apr. 1946; Orr article for *Daily Herald*, 29 Dec. 1943, Orr papers, box 1, folder 3, NLS; "Task for FAO," *London Times*, 4 Apr. 1946; and "Food and the World Crisis," Orr speech at Princeton Bicentennial Conference, 11 Oct. 1946, and "The Job of the FAO Preparatory Commission," Orr remarks at first meeting, Preparatory Commission document 3, 26 Oct. 1946, RG 59, Decimal File 1945–49, 501.SA, box 2298, NACP.

14. "Proposals for a World Food Board," FAO memorandum to member nations, 2 Sept. 1946, T 236/92, PRO.

For WWII comparisons see also "The Choice Ahead: One World or None," Orr address, 14 Dec. 1946, and "American Farmers Are Important to Peace," Orr article, Mar. 1948, both RG 1.1, series D1, FAOA; notes on Sir John's press conference, 2 Apr. 1948, RG 1.1, series E1, FAOA; Orr BBC broadcast, 5 Nov. 1945, RG 1.1, series H1, FAOA; James Rorty, "Man against Hunger," Oct. 1949 newspaper article, RG 1.1, series J1, FAOA; Orr, *As I Recall*, 160; Sir John Orr, *Fighting for What? To "Billy Boy" and All the Other Boys Killed in the War* (London: Macmillan, 1942); and Orr remarks to Copenhagen Conference, 30 Aug. 1946, and Orr speech presenting the world food board proposals, 4 Sept. 1946, both RG 59, Decimal File 1945–49, 501.SA, box 2296, NACP.

15. Yates, *So Bold an Aim*, 57. See also ibid., 80–81; *Functions of a World Food Reserve*, 8–9, 47; and Rorty, "Man against Hunger," Oct. 1949 newspaper article, RG 1.1, series J1, FAOA.

16. Washington embassy telegram to Foreign Office, 25 July 1946, T 236/92, PRO. See also "Proposals for a World Food Board," confidential, restricted document for Second Session of FAO Conference, undated, ibid.; Thomas W. Zeiler, *Free Trade, Free World: The Advent of GATT* (Chapel Hill: Univ. of North Carolina Press, 1999), 1–88; Orr, *As I Recall,* 172–74, 192–94; Yates, *So Bold an Aim,* 80; Leffler, *Preponderance of Power,* 2–3, 10, 12–14, 16–20, 24; "F.A.O. Director Speaks out," *Winnipeg Free Press,* 6 May 1948; Vernon W. Ruttan, "The Politics of U.S. Food Aid Policy: A Historical Review," in *Why Food Aid?* ed. Vernon W. Ruttan (Baltimore, Md.: Johns Hopkins Univ. Press, 1993), 2–36; and Rachel Garst and Tom Barry, *Feeding the Crisis: U.S. Food Aid and Farm Policy in Central America* (Lincoln: Univ. of Nebraska Press, 1990).

17. Washington embassy telegrams to Foreign Office, 1 and 6 Aug. 1946, T 236/92, PRO; USDA Office of Information fact sheet, "FAO Copenhagen Conference," 15 Aug. 1946, Dean Acheson, Acting U.S. Secretary of State, memorandum to President Harry S. Truman, 2 Aug. 1946, and Acheson instructions to Norris E. Dodd, Undersecretary of Agriculture, 29 Aug. 1946, all RG 59, Decimal File 1945–49, 501.SA, box 2296, NACP.

18. Washington embassy telegram to Foreign Office, 1 Aug. 1946, T 236/92, PRO. See also "Remarks by United Kingdom Member," restricted summary minutes of joint meeting of Committees I and II, Preparatory Commission document 177, 10 Dec. 1946, RG 59, Decimal File 1945–49, 501.SA, box 2297, NACP.

19. "The Background for Forthcoming International Discussions on Commodity Policy," 1st draft, 1 Oct. 1946, T 236/93, PRO. See also Washington embassy telegram to Foreign Office, 1 Aug. 1946, note of a meeting on FAO proposals for a World Food Board, 15 Aug. 1946, and R. W. [Richard William] B. Clarke, British Treasury Assistant Secretary, memorandum to Sir Ernest Rowe-Dutton, British Treasury Principal Secretary, and Sir [Sigismund] David Waley, British Treasury Undersecretary, 9 Aug. 1946, all T 236/92, PRO; and "Relation of Increasing Agricultural Production to Costs," restricted summary minutes of joint meeting of Committees I and II, Preparatory Commission document 177, RG 59, Decimal File 1945–49, 501.SA, box 2297, NACP.

20. Secret annex II, "Comments on the FAO World Food Survey," attached to Acheson instructions to Dodd, 29 Aug. 1946, RG 59, Decimal File 1945–49, 501.SA, box 2296, NACP; T. Wilson memorandum to Rowe-Dutton, 26 July 1946, unattributed memorandum to Waley, 6 Aug. 1946, Washington embassy telegrams to Foreign Office, 25 July and 1 Aug. 1946, "The Orr Plan: Some Would-Be Constructive Suggestions for the U.K. Line," unattributed [Clarke] memorandum, undated [approx. 9 Aug. 1946], Waley letter to Sir Percivale Liesching, British Board of Trade Second Secretary, 13 Aug. 1946, note of a meeting on FAO proposals for a World Food Board, 15 Aug. 1946, and draft Foreign Office telegram to Washington embassy, 16 Aug. 1946, all T 236/92, PRO.

21. FAO Standing Advisory Committee on Economics and Marketing, "First Report to the Director-General," 28 Aug. 1946, microfilm 253, FAOA, and T 236/92, PRO; FAO press release, "Standing Economics Advisory Committee Issues Report," 31 Aug. 1946, RG 59, Decimal File 1945–49, 501.SA, box 2296, NACP.

22. "Reply by Sir John Boyd Orr," *Conference of the FAO Journal* 2 (3 Sept. 1946), microfilm 253, FAOA.

23. "Seventh Plenary Meeting" (6 Sept. 1946), proceedings of the Second Plenary Meeting, 2 Sept. 1946, and "Eighth Plenary Meeting," *Conference of the FAO Journal* 2 (6 Sept. 1946),

all microfilm 253, FAOA. See also Orr, *As I Recall*, 175–76; "F.A.O. in a Nutshell," 1946, Orr papers, box 2, folder 3, NLS; telegram from U.S. embassy in London to State Department, 3 Sept. 1946, RG 59, Decimal File 1945–49, 501.SA, box 2295, NACP; and FAO press release, "Talk by Professor André Mayer of France, Chairman of the Executive Committee," 31 Aug. 1946, RG 59, Decimal File 1945–49, 501.SA, box 2296, NACP.

24. Telegram from U.S. embassy in Copenhagen to State and Agriculture departments, 4 Sept. 1946, RG 59, Decimal File 1945–49, 501.SA, box 2295, NACP. See also "Fifth Plenary Session," *Conference of the FAO Journal* 2 (5 Sept. 1946), microfilm 253, FAOA; Orr, *As I Recall*, 175–78; and "Proposals for a Positive Commodity Policy," Preparatory Commission on the FAO Working Party memorandum, 19 Oct. 1946, T 236/93, PRO.

25. "The Background for Forthcoming International Discussions on Commodity Policy," 1st draft, 1 Oct. 1946, T 236/93, PRO; Waley letter to C. F. Cobbold, Bank of England, 25 Sept. 1946, T 236/92, PRO. See also "Proposals for a Positive Commodity Policy," Preparatory Commission on the FAO Working Party memorandum, 19 Oct. 1946, "International Commodity Policy," 2d revise, unattributed memorandum, undated [approx. Oct. 1946], "Finance of Buffer Stocks," Waley memorandum, 2 Oct. 1946, Foreign Office telegram to Washington embassy, 3 Oct. 1946, and minutes of the third and fourth meetings of the Working Party on the FAO Preparatory Commission, 3 and 5 Oct. 1946, all T 236/93, PRO; "International Commodity Policy," Board of Trade and Ministry of Food memorandum for the Preparatory Commission of the FAO Working Party, 24 Sept. 1946, T 236/92, PRO; and Washington embassy telegram to Foreign Office, 4 Oct. 1946, and Clarke memorandum to Rowe-Dutton and Waley, 17 Oct. 1946, both T 236/95, PRO.

26. "Statement by the United States Delegate to the Food and Agriculture Organization Preparatory Commission on World Food Proposals (Dodd), December 21, 1946 (Excerpts)," in *Documents on American Foreign Relations*, vol. 8: *July 1, 1945–December 31, 1946*, ed. Raymond Dennett and Robert K. Turner (Princeton, N.J.: Princeton Univ. Press for the World Peace Foundation, 1948), 699–703; O. L. Williams, Treasury and UK delegate to World Food Board Preparatory Commission, letters to W. H. Fisher, Treasury, 7 and 21 Nov. 1946, T 236/95, PRO; Inverchapel, Washington embassy, letter to Ernest Bevin, Foreign Minister, 4 Mar. 1947, FO 371/62863, PRO; Orr, *As I Recall*, 191–92; Washington embassy telegram to Foreign Office, 17 Oct. 1946, T 236/94, PRO; William L. Clayton, Undersecretary for Economic Affairs, letter to Clinton P. Anderson, Secretary of Agriculture, 27 Sept. 1946, Wilcox, State Department, memorandum to Clayton, 2 Oct. 1946, and confidential James F. Byrnes, Secretary of State, instructions to Dodd, 29 Oct. 1946, all RG 59, Decimal File 1945–49, 501.SA, box 2296, NACP.

27. Restricted note by the ECOSOC representative on discussions and proposals relevant to the work of the UN Subcommission on Economic Development, Preparatory Commission document 88, 20 Nov. 1946, and restricted report to Committee I from the working party on FAO activities, Preparatory Commission document 183, 17 Dec. 1946, both Mordecai Ezekiel papers, box 21, folder 8, FDRL; notes on speech by Viscount Bruce of Melbourne, FAO Council Chair, 16 Nov. 1948, RG 31.0, series K11, FAOA; *Functions of a World Food Reserve*, 47–48; confidential Byrnes instructions to Dodd, 29 Oct. 1946, RG 59, Decimal File 1945–49, 501.SA, box 2296, NACP; "Statement of the Netherlands Delegate," restricted summaries of ninth meeting of Committee I, Preparatory Commission document 159, 29 Nov. 1946, restricted draft report of Joint Committee on Industrial Development,

Preparatory Commission document 118, 29 Nov. 1946, "Statement by G. S. H. Barton, Delegate for Canada," restricted minutes of eighth meeting of Committee II, Preparatory Commission document 100, 3 Dec. 1946, "Industrialization and General Economic Development" and "Financing of Development," restricted first draft reports of FAO Preparatory Commission on World Food Proposals, Preparatory Commission documents 236 and 237, 10 Jan. 1947, and restricted summary minutes of eighth meeting of Subcommittee C, Preparatory Commission document 178, 7 Dec. 1946, all RG 59, Decimal File 1945–49, 501. SA, box 2297, NACP.

28. Williams letter to Fisher, 21 Nov. 1946, T 236/95, PRO. See also restricted statement by U.S. delegation concerning supplemental food programs for vulnerable groups, Preparatory Commission document 197, 20 Dec. 1946, restricted Dodd statement before the joint meeting of Committees 1 and 2, Preparatory Commission document 200, and "Agricultural and Nutritional Programs," restricted first draft report of FAO Preparatory Commission on World Food Proposals, Preparatory Commission document 235, 10 Jan. 1947, all RG 59, Decimal File 1945–49, 501.SA, box 2297, NACP; and Inverchapel letter to Bevin, 4 Mar. 1947, FO 371/62863, PRO.

29. "Remarks by Dr. Rao of the Indian Delegation," restricted summary minutes of joint meeting of Committees I and II, Preparatory Commission document 177, 10 Dec. 1946, RG 59, Decimal File 1945–49, 501.SA, box 2297, NACP. See also restricted minutes of eighth meeting of Committee 2, Preparatory Commission document 100, 3 Dec. 1946, "Regional Prices," restricted memorandum, Preparatory Commission document 147, 6 Dec. 1946, restricted Indian delegation memorandum on prices, Preparatory Commission document 146, 6 Dec. 1946, and "Position of the Egyptian Delegation," restricted summary of the ninth meeting of Committee 1, Preparatory Commission document 159, 29 Nov. 1946, all ibid.; Indian representative statement to plenary meeting, Preparatory Commission document 13, 29 Oct. 1946, RG 59, Decimal File 1945–49, 501.SA, box 2298, NACP; restricted Indian delegation supplementary paper on regional prices, Preparatory Commission document 176, 14 Dec. 1946, Ezekiel papers, box 22, folder "UN: FAO Preparatory Commission, World Food Proposals, 1946–48," FDRL; and Williams letters to Fisher, 7 and 21 Nov. 1946, T 236/95, PRO.

30. "Report of the Executive Committee on the Recommendations of the Preparatory Commission on World Food Proposals," 8 Mar. 1947, RG 59, Decimal File 1945–49, 501. SA, box 2310, NACP. See also Inverchapel letter to Bevin, 4 Mar. 1947, FO 371/62863, PRO; restricted second revised draft of the working party on intergovernmental consultation on agricultural and nutrition programs and World Food Council, 9 Jan. 1947, Ezekiel papers, box 21, folder 8, FDRL; Yates, *So Bold an Aim*, 81–82; confidential memorandum of conversation between L. A. Wheeler, Director of Office of Foreign Agricultural Relations, and Edward G. Cale, State Department, 26 Aug. 1946, and Wilcox memorandum to Clayton, 26 Aug. 1946, both RG 59, Decimal File 1945–49, 501.SA, box 2296, NACP; and W. R. Ogg, American Farm Bureau Federation, report on FAO Geneva Conference, 10 Dec. 1947, RG 59, Decimal File 1945–49, 501.SA, box 2309, NACP.

31. For the World Food Council see *Functions of a World Food Reserve*, 47–48; Yates, *So Bold an Aim*, 82–83; Inverchapel letter to Bevin, 4 Mar. 1947, Caplan memorandum to Helmore on Commodity Policy of the Interim Committee, 15 Mar. 1947, and Neil Caflan, Board of Trade, letter to Colin T. Crow, Foreign Office, 9 May 1947, all FO 371/62863, PRO; H. H. Hannam, President of the Canadian Farmers Association (CFA) and Third Vice-

President of the International Federation of Agricultural Producers (IFAP), restricted statement to the FAO Preparatory Commission on World Food Proposals, 20 Dec. 1946, RG 5, box 4, folder 6, FAOA [note: this document is currently misfiled]; "The New World Food Proposals," Orr address to the CFA, 29 Jan. 1947, RG 1.1, series H1, FAOA; Sir John Boyd Orr, "The New Council of FAO," *United Nations Weekly Bulletin* 3 (23 Sept. 1947): 382–84; Sir John Boyd Orr, "FAO: The Year Past, the Year Ahead," *United Nations Bulletin* 4 (1 Jan. 1948): 17–19; Ralph W. Phillips, *The World Was My Barnyard* (Parsons, W.Va.: McClain, 1984), 127; Orr, *As I Recall,* 192–94; memorandum of conversation between Farmers' Union and State Department representatives, 2 Aug. 1946, RG 59, Decimal File 1945–49, 501. SA, box 2296, NACP; Farmers Union Grain Terminal Association resolution, Preparatory Commission document 205, 9 Jan. 1947, RG 59, Decimal File 1945–49, 501.SA, box 2297, NACP; and Ogg report on Geneva FAO Conference, 10 Dec. 1947, RG 59, Decimal File 1945–49, 501.SA, box 2309, NACP.

For Geneva Conference see Phillips, *The World Was My Barnyard,* 127; Orr, *As I Recall,* 192–94; and Caplan memorandum to Helmore on Commodity Policy of the Interim Committee, 15 Mar. 1947, and Caflan letter to Crow, 9 May 1947, both FO 371/62863, PRO.

32. FAO, *Program of Work for 1949* (Washington, D.C.: FAO, 15 Nov. 1948), 16, 2. See also Yates, *So Bold an Aim,* 95–96, 112–13; Orr, *As I Recall,* 181–82, 196–200; Noble Clark, "Hungry Poland," *Survey Graphic* 37 (Mar. 1948): 116–18; "International Commodity Arrangements Are Emphasized at FAO World Conference" and "FAO Conference Completes First Phase in Its Analysis of World Food Situation," FAO press releases, 17 and 18 Nov. 1948, both RG 59, Decimal File 1945–49, 501.SA, box 2317, NACP; FAO, *1947 State of Food and Agriculture,* 9–10; agreement between FAO and Ethiopian government, 10 Dec. 1947, RG 59, Decimal File 1945–49, 501.SA, box 2309, NACP; and first report of the Standing Advisory Committee on Statistics to Orr, 28 Aug. 1946, RG 59, Decimal File 1945–49, 501.SA, box 2305, NACP.

33. Orr, *As I Recall,* 203.

34. For Dodd's outlook see McDougall comment in "Someone to Speak to Mr. Dodd," 26 Feb. 1954, Dodd papers, box 1, folder 1, HIWRP; "Food, Farming and Peace," Dodd address at Bunker Hill, 19 July 1948, Dodd papers, box 1, folder 7, HIWRP; and "The Faith, Philosophy and Work of FAO," Dodd speech to the International Seminar on FAO, Dec. 1951, and Dodd remarks at United States meeting, 8 Nov. 1950, both Dodd papers, box 1, folder 5, HIWRP.

For shifting global conditions see "International Commodity Arrangements are Emphasized at FAO World Conference," FAO press release, 17 Nov. 1948, RG 59, Decimal File 1945–49, 501.SA, box 2317, NACP; and Indian representative statement to plenary meeting of FAO Preparatory Commission, Preparatory Commission document 13, 29 Oct. 1946, RG 59, Decimal File 1945–49, 501.SA, box 2298, NACP.

For racial difficulties at D.C. office see Orr, *As I Recall,* 202.

35. FAO Committee on Commodity Problems, report of special rice meeting at Bangkok, 5–16 Jan. 1953, microfilm roll 108, FAOA. For Dodd's philosophy in leading the FAO see also "FAO: Prospects and Problems," Dodd papers, box 1, folder 5, HIWRP; "Progress and Accomplishments of FAO," Dodd address to representatives of Washington church and civic organizations, 1 May 1948, and "Food, Farming and Peace," Dodd address at Bunker Hill, 19 July 1948, both Dodd papers, box 1, folder 7, HIWRP; and "Summary of First Week of FAO Conference," FAO press release, 20 Nov. 1948, RG 59, Decimal File 1945–49, 501.SA, box 2317, NACP.

36. Dr. F. T. Wahlen comments, "Someone to Speak to Mr. Dodd," 26 Feb. 1954, Dodd papers, box 1, folder 1, HIWRP. For Dodd's down-to-earth nature see also "The Faith, Philosophy and Work of FAO," Dodd speech to the International Seminar on FAO, Dec. 1951, and Dodd statement at the Opening Plenary Session of the IFAP, Rome, 5 June 1953, both Dodd papers, box 1, folder 5, HIWRP.

For staff's affection for Dodd see "Someone to Speak to Mr. Dodd," 26 Feb. 1954, Dodd papers, box 1, folder 1, HIWRP.

For Dodd's visits with the world's farmers see Marc Viellet-Lavallée comments, "Someone to Speak to Mr. Dodd," 26 Feb. 1954, Dodd papers, box 1, folder 1, HIWRP; "The Faith, Philosophy and Work of FAO," Dodd speech to the International Seminar on FAO, Dec. 1951, and Dodd address to the National Farmers Union Convention, Denver, 16 Mar. 1954, both Dodd papers, box 1, folder 5, HIWRP; and Dodd report to FAO Council on recent mission to Mediterranean basin, Near East, Asia, and the Far East, 20 May 1949, RG 59, Decimal File 1945–49, 501.SA, box 2326, NACP.

37. Frank Shefrin and Howard Trueman, *Canada and FAO* (Ottawa: Canadian Department of Agriculture, 1971), 13–14; Yates, *So Bold an Aim,* 58, 83–85; Marchisio and di Blase, *Food and Agriculture Organization,* 24–25; "FAO: Prospects and Problems," restricted statement by Dodd to the U.S. Inter-Agency Committee, 25 July 1950, Dodd interview by Grant Salisbury, Radio Farm Director at WKAR, Michigan State College, 14 June 1950, and Dodd address to the National Farmers Union Convention, Denver, 16 Mar. 1954, all Dodd papers, box 1, folder 5, HIWRP; and "Progress and Accomplishments of FAO," Dodd address to representatives of Washington church and civic organizations, 1 May 1948, "Food, Farming and Peace," Dodd address at Bunker Hill, 19 July 1948, and "World Food and Peace," Dodd address to the National Catholic Rural Life Conference meeting, 7 Nov. 1949, all Dodd papers, box 1, folder 7, HIWRP.

38. For rejection of the ICCH proposals see Marchisio and di Blase, *Food and Agriculture Organization,* 24–25; Yates, *So Bold an Aim,* 84–85; Salisbury interview of Dodd, 14 June 1950, Dodd papers, box 1, folder 5, HIWRP; Shefrin and Trueman, *Canada and FAO,* 13; "Panel: The Role of Food in Future World Peace," in *The Role of Food in World Peace: An International Symposium in Observance of the Land-Grant Centennial* (Columbus: Ohio State Univ., 1962), 30; *Development through Food: A Strategy for Surplus Utilization,* FFHC Basic Studies 2 (Rome: FAO, 1962), 14; confidential memorandum to Thorp, State Department, from Brown, State Department, and Knapp, State Department, 14 Oct. 1949, RG 59, Decimal File 1945–49, 501.SA, box 2325, NACP; secret State Department memorandum of conversation, 27 Oct. 1949, RG 59, Decimal File 1945–49, 501.SA, box 2326, NACP; and Charles F. Brannan, Agriculture Secretary, statement before Commission I of FAO Conference, 5 Dec. 1949, and Report of Commission I, FAO Conference, 2 Dec. 1949, both RG 59, Decimal File 1945–49, 501.SA, box 2327, NACP.

For creation and operation of CCP see Yates, *So Bold an Aim,* 85–87; Shefrin and Trueman, *Canada and FAO,* 13–14; Marchisio and di Blase, *Food and Agriculture Organization,* 26–32; Dodd address to the National Farmers Union Convention, Denver, 16 Mar. 1954, Dodd papers, box 1, folder 5, HIWRP; and Report of Commission I, FAO Conference, 2 Dec. 1949, RG 59, Decimal File 1945–49, 501.SA, box 2327, NACP. The CCP initially consisted of fourteen members in all but was expanded to twenty in 1953.

39. For the basics of PL 480 and earlier surplus disposal programs see Robert G. Stanley, *Food for Peace: Hope and Reality of U.S. Food Aid* (New York: Gordon and Breach, 1973), ix,

59, 108, 118–19; David S. McLellan and Donald Clare, *Public Law 480: The Metamorphosis of a Law,* Eagleton Institute Studies in Practical Politics, no. 36 (New York: McGraw-Hill, 1965), 2–3, 5, 11; Kaufman, *Trade and Aid,* 27; and "A Policy for Export Surplus Disposal Plans," confidential State Department memorandum, 14 Oct. 1949, RG 59, Decimal File 1945–49, 501.SA, box 2325, NACP.

For concerns about PL 480 see Kaufman, *Trade and Aid,* 28–29, 33, 76; Trudy Huskamp Peterson, *Agricultural Exports, Farm Income, and the Eisenhower Administration* (Lincoln: Univ. of Nebraska Press, 1979); *New York Times,* 20 Jan. 1954, 3 Feb. 1955, and 25 Jan. 1956; McLellan and Clare, *Public Law 480,* 4, 6–7; Stanley, *Food for Peace,* 79; and George R. Zachar, *A Political History of Food for Peace,* Cornell Agricultural Economics Staff Paper, no. 77-18 (Ithaca, N.Y.: Cornell Univ., May 1977), 11–12.

For its political popularity see Stanley, *Food for Peace,* 65, 121; Kaufman, *Trade and Aid,* 76–77, 148–51, 189; McClellan and Clare, *Public Law 480,* 2–4, 11; Elmer L. Menzie and Robert G. Crouch, *Political Interests in Agricultural Export Surplus Disposal through Public Law 480,* Technical Bulletin 161 (Tucson: Univ. of Arizona Experiment Station, Sept. 1964), 9–10; Zachar, *A Political History,* 9; and Frances Moore Lappé, Joseph Collins, and David Kinley, *Aid as Obstacle: Twenty Questions about Our Foreign Aid and the Hungry* (San Francisco, Calif.: Institute for Food and Development Policy, 1980), 98.

40. Dodd statement to UN General Assembly, 9 Nov. 1951, Dodd papers, box 1, folder 5, HIWRP. For FAO technical assistance see also "The Faith, Philosophy and Work of FAO," Dodd speech to the International Seminar on FAO, Dec. 1951, and "FAO: Prospects and Problems," restricted Dodd statement to the U.S. Inter-Agency Committee, 25 July 1950, both Dodd papers, box 1, folder 5, HIWRP; "International Commodity Arrangements Are Emphasized at FAO World Conference," "Summary of First Week of FAO Conference," and "Summary of the Second Week of FAO Conference," FAO press releases, 17, 20, and 27 Nov. 1948, all RG 59, Decimal File 1945–49, 501.SA, box 2317, NACP; and Dodd report to Council on recent mission to Mediterranean basin, Near East, Asia, and Far East, 20 May 1949, RG 59, Decimal File 1945–49, 501.SA, box 2326, NACP.

41. "Some Things That Need to be Said," Dodd address at the U.S.-FAO dinner, 16 Feb. 1953, Dodd papers, box 1, folder 5, HIWRP. See also Dodd statement in Rome, Italy, 7 Aug. 1952, ibid.; and Orr, *As I Recall,* 207.

42. "FAO/UNICEF Cooperation: Past and Future," FAO memorandum, Apr. 1954, attached to Cardon letter to Maurice Pate, UNICEF Executive Director, 29 Apr. 1954, RG 1.3, series A2, FAOA.

43. Dodd statement in Rome, Italy, 7 Aug. 1952, and Dodd address to the National Farmers Union Convention, Denver, 16 Mar. 1954, both Dodd papers, box 1, folder 5, HIWRP.

For international flavor of FAO technical assistance see also "World Food Problems and the Inter-Dependence of Rural and Urban Regions," Dodd address to the World Assembly of Youth, Rome, 7 Sept. 1953, ibid.; and Cardon letter to the Soviet Permanent Representative to the UN, 15 July 1955, RG 1.3, series A3, folder 3, FAOA.

For FAO aid vs. national aid see also "Some Things That Need to be Said," Dodd address at the U.S.-FAO dinner, 16 Feb. 1953, and "FAO: Prospects and Problems," restricted Dodd statement to the U.S. Inter-Agency Committee, 25 July 1950, both Dodd papers, box 1, folder 5, HIWRP; Shefrin and Trueman, *Canada and FAO,* 6; and "Summary of First Week of FAO Conference," FAO press release, 20 Nov. 1948, RG 59, Decimal File 1945–49, 501.SA, box 2317, NACP.

44. For the work of the International Rice Commission see Dodd address to the inaugural session of the International Rice Commission, Bangkok, Thailand, 1949, Dodd papers, box 1, folder 7, HIWRP; and Dodd report to Council on recent mission to Mediterranean basin, Near East, Asia, and Far East, 20 May 1949, RG 59, Decimal File 1945–49, 501.SA, box 2326, NACP. The original members of the commission were Burma, Ceylon, Cuba, the Dominican Republic, Ecuador, Egypt, France, India, Italy, Mexico, the Netherlands, Pakistan, Paraguay, the Philippine Republic, Siam [Thailand], the United Kingdom, and the United States.

For locust control efforts see "World Food Problems and the Inter-Dependence of Rural and Urban Regions," Dodd address to the World Assembly of Youth, Rome, 7 Sept. 1953, Dodd papers, box 1, folder 5, HIWRP.

For rinderpest vaccinations see "Food, Farming and Peace," Dodd address at Bunker Hill, 19 July 1948, Dodd papers, box 1, folder 7, HIWRP; and Dodd report to Council on recent mission to Mediterranean basin, Near East, Asia, and Far East, 20 May 1949, RG 59, Decimal File 1945–49, 501.SA, box 2326, NACP.

For introduction of hybrid maize see Cardon letter to the editor of the *Saginaw (Michigan) News,* 13 Mar. 1954, RG 1.3, series A1, FAOA.

45. "FAO/UNICEF Cooperation: Past and Future," FAO memorandum, Apr. 1954, attached to Cardon letter to Pate, 29 Apr. 1954, RG 1.3, series A2, FAOA.

46. For Dodd's emphasis on information services see Marchisio and di Blase, *Food and Agriculture Organization,* 23–24; Yates, *So Bold an Aim,* 97–98, 103–106; Duncan Wall, Director of FAO Information Division, statement to Commission II on Program of Work, 21 Nov. 1948, RG 59, Decimal File 1945–49, 501.SA, box 2317, NACP.

47. Dodd statement to UN General Assembly, 9 Nov. 1951, Dodd papers, box 1, folder 5, HIWRP. See also "The Faith, Philosophy and Work of FAO," Dodd speech to the International Seminar on FAO, Dec. 1951, "World Food Problems and the Inter-Dependence of Rural and Urban Regions," Dodd address to the World Assembly of Youth, Rome, 7 Sept. 1953, and Dodd address to the National Farmers Union Convention, Denver, 16 Mar. 1954, all Dodd papers, ibid.; Marchisio and di Blase, *Food and Agriculture Organization,* 33–38; Cardon letter to Harry Hunt, President of the European Farm Radio and Television Association, May 1954, RG 1.3, series A1, FAOA; Cardon letter to the editor of the *Saginaw (Michigan) News,* 13 Mar. 1954, RG 1.3, series A1, FAOA; and Dodd report to Council on recent mission to Mediterranean basin, Near East, Asia, and Far East, 20 May 1949, RG 59, Decimal File 1945–49, 501.SA, box 2326, NACP.

48. For Cardon's lack of solidarity with staff see Cardon letter to the editor of the *Saginaw (Michigan) News,* 13 Mar. 1954, RG 1.3, series A1, FAOA; and Cardon letter to Secretary of State for the British Colonies, 24 June 1954, RG 1.3, series A3, folder 1, FAOA.

For Cardon's penchant for citing and obeying precedent see, e.g., Cardon letters to Hammarskjöld, 8 Mar. 1954, 11 Mar. and 8 June 1955, all RG 1.3, series A2, FAOA.

49. Cardon letter to Morse, 22 June 1955, RG 1.3, series A2, FAOA. For Cardon's limitation of FAO activities due to budget considerations see also Cardon letter to Morse, 16 Sept. 1955, Cardon letters to Pate, 29 Apr. 1954 and 21 Feb. and 20 June 1955, Cardon letter to Hammarskjöld with attached memorandum, "FAO Comments on Studies Recommended by the Committee of Experts on Population Trends and Economic and Social Conditions," 15 Mar. 1955, "Food and Agriculture Organization: 1955 Budget" [approximately Sept. 1954], and Cardon letter to Evans, 15 July 1955, all RG 1.3, series A2, FAOA.

For breakdown in locust control operations see Cardon letter to the Secretary of State for the British Colonies, 24 June 1954, RG 1.3, series A3, folder 1, FAOA; and Cardon letter to Shri N. T. Gulrajani, Deputy Secretary in the Indian Ministry of Food and Agriculture, 2 Mar. 1955, RG 1.3, series A3, folder 3, FAOA.

50. "The Job of the FAO Preparatory Commission," Orr remarks at first meeting, Preparatory Commission document 3, 26 Oct. 1946, and Indian representative statement to plenary, Preparatory Commission document 13, 29 Oct. 1946, both RG 59, Decimal File 1945–49, 501.SA, box 2298, NACP.

51. Sen introductory statement to 1959 FAO Conference plenary as quoted in Gertrud Baer, permanent representative to the UN for the Women's International League for Peace and Freedom (WILPF), report to WILPF executive committee and national sections, Nov./Dec. 1959, RG 12, box 1, folder 6, FAOA. For 1950s' food situation see Marchisio and di Blase, *Food and Agriculture Organization*, 42.

7. Redefining an International Role for the Food and Agriculture Organization

1. Sen introductory statement to plenary of 1959 Conference, as quoted in Baer report to WILPF executive committee and national sections, Nov./Dec. 1959, RG 12, box 1, folder 6, FAOA. See also Marchisio and di Blase, *Food and Agriculture Organization*, 41–44; and Cardon, letter to Pakistani Minister of Foreign Affairs and Commonwealth Relations, 23 Oct. 1954, RG 1.3, series A3, folder 2, FAOA.

2. Draft "Project for a 'Free the World from Hunger Year,'" 16 July 1958, RG 12, box 1, folder 9, FAOA. See also "Freedom-from-Hunger Campaign: Strength and Weaknesses," memorandum by R. L. Savary, Special Assistant to Sen, 1 Apr. 1960, RG 12, box 2, folder 7, FAOA; "Positive Achievements in the Fight against Hunger," draft article by F. W. Parker, Assistant Director-General of FAO Technical Department, 21 Aug. 1961, RG 12, box 1, folder 11, FAOA; and Resolution No. 13/59 on the Freedom from Hunger Campaign, 27 Oct. 1960, as printed in B. R. Sen, *Towards a Newer World* (Dublin, Ire.: Tycooly, 1982), 305–307.

For the state of global nutrition see Food and Agriculture Organization, *Second World Food Survey* (Rome: FAO, 1952); "Consultations held by the Director-General on 'Free the World from Hunger' Year," 14 Nov. 1958, RG 12, box 2, folder 5, FAOA; revised working paper for FAO Council ad hoc committee on Free the World from Hunger Campaign, Apr. 1959, RG 12, box 1, folder 7, FAOA; report of the FAO Council ad hoc committee on Free the World from Hunger Campaign, Apr. 1959, RG 12, box 1, folder 3, FAOA; "Freedom-from-Hunger Campaign," 6 Aug. 1959, RG 12, box 1, folder 4, FAOA; draft "Project for a 'Free the World from Hunger Year,'" 16 July 1958, and minutes of meeting on a third world food survey, 10 Sept. 1958, both RG 12, box 1, folder 9, FAOA; Sen, *The Basic Freedom*, 4; "Freedom-from-Hunger Campaign: Strength and Weaknesses," Savary memorandum, 1 Apr. 1960, RG 12, box 2, folder 7, FAOA; memorandum to Sen from M. Moulik, Acting Director of FAO Public Information Service, 5 Dec. 1960, RG 12, box 3, folder 16, FAOA; Sen, *Towards a Newer World*, 140–41; and Arthur Hopcraft, *Born to Hunger* (London: Heinemann, 1968).

For Sen's ideas about hunger and the role of the FAO in alleviating it see first draft of "Outline of a Field Program under the Freedom from Hunger Campaign," 4 Dec. 1959, RG 12, box 1, folder 3, FAOA; Sen, *The Basic Freedom*, 4, 10, "The Nutritional State of the

World," in *Role of Food in World Peace*, 20–22, and *Towards a Newer World*, 24, 137; and Earl de la Warr, "The Freedom from Hunger Campaign," in *Gazebo: A Collection of Writings and Illustrations Edited and Published at Kingswood School as a Contribution to the Freedom from Hunger Campaign*, ed. Neal J. Clough (Plaistow, UK: Curwen, 1963), 6.

3. "Director-General's Proposal for a 'Free-the-World-from-Hunger' Year," 6 Oct. 1958, RG 12, box 2, folder 4, FAOA.

For initial planning see draft "Project for a 'Free the World from Hunger Year,'" 16 July 1958, Sen letter to Sir Herbert Broadley, FAO Deputy Director-General, 18 June 1958, and Rainer Schickele memorandum to Mordecai Ezekiel, Acting Director of FAO Economics Division, 3 July 1958, all RG 12, box 1, folder 9, FAOA.

For the campaign's faith in the potential of facts to prompt action see *Achievement: The W. I. Contribution to the Freedom from Hunger Campaign* (London: National Federation of Women's Institutes, Apr. 1967), 1; Sen, *Towards a Newer World*, 144; and Guilielma Maw, "Foreword," in *Gazebo*, ed. Clough, 3.

For work with other UN specialized agencies see also "Freedom-from-Hunger Campaign," 6 Aug. 1959, RG 12, box 1, folder 4, FAOA; memorandum from A. G. Orbaneja, Chief of FAO International Agency Liaison Service, to Ezekiel, 27 Nov. 1958, Ezekiel memorandum to Sen, 1 Dec. 1958, and abstract of discussion at UNESCO, 17 Mar. 1959, all RG 12, box 2, folder 12, FAOA; report of second session of FFHC advisory committee of NGOs, annex 5 to report of the third session of the government advisory committee on the FFHC, 20 June 1961, RG 12, box 3, folder 3, FAOA; Steele, *Animal Disease and Human Health*, 2; and Sen, *Towards a Newer World*, 142.

For ECOSOC see also memorandum to FAO Conference on Freedom-from-Hunger Campaign, 6 Aug. 1959, RG 12, box 1, folder 4, FAOA; and Sen, *Towards a Newer World*, 138.

4. Sen's draft opening statement to council's ad hoc committee, 13 Apr. 1959, RG 12, box 1, folder 5, FAOA. See also extract from provisional report of the tenth session of the conference, Nov. 1959, and Ezekiel memorandum to Sen, 12 Nov. 1959, both RG 12, box 1, folder 1, FAOA; record of first meeting of interdivisional working party, 4 Sept. 1958, RG 12, box 1, folder 9, FAOA; Moulik memorandum to Ezekiel, 9 Feb. 1960, RG 12, box 1, folder 3, FAOA; draft memorandum "Expected Participation by Non-Governmental Organizations in the Freedom from Hunger Campaign," 23 Mar. 1960, RG 12, box 2, folder 7, FAOA; Norman C. Wright, FAO Deputy Director-General, letter to Islamic Conference, 8 Apr. 1960, RG 12, box 3, folder 6, FAOA; "How to Start an Educational and Informational Campaign," Ezekiel draft article for Freedom-from-Hunger Campaign monthly letter, 25 May 1960, RG 12, box 3, folder 4, FAOA; "Report of the Director-General on the Progress of the Freedom-from-Hunger Campaign," 17 May 1961, RG 12, box 3, folder 3, FAOA; "Panel: The Role of Food in Future World Peace," in *Role of Food in World Peace*, 30; Victor Gollancz, "Messages," de la Warr, "Freedom from Hunger Campaign," and Michael Tippett, "Then and Now," in *Gazebo*, ed. Clough, 5, 6, 26; Sen, *Towards a Newer World*, 14, 149; and *Freedom from Hunger Campaign National Action Projects: A Selection* (Rome: FAO, 1960), v.

5. Sen address to the Società Italiana per l'Organizzazione Internazionale, 22 Jan. 1959, RG 12, box 2, folder 13, FAOA. See also notes on fourth meeting of NGOs to discuss the FFHC, 19 Jan. 1960, and Baer memorandum to members of WILPF, Nov./Dec. 1959, both RG 12, box 1, folder 6, FAOA; "Panel: The Role of Food in Future World Peace," in *Role of Food in World Peace*, 30; Angus Archer, "Methods of Multilateral Management: The Interrelationship of International Organizations and Nongovernmental Organizations," in *The*

U.S., the U.N., and the Management of Global Change, ed. Toby Trister Gati (New York: New York Univ. Press, 1983), 309, 312; and Hopcraft, *Born to Hunger,* 1.

6. Confidential Veillet-Lavallée aide-mémoire, 2 Oct. 1959, RG 12, box 3, folder 17, FAOA. For the FAO's appeal to NGOs see also Savary memorandum, "Freedom-from-Hunger Campaign," 1 Apr. 1960, RG 12, box 2, folder 7, FAOA; and Oyvind Gulbrandsen, *The Freedom from Hunger Campaign (FFHC) Outboard Mechanization Projects in Dahomey and Togo* (Rome: FAO, Dec. 1968), 4.

For NGO participation see Sen, *Towards a Newer World,* 144, 161–63, 279; first progress report to council's ad hoc committee, 8 Dec. 1958, RG 12, box 1, folder 5, FAOA; memorandum to W. G. Casseres, Director of FAO Information and Public Relations Service, from Norman Michie, Chief of FAO Press Section, 17 Nov. 1958, RG 12, box 2, folder 4, FAOA; "Reports Made by Representatives of Non-Governmental Organizations on their Activities," 15 Sept. 1960, RG 12, box 1, folder 10, FAOA; and Sen opening address, appendix 2 to report of the third session of the government advisory committee on FFHC, 20 June 1961, RG 12, box 3, folder 3, FAOA.

Early NGO respondents to the FFHC included the Catholic International Union for Social Service, Commission of the Churches on International Affairs, Conservation Foundation, European Confederation of Agriculture (ECA), Heifer Project, Inc., International Confederation of Agricultural Economists, International Co-Operative Alliance (ICA), IFAP, International Federation of Christian Agricultural Workers Unions, Land Grant College Association, League of Red Cross Societies (LRCS), United Nations Association of Great Britain and Northern Ireland, WILPF, World Confederation of Organizations of the Teaching Professions, World Council of Churches (WCC), and World Federation of United Nations Associations (WFUNA).

The following organizations sent representatives to an 18 Jan. 1960 meeting at FAO headquarters: Associated Country Women of the World, Catholic International Union for Social Service, Committee of the Churches on International Affairs, ECA, International Commission of Rural Life, International Confederation of Christian Trade Unions, International Confederation of Free Trade Unions, International Confederation of Technical Agriculturists, International Conference of Catholic Charities, ICA, International Council of Women, International Dairy Federation, IFAP, International Landworkers Federation, International Union of Biological Sciences, LRCS, Movement Internationale de la Jeunesse Agricole et Rural Catholique [International Movement of Catholic Agricultural and Rural Youth], Unione Mondiale des Organisations Feminines Catholiques [World Union of Catholic Women's Organizations], WILPF, World Assembly of Youth, WCC, World Federation of Trade Unions, WFUNA, World Veterans Federation, World Veterinary Association, and World YWCA.

7. Record of meeting of interdivisional working party on Free the World from Hunger Year, 31 Mar. 1959, RG 12, box 2, folder 11, FAOA; Ezekiel memorandum to Sen, 14 Apr. 1959, RG 12, box 1, folder 9, FAOA; "Extract from Draft Report of Fourth FAO Regional Conference for the Near East," appendix 2 to working paper for meeting of FAO Council ad hoc committee, Apr. 1959, RG 12, box 1, folder 7, FAOA; *FFHC National Action Projects,* v.

For development of the action component see also Sen speech to the Societá Italiana per l'Organizzazione Internazionale, 22 Jan. 1959, RG 12, box 2, folder 13, FAOA; FAO Council ad hoc committee on FFHC report, Apr. 1959, RG 12, box 1, folder 3, FAOA; draft memorandum, "Expected Participation by Non-Governmental Organizations in the Freedom from Hunger Campaign," 23 Mar. 1960, RG 12, box 2, folder 7, FAOA; statement by Indian delegate to FAO Council ad hoc committee on the FFHC, Apr. 1959, RG 12, box 1, folder 7, FAOA; and extract from provisional report of the tenth session of the Conference, Nov. 1959, and Ezekiel memorandum to Sen, 12 Nov. 1959, both RG 12, box 1, folder 1, FAOA.

For the importance of governments' cooperation see *FFHC National Action Programs,* v; Hopcraft, *Born to Hunger,* 3; *Development through Food,* 1, 11; draft memorandum "Expected Participation by Non-Governmental Organizations in the Freedom from Hunger Campaign," 23 Mar. 1960, RG 12, box 2, folder 7, FAOA; FAO Council ad hoc committee report, Apr. 1959, RG 12, box 1, folder 3, FAOA; and Sen speech to Societá Italiana per l'Organizzazione Internazionale, 22 Jan. 1959, RG 12, box 2, folder 13, FAOA.

For importance of FFHC to governments see report of FAO Council ad hoc committee, Apr. 1959, RG 12, box 1, folder 3, FAOA; and extract from provisional report of the tenth session of the conference, Nov. 1959, RG 12, box 1, folder 1, FAOA.

For hopes of an increased budget see record of meeting of interdivision working party on Free the World from Hunger Year, 6 Apr. 1959, RG 12, box 2, folder 11, FAOA; Sen's draft opening statement to council's ad hoc committee, 13 Apr. 1959, RG 12, box 1, folder 5, FAOA; and report of FAO Council ad hoc committee, Apr. 1959, RG 12, box 1, folder 3, FAOA.

For FAO thinking on new development efforts see report of FAO Council ad hoc committee, Apr. 1959, and memorandum from A. Szarf to Gerda Blau, 12 May 1959, both RG 12, box 1, folder 3, FAOA.

8. For rural development ideas see memorandum from R. O. Whyte, Chief of FAO Crop Production and Improvement Branch, to W. H. Pawley, Chief of FAO Program Liaison Branch, 23 July 1959, RG 12, box 1, folder 3, FAOA; memorandum to FAO Conference on FFHC, 6 Aug. 1959, RG 12, box 1, folder 4, FAOA; and Steele, *Animal Disease and Human Health,* 38.

For advantages of rural development see "Panel: The Role of Food in Future World Peace," in *Role of Food in World Peace,* 30.

9. For approval of campaign but lack of budget see extract from provisional report of the tenth session of the FAO Conference, Nov. 1959, RG 12, box 1, folder 1, FAOA; and memorandum to FAO Conference, 6 Aug. 1959, RG 12, box 1, folder 4, FAOA.

For interim FFHC funding see also Ezekiel letters to Harvey B. Matthews Jr., Assistant to the President of the Ford Foundation, 17 Dec. 1959 and 2 Mar. 1960, RG 12, box 2, folder 3, FAOA; revised working paper for FAO Council ad hoc committee, Apr. 1959, RG 12, box 1, folder 7, FAOA; report of FAO Council ad hoc committee, Apr. 1959, RG 12, box 1, folder 3, FAOA; Ezekiel letter to Sen, 14 May 1959, RG 12, box 2, folder 5, FAOA; "Freedom-from-Hunger Campaign," 6 Aug. 1959, RG 12, box 1, folder 4, FAOA; Sen letter to Your Grace, 2 Nov. 1959, RG 12, box 2, folder 2, FAOA; extract from provisional report of the tenth session of the conference, Nov. 1959, RG 12, box 1, folder 1, FAOA; and Ezekiel memorandum to Sen, 24 Feb. 1960, RG 12, box 3, folder 4, FAOA.

For staff reaction to lack of funds see "Freedom-from-Hunger Campaign," 6 Aug. 1959, RG 12, box 1, folder 4, FAOA; Walter M. Kotschnig, UN Rapporteur, consolidated draft report, "Programme Appraisal, 1959–1964," 23 Jan. 1960, RG 12, box 3, folder 11, FAOA; Baer report to WILPF, Nov./Dec. 1959, RG 12, box 1, folder 6, FAOA; minutes of the thirteenth meeting of the FFHC policy committee, 25 Nov. 1960, RG 12, box 3, folder 16, FAOA; and Sen, *Towards a Newer World,* 139, 143.

10. FFHC projects suggested by U.S. delegate to FAO Council ad hoc committee on

FFHC, Apr. 1959, RG 12, box 1, folder 3, FAOA. See also Ezekiel memorandum to Sen, 22 July 1959, RG 12, box 1, folder 17, FAOA; aide-mémoire on meeting with U.S. delegation, 24 June 1959, RG 12, box 2, folder 5, FAOA; "Programme Appraisal, 1959–1964," draft of Kotschnig consolidated report, RG 12, box 3, folder 11, FAOA; and report of the FAO Council ad hoc committee, Apr. 1959, RG 12, box 1, folder 3, FAOA.

11. "General Statement on Agricultural Policy by Ezra Taft Benson," 5 Feb. 1953, Benson Papers, Dwight D. Eisenhower Presidential Library, Abilene, KS, as quoted in Edward L. Schapsmeier and Frederick H. Schapsmeier, "Eisenhower and Ezra Taft Benson: Farm Policy in the 1950s," *Agricultural History* 44 (Oct. 1970): 370.

For the motive forces behind Eisenhower's agricultural policy see also Mervi Gustafsson, *Food Aid in International Relations: The Case of the United States* (Tampere, Fin.: Peace Research Institute, 1977), 15–18, 70–73; "Use of Agricultural Commodities to Improve the Foreign Relations of the United States," 28 July 1953, *Congressional Record: House,* vol. 99, pt. 8, 10077–88; "Agricultural Trade Development and Assistance Act of 1954," 15 June 1954, *Congressional Record: House,* vol. 100, pt. 6, 8268–301; *Food for Freedom, New Emphasis on Self-Help: 1967 Annual Report on Public Law 480* (Washington, D.C.: GPO, 1968), 1–2; Stanley, *Food for Peace,* 63; Kaufman, *Trade and Aid,* 27; Zachar, *A Political History,* 1; *United States Food for Peace Program,* 10; and Department of Agriculture with the State Department and International Cooperation Administration, *How America's Abundance Works for Peace* (Washington, D.C.: GPO, Oct. 1960), 1.

12. For the Eisenhower administration's new approach to foreign aid policy see Kaufman, *Trade and Aid,* 151; Zachar, *A Political History,* 16; Peter A. Toma, *The Politics of Food for Peace: Executive-Legislative Interaction* (Tucson: Univ. of Arizona Press, 1967), 58; Mitchel B. Wallerstein, *Food for War—Food for Peace: United States Aid in a Global Context* (Cambridge, Mass.: MIT Press, 1980), 181; McLellan and Clare, *Public Law 480,* 9–10; and USDA et al., *How America's Abundance Works for Peace,* 1.

For the economic motivations behind Food for Peace see Kaufman, *Trade and Aid,* 189; Zachar, *A Political History,* 14; and USDA et al., *How America's Abundance Works for Peace,* 1, 10, 12, 14.

13. FAO North American Regional Office press release, 6 May 1959, RG 12, box 2, folder 5, FAOA. See also memorandum from I. H. Ergas, Chief of FAO Program and Policy Section, to A. C. Janssen, Chief of FAO Agricultural Development Analysis Branch, 8 Dec. 1959, RG 12, box 1, folder 3, FAOA; personal letter to Gordon Evans, Secretary for UN Association for Great Britain and Northern Ireland, from Stefano D'Amico, Chief of FAO Commodity Policy Section, with attached "British Farming and World Hunger" memorandum by J. W. Murray, 7 May 1959, RG 12, box 1, folder 18, FAOA; "Freedom-from-Hunger Campaign," 6 Aug. 1959, RG 12, box 1, folder 4, FAOA; Wright letter to James G. Patton, President of the National Farmers Union, 19 Dec. 1960, RG 12, box 2, folder 5, FAOA; Sen letter to W. J. Luxton, Director of the Federation of Commonwealth and British Empire Chambers of Commerce, 21 Mar. 1961, RG 12, box 3, folder 20, FAOA; Ezekiel letter to Vogel, 8 June 1961, RG 12, box 1, folder 11, FAOA; Sen, *The Basic Freedom,* 23; *FFHC National Action Projects,* 81; and *Development through Food,* 3.

14. For Eisenhower's UN initiative and the response of the UN General Assembly and FAO see Wright letter to Patton, 19 Dec. 1960, RG 12, box 2, folder 5, FAOA; Wallerstein, *Food for War,* 92–93, 167; and "United Nations General Assembly Res. 1496 (XV)," as printed in *Development through Food,* 65–68.

For McGovern initiative see George S. McGovern, *War Against Want: America's Food for Peace Program* (New York: Walker, 1964), 108–109; "Statement by George S. McGovern at 10 Apr. 1961 Meeting of the Intergovernmental Advisory Committee," as printed in *Development through Food*, 121–22; Wallerstein, *Food for War*, 168–70; Sen, *Towards a Newer World*, 202; and *Food for Peace, 1965: Annual Report on Public Law 480* (Washington, D.C.: GPO, 1966), 83.

For the WFP see "United Nations General Assembly Res. 1714 (16), 19 Dec. 1961," as printed in *Development through Food*, xii, 157–62; *Food for Peace, 1965*, 83; Wallerstein, *Food for War*, 94–95; *Food for Peace* 3 (May 1963): 2, and 9 (Dec. 1963): 6; Gustafsson, *Food Aid in International Relations*, 29–30; *The Food Aid Program, 1966: Annual Report on Public Law 480* (Washington, D.C.: GPO, 1966), 46; and Sen, *Towards a Newer World*, 195.

15. For WFP see Sen, *Towards a Newer World*, 196; and Wallerstein, *Food for War*, 94–97, 242–44.

16. For JFK's approach see McGovern, *War Against Want*, xiii; James N. Giglio, *The Presidency of John F. Kennedy* (Lawrence: Univ. Press of Kansas, 1991), 115–17; Stanley, *Food for Peace*, 71–72; *Food for Peace* 1 (Mar. 1963): 1–2; Wallerstein, *Food for War*, 182; *New York Times*, 17 Mar. 1961; *United States Food for Peace Program*, 10; Arthur M. Schlesinger Jr., *A Thousand Days: John F. Kennedy in the White House* (Boston, Mass.: Houghton Mifflin, 1965), 162; and Zachar, *Political History*, 21.

For Food for Peace development projects see *Food for Peace* 1 (Mar. 1963): 2; 2 (Apr. 1963): 8, 9; 3 (May 1963): 4; 5 (July 1963): 5, 8; 6 (Aug.–Sept. 1963): 2, 4; 7 (Oct. 1963): 1, 4–6; 9 (Dec. 1963): 4, 5, 19; and 10 (Jan. 1964): 6.

For FAO's work in developing such food-for-development schemes see Gerda Blau, *Disposal of Agricultural Surpluses*, FAO Commodity Policy Studies, no. 5 (Rome: FAO, June 1954); *Uses of Agricultural Surpluses to Finance Economic Development in Under-Developed Countries: A Pilot Study in India*, FAO Commodity Policy Studies, no. 6 (Rome: FAO, June 1955); and *FFHC National Action Projects*, 97.

For subjugation of food aid to U.S. economic and diplomatic imperatives see *Food for Peace* 1 (Mar. 1963): 2; 2 (Apr. 1963): 2; 3 (May 1963): 1; 5 (July 1963): 7; 6 (Aug.–Sept. 1963): 5, 8–9; 7 (Oct. 1963): 5; 8 (Nov. 1963): 1–2, 4, 6; 12 (Mar. 1964): 9; Wallerstein, *Food for War*, 169–70; Toma, *Politics of Food for Peace*, 62–63; Zachar, *A Political History*, 21, 23–24; and *Food for Peace: Proceedings of the National Conference of the American Food for Peace Council* (Washington, D.C.: U.S. Department of State, 30 Sept. 1963), esp. 3–10.

17. First draft of "Outline of a Field Action Program under the Freedom from Hunger Campaign," 4 Dec. 1959, RG 12, box 1, folder 3, FAOA. For focus on rural development see also "Note on the Problem of Education and Training in Nutrition for FFHC," FAO Nutrition Division memorandum, 14 Oct. 1960, RG 12, box 1, folder 10, FAOA; *Freedom from Hunger: Outline of a Campaign*, 6–7, 14; *FFHC National Action Projects*, ix; Freedom from Hunger Campaign, *Report on the Food and Agriculture Organization/National Farm Broadcasting Seminar for Malaysia* (Rome: FAO, 1968), 3–4; "Programme Appraisal, 1959–1964," first draft of Kotschnig consolidated report, 23 Jan. 1960, RG 12, box 3, folder 11, FAOA; "Possibilities of Increasing World Food Production," Barton memorandum, 30 Jan. 1961, RG 12, box 3, folder 19, FAOA; Charles H. Weitz, FFHC Coordinator, letter to P. Bertrand, Director of UNESCO Division of Relations with International Organizations, 14 Mar. 1961, RG 12, box 1, folder 10, FAOA; report of the second session of the advisory committee of NGOs on the FFHC, appendix 4 to report of the third session of the government advi-

sory committee on the FFHC, 20 June 1961, RG 12, box 3, folder 3, FAOA; Parker, "Positive Achievements in the Fight against Hunger," draft article, 21 Aug. 1961, RG 12, box 1, folder 11, FAOA; and Sen, *Towards a Newer World,* 143.

For emphasis on human solidarity see Sen letter to national governments with attached "Principles and Methods Governing the Freedom-from-Hunger Campaign," 8 Mar. 1960, RG 12, box 2, folder 3, FAOA; and report of the second session of the advisory committee of NGOs, appendix 4, and FFHC meeting of information and education officers of NGOs, annex 4 to report of the third session of the government advisory committee, 20 June 1961, both RG 12, box 3, folder 3, FAOA.

18. Veillet-Lavallée confidential memorandum to Parker, Ezekiel, Weisl, Vogel, and Dey, 1 Feb. 1960, RG 12, box 1, folder 1, FAOA; *FFHC National Action Projects,* vi.

See also "Report of the Director-General on the Progress of the Freedom-from-Hunger Campaign," 17 May 1961, RG 12, box 3, folder 3, FAOA; memorandum "Freedom-from-Hunger Campaign: Strength and Weaknesses," 1 Apr. 1960, and Ezekiel letter to Wright, 2 Apr. 1960, both RG 12, box 2, folder 7, FAOA; Moulik memorandum to Sen, 5 Dec. 1960, RG 12, box 3, folder 16, FAOA; Ezekiel memorandum to Weitz, 18 Jan. 1961, RG 12, box 3, folder 19, FAOA; Sen opening address, appendix 2, "Report by the Coordinator on Progress and Development," annex 3 (report of the second session of the advisory committee of NGOs on the FFHC), appendix 4, and FFHC meeting of information and education officers of NGOs, annex 4 to report of the third session of the government advisory committee on the FFHC, 20 June 1961, all RG 12, box 3, folder 3, FAOA; first draft of "Outline of a Field Action Program under the Freedom from Hunger Campaign," 4 Dec. 1959, RG 12, box 1, folder 3, FAOA; Veillet-Lavallée memorandum to Sen, 23 Nov. 1959, and unattributed "Report on visit to Germany and Switzerland," Feb. 1960, both RG 12, box 2, folder 2, FAOA; Ezekiel memorandum to Parker, 12 Feb. 1960, RG 12, box 2, folder 1 and box 3, folder 4, FAOA; Savary memorandum "Freedom-from-Hunger Campaign: Strength and Weaknesses," 1 Apr. 1960, draft memorandum "Expected Participation by Non-Governmental Organizations in the Freedom from Hunger Campaign," 23 Mar. 1960, and Ezekiel letter to Savary, 2 Apr. 1960, all RG 12, box 2, folder 7, FAOA; FFHC meeting of information and education officers of NGOs, annex 4 to report of the third session of the government advisory committee on the FFHC, 20 June 1961, RG 12, box 3, folder 3, FAOA; and Sen, *Freedom from Hunger,* 20, and *Towards a Newer World,* 139.

19. Sen, *Freedom from Hunger,* 20–22; draft memorandum "Expected Participation by Non-Governmental Organizations in the Freedom from Hunger Campaign," 23 Mar. 1960, RG 12, box 2, folder 7, FAOA; Sen, "Nutritional State," in *Role of Food in World Peace,* 23; Veillet-Lavallée memorandum to Sen, 14 Sept. 1959, RG 12, box 1, folder 18, FAOA; Sen letter to Hammarskjöld, 18 Sept. 1959, RG 12, box 2, folder 12, FAOA; Baer report to WILPF, Nov./Dec. 1959, and notes on fifth meeting of NGOs on FFHC, 20 Jan. 1960, both RG 12, box 1, folder 6, FAOA; Ezekiel letter to Matthews, 26 Jan. 1960, RG 12, box 2, folder 2, FAOA; Ezekiel letter to Matthews, 2 Feb. 1960, RG 12, box 2, folder 3, FAOA; Ezekiel memorandum to Sen, 24 Feb. 1960, RG 12, box 3, folder 4, FAOA; "Reports Made by Representatives of Non-Governmental Organizations on Their Activities," 15 Sept. 1960, RG 12, box 1, folder 10, FAOA; report of the second session of the advisory committee of NGOs on the FFHC, appendix 4, and FFHC meeting of NGO Information and Education Officers, annex 4 to report of the third session of the government advisory committee on the FFHC, 20 June

1961, RG 12, box 3, folder 3, FAOA; Archer, "Methods of Multilateral Management," 312; *FFHC National Action Projects,* 125; Sen, *Towards a Newer World,* 139.

Organizations represented on the FFHC Advisory Committee on Non-Governmental Organizations included the Associated Country Women of the World, Commission of the Churches on International Affairs, International Confederation of Free Trade Unions, International Conference of Catholic Charities, IFAP, Islamic Congress, World Assembly of Youth, World Confederation of Organizations of the Teaching Profession, World Federation of Trade Unions, and WFUNA. Organizations sending observers included the Catholic International Union for Social Services, Intercontinental Centre of Biological Research, International Centre for Technical and Practical Studies, International Council of Catholic Men, International Federation of Margarine Associations, International Organization for Rural Development, Lutheran World Federation, Salvation Army, and World YMCA ("Freedom from Hunger Campaign Advisory Committee of Non-Governmental Organizations, Second Session," annex 1 to report of the third session of the government advisory committee on the FFHC, 20 June 1961, RG 12, box 3, folder 3, FAOA).

20. Report of the third session of the government advisory committee on the FFHC, 20 June 1961, RG 12, box 3, folder 3, FAOA. For role of youth in development efforts see also Sen opening address, appendix 2, "Report by the Coordinator on Progress and Development," annex 3, and "Report on the Employment of Peace Corps Volunteers," appendix 5 to report of the third session of the government advisory committee on the FFHC, ibid.; "Reports Made by Representatives of Non-Governmental Organizations on Their Activities," 15 Sept. 1960, RG 12, box 1, folder 10, FAOA; and Gollancz, "Messages," in *Gazebo,* ed. Clough, 5.

For calls to divert arms race expenditures to the fight against hunger see Sybil Thorndike, "Messages," in *Gazebo,* ed. Clough, 5.

For the growing interest of the world's youth in development efforts such as the Peace Corps see Elizabeth Cobbs Hoffman, *All You Need Is Love: The Peace Corps and the Spirit of the 1960s* (Cambridge, Mass.: Harvard Univ. Press, 1998).

21. Ezekiel memorandum to Parker, 12 Feb. 1960, and FAO press release, 12 May 1960, both RG 12, box 2, folder 1, FAOA; Parker memorandum to Wright, 2 Mar. 1960, and "Report of the Informal Meeting of the FAO Fertilizer Survey Team with Representatives from Fertilizer Associations," Dec. 1959, both RG 12, box 2, folder 3, FAOA; minutes of working group on FFHC fertilizer program, 17 June 1960, RG 12, box 2, folder 1 or box 1, folder 11, FAOA; "Report of the Director-General on the Progress of the Freedom-from-Hunger Campaign," 17 May 1961, RG 12, box 3, folder 3, FAOA.

22. For industry involvement in the FFHC see Savary memorandum to Wright, 23 Mar. 1960, RG 12, box 2, folder 7, FAOA; and "Report of the Director-General on the Progress of the Freedom-from-Hunger Campaign," 17 May 1961, and "Report of the Third Session of the Government Advisory Committee on the Freedom-from-Hunger Campaign," both RG 12, box 3, folder 3, FAOA.

For the Near East wheat and barley project see "Dutch Housewives Back Freedom-from-Hunger Campaign," FAO press release, 12 May 1960, RG 12, box 2, folder 1, FAOA; and "Report of the Director-General on the Progress of the Freedom-from-Hunger Campaign," and reports of national committees on activities in support of the FFHC, annex 3 to report of meeting of European representatives of FFHC committees, 10 Nov. 1961, both RG 12, box 3, folder 3, FAOA.

23. Draft memorandum, "Expected Participation by Non-Governmental Organizations in the Freedom from Hunger Campaign," 23 Mar. 1960, RG 12, box 2, folder 7, FAOA. See also confidential memorandum from Veillet-Lavallée to Parker, Ezekiel, Weisl, Vogel, and Dey, 1 Feb. 1960, RG 12, box 1, folder 1, FAOA; "Principles and Methods Governing the Freedom-from-Hunger Campaign," attached to Sen letter to national governments, 8 Mar. 1960, RG 12, box 2, folder 3, FAOA; confidential Ezekiel memorandum to Addeke Henrik Boerma, 18 July 1960, RG 12, box 3, folder 4, FAOA; "FFHC Publicity Program for 1961," attached to Moulik memorandum to Sen, 5 Dec. 1960, RG 12, box 3, folder 16, FAOA; Sen, *Freedom from Hunger*, 17, 20, 23; first draft, "Outline of a Field Action Program under the Freedom from Hunger Campaign," 4 Dec. 1959, RG 12, box 1, folder 3, FAOA; draft memorandum to Sen from special group on FFHC budget, 14 Oct. 1959, and extract from provisional report of the tenth session of the conference, Nov. 1959, both RG 12, box 1, folder 1, FAOA; Sen, *The Basic Freedom*, 17; *FFHC National Action Projects*, x; and *Achievement*, 2.

24. "Report of the Director-General on the Progress of the Freedom-from-Hunger Campaign," 17 May 1961, box 3, folder 3, FAOA. For reaction of national governments to the FFHC see also unattributed "Report on visit to Germany and Switzerland," Feb. 1960, RG 12, box 2, folder 2, FAOA; Ezekiel memorandum to Sen, 24 Feb. 1960, RG 12, box 3, folder 4, FAOA; Sen letter to national governments with attached "Principles and Methods Governing the Freedom-from-Hunger Campaign," 8 Mar. 1960, RG 12, box 2, folder 3, FAOA; *Food for Peace* 3 (May 1963): 4; draft memorandum "Expected Participation by Non-Governmental Organizations in the Freedom from Hunger Campaign," 23 Mar. 1960, RG 12, box 2, folder 7, FAOA; Savary memorandum to Wright, 23 Mar. 1960, and Savary memorandum "Freedom-from-Hunger Campaign: Strength and Weaknesses," 1 Apr. 1960, both RG 12, box 2, folder 7, FAOA; "Reports Made by Representatives of Non-Governmental Organizations on their Activities," 15 Sept. 1960, RG 12, box 1, folder 10, FAOA; "FFHC Publicity Program for 1961," attached to Moulik memorandum to Sen, 5 Dec. 1960, RG 12, box 3, folder 16, FAOA; Weitz letter to R. Gachot, FAO Regional Officer for Latin America–Eastern Zone, 18 July 1961, and reports by national committees on activities in support of the FFHC, annex 3 to report of meeting of European representatives of FFHC committees, 10 Nov. 1961, both RG 12, box 3, folder 3, FAOA; Sen, *Towards a Newer World*, 128, 145, 152–53; Archer, "Methods of Multilateral Management," 312; and Gerald Furnivall and Alison Clarke, *Impact: The Freedom from Hunger Campaign in Relation to School Curricula and Examinations* (London: Education Department, Sept. 1965), 30.

For FFHC national committees see report of the third session of the government advisory committee on FFHC, 20 June 1961, RG 12, box 3, folder 3, FAOA; Sen opening address, appendix 2, and "Report by the Coordinator on Progress and Development," annex 3 to ibid.; and reports presented by national committees on activities in support of the FFHC, annex 3 to report of meeting of European representatives of FFHC committees, 10 Nov. 1961, RG 12, box 3, folder 3, FAOA.

25. De la Warr, "Freedom from Hunger Campaign," in *Gazebo*, ed. Clough, 8.

For UK enthusiasm and launch of campaign see Moulik report on visit to London, 28 Jan. 1960, RG 12, box 3, folder 4, FAOA; "Report of the Third Session of the Government Advisory Committee on the Freedom-from-Hunger Campaign," 20 June 1961, RG 12, box 3, folder 3, FAOA; Moulik memorandum to Ezekiel, 9 Feb. 1960, RG 12, box 1, folder 3, FAOA; and Sen, *Towards a Newer World*, 146.

26. For fund-raising efforts see Clough, "Introduction," in *Gazebo,* ed. Clough, 4; and "Report of the Third Session of the Government Advisory Committee on the Freedom-from-Hunger Campaign," 20 June 1961, RG 12, box 3, folder 3, FAOA.

For review procedure see Moulik memorandum to Ezekiel, 9 Feb. 1960, RG 12, box 1, folder 3, FAOA; de la Warr, "Freedom from Hunger Campaign," in *Gazebo,* ed. Clough, 7; and report of the third session of the government advisory committee on the FFHC, 20 June 1961, RG 12, box 3, folder 3, FAOA.

For educational efforts see de la Warr, "Freedom from Hunger Campaign," in *Gazebo,* ed. Clough, 6–7; Furnivall and Clarke, *Impact,* 4, 6; and "Report of the Third Session of the Government Advisory Committee on the Freedom-from-Hunger Campaign," and reports presented by national committees on activities in support of the FFHC, annex 3 to report of meeting of European representatives of the FFHC committees, 10 Nov. 1961, both RG 12, box 3, folder 3, FAOA.

27. "Panel: The Role of Food in Future World Peace," in *Role of Food in World Peace,* 28. See also "Principles and Methods Governing the Freedom-from-Hunger Campaign," attached to Sen letter to national governments, 8 Mar. 1960, RG 12, box 2, folder 3, FAOA; report by Dr. R. N. Poduval, Economic and Statistical Adviser to the Indian Ministry of Food and Agriculture, 13 June 1961, report of the third session of the government advisory committee on the FFHC, 20 June 1961, report of meeting of European FFHC committees, 10 Nov. 1961, and reports by national committees on activities in support of the FFHC, annex 3 to report of meeting of European representatives of FFHC committees, 10 Nov. 1961, all RG 12, box 3, folder 3, FAOA; draft memorandum, "Expected Participation by Non-Governmental Organizations in the Freedom from Hunger Campaign," 23 Mar. 1960, RG 12, box 2, folder 7; "Possibilities of Increasing World Food Production," Barton memorandum, 30 Jan. 1961, RG 12, box 3, folder 19, FAOA; "Positive Achievements in the Fight against Hunger," Parker draft article, 21 Aug. 1961, RG 12, box 1, folder 11, FAOA; Sen, *The Basic Freedom,* 17–18; *FFHC National Action Projects,* vi, ix, xiii, 147, 149; *Plan of Operations for the Programme of Protection of Pre-school Children which Will Be Carried out by the Ministry of Public Health and the National Institute of Nutrition, with Financial Cooperation from the United Kingdom Committee of the Freedom from Hunger Campaign: Supported by the National Federation of Women's Institutes* (Bogotá: Colombian National Institute of Nutrition, 1965); and *Development through Food,* 4.

28. For emphasis on education see "Possibilities of Increasing World Food Production," Barton memorandum, 30 Jan. 1961, RG 12, box 3, folder 19, FAOA; Sen, *The Basic Freedom,* 15; *FFHC National Action Projects,* ix, 5, 17, 25, 49, 63, 139, 147; FFHC, *Report on the FAO/National Farm Broadcasting Seminar,* 6; "Report of the Director-General on the Progress of the Freedom-from-Hunger Campaign," 17 May 1961, RG 12, box 3, folder 3, FAOA; Gulbrandsen, *Outboard Mechanization Projects,* 7; *Achievement,* 8; and Sen, *Towards a Newer World,* 154.

For radio work see *Report on the FAO Near East Farm Broadcasting Seminar* (Rome: FAO, 1963); and FFHC, *Report on the FAO/National Farm Broadcasting Seminar.*

29. *Development through Food,* 4. For protein-enrichment projects see also "Report of the Director-General on the Progress of the Freedom-from-Hunger Campaign," 17 May 1961, RG 12, box 3, folder 3, FAOA; *FFHC National Action Projects,* 21, 31; *Plan of Operations;* Freedom from Hunger Campaign, *Report to the Government of India: The Establishment of a Model Piggery* (Rome: FAO, 1971); and confidential Ezekiel memorandum to Boerma, 18 July 1960, RG 12, box 3, folder 4, FAOA.

For the outboard motor projects see minutes of the thirteenth meeting of the FFHC Policy Committee, 25 Nov. 1960, RG 12, box 3, folder 16, FAOA; "Report of the Director-General on the Progress of the Freedom-from-Hunger Campaign," 17 May 1961, RG 12, box 3, folder 3, FAOA; *FFHC National Action Projects,* 41, 53; Gulbrandsen, *Outboard Mechanization Projects;* and *Achievement,* 15.

30. "Possibilities of Increasing World Food Production," Barton memorandum, 30 Jan. 1961, RG 12, box 3, folder 19, FAOA; *FFHC National Action Projects,* 47, 49, 53, 69; J. C. Abbott, *Marketing: Its Role in Increasing Productivity,* FFHC Basic Study no. 4 (Rome: FAO, 1962).

31. Maw, "Foreword," in *Gazebo,* ed. Clough, 3; *Achievement,* 1–2, 8, 11–13; B. L. Amla, *Seventh Report of FAO International Food Technology Training Centre at the Central Food Technological Research Institute, Mysore City, India* (Rome: FAO, 1976).

32. Baer report to WILPF, Nov./Dec. 1959, RG 12, box 1, folder 6, FAOA. See also "Reports Made by Representatives of Non-Governmental Organizations on Their Activities," 15 Sept. 1960, RG 12, box 1, folder 10, FAOA; report of the third session of the government advisory committee on the FFHC, 20 June 1961, RG 12, box 3, folder 3, FAOA; report of the second session of the advisory committee of NGOs on the FFHC, appendix 4, and FFHC meeting of NGO information and education officers, annex 4 to report of the third session of the government advisory committee on the FFHC, 20 June 1961, both RG 12, box 3, folder 3, FAOA; Maw, "Foreword," in *Gazebo,* ed. Clough, 3; *Report on the FAO Near East Farm Broadcasting Seminar,* 7; *FFHC National Action Projects,* 47, 63, 109; and *Achievement,* 3–4, 7.

33. Sen, *Towards a Newer World,* 150.

For World Food Congress plans see "First Draft Proposals: World Food Congress," Ezekiel memorandum, 30 Mar. 1961, RG 12, box 1, folder 10, FAOA; draft proposals "World Food Congress," 14 June 1961, RG 12, box 1, folder 1, FAOA; position paper on World Food Congress for FFHC government advisory committee, 15 June 1961, RG 12, box 3, folder 23, FAOA; report of the third session of the government advisory committee on the FFHC, 20 June 1961, RG 12, box 3, folder 3, FAOA; and minutes of the third meeting of the working group on the World Food Congress, 9 Aug. 1961, "Suggested Syllabus of the Section on Development of Land, Water and Forestry Resources of the Technical Commission," Schickele memorandum, 16 Aug. 1961, Parker memorandum to Wright, 22 Aug. 1961, Dey memorandum to R. C. Fortunescu, Operations Officer of the FFHC Coordinator's Office, 22 Aug. 1961, and Ezekiel memorandum to Weitz, 27 Oct. 1961, all RG 12, box 3, folder 23, FAOA.

For lead-up to the campaign see also Sen, *Towards a Newer World,* 152–53, 162–63; draft memorandum "Expected Participation by Non-Governmental Organizations in the Freedom from Hunger Campaign," 23 Mar. 1960, RG 12, box 2, folder 7, FAOA; and reports by national committees of activities in support of the FFHC, annex 3 to report of meeting of European representatives of FFHC committees, 10 Nov. 1961, and report of the third session of the government advisory committee on the FFHC, 20 June 1961, both RG 12, box 3, folder 3, FAOA.

34. John F. Kennedy, "We Have the Means . . . We Need Only the Will," *Freedom from Hunger Campaign News* 4 (Sept. 1963): 2; *Food for Peace* 5 (July 1963): 3, 4; Sen, *Towards a Newer World,* 155. See also Sen, *Towards a Newer World,* 145–55, 158–59; *Food for Peace* 1 (Mar. 1963): 3–4; and 5 (July 1963): 1.

35. "First World Food Congress . . . An End and a Beginning," *Freedom from Hunger Campaign News* 4 (Sept. 1963): 11. See also Archer, "Methods of Multilateral Management," 312; Sen, *Towards a Newer World,* 155, 157–58, 235; and "Exhibit: How the Job Can be Done,"

"Editorial," and "First World Food Congress," *Freedom from Hunger Campaign News* 4 (Sept. 1963): ii, 1, 10, resp.

36. "Declaration of the World Food Congress," *Freedom from Hunger Campaign News* 4 (Sept. 1963): 12–13. See also *Food for Peace* 5 (July 1963): 2; Sen, *Towards a Newer World*, 155, 159, 210; and Archer, "Methods of Multilateral Management," 309, 311.

37. Sen, *Towards a Newer World*, 158, 160, 210–15, 218; report of the third session of the government advisory committee on FFHC, 20 June 1961, RG 12, box 3, folder 3, FAOA.

38. Sen, *Towards a Newer World*, 212. See also ibid., 210–14.

39. Ibid., 279.

40. Marchisio and di Blase, *Food and Agriculture Organization*, 67–91; Ross B. Talbot and H. Wayne Moyer, "Who Governs the Rome Food Agencies?" in *Peace by Pieces–United Nations Agencies and Their Roles: A Reader and Selective Bibliography*, ed. Robert N. Wells Jr. (Metuchen, N.J.: Scarecrow, 1991), 40–65.

8. The Growth of International Cooperation in Medicine

1. J. Bouillaud, *Essai sur la Philosophie Médicale, et sur les Generalites de la Clinique Medicale* (Paris: Rouvier et le Bouvier, 1836), 96–97, as cited in Richard Harrison Shryock, *The Development of Modern Medicine: An Interpretation of the Social and Scientific Factors Involved*, 2d ed. (New York: Knopf, 1947), 167.

For the growing emphasis on clinical and scientific medicine between 1800 and 1850 generally see also, e.g., Shryock, *Development of Modern Medicine*, 151–77, 185–87; Edward Kremers and George Urdang, *History of Pharmacy: A Guide and a Survey*, 2d rev. and enlarged ed. (Philadelphia, Pa.: Lippincott, 1951); John E. Lesch, "The Paris Academy of Medicine and Experimental Science, 1820–1848," in *The Investigative Enterprise: Experimental Physiology in Nineteenth-Century Medicine*, ed. William Coleman and Frederic L. Holmes (Berkeley: Univ. of California Press, 1988), 100–38; John E. Lesch, *Science and Medicine in France: The Emergence of Experimental Physiology, 1790–1855* (Cambridge, Mass.: Harvard Univ. Press, 1984); S. Leff and Vera Leff, *From Witchcraft to World Health* (New York: Macmillan, 1958), 151–55; Fielding H. Garrison, *An Introduction to the History of Medicine*, 4th rev. and enlarged ed. (Philadelphia, Pa.: W. B. Saunders, 1929), 465–67; and Owsei Temkin, "The Scientific Approach to Disease: Specific Entity and Individual Illness," in *Scientific Change: Historical Studies in the Intellectual, Social and Technical Conditions for Scientific Discovery and Technical Invention, from Antiquity to the Present*, ed. A. C. Crombie (New York: Basic, 1963), 629–47.

For the "numerical method" see P. C. A. Louis, *Recherches sur les Effets de la Saignée dans Quelques Maladies Inflammatoires* (Paris: J. B. Bailliere, 1835); Lester S. King, *Transformations in American Medicine: From Benjamin Rush to William Osler* (Baltimore, Md.: Johns Hopkins Univ. Press, 1991), 190–95; and Garrison, *Introduction to the History of Medicine*, 410–11.

For the invention of new clinical tools see Martin Duke, *The Development of Medical Techniques and Treatments: From Leeches to Heart Surgery* (Madison, Conn.: International Universities Press, 1991), 31–54; Stanley Joel Reiser, *Medicine and the Reign of Technology* (Cambridge, UK: Cambridge Univ. Press, 1978), 23–44; and Sherwin B. Nuland, *Doctors: A Biography of Medicine* (New York: Knopf, 1988), 200–37.

2. For public health work see James H. Cassedy, *Charles V. Chapin and the Public Health*

Movement (Cambridge, Mass.: Harvard Univ. Press, 1962); James G. Burrow, *Organized Medicine in the Progressive Era: The Move toward Monopoly* (Baltimore, Md.: Johns Hopkins Univ. Press, 1977), 88–102; Judith Walzer Leavitt, "Public Health and Preventive Medicine," in *The Education of American Physicians: Historical Essays,* ed. Ronald L. Numbers (Berkeley: Univ. of California Press, 1980), 250–72; Wilson G. Smillie, *Public Health, Its Promise for the Future: A Chronology of the Development of Public Health in the United States, 1607–1914* (New York: Macmillan, 1955), 228–70, 284–458; Richard A. Meckel, *Save the Babies: American Public Health Reform and the Prevention of Infant Mortality, 1850–1929* (Baltimore, Md.: Johns Hopkins Univ. Press, 1990); and Rosenberg, *No Other Gods,* 109–22.

For the growing emphasis on clinical and scientific medical education between 1800 and 1850 see, e.g., Thomas Neville Bonner, *Becoming a Physician: Medical Education in Britain, France, Germany, and the United States, 1750–1945* (New York: Oxford Univ. Press, 1995), 99–103, 142, 158–82, 203, 231; Jeffrey Lionel Berlant, *Profession and Monopoly: A Study of Medicine in the United States and Great Britain* (Berkeley: Univ. of California Press, 1975), 153–61; Richard Harrison Shryock, *Medical Licensing in America, 1650–1965* (Baltimore, Md.: Johns Hopkins Press, 1967); Robert C. Derbyshire, *Medical Licensure and Discipline in the United States* (Baltimore, Md.: Johns Hopkins Press, 1969), 3–6; and Charles Newman, *The Evolution of Medical Education in the Nineteenth Century* (London: Oxford Univ. Press, 1957), 82–248.

For the debates over the origin of disease see Charles-Edward Amory Winslow, *The Conquest of Epidemic Disease: A Chapter in the History of Ideas* (Princeton, N.J.: Princeton Univ. Press, 1943; reprint, Madison: Univ. of Wisconsin Press, 1980).

3. For Panum's work see Winslow, *Conquest of Epidemic Disease,* 265–71; William M. Gafafer, "Peter Ludwig Panum's 'Observations on the Contagium of Measles,'" *Isis* 24 (Dec. 1935): 90–101; and P. L. Panum, *Observations Made during the Epidemic of Measles on the Faroe Islands in the Year 1846,* trans. A. S. Hatcher (New York: Delta Omega Society, 1940).

For Snow's work see Winslow, *Conquest of Epidemic Disease,* 265, 270–79, 290; and J. Snow, *On the Mode of Communication of Cholera* (London: J. Churchill, 1849).

For Budd's work see Winslow, *Conquest of Epidemic Disease,* 265, 270–71, 279–90; William Budd, *Typhoid Fever: Its Nature, Mode of Spreading, and Prevention* (London: Longmans, Green, 1873).

For the general neglect of the importance of this work see Norman Howard-Jones, *The Scientific Background of the International Sanitary Conferences, 1851–1938* (Geneva: WHO, 1975), 17–21, 27–28, 34, 42–43, 56–57, 69. This was also printed serially in *Chronicle of the World Health Organization* 28 (1974): 159–71, 229–47, 348–69, 414–26, 455–70, 495–508.

4. For the microscope's role in establishing germ theory see Winslow, *Conquest of Epidemic Disease,* 293; Shryock, *Development of Modern Medicine,* 201–203; Reiser, *Medicine and the Reign of Technology,* 69–90; Ann La Berge, "Medical Microscopy in Paris, 1830–1855," in *French Medical Culture in the Nineteenth Century,* ed. Ann La Berge and Mordechai Feingold (Amsterdam: Editions Rodopi B. V., 1994), 296–326; Nuland, *Doctors,* 304–42; and Lester S. King, *The Growth of Medical Thought* (Chicago, Ill.: Univ. of Chicago Press, 1963), 175–219.

For Pasteur see Winslow, *Conquest of Epidemic Disease,* 291–310; E. Duclaux, *Pasteur: The History of a Mind,* trans. E. F. Smith and F. Hedges (Philadelphia, Pa.: W. B. Saunders, 1920); and R. Vallery-Radot, *The Life of Pasteur,* trans. R. L. Devonshire, 2 vols. (New York: McClure, Philips, 1902).

For Lister see Winslow, *Conquest of Epidemic Disease,* 301–303, 307, 310; J. Lister, *The Collected Papers of Joseph, Baron Lister,* 2 vols. (Oxford, UK: Clarendon, 1909); Frederick F. Cartwright, *The Development of Modern Surgery* (New York: T. Y. Crowell, 1967); Lindsay Granshaw, "'Upon This Principle I Have Based a Practice': The Development and Reception of Antisepsis in Britain, 1867–90," in *Medical Innovations in Historical Perspective,* ed. John V. Pickstone (New York: St. Martin's, 1992), 17–46; Nuland, *Doctors,* 343–85; and F. F. Cartwright, "Antiseptic Surgery," and John Shepherd, "Lister and the Development of Abdominal Surgery," in *Medicine and Science in the 1860s,* ed. F. N. L. Poynter (London: Wellcome Institute for the History of Medicine, 1968), 77–103, 105–15.

For Koch see Winslow, *Conquest of Epidemic Disease,* 307–10; Garrison, *Introduction to the History of Medicine,* 578–80; and Howard-Jones, *Scientific Background of the International Sanitary Conferences,* 47–51. Howard-Jones points out in *Scientific Background of the International Sanitary Conferences* that the Florentine microscopist Filippo Pacini actually discovered and identified the cholera vibrio thirty years before Koch, but this finding was ignored by the scientific medical community (17, 20, 28, 35).

5. For the shift toward laboratory training of doctors see Bonner, *Becoming a Physician,* 231–308, 347; Arleen M. Tuchman, "From the Lecture to the Laboratory: The Institutionalization of Scientific Medicine at the University of Heidelberg," in *The Investigative Enterprise,* ed. Coleman and Holmes, 65–99; Newman, *Evolution of Medical Education,* 265–310; Martha L. Hildreth, *Doctors, Bureaucrats, and Public Health in France, 1888–1902* (New York: Garland, 1987), 36–163; Theodor Billroth, *The Medical Sciences in the German Universities: A Study in the History of Civilization* (New York: Macmillan, 1924), 1–42; Burrow, *Organized Medicine in the Progressive Era,* 31–51; and Morris J. Vogel, "The Transformation of the American Hospital, 1850–1920," in *Health Care in America: Essays in Social History,* ed. Susan Reverby (Philadelphia, Pa.: Temple Univ. Press, 1979), 108–12.

For the growing public confidence in physicians see Samuel Haber, *The Quest for Authority and Honor in the American Professions, 1750–1900* (Chicago, Ill.: Univ. of Chicago Press, 1991), 319–58; and Noel Parry and José Parry, *The Rise of the Medical Profession: A Study of Collective Social Mobility* (London: Croom Helm, 1976), 131–61.

6. For short overview of the great changes in American medicine see Burrow, *Organized Medicine in the Progressive Era,* 3–13.

For the creation of Johns Hopkins specifically see Bonner, *Becoming a Physician,* 267, 292–93, 298; Haber, *Quest for Authority and Honor,* 321–26; John S. Billings, "The Plans and Purposes of the Johns Hopkins Hospital," *Medical News* 54 (1 May 1889): 505–10; Alan Mason Chesney, *The Johns Hopkins Hospital and the Johns Hopkins University School of Medicine: A Chronicle,* vol. 1: *Early Years: 1867–1893,* vol. 2: *1893–1905,* vol. 3: *1905–1914* (Baltimore, Md.: Johns Hopkins Univ. Press, 1943–1963); Harvey W. Cushing, *The Life of Sir William Osler,* 2 vols. (London: Oxford Univ. Press, 1940); Donald Harnish Fleming, *William H. Welch and the Rise of Modern Medicine* (Boston, Mass.: Little, Brown, 1954); Richard H. Shryock, *The Unique Influence of the Johns Hopkins University in American Medicine* (Copenhagen: Munksgaard, 1953); Nuland, *Doctors,* 386–421; and A. McGehee Harvey, *Science at the Bedside: Clinical Research in American Medicine, 1905–1945* (Baltimore, Md.: Johns Hopkins Univ. Press, 1981), 63–103, 153–83.

For emulators of the Hopkins model see Harvey, *Science at the Bedside,* 189–399; Horace W. Davenport, *Fifty Years of Medicine at the University of Michigan, 1891–1941* (Ann Arbor: Univ. of Michigan Medical School, 1986), 1–35; Henry K. Beecher and Mark D. Altschule,

Medicine at Harvard: The First Three Hundred Years (Hanover, N.H.: Univ. Press of New England, 1977), 175–213; and Timothy C. Jacobson, *Making Medical Doctors: Science and Medicine at Vanderbilt since Flexner* (Tuscaloosa: Univ. of Alabama Press, 1987).

For licensing and the rising influence of professional associations see Derbyshire, *Medical Licensure,* 6–10; Shryock, *Medical Licensing;* Berlant, *Profession and Monopoly,* 167–76; 180–81, 234–50; Haber, *Quest for Authority and Honor,* 329–32, 336–42; Burrow, *Organized Medicine in the Progressive Era,* 14–28; Samuel L. Baker, "Physician Licensure Laws in the United States, 1865–1915," *Journal of the History of Medicine and Allied Sciences* 39 (1984): 173–94; William Osler, "The License to Practice," *Journal of the American Medical Association* 12 (1889): 649–54; Ernest Muirhead Little, *History of the British Medical Association, 1832–1932* (London: British Medical Association, 1932); and Elton Rayack, *Professional Power and American Medicine: The Economics of the American Medical Association* (Cleveland, Ohio: World Publishing, 1967), 66–106.

For the exclusion of African Americans and women see Thomas Neville Bonner, *To the Ends of the Earth: Women's Search for Education in Medicine* (Cambridge, Mass.: Harvard Univ. Press, 1992); Mary Roth Walsh, *"Doctors Wanted–No Women Need Apply": Sexual Barriers in the Medical Profession, 1835–1975* (New Haven, Conn.: Yale Univ. Press, 1975), esp. 178–225; Herbert M. Morais, *The History of the Negro in Medicine* (New York: Publishers Company, 1967), 39–130; Gloria Moldow, *Women Doctors in Gilded-Age Washington, D.C.: Race, Gender, and Professionalization* (Urbana: Univ. of Illinois Press, 1987); W. Montague Cobb, *The First Negro Medical Society: A History of the Medico–Chirurgical Society of the District of Columbia, 1884–1939* (Washington, D.C.: Associated Publishers, 1939); Gulielma Fell Alsop, *History of the Woman's Medical College, Philadelphia, Pennsylvania, 1850–1950* (Philadelphia, Pa.: Lippincott, 1950), 1–37, 45–74, 95–229; Regina Markell Morantz, "Feminism, Professionalism, and Germs," *American Quarterly* 34 (Winter 1982): 460–78; and Mary Roth Walsh, "Women in Medicine Since Flexner," and Todd L. Savitt, "Abraham Flexner and the Black Medical Schools," in *Beyond Flexner: Medical Education in the Twentieth Century,* ed. Barbara Barzansky and Norman Gevitz (New York: Greenwood, 1992), 51–63, 65–81.

For the exclusion of other types of medical education see John S. Haller Jr., *Medical Protestants: The Eclectics in American Medicine, 1825–1939* (Carbondale: Southern Illinois Univ. Press, 1994), 198–251; Martin Kaufman, *Homeopathy in America: The Rise and Fall of a Medical Heresy* (Baltimore, Md.: Johns Hopkins Univ. Press, 1971), esp. 156–73; and William G. Rothstein, *American Physicians in the Nineteenth Century: From Sects to Science* (Baltimore, Md.: Johns Hopkins Univ. Press, 1972), 152–74, 217–46, 298–326.

For the development of the new ideal in medical education see Bonner, *Becoming a Physician,* 304–43, 347.

7. For the international training of many physicians see Bonner, *Becoming a Physician,* 164, 178–79, 242, 244, 248–49, 264, 292, 308, 313, 336; Winslow, *Conquest of Epidemic Disease,* 267–68, 280, 308; Deborah C. Brunton, "The Transfer of Medical Education: Teaching at the Edinburgh and Philadelphia Medical Schools," in *Scotland and America in the Age of the Enlightenment,* ed. Richard B. Sher and Jeffrey R. Smitten (Princeton, N.J.: Princeton Univ. Press, 1990), 242–58; Stephen Jacyna, "Robert Carswell and William Thomson at the Hôtel-Dieu of Lyons: Scottish Views of French Medicine," in *British Medicine in an Age of Reform,* ed. Roger French and Andrew Wear (London: Routledge, 1991), 110–35; Bonner, *To the Ends of the Earth,* 31–80; Thomas Neville Bonner, *American Doctors and German*

Universities: A Chapter in International Intellectual Relations, 1870–1914 (Lincoln: Univ. of Nebraska Press, 1987); Martin David Dubin, "The League of Nations Health Organisation," in *International Health Organisations and Movements, 1918–1939,* ed. Paul Weindling (Cambridge, UK: Cambridge Univ. Press, 1995), 66; Francis R. Packard, *History of Medicine in the United States,* vol. 2 (New York: Paul B. Hoeber, 1931), 949–1052; Russell M. Jones, ed., *The Parisian Education of an American Surgeon: Letters of Jonathan Mason Warren, 1832–1835* (Philadelphia, Pa.: American Philosophical Society, 1978); and Owsei Temkin, *The Double Face of Janus and Other Essays in the History of Medicine* (Baltimore, Md.: Johns Hopkins Univ. Press, 1977), 252–68.

For Billings and the *Index Medicus* see Shryock, *Development of Modern Medicine,* 182–83; Harry Miller Lydenberg, *John Shaw Billings, Creator of the National Medical Library and Its Catalogue* (Chicago, Ill.: American Library Assoc., 1924); and Garrison, *Introduction to the History of Medicine,* 668–69.

8. Evan Schofer, "Science Associations in the International Sphere, 1875–1990: The Rationalization of Science and the Scientization of Society," in *Constructing World Culture: International Nongovernmental Organizations since 1875,* ed. John Boli and George M. Thomas (Stanford, Calif.: Stanford Univ. Press, 1999), 249–66; Elisabeth Crawford, *Nationalism and Internationalism in Science, 1880–1939* (Cambridge, UK: Cambridge Univ. Press, 1992).

For Farr and the International Statistical Congresses see John M. Eyler, *Victorian Social Medicine: The Ideas and Methods of William Farr* (Baltimore, Md.: Johns Hopkins Univ. Press, 1979); P. H. Eijkman, *L'Internationalisme Médical* (Amsterdam: F. Van Rossen for the Fondation pour l'Internationalisme, 1910), notes 152–54; and Donald A. Mackenzie, *Statistics in Britain, 1865–1930: The Social Construction of Scientific Knowledge* (Edinburgh, UK: Edinburgh Univ. Press, 1981).

For the International Congress of Medicine see Eijkman, *L'Internationalisme Médical,* note 1. For the International Congress on Hygiene and Demography see Howard-Jones, *Scientific Background of the International Health Conferences,* 75–77; and Eijkman, *L'Internationalisme Médical,* note 69.

For international specialist medical organizations see Eijkman, *L'Internationalisme Médical;* and Norman Howard-Jones, *International Public Health between the Two World Wars: The Organizational Problems* (Geneva: WHO, 1978), 30. This last was also published serially in *Chronicle of the World Health Organization* 31 and 32 (1977 and 1978): 391–403, 449–60, 26–38, 63–75, 114–25, 156–66. Among the specialist groups that met in international medical congresses at least twice before the outbreak of World War I were the anatomists, physiologists, pharmacists, physiotherapists, radiologists, gynecologists and obstetricians, ophthalmologists, psychologists, experimental psychologists, dermatologists, nose and throat specialists, ear specialists, dentists, applied chemists, specialists on leprosy, specialists on tuberculosis, and nurses.

9. For the Conseil Supérieur de Santé de Constantinople see Oleg P. Schepin and Waldemar V. Yermakov, *International Quarantine,* trans. Boris Meerovich and Vladimir Bobrov (Madison, Conn.: International Universities Press, 1991), 51–59; and Norman Howard-Jones, *The Pan American Health Organization: Origins and Evolution* (Geneva: WHO, 1981), 19. The Howard-Jones piece was first published serially in *Chronicle of the World Health Organization* 34 (1980): 367–75, 419–26.

For origins of the sanitary conferences see Howard-Jones, *Scientific Background of the International Sanitary Conferences,* 9–16; Javed Siddiqi, *World Health and World Politics:*

The World Health Organization and the UN System (Columbia: Univ. of South Carolina Press, 1995), 14–16; and George Rosen, *A History of Public Health,* expanded ed. (Baltimore, Md.: Johns Hopkins Univ. Press, 1958), 266–69. Austria-Hungary, France, Great Britain, Greece, the Papal States, Portugal, Russia, Sardinia, the Two Sicilies, Spain, Turkey, and Tuscany were the participants in the first International Sanitary Conference.

10. Howard-Jones, *Scientific Background of the International Sanitary Conferences,* 17–57; Schepin and Yermakov, *International Quarantine,* 74–123.

11. For the Egyptian Council see LaVerne Kuhnke, *Lives at Risk: Public Health in Nine-teenth-Century Egypt* (Berkeley: Univ. of California Press, 1990), 92–110.

For international sanitary conferences and conventions and OIHP see Howard-Jones, *Scientific Background of the International Sanitary Conferences,* 58–98; Siddiqi, *World Health,* 17–19; Schepin and Yermakov, *International Quarantine,* 125–58, 169–210; and Rosen, *History of Public Health,* 269.

12. Schepin and Yermakov, *International Quarantine,* 159–68; Howard-Jones, *Pan American Health Organization,* 5, 7–16; Fred Lowe Soper, *Ventures in World Health: The Memoirs of Fred Lowe Soper* (Washington, D.C.: PAHO, 1977), 313, 315; "El Dr. John D. Long entra en el Servicio del Gobierno de Chile como Asesor Sanitario," *Boletín de la Oficina Sanitaria Panamericana* 8 (1925): 283–84; "Fourth Meeting," in WHOIC, *Minutes of the Technical Preparatory Committee,* 14.

13. Howard-Jones, *Scientific Background of International Sanitary Conferences,* 86–88, 93, and *International Public Health between the Two World Wars,* 13–15.

14. Siddiqi, *World Health,* 19–20; League of Nations, *Ten Years of World Co-operation* (London: Hazell, Watson, and Viney for League Secretariat, 1930), 232; Howard-Jones, *Scientific Background to the International Sanitary Conferences,* 93, and *International Public Health between the Two World Wars,* 14–15, 17–19.

15. For the work of the epidemic commission see Dubin, "League of Nations Health Or-ganisation," and Marta Aleksandra Balinska, "Assistance and Not Mere Relief: The Epidem-ic Commission of the League of Nations, 1920–1923," in *International Health Organisations and Movements,* ed. Weindling, 67–68, 81–108; League of Nations, *Report of the Epidemic Commission of the League of Nations* (Geneva: Imprimerie Atar for League, 1921, 1922); League, *Ten Years of World Co-operation,* 232–33, 235–36; and Howard-Jones, *International Public Health between the Two World Wars,* 19–20, 36, 38.

For LRCS work see Howard-Jones, *International Public Health between the Two World Wars,* 9–15, 17, 19–20, 23–26, 34, 36–37, 44–45; and Bridget Towers, "Red Cross Organisa-tional Politics, 1918–1922: Relations of Dominance and the Influence of the United States," in *International Health Organisations and Movements,* ed. Weindling, 36–55.

For subsequent LNHO emergency work see "The Floods in China: Report by the Medical Director of the Health Organisation of the Work Undertaken to Co-Ordinate the Campaign against Epidemics," *Quarterly Bulletin of the Health Organisation* 1 (Mar. 1932): 142–57.

16. League, *Ten Years of World Co-operation,* 233–35, 245; Dubin, "League of Nations Health Organisation," in *International Health Organisations and Movements,* ed. Wein-dling, 58–59, 62–71; Howard-Jones, *International Public Health between the Two World Wars,* 35–36.

17. Dubin, "League of Nations Health Organisation," in *International Health Organisa-tions and Movements,* ed. Weindling, 59–60, 64–69, 72–73; Charles W. Popkin, *The Interchange*

of Public Health Personnel under the Health Organisation of the League of Nations: A Study in the Creation of an International Standard of Public Health Administration (Geneva: League of Nations Non-Partisan Association, 1928).

18. For the League's epidemiological work see League, *Ten Years of World Co-operation,* 236–37, 240–41; Schepin and Yermakov, *International Quarantine,* 211–29; "Report of the Health Organisation for the Period October 1932 to September 1933," *Quarterly Bulletin of the Health Organisation* 2 (Sept. 1933): 543–45; and "Report on the Work of the Health Organisation between June 1937 and May 1938," 656–58.

For the relationship between the LNHO and the OIHP see Howard-Jones, *Scientific Background of the International Sanitary Conferences,* 94–95; and League, *Ten Years of World Co-operation,* 238–39.

For the Singapore bureau see League, *Ten Years of World Co-operation,* 239; Lenore Manderson, "Wireless Wars in the Eastern Arena: Epidemiological Surveillance, Disease Prevention and the Work of the Eastern Bureau of the League of Nations Health Organisation, 1925–1942," in *International Health Organisations and Movements,* ed. Weindling, 109–33; R. Gautier, "Tropical Pneumonia," *Quarterly Bulletin of the Health Organisation* 1 (Mar. 1932): 64–109; and "Report of the Health Organisation for the Period October 1932 to September 1933," 546.

For LNHO in Asia, Latin America, and Africa see "Report of the Health Organisation for the Period October 1932 to September 1933," 497–514; "Report of the International Conference of Representatives of the Health Services of Certain African Territories and British India, held at Cape Town, November 15th to 25th, 1932," *Quarterly Bulletin of the Health Organisation* 2 (Mar. 1933): 3–115; and Dubin, "League of Nations Health Organisation," in *International Health Organisations and Movements,* ed. Weindling, 60, 63.

19. League, *Ten Years of World Co-operation,* 242–45; R. Burri, "The Milk Supply of North-American Cities: Impressions from a Study Tour undertaken under the Auspices of the Health Organisation of the League of Nations," *Quarterly Bulletin of the Health Organisation* 1 (Mar. 1932): 7–45; "Report on the Health Organisation for the Period October 1932 to September 1933," 519; "Current Notes on the Work of the Health Organisation: The Twentieth Session of the Health Committee," *Quarterly Bulletin of the Health Organisation* 2 (Dec. 1933): 752; "Report on the Work of the Health Organisation between June 1937 and May 1938," 652–56; Dubin, "League of Nations Health Organisation," in *International Health Organisations and Movements,* ed. Weindling, 72–73.

20. League, *Ten Years of World Co-operation,* 245–60; Howard-Jones, *International Public Health between the Two World Wars,* 36–38; and from *Quarterly Bulletin of the Health Organisation:* "Immunisation against Diphtheria: Resolutions of the Conference Held in London in June 1931," and A. G. McKendrick, "A Second Analytical Review of Reports from Pasteur Institutes on the Results of Anti-Rabies Treatment," 1 (Mar. 1932): 1–6, 110–41, resp.; "Commission on the Fumigation of Ships," Ludwik Anigstein, "Malaria and Anophelines in Siam: Report on a Study Tour," and "Current Notes on the Work of the Health Organisation," 1 (June 1932): 208–32, 233–308, 309–11, resp.; "The Most Suitable Methods of Detecting Malnutrition due to the Economic Depression," and "Typhoid Fever in Rural Areas," 2 (Mar. 1933): 116–29, 154–75 resp.; "The Therapeutics of Malaria: Third General Report of the Malaria Commission," and "Report on the Best Methods of Safeguarding the Public Health during the Depression," 2 (June 1933): 181–285, 286–332, resp.; S. R. Christophers and A. Missiroli, "Report on Housing and Malaria," J. Tandler, "The Reform of

Medical Education," and "Report of the Health Organisation for the Period, October 1932 to September 1933," 2 (Sept. 1933): 355–482, 483–94, 495–549, resp.; A. G. McKendrick, "A Fourth Analytical Review of Reports from Pasteur Institutes on the Results of Anti-Rabies Treatment," Friedrich Schmidt, "Suburban Settlements for Unemployed in Germany," and "Current Notes on the Work of the Health Organisation," 2 (Dec. 1933): 585–99, 600–19, 750–52, resp.; and "Report of the Group of Experts on the Commission on Physical Education," "Report on the Work of the Health Organisation between June 1937 and May 1938," "Technical Commission on Nutrition: Report by a Special Committee Which Met in Geneva from August 22d to 24th, 1938," and J. Orskov, "Some Preliminary Remarks on the Question of the Standardisation of Smallpox Vaccine," 7 (Aug. 1938): 609–21, 622–65, 666–78, 679–81, resp.

21. For the League's standardization and statistical work see "Report of the Health Organisation for the Period October 1932 to September 1933," 520–22; "Report on the Work of the Health Organisation between June 1937 and May 1938," 631–36; "Report on the Meeting of Serologists of the Permanent Commission on Biological Standardisation," *Quarterly Bulletin of the Health Organisation* 7 (Oct. 1938): 683–88; Dubin, "League of Nations Health Organisation," in *International Health Organisations and Movements,* ed. Weindling, 59–60; and W. C. Cockburn, "The International Contribution to the Standardization of Biological Substances. 1. Biological Standards and the League of Nations, 1921–1946," *Biologicals* 19 (1991): 161–69. The subjects of such standardization included antitoxins, hormones, vitamins, tuberculin, agglutination tests, and sera.

22. "Joint Declaration by the Delegations of Brazil and China," printed as appendix I in Szeming Sze, *The Origins of the World Health Organization: A Personal Memoir, 1945–1948* (Boca Raton, Fla.: LISZ, 1982), 27 and as "Annex 1: San Francisco Resolution and Summary of Events Leading up to the Meeting of the Technical Preparatory Committee," in WHOIC, *Minutes of the Technical Preparatory Committee,* 39.

For the work of the UNRRA health section see "Fourth Meeting," and "Annex 9: Suggestions Relating to the Constitution of an International Health Organization (Submitted by Dr. A. Stampar, Yugoslavia)," in *Minutes of the Technical Preparatory Committee,* 13–14, 56–57; and note on the organization and activities of the UNRRA Health Division by Dr. Wilbur A. Sawyer, UNRRA Director of Health, 26 June 1946, World Health Organization Archives, Geneva, Switzerland [hereafter WHOA], microform: International Health Conference: Committees Documents [hereafter IHC: CD], card 13.

For the development of the San Francisco resolution see Sze, *Origins of the World Health Organization,* 1–9.

23. "Third Meeting," "Fourth Meeting," and "Annex 10: Draft of 'Preamble' to the Convention of the World Health Organization (Submitted by the Sub-Committee)," in WHO-IC, *Minutes of the Technical Preparatory Committee,* 12, 13, 61.

For ECOSOC work on the WHO see "Resolution on the Calling of an International Health Conference," printed as appendix 2 in Sze, *Origins of the World Health Organization,* 28–29; and "Annex 2: Resolution of the Economic and Social Council of the United Nations of 15 Feb. 1946," in WHOIC, *Minutes of the Technical Preparatory Committee,* 39–40.

For the belief that the WHO should have a broad mandate see also "Sixth Meeting," "Annex 8: Proposal for an International Convention Establishing the International Health Organization (Submitted by Dr. A. Cavaillon and Dr. X. Leclainche, France)," and "Annex 12: Modifications to the Section on 'Functions' as Defined in the Text by Surgeon-General

Parran (Submitted by the Sub-Committee on Aims and Objectives)," WHOIC, Minutes of the Technical Preparatory Committee, 17, 50, 62.

For emphasis on positive health see also "Sixth Meeting," "Eighth Meeting," "Annex 7: Proposals for the Establishment of an International Health Organization (Submitted by Surgeon-General T. Parran, United States of America)," and "Annex 11: Draft of 'Aims and Objectives' (Submitted by the Sub-Committee)," ibid., 17–18, 19, 46, 62.

For the preamble see also "Sixth Meeting," and "Seventh Meeting," ibid., 17, 19.

24. For the general work and character of the Technical Preparatory Committee see Sze, *Origins of the World Health Organization,* 13–16; and "Third Meeting," in WHOIC, *Minutes of the Technical Preparatory Committee,* 21.

For the draft constitutions see "Annex 6: Proposals for the Establishment of an International Health Organization (Submitted by Sir Wilson Jameson, United Kingdom); "Annex 7," "Annex 8," and "Annex 9," in WHOIC, *Minutes of the Technical Preparatory Committee,* 42–45, 46–49, 49–53, 54–61; and Soper, *Ventures in World Health,* 310.

For the WHO organizational structure see "Nineteenth Meeting," "Annex 6," "Annex 7," "Annex 8," "Annex 13: Draft of the Sections on the 'Governing Body and Executive Council' (Submitted by the Sub-Committee of the Governing Body)," "Annex 14: Modifications to the Sections on the 'Governing Board and Executive Organ' in the Text by Surgeon-General Parran (Submitted by the Sub-Committee for the Executive Organ)," "Annex 15: Draft of the Section dealing with the 'Director-General' (Submitted by the Sub-Committee)," and "Annex 23: Proposals for the Constitution of the World Health Organization (As submitted to the Economic and Social Council)," in WHOIC, *Minutes of the Technical Preparatory Committee,* 33, 43–44, 47–48, 50–52, 62–63, 63–64, 64–65, 71–72.

For emphasis on secretariat's technical proficiency see "Second Meeting," "Third Meeting," "Tenth Meeting," and "Annex 15," ibid., 10–11, 12, 22, 64.

For emphasis on assembly delegates being national public health administrators see "Second Meeting," "Sixth Meeting," "Ninth Meeting," "Annex 6," "Annex 7," and "Annex 8," ibid., 11, 16, 21, 43, 47, 50.

For emphasis on cooperation with other intergovernmental organizations and NGOs see "Second Meeting," "Third Meeting," "Eighth Meeting," "Twelfth Meeting," "Annex 6," and "Annex 8," ibid., 10–11, 12, 19–20, 24–25, 43–44, 53.

For emphasis on universal membership see "Second Meeting," "Fourth Meeting," "Twentieth Meeting," "Twenty-second Meeting," "Annex 6," "Annex 8," "Annex 18: Draft of the Section Dealing with 'Membership' (Submitted by the Drafting Sub-Committee)," and "Annex 24: Resolutions (As adopted by the Technical Preparatory Committee on 5 April 1946)," ibid., 11, 14, 34, 35, 42, 50, 66, 75.

For questions left to conference to resolve see "Ninth Meeting," "Eleventh Meeting," and "Twenty-first Meeting," ibid., 21, 23, 34.

25. "Second Meeting," "Seventeenth Meeting," "Annex 21: Alternative Proposals relating to 'Regionalization,'" and "Annex 22: Note on 'Regionalization in World Health Affairs' (Submitted by Surgeon-General T. Parran, United States of America)," ibid., 10, 30, 67, 68–69.

For the dispute over regional organization see also "Fourth Meeting," "Eighth Meeting," "Fourteenth Meeting," "Sixteenth Meeting," "Seventeenth Meeting," "Eighteenth Meeting," "Nineteenth Meeting," "Annex 6," "Annex 19: Proposals on 'Regional Arrangements' (Submitted by Dr. C. Mani and Dr. S. Sze)," "Annex 20: Amendment to the Proposals of Dr. Mani and Dr. Sze (Suggested by Surgeon-General T. Parran)," "Annex 21," "Annex 22," and

"Annex 23," ibid., 14, 19, 27–28, 29–30, 30–31, 31, 32, 44–45, 66, 66, 67, 67–69, 73–74; Sze, *Origins of the World Health Organization,* 15; and Howard-Jones, *Pan American Health Organization,* 17.

For agreement on WHO absorption of OIHP, LNHO, and UNRRA Health Section see "Annex 6," and "Annex 24," in WHOIC, *Minutes of the Technical Preparatory Committee,* 45, 76.

26. "Remarks of Surgeon General Thomas Parran," 20 June 1946, RG 59, Decimal File 1945–49, 501.NA, box 2222, NACP.

For WHO as pioneering organization see also speech by Professor Henry Laugier, Assistant Secretary-General of the UN in charge of the Department of Social Affairs at the opening session of the International Health Conference, 19 June 1946, RG 59, Decimal File 1945–49, 501.NA, box 2223, NACP.

For WHO as building block of peace see also comments of Parran, U.S. Surgeon General, and E. L. Bishop, Tennessee Valley Authority [TVA] Director of Health, "Advisory Health Group," confidential State Department report, 11 Oct. 1945, RG 59, Decimal File 1945–49, 501.NA, box 2229, NACP.

27. For discussion of universal membership see Articles 3–6 and 8 of the WHO Constitution; WHOIC, *Summary Report on Proceedings, Minutes and Final Acts of the International Health Conference, Held in New York from 19 June to 22 July 1946,* Official Records of the World Health Organization, no. 2 (New York: WHOIC, June 1948), 18; statement on membership by the U.S. delegate to Committee III, 27 June 1949, and summary record of the sixth meeting of Committee 3, 11 July 1946, both microform: IHC: CD, card 9, WHOA; and restricted Acheson letter to Parran, 15 June 1946, memorandum from John C. Dreier, U.S. State Department Division of Special Inter-American Affairs, to Butler and Briggs, 19 July 1946, telegram to Secretary of State from International Health Conference, 17 July 1946, and "Statement on Membership by the Delegate of the United States, Committee III," 27 June 1946, all RG 59, Decimal File 1945–49, 501.NA, box 2222, NACP.

For exclusion of fascist powers see Dreier memorandum to Butler and Briggs, 19 July 1946, and summary record of meeting of U.S. delegation, 29 June 1946, both RG 59, Decimal File 1945–49, 501.NA, box 2222, NACP.

For the debate surrounding the name of the WHO see WHOIC, *Summary Report on the International Health Conference,* 16; unattributed memorandum on the proposed WHO emblem, undated [approx. Feb. 1948], microform 1-1-5, WHOA; Sze, *Origins of the World Health Organization,* 17; "Sixth Meeting," and "Seventh Meeting," in WHOIC, *Minutes of the Technical Preparatory Committee,* 17, 19; Proposals submitted by the UK delegation concerning the title, preamble, aims and objectives, and functions, 1 July 1946, microform: IHC: CD, card 1, WHOA; summary record of third meeting of Committee I, 5 July 1946, mircoform: IHC: CD, cards 1 and 2, WHOA; and restricted letter from Acheson to Parran, Chairman of U.S. Delegation to International Health Conference, 15 June 1946, Decimal File 1945–49, 501.NA, box 2222, RG 59, NACP.

For attendance by non-UN members see WHOIC, *Summary Report on the International Health Conference,* 12, 18; UK health delegation telegram to Foreign Office, 5 June 1946, FO 371/59613, PRO; Sze, *Origins of the World Health Organization,* 16; and statement on membership by the U.S. delegate to Committee III, 27 June 1949, microform: IHC: CD, card 9, WHOA.

For debate over associate membership see WHOIC, *Summary Report on the International*

Health Conference, 18–19, 24; Sze, *Origins of the World Health Organization,* 17–18; minutes, 7 June 1946, FO 371/59613, PRO; "Sixteenth Meeting," and "Annex 6," in WHOIC, *Minutes of the Technical Preparatory Committee,* 30, 43; summary record of fifth meeting of Committee III, 6 July 1946, and summary record and approved draft of first meeting of joint harmonizing subcommittee of Committees 3 and 5, 9 July 1946, both microform: IHC: CD, card 9, WHOA; summary record of the seventh meeting, 11 July 1946, and summary record of the second meeting of the joint harmonizing subcommittee of Committee 3 and 5, 9 July 1946, both microform IHC: CD, card 11; Winant telegram to Secretary of State, 18 July 1946, and summary report of fifth meeting of Committee 3, 18 July 1946, both RG 59, Decimal File 1945–49, 501. NA, box 2222, NACP.

28. For WHO objective see Article 1 of the WHO Constitution; and WHOIC, *Summary Report on the International Health Conference,* 16.

For WHO preamble see WHOIC, *Summary Report on the International Health Conference,* 16; and summary record of third meeting of Committee I, 5 July 1946, microform: IHC: CD, cards 1 and 2, WHOA.

For WHO functions see Article 2 of the WHO Constitution; and WHOIC, *Summary Report on the International Health Conference,* 17–18, 20–21.

For the WHO's coordinative and cooperative function specifically see amendments to chapter 3 submitted by the Belgian and Chilean delegations, 1 July 1946, card 1, summary record of tenth meeting of Committee 2, 3 July 1946, card 6, summary record of first meeting of Committee IV, 26 June 1946, card 13, and summary record of second meeting of Committee IV, 1 July 1946, card 14, all microform: IHC: CD, WHOA; and WHOIC, *Summary Report on the International Health Conference,* 25–26.

For the WHO's research function specifically see draft list of WHO activities, 5 Dec. 1947, and letter to Stampar from Ferenc Horvath, Munich, with attached "Proposal Concerning the Establishment of a General Institute for Research," 3 Oct. 1948, microform 1-1-2, card 1, WHOA; summary record of third meeting of Committee I, 5 July 1946, microform: IHC: CD, cards 1 and 2, WHOA; and proposal by the Mexican delegation, 1 July 1946, microform IHC: CD, card 3, WHOA.

For WHO's technical services see proposed amendment submitted by the Polish Delegation, 2 July 1946, microform: IHC: CD, card 1, WHOA; and unattributed memorandum on the functions of the International Health Organisation, 13 May 1946, FO 371/59613, PRO.

For the WHO's educational function see proposal of amendment to the report of the Technical Preparatory Committee submitted by the Chinese delegation, 1 July 1946, and additions proposed by the Venezuelan delegation, 2 July 1946, both microform: IHC: CD, card 1, WHOA.

For the organizational structure see chapters 4–7 of the WHO Constitution; and WHOIC, *Summary Report on the International Health Conference,* 19–22.

For automatic ratification see restricted Acheson letter to Parran, 15 June 1946, RG 59, Decimal File 1945–49, 501.NA, box 2222, NACP; executive secretary report, 6 Mar. 1947, microform 312-1-1, WHOA; Peruvian proposal to revise the International Sanitary Conventions, 3 Apr. 1947, and U.S. note to WHOIC Committee on Technical Questions, 3 Sept. 1947, both microform 468-3-1, WHOA; "First World Health Assembly," *Chronicle of the WHO* 2 (Aug.–Sept. 1948): 186; "Towards New International Sanitary Regulations: First Session of the Expert Committee on International Epidemiology and Quarantine," *Chronicle of the WHO* 3 (Jan. 1949): 1–8; *Official Records of the WHO,* vol. 11, p. 21; "International

Sanitary Conventions," *British Medical Journal* 4591 (1 Jan. 1949): 22–23; "Second World Health Assembly: General Account," *Chronicle of the WHO* 3 (Oct. 1949): 173; and "International Sanitary Regulations: World Health Organization Regulations No. 2," *WHO Technical Report Series* 41 (July 1951).

29. Restricted Acheson letter to Parran, 15 June 1946, RG 59, Decimal File 1945–49, 501. NA, box 2222, NACP; memorandum to Dr. Kelchner, U.S. State Department, to Dr. L. L. Williams, U.S. State Department, 7 Oct. 1946, RG 59, Decimal File 1945–49, 501.NA, box 2227, NACP; Article 54 of the WHO Constitution.

For change in U.S. position see also memorandum of conversation between Roger Makins, British Embassy in Washington, and Stinebower, State Department Office of International Trade Policy, 3 July 1946, memorandum to Dreier from Wainhouse, U.S. State Department Division of British Commonwealth Affairs, 2 July 1946, memorandum from Dreier to Briggs, Butler, and Spaeth, U.S. State Department, 25 July 1946, summary record of meetings of U.S. delegation, 24 and 25 June 1946, and "Statement by the Chairman, Delegation of the United States of America," 27 June 1946, all RG 59, Decimal File 1945–49, 501.NA, box 2222, NACP.

For Cumming's opposition see also Halle memorandum to Spruille Braden, 21 Aug. 1946, circular airgram from State Department to U.S. diplomatic missions in Latin America, 18 Sept. 1946, and "Meeting of the Subcommittee on the PASB and the WHO," 24 Sept. 1946, all RG 59, Decimal File 1945–49, 501.NA, box 2224, NACP.

For conference debates on this provision see WHOIC, *Summary Report of the International Health Conference,* 23–24; minutes, 7 June 1946, FO 371/59613, PRO; Sze, *Origins of the World Health Organization,* 18; summary record of the sixteenth meeting of Committee II, 9 July 1946, microform: IHC: CD, card 4, WHOA; proposal on regional arrangements submitted by the Brazilian delegation, 20 June 1946, microform: IHC: CD, card 13, WHOA; summary record of the second meeting of Committee V, 28 June 1946, proposed amendment to Section XII and statement made by Brazilian delegate Dr. Geraldo H. de Paula Souza, 1 July 1946, and proposals submitted by the United Kingdom delegation, 1 July 1946, all microform: IHC: CD, card 16, WHOA; summary record of the third meeting of Committee V, 29 June 1946, microform: IHC: CD, cards 16–17, WHOA; summary records of the fourth, fifth, sixth, and seventh meetings of Committee V, 1, 2, 8, and 11 July 1946, and report by Major C. Mani, Rapporteur, on the work of the harmonizing subcommittee, 6 July 1946, both microform: IHC: CD, card 17, WHOA; and summary record of harmonizing subcommittee's first and second meetings, 2 and 3 July 1946, microform: IHC: CD, card 19, WHOA.

For WHO absorption of the OIHP, LNHO, and UNRRA Health Section see Article 72 of the WHO Constitution; "Arrangement Concluded by the Governments Represented at the International Health Conference" and "Protocol Concerning the Office International d'Hygiène Publique," both in WHOIC, *Summary Report on the International Health Conference,* 110–12, 113, resp.; report of the legal commission on the OIHP, 13 June 1946, statement by Dr. Gaud, OIHP representative, 3 July 1946, and summary record of fourth meeting of Committee III, 3 July 1946, all microform: IHC: CD, card 9, WHOA; and summary record of the second meeting of Committee IV, 1 July 1946, microform: IHC: CD, card 14, WHOA.

30. For headquarters site see Article 43 of the WHO Constitution; WHOIC, *Summary Report on the International Health Conference,* 23; and summary record of eleventh meeting of Committee II, 5 July 1946, card 4, summary record of twelfth and thirteenth meetings of Committee II, 5 and 6 July 1946, card 5, and summary record of the fourteenth meeting of

Committee II, 8 July 1946, card 6, all microform: IHC: CD, WHOA.

For establishment of interim commission and its responsibilities see "Arrangement Concluded by the Governments Represented at the International Health Conference," in WHOIC, *Summary Report on the International Health Conference,* 110–12.

9. Constructing International Authority in the World Health Organizaition

1. WHO staff members who studied abroad included Andrija Stampar (University of Vienna), Sir Aly Tewfik Shousha (University of Berlin), and Dr. D. K. Viswanathan (Johns Hopkins University).

WHO staff members who held positions abroad included Stampar (University of California), Shousha (University of Zurich), and Brock Chisholm (Yale University and British National Hospital for Nervous Diseases).

WHO staff members who worked for international health organizations before joining the WHO included Stampar (LNHO), Emilio Pampana (LNHO), Raymond Gautier (LNHO), Antoine Zarb (OIHP), Georges de Brancion (OIHP), and Neville M. Goodman (OIHP, LNHO, UNRRA).

2. This philosophy is summed up operationally in "Draft of a Ten Year Programme," [approx. Aug. 1949], microform 1-1-8, card 1, WHOA; and letter to WHO Director-General Brock Chisholm from Dr. José Zozaya, Mexican member of the WHO Executive Board, 21 Oct. 1949, microform 1-1-8, card 2, WHOA.

3. "Fifth Session of the Interim Commission: Geneva, 22 Jan. to 7 February," *Chronicle of the WHO* 2 (Mar. 1948): 29. For similar expressions of goodwill among the WHOIC see personal letter from H. van Zile Hyde, U.S. representative to WHOIC, to Chisholm, WHO-IC Executive Secretary, 12 May 1947, microform 1-1-2, card 1, WHOA; and "The World Health Organization," unidentified general memorandum, 28 Jan. 1949, RG 25, External Affairs, series G-2, vol. 3684, file: 5475-K-40, CNA. For indications of some strife among the staff see Sze, *Origins of the WHO,* 20–26.

For the functions of the interim commission see Sze, *Origins of the WHO,* 20–26; "Annex 24: Resolutions (as Adopted by the Technical Preparatory Committee on 5 April 1946)," in WHOIC, *Minutes of the Technical Preparatory Committee,* 75–76; and telegram from van Zile Hyde, WHO Executive Board, to Williams, 13 Apr. 1947, RG 59, Decimal File 1945–49, 501.NA, box 2224, NACP.

For the prolonged life of the interim commission see "Work of the Interim Commission," *Chronicle of the WHO* 2 (May 1948): 77; "Ratification of the World Health Organization Constitution: The Present Position," ibid. 1 (July–Aug. 1948): 116; and "Ratification of the Constitution of the WHO: The Present Position," ibid. 2 (Feb. 1948): 27.

For the size of the Interim Commission see "Work of the Interim Commission," 78–79; and "First World Health Assembly," ibid. 2 (Aug.–Sept. 1948): 163.

4. For the integration of OIHP activities see "Work of the Interim Commission," 82; and "WHO Publications," *Chronicle of the WHO* 3 (Jan. 1949): 18.

For WHO's takeover of epidemiological reporting see executive secretary report, 6 Mar. 1947, and summary of conversation, 9 May 1947, both microform 312-1-1, WHOA.

For the interim commission's assumption of League health activities see "Work of the Interim Commission," 82–83, 85–87; "First World Health Assembly," 196; and "Second

World Health Assembly: Technical Questions," *Chronicle of the WHO* 3 (Oct. 1949): 205.

For PASB integration process see personal van Zile Hyde letter to Chisholm, 12 May 1947, microform 1-1-2, card 1, WHOA; "Second Session of the Executive Board: Geneva, 25 October–11 November," *Chronicle of the WHO* 2 (Nov. 1948): 247; "Fifty-eight Nations Members of WHO," ibid. 3 (Jan. 1949): 20; "Second World Health Assembly: Organizational Problems," ibid. 3 (Oct. 1949): 212; executive secretary report, 6 Mar. 1947, microform 312-1-1, WHOA; and confidential Halle memorandum to Barber, U.S. State Department, 8 Nov. 1946, RG 59, Decimal File 1945–49, 501.NA, box 2224, NACP.

For new approaches to epidemiology see "Work of the Interim Commission," 84–85; "First World Health Assembly," 188; "Towards New International Sanitary Regulations," 1–8; "Epidemiological Radio-Broadcasts from Geneva," *Chronicle of the WHO* 3 (Feb. 1949): 35–38; "International Quarantine Messages by Radio," and "Disinsectization of Aircraft," ibid. 3 (July 1949): 158–60, 160–62; and "Fourth Session of the Executive Board," ibid. 3 (Nov. 1949): 243.

5. "Work of the Interim Commission," 89; "Cholera in Egypt," *Chronicle of the WHO* 1 (Nov. 1947): 157–61; "Quarantine Measures during the Cholera Epidemic," ibid. 2 (Mar. 1948): 43; "First World Health Assembly," 163; Robert Baker, "Two Millions Call Him Doctor," *Maclean's Magazine* (1 May 1950): 47.

6. For the new offensive philosophy see Dr. N. Vinogradov and Dr. J. N. Togba as quoted in "First World Health Assembly," 201–202; "Inaugural Address by Dr. Karl Evang, President of the Second World Health Assembly," WHO press release, 14 June 1949, microform 102-1-13, WHOA; "Landmark in World Health," *Chronicle of the WHO* 2 (Apr. 1948): 51; "Towards New International Sanitary Regulations: First Session of the Expert Committee on International Epidemiology and Quarantine," ibid. 3 (Jan. 1949): 1, 5; "Second World Health Assembly: General Account," and Dr. M. Cotellessa as quoted in "Points from Speeches," ibid. 3 (Oct. 1949): 165–66, 168, 217; and "Introductory Statement by the Director-General," in WHO, *Programme and Budget Estimates for 1950*, Official Records of the WHO, no. 18 (Geneva: WHO, Apr. 1949), 1.

For the setting of priorities see "Work of the Interim Commission," 78, 87–88; WHO, *The First Ten Years of the World Health Organization* (Geneva: WHO, 1958), 73; "First World Health Assembly," 171–75; and van Zile Hyde letter to Chisholm with attached "World Health Organization Six-Year Plan," 27 Sept. 1949, microform 1-1-8, card 1, WHOA.

For tuberculosis plan of attack see "First World Health Assembly," 174, 194–95; and van Zile Hyde comments to NGOs, 21 Oct. 1948, attached to Chester S. Williams, State Department Public Liaison Officer, letter to Margaret R. T. Carter, Chief of State Department Division of Public Liaison, 29 Oct. 1948, RG 59, Decimal File 1945–49, 501.NA, box 2229, NACP.

For venereal disease plan of attack see "First World Health Assembly," 174–75, 195; and "Penicillin in Venereal Diseases," *Chronicle of the WHO* 3 (Jan. 1949): 15–16.

For the establishment of expert committees on these diseases see WHO, *First Ten Years*, 74; and "First Session of the Executive Board (Geneva, 16–26 July 1948)," *Chronicle of the WHO* 2 (Aug.–Sept. 1948): 207.

7. WHO, *First Ten Years*, 164. For European conditions and needs see also "European Health Conference," *Chronicle of the WHO* 2 (Dec. 1948): 275–76; and "Second World Health Assembly: General Account," 170.

For health missions see letter to Canadian Secretary for External Affairs from Canadian

Ambassador to Greece, 28 June 1949, RG 25, External Affairs, series G-2, vol. 3684, file: 5475-K-40, CNA; "The Health Missions of the WHO," *Chronicle of the WHO* 1 (Dec. 1947): 173–86; and J. B. McDougall, "Tuberculosis in Greece: An Experiment in the Relief and Rehabilitation of a Country," *Bulletin of the WHO* 1 (1947/48): 103–96.

For fellowships see "Work of the Interim Commission," 91; "Health Missions," 177, 179; Stampar letter to Chisholm, 1 Jan. 1947, Stampar letter to Dr. Y. M. Biraud, WHOIC Adjunct Executive Secretary, 10 Jan. 1947, and letter to Stampar from Frank A. Calderone, Director of WHO Headquarters Office in New York, 8 Feb. 1947, all microform 2-1-4, WHOA; "Reports from WHO Fellows: Cancer Treatment in the United States," *Chronicle of the WHO* 3 (Feb. 1949): 39–40; "Reports from WHO Fellows: Cardiology in France and the United Kingdom," ibid. 3 (June 1949): 130–31; "Reports from WHO Fellows: Psychiatry in England," ibid. 3 (July 1949): 162–64; and Stampar as quoted in "Points in Speeches," ibid. 3 (Oct. 1949): 218.

For study tours see WHO, *First Ten Years*, 165; and Erwin Kohl, *Medical Mission to Austria: July 1–August 8, 1947* (Boston, Mass.: Unitarian Service Committee, 1947).

8. *Journal of the First World Health Assembly*, no. 28 (24 July 1948), RG 59, Decimal File 1945–49, 501.NA, box 2228, NACP.

For Stampar see "First World Health Assembly," 164, 204–205.

For the selection of Geneva see ibid., 197; Candau, "Foreword," vii–viii; and *Journal of the First World Health Assembly*, no. 7 (1 July 1948), RG 59, Decimal File 1945–49, 501.NA, box 2228, NACP.

9. Albania, Australia, Austria, the Byelosrussian Soviet Socialist Republic, Canada, China, Czechoslovakia, Egypt, Ethiopia, Finland, Greece, Haiti, India, Iran, Iraq, Ireland, Italy, Liberia, Mexico, the Netherlands, New Zealand, Norway, Portugal, Saudi Arabia, Siam (present-day Thailand), the Soviet Union, Sweden, Switzerland, Syria, Transjordan, Turkey, the Ukrainian Soviet Socialist Republic, the Union of South Africa, the United Kingdom, and Yugoslavia officially belonged to the WHO when its constitution came into force. Before the WHA convened, an additional twenty-eight states had ratified the constitution. For WHA membership see "Landmark in World Health," 52; "Ratifications," *Chronicle of the WHO* 2 (June 1948): 131; and "First World Health Assembly," 164.

For the duties and character of the WHA see WHO, *First Ten Years*, 84, 86, 91.

For the interim commission's contributions to the work of the first WHA see "Work of the Interim Commission," 79, 82; "Fifth Session of the Interim Commission: Geneva, 22 Jan. to 7 February," *Chronicle of the WHO* 2 (Mar. 1948): 31; and "First World Health Assembly," 165–66.

For voting procedures for first WHA see "Landmark in World Health," 52; and Siddiqi, *World Health*, 118.

The countries that belonged to the WHO but not the UN in 1948 included Albania, Bulgaria, Ireland, Portugal, Romania, and Switzerland (off-the-record meeting between van Zile Hyde and NGOs, 21 Oct. 1948, attached to letter from Williams to Carter, 29 Oct. 1948, RG 59, Decimal File 1945–49, 501.NA, box 2229, NACP).

10. *Journal of the First World Health Assembly*, no. 9 (3 July 1948), RG 59, Decimal File 1945–49, 501.NA, box 2228, NACP.

For U.S. reservations see memorandum concerning deposit of signature to constitution by United States, 23 June 1948, microform 102-1-6, WHOA; Siddiqi, *World Health*, 102; and Calderwood, U.S. State Department, memorandum to Sandifer, State Department's United

Nations Affairs division, 18 Feb. 1948, restricted State Department telegram to Tomlinson, American Consul in Geneva, 5 June 1948, unattributed "History of Withdrawal Provision in U.S. Acceptance of World Health Constitution," 18 June 1948, restricted State Department telegram to van Zile Hyde, U.S. delegation to WHA, 21 June 1948, and "Congressional Conference Report on U.S. Membership in the World Health Organization," submitted to WHA, 23 June 1948, all RG 59, Decimal File 1945–49, 501.NA, box 2228, NACP.

For the work of the credentials committee and WHA see also Siddiqi, *World Health,* 103–104; "Canada's Responsibility in World Health," Chisholm address to the Eighth Annual Conference of the Institute of Public Administration of Canada, Chisholm papers, vol. 2, folder 146–64, CNA; and confidential telegram from U.S. delegation to WHA to Secretary of State George C. Marshall, 25 June 1948, confidential Marshall telegram to U.S. delegation to WHA, 28 June 1948, and Parran telegram to Marshall, 2 July 1948, all RG 59, Decimal File 1945–49, 501.NA, box 2227, NACP.

For a different, more legalistic interpretation of the U.S. reservations see letters to Miss J. Murray, British Foreign Office United Nations Department, from C. H. K. Edmonds, British Ministry of Health, 24 Oct. and 5 Nov. 1947, Murray letter to Edmonds, 3 Nov. 1947, letter from E. B. Boothby, Foreign Office, to Edmonds, 11 Nov. 1947, confidential Washington embassy letter to Foreign Office United Nations Department, 8 Dec. 1947, and Washington embassy aide mémoire to State Department, 3 Dec. 1947, all FO 371/67596, PRO.

11. Evang, as quoted in "First World Health Assembly," 200.

For the expanded program of work see "First World Health Assembly," 179–80, 182–85; and letter to Chisholm from Melville Mackenzie, British Ministry of Health, 7 Oct. 1949, microform 1-1-8, card 2, WHOA.

For budget assessments see WHO, *First Ten Years,* 121–22; and memorandum of conversation between Lord Jellicoe, British Embassy, Calderwood, and Miss Maylott, U.S. State Department, 1 June 1948, RG 59, Decimal File 1945–40, 501.NA, box 2227, NACP.

12. "Second World Health Assembly: Organizational Problems," 211. See also ibid., 209–11; "Canada's Responsibility in World Health," Chisholm address to the Eighth Annual Conference of the Institute of Public Administration of Canada, Chisholm papers, vol. 2, folder 146–164, CNA; "Explanatory Memorandum on the Amendments Proposed by the Government of Australia to Articles 24 and 55 of the Constitution of the World Health Organization," attached to letter to A. D. P. Heeney, Canadian Secretary of State for External Affairs, from Dr. R. Gautier, acting WHO director-general, 20 Dec. 1949, letter from G. D. W. Cameron, Canadian Deputy Minister of National Health, to J. W. Holmes, Canadian Under-Secretary of State for External Affairs, 3 June 1949, memorandum for Holmes from the European, British Commonwealth, American, and Far Eastern divisions, 2 June 1949, and confidential outward saving telegram from the Commonwealth Relations Office to Acting UK High Commissioner in Canada, 19 May 1949, all RG 25, External Affairs, series G-2, vol. 3684, file: 5475-K-40, CNA; "First World Health Assembly," 167, 169; WHO, *First Ten Years,* 92–95, 98; "First Session of the Executive Board," 206–207; and "Fourth Session of the Executive Board," 237.

13. Jeannine Locke, "Brock Chisholm Speaks Out!" *Star Weekly Magazine,* 26 Jan. 1963, 1–5, "Lt.-Col. G. B. Chisholm Heads Halton Rifles," undated, unidentified newspaper article, "British Military Authorities Adopt Pulhems Profile Test," *Ottawa Globe and Mail,* undated [approx. Oct. 1943], and Corolyn Cox, "Gen. Chisholm Will Cure Psychic Ills of Civil Life as of Army," *(Toronto) Saturday Night,* 30 Dec. 1944, all Chisholm papers, vol. 5,

folder: special articles (1), CNA; The Man with a Notebook, "Backstage at Ottawa: Can a Civil Servant Say What He Thinks?" *Maclean's Magazine,* 1 Jan. 1946; Baker, "Two Millions Call Him Doctor," 21, 45, 47–49; Charles S. Ascher, "Chisholm of WHO," *The Survey* (Feb. 1952), and 1952 tribute to Chisholm by B.U., both Chisholm papers, vol. 5, folder: special articles (2); "First World Health Assembly," 170, 205–206; and microform 14-1-2, WHOA.

The Pulhems Profile correlated physique, upper limbs, lower limbs, hearing, eyesight, mentality, and stability (hence the profile's acronymic name) to military work.

14. As quoted in Leonard A. Scheele, U.S. Surgeon General, "Report of the Chairman of the United States Delegation," attached to Scheele letter to Secretary of State, 12 Oct. 1953, RG 59, Decimal File 1950–54, 398.55-WHO, box 1634, NACP. Also see this document for reservations about Candau as director-general.

For Candau see restricted Blaisdell dispatch to State Department, 6 Feb. 1953, and restricted position paper, "Appointment of a New Director General," 5 May 1953, both RG 59, Decimal File 1950–54, 398.55-WHO, box 1634, NACP. The vote in the private plenary session was forty-seven in favor of Candau's nomination, sixteen against, and one abstention.

15. Executive Orders 10422 and 10459 dealt with U.S. employees of international organizations.

For Chisholm's refusal to comply with U.S. loyalty regulations see restricted telegram to Secretary of State from Lodge, New York, 18 Feb. 1953, and letter to Chisholm from John D. Hickerson, Assistant Secretary of State, 13 Mar. 1953, both RG 59, Decimal File 1950–54, 398.55-WHO, box 1633, NACP; and restricted dispatch from Donald C. Blaisdell, U.S. representative for International Organization Affairs, to State Department, 22 May 1953, confidential airgram from Dulles to R. E. Ward Jr., American Consul General and Assistant to the Chief of the Resident Delegation in Geneva, 12 June 1953, and confidential dispatch to State Department from Henry F. Nichol, Conference Attaché in Geneva, 27 July 1953, all RG 59, Decimal File 1950–54, 398.55-WHO, box 1634, NACP.

For pressure to exempt appointees to WHO expert committees see Chisholm letter, 30 June 1953, as quoted in Ward dispatch to State Department, 1 July 1953, unattributed, restricted dispatch from U.S. resident delegation in Geneva to State Department, 21 July 1953, restricted Nichol dispatch to State Department, 31 July 1953, Ward dispatch to State Department, 10 Aug. 1953, and letter to Dulles from John T. Edsall, Harvard University Laboratory of Physical Chemistry, 23 Oct. 1953, all RG 59, Decimal File 1950–54, 398.55-WHO, box 1634, NACP.

16. "Draft Staff Rules and Regulations," WHOIC Committee on Administration and Finance, 5 Aug. 1947, RG 59, Decimal File 1945–49, 501.NA, box 2226, NACP; Baker, "Two Millions Call Him Doctor," 45.

For staff ésprit see letter from Edric A. Weld Jr., Paris, to Chisholm, 25 July 1949, and Chisholm letter to Weld, 1 Aug. 1949, both microform 1-1-2, card 2, WHOA; and "Director-General's Circular No. 2" to staff members, 4 Aug. 1948, microform 300-1-14, WHOA.

17. Confidential memorandum of conversation between Chisholm, Murphy, State Department, and Ingram, State Department Office of International Affairs, 8 Dec. 1953, RG 59, Decimal File 1950–54, 398.55-WHO, box 1634, NACP. The only staff members subjected to this treatment were Sir Sahib Singh Soklhey of India and Dr. C. K. Chu of China.

18. WHO, *First Ten Years,* 109, 108. For other expressions of support for international civil service see minutes of conference of the working party on the formation of an international civil service commission, 5 May 1947, report to the ECOSOC Bureau of Personnel on the International Centre for Training in Public Administration, 19 Oct. 1946, and

Secretary-General's report to the third session of the fifth committee of the UN General Assembly on the International Centre for Training in Public Administration, 8 Nov. 1948, all microform 301-1-9, card 1, WHOA.

For the international character and loyalty of the staff see WHO, *First Ten Years,* 106–109, 111; Evang as quoted in "First World Health Assembly," 198; memorandum from Dr. Williams to Dallas Dort, State Department Division of Economic Affairs, 23 Mar. 1949, RG 59, Decimal File 1945–49, 501.NA, box 2230, NACP; and Chisholm statement to the Carnegie Conference on Human Relations in International Administration, 15 Feb. 1957, Chisholm papers, vol. 2, folder 168–183, CNA.

For the method of selecting staff see Stampar letters to Biraud, 11 Dec. 1946 and 10 Jan. 1947, microform 2-1-4, WHOA; minutes of conference of the working party on the formation of an international civil service commission, 5 May 1947, microform 301-1-9, card 1, WHOA; note by secretary, 25 Feb. 1949, microform 301-1-9, cards 1 and 2, WHOA; and Calderone memorandum to Chisholm, with attached "Personnel Regulations: General Character and Objective of Regulations," 11 Feb. 1947, and Calderone memorandum to Chisholm with attached "Provisional Staff Regulations," 8 Mar. 1947, both microform 301-2-1, card 1, WHOA.

For staff turnover see WHO, *First Ten Years,* 107, 110.

In 1949 the top forty WHO posts were filled with citizens of Canada, China, Czechoslovakia, Egypt, Finland, France, Greece, India, Italy, Netherlands, New Zealand, Norway, Poland, Romania, Spain, Sweden, Switzerland, the United Kingdom, and the United States.

19. Off-the-record van Zile Hyde meeting with NGOs, 21 Oct. 1948, attached to Williams letter to Carter, 29 Oct. 1948, RG 59, Decimal File 1945–49, 501.NA, box 2229, NACP; Baker, "Two Millions Call Him Doctor," 21, 45, 47–49. See also "Responsibility for Health," Chisholm address to the International Federation of Sanitarians Organization, 17 July 1957, Chisholm papers, vol. 2, folder 168–183, CNA; and "No 'Iron Curtain' Here," editorial in *Toronto Daily Star,* 22 May 1948, and Charles S. Ascher, "Chisholm of WHO," *The Survey* (Feb. 1952), both Chisholm papers, vol. 5, folder: special articles (2), CNA.

20. Dr. R. B. Fosdick, President of the Rockefeller Foundation, in Rockefeller Foundation, *Annual Report* (New York: Rockefeller Foundation, 1947), 12. For this functional belief that international health cooperation would lead to broader international cooperation see also Dr. J. Salcedo, President of the Manila Medical Society, *Journal of the Philippine Medical Association* 25 (1949): 31.

For sense of international fellowship among medical community see "Second World Health Assembly: General Account," 165; and Expert Committee on Biological Standardization, "Report on the Third Session," *WHO Technical Report Series* 2 (Feb. 1950): 3.

21. Salcedo, 31. For the conviction that world health would bring world peace see also "Second World Health Assembly: General Account," 166; and letter to Secretary of State from van Zile Hyde, U.S. alternate to WHOIC, 20 Feb. 1948, RG 59, Decimal File 1945–49, 501.NA, box 2227, NACP.

22. British delegation paper on Article 8, 5 July 1948, RG 59, Decimal File 1945–49, 501. NA, box 2228, NACP; Charles S. Ascher, "Chisholm of WHO," *The Survey* (Feb. 1952), Chisholm papers, vol. 5, folder: special articles (2).

For associate membership see also WHO, *First Ten Years,* 81; "First World Health Assembly," 191n; and "Chisholm Reveals Plan to Offset Food Shortages," AP newspaper article, 9 Nov. 1948, Chisholm papers, vol. 5, folder: special articles (2), CNA.

For adamance regarding universal membership see Siddiqi, *World Health,* 25, 101.

23. For early organizational debates about the degree of decentralization/centralization see WHO, *First Ten Years,* 101–102; Siddiqi, *World Health,* 118; "First World Health Assembly," 191; Dr. L. A. Scheele, Dr. A. H. Radji, and Dr. F. U. Kazi as quoted in "Points from Speeches," *Chronicle of the WHO* 3 (Oct. 1949): 217, 221; "The World Health Organization," unidentified general memorandum, 28 Jan. 1949, RG 25, External Affairs, series G-2, vol. 3684, file: 5475-K-40, CNA; Stampar letter to Chisholm, 2 Sept. 1949, microform 1-1-8, card 1, WHOA; and "Inaugural Address by Dr. Karl Evang, President of Second World Health Assembly," WHO press release, 14 June 1949, microform 102-1-13, WHOA.

For WHO's balancing act see, e.g., Charles S. Ascher, "Chisholm of WHO," *The Survey* (Feb. 1952), Chisholm papers, vol. 5, folder: special articles (2), CNA.

For "rotation" system see WHO, *First Ten Years,* 106, 110.

24. For regional grouping rationale see WHO, *First Ten Years,* 75–76; "First World Health Assembly," 193; secret Boothby letter to Edmonds, 21 July 1947, FO 371/67595, PRO; and "Eastern Mediterranean Conference," *Chronicle of the WHO* 3 (Jan. 1949): 13n.

For Southeast Asian Regional Office (SEARO) see "Second Session of the Executive Board," 246–47; WHO, *First Ten Years,* 77; and "First WHO South-East Asia Regional Conference," *Chronicle of the WHO* 2 (Oct. 1948): 225–26.

For Eastern Mediterranean Regional Office (EMRO) see "First World Health Assembly," 193; confidential brief for UK delegation to fourth session of WHOIC [approx. Aug. 1947], FO 371/67596, PRO; "Eastern Mediterranean Conference," 13; "Eastern Mediterranean Regional Conference," *Chronicle of the WHO* 3 (Mar. 1949): 48–52; and "Pre-Existing Regional Organizations," in WHOIC, *Supplementary Report of the Interim Commission to the World Health Assembly,* Official Records of the WHO, no. 12 (Geneva: WHO, Dec. 1948), 65.

25. "Inaugural Address by Dr. Karl Evang," WHO press release, 14 June 1949, microform 102-1-13, WHOA. For emphasis on apolitical nature of WHO see also Siddiqi, *World Health,* 6, 49.

26. Sixth World Health Assembly as quoted in Siddiqi, *World Health,* 87–92, 119.

For WHO assistance to Palestinian refugees see WHO, *First Ten Years,* 135–36; "WHO Representative for Palestine Relief," *Chronicle of the WHO* 3 (Jan. 1949): 21; "Malaria Control in Europe and Asia: Palestine Refugee Camps," ibid., 3 (June 1949): 136; "Second World Health Assembly: Technical Questions," 206; and "Nutritional Problems among Palestine Arab Refugees," report by Dr. R. C. Burgess, WHO Nutrition Section Chief, and Dr. A. G. van Veen, FAO Nutrition Division Senior Supervisory Officer, June 1954, microform FN 7 UNRWA, WHOA.

For Israel and WHO regional assignment see Siddiqi, *World Health,* 87–92, 119.

For a later, somewhat parallel incident see WHO's reaction to the request for the transfer of the EMRO headquarters from Alexandria, Egypt, after the signing of the Camp David Accords (Siddiqi, *World Health,* 93–100, 119).

27. "Integration of Pan American Sanitary Organization with WHO," *Chronicle of the WHO* 3 (June 1949): 131–32; WHO, *First Ten Years,* 159–62.

28. For WHO work in the African region see WHO, *First Ten Years,* 156–58; "Report on the Malaria Conference in Equatorial Africa," *WHO Technical Report Series* 38 (Apr. 1951); and "Bilharzia Snail Vector Identification and Classification (Equatorial and South Africa): Report of a Study-Group," *WHO Technical Report Series* 90 (Nov. 1954).

For delay in formation of African regional office see "Second World Health Assembly: Organizational Problems," 213. For the Western Pacific region, see ibid., 212.

29. As quoted in Siddiqi, *World Health,* 105. For Soviet bloc motives and withdrawal see also ibid., 104–106; WHO, *First Ten Years,* 79; Alieh Dadashi, "Soviet Policy in the World Health Organization" (M.A. thesis, Univ. of Washington, 1978), 12–25; Chris Osakwe, *The Participation of the Soviet Union in Universal International Organizations: A Political and Legal Analysis of Soviet Strategies and Aspirations inside ILO, UNESCO, and WHO* (Leiden, Neth.: A. W. Sijthoff, 1972), 101–31; telegram from van Zile Hyde to Williams, 9 Apr. 1947, RG 59, Decimal File 1945–49, 501.NA, box 2224, NACP; and *Journal of the First World Health Assembly,* nos. 4, 5, and 6 (28, 29, and 30 June 1948), RG 59, Decimal File 1945–49, 501.NA, box 2228, NACP.

For differing philosophies on WHO provision of health supplies see "Second World Health Assembly: General Account," 173; "Second World Health Assembly: Technical Questions," 182–85; Sir Aly Tewfik Shousha, "Transmittal of the Proposed Programme and Budget Estimates to the Second World Health Assembly by the Executive Board," *Programme and Budget Estimates for 1950,* v; and J. Plojhar as quoted in "Points from Speeches," *Chronicle of the WHO* 3 (Oct. 1949): 219.

For WHO reaction see Siddiqi, *World Health,* 107, 119; "Inaugural Address by Dr. Karl Evang," WHO press release, 14 June 1949, microform 102-1-13, WHOA; letter to the head of the Canadian delegation to the second WHA from Heeney, 17 June 1949, and letter from J. H. Halstead, Office of the British High Commissioner for Canada, to Heeney, 25 Feb. 1949, both RG 25, External Affairs, series G-2, vol. 3684, file: 5475-K-40, CNA; WHO, *First Ten Years,* 79–80; "Second World Health Assembly: Organizational Problems," 209; and "Thirteenth Meeting," in *Minutes of the Technical Preparatory Committee,* 26.

Albania, Bulgaria, Poland, and the Soviet Union attended the 1957 WHA as members. Czechoslovakia and Romania became active members again the next year, and Hungary finally returned in 1963 (Siddiqi, *World Health,* 80).

30. Private and confidential Calderone letter to Chisholm, 12 Nov. 1947, microform 1-1-2, card 1, WHOA. See also WHO, *First Ten Years,* 81; Siddiqi, *World Health,* 110–14; and *The Bonn Policy of Coercion Is Doomed to Failure: Government of the FRG Again Prevents Membership of the GDR in the World Health Organization (WHO) on a Basis of Equality* (Dresden: Verlag Zeit im Bild, undated [approx. 1972]). Spain was finally admitted to the WHO in 1951, the PRC in 1971, and North Korea in 1973.

31. Restricted position paper, "Budget for 1950," 14 June 1949, RG 59, Decimal File, 1945–49, 501.NA, box 2230, NACP. For the 1950 budget see also Ingram memo to Sandifer, Hall (State Department), Kotschnig, van Zile Hyde, Calderwood, and Anderson (State Department), 4 Feb. 1949, ibid.; and Halstead letter to Heeney, 25 Feb. 1949, RG 25, External Affairs, series G-2, vol. 3684, file: 5475-K-40, CNA.

For 1948 meeting and 1949 budget see Marshall telegram to U.S. Embassy in London and Paris and U.S. delegation to WHA, 16 July 1948, confidential telegram from Douglas, London, to Secretary of State, 17 July 1948, and secret telegram to Marshall from Caffery, Paris, 19 July 1948, all RG 59, Decimal File 1945–49, 501.NA, box 2227, NACP; and Ingram memo to Sandifer, Hall, Kotschnig, van Zile Hyde, Calderwood, and Anderson, 4 Feb. 1949, RG 59, Decimal File 1945–49, 501.NA, box 2230, NACP.

For 1952 budget battles see Scheele, "Report of the Chairman of the United States Delegation," attached to Scheele letter to Secretary of State, 12 Oct. 1953, RG 59, Decimal File 1945–49, 501. NA, box 2230, NACP.

32. Scheele, "Report of the Chairman of the United States Delegation," attached to Scheele letter to Secretary of State, 12 Oct. 1953, and unattributed, restricted dispatch from

U.S. resident delegation in Geneva to State Department, 21 July 1953, both RG 59, Decimal File 1950–54, 398.55-WHO, box 1634, NACP; undated [approx. Sept. 1959] position paper on malaria eradication for the tenth session of the WHO's Western Pacific Regional Committee, RG 59, Decimal File 1955–59, 398.55-WHO, box 1578, folder 7–159, NACP.

33. Memorandum of conversation between Miss Barbara Salt, First Secretary of British Embassy in Washington, and Joseph S. Henderson, State Department, 24 June 1952, RG 59, Decimal File 1950–54, 398.55-WHO, box 1633, NACP.

For Chisholm and the budget see restricted Blaisdell dispatch to State Department, 6 Feb. 1953, RG 59, Decimal File 1950–54, 398.55-WHO, box 1633, NACP; and "Canada's Responsibility in World Health," Chisholm address to the Eighth Annual Conference of the Institute of Public Administration of Canada, Chisholm papers, vol. 2, folder 146–164, CNA.

For 1953–54 budget discussions see restricted dispatch from U.S. Delegation to WHA to State Department, 9 May 1953, dispatch from Scheele, Chairman of U.S. delegation to WHA, to State Department, 19 May 1953, and Scheele, "Report of the Chairman of the United States Delegation," attached to Scheele letter to Secretary of State, 12 Oct. 1953, all RG 59, Decimal File 1950–54, 398.55-WHO, box 1634, NACP.

34. Position paper on WHO program and budget estimates for 1957, 30 Apr. 1956, RG 59, Decimal File 1955–59, 398.55-WHO, box 1578, folder 5–456, NACP.

For 1955 budget debate see letter to David McK. Key, Assistant Secretary of State for United Nations Affairs, from van Zile Hyde, Public Health Service Medical Director, 19 Mar. 1954, RG 59, Decimal File 1950–54, 398.55-WHO, box 1635, NACP.

For State Department desire to play a more positive role in the WHO see off-the-record van Zile Hyde comments to NGOs, 21 Oct. 1948, attached to Williams letter to Carter, 29 Oct. 1948, RG 59, Decimal File 1945–49, 501.NA, box 2229, NACP; Ingram memo to Sandifer, Hall, Kotschnig, Hyde, Calderwood, and Anderson, 4 Feb. 1949, and restricted position paper, "Budget for 1950," 14 June 1949, both RG 59, Decimal File 1945–49, 501.NA, box 2230, NACP.

For 1958 budget and 1959 efforts see undated [approx. Sept. 1959], position paper on malaria eradication for the tenth session of the WHO's Western Pacific Regional Committee, RG 59, Decimal Files 1955–59, 398.55-WHO, box 1578, folder 7–159, NACP.

35. World Health Organization, *Handbook of Resolutions and Decisions of the World Health Assembly and the Executive Board,* 8th ed. (Geneva: WHO, Nov. 1965), 288–89; and World Health Organization, *The Second Ten Years of the World Health Organization, 1958–1967* (Geneva: WHO, 1968), 308.

36. For WHO emphasis on cooperation with a broad range of organizations see Article 2 of the WHO Constitution; and WHO, *First Ten Years,* 129–30.

For WHO collaborative efforts with UNICEF see WHO, *First Ten Years,* 97, 132–35; "First Session of the Executive Board," 207; "Expert Advice on Child Nutrition," *Chronicle of the WHO* 2 (Jan. 1948): 6–8; Ritchie Calder, *Growing Up with UNICEF,* Public Affairs Pamphlet 330; Maggie Black, *The Children and the Nations: The Story of Unicef* (Geneva: UNICEF, 1986), 87–190; letter to Holmes from George F. Davidson, Deputy Minister of Welfare, 1 June 1949, RG 25, External Affairs, series G-2, vol. 3684, file: 5475-K-40, CNA; and "Fourth Session of the Executive Board," 237, 240–41.

37. For FAO-WHO work on malaria and agricultural productivity see "Proposal for a Joint Action Programme to Increase World Food Production and Raise Standards of Health," presented by FAO and WHO to the UNRRA Central Committee, Nov. 1948, and

report to the director-general by the third meeting of the Standing Advisory Committee on Nutrition, 7 Dec. 1948, both microform 803-1-3, WHOA; FAO Agriculture Division memorandum, 20 Aug. 1948, and "Collaboration between FAO and WHO on a Joint Action Program to Establish Demonstration Areas for the Control of Malaria, to Increase Food Production and Raise Standards of Living," memorandum to the Director-General from the FAO Inter-Division Working Party, Dec. 1948, both microform 453-4-21, WHOA; Chisholm letter to Lester B. Pearson, Canadian Under-Secretary of State for External Affairs, 26 Aug. 1948, RG 25, External Affairs, series G-2, vol. 3684, file: 5475-K-40, CNA; "Second World Health Assembly: General Account," 172; and "Second World Health Assembly: Technical Questions," 175–77.

For FAO-WHO work on nutrition and food in general see memorandum to D. W. M. Bonne, Director of the WHO Division of Planning, from F. W. Clements, Chief of FAO Nutrition Division, microform 803-1-3, WHOA; "Proposal for a Joint WHO/FAO Nutrition Training Centre in the Middle East: Comments on the Colonial Nutrition Aspect of the Proposal," Nov. 1949, microform 803-1-14, WHOA; Reports of Joint FAO/WHO Expert Committee on Nutrition, WHO Technical Report Series 16, 44, 97, 149; and "Prevention and Treatment of Severe Malnutrition in Times of Disaster: Report Approved by the Joint FAO/WHO Expert Committee on Nutrition and Presented to the Fourth World Health Assembly," 45 (Nov. 1951), Joint FAO/WHO Expert Committee on Meat Hygiene, "First Report," 99 (Dec. 1955), Joint FAO/WHO Conference on Food Additives, "Report," 107 (July 1956), Joint FAO/WHO Expert Committee on Milk Hygiene, "First Report," 124 (1957), and "General Principles Governing the Use of Food Additives: First Report of the Joint FAO/WHO Expert Committee on Food Additives," 129 (1957), all WHO Technical Report Series.

For FAO-WHO work on brucellosis and other zoonoses see "World Brucellosis Centre," Chronicle of the WHO 2 (Dec. 1948): 281–82; and Joint FAO/WHO Expert Panel on Brucellosis, "Report on the First Session," 37 (May 1951), "Second Report," 67 (May 1953), and "Third Report," 148 (1958), and Joint FAO/WHO Expert Group on Zoonoses, "Report on the First Session," 40 (May 1951), all WHO Technical Report Series.

38. Such panels included joint FAO/WHO expert committees on brucellosis, food additives, meat and milk hygiene, nutrition, and zoonoses; joint ILO/WHO committees on the hygiene of seafarers and occupational health; joint UN/WHO meeting of experts on the mental-health aspects of adoption; joint expert committees on WHO, UN, ILO, and UNESCO representatives on the mentally subnormal child and the physically handicapped child; the Joint WHO/UNESCO Expert Committee; the joint expert committee of WHO, UN, FAO, ILO, and UNICEF representatives on the care of well children in day-care centers and institutions; and the WHO/UNESCO Council of International Organizations of Medical Sciences.

For WHO work with specialized agencies see "First Session of the Executive Board," 207; "WHO and Medical Science Congresses," Chronicle of the WHO 2 (Mar. 1948): 38–39; "Towards the Co-ordination of Medical Congresses," 2 ibid. (Apr. 1948): 63; "Co-ordination of Medical Congresses," 3 ibid. (Feb. 1949): 41–42; WHO, First Ten Years, 139–40, 144; "Agreement between the International Labour Organisation and the World Health Organization," "Agreement between the Food and Agriculture Organization and the World Health Organization," "Agreement between the United Nations Educational, Scientific and Cultural Organization and the World Health Organization," and "Agreement between the International Atomic Energy Agency and the World Health Organization," all in WHO, Basic Documents,

13th ed. (Geneva: WHO, Dec. 1962), 50–53, 54–57, 58–61, 62–66, resp.; "First World Health Assembly," 197; "Second World Health Assembly: Technical Questions," 194, 207–208; and "Fourth Session of Executive Board," 239.

The WHO undertook similar work for a number of intergovernmental organizations, such as the Colombo Plan Bureau, the Committee for Technical Co-operation in Africa South of the Sahara, the Council of Europe, the Intergovernment Committee for European Migration, the League of Arab States, and the Office International des Epizooties (WHO, *First Ten Years,* 141).

39. WHO, *First Ten Years,* 142. For NGO-WHO relationship see also ibid., 142–44; "Relations with Non-Governmental Organizations," *Chronicle of the WHO* 2 (Mar. 1948): 41–42; and "Relations with Non-Governmental Organizations," in WHO, *Basic Documents,* 67–69.

Between 1947 and 1965, the WHO established expert committees or study groups to investigate the following areas: accidents in childhood, African rickettsioses, alcoholism, antibiotics, arthropod-borne viruses, ataractic and hallucinogenic drugs in psychiatry, bilharziasis, biological standardization, brucellosis, cancer, Chagas's disease, cholera, dental health, drug addiction, environmental sanitation, fellowships, filariasis, general medical practice, health education of the public, health laboratory methods, health statistics, heart disease, hepatitis, human genetics, immunological and hematological surveys, influenza, insecticides, international sanitary regulations, iron deficiency anaemia, juvenile epilepsy, leprosy, leptospirosis, malaria, maternal and child health, the measurement of levels of health, medical education, medical rehabilitation, mental health, the mental health aspects of the peaceful uses of atomic energy, the mental health problems of automation, midwifery training, nursing, nutrition, onchocerciasis, the organization of medical care, paediatric education, plague, poliomyelitis, premature births, professional and technical education of medical and auxiliary personnel, public health administration, the public health aspects of housing, the public health aspects of the use of antibiotics in food and feedstuffs, rabies, radiation, respiratory virus diseases, rheumatic diseases, school health services, trachoma, tuberculosis, trypanosomiasis, the unification of pharmacopoeias, vaccinations, venereal infections and treponematoses, and yellow fever.

For the consensus-building potential of the expert committees see "Second Session of the Executive Board," 251.

For WHO efforts to incorporate NGOs into its mission see WHO, *First Ten Years,* 96; personal van Zile Hyde letter to Chisholm, 12 May 1947, microform 1-1-2, card 1, WHOA; and Joint FAO/WHO Expert Committee on Nutrition, "Report on the First Session," *WHO Technical Report Series* 16 (June 1950): 22–23.

Some NGOs attached to the WHO included the Federation Dentaire Internationale, the International Committee of Catholic Nurses, the International Committee of the Red Cross and the League of Red Cross Societies, the International Council of Nurses, the International Leprosy Association, the International Organization against Trachoma, the International Tuberculosis Campaign, the World Federation for Mental Health, the World Federation of United Nations Associations, and the World Medical Association.

40. For WHO philosophy about research laboratories see WHO, *First Ten Years,* 154–55; and "Second World Health Assembly: Technical Questions," 204–205.

For WHO reference laboratories see WHO, *First Ten Years,* 154; "Laboratories Approved for Testing Yellow-Fever Vaccines," *Chronicle of the WHO* 2 (Mar. 1948): 43; "Fourth Session of the Executive Board," 242–43; and Candau memorandum to the Assistant Director-Generals

(Drs. O. V. Baroyan, F. Grundy, and P. M. Kaul) with attached "WHO International Reference Centres," 14 Dec. 1962, file M 2/286/12, WHOA.

For influenza centers see "International Influenza Centre," 2 (Mar. 1948): 44, "Influenza in Europe," 3 (Jan. 1949): 12, and "Influenza Epidemic of 1948/49 in Europe," 3 (June 1949): 129, all *Chronicle of the WHO*; WHO, *First Ten Years,* 211–17; Expert Committee on Influenza, "First Report," *WHO Technical Report Series* 64 (Apr. 1953); "Influenza in Europe," *Relevé Épidémiologique Hebdomadaire/Weekly Epidemiological Record* 24 (12 Jan. 1949): 18; and *New England Journal of Medicine* 240 (1949): 313.

For other international research laboratories see Expert Committee on Tuberculosis, "Report on the Fourth Session," 7 (Apr. 1950): 10–11, and "Report on the Fifth Session," 32 (Apr. 1951): 10, both *WHO Technical Report Series.*

For training role of such laboratories see "Fellowships in Venereal Diseases," *Chronicle of the WHO* 3 (Feb. 1949): 42; and Expert Committee on Influenza, "First Report," 17.

41. For international pharmacopoeia see Expert Committee on the Unification of Pharmacopoeias, "Report on the Fourth Session," "Report on the Fifth Session," 12 (May 1950), "Report on the Sixth Session," 29 (Oct. 1950), "Report on the Seventh Session," 35 (Apr. 1951), "Report on the Eighth Session," 43 (Nov. 1951); and "Ninth Report," 50 (May 1952), all *WHO Technical Report Series*; "Unification of Pharmacopoeias," *Chronicle of the WHO* 3 (June 1949): 120–22; and "Fourth Session of the Executive Board," 238–39.

For biological standardization work see "Biological Standardization: Third Session of the Expert Committee" and "Biological Standardization," *Chronicle of the WHO* 3 (July 1949): 141–48, 164; letter from N. K. Jerne, Acting Chief of the WHO Department of Biological Standardisation, to Professor J. Tréfouël, Director of the Paris Pasteur Institute, 26 Feb. 1949, microform 751-1-4, WHOA; and Expert Committee on Biological Standardization, "Report on the Third Session," "Report of the Subcommittee on Fat-Soluble Vitamins," 3 (Feb. 1950), "Report on the Fourth Session," 36 (Apr. 1951), "Fifth Report," 56 (July 1952), "Sixth Report," 68 (Apr. 1953), "Seventh Report," 86 (June 1954), "Eighth Report," 96 (July 1955), "Ninth Report," 108 (July 1956), "Tenth Report," 127 (1957), "Eleventh Report," 147 (1958), "Diphtheria and Pertussis Vaccination: Report of a Conference of Heads of Laboratories Producing Diphtheria and Pertussis Vaccines," 61 (May 1953), and Expert Committee on Tuberculosis, "Report on the Fifth Session," 10, all *WHO Technical Report Series.*

For standardization of causes of death see World Health Organization, *Manual of the International Classification of Diseases, Injuries and Causes of Death* (Geneva: WHO, 1949); and "WHO Publications," 17–18.

42. For concern over the lack of health statistics see WHO, *First Ten Years,* 163, 167–68, 170; letter to Chisholm from Sao Paulo, Brazil, 1 Oct. 1949, microform 1-1-8, card 2, WHOA; E. Claveaux as quoted in "Points from Speeches," *Chronicle of the WHO* 3 (Oct. 1949): 218; and Expert Committee on Health Statistics, "Report on the First Session," *WHO Technical Report Series* 5 (Mar. 1950): 9.

For WHO efforts to remedy the situation see WHO, *First Ten Years,* 167; "Second World Health Assembly: Technical Questions" and "Improvement of Medical Statistics: First Session of the Expert Committee on Health Statistics," *Chronicle of the WHO* 3 (Nov. 1949): 198–99, 246–51, resp.; Expert Committee on Health Statistics, "Report on the First Session," esp. 4–5; "Report on the Second Session," 25 (Oct. 1950), "Third Report," 53 (July 1952), "Fifth Report," 133 (1957), and First International Conference of National Committees on Vital and Health Statistics, "Report," 85 (June 1954), all *WHO Technical Report Series.*

For standardized causes of death see "Fourth Session of the Executive Board," 246.

For national committees on vital and health statistics see "Report of the International Conference for the Sixth Decennial Revision of the International Lists of Diseases and Causes of Death," in WHOIC, *Reports of the Expert Committees and Other Advisory Bodies to the Interim Commission,* Official Records of the WHO, no. 11 (Geneva: WHO, Dec. 1948), 25, 30; "Fourteenth Plenary Session" and "Committee on Programme: Second Report," in WHO, *First World Health Assembly,* Official Records of the WHO, no. 13 (Geneva: WHO, Dec. 1948), 97, 304; Expert Committee on Health Statistics, "Report on the First Session," 3–4; and First International Conference of National Committees on Vital and Health Statistics, "Report."

43. For first-year budget and requests see "Second Session of the Executive Board," 249–50; and letter to the British High Commissioner for Canada from the Canadian Secretary for External Affairs, 14 Dec. 1948, RG 25, External Affairs, series G-2, vol. 3684, file: 5475-K-40, CNA.

44. For emphasis on international training centers in Third World see "Second World Health Assembly: General Account," 171, 181; and Rajkumari Amrit Kaur as quoted in "Points from Speeches," *Chronicle of the WHO* 3 (Oct. 1949): 218.

For auxiliary personnel training see "Second World Health Assembly: Technical Questions," 180–82; and Expert Committee on Professional and Technical Education of Medical and Auxiliary Personnel, "Report on the First Session," 22 (Dec. 1950), "Second Report," 69 (June 1953), and "Third Report," 109 (May 1956), all *WHO Technical Report Series.*

45. "Second World Health Assembly: General Account," 172. See also "Second World Health Assembly: Technical Questions," 177–78.

46. For priority work in these fields see "Five Year Plan," Maternal and Child Health Section memorandum, 10 May 1949, memorandum to Bonne from Dr. Guthe, WHO Venereal Disease Section, 16 May 1949, "Five-Year Plan of the Public Health Administration Section," [approx. May 1949], memorandum from Leclainche, WHO Public Health Administration Section, to Dr. G. W. Miller, 22 June 1949, and "Malaria: Five Year Plan, 1950–1954" [approx. June 1949], all microform 1-1-8, card 1, WHOA.

For EPTA funds see WHO, *First Ten Years,* 125–26; and "Second World Health Assembly: General Account," 166, 168–70.

47. For commission program in maternal and child health see "Programme for Maternal and Child Health," 2 (Mar. 1948): 39–40, and "Maternal and Child Health," 3 (Mar. 1949): 43–48, both *Chronicle of the WHO;* and "First World Health Assembly," 171, 175, 195.

For nutrition see "First World Health Assembly," 172–73, 177–78.

For sanitary engineering see "First World Health Assembly," 172–73, 177–78; and Stampar letter, 25 Jan. 1947, microform 2-1-4, WHOA.

48. For maternal and child health activities see "Second World Health Assembly: Technical Questions," 188–89; "Maternal and Child Health," *Programme and Budget Estimates for 1950,* 65; "Active Immunization against Common Communicable Diseases of Childhood: Report of a Group of Consultants convened by the Director-General," 6 (Mar. 1950), Expert Group of Prematurity, "Final Report," 27 (Oct. 1950), Expert Committee on School Health Services, "Report on the First Session," 30 (Apr. 1951), Expert Committee on Maternity Care, "First Report: A Preliminary Survey," 51 (June 1952), Joint Expert Committee on the Physically Handicapped Child, "First Report," 58 (Dec. 1952), "The Mentally Subnormal Child: Report of a Joint Expert Committee convened by WHO with the participation

of United Nations, ILO, and UNESCO," 75 (Apr. 1954), Expert Committee on Midwifery Training, "First Report," 93 (July 1955), "Administration of Maternal and Child Health Services," 115 (Feb. 1957), "Accidents in Childhood, Facts as a Basis for Prevention: Report of an Advisory Group," 118 (1957), and Study Group of Paediatric Education, "Report," 119 (1957), all *WHO Technical Report Series.*

For WHO nutrition program see "Second World Health Assembly: Technical Questions," 202; "Nutrition," *Programme and Budget Estimates,* 108; Joint FAO/WHO Expert Committee on Nutrition, "Report on the First Session," 4–8; and "Third Report," *WHO Technical Report Series* 72 (Dec. 1953).

For WHO environmental sanitation work see Expert Committee on Environmental Sanitation, "Report on the First Session," 10 (May 1950), "Second Report," 47 (June 1952), "Third Report," 77 (Apr. 1954), and "Food Hygiene: Fourth Report of the Expert Committee on Environmental Sanitation," 104 (June 1956), all *WHO Technical Report Series.*

49. For WHO role in the European BCG campaign see "Work of the Interim Commission," 89; "Second Session of the Executive Board," 248; "Second World Health Assembly: Technical Questions," 190; Expert Committee on Tuberculosis, "Report on the Fifth Session," 32 (Apr. 1951): 9–10, and "Tuberculosis Control: Plans for Intensified Inter-Country Action in Europe, Report of a Study-Group," 112 (Sept. 1956), both *WHO Technical Report Series.*

For the global TB campaign see "Second World Health Assembly: Technical Questions," 189–91; "Fourth Session of the Executive Board," 242; Expert Committee on Tuberculosis, "Report on the Fourth Session," *WHO Technical Report Series* 7 (Apr. 1950); "Vaccination against Tuberculosis: Sixth Report of the Expert Committee on Tuberculosis," 88 (Oct. 1954): esp. 3, 5, and "Chemotherapy and Chemoprophylaxis in Tuberculosis Control: Report of a Study Group," 141 (1957), both *WHO Technical Report Series*; and Expert Committee on Tuberculosis, "Report on the Fifth Session."

For WHO consultants see "Tuberculosis," *Chronicle of the WHO* 3 (June 1949): 132–33.

50. For work of expert committee see "Second World Health Assembly: General Account," 171; "Second World Health Assembly: Technical Questions," 193; Expert Committee on Venereal Infections, "Report on the Third Session," 13 (May 1950), and "Report on the First Session of the Subcommittee on Serology and Laboratory Aspects," 14 (May 1950), WHO Syphilis Study Commission, "Venereal-Disease Control in the USA, with Special Reference to Penicillin in Early, Prenatal, and Infantile Syphilis," 15 (May 1950), Expert Committee on Venereal Infections and Treponematoses, "Report on the Second Session of the Subcommittee and Laboratory Aspects," 33 (Apr. 1951): esp. 4, 7, and "Fourth Report," 63 (May 1953), and Expert Committee on Venereal Infections and Treponematoses, Subcommittee on Serology and Laboratory Aspects, "Third Report," 79 (Oct. 1954), all *WHO Technical Report Series.*

For WHO advisory services on venereal diseases in Europe see "Venereal-Disease Control in Poland," 3 (Feb. 1949): 29–32, and "Venereal Diseases," 3 (June 1949): 133–34, both *Chronicle of the WHO*; and "Second World Health Assembly: Technical Questions," 191–93.

For Third World antivenereal disease campaigns specifically see "Venereal Diseases," 133–34; "Second World Health Assembly: Technical Questions," 192; and Expert Committee on Venereal Diseases, "Report on the Second Session," *Reports of Expert Committees to the Executive Board,* Official Records of the WHO, no. 15 (Geneva: WHO, Apr. 1949), 29.

For contribution of pharmaceutical industry see "Venereal Diseases," 134.

10. Exercising International Authority

1. Malaria is an infection with any one of a family of parasites, of which *Plasmodium falciparum* and *P. vivax* are the most common. For more extensive information about malaria see Emilio Pampana, *A Textbook of Malaria Eradication*, 2d ed. (London: Oxford Univ. Press, 1969), 11–31.

For the devastation of malaria see Paul Farr Russell, *Malaria: Basic Principles Briefly Stated* (Oxford, UK: Blackwell Scientific, 1952); Siddiqi, *World Health*, 126, 150; Indian Central Health Education Bureau, *Malaria Eradication in India* (New Delhi: Government of India Press, 1961), 1; "After Effects of Malaria Eradication: Its Gains and Challenges: With Socio-Economic Approaches," interim report by Dr. S. Dakshinamurty, Emeritus Professor of Preventative and Social Medicine at Andhra Medical College in Visakhapatnam, India, Apr. 1968, file M 2/180/4, J2, WHOA; and D. P. Karmarkar, Indian Minister of Health, letter, and M. G. Candau, "World Health Day: 'Malaria Eradication–A World Challenge,' 7th April, 1960," in *World Health Day Souvenir*, ed. G. Kameswara Rao (Hyderabad, India: Public Health Department, 1960), vii, 8.

2. For early malaria control efforts see Paul Farr Russell, *Man's Mastery of Malaria* (London: Oxford Univ. Press, 1955); League, *Ten Years of World Co-operation*, 245–48; Leonard J. Bruce-Chwatt, "Malaria in Nigeria," 4 (1951): 310, and Samuel W. Simmons and William M. Upholt, "Disease Control with Insecticides: A Review of the Literature," 3 (1951): 535–38, both *Bulletin of the WHO*; Leonard J. Bruce-Chwatt and James Haworth, "Malaria Eradication: Its Present Status," *Israel Journal of Medical Sciences* 1 (Mar. 1965): 284–85; Indian Central Health Education Bureau, *Malaria Eradication in India*, 4; and Howard-Jones, *Scientific Background to International Sanitary Conferences*, 84.

For the invention of DDT, its properties, and use see T. F. West and G. A. Campbell, *DDT and the Newer Persistent Insecticides*, 2d ed. (New York: Chemical Publishing, 1952); Paul F. Russell, "World-Wide Malaria Eradication," Delta Omega Lecture at the University of Michigan School of Public Health, 11 Feb. 1958, 3–4; Rita Gray Beatty, *The DDT Myth: Triumph of the Amateurs* (New York: John Day, 1973); United Nations Environment Programme, the International Labour Organisation, and the WHO, *DDT and Its Derivatives: Environmental Aspects*, Environmental Health Criteria Series, no. 83 (Geneva: WHO, 1989); Harold Farnsworth Gray, "Some Newer Ideas in Mosquito Control," 27 (Apr. 1948): 321–25, and L. Vargas, "DDT: Información General," 27 (June 1948): 531–42, both *Boletín de la Oficina Sanitaria Panamericana;* and Kenneth S. Davis, "The Deadly Dust: The Unhappy History of DDT," *American Heritage* 22 (Feb. 1971): 45.

3. Davis, "Deadly Dust," 45–47.

4. For the development of a theory of malaria eradication through DDT use see Siddiqi, *World Health*, 126; WHO, *First Ten Years*, 173; G. Macdonald and G. W. Göckel, "The Malaria Parasite Rate in Interruption of Transmission," *Bulletin of the WHO* 31 (1964): 365–77; and "Mosquitos," *Boletín de la Oficina Sanitaria Panamericana* 26 (Apr. 1947): 356–59.

For the per capita cost of malaria eradication see draft "Director-General's Report to ECOSOC," 6 Oct. 1959, file M 2/180/5, WHOA; C. M. J. Jaujou, "La Lutte Antipaludique en Corse" [The Antimalarial Campaign in Corsica], *Bulletin of the WHO* 11 (1954): 635–77; and "Paludismo" [Malaria], *Boletín de la Oficina Sanitaria Panamericana* 26 (Apr. 1947): 349.

5. Siddiqi, *World Health*, 24, 123, 125.

6. As quoted in Davis, "Deadly Dust," 46.

7. For the invention, World War II use, and initial experimentation with DDT see West and Campbell, *DDT;* Siddiqi, *World Health,* 129; J. B. Graham, B. V. Travic, F. A. Morton, and A. W. Lindquist, "DDT as a Residual-Type Treatment to Control *Anopheles quadrimaculatus:* Practical Tests," *Journal of Economic Entomology* 38 (1945): 231–35; and P. A. Harper, E. T. Lisansky, and B. E. Sasse, "Malaria and Other Insect-Borne Diseases in the South Pacific Campaign, 1942–1945: General Aspects and Control Measures," *American Journal of Tropical Medicine* 27: supplement to 3 (May 1947): 1–68.

For the Italian field tests see Fred Soper, F. W. Knipe, G. Casini, Louis A. Riehl, and A. Rubino, "Reduction of Anopheles Density Effected by the Pre-Season Spraying of Building Interiors with DDT in Kerosene, at Castel Volturno, Italy, in 1944–1945 and in the Tiber Delta in 1945," *American Journal of Tropical Medicine* 27 (Mar. 1947): 177–200; and Russell, "World-Wide Malaria Eradication," 5–6.

8. For early malaria control programs using DDT see, e.g., undated draft letter from Indonesian Minister for Health to the Indonesian Prime Minister, attached to memorandum to the WHO Assistant Director-General from Regional Director of the WHO Southeast Asian Regional Office (SEARO), 18 Aug. 1958, file M 2/180/4, J1, WHOA; Siddiqi, *World Health,* 130–31, 133; Carlos A. Alvarado and Héctor A. Coll, "Programa para la Erradicación del Paludismo en la República Argentina" [Program for the Eradication of Malaria in Argentina], "Guyana Inglesa" [British Guiana], and "Paludismo," 27 (July 1948): 585–602, 660–61, 654–55, resp., Arnoldo Gabaldón, "Enseñanzas para la Accion Sanitaria en la America Latina Derivadas de la Lucha Antimalarica en Venezuela" [Lessons for Sanitary Action in Latin America Derived from the Antimalaria Campaign in Venezuela], 38 (Mar. 1955): 259–65, and "Paludismo," 26 (Apr. 1947): 349, all *Boletín de la Oficina Sanitaria Panamericana;* Bruce-Chwatt, "Malaria in Nigeria," 321–24; Simmons and Upholt, "Disease Control with Insecticides," 539–43, G. Davidson, "Results of Recent Experiments on the Use of DDT and BHC against Adult Mosquitos at Taveta, Kenya," and Botha de Meillon, "Malaria Survey of South-West Africa," 4 (1951): 329, 444, P. C. Issaris, "Malaria Transmission in the Tarai, Naini Tal District, Uttar Pradesh, India," 9 (1953): 311–33, C. Garrett-Jones, "An Experiment in Trapping and Controlling *Anopheles maculipennis* in North Iran," 4 (1951): 547–62, M. Ciuca, "Le Paludisme en Roumanie de 1949 a 1955" [Malaria in Romania, 1949–1955], 15 (1956): 725–51, P. H. van Thiel and D. Metselaar, "A Pilot Project of Residual-Insecticide Spraying to Control Malaria Transmitted by the Anopheles punctulatus Group in Netherlands New Guinea," J. Hamon and G. Dufour, "La Lutte Antipaludique a la Réunion" [The Antimalarial Campaign in Réunion], H. Floch, "La Lutte Antipaludique en Guyane Française" [The Antimalarial Campaign in French Guiana], F. J. Dy, "Present Status of Malaria Control in Asia," and G. Giglioli, "Malaria Control in British Guiana," 11 (1954): 521–24, 525–56, 579–633, 635–77, 725–63, 849–53, resp., and H. Floch and P. Fauran, "Sensibilité aux Insecticides Chlorés des Larves de *Culex fatigans* et d'*Anopheles aquasalis* en Guyane Française" [Susceptibility of the larvae of *Culex fatigans* and *Anopheles aquasalis* in French Guiana to Chlorinated Insecticides], 18 (1958): 667–73, all *Bulletin of the WHO;* Jaujou, "La Lutte Antipaludique en Corse"; M. A. C. Dowling, *The Malaria Eradication in Mauritius, 1948–52* (Port Louis, Mauritius: Medical and Health Department, 1953); G. Giglioli, *Malaria, Filariasis and Yellow Fever in British Guiana: Control by Residual D.D.T. Methods* (Georgetown, British Guiana, 1948); Harper, Lisansky, and Sasse, "Malaria and Other Insect-Borne Diseases in the South Pacific Campaign, 1942–1945," 1–128; and Arnoldo Gabaldón, "The Nation-Wide Campaign against Malaria in Venezuela," *Transactions of the Royal Society of Tropical Medicine and Hygiene* 43 (Sept. 1949): 113–60.

For early WHO antimalarial work see draft Chisholm letter, 13 Aug. 1948, microform 453-2-14, WHOA; memoranda from Dr. E. J. Pampana, WHO Expert Committee on Malaria, to Chisholm [approx. Oct. 1948], microform 453-2-15, WHOA; "Rural Malaria Control Demonstration Projects in the Far East," report by H. G. S. Morin, WHO malariologist attached to the Far East Headquarters of UNICEF [approx. 1947], microform 453-4-4, WHOA; "A Note on the Present Status of Malaria Control Programme in India," in Proceedings of Antimalaria Coordination Conference on Indo-Burma Border, 15–17 Jan. 1957, microform M 2/86/4 SEARO, card 1, WHOA; Siddiqi, *World Health*, 128–29; Russell, "World-Wide Malaria Eradication," 11; WHO, *First Ten Years*, 172–75; "Review of the Malaria Programme in the African Region," Dowling memorandum, 23 Oct. 1959, file M 2/372/3 AFRO, J2, WHOA; and L. Mara, "Malaria Control in South Malabar, Madras State," *Bulletin of the WHO* 11 (1954): 679–723.

For optimism engendered by DDT spraying see "Malaria Conference in Equatorial Africa," *Bulletin of the WHO* 4 (1951): 299.

9. Expert Committee on Malaria, "Fifth Report," *WHO Technical Report Series* 80 (June 1954): 24. See also E. J. Pampana, "Changing Strategy in Malaria Control," 11 (1954): 515, "Introduction" and G. Macdonald, "Theory of the Eradication of Malaria," 15 (1956): 361–64, 369–87, all *Bulletin of the WHO;* WHO, *First Ten Years*, 175; and Bruce-Chwatt and Haworth, "Malaria Eradication," 285.

10. For the development of insecticide resistance see Expert Committee on Insecticides, "Sixth Report," *WHO Technical Reports Series* 110 (Oct. 1956); G. Macdonald, *The Epidemiology and Control of Malaria* (London: Oxford Univ. Press, 1957); Siddiqi, *World Health*, 135; Russell, "World-Wide Malaria Eradication," 8–10; draft "Director-General's Report to ECO-SOC," 6 Oct. 1959, file M 2/180/5, WHOA; G. A. Livadas and G. Georgopoulos, "Development of Resistance to DDT by *Anopheles sacharovi* in Greece," 8 (1953): 497–511, A. W. A. Brown, "DDT-Dehydrochlorinase Activity in Resistant Houseflies and Mosquitos," 14 (1956): 807–12, and "The Insecticide-Resistance Problem: A Review of Developments in 1956 and 1957," 18 (1958): 309–21, L. E. Chadwick, "Progress in Physiological Studies of Insecticide Resistance," 16 (1957): 1203–18, G. Davidson, "Studies on Insecticide Resistance in Anopheline Mosquitos," S. Y. Liu, "A Summary of Recent Insecticidal Tests on Some Insects of Medical Importance in Taiwan," J. R. Busvine and W. Z. Coker, "Resistance Patterns in DDT-Resistant *Aëdes aegypti,*" R. H. Wharton, "Dieldrin Resistance in *Culex pipiens fatigans* in Malaya," and Marshall Laird, "Susceptibility of Adults of a Malayan Strain of *Culex pipiens fatigans* Wiedemann to DDT and Dieldrin," 18 (1958): 579–621, 623–49, 651–56, 657–65, 681–83, resp., E. Mosna, L. Rivosecchi, and K. R. S. Ascher, "Studies on Insecticide-Resistant Anophelines," G. Gramiccia, B. de Meillon, J. Petrides, and A. M. Ulrich, "Resistance to DDT in *Anopheles stephensi* in Southern Iraq," and M. Qutubuddin, "The Inheritance of DDT-Resistance in a Highly Resistant Strain of *Aëdes aegypti* (L.)," 19 (1958): 297–301, 1102–4, 1109–12, resp., D. W. Micks, "Insecticide-Resistance: A Review of Developments in 1958 and 1959," 22 (1960): 519–29, George R. Shidrawi, "Laboratory Tests on Mosquito Tolerance to Insecticides and the Development of Resistance by *Aëdes aegypti,*" 17 (1957): 377–411, A. Smith, "Results of Screening *Anopheles gambiae* for Resistance to Dieldrin in the Pare Area of North-East Tanganyika," 21 (1959): 239–40; R. L. Peffly, "Insecticide Resistance in Anophelines in Eastern Saudi Arabia," R. Elliott, "Insecticide Resistance in Populations of *Anopheles gambiae* in West Africa," and Julian de Zulueta, "Insecticide Resistance in *Anopheles sacharovi,*" 20 (1959): 757–76, 777–96, 797–822, resp., G. D. Georgopoulos, "Extension to Chlordane of the Resistance to DDT Observed in *Anopheles sa-*

charovi," 11 (1954): 855–64, C. Garrett-Jones and C. Gramiccia, "Evidence of the Development of Resistance to DDT by *Anopheles sacharovi* in the Levant," and Harold Trapido, "Recent Experiments on Possible Resistance to DDT by *Anopheles albimanus* in Panama," 11 (1954): 865–83, 885–89, all *Bulletin of the WHO;* "Insecticide Resistance," 11 (Sept. 1957): 287–88, and "Resistance of Insects to Insecticides," 8 (Jan. 1954): 3–6, both *Chronicle of the WHO; Report on the Status of Malaria Eradication in the Americas: XIV Report* (Washington, D.C.: Pan American Sanitary Conference, 16 Aug. 1966), 2; and James R. Busvine, "Insecticide-Resistant Strains of Insects of Public Health Importance," *Transactions of the Royal Society of Tropical Medicine and Hygiene* 51 (Jan. 1957): 11–31.

For the impetus that resistance gave to the eradication campaign see Pampana, "Changing Strategy in Malaria Control," 517; "Introduction," 20 (1959): 751, "Introduction," 15 (1956): 361–62, and J. R. Busvine, "The Significance of Insecticide-Resistant Strains: With Special Reference to Pests of Medical Importance," Gregory A. Livadas and Kyriacos Thymakis, "Susceptibility of Malaria Vectors to DDT in Greece," George D. Belios and George Fameliaris, "Resistance of Anopheline Larvae to Chlordane and Dieldrin," and P. M. Bernard, "La Lutte Contre le Paludisme en Afrique Tropicale" [The Campaign against Malaria in Tropical Africa], 15 (1956): 389–401, 403–13, 415–23, 627–34, resp., all *Bulletin of the WHO;* WHO, *First Ten Years,* 175–76; "A Brief Statement Regarding the Presumed Effects of Malaria Eradication on Economic and Social Conditions," memorandum for Marcolino Candau, WHO Director-General, from Paul F. Russell, staff member of the Rockefeller Foundation and WHO medical consultant, 15 July 1959, and draft "Director-General's Report to ECOSOC," 6 Oct. 1959, both file M 2/180/5, WHOA; undated draft letter from Indonesian Minister for Health to the Indonesian Prime Minister, attached to SEARO Regional Director memorandum to Assistant Director-General, 18 Aug. 1958, file M 2/180/4, J1, WHOA; "Review of the Malaria Programme in the African Region"; and *Report on the Status of Malaria Eradication in the Americas,* 2.

11. For cost-benefit analyses of MEPs see also Russell, "World-Wide Malaria Eradication," 12; "Approximate Estimates of the Economic Loss Caused by Malaria with Some Estimates of the Benefits of MEP in Iraq," memorandum by Dr. Amjad Dauod Niazi, attached to letter from L. J. Bruce-Chwatt, Professor of Tropical Hygiene at the London School of Hygiene and Tropical Medicine, to Dr. James Haworth, Research and Technical Intelligence Section of WHO Division of Malaria Eradication, 24 Mar. 1970, and draft "Director-General's Report to ECOSOC," 6 Oct. 1959, both file M 2/180/5, WHOA; Malaria Conference for the Western Pacific and South-East Asia Regions, "Report," *WHO Technical Report Series* 103 (May 1956): 16–22; "Facts and Figures Concerning the Economic Damage Caused by Malaria in Some Countries," 1 July 1957, attached to SEARO Regional Director memorandum to Assistant Director-General, 18 Aug. 1958, file M 2/180/4, J1, WHOA; Pampana, *Textbook of Malaria Eradication,* 481–91; Robin Barlow, *The Economic Effects of Malaria Eradication* (Ann Arbor: Univ. of Michigan School of Public Health, 1968); and C.-E. A. Winslow, *The Cost of Illness and the Price of Health,* WHO Monograph Series, no. 7 (Geneva: WHO, 1951), 20–27, 75–77.

For the savings of malaria eradication over control see also Russell, "World-Wide Malaria Eradication," 2, 8; Siddiqi, *World Health,* 135, 148–50; "A Brief Statement Regarding the Presumed Effects of Malaria Eradication on Economic and Social Conditions," and draft "Director-General's Report to ECOSOC," 6 Oct. 1959, both file M 2/180/5, WHOA; and de Meillon, "Malaria Survey of South-West Africa," 414.

For the creation of a rural, public health corps through the MEP see Siddiqi, *World Health*, 137; Bruce-Chwatt and Haworth, "Malaria Eradication," 286; Dowling memorandum to Chief of Policy and Planning in WHO Malaria Eradication Division, 7 Oct. 1960, file M 2/372/3 AFRO, J2, WHOA; and Indian Central Health Education Bureau, *Malaria Eradication in India*, 9.

For the argument that malaria eradication would spur economic development see secret "Draft Report of the Appraisal Committee on Malaria Eradication Programme," Jan. 1967, file M 2/180/4, J2, WHOA; Siddiqi, *World Health*, 137, 151; "A Brief Statement Regarding the Presumed Effects of Malaria Eradication on Economic and Social Conditions," "Approximate Estimates of the Economic Loss Caused by Malaria with Some Estimates of the Benefits of MEP in Iraq," and draft "Director-General's Report to ECOSOC," 6 Oct. 1959, all file M 2/180/5, WHOA; "The Urgent Need for a Study of the Economics of Malaria Eradication," National Institutes of Health (NIH) grant application by P. H. Nathan, University of Michigan School of Public Health, 30 Dec. 1960, and "Facts and Figures Concerning the Economic Damage Caused by Malaria in Some Countries," both file M 2/180/4, J1, WHOA; Bruce-Chwatt and Haworth, "Malaria Eradication," 284; and Dy, "Present Status of Malaria Control in Asia," 725–63.

12. For the PAHO initiatives on eradication see *Report on the Status of Malaria Eradication in the Americas*, 1; Bruce-Chwatt and Haworth, "Malaria Eradication," 285; Siddiqi, *World Health*, 134, 141; Russell, "World-Wide Malaria Eradication," 11; and Fred L. Soper, "La Erradicacion de la Malaria en el Hemisferio Occidental" [The Eradication of Malaria in the Western Hemisphere] *Boletín de la Oficina Sanitaria Panamericana* 38 (Mar. 1955): 231–39.

13. "Malaria Eradication," report of special committee of the international development advisory board, 13 Apr. 1956, RG 59, Decimal File 1955–1959, 398.55-WHO, box 1575, folder 5-456, NACP.

For WHA action see Shri M. Roshan Ali Khan, "Malaria: A World Menace," and Candau, "World Health Day," in *World Health Day Souvenir*, ed. Rao, 4, 8; and WHO, *First Ten Years*, 176.

For the beginning of the WHO campaign see draft "Director-General's Report to ECOSOC on Malaria Eradication," 6 Oct. 1959, file M 2/180/5, WHOA; and WHO, *First Ten Years*, 119.

For the eradication blueprint see Expert Committee on Malaria, "Sixth Report," *WHO Technical Report Series* 123 (1957); and Siddiqi, *World Health*, 152.

14. For an overview of the process see Expert Committee on Malaria, "Sixth Report"; draft "Director-General's Report to ECOSOC," 6 Oct. 1959, file M 2/180/5, WHOA; Bruce-Chwatt and Haworth, "Malaria Eradication," 286; Pampana, *Textbook of Malaria Eradication*, 275–449, 457–63; and C. Simic, "Le Paludisme en Yougoslavie" [Malaria in Yugoslavia], *Bulletin of the WHO* 15 (1956): 753–66.

For the preparatory phase specifically see de Meillon, "Malaria Survey of South-West Africa," 333–35, 412–13; Pampana, *Textbook of Malaria Eradication*, 319–44; "Review of the Malaria Programme in the African Region," Dowling memorandum, 23 Oct. 1959, and memorandum on WHO assistance to African MEPs, May 1960, both file M 2/372/3 AFRO, J2, WHOA; Dorothy Bird Nyswander, *Education Approaches in the Malaria Eradication Program* (Washington, D.C.: ICA, 1959); memorandum to Malaria Eradication Division Director from F. J. C. Cambournac, Director of WHO African Regional Office (AFRO), 7

Sept. 1960, file M 2/372/3 AFRO, J2, WHOA; and "Paludismo," *Boletín de la Oficina Sanitaria Panamericana* 27 (July 1948): 655–56.

For the consolidation phase see draft "Director-General's Report to ECOSOC," 6 Oct. 1959, file M 2/180/5, WHOA; Pampana, *Textbook of Malaria Eradication,* 402–49; and memorandum on WHO assistance to African MEPs, May 1960, file M 2/372/3 AFRO, J2, WHOA.

15. For MEP minimum provisions see memorandum of conversation between Cambournac and C. A. Alvarado, Director of Malaria Eradication Division, 10 Nov. 1960; memorandum on WHO assistance to African MEPs, May 1960, and Cambournac memorandum to Malaria Eradication Division Director, 13 Oct. 1960, all file M 2/372/3 AFRO, J2, WHOA; and Pampana, *Textbook of Malaria Eradication,* 275–77.

For military metaphors see "The Approach to the Problem of the Control of Malaria in Tropical Africa," restricted memorandum approved by Candau, May 1957, file M 2/372/3 AFRO, J1, WHOA; undated draft letter from Indonesian Minister for Health to the Indonesian Prime Minister, attached to SEARO Regional Director memorandum to Assistant Director-General, 18 Aug. 1958, file M 2/180/4, J1, WHOA; and Shri P. V. G. Raju, "An Appeal to the People of Andhra Pradesh," in *World Health Day Souvenir,* ed. Rao, xiii.

For similar military analogies see *Report on the Status of Malaria Eradication in the Americas,* 2; Indian Central Health Education Bureau, *Malaria Eradication in India,* 20, 23; and Mani (WHO Southeast Asia Regional Director) letter, quote from Pampana, Dr. D. K. Viswanathan (SEARO Regional Director), "Malaria Eradication in S. E. Asia is an Investment. Yield: Health Plus 30 p. c. Cash Dividend," and "Where Greece has Led the Way," in *World Health Day Souvenir,* ed. Rao, ix, 5, 25, 27.

16. For the WHO standardization of terminology and statistical methods see Sir Gordon Covell, Paul F. Russell, and N. H. Swellengrebel, *Malaria Terminology: Report of a Drafting Committee Appointed by the World Health Organization,* WHO Monograph Series, no.13 (Geneva: WHO, 1953); WHO, *Terminology of Malaria and of Malaria Eradication: Report of a Drafting Committee* (Geneva: WHO, 1963); Sir Gordon Covell, G. Robert Coatney, John W. Field, and Jaswant Singh, *Chemotherapy of Malaria,* WHO Monograph Series, no. 27 (Geneva: WHO, 1955); Satya Swaroop, *Statistical Methods in Malaria Eradication* (Geneva: WHO, 1960, 1966); and WHO, *First Ten Years,* 181–82.

For standardization of equipment and testing methods see "The Approach to the Problem of the Control of Malaria in Tropical Africa"; WHO Division of Malaria Eradication, *Practical Entomology in Malaria Eradication,* part 1: *Field and Laboratory Techniques* and part 2: *The Practical Application of Entomological Methods, with Special Reference to the Planning of Investigations, the Selection of Techniques and the Interpretation of Data* (Geneva: WHO Division of Malaria Eradication, Apr. 1963); WHO Malaria Eradication Division, *Manual for the Processing and Examination of Blood Slides in Malaria Eradication Programs* (Geneva: WHO, 1960), and *Manual on Preparation of Malaria Eradication Programs* (Geneva: WHO, 1961); *Handbook on Malaria Training: Report on a Secretariat Meeting on Training in Malaria Eradication* (Geneva: WHO, 1966); *Insecticides: Manual of Specifications for Insecticides and for Spraying and Dusting Apparatus* (Geneva: WHO, 1953); *Manual on Epidemiological Evaluation and Surveillance in Malaria Eradication* (Geneva: WHO, 1962); "Specifications for Insecticides and Methods of Application," *Chronicle of the WHO* 5 (June 1951): 147; *Report on the Status of Malaria Eradication in the Americas,* 130–31; and Floch and Fauran, "Sensibilité aux Insecticides Chlorés," 667–73.

For WHO journal articles contributing to a standardization of MEP methods see Edward I. Coher, "A Technique for the Collection of Adult Mosquitos for Study," 21 (1959): 787–88, Maria E. Alessandrini, "Residual DDT Content: A Rapid Method for the Detection and Determination of Small Quantities of DDT on Sprayed Surfaces," 2 (1950): 629–36, Humberto Romero Alvarez and Rafael Miranda Franco, "Measurement of Insecticides for House Spraying," Roy Fritz and Donald J. Pletsch, "A Practical Device for Weighing Insecticides in Malaria Eradication Programmes," and W. N. Beklemishev, T. S. Detinova, and V. P. Polovodova, "Determination of Physiological Age in Anophelines and of Age Distribution in Anopheline Populations in the USSR," 21 (1959): 207–10, 211–14, 223–32, resp., A. W. A. Brown, "Methods Employed for Determining Insecticide Resistance in Mosquito Larvae," Fred W. Knipe, "Nozzle Tip Erosion Resistance Tests," "Pressure Regulators and Gauges on Hand-Compression Insecticide Sprayers: Some Causes of Failure and Suggestions for Improvement," and Ernest Paulini and Sergio Roubaud Reis, "A Colorimetric Method for Estimation of DDT and BHC," 16 (1957): 201–204, 211–25, 208–11, resp., R. W. Fay, J. W. Kilpatrick, R. L. Crowell, and K. D. Quarterman, "A Method for Field Detection of Adult-Mosquito Resistance to DDT Residues," 9 (1953): 345–51, R. A. Fitzjohn and P. A. Stevens, "Field Tests of Rubber Disc Flow-Regulators on Compression Sprayers," 29 (1963): 375–86, W. L. French and J. B. Kitzmiller, "Time in Concentration: A Simple Technique for the Accurate Detection of Resistance in Mosquito Larvae," 32 (1965): 133–42, Lawrence B. Hall, "Suggested Techniques, Equipment, and Standards for the Testing of Hand Insecticide-Spraying Equipment," and Fred W. Knipe, "Nozzles of Insecticide Sprayers: Comments from the Point of View of Malaria Control," 12 (1955): 371–400, 401–409, "Characteristics of Nozzle Tips Used on Mosquito-Control Equipment: A Measurement of Materials Lost through Rebound and Atomization," 13 (1955): 337–44, Richard P. Lonergan and Lawrence B. Hall, "A Method of Predicting the Effect of Nozzle Erosion from Water-Wettable Insecticides on the Discharge Rates of Nozzles," and R. C. Muirhead-Thomson, "A Pit Shelter for Sampling Outdoor Mosquito Populations," 19 (1958): 1073–83, 1116–18, and J. M. Press, "Measurement of Adsorption of Residual Insecticides using Flowing Chromatography," 20 (1959): 153–62, all *Bulletin of the WHO*.

17. For WHO short-term, expert consultants see AFRO Regional Director memorandum to Assistant Director-General of the WHO Department of Advisory Services, 14 June 1955, file M 2/372/3 AFRO, J1, WHOA; memorandum on WHO assistance to African MEPs, May 1960, file M 2/372/3 AFRO, J2, WHOA; and *Report on the Status of Malaria Eradication in the Americas,* 10.

For activities of the WHO Malaria Division see memorandum to Alvarado from Kaul, 29 Jan. 1962, file M 2/370/6, WHOA; and memorandum on WHO assistance to African MEPs, May 1960, file M 2/372/3 AFRO, J2, WHOA.

18. Letter to Cambournac, 19 Nov. 1957, file M 2/372/3 AFRO, J1, WHOA.

For WHO malaria training centers and courses see Cambournac memoranda to Alvarado, 7 Sept. and 13 Oct. 1960, file M 2/372/3 AFRO, J2, WHOA; Pampana memorandum of a meeting with AFRO Regional Director, 5 June 1957, file M 2/372/3 AFRO, J1, WHOA; "Contribution to the Annual Report of the Director-General to the World Health Assembly and to the United Nations in 1973," and memorandum from Dr. G. Houel to Dr. T. Lepes and Haworth, 13 Aug. 1973, both file M 2/370/16, J2, WHOA; "Review of the Malaria Programme in the African Region," Dowling memorandum, 23 Oct. 1959, and memorandum on WHO assistance to African MEPs, May 1960, both file M 2/372/3 AFRO, J2, WHOA;

"Malaria Course Programme for the Medical Officers at the Malaria Institute of India," Jan. 1949, microform 453-4-14, WHOA; *Report on the Status of Malaria Eradication in the Americas*, 2, 137; and "Curso Internacional de Malaria" [International Malaria Course], *Boletín de la Oficina Sanitaria Panamericana* 27 (June 1948): 572–73.

For WHO fellowships for malaria study see AFRO Regional Director memorandum to Assistant Director-General of Department of Advisory Services, 14 June 1955, file M 2/372/3 AFRO, J1, WHOA; and *Report on the Status of Malaria Eradication in the Americas*, 137.

19. For the WHO's promotion efforts and funding difficulties see undated [approx. Sept. 1959] position paper on malaria eradication for the tenth session of the WHO's Western Pacific Regional Committee, RG 59, Decimal File 1955–1959, 398.55-WHO, box 1577, folder 7–159, NACP.

20. For regional meetings of malaria eradication personnel see Candau memorandum to Budget Department, 27 June 1955, AFRO Regional Director memorandum to Assistant Director-General of Department of Advisory Services, 14 June 1955, and personal Dowling letter to Pampana, Chief of the WHO Malaria Section, 13 June 1957, all file M 2/372/3 AFRO, J1, WHOA; "Contribution to the Annual Report of the Director-General to the World Health Assembly and to the United Nations in 1973," Houel memorandum to Lepes and Haworth, 13 Aug. 1973, file M 2/370/16, J2, WHOA; "Review of the Malaria Programme in the African Region," Dowling memorandum, 23 Oct. 1959, and memorandum on WHO assistance to African MEPs, May 1960, both file M 2/372/3 AFRO, J2, WHOA; African Malaria Conference, *Malaria Eradication: Report of the Third African Malaria Conference* (Geneva: WHO, 1963); "Antimalaria Co-ordination in Asia," *Chronicle of the WHO* 11 (Jan. 1957): 3–6; Malaria Conference of Equatorial Africa, "Report," *WHO Technical Report Series* 38 (1951); Burma-India-Pakistan Malaria Eradication Coordination Conference, *Report on Malaria Eradication Program, East Pakistan, for Presentation to Burma-India-Pakistan Malaria Eradication Coordination Conference* (1966); European Conference on Malaria Eradication, *Malaria Eradication: Report on the Second European Conference* (Copenhagen: WHO Regional Office for Europe, 1962); and *Report on the Status of Malaria Eradication in the Americas*, 10, 12.

For WHO regional offices' role in transmitting relevant MEP information between meetings see AFRO Regional Director memorandum to Assistant Director-General, Department of Advisory Services, 14 June 1955, and personal letter to Pampana and Dowling, 13 June 1957, both file M 2/372/3 AFRO, J1, WHOA.

21. For Third World nations' desire to cooperate with neighboring nations in formulating regional MEPs see undated draft letter from Indonesian Minister for Health to the Indonesian Prime Minister, attached to SEARO Regional Director memorandum to Assistant Director-General, 18 Aug. 1958, file M 2/180/4, J1, WHOA.

For functionalism see Ernst Haas, *Beyond the Nation State: Functionalism and International Organization* (Stanford, Calif.: Stanford Univ. Press, 1964); and Zahra Moazami, "The Functional Approach to Integration: A Case Study of the World Health Organization," (M.A. thesis: Tulane Univ., 1979).

For intercountry regional MEPs see memorandum on WHO assistance to African MEPs, May 1960, and Cambournac memorandum to Alvarez, 7 Sept. 1960, both file M 2/372/3 AFRO, J2, WHOA; *Report on the Status of Malaria Eradication in the Americas*, 12, 28; and "Sanitary Convention among the Republics of Peru, Bolivia, and Chile," *Boletín de la Oficina Sanitaria Panamericana* 27 (Jan. 1948): 5–8.

22. For WHO's role in managing global malaria research see Expert Committee on Insecticides, "Sixth Report," *WHO Technical Report Series* 110 (Oct. 1956).

For WHO laboratory arrangements see "The Approach to the Problem of the Control of Malaria in Tropical Africa."

For cooperative measures in research projects see Bruce-Chwatt and Haworth, "Malaria Eradication," 289; Cambournac memorandum to Alvarez, 7 Sept. 1960, file M 2/372/3 AFRO, J2, WHOA; letter to Dr. A. A. MacKelvie, Chief Medical Adviser of the Sierra Leone Development Company, from Bruce-Chwatt, Chief of the Planning Section of the WHO Division of Malaria Eradication, 11 June 1958, file M 2/372/3 AFRO, J1, WHOA; memorandum on WHO assistance to African MEPs, May 1960, file M 2/372/3 AFRO, J2, WHOA; C. P. Pant and L. S. Self, "Field Trials of Bromophos and Schering 34615 Residual Sprays and of Cheesecloth Impregnated with Bayer 39007 for Control of *Anopheles gambiae* and *A. funestus* in Nigeria," 35 (1966): 709–19, A. Smith, P. O. Park, and K. S. Hocking, "Assessment of the Kill of *Anopheles gambiae* by the Fumigant Insecticide Dichlorvos in Experimental Huts," 31 (1964): 399–409, M. Soerono, G. Davidson, and D. A. Muir, "The Development and Trend of Insecticide-Resistance in *Anopheles aconitus* Dönitz and *Anopheles sundaicus* Rodenwaldt," 32 (1965): 161–68, and "Field Trials of Insecticides," 30 (1964): 862–67, all *Bulletin of the WHO;* and *Report on the Status of Malaria Eradication in the Americas,* 134–35.

23. For UNICEF contributions to the campaign see "A Brief Statement Regarding the Presumed Effects of Malaria Eradication on Economic and Social Conditions"; Siddiqi, *World Health,* 134, 142; Russell, "World-Wide Malaria Eradication," 12; Dowling memorandum for Malaria Eradication Section's Chief of Policy and Planning, 7 Oct. 1960, file M 2/372/3 AFRO, J2, WHOA; personal Dowling letter to Pampana, 13 June 1957, file M 2/372/3 AFRO, J1, WHOA; Maggie Black, *Children First: The Story of UNICEF, Past and Present* (Oxford, UK: Oxford Univ. Press for UNICEF, 1996), 8–9, and *Children and the Nations;* and S. M. Keeny, *Half the World's Children: A Diary of UNICEF at Work in Asia* (New York: Association Press, 1957), 30, 49, 68, 74–75, 79, 110-11, 162–64, 221, 242–43.

For U.S. contributions to the campaign and its motives see Siddiqi, *World Health,* 134, 141–43; WHO, *First Ten Years,* 119; Russell, "World-Wide Malaria Eradication," 12–13; "Malaria Eradication Program," Malaria Eradication Branch memorandum, Sept. 1963, file M 2/370/16, J2, WHOA; and position paper on malaria eradication for Eleventh WHA, 19 May 1958, and position paper on two-thirds vote on WHO budget level for Eleventh WHA, 29 Apr. 1958, both RG 59, Decimal File 1955–59, 398.55-WHO, box 1575, folder 5–235, NACP.

For impact of malaria on children see Bruce-Chwatt, "Malaria in Nigeria," 314–16; draft "Director-General's Report to ECOSOC," 6 Oct. 1959, file M 2/180/5, WHOA; Bruce-Chwatt and Haworth, "Malaria Eradication," 286; and A. J. W. Spitz, "Malaria Infection of the Placenta and Its Influence on the Incidence of Prematurity in Eastern Nigeria," 21 (1959): 242–44, and Leonard J. Bruce-Chwatt, "Biometric Study of Spleen- and Liver-Weights in Africans and Europeans with Special Reference to Endemic Malaria," 15 (1956): 513–48, both *Bulletin of the WHO.*

For the role of aid money in promoting the establishment of MEPs see undated draft letter from Indonesian Minister for Health to the Indonesian Prime Minister, attached to SEARO Regional Director memorandum to Assistant Director-General, 18 Aug. 1958, file M 2/180/4, J1, WHOA; and "WHO/PAHO/UNICEF Expenditure on Malaria Eradication

1957 through 1964," Administrative Officer of the Malaria Eradication Division memorandum for Division Director, 7 Dec. 1964, file M 2/370/16, J2, WHOA.

24. Indian Central Health Education Bureau, *Malaria Eradication in India*, 15; "Broadcast Talk by Shri Bhimsen Sachar, Governor of Andhra Pradesh in Connection with the Celebration of the World Health Day on the 7th Apr. 1960," and Mani letter in *World Health Day Souvenir*, ed. Rao, iii, ix; Pampana letter to Morin, Director of the Pasteur Institute of Indochina, 13 May 1947, microfilm 453-4-5, WHOA; and "A Note on the Present Status of Malaria Control Programme in India," in Proceedings of Antimalaria Coordination Conference on Indo-Burma Border, 15–17 Jan. 1957, microform M 2/86/4 SEARO, card 1, WHOA.

25. For national malaria control program see Indian Central Health Education Bureau, *Malaria Eradication in India*, 3, 5, 7, 9; and "Report on Antimalaria Coordination Conference on the Burma-Thailand Border," 27–29 Aug. 1956, and "A Note on the Present Status of Malaria Control Programme in India," in proceedings of Antimalaria Coordination Conference on Indo-Burma Border, 15–17 Jan. 1957, both microform M 2/86/4 SEARO, card 1, WHOA.

For U.S. aid contribution see "Broadcast Talk by Shri Bhimsen Sachar," and Viswanathan, "Malaria Eradication in S.E. Asia Is an Investment," in *World Health Day Souvenir*, ed. Rao, iv, 23; and "A Note on the Present Status of Malaria Control Programme in India," in Proceedings of Antimalaria Coordination Conference on Indo-Burma Border, 15–17 Jan. 1957, microform M 2/86/4 SEARO, card 1, WHOA.

26. Indian Central Health Education Bureau, *Malaria Eradication in India*, 20. See also "Broadcast Talk by Shri Bhimsen Sachar" and D. P. Karmarkar, Indian Minister of Health, letter, in *World Health Day Souvenir*, ed. Rao, iv, vii; "DDT Resistance in *Anopheles stephensi* in India," 12 (June 1958): 207 and "Malaria Eradication Plan for India," 12 (October 1958): 352–53, both *Chronicle of the WHO;* "Malaria Course Programme for the Medical Officers at the Malaria Institute of India," January 1949, microform 453-4-14, WHOA; and "A Note on the Present Status of Malaria Control Programme in India," microform M 2/86/4 SEARO, card 1, WHOA.

27. Indian Central Health Education Bureau, *Malaria Eradication in India*, 13–14, 21–22; Dr. S. P. Ramakrishnan (Director of Malaria Institute of India) letter, Rajun "An Appeal to the People of Andhra Pradesh," Viswanathan, "Malaria Eradication in S. E. Asia," "Eradication of Malaria: Do's and Don't's for the Public," and Dr. V. Raghvender Rao, "Field Experiences," in *World Health Day Souvenir*, ed. Rao, xi, xiii, 26, 27, 32–35, resp.; and "Proceedings of the Second Indo-Burma Border Antimalaria Coordination Conference, Myitkyina, 8–9 December 1958," and "Address by Shri P. C. Mathew, Chief Commissioner, Manipur, India," in proceedings of Antimalaria Coordination Conference on Indo-Burma Border, 15–17 Jan. 1957, both microform M 2/86/4 SEARO, card 1, WHOA.

28. Indian Central Health Education Bureau, *Malaria Eradication in India*, 17–22; and "Eradication of Malaria: Do's and Don't's for the Public," N. L. Mukherji, "Give Us a Drop of Your Blood," and Rao, "Field Experiences," in *World Health Day Souvenir*, ed. Rao, 27, 28–29, 34.

29. For ways in which the momentum of eradication slowed recognition of its obstacles see Siddiqi, *World Health*, 144–45; and memorandum to Miller from G. E. Hill, 25 Aug. 1949, microform 453-4-11, WHOA.

For early warnings of potential problems with the MEP see Russell, "World-Wide Malaria Eradication," 6; Siddiqi, *World Health,* 132; WHO, *First Ten Years,* 175; and M. A. Farid, "Ineffectiveness of DDT Residual Spraying in Stopping Malaria Transmission in the Jordan Valley," *Bulletin of the WHO* 11 (1954): 765–83.

For studies on mosquito exophily see W. Büttiker, A. W. A. Brown, "Laboratory Studies on the Behaviouristic Resistance of *Anopheles albimanus* in Panama," and "Observations on the Physiology of Adult Anophelines in Asia," *Bulletin of the WHO* 19 (1958): 1053–61, 1063-71, resp.

30. "Review of the Malaria Programme in the African Region," Dowling memorandum, 23 Oct. 1959, file M 2/372/3 AFRO, J2, WHOA.

For initial exclusion of Africa see also report to John Foster Dulles, U.S. Secretary of State, by Charles W. Mayo and Frederick J. Brady, chairmen of the U.S. delegation to the Eighth WHA, 3 Nov. 1955, RG 59, Decimal File 1955–1959, 398.55-WHO, box 1573, NACP.

For the unique challenges presented by African MEPs see Russell, "World-Wide Malaria Eradication," 10; WHO, *First Ten Years,* 181, 186; Bruce-Chwatt and Haworth, "Malaria Eradication," 285, 288–89; "Review of the Malaria Programme in the African Region," Dowling Memorandum, 23 Oct. 1959, file M 2/372/3 AFRO, J2, WHOA; "The Approach to the Problem of the Control of Malaria in Tropical Africa," restricted memorandum approved by Candau, May 1957, file M 2/372/3 AFRO, J1, WHOA; G. Macdonald, "Epidemiological Basis of Malaria Control," *Bulletin of the WHO* 15 (1956): 613–26; and undated [approx. Sept. 1959] position paper on malaria eradication for the tenth session of the WHO's Western Pacific Regional Committee, RG 59, Decimal File 1955–1959, 398.55-WHO, box 1577, folder 7-159.

For malaria immunity see de Meillon, "Malaria Survey," 413; and Pampana, *Textbook of Malaria Eradication,* 56-71.

For mosquito species in Africa see de Meillon, "Malaria Survey," 419, 437–38, 444; memorandum on WHO assistance to African MEPs, May 1960, and Cambournac memoranda to Malaria Eradication Division Director, 7 Sept. and 13 Oct. 1960, both file M 2/372/3 AFRO, J2, WHOA; and G. Davidson, "Anopheles gambiae, a Complex of Species," and H. E. Paterson, "'Saltwater Anopheles gambiae' on Mauritius," 31 (1964): 625–34, 635–44 resp., J. Sautet, "Exophilie et Migrations chez les Anophèles, en Particulier chez Anopheles gambiae" ["Anophelic Exophily and Migration, particularly among Anopheles gambiae"], 17 (1957): 367–76; and G. Frizzi and M. Holstein, "Étude Cytogénétique d'Anopheles gambiae" ["A Cytogenetic Study of Anopheles gambiae"], G. Giglioli, "Biological Variations in Anopheles darlingi and Anopheles gambiae," and J. Hamon, J. P. Adam, and A. Grjebine, "Observations sur la Répartition et le Comportement des Anophèles de l'Afrique-Équatoriale Française, du Cameroun et de l'Afrique Occidentale" ["Observations on the Distribution and Behaviour of Anophelines in French Equatorial Africa, from Cameroon and West Africa"], 15 (1956): 425–35, 461–71, 549–91, resp., all *Bulletin of the WHO.*

For lack of adequate African medical or transportation infrastructure see "Malaria Eradication Program," Malaria Eradication Branch memorandum, Sept. 1963, file M 2/370/16, J2, WHOA; Bruce-Chwatt and Haworth, "Malaria Eradication," 288; personal Dowling letter to Pampana, 13 June 1957, and "The Approach to the Problem of the Control of Malaria in Tropical Africa," restricted memorandum approved by Candau, May 1957, both file M 2/372/3 AFRO, J1, WHOA; and "Review of the Malaria Programme in the African Region," Dowling memorandum, 23 Oct. 1959, memorandum on WHO assistance to African MEPs,

May 1960, and Cambournac memoranda to Malaria Eradication Division Director, 7 Sept. and 13 Oct. 1960, all file M 2/372/3 AFRO, J2, WHOA.

For the lack of reliable scienctific information prior to the MEP see personal Dowling letter to Pampana, 13 June 1957, and Bruce-Chwatt letter to MacKelvie, 11 June 1958, both file M 2/372/3 AFRO, J1, WHOA; and memorandum on WHO assistance to African MEPs, May 1960, file M 2/372/3 AFRO, J2, WHOA.

31. For excito-repellency of DDT see R. C. Muirhead-Thomson, "DDT and Gammexane as Residual Insecticides against *Anopheles gambiae* in African Houses," *Transactions of the Royal Society of Tropical Medicine and Hygiene* 43 (Jan. 1950): 401–12; Pampana, *Textbook of Malaria Eradication,* 183–86; and G. H. S. Hooper and A. W. A. Brown, "A Case of Developed Irritability to Insecticides," 32 (1965): 131–32, M. T. Gillies, "The Problem of Exophily in *Anopheles gambiae,*" and Davidson, "Studies on Insecticide Resistance," 15 (1956): 437–49, 614, all *Bulletin of the WHO.*

For insecticide absorption into mud walls see Pampana, *Textbook of Malaria Eradication,* 161–72; Davidson, "Results of Recent Experiments," 330–31; E. Bordas, W. G. Downs, and L. Navarro, "Inactivation of DDT Deposits on Mud Surfaces," 9 (1953): 39–57, and A. B. Hadaway, "Assessment of Two Possible Pretreatment Methods of Preventing Sorption of Insecticide Residues by Dried Mud," 32 (1965): 585–90, both *Bulletin of the WHO;* Press, "Measurement of Adsorption," 153–62; "The Sorption of Insecticides on Mud Walls," *Chronicle of the WHO* 11 (Dec. 1957): 371–74; and "The Approach to the Problem of the Control of Malaria in Tropical Africa," restricted memorandum approved by Candau, May 1957, file M 2/372/3AFRO, J1, WHOA.

For slow progress of malaria eradication in Africa see "Malaria Eradication Program," Malaria Eradication Branch memorandum, Sept. 1963, file M 2/370/16, J2, WHOA.

For failures to stop transmission despite spraying operations see personal Dowling letter to Pampana, 13 June 1957, file M 2/372/3 AFRO, J1, WHOA; and memorandum on WHO assistance to African MEPs, May 1960, file M 2/372/3 AFRO, J2, WHOA.

32. For WHO staff optimism see dispatch from Richard L. Jones, American Embassy in Monrovia, to State Department, 23 June 1959, RG 59, Decimal Files 1955–1959, 398.55-WHO, box 1575, folder 5–1359, NACP.

For the development of double resistance see *Report on the Status of Malaria Eradication in the Americas,* 10; and Bruce-Chwatt and Haworth, "Malaria Eradication," 287.

For the new insecticides and their drawbacks see Bruce-Chwatt and Haworth, "Malaria Eradication: Its Present Status"; J. M. Barnes, W. J. Hayes, and Kingsley Kay, "Control of Health Hazards Likely to Arise from the Use of Organo-Phosphorus Insecticides in Vector Control," and A. W. Lindquist, "Effectiveness of Organo-Phosphorus Insecticides against Houseflies and Mosquitos," 16 (1957): 33–39, 41–61, resp., A. B. Hadaway, "The Toxicity of Three Organic Phosphorus Insecticides to Houseflies and Mosquitos," 16 (1957): 870–73, H. F. Jung, "A New Phosphoric Ester Residual Insecticide with a Low Order of Toxicity," 21 (1959): 215–21, and Homer R. Wolfe, Kenneth C. Walker, Joseph W. Elliott, and William F. Durham, "Evaluation of the Health Hazards Involved in House-Spraying with DDT," 20 (1959): 1–14, all *Bulletin of the WHO;* and *Report on the Status of Malaria Eradication in the Americas,* 10–11, 132, 134.

For antilarval operations see Expert Committee on Malaria, "Eleventh Report," *WHO Technical Report Series* 291 (1964): 40; WHO, *Field Manual for Antilarval Operations in Malaria Eradication Programmes* (Geneva: WHO, 1969), 1, 29; and *Report on the Status of Malaria Eradication in the Americas,* 11, 13, 132.

For experimental mosquito control methods see Carroll N. Smith, "Repellents for Anopheline Mosquitos," G. Davidson and J. B. Kitzmiller, "Application of New Procedures to Control: Genetic Control of Anophelines," and George B. Craig Jr., "Hormones for Control of Anopheles," *Miscellaneous Publications of the Entomological Society of America 7* (May 1970): 99–117, 118–29, and 130–33, resp.

33. For problems caused by new buildings, painting, and soot see *Report on the Status of Malaria Eradication in the Americas,* 2.

For the difficulties posed by nomadic or migratory populations see de Meillon, "Malaria Survey," 412–13; William Alves, "Malaria Parasite Rates in Southern Rhodesia: May–September 1956," *Bulletin of the WHO* 19 (1958): 69–74; memorandum of conversation between Cambournac and Alvarado, 10 Nov. 1960, "Review of the Malaria Programme in the African Region," Dowling memorandum, 23 Oct. 1959, and memorandum on WHO assistance to African MEPs, May 1960, all file M 2/372/3 AFRO, J2, WHOA; and *Report on the Status of Malaria Eradication in the Americas,* 10, 131.

For chemoprophylactic experiments see personal Dowling letter to Pampana, 13 June 1957, and "The Approach to the Problem of the Control of Malaria in Tropical Africa," both file M 2/372/3 AFRO, J1, WHOA; Pampana, *Textbook of Malaria Eradication,* 221–72; "Review of the Malaria Programme in the African Region," Dowling memorandum, 23 Oct. 1959, and memorandum on WHO assistance to African MEPs, May 1960, both file M 2/372/3 AFRO, J2, WHOA; D. F. Clyde, "Suppression of Malaria in Tanzania with the Use of Medicated Salts," 35 (1966): 962–68, G. Robert Coatney, Olaf Mickelsen, Robert W. Burgess, Martin D. Young, and Carl I. Pirkle, "Chloroquine or Pyrimethamine in Salt as a Suppressive against Sporozoite-Induced Vivax Malaria (Chesson Strain)," 19 (1958): 53–67, "Introduction," 20 (1959): 753, I. H. Vincke, "Prophylaxie Médicamenteuse du Paludisme en Zone Rurale" [Medical Prophylaxis of Malaria in Rural Areas], 11 (1954): 785–92, and G. Joncour, "La Lutte Contre le Paludisme a Madagascar" [The Antimalarial Campaign in Madagascar], Guy Houel, "La Prophylaxie Antipaludique au Maroc par Administration Mensuelle de Divers Médicaments" [Antimalarial Prophylaxis in Morocco by Monthly Administration of Diverse Medications], and H. Munro Archibald and Leonard J. Bruce-Chwatt, "Suppression of Malaria with Pyrimethamine in Nigerian Schoolchildren," 15 (1956): 711–23, 767–74, 775–84, resp., all *Bulletin of the WHO;* Covell et al., *Chemotherapy of Malaria;* G. Robert Coatney, "Chemotherapy of Malaria," *Boletín de la Oficina Sanitaria Panamericana* 28 (Jan. 1949): 27–36; *Report on the Status of Malaria Eradication in the Americas,* 136; and undated [approx. Sept. 1959] position paper on malaria eradication for the tenth session of the WHO's Western Pacific Regional Committee, RG 59, Decimal File 1955–1959, 398.55-WHO, box 1577, folder 7–159, NACP.

For the shortcomings of these experiments see personal Dowling letter to Pampana, 13 June 1957, file M 2/372/3 AFRO, J1, WHOA; "Review of the Malaria Programme in the African Region," Dowling memorandum, 23 Oct. 1959, memorandum on WHO assistance to African MEPs, May 1960, and Cambournac memorandum to Malaria Eradication Division Director, 7 Sept. 1960, all file M 2/372/3 AFRO, J2, WHOA; *Report on the Status of Malaria Eradication in the Americas,* 11, 13–14, 133–34, 136; and M.-E. Farinaud and R. Choumara, "La Prophylaxie du Paludisme dans les Pays Montagnards du Sud Viet-Nam" [Malaria Prophylaxis in the Montagnard Areas of South Vietnam], *Bulletin of the WHO* 11 (1954): 793–838.

For the development of resistance in the malaria parasite see personal Dowling letter to Pampana, 13 June 1957, file M 2/372/3 AFRO, J1, WHOA; memorandum on WHO assistance to African MEPs, May 1960, file M 2/372/3 AFRO, J2, WHOA; G. M. Jeffery and F. D. Gibson, "Studies on Chloroquine-Resistance of *Plasmodium falciparum* in Upper Volta and Liberia, West Africa," 35 (1966): 441–49, and Martin D. Young and Robert W. Burgess, "Pyrimethamine Resistance in *Plasmodium vivax* Malaria," and "The Development of Pyrimethamine Resistance in *Plasmodium falciparum*," 20 (1959): 27–36, 37–46, all *Bulletin of the WHO*; and *Report on the Status of Malaria Eradication in the Americas*, 10–11, 131, 136.

For drug treatment of immigrants and nomads see memorandum on WHO assistance to African MEPs, May 1960, file M 2/372/3 AFRO, J2, WHOA; and Alves, "Malaria Parasite Rates in Southern Rhodesia," 69–74.

34. For the primary importance of financial and administrative difficulties see *Report on the Status of Malaria Eradication in the Americas*, 12.

For the failure to create indigenous public health systems able to cope with MEP surveillance see Siddiqi, *World Health*, 138; "After Effects of Malaria Eradication: Its Gains and Challenges—With Socio-Economic Approaches," Dakshinamurty interim report, Apr. 1968, file M 2/180/4, J2, WHOA; personal Dowling letter to Pampana, 13 June 1957, file M 2/372/3 AFRO, J1, WHOA; "Review of the Malaria Programme in the African Region," Dowling memorandum, 23 Oct. 1959, memorandum on WHO assistance to African MEPs, May 1960, and Cambournac memorandum to Malaria Eradication Division Director, 13 Oct. 1960, all file M 2/372/3 AFRO, J2, WHOA; *Report on the Status of Malaria Eradication in the Americas*, 12; undated [approx. Sept. 1959] position paper on malaria eradication for the tenth session of the WHO's Western Pacific Regional Committee, RG 59, Decimal File 1955–1959, 398.55-WHO, box 1577, folder 7–159, NACP; and dispatch from Richard L. Jones, American Embassy in Monrovia, to State Department, 23 June 1959, RG 59, Decimal File 1955–1959, 398.55-WHO, box 1575, folder 5–1359, NACP.

35. For the situation between India and Pakistan see "After Effects of Malaria Eradication: Its Gains and Challenges—With Socio-Economic Approaches," file M 2/180/4, J2, WHOA; and "Socio-Economic Benefits of Malaria Eradication," attached to letter from M. K. Q. Hashmi, Director of Pakistani MEP, to Dr. A. H. Taba, WHO EMRO Regional Director, 21 Oct. 1966, file M 2/180/4, J1, WHOA.

For similar budget crises in other nations and their effect on MEPs see *Report on the Status of Malaria Eradication in the Americas*, 10, 13–14, 21, 29; and "The Urgent Need for a Study of the Economics of Malaria Eradication," Nathan NIH grant application, 30 Dec. 1960, file M 2/180/4, J1, WHOA.

For concerns over post-attack stages see George D. Belios, "Mental Attitudes during the Later Phases of a Malaria Eradication Program," *Israel Journal of Medical Sciences* 1 (Mar. 1965): 290–93; "After Effects of Malaria Eradication: Its Gains and Challenges—With Socio-Economic Approaches," file M 2/180/4, J2, WHOA; and "The Urgent Need for a Study of the Economics of Malaria Eradication," file M 2/180/4, J1, WHOA.

36. Robert C. Cook, *Human Fertility: The Modern Dilemma* (New York: William Sloane Associates, 1951), 11, and "World-Wide War on Malaria: Prelude to a Greater Challenge," *Population Bulletin* 14 (Mar. 1958): 1–15.

For the new demands fueled by MEP success see "After Effects of Malaria Eradication: Its Gains and Challenges—With Socio-Economic Approaches," file M 2/180/5, WHOA; and Dakshinamurty letter to Dr. N. Jungalwalla, Director of WHO Division of Public Health Services, 16 Dec. 1969, file M 2/180/4, J2, WHOA.

For government reluctance to fund malaria eradication see "A Brief Statement Regarding the Presumed Effects of Malaria Eradication on Economic and Social Conditions," Russell memorandum for Candau, 15 July 1959, file M 2/180/5, WHOA; and "Socio-Economic Benefits of Malaria Eradication," attached to Hashmi letter to Taba, 21 Oct. 1966, file M 2/180/4, J1, WHOA.

For WHO-commissioned studies on the monetary benefits of MEPs see "A Brief Statement Regarding the Presumed Effects of Malaria Eradication on Economic and Social Conditions," Russell memorandum for Candau, 15 July 1959, file M 2/180/5, WHOA; memorandum from Dr. A. P. Ruderman, PAHO Economic Adviser, to Dr. Abraham Horwitz, Dr. A. Drobny, and Dr. Victor A. Sutter, 4 Jan. 1967, and "After Effects of Malaria Eradication: Its Gains and Challenges—With Socio-Economic Approaches," both file M 2/180/4, J2, WHOA; Hashmi letter to Taba, 21 Oct. 1966, file M 2/180/4, J1, WHOA; and undated [approx. Sept. 1959] position paper on malaria eradication for the tenth session of the WHO's Western Pacific Regional Committee, RG 59, Decimal File 1955–1959, 398.55-WHO, box 1577, folder 7–159, NACP.

37. Malaria Conference for the Western Pacific and South-East Asia Regions, "Report," *WHO Technical Report Series* 103 (May 1956): 20. For other similar forewarnings see "After Effects of Malaria Eradication: Its Gains and Challenges—With Socio-Economic Approaches," Dakshinamurty interim report, Apr. 1968, and Dakshinamurty letter to Jungalwalla, 16 Dec. 1969, file M 2/180/4, J2, WHOA; "The Urgent Need for a Study of the Economics of Malaria Eradication," file M 2/180/4, J1, WHOA; and Winslow, *The Cost of Sickness*, 77–80.

For taboo on discussion of population issues in WHO see "Dangerous Complacency," Chisholm address to the American Humanist Association, 28 Feb. 1959, Chisholm papers, box 56, vol. 3, folder 184–200.

For optimistic appraisals of the MEP's effect on Third World development see Norman S. Buchanan and Howard S. Ellis, *Approaches to Economic Development* (New York: Twentieth Century Fund, 1955), 12–13; Joseph J. Spengler, "Economic Factors in the Development of Densely Populated Areas," *Proceedings of the American Philosophical Society* (Feb. 1951): 38–39; and John D. Durand, "World Population: Trend and Prospect," in *Population and World Politics,* ed. P. M. Hauser (Glencoe, Ill.: Free Press, 1958): 27–37; and "A Brief Statement Regarding the Presumed Effects of Malaria Eradication on Economic and Social Conditions," Russell memorandum for Candau, 15 July 1959, file M 2/180/5, WHOA.

For the other inputs to population growth and the contention that such growth would not continue unabated see Peter Newman, *Malaria Eradication and Population Growth: With Special Reference to Ceylon and British Guiana,* Bureau of Public Health Economics Research Series, no. 10 (Ann Arbor: Univ. of Michigan School of Public Health, 1965), esp. 1–10, 117, 197; "A Brief Statement Regarding the Presumed Effects of Malaria Eradication on Economic and Social Conditions," Russell memorandum for Candau, 15 July 1959, file M 2/180/5, WHOA; Dakshinamurty letter to Jungalwalla, 16 Dec. 1969, file M 2/180/4, J2, WHOA; "Socio-Economic Benefits of Malaria Eradication," attached to Hashmi letter to Taba, 21 Oct. 1966, file M 2/180/4, J1, WHOA; and Fred Sukdeo, *Malaria Eradication and Population Growth in Guyana, 1973* (Georgetown: University of Guyana, n.d.).

38. For early declarations that DDT was nontoxic see West and Campbell, *DDT,* 2, 5.

For environmental and health concerns relating to DDT see UN Environment Programme et al., *DDT and Its Derivatives,* 8–11, 76–78; Rachel Carson, *Silent Spring* (Boston,

Mass.: Houghton Mifflin, 1962); Harmon Henkin, Martin Merta, and James Staples, *The Environment, the Establishment, and the Law* (Boston, Mass.: Houghton Mifflin, 1971), 185–86; and "Petition of Citizens Natural Resources Association, Inc., Wisconsin Division, Izaak Walton League of America, Inc. for a declaratory ruling on the use of dichloro-diphenyl-trichloro-ethane, commonly known as DDT, in the state of Wisconsin," as printed in ibid., 191–206.

39. Note on the use of super-insecticides by H. de Saeger, Secretary-General of the Belgian Congo National Parks Institute, for the International Technical Conference on the Protection of Nature, sponsored by UNESCO and the International Union for the Protection of Nature, 14 June 1949, microform 453-4-11, WHOA. For other early warnings about DDT see also Joseph P. Linduska, "DDT and the Balance of Nature," and C. H. Curran, "DDT and Other Pest Control Chemicals," for International Technical Conference on the Protection of Nature, Aug. 1949, ibid.; and C. S. Leete, Chief Milk Inspector of the New York State Department of Health, "El DDT: Su Uso y Abuso" [DDT: Its Use and Abuse], *Boletín de la Oficina Sanitaria Panamericana* 26 (June 1947): 512–13.

For DDT's general lack of selectivity see UN Environment Programme et al., *DDT and Its Derivatives,* 77; and Henkin, Merta, and Staples, *The Environment, the Establishment, and the Law,* 185.

40. For refusal to open homes for spraying see memorandum on WHO assistance to African MEPs, May 1960, file M 2/372/3 AFRO, J2, WHOA; and Liu, "A Summary of Recent Insecticidal Tests," 624.

For the development of insecticide resistance in other insects see James R. Busvine, "Insecticide-Resistance in Bed-Bugs," 19 (1958): 1041–52, and Marshall Hertig, "Observations on the Density of Phlebotomus Populations following DDT Campaigns," 2 (1950): 621–28, both *Bulletin of the WHO;* Brown, "The Insecticide-Resistance Problem," 310–11, 313, 315; and Liu, "A Summary of Recent Insecticidal Tests," 624, 648.

41. Siddiqi, *World Health,* 125–26; "WHO/PAHO/UNICEF Expenditure on Malaria Eradication, 1957 though 1964," Malaria Eradication Division administrative officer memorandum for Malaria Eradication Division Director, 7 Dec. 1964, file M 2/70/16, J2, WHOA.

Conclusion

1. For the International Red Cross see Henri Coursier, *The International Red Cross* (Geneva: International Committee of the Red Cross, 1961).

For two recent studies on missionaries' influence and agenda see, e.g., Carol C. Chin, "Beneficent Imperialists: American Women Missionaries in China at the Turn of the Twentieth Century," *Diplomatic History* 27 (June 2003): 327–52; and Charles M. Good, *The Steamer Parish: The Rise and Fall of Missionary Medicine on an African Frontier* (Chicago, Ill.: Univ. of Chicago Press, 2004).

For nutrition see League of Nations, *The Problem of Nutrition,* vol. 3: *Nutrition in Various Countries* (Geneva: League of Nations, 1936), and *Nutrition: Final Report of the Mixed Committee of the League of Nations on the Relation of Nutrition to Health, Agriculture and Economic Policy* (Geneva: League of Nations, 1937).

2. Mason and Asher, *The World Bank since Bretton Woods,* 473–87; Jochen Kraske with William H. Becker, William Diamond, and Louis Galambos, *Bankers with a Mission: The*

Presidents of the World Bank, 1946–91 (Oxford, UK: Oxford Univ. Press for the World Bank, 1996), 115–200; Shapley, *Promise and Power,* 461–580.

3. Francisco H. G. Ferreira and Louise C. Keely, "The World Bank and Structural Adjustment: Lessons from the 1980s," in *The World Bank: Structure & Policies,* ed. Christopher L. Gilbert and David Vines (Cambridge, UK: Cambridge Univ. Press, 2000), 159–195.

For the World Bank's response to the debt crisis and its detractors see, e.g., Kraske, *Bankers with a Mission,* 200–79; Jeffrey D. Sachs, ed., *Developing Country Debt and the World Economy* (Chicago, Ill.: Univ. of Chicago Press for the National Bureau of Economic Research, 1989); George and Sabelli, *Faith and Credit,* 55–72; Peter Kenen, "A Bailout for the Banks," *New York Times,* 6 March 1983; Bela Balassa, "Adjustment Policies in Developing Countries: A Reassessment," *World Development* 12 (Sept. 1984): 955–72; and Danaher, ed., *50 Years Is Enough.*

4. Kraske, *Bankers with a Mission,* 213–79; Dharam Ghai, ed., *Development and Environment: Sustaining People and Nature* (Oxford, UK: Blackwell for the United Nations Research Institute for Social Development, 1994); George and Sabelli, *Faith and Credit,* 162–83; Danaher, ed., *50 Years Is Enough.*

5. Marchisio and di Blase, *Food and Agriculture Organization,* 67–86.

6. Ibid., 74–91; Ross B. Talbot and H. Wayne Moyer, "Who Governs the Rome Food Agencies?" in *Peace by Pieces,* ed. Wells, 47–48, 55–59; John Andrews King, "The International Fund for Agricultural Development: The First Six Years," in ibid., 161–80; and *Report of the World Food Conference: Rome, 5–16 November 1974* (New York: United Nations, 1975).

7. Marchisio and di Blase, *Food and Agriculture Organization,* 86–91; Talbot and Moyer, "Who Governs?" in *Peace by Pieces,* ed. Wells, 48–50; Graham Hancock, *Lords of Poverty: The Power, Prestige, and Corruption of the International Aid Business* (New York: Atlantic Monthly, 1989), 84–88; Roberto Suro, "Food Agency Chief Wins a Bitter Vote," *New York Times,* 10 Nov. 1987, p. 3; Loren Jenkins, "U.S. Holds Bank Funds to Press Changes at FAO," *Washington Post,* 13 Feb. 1988, p. G3; "No Sheltering Tree," *The Economist (U.S.)* 329 (30 Oct. 1993): 50; "New F.A.O. Director Committed to Boost Third World Food Output," *Milling and Baking News* 72 (23 Nov. 1993): 40.

8. "New F.A.O. Director," 40; "FAO: Harvesting Votes," *The Economist (U.S.)* 351 (15 May 1999): 48.

9. Justin Gillis, "Biotech Crops Could Help Poor Farmers, U.N. Says," Washingtonpost. com, 16 May 2004; Stephen Clapp, "FAO Chief Responds to Criticism of Biotech Report," *Pesticide and Toxic Chemical News* 32 (28 June 2004): 16; Grain, "FAO Declares War on Farmers, Not on Hunger," press release, www.grain.org/front/?id=24> [accessed 5 Sept. 2004].

10. World Health Organization, *Four Decades of Achievement: Highlights of the Work of WHO* (Geneva: WHO, 1988), 7–22; Rolf Myller, "Worldwide Vaccination Progresses," *Washington Post,* 9 Oct. 1991, p. A16; Peter Passell, "Problems May Be Ahead for the World's Vaccine Program," *New York Times,* 26 Sept. 1996, p. C2; "African Countries Bracing for Worst Polio Outbreak," *Modern Healthcare* 34 (28 June 2004): 54.

11. D. N. Durrheim and R. Speare, "Global Leprosy Elimination: Time to Change More than the Elimination Target Date: Contentious Elimination Target Requires Rethinking," *Journal of Epidemiology and Community Health* 57 (May 2003): 316–18.

12. Richard Horton, "WHO's Mandate: A Damaging Reinterpretation Is Taking Place," *Lancet* 360 (28 Sept. 2002): 960; Kathryn Sikkink, "Codes of Conduct for Transnational Corporations: The Case of the WHO/UNICEF Code," in *Peace by Pieces,* ed. Wells, 335–71;

Gerald Caiden and German Retana, "What Will Work? The Costa Rican Experience Using SILOS in Achieving Universal Health Care 2000," *International Journal of Public Administration* 21 (Dec. 1998): 1863–85; Michael Backman, "Sars: A WHO-Induced Panic?" *Far Eastern Economic Review* 166 (22 May 2003): 21.

13. Denis Aitken, "WHO Responds," *British Medical Journal* 326 (25 Jan. 2003): 217. See also ibid., 217–19.

14. For felon enfranchisement issues see, e.g., Marc Mauer, "Mass Imprisonment and the Disappearing Voters," in *Invisible Punishment: The Collateral Consequences of Mass Imprisonment*, ed. Marc Mauer and Meda Chesney-Lind (New York: New Press, 2002), 50–58; and Save Our Cumberland Mountains (SOCM), "Social Progress Committee: Voter Rights," available at www.socm.org/racism.html#voterrights [accessed 13 July 2004].

For voter registration and civic engagement projects focused on young people see, e.g., MTV, "Rock the Vote," available at www.rockthevote.org/rtv_about.php and www.rockthevote.org/rtv_timeline.php [accessed 13 July 2004]; FinD 18: Faith IN Democracy, "Have Faith in Democracy!" available at www.find18.org [accessed 13 July 2004]; and American Association of State Colleges and Universities, "American Democracy Project," available at aascu.org/programs/adp/about/default.htm [accessed 13 July 2004].

15. For some other examples of innovative development funding during the fifties and sixties see Tim Büthe, review of *Banker to the Poor: Micro-Lending and the Battle against World Poverty*, by Muhammad Yunus, *Journal of International Affairs* 53 (Spring 2000): 741–42.

For the Green Revolution see Nick Cullather, "Miracles of Modernization: The Green Revolution and the Apotheosis of Technology," *Diplomatic History* 28 (Apr. 2004): 227–54.

16. Arturo Escobar, "Imagining a Post-Development Era," in *Power of Development*, ed. Jonathan Crush (London: Routledge, 1995), 211–27; Majid Rahnema and Victoria Bawtree, eds., *The Post-Development Reader* (London: Zed Books, 1997).

17. While Americans are more familiar with the word "untouchable," these Indians tend to prefer the word *dalit*, which roughly translates as "the oppressed." Mahatma Gandhi called them *harijan*, "children of God."

18. Sundaramma as quoted in Caspar Henderson, "Turning the World Upside Down," available at www.ddsindia.com/turningupside.htm [accessed 19 Nov. 2003].

For basic information on the Deccan Development Society see Deccan Development Society, "About Us," available at ddsindia.com/aboutus [accessed 9 Aug. 2003]. For information specifically about the *sanghams* see Jagannadha Reddy, Jayappa, Padma, Baliah and other Sangham staff, "Sanghams: Experiences, Expectations," available at ddsindia.org.in/sanghams.htm [accessed 9 Aug. 2003]. In addition to the cited material on the Deccan Development Society, I am drawing on my own observations during a visit to one of its villages during a Council for International Educational Exchange Faculty Development Seminar in Hyderabad during the summer of 2003.

19. P. V. Satheesh, Jagannadha Reddy, and Jayappa, "Food Security: Four Major Steps," available at www.ddsindia.com/foodsec_4steps.htm [accessed 12 July 2004], "Food Security for Dryland Communities," available at www.ddsindia.com/feedsec_dryland.htm [accessed 12 July 2004]; "People's Voices: Land Lease Groups," available at www.ddsindia.com/Land%20Lease.htm [accessed 12 July 2004].

20. For the seed bank component of food sovereignty see Menna Menon, "The Crops of Truth," available at www.ddsindia.com/cropstruth.htm [accessed 19 Nov. 2003]; P. V. Satheesh, "The Crops of Truth: Farmers' Perception of Agrodiversity in the Deccan Region of

South India," available at www.ddsindia.com/cropstruth_pvs.htm [accessed 19 Nov. 2003]; and Katharine Ainger, "The Market and the Monsoon. Part 2: Crops of Truth," *New Internationalist* 353 (Jan.–Feb. 2003), available at www.newint.org/issue353/part2.htm [accessed 19 Nov. 2003].

For the public distribution system component see Community Media Trust video, "PDS," available at www.dds.india.com/videogallery.htm [accessed 12 July 2004]; Ch. Srinivas and S. Abdul Thaha, *A Study on Alternative Public Distribution System: A Novel Initiative of Deccan Development Society* (Hyderabad, India: Booksline for the Deccan Development Society, 2004), available at www.ddsindia.com/PDF/dds_pds%20text.pdf [accessed 12 July 2004]; and P. V. Satheesh, "How to Make PDS Work for the Poor," paper presented in an Action Aid seminar on Food Security, Hyderabad, India, 26–27 Oct. 1998, available at www.ddsindia.com/howtopds.htm [accessed 12 July 2004].

21. For *balwadis* see Kesamma Rama and Leader Narsimlu, "Balwadis: Through a Crisis, Strongly," available at www.ddsindia.com/balwadies.htm [accessed 22 Nov. 2003]; Community Media Trust video, "Balwadi," available at www.ddsindia.com/videogallery.htm [accessed 12 July 2004]; and Lakshmi Krishnamurty, "Balwadis of the Deccan Development Society: A Reflective Study," Mar. 2003, available at www.ddsindia.com/PDF/Balwadievaluation.pdf [accessed 12 July 2004].

For the "green school" (Pachasaale) see Henderson, "Turning the World Upside Down" and "Pachasaale—The Green School," available at www.ddsindia.com/psaale.htm [accessed 12 July 2004].

22. Reddy et al., "Sanghams"; "People's Voices: Health," available at www.ddsindia.com.Health.htm [accessed 12 July 2004].

23. Reddy et al., "Sanghams"; B. Suresh Reddy, "Non-Pesticidal Management of Gram Pod Borer in Pigeon Pea and Chick Pea by Farmers of the Zaheerabad Region in Deccan Plateau," available at www.ddsindia.com/npm.htm [accessed 12 July 2004].

24. For information about their programs of food security and food sovereignty see DDS, "About Us: Autonomy over Food Production and Food Security," www.ddsindia.org/aboutus.htm [accessed 12 July 2004].

For festivals in particular see Community Media Trust, "Bio-diversity Festival" video, available at www.ddsindia.com/videogallery.htm [accessed 12 July 2004]; and "Mobile Biodiversity Festival 2003," available at www.ddsiindia.com/mbf.htm [accessed 12 July 2004].

25. R. Akhileshwari, "Virtual Voice: Community Media Trust," *Deccan (Hyderabad, India) Herald,* 21 Oct. 2001, available at www.ddsindia.com/cmt.htm [accessed 19 Nov. 2003]; Community Media Trust video, "The Sangham Shot," available at www.ddsindia.com/videogallery.htm [accessed 12 July 2004]; P. V. Satheesh, "DDS and Community Radio," available at www.ddsindia.com/radiostn.htm [accessed 12 July 2004]; P. V. Satheesh, "An Entitlement Refused: The Story of DDS Radio," available at www.ddsindia.com/undp.htm [accessed 12 July 2004]; "Participation and Beyond: Handing Over the Camera," available at www.ddsindia.com/ppvideo.htm [accessed 12 July 2004].

26. Michel P. Pimbert and Tom Wakeford, *Prajateerpu: A Citizens Jury/Scenario Workshop on Food and Farming Futures for Andhra Pradesh, India* (London: International Institute for Environment and Development and Institute for Development Studies, 2002); "UK Funds Scheme to Throw 20 Million Indian Farmers Off Their Land: Farmers Come to UK Parliament to Make Their Case," press release, 18 Mar. 2003, available at www.mindfully.org/GE/GE4/20M-Indian-Farmers18mar02.htm [accessed 19 Nov. 2003]; "Conclusions

and Recommendations from NGO Perspectives: How TRIPs Threatens Biodiversity and Food Sovereignty: The Power of People's Traditional Knowledge," 21 June 2003, Hyderabad, India, available at www.ddsindia.com/pdf/hyderabad_declaration.pdf [accessed 19 Nov. 2003].

27. Abdul Qayum and Kiran Sakkhari, "Did Bt Cotton Save Farmers in Warangal? A Season Long Impact Study of Bt Cotton: Kharif 2002 in Warangal District of Andhra Pradesh" (Hyderabad, India: AP Coalition in Defence of Diversity and Deccan Development Society, 2002), 28, available at www.ddsindia.com/pdf/English%20Report.pdf [accessed 12 July 2004].

28. David Bornstein, *The Price of a Dream: The Story of the Grameen Bank and the Idea That Is Helping the Poor to Change Their Lives* (New York: Simon and Schuster, 1996), 93; Büthe review, 743.

For the origins and structure of Grameen see Muhammad Yunus, with Alan Jolis, *Banker to the Poor: Micro-Lending and the Battle against World Poverty* (New York: Public Affairs, 1999), 45–58, and "Empowerment of the Poor: Eliminating the Apartheid Practiced by Financial Institutions," *Humanist* 57 (July–Aug. 1997): 25–27; and Bornstein, *Price of a Dream,* 42–47, 92–103.

For Grameen lending statistics see Yunus, "Empowerment of the Poor," 28; and Muhammad Yunus, founder and managing director of the Grameen Bank of Bangladesh, "Acceptance Speech on Petersberg Prize, 2004," presented on 27 June 2004, at the Development Gateway Forum, in Konigswinter, Germany, available at www.grameen-info.org/bank/Acceptance.html [accessed 30 June 2004].

29. Yunus, *Banker to the Poor,* 135–36; or Bornstein, *Price of a Dream,* 97.

For family planning and other social improvements see also Yunus, "Empowerment of the Poor," 28, and *Banker to the Poor,* 133–37.

30. Farid Ahmed, "'Hello, I'm Calling from Parulia . . .'" *Unesco Courier* (July–Aug. 2000): 67–68; Yunus, "Acceptance Speech on Petersberg Prize, 2004"; Edna F. Einsiedel and Melissa P. Innes, "Communications and Development: Challenges of the New Information and Communication Technologies," in *Transforming Development: Foreign Aid for a Changing World,* ed. Jim Freedman (Toronto, Can.: Univ. of Toronto Press, 2000), 263.

31. Yunus, *Banker to the Poor,* 247.

For new credit program for beggars see Yunus, "Acceptance Speech on Petersberg Prize, 2004."

For critiques of the Grameen model and its adaptability see Morgan Brigg, "Empowering NGOs: The Microcredit Movement through Foucault's Notion of *Dispositif,*" *Alternatives: Global, Local, Political* 26 (July–Sept. 2001): 233–58; Kathleen Pickering and David W. Mushinski, "Cultural Aspects of Credit Institutions: Transplanting the Grameen Bank Credit Group Structure to the Pine Ridge Indian Reservation," *Journal of Economic Issues* 35 (June 2001): 459–67; Jonathan Conning, "Outreach, Sustainability and Leverage in Monitored and Peer-Monitored Lending," *Journal of Development Economics* 60 (1999): 51–77; and Kavaljit Singh and Daphne Wysham, "Micro Credit: Band-Aid or Wound?" *Ecologist* 27 (1997): 42–43.

Yunus and his converts, however, point out a number of successes in the application of the Grameen model in a variety of national contexts: Yunus, *Banker to the Poor,* 155–92; David S. Gibbons, *The Grameen Reader: Training Materials for the International Replication of the Grameen Bank Financial System for Reduction of Rural Poverty* (Bangladesh: Grameen

Bank, 1992); and Alex Counts, *Give Us Credit* (New York: Times, 1996).

32. Anna K. Dickson, *Development and International Relations* (Cambridge, UK: Polity, 1997), 85; Amartya Sen, *Development as Freedom* (New York: Anchor, 1999), 5.

For scholars who argue that "development" should be abandoned altogether see Thomas W. Dichter, *Despite Good Intentions: Why Development Assistance to the Third World Has Failed* (Amherst: Univ. of Massachusetts Press, 2003), 286–96; and Rist, *The History of Development*, 238–58.

33. For disagreements see Yunus, *Banker to the Poor,* 142–51, and "Empowerment of the Poor," 28.

For areas of cooperation see Yunus, *Banker to the Poor,* 142–43, 148, 158, 164, 166, 168.

34. As quoted in Geoffrey Cowley, "Medicine without Doctors," *Newsweek,* 19 July 2004.

35. "Prescription for Survival," Chisholm address for United Nations Radio, 1 Nov. 1957, Chisholm papers, box 56, vol. 3, folder 168–183, CNA. See also "Dangerous Complacency," Chisholm address to the American Humanist Association, 28 Feb. 1959, Chisholm papers, box 56, vol. 4, folder 201–213, CNA.

Bibliography

Archives

World Bank Group Archive, Washington, D.C.
Food and Agriculture Organization of the United Nations Archive, Rome, Italy
World Health Organization Archive, Geneva, Switzerland
U.S. National Archives, College Park, Maryland
British Public Records Office, Kew, United Kingdom
Canadian National Archive, Ottawa
National Library of Scotland, Edinburgh
Franklin D. Roosevelt Presidential Library, Hyde Park, New York
Hoover Institution on War, Revolution and Peace, Stanford, California
Columbia Oral History Project, New York, New York
University of Georgia Archive, Athens

Published Government, United Nations, and Other Official Documents

Abbott, J. C. *Marketing: Its Role in Increasing Productivity.* FFHC Basic Study, no. 4. Rome: FAO, 1962.
African Malaria Conference. *Malaria Eradication: Report of the Third African Malaria Conference.* Geneva: WHO, 1963.
American Engineering Council, Committee on Elimination of Waste in Industry, and Federated American Engineering Societies. *Waste in Industry.* New York: McGraw-Hill, 1921.
Amla, B. L. *Seventh Report of FAO International Food Technology Training Centre at the Central Food Technological Research Institute, Mysore City, India.* Rome: FAO, 1976.
Aziz, Mehmed. *Report on the Anopheles (Malaria) Eradication Scheme.* Nicosia: Cyprus Government Printing Office, 1947.
Bhattacharjee, B. N., ed. *Health Education in Malaria Eradication Program (India).* New Delhi: National Health Program Division, 1972.

Blau, Gerda. *Disposal of Agricultural Surpluses*. FAO Commodity Policy Studies, no. 5. Rome: FAO, June 1954.

British Honduras Health Department. *Plan of Operation for the Malaria Eradication Program in British Honduras*. Belize: Health Department, 1954.

Burma-India-Pakistan Malaria Eradication Coordination Conference. *Report on Malaria Eradication Program, East Pakistan, for Presentation to Burma-India-Pakistan Malaria Eradication Coordination Conference*. N.p., 1966.

Calder, Ritchie. *The Lamp Is Lit: The Story of WHO*. Geneva: WHO Division of Public Information, May 1951.

Charts Relating to the Bretton Woods Proposals: The Danger that Restrictive and Discriminatory Currency Practices Will Be Resumed and Intensified after the War Makes International Monetary Cooperation Essential. Washington, D.C.: U.S. Treasury, 30 Apr. 1945.

Chen, Wan-i. *The Prospect of Malaria Eradication in Taiwan*. Geneva: WHO, 1963.

Commission Internationale d'Agriculture. *XIE Congrès International d'Agriculture: Paris, 22 au 28 Mai 1923*. Paris: Librairie Agricole de la Maison Rustique, 1923.

Congrès Agricole International de Budapest. *Procès-Verbal*. Budapest: Otto Bròzsa, 1886.

Covell, Sir Gordon, Paul F. Russell, and N. H. Swellengrebel. *Malaria Terminology: Report of a Drafting Committee Appointed by the World Health Organization*. WHO Monograph Series, no. 13. Geneva: WHO, 1953.

Covell, Sir Gordon, G. Robert Coatney, John W. Field, and Jaswant Singh. *Chemotherapy of Malaria*. WHO Monograph Series, no. 27. Geneva: WHO, 1955.

Dennett, Raymond, and Robert K. Turner, eds. *Documents on American Foreign Relations*. Vol. 8: *July 1, 1945–December 31, 1946*. Princeton, N.J.: Princeton Univ. Press for the World Peace Foundation, 1948.

Development through Food: A Strategy for Surplus Utilization. FFHC Basic Studies, no. 2. Rome: FAO, 1962.

Dop, Louis J. *Le Présent et l'Avenir de l'Institut International d'Agriculture*. Rome: International Institute of Agriculture, 1912.

Dowling, M. A. C. *The Malaria Eradication Experiment in Mauritius, 1948–52*. Port Louis, Mauritius: Medical and Health Department, 1953.

Environment and Development in Latin America and the Caribbean: The Role of the World Bank. Washington, D.C.: World Bank, 1992.

European Conference on Malaria Eradication. *Malaria Eradication: Report on the Second European Conference*. Copenhagen: WHO Regional Office for Europe, 1962.

The Food Aid Program, 1966: Annual Report on Public Law 480. Washington, D.C.: GPO, 1967.

Food and Agriculture Organization of the United Nations. *Proposals for a World Food Board*. Washington, D.C.: FAO, 5 July 1946.

———. *The State of Food and Agriculture: 1947*. Geneva: FAO, Aug. 1947.

———. *Programme of Work for 1949*. Washington, D.C.: FAO, 15 Nov. 1948.

———. *Second World Food Survey*. Rome: FAO, 1952.

Food for Freedom, New Emphasis on Self-Help: 1967 Annual Report on Public Law 480. Washington, D.C.: GPO, 1968.

Food for Peace, 1965: Annual Report on Public Law 480. Washington, D.C.: GPO, 1966.

Freedom from Hunger Campaign. *Report on the Food and Agriculture Organization/National Farm Broadcasting Seminar for Malaysia*. Rome: FAO, 1968.

———. *Report to the Government of India: The Establishment of a Model Piggery.* Rome: FAO, 1971.

Freedom from Hunger Campaign National Action Projects: A Selection. Rome: FAO, 1960.

Freedom from Hunger: Outline of a Campaign. Rome: FAO, 1960.

Functions of a World Food Reserve: Scope and Limitations. FAO Commodity Policy Studies, no. 10. Rome: FAO, 1956.

Furnivall, Gerald, and Alison Clarke. *Impact: The Freedom from Hunger Campaign in Relation to School Curricula and Examinations.* London: Education Department, Sept. 1965.

Geographical Reconnaissance for Malaria Eradication Programs. Geneva: WHO, 1965.

Gulbrandsen, Oyvind. *The Freedom from Hunger Campaign (FFHC) Outboard Mechanization Projects in Dahomey and Togo.* Rome: FAO, Dec. 1968.

Handbook on Malaria Training: Report on a Secretariat Meeting on Training in Malaria Eradication. Geneva: WHO, 1966.

Hemming, James. *A Strategy for World Health.* London: WHO Division of Public Information, 1955.

India Special Committee to Review the Working of the National Malaria Eradication Program and to Recommend Measures for Improvement. New Delhi: Ministry of Health, Family Planning, and Urban Development, 1970.

Indian Central Health Education Bureau. *Malaria Eradication in India.* New Delhi: Government of India Press, 1961.

Insecticides: Manual of Specifications for Insecticides and for Spraying and Dusting Apparatus. Geneva: WHO, 1953.

Interim Co-ordinating Committee for International Commodity Arrangements. *Review of International Commodity Problems, 1948.* Lake Success, N.Y.: United Nations, Nov. 1948.

International Development Advisory Board. *Partners in Progress: A Report to the President.* Washington, D.C.: GPO, Mar. 1951.

International Labour Office. *Intergovernmental Commodity Control Agreements.* Montreal, Can.: ILO, 1943.

———. *Workers' Nutrition and Social Policy.* Studies and Reports Series B, no. 23. Geneva: ILO, 1936.

———. *Intergovernmental Commodity Control Agreements.* Montreal: ILO, 1943.

Joint Statement by Experts on the Establishment of an International Monetary Fund of the United and Associated States. Washington, D.C.: U.S. Treasury, 21 Apr. 1944.

Knoblauch, H. C., et al. *State Agricultural Experiment Stations: A History of Research Policy and Procedure.* USDA Miscellaneous Publication, no. 904. Washington, D.C.: USDA, May 1962.

League of Nations. *Proceedings of the Conference.* Vol. 1: *Report of the Conference.* Geneva: League of Nations, 1920.

———. *Ten Years of World Co-operation.* London: Hazell, Watson and Viney for League Secretariat, 1930.

———. *Report of the Epidemic Commission of the League of Nations.* Geneva: Imprimerie Atar for League, 1921, 1922.

———. *The Problem of Nutrition.* Vol. 3: *Nutrition in Various Countries.* Geneva: League of Nations, 1936.

———. *Nutrition: Final Report of the Mixed Committee of the League of Nations on the Relation of Nutrition to Health, Agriculture and Economic Policy.* Geneva: League of Nations, 1937.

League of Nations Economic and Financial Section, *Report and Proceedings of the World Economic Conference held at Geneva, May 4th to 23rd, 1927*. Vol. 1. Geneva: League of Nations, 1927.

League of Nations Economic Committee. *The Agricultural Crisis*. Vol. 1. Geneva: League of Nations, 1931.

Lubin, David. *The International Institute of Agriculture and Its Influence on Economic Welfare: Reply to Some Comments Made by the Minister of Agriculture of France*. Rome: International Institute of Agriculture, 2 Mar. 1911.

Main Reports of 18th Congrès International d'Agriculture. Berlin: Reichsnährstand Verlags-Ges, 1939.

Malaria Eradication in the Americas: The First Six Years in the Hemisphere-Wide Campaign. Washington, D.C.: Pan American Health Organization, 1960.

Manual on Epidemiological Evaluation and Surveillance in Malaria Eradication. Geneva: WHO, 1962.

National Malaria Eradication Program, Rajasthan, 1959. Jaipur, India, 1960.

National Malaria Eradication Project Plan of Operations: Royal Government of Thailand in Cooperation with WHO. Bangkok: U.S. Operations Mission to Thailand, 1966.

National Malaria Eradication Project. *Plan of Operations*. Royal Government of Thailand in cooperation with the WHO, June 1965.

Nyswander, Dorothy Bird. *Education Approaches in Malaria Eradication Programs*. Washington, D.C.: International Cooperation Administration, 1959.

Orr, Sir John Boyd. "The New Council of FAO." *United Nations Weekly Bulletin* 3 (23 Sept. 1947): 382–84.

———. "FAO: The Year Past, the Year Ahead." *United Nations Weekly Bulletin* 4 (1 Jan. 1948): 17–19.

Pan American Health Organization. *Register on Malaria Eradication of Dominica, West Indies*. Washington, D.C.: PAHO, 1966.

———. *Health Conditions in the Americas, 1961–1964*. Scientific Publication 138. Washington, D.C.: PAHO, Aug. 1966.

Plan of Operations for the Programme of Protection of Pre-school Children which Will Be Carried out by the Ministry of Public Health and the National Institute of Nutrition, with Financial Cooperation from the United Kingdom Committee of the Freedom from Hunger Campaign: Supported by the National Federation of Women's Institutes. Bogotá: Colombia National Institute of Nutrition, 1965.

Pletsch, Donald J., F. E. Gatrell, and E. Harold Hinman. *A Critical Review of the National Malaria Eradication Program of India*. New Delhi: Health Division of U.S. Technical Cooperation Mission to India, Nov. 1960.

Program of Malaria Eradication in Ceylon. Colombo, 1963.

Rao, G. Kameswara, ed. *World Health Day Souvenir*. Hyderabad, India: Public Health Department, 1960.

Report of an Assessment of the National Malaria Eradication Program of Thailand. Bangkok: U.S. Agency for International Development, 1964.

Report of the Indonesia Malaria Assessment Team. Indonesia, 1961.

Report on Malaria Eradication in Venezuela: Study Carried out under the Auspices of the Pan American Health Organization. N.p., 1974.

Report on Progress of Malaria Eradication Scheme. Port Louis, Mauritius: Felix, 1949.

Report on the FAO Near East Farm Broadcasting Seminar. Rome: FAO, 1963.

Report on the Status of Malaria Eradication in the Americas: XIV Report. Washington, D.C.: Pan American Sanitary Conference, 16 Aug. 1966.

Rockefeller Foundation. *Annual Report.* New York: Rockefeller Foundation, 1947.

Saint Lucia Medical Department. *Report of the Malaria Eradication Program for the Year 1956.* Castries: Saint Lucia Medical Department, 1958.

Sen, B. R. *The Basic Freedom: Freedom from Hunger.* Rome: FAO, 1960.

Steele, James H. *Animal Disease and Human Health.* FFHC Basic Studies, no. 3. Rome: FAO, 1962.

Sukdeo, Fred. *Malaria Eradication and Population Growth in Guyana, 1973.* Georgetown, Guyana: University of Guyana, n.d.

Summary Proceedings of the Annual Meeting of the Board of Governors of the International Bank for Reconstruction and Development. Washington, D.C.: World Bank, 1947–64.

Swaroop, Satya. *Statistical Methods in Malaria Eradication.* Geneva: WHO, 1960 and 1966.

True, Alfred Charles. *A History of Agricultural Experimentation and Research in the United States, 1607–1925, including a History of the United States Department of Agriculture.* USDA Miscellaneous Publication, no. 251. Washington, D.C.: USDA, 1937.

U.S. Congress. House. Committee on Agriculture. *Report of the Delegation of the United States to the General Assembly to the International Institute of Agriculture, 1911.* 62d Cong., 2d sess., 1911.

U.S. Congress. House. Committee on Banking and Currency. *Report to Accompany H.R. 3314: Participation of the United States in the International Monetary Fund and the International Bank for Reconstruction and Development.* 79th Cong., 1st sess., 1945.

U.S. Congress. Senate. Committee on Agriculture and Forestry. *Food and Fiber as a Force for Freedom.* Report prepared by Hubert H. Humphrey. 83d Cong., 21 Apr. 1958.

U.S. Congress. Senate. Subcommittee on Reorganization and International Organization. *The United States and the World Health Organization: Teamwork for Mankind's Well-Being.* Report by Hubert H. Humphrey. 11 May 1959.

U.S. Department of Agriculture. *Farmers in a Changing World: Yearbook of Agriculture, 1940.* Washington, D.C.: GPO, 1940.

———. *Yearbook of the U.S. Department of Agriculture, 1937.* Washington, D.C.: USDA, 1937.

———, with the State Department and International Cooperation Administration. *How America's Abundance Works for Peace.* Washington, D.C.: GPO, Oct. 1960.

U.S. Department of State. *Proceedings and Documents of the United Nations Monetary and Financial Conference, Bretton Woods, New Hampshire, July 1–22, 1944.* 2 vols. Washington, D.C.: GPO, 1945.

U.S. Department of State. *Proceedings of the National Conference, American Food for Peace Council.* Washington, D.C.: State Department, 30 Sept. 1963.

U.S. Department of State. *Point Four: A Selected Bibliography of Materials on Technical Cooperation with Foreign Governments.* Washington, D.C.: Department of State, 15 Nov. 1950.

United Nations. *Aspects of Economic Development: The Background to Freedom from Hunger.* FFHC Basic Studies, no. 8. New York: UN Office of Public Information, 1963.

United Nations Conference on Food and Agriculture. "Text of the Final Act." *American Journal of International Law* 37 supplement (1943): 159–92.

United Nations Department of International Economic and Social Affairs. *World Survey on the Role of Women in Development.* New York: United Nations, 1986.

United Nations Educational, Scientific and Cultural Organization. *Women in the Villages, Men in the Towns.* Paris: UNESCO, 1984.

United Nations Environment Programme, the International Labour Organisation, and the World Health Organization. *DDT and Its Derivatives: Environmental Aspects.* Environmental Health Criteria Series, no. 83. Geneva: WHO, 1989.

United Nations Interim Commission on Food and Agriculture. *The Work of FAO.* Washington, D.C.: UNICFA, 20 Aug. 1945.

Uses of Agricultural Surpluses to Finance Economic Development in Under-Developed Countries: A Pilot Study in India. FAO Commodity Policy Studies, no. 6. Rome: FAO, June 1955.

VI^E Congrès International d'Agriculture: Paris, 1er au 8 Juillet 1900. Paris: Masson, 1900.

Visvalingam, T. *Report of the Assessment of the Malaria Eradication Program in Ceylon.* New Delhi: WHO Southeast Asian Regional Office, 1972.

Winslow, Charles-Edward Amory. *The Cost of Illness and the Price of Health.* WHO Monograph Series, no. 7. Geneva: WHO, 1951.

World Bank. *The World Environment and the World Bank.* Washington, D.C.: World Bank, 1972.

World Bank Group Staff Association's Status of Women Working Group. *Report on the Status of Women in the Bank.* Washington, D.C.: World Bank, 1981.

World Health Organization. *First World Health Assembly.* Official Records of the World Health Organization, no. 13. Geneva: WHO, Dec. 1948.

———. *Programme and Budget Estimates for 1950.* Official Records of the World Health Organization, no. 18. Geneva: WHO, Apr. 1949.

———. *Reports of Expert Committees and Executive Board.* Official Records of the World Health Organization, no. 15. Geneva: WHO, Apr. 1949.

———. *Manual of the International Classification of Diseases, Injuries and Causes of Death.* Geneva: WHO, 1949.

———. *Malaria: Eradication, Insecticide Resistance, Entomological Investigations, Epidemiology, Control, Prophylaxis.* Geneva: WHO, 1956.

———. *Malaria Eradication: A Plea for Health.* Geneva: WHO, 1958.

———. *The First Ten Years of the World Health Organization.* Geneva: WHO, 1958.

———. *First Report on the World Health Situation, 1954–1956.* Official Records of the WHO, no. 94. Geneva: WHO, 1959.

———. *Basic Documents.* 13th ed. Geneva: WHO, Dec. 1962.

———. *Terminology of Malaria and of Malaria Eradication: Report of a Drafting Committee.* Geneva: WHO, 1963.

———. *Handbook of Resolutions and Decisions of the World Health Assembly and the Executive Board.* 8th ed. Geneva: WHO, Nov. 1965.

———. *Twenty Years in South-East Asia, 1948–1967.* New Delhi: WHO Regional Office for South-East Asia, 1967.

———. *The Second Ten Years of the World Health Organization, 1958–1967.* Geneva: WHO, 1968.

———. *Field Manual for Antilarval Operations in Malaria Eradication Programmes.* Geneva: WHO, 1969.

———. *Four Decades of Achievement: Highlights of the Work of WHO.* Geneva: WHO, 1988.

World Health Organization Interim Commission. *Minutes of the Second Session of the Interim Commission, Held in Geneva from 4 to 13 November 1946.* New York and Geneva: WHOIC, Feb. 1947.

———. *Minutes of the First Session of the Interim Commission, Held in New York from 19 to 23 July 1946.* New York and Geneva: WHOIC, June 1947.

———. *Minutes of the Technical Preparatory Committee for the International Health Conference, Held in Paris from 18 March to 5 April 1946.* Official Records of the World Health Organization, no. 1. New York and Geneva: WHOIC, Oct. 1947.

———. *Summary Report on Proceedings, Minutes and Final Acts of the International Health Conference, Held in New York from 19 June to 22 July 1946.* Official Records of the World Health Organization, no. 2. New York and Geneva: WHOIC, June 1948.

———. *Reports of Expert Committees and Other Advisory Bodies to the Interim Commission.* Official Records of the World Health Organization, no. 11. Geneva: WHO, Dec. 1948.

———. *Supplementary Report of the Interim Commission to the World Health Assembly.* Official Records of the World Health Organization, no. 12. Geneva: WHO, Dec. 1948.

World Health Organization Malaria Eradication Division. *Manual for the Processing and Examination of Blood Slides in Malaria Eradication Programs.* Geneva: WHO, 1960.

———. *Manual on Preparation of Malaria Eradication Programs.* Geneva: WHO, 1961.

———. *Practical Entomology in Malaria Eradication.* 2 Parts. Geneva: WHO, Apr. 1963.

Yates, P. Lamartine. *So Bold an Aim: Ten Years of International Co-operation toward Freedom from Want.* Rome: FAO, 1955.

Memoirs, Diaries, and Contemporary Accounts

Achievement: The W. I. Contribution to the Freedom from Hunger Campaign. London: National Federation of Women's Institutes, Apr. 1967.

Baker, Robert. "Two Millions Call Him Doctor." *Maclean's Magazine* (1 May 1950): 21, 45, 47–49.

Belios, George D. "Mental Attitudes during the Later Phases of a Malaria Eradication Program." *Israel Journal of Medical Sciences* 1 (Mar. 1965): 290–93.

Billings, John S. "The Plans and Purposes of the Johns Hopkins Hospital." *Medical News* 54 (1 May 1889): 505–10.

Black, John D. "The International Food Movement." *American Economic Review* 33 (Dec. 1943): 791–811.

———. *Agricultural Reform in the United States.* New York: McGraw-Hill, 1929.

———. *Federal-State-Local Relations in Agriculture.* Washington, D.C.: National Planning Association, 1950.

———, ed. "Nutrition and Food Supply: The War and After." *Annals of the American Academy of Political and Social Science* 225 (Jan. 1943).

———, ed. *Research in Farm Management: Scope and Method.* New York: Social Science Research Council, 1932.

Boudreau, Frank G. "Food and Nutrition: Basic Factors in International Relations." *Nutrition Reviews* 1 (Mar. 1943): 129–30.

———. "The Food Conference at Hot Springs." *Nutrition Reviews* 1 (Sept. 1943): 321–26.

————. "The UN and the World's Health." *Proceedings of the Academy of Political Science* 25 (Jan. 1953): 2–11.

Bouillaud, J. *Essai sur la Philosophie Médicale, et sur les Generalites de la Clinique Medicale.* Paris: Rouvier et le Bouvier, 1836.

Braddon, Russell. *Suez: Splitting of a Nation.* London: Collins, 1973.

Bruce-Chwatt, Leonard J. "Malaria Research for Malaria Eradication." *Transactions of the Royal Society of Tropical Medicine and Hygiene* 59 (Mar. 1965): 105–37.

————. "Towards Malaria Eradication." *Span* 7 (1964): 11–14.

————. "Malaria Eradication: A Tangled Web." *Annales des Sociétés Belges de Médecine Tropicale de Parasitologie et de Mycologie* 51 (1971): 615–21.

————. "Twenty Years of Malaria Eradication." *British Journal of Hospital Medicine* 12 (Sept. 1974): 381–82, 384, 387–88.

Bruce-Chwatt, Leonard J., and James Haworth. "Malaria Eradication: Its Present Status." *Israel Journal of Medical Sciences* 1 (Mar. 1965): 284–89.

Budd, William. *Typhoid Fever: Its Nature, Mode of Spreading, and Prevention.* London: Longmans, Green, 1873.

Busvine, James R. "Insecticide-Resistant Strains of Insects of Public Health Importance." *Transactions of the Royal Society of Tropical Medicine and Hygiene* 51 (Jan. 1957): 11–31.

Chisholm, Brock. "Barriers to World Health." *International Conciliation* 491 (May 1953): 260–66.

————. "The Role of WHO: Past, Present and Future." *American Journal of Public Health* 41 (Dec. 1951): 1460–63.

————. *Nations Are Learning to Live Together.* Vancouver, Can.: Univ. of British Columbia, 1954.

Clough, Neal J., ed. *Gazebo: A Collection of Writings and Illustrations Edited and Published at Kingswood School as a Contribution to the Freedom from Hunger Campaign.* Plaistow, UK: Curwen, 1963.

Commons, John R. *Myself.* New York: Macmillan, 1934.

————. *Labor and Administration.* New York: Macmillan, 1913.

Crawford, Arthur W. *The Bretton Woods Proposals.* Washington, D.C.: Finance Department of the U.S. Chamber of Commerce, Feb. 1945.

Crutchfield, J. S. "Food in the Reconstruction Period." *Annals of the American Academy of Political and Social Science* 82 (Mar. 1919): 7–10.

Davis, Chester C. "The Agricultural Administration Act and National Recovery." *Journal of Farm Economics* 18 (1936): 229–43.

Davis, Joseph S. *On Agricultural Policy, 1926–1938.* Stanford, Calif.: Food Research Institute, 1939.

de Huszar, George B. *Persistent International Issues.* New York: Harper, 1947.

Eden, Anthony. *The Memoirs of Anthony Eden, Earl of Avon.* Vol. 4: *Full Circle.* London: Cassell, 1960.

Eisenhower, Dwight D. *The White House Years.* Vol. 2: *Waging Peace, 1956–1961.* Garden City, N.Y.: Doubleday, 1965.

Evang, Karl. *Norway's Food in Peace and War.* Washington, D.C.: 1942.

Flexner, Abraham. *Medical Education in the United States and Canada: A Report to the Carnegie Foundation for the Advancement of Teaching.* New York: Carnegie Foundation, 1910.

————. *Medical Education: A Comparative Study.* New York: Macmillan, 1925.

"Food and Agriculture Organization Looks Ahead." *Nutrition News* 9 (Feb. 1946): 1.

Food for Peace: Proceedings of the National Conference of the American Food for Peace Council. Washington, D.C.: U.S. Department of State, 30 Sept. 1963.

Gabaldón, Arnoldo. "Global Eradication of Malaria: Changes of Strategy and Future Outlook." *American Journal of Tropical Medicine and Hygiene* 18 (Sept. 1969): 641–56.

———. "The Nation-Wide Campaign against Malaria in Venezuela." *Transactions of the Royal Society of Tropical Medicine and Hygiene* 43 (Sept. 1949): 113–60.

Gaer, Joseph. *Bretton Woods Is No Mystery.* Pamphlets of the Congress of Industrial Organizations' Political Action Committee, no. 1. New York: Pamphlet Press, 1945.

Georges-Picot, Jacques. *The Real Suez Crisis: The End of a Great Nineteenth Century Work.* Translated by W. G. Rogers. New York: Harcourt Brace Jovanovich, 1975.

Giglioli, G. *Malaria, Filariasis and Yellow Fever in British Guiana: Control by Residual D.D.T. Methods.* Georgetown, British Guiana: 1948.

Gilroy, A. B. *Increasing Malaria during an Eradication Program: A Study of the Tea Estates of Assam, 1964–68.* N.p., 1970.

———. *The Role of Drugs in Malaria Eradication in Southeast Asia.* Lisbon: Casa Portuguesa, 1958.

Gockel, G. W. "Methodology of Epidemiological Assessment of the Malaria Situation throughout a Malaria Eradication Program." *Journal of Tropical Medicine* 64 (Sept. 1961).

Graham, J. B., B. V. Travic, F. A. Morton, and A. W. Lindquist. "DDT as a Residual-Type Treatment to Control *Anopheles quadrimaculatus*: Practical Tests." *Journal of Economic Entomology* 38 (1945): 231–35.

Hambidge, Gove. "The Food and Agriculture Organization at Work." *International Conciliation* 432 (Dec. 1947): 347–422.

———. *The Story of FAO.* Toronto: D. Van Nostrand, 1955.

Hansen, Alvin H. *After the War: Full Employment.* Washington, D.C.: National Resources Planning Board, Jan. 1942.

Hayes, Wayland J., Jr. "The Current State of Our Knowledge of DDT Intoxication." *American Journal of Public Health* 45 (Apr. 1955): 478–85.

Hobson, Asher. *The International Institute of Agriculture: An Historical and Critical Analysis of Its Organization, Activities, and Policies of Administration.* Berkeley: Univ. of California Press, 1931.

Hopcraft, Arthur. *Born to Hunger.* Sponsored by the Freedom from Hunger Campaign. London: Heinemann, 1968.

Howson, Susan, and Donald Moggridge, eds. *The Wartime Diaries of Lionel Robbins and James Meade, 1943–45.* London: Macmillan, 1990.

Johannsen, Ernst. *Four Infantrymen on the Western Front.* London: Methuen, 1929.

Jones, Russell M., ed. *The Parisian Education of an American Surgeon: Letters of Jonathan Mason Warren, 1832–1835.* Philadelphia, Pa.: American Philosophical Society, 1978.

Kelsey, Carl, ed. "Mobilizing America's Resources for the War." *Annals of the American Academy of Political and Social Science* 78 (July 1918).

Keynes, John Maynard. *The Economic Consequences of the Peace.* London: Macmillan, 1919.

———. *The General Theory of Employment, Interest and Money.* New York: Harcourt, Brace, and World, 1936.

Lilienthal, David E. *TVA: Democracy on the March.* New York: Harper, 1944.

————. *The Journals of David E. Lilienthal.* Vol. 1: *The TVA Years, 1938–1945.* New York: Harper and Row, 1964.

————. *The Journals of David E. Lilienthal.* Vol. 3: *Venturesome Years, 1950–1955.* New York: Harper and Row, 1966.

Lister, J. *The Collected Papers of Joseph, Baron Lister.* 2 vols. Oxford, UK: Clarendon, 1909.

Livadas, Gregory A. *The Economic Benefits of Malaria Eradication in Greece.* N.p., 1963.

Lloyd, Selwyn. *Suez 1956: A Personal Account.* London: Jonathan Cape, 1978.

Louis, P. C. A. *Recherches sur les Effets de la Saignée dans Quelques Maladies Inflammatoires.* Paris: J. B. Bailliere, 1835.

Macdonald, G. *The Epidemiology and Control of Malaria.* London: Oxford Univ. Press, 1957.

Malaria Institute of India. *Manual of the Malaria Eradication Operation.* Delhi: National Malaria Eradication Program, 1958, 1960.

May, H. J. "The International Co-operative Alliance: Its History, Aims, Constitution and Government." Pamphlet of the International Co-operative Alliance. London, n.d.

McDougall, F. L. "Food and Welfare." *Geneva Studies* 9 (Nov. 1938): 7–56.

McGovern, George S. *War Against Want: America's Food for Peace Program.* New York: Walker, 1964.

Mendès-France, Pierre. *Oeuvres Complètes.* Vol. 2: *Une Politique de l'Économie, 1945–1954.* Paris: Gallimard, 1985.

Moggridge, Donald, ed. *The Collected Writings of John Maynard Keynes.* Vol. 26: *Activities, 1941–1946: Shaping the Post-War World, Bretton Woods and Reparations.* London: Macmillan, 1980.

Morgenthau, Henry, Jr. "Bretton Woods and International Coöperation." *Foreign Affairs* 24 (July 1946): 182–94.

Muirhead-Thomson, R. C. "DDT and Gammexane as Residual Insecticides against *Anopheles gambiae* in African Houses." *Transactions of the Royal Society for Tropical Medicine and Hygiene* 43 (Jan. 1950): 401–12.

Nasser, Gamal Abdel. *President Gamal Abdel-Nasser's Speeches and Press Interviews, 1959.* Vol. 2. Cairo: United Arab Republic Information Department, n.d.

————. *The Philosophy of Revolution.* Translated by Dar Al-Maaref. Buffalo, N.Y.: Economica Books, 1959.

————. "The Egyptian Revolution." *Foreign Affairs* 33 (Jan. 1955): 199–211.

Niebuhr, Reinhold. *Christianity and Power Politics.* New York: Scribner's, 1940.

Nourse, Edwin G., Joseph S. Davis, and John D. Black. *Three Years of the Agricultural Adjustment Administration.* Washington, D.C.: Brookings Institution, 1937.

Nutting, Anthony. *No End of a Lesson: The Story of Suez.* New York: Clarkson N. Potter, 1967.

Oliver, Robert W. *Conversations about George Woods and the World Bank.* Pasadena: California Institute of Technology Division of the Humanities and Social Sciences, 1985.

Orr, John Boyd. *Food, Health and Income: Report on a Survey of Adequacy of Diet in Relation to Income.* London: Macmillan, 1936.

Orr, Lord Boyd. *As I Recall.* London: MacGibbon and Kee, 1966.

Orr, Sir John [Boyd]. *Fighting for What? To "Billy Boy" and All the Other Boys Killed in the War.* London: Macmillan, 1942.

————. *Food: The Foundation of World Unity.* Towards World Government, no. 1. London: National Peace Council, July 1948.

Orr, Sir John, and David Lubbock. *Feeding the People in War-Time.* London: Macmillan, 1940.

Osler, William. "The License to Practice." *Journal of the American Medical Association* 12 (1889): 649–54.

Pampana, Emilio J. *A Textbook of Malaria Eradication.* 2d edition. London: Oxford Univ. Press, 1969.

———. "Malaria in Europe, 1938–1947." *Epidemiological and Vital Statistics Report* 1 (1948): 392–400 (supplement to no. 18).

———, and P. F. Russell. *Malaria: A World Problem.* Geneva: WHO, 1955.

Panum, P. L. *Observations Made during the Epidemic of Measles on the Faroe Islands in the Year 1846.* Translated by A. S. Hatcher. New York: Delta Omega Society, 1940.

Phillips, Ralph W. *The World Was My Barnyard.* Parsons, W.Va.: McClain, 1984.

Remarque, Erich Maria. *All Quiet on the Western Front.* Translated by A. W. Wheen. New York: Ballantine, 1987.

Report of the World Food Conference: Rome, 5–16 November 1974. New York: United Nations, 1975.

Richardson, H. L. *Developments in the F.A.O. Fertiliser Programme under the Freedom from Hunger Campaign.* London: Fertiliser Society, 1962.

Roemer, Milton I., ed. *Henry E. Sigerist on the Sociology of Medicine.* New York: MD, 1960.

The Role of Food in World Peace: An International Symposium in Observance of the Land-Grant Centennial. Columbus: Ohio State Univ., 1962.

Roll, Erich. *The Combined Food Board: A Study in Wartime International Planning.* Stanford, Calif.: Stanford Univ. Press, 1956.

Russell, Paul Farr. "World-Wide Malaria Eradication." Delta Omega Lecture at the University of Michigan School of Public Health, 11 Feb. 1958.

———. *Malaria: Basic Principles Briefly Stated.* Oxford, UK: Blackwell Scientific, 1952.

———. *Man's Mastery of Malaria.* London: Oxford Univ. Press, 1955.

———. *Worldwide Malaria Eradication.* Ann Arbor: Univ. of Michigan School of Public Health, 1958.

———. *Malaria and Malaria Eradication.* New York, 1959.

Schultz, Theodore W., ed. *Food for the World.* Chicago, Ill.: Univ. of Chicago Press, 1945.

Sen, B. R. *Towards a Newer World.* Dublin, Ire.: Tycooly, 1982.

Snow, J. *On the Mode of Communication of Cholera.* London: J. Churchill, 1849.

Soper, Fred Lowe. *Ventures in World Health: The Memoirs of Fred Lowe Soper.* Washington, D.C.: Pan American Health Organization, 1977.

———, F. W. Knipe, G. Casini, Louis A. Riehl, and A. Rubino. "Reduction of Anopheles Density Effected by the Pre-Season Spraying of Building Interiors with DDT in Kerosene, at Castel Volturno, Italy, in 1944–1945 and in the Tiber Delta in 1945." *American Journal of Tropical Medicine* 27 (Mar. 1947): 177–200.

Sze, Szeming. *The Origins of the World Health Organization: A Personal Memoir, 1945–1948.* Boca Raton, Fla.: LISZ, 1982.

Tennessee Valley Authority. *The TVA Fertilizer Program.* Knoxville, Tenn.: TVA, Sept. 1965.

Testimony of Leon Fraser on the Bretton Woods Agreements Act. New York: First National Bank of the City of New York, 1945.

Thomas, Hugh. *Suez.* New York: Harper and Row, 1966.

Vinson, Fred. "After the Savannah Conference." *Foreign Affairs* 24 (July 1946): 622–32.

Watts, V. Orval. *The Bretton Woods Agreements.* Los Angeles, Calif.: Los Angeles Chamber of Commerce, 1945.

Wells, H. G. *An Englishman Looks at the World: Being a Series of Unrestrained Remarks on Contemporary Matters.* London: Cassell, 1914.

White, H. D. "The Monetary Fund: Some Criticisms Examined." *Foreign Affairs* 23 (Jan. 1945): 195–210.

Yates, P. Lamartine. "Trade and Aid: The Aims of the World Food Programme." *Span* 7 (1964): 123–26.

Younis, Mahmoud. "The Future of Suez." *World Petroleum* (Apr. 1958).

Yunus, Muhammad, with Alan Jolis. *Banker to the Poor: Micro-Lending and the Battle against World Poverty.* New York: PublicAffairs, 1999.

———. "Empowerment of the Poor: Eliminating the Apartheid Practiced by Financial Institutions." *Humanist* 57 (July–Aug. 1997): 25–27.

———. "Acceptance Speech on Petersberg Prize, 2004." www.grameen-info.org/bank/Acceptance.html. Accessed 30 June 2004.

Contemporary Periodicals

Boletín de la Oficina Sanitaria Panamericana, 1925, 1947–55.

British Medical Journal, 2003.

Bulletin of the World Health Organization, 1947–66.

Buffalo (N.Y.) Evening News, 1960.

Business Week, 1947.

Christian Science Monitor, 1989.

Chronicle of the World Health Organization, 1947–58, 1977–78.

Congressional Record, 1953–54.

Economist (U.S.), 1993-99.

Egyptian Gazette, 1957–59.

Engineering News-Record, 1960.

Far Eastern Economic Review, 2003.

Finance and Development, 1991.

Food for Peace, 1963.

Fortune, 1943.

Freedom from Hunger Campaign News, 1963.

Journal of the Philippine Medical Association, 1949.

Lancet, 2002.

Life, 1943.

London Investor's Review, 1960.

London Times, 1944–46, 1954–60.

Maclean's Magazine, 1946–50.

Milling and Baking News, 1993.

Modern Healthcare, 2004.

New England Journal of Medicine, 1949.

Newsweek, 2004.

New York Times, 1944, 1951–59, 1961, 1983–87, 1996.

Norfolk Virginian-Pilot, 1957.

Peoria (Ill.) Journal Star, 1957.

Pesticide and Toxic Chemical News, 2004.

Quarterly Bulletin of the Health Organisation, 1932–38.

Time, 1945–49.

U.S. News, 1947.

Wall Street Journal, 1944.

Washington News, 1961.

Washington Post, 1944, 1958, 1988–91.

Waycross (GA) Journal-Herald, 1957.

Winnipeg Free Press, 1948.

World Health Organization Technical Report Series, 1950–64.

Secondary Sources

BOOKS

Abel, Wilhelm. *Agricultural Fluctuations in Europe: From the Thirteenth to the Twentieth Centuries.* Translated by Olive Ordish. London: Methuen, 1980.

Adams, John A., Jr. *Damming the Colorado: The Rise of the Lower Colorado River Authority, 1933–1939.* College Station: Texas A&M Univ. Press, 1990.

Agresti, Olivia Rossetti. *David Lubin: A Study in Practical Idealism.* Berkeley: Univ. of California Press, 1941.

Agudelo, Saul Franco. *El Paludismo en América Latina.* Guadalajara, Mex.: Editorial Universidad de Guadalajara, 1990.

Agulhon, Maurice. *The French Republic, 1879–1992.* Translated by Antonia Neville. Cambridge, Mass.: Blackwell, 1993.

Albert, Michael, and Robin Hahnel. *Looking Forward: Participatory Economics for the Twenty-First Century.* Boston, Mass.: South End, 1991.

Alchon, Guy. *The Invisible Hand of Planning: Capitalism, Social Science, and the State in the 1920s.* Princeton, N.J.: Princeton Univ. Press, 1985.

Alsop, Gulielma Fell. *History of the Woman's Medical College, Philadelphia, Pennsylvania, 1850–1950.* Philadelphia, Pa.: Lippincott, 1950.

An Analysis of the Brannan Plan. Economic Policy Division Series, no. 17. New York: National Association of Manufacturers, Oct. 1949.

Anderson, Benedict. *Imagined Communities: Reflections on the Origin and Spread of Nationalism.* Revised and extended edition. London: Verso, 1991.

Andrews, Gregg. *Shoulder to Shoulder? The American Federation of Labor, the United States, and the Mexican Revolution, 1910–1924.* Berkeley: Univ. of California Press, 1991.

Angle, Paul M., ed. *Created Equal? The Complete Lincoln-Douglas Debates of 1858.* Chicago, Ill.: Univ. of Chicago Press, 1958.

Anning, S. T., and W. K. J. Walls. *A History of Leeds School of Medicine: One and a Half Centuries, 1831–1981.* Leeds, UK: Leeds Univ. Press, 1982.

Annis, Sheldon, and Peter Hakim, eds. *Direct to the Poor: Grassroots Development in Latin America.* Boulder, Colo.: Lynne Rienner, 1988.

Armstrong, David, Lorna Lloyd, and John Redmond. *From Versailles to Maastricht: International Organisation in the Twentieth Century.* New York: St. Martin's, 1996.

Arndt, Richard T., and David Lee Rubin, eds. *The Fulbright Difference, 1948–1992.* New Brunswick: Transaction, 1993.

Azimi, Fakhreddin. *Iran: The Crisis of Democracy.* London: I. B. Tauris, 1989.

Backman, Jules. *Rationing and Price Control in Great Britain.* Washington, D.C.: Brookings Institution, 1943.

Badger, Anthony J. *The New Deal: The Depression Years, 1933–1940.* New York: Hill and Wang, 1989.

Bailey, Joseph C. *Seaman A. Knapp: Schoolmaster of American Agriculture.* New York: Columbia Univ. Press, 1945.

Baker, Gladys L., Wayne D. Rasmussen, Vivian Wiser, and Jane M. Porter. *Century of Service: The First 100 Years of the United States Department of Agriculture.* Washington, D.C.: GPO for the U. S. Department of Agriculture Centennial Committee, 1963.

Bane, Suda Lorena, and Ralph Haswell Lutz, eds. *Organization of American Relief in Europe, 1918–1919.* Stanford, Calif.: Stanford Univ. Press, 1943.

Baratta, Joseph Preston. *United Nations System.* International Organizations Series, edited by Robert G. Neville, vol. 10. New Brunswick, N.J.: Transaction, 1995.

Barber, William J. *Designs within Disorder: Franklin D. Roosevelt, the Economists, and the Shaping of American Economic Policy, 1933–1945.* Cambridge, UK: Cambridge Univ. Press, 1996.

Barlow, Robin. *The Economic Effects of Malaria Eradication.* Ann Arbor: Univ. of Michigan School of Public Health, 1968.

Barnet, Richard J., and John Cavanagh. *Global Dreams: Imperial Corporations and the New World Order.* New York: Touchstone, 1994.

Barzansky, Barbara, and Norman Gevitz, eds. *Beyond Flexner: Medical Education in the Twentieth Century.* New York: Greenwood, 1992.

Basch, Paul F. *Textbook of International Health.* New York: Oxford Univ. Press, 1990.

———. *International Health.* New York: Oxford Univ. Press, 1978.

Beatty, Rita Gray. *The DDT Myth: Triumph of the Amateurs.* New York: John Day, 1973.

Becker, William H. *The Dynamics of Business-Government Relations: Industry and Exports, 1893–1921.* Chicago, Ill.: Univ. of Chicago Press, 1982.

Beecher, Henry K., and Mark D. Altschule. *Medicine at Harvard: The First Three Hundred Years.* Hanover, N.H.: Univ. Press of New England, 1977.

Beloff, Max. *Dream of Commonwealth, 1921–42.* Dobbs Ferry, N.Y.: Sheridan, 1989.

Benedick, Richard Elliot. *Ozone Diplomacy: New Directions in Safeguarding the Planet.* Cambridge, Mass.: Harvard Univ. Press, 1991.

Bennett, Jon. *The Hunger Machine: The Politics of Food.* Cambridge, UK: Polity, 1987.

Berkov, Robert. *The World Health Organization: A Study in Decentralized International Administration.* Geneva: Librairie E. Droz, 1957.

Berlant, Jeffrey Lionel. *Profession and Monopoly: A Study of Medicine in the United States and Great Britain.* Berkeley: Univ. of California Press, 1975.

Berman, Edward H. *The Ideology of Philanthropy: The Influence of the Carnegie, Ford, and Rockefeller Foundations on American Foreign Policy.* Albany: State Univ. of New York Press, 1983.

Bess, Michael. *Realism, Utopia, and the Mushroom Cloud: Four Activist Intellectuals and Their Strategies for Peace, 1945–1989.* Chicago, Ill.: Univ. of Chicago Press, 1993.

Billroth, Theodor. *The Medical Sciences in the German Universities: A Study in the History of Civilization.* New York: Macmillan, 1924.

Bird, Kai. *The Chairman, John J. McCloy: The Making of the American Establishment.* New York: Simon and Schuster, 1992.

Black, John D. *Parity, Parity, Parity.* New York: Da Capo, 1972.

Black, Maggie. *Children First: The Story of UNICEF, Past and Present.* Oxford, UK: Oxford Univ. Press for UNICEF, 1996.

———. *The Children and the Nations: The Story of Unicef.* Geneva: UNICEF, 1986.

Blaugh, Mark. *Great Economists before Keynes.* New York: Cambridge Univ. Press, 1986.

Bledstein, Burton J. *The Culture of Professionalism: The Middle Class and the Development of Higher Education in America.* New York: Norton, 1976.

Block, Fred L. *The Origins of International Economic Disorder: A Study of United States International Monetary Policy from World War II to the Present.* Berkeley: Univ. of California Press, 1977.

Boli, John, and George M. Thomas, eds. *Constructing World Culture: International Nongovernmental Organizations since 1875.* Stanford, Calif.: Stanford Univ. Press, 1999.

Bonanno, Alessandro, and Douglas Constance. *Caught in the Net: The Global Tuna Industry, Environmentalism, and the State.* Lawrence: Univ. Press of Kansas, 1996.

The Bonn Policy of Coercion Is Doomed to Failure: Government of the FRG Again Prevents Membership of GDR in the World Health Organization (WHO) on a Basis of Equality. Dresden: Verlag Zeit im Bild, [1972].

Bonner, Thomas Neville. *Becoming a Physician: Medical Education in Britain, France, Germany, and the United States, 1750–1945.* New York: Oxford Univ. Press, 1995.

———. *American Doctors and German Universities: A Chapter in International Intellectual Relations, 1870–1914.* Lincoln: Univ. of Nebraska Press, 1987.

———. *To the Ends of the Earth: Women's Search for Education in Medicine.* Cambridge, Mass.: Harvard Univ. Press, 1992.

Bornstein, David. *The Price of a Dream: The Story of the Grameen Bank and the Idea That Is Helping the Poor to Change Their Lives.* New York: Simon and Schuster, 1996.

Boserup, Ester. *Woman's Role in Economic Development.* London: Allen and Unwin, 1970.

Brand, Jeanne L. *Doctors and the State: The British Medical Profession and Government Action in Public Health, 1870–1912.* Baltimore, Md.: Johns Hopkins Univ. Press, 1965.

Brecher, Jeremy, and Tim Costello. *Global Village or Global Pillage: Economic Reconstruction from the Bottom Up.* Boston, Mass.: South End, 1994.

———, John Brown Childs, and Jill Cutler, eds. *Global Visions: Beyond the New World Order.* Boston, Mass.: South End, 1993.

Breit, William, and Roger L. Ransom. *The Academic Scribblers: American Economists in Collision.* New York: Holt, Rinehart, and Winston, 1971.

Brenton, Tony. *The Greening of Machiavelli: The Evolution of International Environmental Politics.* Washington, D.C.: Brookings Institution, 1994.

Britnell, G. E., and V. C. Fowke. *Canadian Agriculture in War and Peace, 1935–50.* Stanford, Calif.: Stanford Univ. Press, 1962.

Brockington, Fraser. *World Health.* London: Penguin, 1958.

Brown, William Adams, Jr. *England and the New Gold Standard, 1919–1926.* London: P. S. King, 1929.

Bruner, David. *Herbert Hoover: A Public Life.* New York: Knopf, 1979.

Buchanan, Norman S., and Howard S. Ellis. *Approaches to Economic Development.* New York: Twentieth Century Fund, 1955.

Buehrig, Edward H. *The UN and the Palestinian Refugees: A Study in Nonterritorial Administration.* Bloomington: Indiana Univ. Press, 1971.

Buenker, John D., John C. Burnham, and Robert M. Crunden. *Progressivism.* Cambridge, Mass.: Schenkman, 1977.

Bull, Hedley, and Adam Watson, eds. *The Expansion of International Society.* Oxford, UK: Clarendon, 1984.

Burrow, James G. *AMA: Voice of American Medicine.* Baltimore, Md.: Johns Hopkins Univ. Press, 1963.

———. *Organized Medicine in the Progressive Era: The Move toward Monopoly.* Baltimore, Md.: Johns Hopkins Univ. Press, 1977.

Buvinic, Mayra, Margaret A. Lycette, and William Paul McGreevey, eds. *Women and Poverty in the Third World.* Baltimore, Md.: Johns Hopkins Univ. Press, 1983.

Calder, Ritchie. *Growing Up with UNICEF.* Public Affairs Pamphlet 330. N.p., n.d.

Caldwell, Lynton K. *International Environmental Policy.* Durham, N.C.: Duke Univ. Press, 1984.

Campbell, David. *Writing Security: United States Foreign Policy and the Politics of Identity.* Minneapolis: Univ. of Minnesota Press, 1992.

Carlton, David. *Britain and the Suez Crisis.* Making Contemporary Britain Series, edited by Anthony Selden. London: Basil Blackwell, 1988.

Carr-Saunders, A. M., and P. A. Wilson. *The Professions.* Oxford, UK: Clarendon, 1933.

Carson, Rachel. *Silent Spring.* Boston, Mass.: Houghton Mifflin, 1962.

Cartwright, Frederick F. *The Development of Modern Surgery.* New York: T. Y. Crowell, 1967.

Cartwright, William H., and Richard L. Watson Jr., eds. *The Reinterpretation of American History and Culture.* Washington, D.C.: National Council for Social Studies, 1973.

Cassedy, James H. *Charles V. Chapin and the Public Health Movement.* Cambridge, Mass.: Harvard Univ. Press, 1962.

Chandler, Alfred D. *The Visible Hand: The Managerial Revolution in American Business.* Cambridge, Mass.: Belknap Press, 1977.

Chandler, Lester V. *Benjamin Strong, Central Banker.* Washington, D.C.: Brookings Institution, 1958.

Chesney, Alan Mason. *The Johns Hopkins Hospital and the Johns Hopkins University School of Medicine: A Chronicle.* 3 vols. Baltimore, Md.: Johns Hopkins Univ. Press, 1943, 1958, 1963.

Chossudovsky, Michel. *The Globalisation of Poverty: Impacts of IMF and World Bank Reforms.* Cape Town, South Africa: IPSR Books, 1997.

Christenson, Reo M. *The Brannan Plan: Farm Politics and Policy.* Ann Arbor: Univ. of Michigan Press, 1959.

Clarke, Sally H. *Regulation and the Revolution in United States Farm Productivity.* Cambridge, UK: Cambridge Univ. Press, 1994.

Clarke, Sir Richard. *Anglo-American Economic Collaboration in War and Peace, 1942–1949.* Oxford, UK: Clarendon, 1982.

Cline, Rodney. *The Life and Work of Seaman A. Knapp.* Nashville, Tenn.: George Peabody College for Teachers, 1936.

Coats, A. W., ed. *Economists in International Agencies: An Exploratory Study.* New York: Praeger, 1986.

Coats, A. W. Bob. *British and American Economic Essays.* Vol. 1: *On the History of Economic Thought.* London: Routledge, 1992.

Cobb, W. Montague. *The First Negro Medical Society: A History of the Medico-Chirurgical Society of the District of Columbia, 1884–1939*. Washington, D.C.: Associated Publishers, 1939.

Cobbs, Elizabeth A. *The Rich Neighbor Policy: Rockefeller and Kaiser in Brazil*. New Haven, Conn.: Yale Univ. Press, 1992.

Cochrane, Willard W. *The Development of American Agriculture: A Historical Analysis*. Minneapolis: Univ. of Minnesota Press, 1993.

———, and Mary E. Ryan. *American Farm Policy, 1948–1973*. Minneapolis: Univ. of Minnesota Press, 1976.

Cohen, Warren. *The Chinese Connection: Roger S. Greene, Thomas W. Lamont, George E. Sokolsky, and American-East Asian Relations*. New York: Columbia Univ. Press, 1978.

Coleman, William, and Frederic L. Holmes, eds. *The Investigative Enterprise: Experimental Physiology in Nineteenth-Century Medicine*. Berkeley: Univ. of California Press, 1988.

Cook, Robert C. *Human Fertility: The Modern Dilemma*. New York: William Sloane Associates, 1951.

Conference on Anopheline Biology and Malaria Eradication: A Symposium at the Walter Reed Army Institute. Baltimore, 1970.

Conkin, Paul K. *The New Deal*. 2d edition. Arlington Heights, Ill.: Harlan Davidson, 1975.

Conner, Valerie Jean. *The National War Labor Board*. Chapel Hill: Univ. of North Carolina Press, 1983.

Corbett, P. E. *Law and Society in the Relations of States*. New York: Harcourt Brace, 1951.

Costigliola, Frank. *Awkward Dominion: American Political, Economic, and Cultural Relations with Europe, 1919–1933*. Ithaca, N.Y.: Cornell Univ. Press, 1984.

Cottrell, J. D. *The Prevention of Tropical Disease and the World Health Organisation's Rural Health Campaigns*. N.p., 5 Sept. 1957.

Counts, Alex. *Give Us Credit*. New York: Times, 1996.

Coursier, Henri. *The International Red Cross*. Geneva: International Committee of the Red Cross, 1961.

Crawford, Elisabeth. *Nationalism and Internationalism in Science, 1880–1939*. Cambridge, UK: Cambridge Univ. Press, 1992.

Cromwell, Lyman. *The Structure of Private International Organizations*. Philadelphia, Pa.: George S. Ferguson, 1933.

Crunden, Robert M. *Ministers of Reform: The Progressives' Achievement in American Civilization, 1889–1920*. Urbana: Univ. of Illinois Press, 1984.

Cueto, Marcos, ed. *Missionaries of Science: The Rockefeller Foundation and Latin America*. Bloomington: Indiana Univ. Press, 1994.

Cuff, Robert D. *The War Industries Board*. Baltimore, Md.: Johns Hopkins Univ. Press, 1973.

Cushing, Harvey W. *The Life of Sir William Osler*. 2 vols. London: Oxford Univ. Press, 1940.

Danaher, Kevin, ed. *50 Years Is Enough: The Case against the World Bank and the International Monetary Fund*. Boston, Mass.: South End, 1994.

Dauber, Roslyn, and Melinda L. Cain, eds. *Women and Technological Change in Developing Countries*. American Association for the Advancement of Science Symposia Series. Boulder, Colo.: Westview, 1981.

Davenport, Horace W. *Fifty Years of Medicine at the University of Michigan, 1891–1941*. Ann Arbor: Univ. of Michigan Medical School, 1986.

Davidson, Bruce R. *European Farming in Australia: An Economic History of Australian Farming.* Amsterdam: Elsevier Scientific, 1981.

Derbyshire, Robert C. *Medical Licensure and Discipline in the United States.* Baltimore, Md.: Johns Hopkins Univ. Press, 1969.

Deutsch, Albert. *The World Health Organization: Its Global Battle against Disease.* New York: Public Affairs Committee, 1958.

Dichter, Thomas W. *Despite Good Intentions: Why Development Assistance to the Third World Has Failed.* Amherst: Univ. of Massachusetts Press, 2003.

Dickson, Anna K. *Development and International Relations: A Critical Introduction.* Cambridge, UK: Polity, 1997.

Divine, Robert A. *Eisenhower and the Cold War.* Oxford, UK: Oxford Univ. Press, 1981.

———. *Blowing on the Wind: The Nuclear Test Ban Debate, 1954–1960.* New York: Oxford Univ. Press, 1978.

Dogra, Bharat. *In the Interests of Interest: Trade, Aid and Debt in an Unequal World.* Asthal Bohar, India: Disha, 1991.

Dowling, M. A. C. *The Malaria Eradication Experiment in Mauritius, 1948–52.* Port Louis, Mauritius: Medical and Health Department, 1953.

Duclaux, E. *Pasteur: The History of a Mind.* Translated by E. F. Smith and F. Hedges. Philadelphia, Pa.: W. B. Saunders, 1920.

Duffy, John. *From Humors to Medical Science: A History of American Medicine.* 2d edition. Urbana: Univ. of Illinois Press, 1993.

Duke, Martin. *The Development of Medical Techniques and Treatments: From Leeches to Heart Surgery.* Madison, Conn.: International Universities Press, 1991.

Dupree, A. Hunter. *Science in the Federal Government: A History of Policies and Activities to 1940.* Cambridge, Mass.: Harvard Univ. Press, 1957.

Eijkman, P. H. *L'Internationalisme Médical.* Amsterdam: F. Van Rossen for the Fondation pour l'Internationalisme, 1910.

Eisenberg, Azriel Louis. *Feeding the World: A Biography of David Lubin.* London: Abelard-Schuman, 1965.

Ellis, Jack D. *The Physician-Legislators of France: Medicine and Politics in the Early Third Republic, 1870–1914.* Cambridge, UK: Cambridge Univ. Press, 1990.

Elm, Mostafa. *Oil, Power, and Principle: Iran's Oil Nationalization and Its Aftermath.* Syracuse, N.Y.: Syracuse Univ. Press, 1992.

Enloe, Cynthia. *Bananas Beaches and Bases: Making Feminist Sense of International Politics.* Berkeley: Univ. of California Press, 1989.

Environment and Development in Latin America and the Caribbean: The Role of the World Bank. Washington, D.C.: World Bank, 1992.

Eyler, John M. *Victorian Social Medicine: The Ideas and Methods of William Farr.* Baltimore, Md.: Johns Hopkins Univ. Press, 1979.

Ferber, Marianne A., and Julie A. Nelson, eds. *Beyond Economic Man: Feminist Theory and Economics.* Chicago, Ill.: Univ. of Chicago Press, 1993.

Fforde, John. *The Bank of England and Public Policy, 1941–1958.* Cambridge, UK: Cambridge Univ. Press, 1992.

Filippelli, Ronald L. *American Labor and Postwar Italy, 1943–1953: A Study of Cold War Politics.* Stanford, Calif.: Stanford Univ. Press, 1989.

Fink, Carole. *The Genoa Conference: European Diplomacy, 1921–1922*. Chapel Hill: Univ. of North Carolina Press, 1984.

Fisher, Jean, ed. *Global Visions: Toward a New Internationalism in the Visual Arts*. London: Kala, 1994.

Fleming, Donald Harnish. *William H. Welch and the Rise of Modern Medicine*. Boston, Mass.: Little, Brown, 1954.

Fosdick, R. *The Story of the Rockefeller Foundation*. New York: Harper, 1952.

Fraenkel, Richard M., Don F. Hadwiger, and William P. Browne, eds. *The Role of U.S. Agriculture in Foreign Policy*. New York: Praeger, 1979.

Fraser, Steve, and Gary Gerstle, eds. *The Rise and Fall of the New Deal Order, 1930–1980*. Princeton, N.J.: Princeton Univ. Press, 1989.

Fuentes, Annette, and Barbara Ehrenreich. *Women in the Global Factory*. Boston, Mass.: South End, 1983.

Furner, Mary O. *Advocacy and Objectivity: A Crisis in the Professionalization of American Social Science, 1865–1905*. Lexington: Univ. Press of Kentucky for the Organization of American Historians, 1975.

——, and Barry Supple, eds. *The State and Economic Knowledge: The American and British Experience*. New York: Cambridge Univ. Press, 1990.

Galbraith, John Kenneth. *The Great Crash, 1929*. Boston, Mass.: Houghton Mifflin, 1988.

Gardner, Lloyd C. *Economic Aspects of New Deal Diplomacy*. Madison: Univ. of Wisconsin Press, 1964.

Gardner, Richard N. *Sterling-Dollar Diplomacy: Anglo-American Collaboration in the Reconstruction of Multilateral Trade*. Oxford, UK: Clarendon, 1956.

Garraty, John A. *The Great Depression*. New York: Doubleday, 1987.

Garrett, Laurie. *Betrayal of Trust: The Collapse of Global Public Health*. New York: Hyperion, 2000.

Garrison, Fielding H. *An Introduction to the History of Medicine*. 4th revised edition. Philadelphia, Pa.: W. B. Saunders, 1929.

Garst, Rachel, and Tom Barry. *Feeding the Crisis: U.S. Food Aid and Farm Policy in Central America*. Lincoln: Univ. of Nebraska Press, 1990.

Gear, H. S., and Z. Deutschman. *Disease Control and International Travel: A Review of the International Sanitary Regulations*. Geneva: WHO, 1956.

Gee, Wilson. *American Farm Policy*. New York: Norton, 1934.

Geertz, Clifford. *Local Knowledge: Further Essays in Interpretative Anthropology*. New York: Basic, 1983.

Geison, Gerald L., ed. *Professions and the French State, 1700–1900*. Philadelphia: Univ. of Pennsylvania Press, 1984.

George, Susan. *Ill Fares the Land: Essays on Food, Hunger, and Power*. Washington, D.C.: Institute for Policy Studies, 1984.

——. *How the Other Half Dies: The Real Reasons for World Hunger*. Montclair, N.J.: Allanheld, Osmun, 1977.

George, Susan, and Fabrizio Sabelli. *Faith and Credit: The World Bank's Secular Empire*. Boulder, Colo.: Westview, 1994.

Ghai, Dharam, ed. *Development and Environment: Sustaining People and Nature*. Oxford, UK: Blackwell for the United Nations Research Institute for Social Development, 1994.

Ghosh, U. N. *The Food Problem in Peace & War in India.* Lahore, India: Minerva, 1943.

Giglio, James N. *The Presidency of John F. Kennedy.* Lawrence: Univ. of Kansas Press, 1991.

Gibbons, David S. *The Grameen Reader: Training Materials for the International Replication of the Grameen Bank Financial System for Reduction of Rural Poverty.* Bangladesh: Grameen Bank, 1992.

Gold, Bela. *Wartime Economic Planning in Agriculture: A Study in the Allocation of Resources.* New York: Columbia Univ. Press, 1949.

Gong, Gerrit W. *The Standard of "Civilization" in International Society.* Oxford, UK: Oxford Univ. Press, 1984.

Good, Charles M. *The Steamer Parish: The Rise and Fall of Missionary Medicine on an African Frontier.* Chicago, Ill.: Univ. of Chicago Press, 2004.

Goodman, Neville M. *International Health Organizations and Their Work.* London: J. and A. Churchill, 1952.

Grabill, James. *Protestant Diplomacy and the Near East: Missionary Influence on American Policy, 1810–1927.* Minneapolis: Univ. of Minnesota Press, 1971.

Graham, Bettie J. *Malaria Eradication/Control Programs in Sub-Sahara Africa: Previous Programs and Factors Which Influence Successful Programs.* Bethesda, Md.: National Institutes of Health, Aug. 1979.

Gramsci, Antonio. *Gramsci's Prison Letters/Lettere dal Carcere.* Translated and introduction by Hamish Henderson. London: Zwan, 1988.

Gruchy, Allan G. *Modern Economic Thought: The American Contribution.* New York: Prentice Hall, 1947.

Gustafsson, Mervi. *Food Aid in International Relations: The Case of the United States.* Tampere, Fin.: Peace Research Institute, 1977.

Gwin, Catherine. *U.S. Relations with the World Bank, 1945–92.* Brookings Occasional Papers. Washington, D.C.: Brookings Institution, 1994.

Haas, Ernst. *Beyond the Nation State: Functionalism and International Organization.* Stanford, Calif.: Stanford Univ. Press, 1964.

Haber, Samuel. *The Quest for Authority and Honor in the American Professions, 1750–1900.* Chicago, Ill.: Univ. of Chicago Press, 1991.

——. *Efficiency and Uplift: Scientific Management in the Progressive Era, 1890–1920.* Chicago, Ill.: Univ. of Chicago Press, 1964.

Habicht, Jean-Pierre, and William P. Butz. *Measurement of Health and Nutrition Effects of Large-Scale Nutrition Intervention Projects.* Santa Monica, Calif.: RAND, October 1980.

Hackney, Sheldon. *Populism to Progressivism in Alabama.* Princeton, N.J.: Princeton Univ. Press, 1969.

Hahn, Peter L. *The United States, Great Britain, and Egypt, 1945–1956: Strategy and Diplomacy in the Early Cold War.* Chapel Hill: Univ. of North Carolina Press, 1991.

Haller, John S., Jr. *Medical Protestants: The Eclectics in American Medicine, 1825–1939.* Carbondale: Southern Illinois Univ. Press, 1994.

Hancock, Graham. *Lords of Poverty: The Power, Prestige, and Corruption of the International Aid Business.* New York: Atlantic Monthly, 1989.

Harden, Victoria A. *Inventing the NIH: Federal Biomedical Research Policy, 1887–1937.* Baltimore, Md.: John Hopkins Univ. Press, 1986.

Harrod, Roy F. *The Life of John Maynard Keynes.* New York: Harcourt, Brace, 1951.

Harvey, A. McGehee. *Science at the Bedside: Clinical Research in American Medicine, 1905–1945.* Baltimore, Md.: Johns Hopkins Univ. Press, 1981.

Hawley, Ellis W. *The Great War and the Search for a Modern Order: A History of the American People and Their Institutions, 1917–1933.* New York: St. Martin's, 1979.

———. *The New Deal and the Problem of Monopoly.* Princeton, N.J.: Princeton Univ. Press, 1966.

———, ed. *Herbert Hoover as Secretary of Commerce, 1921–1928: Studies in New Era Thought and Practice.* Iowa City: Univ. of Iowa Press, 1981.

Hayami, Yujiro, and Vernon W. Ruttan. *Agricultural Development: An International Perspective.* Baltimore, Md.: Johns Hopkins Univ. Press, 1971.

Hayes, E. P. *Activities of the President's Emergency Committee for Employment.* Concord, N.H.: Rumford, 1936.

Hayes, Herbert Kendall. *A Professor's Study of Hybrid Corn Makers: Prophets of Plenty.* New Brunswick, N.J.: Rutgers Univ. Press, 1947.

Hays, Samuel P. *The Response to Industrialism, 1885–1914.* 2d edition. Chicago, Ill.: Univ. of Chicago Press, 1995.

———. *Conservation and the Gospel of Efficiency: The Progressive Conservation Movement, 1890–1920.* Cambridge, Mass.: Harvard Univ. Press, 1959.

Heintz, F. J., Jr. *Regionalism in International Political Organizations.* Washington, D.C.: Catholic Univ. Press, 1953.

Heiss, Mary Ann. *Empire and Nationhood: The United States, Great Britain, and Iranian Oil, 1950–1954.* New York: Columbia Univ. Press, 1997.

Henderson, Willie, Tony Dudley-Evans, and Roger Backhouse, eds. *Economics and Language.* London: Routledge, 1993.

Henkin, Harmon, Martin Merta, and James Staples. *The Environment, the Establishment, and the Law.* Boston, Mass.: Houghton Mifflin, 1971.

Hervé, Gustave. *L'Internationalisme.* Paris: V. Giard and E. Brière, 1910.

Hickman, C. Addison. *Our Farm Program and Foreign Trade: A Conflict of National Policies.* New York: Council on Foreign Relations, 1949.

Hildreth, Martha L. *Doctors, Bureaucrats, and Public Health in France, 1888–1902.* New York: Garland, 1987.

Hill, Patricia. *The World Their Household: The American Women's Foreign Mission Movement and Cultural Transformation, 1870–1920.* Ann Arbor: Univ. of Michigan Press, 1985.

Himmelberg, Robert F. *The Origins of the National Recovery Administration: Business, Government, and the Trade Association Issue, 1921–1933.* New York: Fordham Univ. Press, 1976.

Hoff, Joan. *Herbert Hoover: Forgotten Progressive.* Boston, Mass.: Little, Brown, 1975.

Hoffman, Elizabeth Cobbs. *All You Need Is Love: The Peace Corps and the Spirit of the 1960s.* Cambridge, Mass.: Harvard Univ. Press, 1998.

Hogan, Michael J. *The Marshall Plan: America, Britain, and the Reconstruction of Europe, 1947–1952.* New York: Cambridge Univ. Press, 1987.

———. *A Cross of Iron: Harry S. Truman and the Origins of the National Security State, 1945–1954.* New York: Cambridge Univ. Press, 1998.

———. *Informal Entente: The Private Structure of Cooperation in Anglo-American Economic Diplomacy, 1918–1929.* Columbia: Univ. of Missouri Press, 1977; revised edition, Chicago, Ill.: Imprint, 1991.

———, ed. *The End of the Cold War: Its Meanings and Implications.* Cambridge, UK: Cambridge Univ. Press, 1992.

Hoole, Francis W. *Politics and Budgeting in the World Health Organization.* Bloomington: Indiana Univ. Press, 1976.

Howard-Jones, Norman. *The Scientific Background of the International Sanitary Conferences, 1851–1938.* Geneva: WHO, 1975.

———. *International Public Health between the Two World Wars: The Organizational Problems.* Geneva: WHO, 1978.

———. *The Pan American Health Organization: Origins and Evolution.* Geneva: WHO, 1981.

Hunt, Michael H. *Frontier Defense and the Open Door: Manchuria in Chinese-American Relations, 1895–1911.* New Haven, Conn.: Yale Univ. Press, 1973.

———. *Ideology and U.S. Foreign Policy.* New Haven, Conn.: Yale Univ. Press, 1987.

Hunter, Jane. *The Gospel of Gentility: American Women Missionaries in Turn-of-the-Century China.* New Haven, Conn.: Yale Univ. Press, 1984.

Iriye, Akira. *Cultural Internationalism and World Order.* Baltimore, Md.: Johns Hopkins Univ. Press, 1997.

———. *Global Community: The Role of International Organizations in the Making of the Contemporary World.* Berkeley: Univ. of California Press, 2002.

Irons, Peter H. *The New Deal Lawyers.* Princeton, N.J.: Princeton Univ. Press, 1982.

Isaacson, Walter, and Evan Thomas. *The Wise Men: Six Friends and the World They Made: Acheson, Bohlen, Harriman, Kennan, Lovett, McCloy.* New York: Simon and Schuster, 1986.

Jacobson, Timothy C. *Making Medical Doctors: Science and Medicine at Vanderbilt since Flexner.* Tuscaloosa: Univ. of Alabama Press, 1987.

Jensen, Einar. *Danish Agriculture, Its Economic Development: A Description and Economic Analysis Centering on the Free Trade Epoch, 1870–1930.* Copenhagen: J. H. Schultz Forlag, 1937.

Johnson, D. Gale, and John A. Schnittker, eds. *U.S. Agriculture in a World Context: Policies and Approaches for the Next Decade.* New York: Praeger for the Atlantic Council of the United States, 1974.

Johnson, Donald P. *Malaria Eradication: What It Has Achieved.* N.p., 1969.

Johnson, James A., and Walter J. Jones. *The American Medical Association and Organized Medicine: A Commentary and Annotated Bibliography.* New York: Garland, 1993.

Jonas, Steven. *Medical Mystery: The Training of Doctors in the United States.* New York: Norton, 1978.

Jordan, Robert S., ed. *Multinational Cooperation: Economic, Social, and Scientific Development.* New York: Oxford Univ. Press, 1972.

Josephson, Harold. *James T. Shotwell and the Rise of Internationalism in America.* Rutherford, N.J.: Fairleigh Dickinson Univ. Press, 1975.

Kadish, Alon. *Historians, Economists, and Economic History.* London: Routledge, 1989.

Käkönen, Jyrki. *The World Bank: A Bridgehead of Imperialism.* Tampere, Fin.: Peace Research Institute, 1975.

Kaltefleiter, Werner, and Robert L. Pfaltzgraff Jr. *The Peace Movement in Europe and the United States.* London: Croom Helm, 1985.

Kapur, Devesh, John P. Lewis, and Richard Webb. *The World Bank: Its First Half Century.* Vol. 1: *History.* Washington, D.C.: Brookings, 1997.

Kapur, Sudarshan. *Raising Up a Prophet: The African-American Encounter with Gandhi.* Boston, Mass.: Beacon, 1992.

Katouzian, Homa. *Musaddiq and the Struggle for Power in Iran*. London: I. B. Tauris, 1990.

———. *The Political Economy of Modern Iran: Despotism and Pseudo-Modernism, 1926–1979*. New York: New York Univ. Press, 1981.

Kaufman, Burton I. *Trade and Aid: Eisenhower's Foreign Economic Policy, 1953–1961*. Baltimore, Md.: Johns Hopkins Univ. Press, 1982.

Kaufman, Martin. *Homeopathy in America: The Rise and Fall of a Medical Heresy*. Baltimore, Md.: Johns Hopkins Univ. Press, 1971.

Keeny, S. M. *Half the World's Children: A Diary of UNICEF at Work in Asia*. New York: Association Press, 1957.

Kennedy, David M. *Over Here: The First World War and American Society*. Oxford, UK: Oxford Univ. Press, 1980.

Keuhl, Warren F. *Seeking World Order: The United States and International Organization to 1920*. Nashville, Tenn.: Vanderbilt Univ. Press, 1969.

Keynes, John Maynard. *Essays in Biography*. London: Macmillan, 1933.

King, Lester S. *Transformations in American Medicine: From Benjamin Rush to William Osler*. Baltimore, Md.: Johns Hopkins Univ. Press, 1991.

———. *The Growth of Medical Thought*. Chicago, Ill.: Univ. of Chicago Press, 1963.

Kirkendall, Richard S. *Social Scientists and Farm Politics in the Age of Roosevelt*. Columbia: Univ. of Missouri Press, 1966.

Kloppenberg, James T. *Uncertain Victory: Social Democracy and Progressivism in European and American Thought, 1870–1920*. New York: Oxford Univ. Press, 1986.

Knock, Thomas J. *To End All Wars: Woodrow Wilson and the Quest for a New World Order*. Princeton, N.J.: Princeton Univ. Press, 1995.

Kohl, Erwin. *Medical Mission to Austria: July 1–August 8, 1947*. Boston, Mass.: Unitarian Service Committee, 1947.

Kolko, Gabriel. *The Triumph of Conservatism: A Reinterpretation of American History, 1900–1916*. New York: Free Press, 1963.

———. *Confronting the Third World: United States Foreign Policy, 1945–1980*. New York: Pantheon, 1988.

Kolko, Joyce. *Restructuring the World Economy*. New York: Pantheon, 1988.

Kraske, Jochen, with William H. Becker, William Diamond, and Louis Galambos. *Bankers with a Mission: The Presidents of the World Bank, 1946–91*. Oxford, UK: Oxford Univ. Press for the World Bank, 1996.

Kremers, Edward, and George Urdang. *History of Pharmacy: A Guide and a Survey*. 2d revised edition. Philadelphia, Pa.: Lippincott, 1951.

Kuhnke, LaVerne. *Lives at Risk: Public Health in Nineteenth-Century Egypt*. Berkeley: Univ. of California Press, 1990.

Kuisel, Richard. *Seducing the French: The Dilemma of Americanization*. Berkeley: Univ. of California Press, 1993.

Kunz, Diane B. *The Battle for Britain's Gold Standard in 1931*. London: Croom Helm, 1987.

———. *The Economic Diplomacy of the Suez Crisis*. Chapel Hill: Univ. of North Carolina Press, 1991.

Kurlansky, Mark. *Cod: A Biography of the Fish That Changed the World*. New York: Walker, 1997.

Kux, Dennis. *India and the United States: Estranged Democracies, 1941–1991*. Washington, D.C.: National Defense Univ. Press, 1992.

Kyle, Keith. *Suez*. New York: St. Martin's, 1991.

Lacey, Michael J., and Mary O. Furner, eds. *The State and Social Investigation in Britain and the United States*. Washington, D.C.: Woodrow Wilson Center, 1993.

LaFeber, Walter. *The New Empire: An Interpretation of American Expansionism, 1860–1898*. Ithaca, N.Y.: Cornell Univ. Press, 1963.

———. *America, Russia, and the Cold War, 1945–1992*. 7th edition. New York: McGraw-Hill, 1993.

———, ed. *John Quincy Adams and American Continental Empire: Letters, Papers and Speeches*. Chicago, Ill.: Quadrangle, 1965.

Langley, Lester D., and Thomas Schoonover. *The Banana Men: American Mercenaries and Entrepreneurs in Central America, 1880–1930*. Lexington: Univ. Press of Kentucky, 1995.

Lappé, Frances Moore, Joseph Collins, and David Kinley. *Aid as Obstacle: Twenty Questions about Our Foreign Aid and the Hungry*. San Francisco, Calif.: Institute for Food and Development Policy, 1980.

Larsen, Egon. *A Flame in Barbed Wire: The Story of Amnesty International*. London: F. Muller, 1978.

Lears, T. J. Jackson. *No Place of Grace: Antimodernism and the Transformation of American Culture, 1880–1920*. Chicago, Ill.: Univ. of Chicago Press, 1981.

Leff, S., and Vera Leff. *From Witchcraft to World Health*. New York: Macmillan, 1958.

Leffler, Melvyn P. *A Preponderance of Power: National Security, the Truman Administration, and the Cold War*. Stanford, Calif.: Stanford Univ. Press, 1992.

Lesch, John E. *Science and Medicine in France: The Emergence of Experimental Physiology, 1790–1855*. Cambridge, Mass.: Harvard Univ. Press, 1984.

Leys, Colin. *The Rise and Fall of Development Theory*. Bloomington: Indiana Univ. Press, 1996.

Little, Ernest Muirhead. *History of the British Medical Association, 1832–1932*. London: British Medical Association, 1932.

Livingston, James. *Origins of the Federal Reserve System: Money, Class, and Corporate Capitalism, 1890–1913*. Ithaca, N.Y.: Cornell Univ. Press, 1986.

Longobardi, Cesare. *International Collaboration in Agriculture*. Rome: Villa Umberto I, 1946.

Louis, William Roger, and Roger Owen, eds. *Suez 1956: The Crisis and Its Consequences*. Oxford, UK: Clarendon, 1989.

Lowitt, Richard. *The New Deal and the West*. Norman: Univ. of Oklahoma Press, 1993.

Lubbock, David. *The Boyd Orr View: From the Old World to the New, with Proposal for Action to Banish Hunger: The Late Lord Boyd Orr's Testament*. Privately published, 1992.

Lucas, W. Scott. *Divided We Stand: Britain, the US and the Suez Crisis*. London: Hodder and Stoughton, 1991.

Lydenberg, Harry Miller. *John Shaw Billings: Creator of the National Medical Library and Its Catalogue*. Chicago, Ill.: American Library Association, 1924.

Lynn, Kenneth S., ed. *The Professions in America*. Boston, Mass.: Beacon, 1963.

Lyons, H. L. S. *Internationalism in Europe, 1815–1914*. Leiden, Neth.: A.W. Sijthoff, 1963.

MacDowell, C. L. *Two Ears of Corn, by Way of the Chemical Kettle: The Life Story of Charles L. MacDowell*. Stonington, Conn.: Pequot, 1954.

Mackenzie, Donald A. *Statistics in Britain, 1865–1930: The Social Construction of Scientific Knowledge*. Edinburgh, UK: Edinburgh Univ. Press, 1981.

Maier, Charles S. *Recasting Bourgeois Europe: Stabilization in France, Germany, and Italy in the Decade after World War I*. Princeton, N.J.: Princeton Univ. Press, 1975.

Malay, Armando, Jr. *P.L. 480: How the U.S. Exports Its Agricultural Crisis to the Third World.* Quezon City, Philippines: Third World Studies, Dec. 1979.

Maloney, John. *Marshall, Orthodoxy and the Professionalisation of Economics.* Cambridge, UK: Cambridge Univ. Press, 1985.

Marchisio, Sergio, and Antonietta di Blase. *The Food and Agriculture Organization (FAO).* International Organization and the Evolution of World Society Series. Dordrecht, Neth.: M. Nijhoff, 1991.

Markham, Jesse W. *The Fertilizer Industry.* Nashville, Tenn.: Vanderbilt Univ. Press, 1958.

Martin, Oscar B. *The Demonstration Work: Dr. Seaman A. Knapp's Contribution to Civilization.* San Antonio, Tex.: Naylor, 1941.

Mason, Edward S., and Robert E. Asher. *The World Bank since Bretton Woods: The Origins, Policies, Operations, and Impact of the International Bank for Reconstruction and Development and the Other Members of the World Bank Group.* Washington, D.C.: Brookings Institution, 1973.

May, Irvin M., Jr. *Marvin Jones: The Public Life of an Agrarian Advocate.* College Station: Texas A&M Univ. Press, 1980.

McClure, Wallace. *World Prosperity, as Sought through the Economic Work of the League of Nations.* New York: Macmillan, 1933.

McConnell, Grant. *The Decline of Agrarian Democracy.* Berkeley: Univ. of California Press, 1953.

McConnell, John W. *Ideas of the Great Economists.* 2d edition. New York: Harper and Row, 1980.

McCormick, John. *Reclaiming Paradise: The Global Environmental Movement.* Bloomington: Indiana Univ. Press, 1989.

McCormick, Thomas. *China Market: America's Quest for Informal Empire, 1893–1901.* Chicago, Ill.: Quadrangle, 1967.

McLellan, David S., and Donald Clare. *Public Law 480: The Metamorphosis of a Law.* Eagleton Institute Studies in Practical Politics, no. 36. New York: McGraw-Hill, 1965.

McMahon, Robert J. *Colonialism and Cold War: The United States and the Struggle for Indonesian Independence, 1945–49.* Ithaca, N.Y.: Cornell Univ. Press, 1981.

Mead, Pauline A. *The Rockefeller Foundation Operations and Research in the Control and Eradication of Malaria.* N.p., 1955.

Meckel, Richard A. *Save the Babies: American Public Health Reform and the Prevention of Infant Mortality, 1850–1929.* Baltimore, Md.: Johns Hopkins Univ. Press, 1990.

Mellanby, Kenneth. *The DDT Story.* Farnham, UK: British Crop Protection Council, 1992.

Mellor, John W. *The Economics of Agricultural Development.* Ithaca, N.Y.: Cornell Univ. Press, 1966.

Menzie, Elmer L., and Robert G. Crouch. *Political Interests in Agricultural Export Surplus Disposal through Public Law 480.* Technical Bulletin 161. Tucson: Univ. of Arizona Experiment Station, Sept. 1964.

Mies, Maria. *Patriarchy and Accumulation on a World Scale: Women in the International Division of Labour.* London: Zed, 1986.

Millett, Allan R. *Military Professionalism and Officership in America.* Mershon Center Briefing Paper 2. Columbus: Mershon Center of the Ohio State Univ., 1977.

Mink, Stephen D. *Poverty, Population, and the Environment.* World Bank Discussion Papers. Washington, D.C.: World Bank, 1992.

Moggridge, D. E. *The Return to Gold 1925: The Formulation of Economic Policy and Its Crit-ics.* University of Cambridge Department of Applied Economics Occasional Paper 19. Cambridge, UK: Cambridge Univ. Press, 1969.

———. *Keynes.* London: Macmillan, 1976.

Moldow, Gloria. *Women Doctors in Gilded-Age Washington, D.C.: Race, Gender, and Profes-sionalization.* Urbana: Univ. of Illinois Press, 1987.

Moll, Aristides A. *The Pan American Sanitary Bureau: Its Origin, Development and Achieve-ments.* Washington, D.C.: Pan American Sanitary Bureau, Dec. 1948.

Morais, Herbert M. *The History of the Negro in Medicine.* New York: Publishers Company, 1967.

Morgenthau, Henry III. *Mostly Morgenthaus: A Family History.* New York: Ticknor and Fields, 1991.

Mowry, George E. *The California Progressives.* Berkeley: Univ. of California Press, 1951.

Narasimham, M.V. V. L. *National Malaria Eradication Program.* New Delhi: National Insti-tute of Health and Family Welfare, 1988.

Newman, Charles. *The Evolution of Medical Education in the Nineteenth Century.* London: Oxford Univ. Press, 1957.

Newman, Peter. *Malaria Eradication and Population Growth, with Special Reference to Cey-lon and British Guiana.* Bureau of Public Health Economics Research Series, no. 10. Ann Arbor: Univ. of Michigan School of Public Health, 1965.

Nourse, Edwin G. *Government in Relation to Agriculture.* Washington, D.C.: Brookings In-stitution, 1940.

Nuland, Sherwin B. *Doctors: A Biography of Medicine.* New York: Knopf, 1988.

O'Brien, D. P., and John R. Presley, eds. *Pioneers of Modern Economics in Britain.* London: Macmillan, 1981.

O'Neill, William L. *The Progressive Years: America Comes of Age.* New York: Harper and Row, 1975.

Onimode, Bade, ed. *The IMF, the World Bank and the African Debt.* Vol. 1: *The Economic Impact.* London: Zed and the Institute for African Alternatives, 1989.

Oncu, Ayse, and Petra Weyland, eds. *Space, Culture and Power: New Identities in Globalizing Cities.* London: Zed, 1997.

Orwin, Christabel S., and Edith H. Whetham. *History of British Agriculture, 1846–1914.* Newton Abbot, UK: David and Charles, 1971.

Osakwe, Chris. *The Participation of the Soviet Union in Universal International Organi-zations: A Political and Legal Analysis of Soviet Strategies and Aspirations inside ILO, UNESCO and WHO.* Leiden, Neth.: A. W. Sijthoff, 1972.

Paarlberg, Don. *American Farm Policy: A Case Study of Centralized Decision-Making.* New York: John Wiley, 1964.

Pach, Chester J., Jr. *Arming the Free World: The Origins of the United States Military Assis-tance Program, 1945–1950.* Chapel Hill: Univ. of North Carolina Press, 1991.

Packard, Francis R. *History of Medicine in the United States.* Vol. 2. New York: Paul B. Hoe-ber, 1931.

Palmer, Bryan D. *Descent into Discourse: The Reification of Language and the Writing of Social History.* Philadelphia, Pa.: Temple Univ. Press, 1990.

Parry, Noel, and José Parry. *The Rise of the Medical Profession: A Study of Collective Social Mobility.* London: Croom Helm, 1976.

Pattullo, Polly. *Last Resorts: The Cost of Tourism in the Caribbean.* New York: Monthly Review, 1998.

Paul, Harry W. *From Knowledge to Power: The Rise of the Science Empire in France, 1860–1939.* Cambridge, UK: Cambridge Univ. Press, 1985.

Perkin, Harold. *The Rise of Professional Society: England since 1880.* London: Routledge, 1989.

Peterson, M. Jeanne. *The Medical Profession in Mid-Victorian London.* Berkeley: Univ. of California Press, 1978.

Peterson, Trudy Huskamp. *Agricultural Exports, Farm Income, and the Eisenhower Administration.* Lincoln: Univ. of Nebraska Press, 1979.

Pike, Fredrick B. *The United States and Latin America: Myths and Stereotypes of Civilization and Nature.* Austin: Univ. of Texas Press, 1992.

Pimbert, Michel P., and Tom Wakeford. *Prajateerpu: A Citizens Jury/Scenario Workshop on Food and Farming Futures for Andhra Pradesh, India.* London: International Institute for Environment and Development and Institute for Development Studies, 2002.

Popkin, Charles W. *The Interchange of Public Health Personnel under the Health Organisation of the League of Nations: A Study in the Creation of an International Standard of Public Health Administration.* Geneva: League of Nations Non-Partisan Association, 1928.

Porter, Gareth, and Janet Welsh Brown. *Global Environmental Politics.* Boulder, Colo.: Westview, 1991.

Poynter, F. N. L., ed. *Medicine and Science in the 1860s.* London: Wellcome Institute for the History of Medicine, 1968.

Prasad, Devki Nandan. *Food For Peace: U.S. Food Assistance to India.* New York: Apt, 1982.

Pratt, Edwin A. *Agricultural Organisation: Its Rise, Principles and Practice Abroad and at Home.* London: P. S. King, 1912.

Purcell, Randall B., and Elizabeth Morrison, eds. *U.S. Agriculture & Third World Development: The Critical Linkage.* Boulder, Colo: Lynne Rienner, 1987.

Pusey, Merlo J. *Eugene Meyer.* New York: Knopf, 1974.

Quandt, Jean B. *From the Small Town to the Great Community: The Social Thought of Progressive Intellectuals.* New Brunswick, N.J.: Rutgers Univ. Press, 1970.

Rahnema, Majid, and Victoria Bawtree, eds. *The Post-Development Reader.* London: Zed, 1997.

Rayack, Elton. *Professional Power and American Medicine: The Economics of the American Medical Association.* Cleveland, Ohio: World, 1967.

Reader, W. J. *Professional Men: The Rise of the Professional Classes in Nineteenth-Century England.* London: Weidenfeld and Nicolson, 1966.

Rees, David. *Harry Dexter White: A Study in Paradox.* New York: Coward, McCann, and Geoghegan, 1973.

Reische, Diana L., ed. *U.S. Agricultural Policy.* New York: H. H. Wilson, 1966.

Reiser, Stanley Joel. *Medicine and the Reign of Technology.* Cambridge, UK: Cambridge Univ. Press, 1978.

Rich, Bruce. *Mortgaging the Earth: The World Bank, Environmental Impoverishment, and the Crisis of Development.* Boston, Mass.: Beacon, 1994.

Rist, Gilbert. *The History of Development: From Western Origins to Global Faith.* Revised edition. Translated by Patrick Camiller. London: Zed, 2002.

Roberts, Richard, and David Kynaston, eds. *The Bank of England: Money, Power and Influence, 1694–1994.* Oxford, UK: Clarendon, 1995.

The Rockefeller Foundation Operations and Research in the Control and Eradication of Malaria. New York: Rockefeller Foundation, 10 Oct. 1955.

Romero, Federico. *The United States and the European Trade Union Movement, 1944–1951.* Translated by Harvey Fergusson II. Chapel Hill: Univ. of North Carolina Press, 1992.

Rosen, George. *A History of Public Health.* New York: MD, 1958; expanded edition, Baltimore, Md.: Johns Hopkins Univ. Press, 1993.

Rosenberg, Charles E. *No Other Gods: On Science and American Social Thought.* Revised and expanded edition. Baltimore, Md.: Johns Hopkins Univ. Press, 1997.

Rosenberg, Emily S. *Spreading the American Dream: American Economic and Cultural Expansion, 1898–1945.* New York: Hill and Wang, 1982.

Rothstein, William G. *American Physicians in the Nineteenth Century: From Sects to Science.* Baltimore, Md.: Johns Hopkins Univ. Press, 1972.

Rupp, Leila J. *Worlds of Women: The Making of an International Women's Movement.* Princeton, N.J.: Princeton Univ. Press, 1997.

Ruttan, Vernon W., ed. *Why Food Aid?* Baltimore, Md.: Johns Hopkins Univ. Press, 1993.

Rydell, Robert. *All the World's a Fair: Visions of Empire at American International Expositions, 1876–1916.* Chicago, Ill.: Univ. of Chicago Press, 1984.

Sachs, Jeffrey D., ed. *Developing Country Debt and the World Economy.* Chicago, Ill.: Univ. of Chicago Press for the National Bureau of Economic Research, 1989.

Sachs, Wolfgang, ed. *Global Ecology: A New Arena of Political Conflict.* London: Zed, 1993.

Sandilands, Roger J. *The Life and Political Economy of Lauchlin Currie: New Dealer, Presidential Adviser, and Development Economist.* Durham, N.C.: Duke Univ. Press, 1990.

Sarup, Madan. *An Introductory Guide to Post-Structuralism and Postmodernism.* 2d edition. Athens: Univ. of Georgia Press, 1993.

Schaeper, Thomas J., and Kathleen Schaeper. *Cowboys into Gentlemen: Rhodes Scholars, Oxford, and the Creation of an American Elite.* Providence, R.I.: Berghahn, 1998.

Schapsmeier, Edward L., and Frederick H. Schapsmeier. *Encyclopedia of American Agricultural History.* Westport, Conn.: Greenwood, 1975.

Schepin, Oleg P., and Waldemar V. Yermakov. *International Quarantine.* Translated by Boris Meerovich and Vladimir Bobrov. Madison, Conn.: International Universities Press, 1991.

Schickele, Rainer. *Agricultural Policy: Farm Programs and National Welfare.* New York: McGraw-Hill, 1954.

Schild, Georg. *Bretton Woods and Dumbarton Oaks: American Economic and Political Postwar Planning in the Summer of 1944.* New York: St. Martin's, 1995.

Schlebecker, John T. *Whereby We Thrive: A History of American Farming, 1607 to 1972.* Ames: Iowa State Univ. Press, 1975.

Schlesinger, Arthur M., Jr. *The Coming of the New Deal: The Age of Roosevelt.* Boston, Mass.: Houghton Mifflin, 1958.

———. *A Thousand Days: John F. Kennedy in the White House.* Boston, Mass.: Houghton Mifflin, 1965.

Schuker, Stephen A. *The End of French Predominance in Europe: The Financial Crisis of 1924 and the Adoption of the Dawes Plan.* Chapel Hill: Univ. of North Carolina Press, 1976.

Schwartz, Thomas Alan. *America's Germany: John J. McCloy and the Federal Republic of Germany.* Cambridge, Mass.: Harvard Univ. Press, 1991.

Sen, Amartya. *Development as Freedom.* New York: Anchor, 1999.

Sen, Gita, and Caren Grown. *Development, Crises, and Alternative Visions: Third World Women's Perspectives.* New York: Monthly Review, 1987.

Shalpen, Robert. *Toward the Well-Being of Mankind: Fifty Years of the Rockefeller Foundation.* New York: Doubleday, 1964.

Shapley, Deborah. *Promise and Power: The Life and Times of Robert McNamara.* Boston, Mass.: Little, Brown, 1993.

Sharp, Walter. *International Technical Assistance: Programs and Organization.* Chicago, Ill.: Public Administration Service, 1952.

Shefrin, Frank, and Howard Trueman. *Canada and FAO.* Ottawa: Canadian Department of Agriculture, 1971.

Shideler, James H. *Farm Crisis, 1919–1923.* Berkeley: Univ. of California Press, 1957.

Shryock, Richard Harrison. *The Development of Modern Medicine: An Interpretation of the Social and Scientific Factors Involved.* New York: Knopf, 1936, 1947.

———. *Medical Licensing in America, 1650–1965.* Baltimore, Md.: Johns Hopkins Univ. Press, 1967.

———. *The Unique Influence of the Johns Hopkins University in American Medicine.* Copenhagen: Munksgaard, 1953.

Siddiqi, Javed. *World Health and World Politics: The World Health Organization and the UN System.* Columbia: Univ. of South Carolina Press, 1995.

Sklair, Leslie. *Sociology of the Global System.* 2d edition, revised and updated. Baltimore, Md.: Johns Hopkins Univ. Press, 1995.

Sklar, Martin J. *The Corporate Reconstruction of American Capitalism, 1890–1916: The Market, the Law, and Politics.* Cambridge, UK: Cambridge Univ. Press, 1988.

Smillie, Wilson G. *Studies on Hookworm Infection in Brazil: 1918–1920.* New York: Rockefeller Institution for Medical Research, 1922.

———. *Public Health, Its Promise for the Future: A Chronology of the Development of Public Health in the United States, 1607–1914.* New York: Macmillan, 1955.

Souchon, A. *Agricultural Societies in France.* Paris: Évreux for Exposition Universelle de San Francisco, 1915.

Sprague, George F., ed. *Corn and Corn Improvement.* New York: Academic, 1955.

Stabile, Donald. *Prophets of Order.* Boston, Mass.: South End, 1984.

Stanley, Robert G. *Food for Peace: Hope and Reality of U.S. Food Aid.* New York: Gordon and Breach, 1973.

Starr, Paul. *The Social Transformation of American Medicine.* New York: Basic, 1982.

Staudt, Kathleen, ed. *Women, International Development, and Politics: The Bureaucratic Mire.* Philadelphia, Pa.: Temple Univ. Press, 1990.

Stienstra, Deborah. *Women's Movements and International Organizations.* New York: St. Martin's, 1994.

Stichter, Sharon, and Jane L. Parpart, eds. *Women, Employment and the Family in the International Division of Labour.* Women in the Political Economy Series, edited by Ronnie J. Steinberg. Philadelphia, Pa.: Temple Univ. Press, 1990.

Strode, G. *Yellow Fever.* New York: McGraw-Hill, 1951.

Sullivan, Denis J. *Private Voluntary Organizations in Egypt: Islamic Development, Private Initiative, and State Control.* Gainesville: Univ. Press of Florida, 1994.

Surface, Frank M., and Raymond L. Bland. *American Food Aid in the World War and Reconstruction Period.* Stanford, Calif.: Stanford Univ. Press, 1931.

Susskind, Lawrence. *Environmental Diplomacy: Negotiating More Effective International Agreements.* New York: Oxford Univ. Press, 1994.

Tabibzadeh, I., and A. Mossadegh. *Study of Malaria Control and Eradication in Iran Up to 1971.* N.p., 1971.

Taylor, Henry C., and Ann Dewees Taylor. *The Story of Agricultural Economics in the United States, 1840–1932: Men, Service, Ideas.* Ames: Iowa State Univ. Press, 1952.

Temkin, Owsei. *The Double Face of Janus and Other Essays in the History of Medicine.* Baltimore, Md.: Johns Hopkins Univ. Press, 1977.

Thompson, Willard. *David Lubin: Sacramento's Pioneer Merchant-Philosopher.* Sacramento, Calif.: Sacramento County Historical Society, 1986.

Tickner, J. Ann. *Gender in International Relations: Feminist Perspectives on Achieving Global Security.* New York: Columbia Univ. Press, 1992.

Toma, Peter A. *The Politics of Food for Peace: Executive-Legislative Interaction.* Tucson: Univ. of Arizona Press, 1967.

Tosi, Luciano. *Alle Origini della FAO: Le relazioni tra l'Instituto Internazionale di Agricoltura e la Società delle Nazioni.* Milan, Italy: Franco Angeli, 1989.

Toward Mankind's Better Heath. UN Study Guide Series, vol. 3. Dobbs Ferry, N.Y.: Oceana, 1963.

Traynor, Dean A. *International Monetary and Financial Conferences in the Interwar Period.* Washington, D.C.: Catholic Univ. of America Press, 1949.

Troen, Selwyn Ilan, and Moshe Shemesh, eds. *The Suez-Sinai Crisis, 1956: Retrospective and Reappraisal.* New York: Columbia Univ. Press, 1990.

Tyrrell, Ian R. *Woman's World, Woman's Empire: The Woman's Christian Temperance Union in International Perspective, 1880–1930.* Chapel Hill: Univ. of North Carolina Press, 1991.

The United States Food for Peace Program, 1954–1984: A Compilation of Informational Materials on United States Public Law 480. Arlington, Va.: International Trade and Development Education Foundation, Spring 1985.

Vallery-Radot, R. *The Life of Pasteur.* Translated R. L. Devonshire. 2 vols. New York: McClure, Philips, 1902.

Van Alstyne, Richard W. *The Rising American Empire.* Oxford, UK: Blackwell, 1960.

Varg, Paul A. *Missionaries, Chinese, and Diplomats: The American Protestant Missionary Movement in China, 1890–1952.* Princeton, N.J.: Princeton Univ. Press, 1958.

Venkataramani, M. S. *Bengal Famine of 1943: The American Response.* Delhi: Vikas, 1973.

Wadham, Samuel. *Australian Farming, 1788–1965.* Melbourne: F. W. Cheshire, 1967.

Wagnleitner, Reinhold. *Coca-Colonization and the Cold War: The Cultural Mission of the United States in Austria after the Second World War.* Translated by Diana M. Wolf. Chapel Hill: Univ. of North Carolina Press, 1994.

Wallerstein, Mitchel B. *Food for War—Food for Peace: United States Aid in a Global Context.* Cambridge, Mass.: MIT Press, 1980.

Walsh, Mary Roth. *"Doctors Wanted—No Women Need Apply": Sexual Barriers in the Medical Profession, 1835–1975.* New Haven, Conn.: Yale Univ. Press, 1975.

Walters, F. P. *A History of the League of Nations.* London: Oxford Univ. Press for the Royal Institute of International Affairs, 1952, 1960.

Ward, Kathryn B. *Women in the World-System: Its Impact on Status and Fertility.* New York: Praeger, 1984.

Waterbury, John. *Hydropolitics in the Nile Valley.* Syracuse, N.Y.: Syracuse Univ. Press, 1979.

Watkins, T. H. *The Great Depression: America in the 1930s.* Boston, Mass.: Little, Brown, 1993.

Watkins, W. P. *The International Co-operative Alliance, 1895–1970.* London: International Co-operative Alliance, 1970.

Weindling, Paul, ed. *International Health Organisations and Movements, 1918–1939.* Cambridge, UK: Cambridge Univ. Press, 1995.

Weinstein, James. *The Corporate Ideal in the Liberal State, 1900–1918.* Boston, Mass.: Beacon, 1969.

Weissman, Steve, and Members of Pacific Studies Center and the North American Congress on Latin America. *The Trojan Horse: A Radical Look at Foreign Aid.* Revised edition. Palo Alto, Calif.: Ramparts, 1975.

Wells, Robert N., Jr., ed. *Peace by Pieces—United Nations Agencies and Their Roles: A Reader and Selective Bibliography.* Metuchen, N.J.: Scarecrow, 1991.

West, T. F., and G. A. Campbell. *DDT and Newer Persistent Insecticides.* 2d edition. New York: Chemical, 1952.

Wheaton, Henry. *Elements of International Law.* 6th edition. Boston, Mass.: Little, Brown, 1906.

White, Hayden. *The Content of the Form: Narrative Discourse and Historical Representation.* Baltimore, Md.: Johns Hopkins Univ. Press, 1987.

White, Richard. *"It's Your Misfortune and None of My Own": A New History of the American West.* Norman: Univ. of Oklahoma Press, 1991.

Wickizer, V. D. *The World Coffee Economy with Special Reference to Control Schemes.* Stanford, Calif.: Food Research Institute, 1943.

Wiebe, Robert H. *The Search for Order, 1877–1920.* New York: Hill and Wang, 1967.

———. *Businessmen and Reform: A Study of the Progressive Movement.* Chicago, Ill.: Quadrangle, 1962, 1968.

Wilkins, Mira. *The Maturing of Multinational Enterprise: American Business Abroad from 1914 to 1970.* Cambridge, Mass.: Harvard Univ. Press, 1974.

Willett, Ralph. *The Americanization of Germany, 1945–1949.* London: Routledge, 1989.

Williams, Greer. *The Plague Killers.* New York: Scribner's, 1967.

Williams, William Appleman. *The Roots of the Modern American Empire: A Study of the Growth and Shaping of Social Consciousness in a Marketplace Society.* New York: Random House, 1969.

———. *The Tragedy of American Diplomacy.* 2d revised and enlarged edition. New York: Dell, 1972.

Wilson, Joan Hoff. *American Business and Foreign Policy, 1920–1933.* Lexington: Univ. Press of Kentucky, 1971.

Wilson, R. Jackson. *In Quest of Community: Social Philosophy in the United States, 1860–1920.* New York: Wiley, 1968.

Winslow, Charles-Edward Amory. *The Conquest of Epidemic Disease: A Chapter in the History of Ideas.* Princeton, N.J.: Princeton Univ. Press, 1943; reprint, Madison: Univ. of Wisconsin Press, 1980.

Wittner, Lawrence S. *The Struggle against the Bomb.* Vol. 1: *One World or None: A History of the World Nuclear Disarmament Movement through 1953.* Vol. 2: *Resisting the Bomb: A History of the World Nuclear Disarmament Movement, 1954–1970.* Stanford, Calif.: Stanford Univ. Press, 1993 and 1997.

Wright, James. *The Progressive Yankees: Republican Reformers in New Hampshire, 1906–1916.* Hanover, N.H.: Univ. Press of New England for Dartmouth College, 1987.

Wynia, Gary W. *Argentina: Illusions and Realities.* New York: Holmes and Meier, 1986.

Yates, P. Lamartine. *Food Production in Western Europe: An Economic Survey of Agriculture in Six Countries.* London: Longmans, Green, 1940.

Yergin, Daniel. *The Prize: The Epic Quest for Oil, Money, and Power.* New York: Simon and Schuster, 1991.

Yohe, Ralph Sandlin. *What Our Farmers Can Learn from Other Lands.* Ames: Iowa State College Press, 1953.

Zachar, George R. *A Political History of Food for Peace.* Cornell Agricultural Economics Staff Paper, no. 77-18. Ithaca, N.Y.: Cornell Univ., May 1977.

Zeiler, Thomas W. *Free Trade, Free World: The Advent of GATT.* Chapel Hill: Univ. of North Carolina Press, 1999.

ARTICLES AND CHAPTERS

Ahmed, Farid. "'Hello, I'm Calling from Parulia . . .'" *Unesco Courier* (July–Aug. 2000): 67–68.

Ainger, Katharine. "The Market and the Monsoon—Part 2: Crops of Truth." *New Internationalist* 353 (Jan.–Feb. 2003). www.newint.org/issue353/part2.htm. Accessed 19 Nov. 2003.

Allen, Charles E. "World Health and World Politics." *International Organization* 4 (Feb. 1950): 27–43.

Anderson, Carol. "From Hope to Disillusion: African Americans, the United Nations, and the Struggle for Human Rights, 1944–1947." *Diplomatic History* 20 (Fall 1996): 531–63.

Anderson, Mary Ann, James E. Austin, Joe D. Wray, and Marian F. Zeitlin. "Supplementary Feeding." In *Nutrition Intervention in Developing Countries,* edited by Harvard Institute for International Development, 25–48. Cambridge, Mass.: Oelgeschlager, Gunn, and Hain, 1981.

Anderson, William G. "Progressivism: An Historiographical Essay." *History Teacher* 6 (May 1973): 427–52.

Archer, Angus. "Methods of Multilateral Management: The Interrelationship of International Organizations and Nongovernmental Organizations." In *The U.S., the U.N., and the Management of Global Change,* edited by Toby Trister Gati, 309–12. New York: New York Univ. Press, 1983.

Ascher, Charles S. "Current Problems in the World Health Organization's Program." *International Organization* 6 (1952): 27–50.

Baker, Samuel L. "Physician Licensure Laws in the United States, 1865–1915." *Journal of the History of Medicine and Allied Sciences* 39 (1984): 173–94.

Baldwin, E. "The International Congresses and Conferences of the Last Century as Forces Working Toward the Solidarity of the World." *American Journal of International Law* 1 (July 1907): 565–78.

Balassa, Bela. "Adjustment Policies in Developing Countries: A Reassessment." *World Development* 12 (Sept. 1984): 955–72.

Barber, William J. "Government as Laboratory for Economic Learning in the Years of the Democratic Roosevelt." In *The State and Economic Knowledge,* edited by Mary O. Furner and Barry Supple, 104–16. New York: Cambridge Univ. Press, 1990.

Beaton, George H., and Hossein Ghassemi. "Supplementary Feeding Programs for Young Children in Developing Countries." *American Journal of Clinical Nutrition* 35 (Apr. 1982): 864–916.

Beckman, Margaret F. "AAA's Ed." *USDA* 3 (2 Oct. 1944).

Beringer, Christoph. "Real Effects of Foreign Surplus Disposal in Underdeveloped Economies: Comment." *Quarterly Journal of Economics* 77 (May 1963): 317–23.

Blair, I. D. "Wartime Problems of English Agriculture." *Agricultural History* 15 (Jan. 1941): 12–19.

Bolles, Blair. "World Nutrition and Agrarian Stability: Proposals for a Food Board." *Foreign Policy Reports* 22 (1 Dec. 1946): 218–27.

Booth, J. F. "Our Hungry World." *Behind the Headlines* 8 (Feb. 1948): 1–17.

Bové, Paul A. "Discourse." In *Critical Terms for Literary Study,* edited by Frank Lentricchia and Thomas McLaughlin, 50–65. Chicago, Ill.: Univ. of Chicago Press, 1990.

Boyce, Robert. "World Depression, World War: Some Economic Origins of the Second World War." In *Paths to War: New Essays on the Origins of the Second World War,* edited by Robert Boyce and Esmonde Robertson, 55–95. Basingstoke, UK: Macmillan, 1989.

Brigg, Morgan. "Empowering NGOs: The Microcredit Movement through Foucault's Notion of *Dispositif.*" *Alternatives: Global, Local, Political* 26 (July–Sept. 2001): 233–58.

"British Food Advisor." *Nutrition Reviews* 1 (Nov. 1942): 31.

Brunton, Deborah C. "The Transfer of Medical Education: Teaching at the Edinburgh and Philadelphia Medical Schools." In *Scotland and America in the Age of the Enlightenment,* edited by Richard B. Sher and Jeffrey R. Smitten, 242–58. Princeton, N.J.: Princeton Univ. Press, 1990.

Büthe, Tim. Review of *Banker to the Poor: Micro-Lending and the Battle against World Poverty,* by Muhammad Yunus. *Journal of International Affairs* 53 (Spring 2000): 741–42.

Butler, Stella V. F. "A Transformation in Training: The Formation of University Medical Faculties in Manchester, Leeds, and Liverpool, 1870–84." *Medical History* 30 (1986): 115–32.

Caiden, Gerald, and German Retana. "What Will Work? The Costa Rican Experience Using SILOS in Achieving Universal Health Care 2000." *International Journal of Public Administration* 21 (Dec. 1998): 1863–85.

Calder, Ritchie. "The Man and His Message." *Survey Graphic* 37 (Mar. 1948): 99–103.

Calderwood, Howard B. "The World Health Organization and Its Regional Organizations." *Temple Law Quarterly* 37 (1963): 15–27.

Campbell, J. Phil. "Action Programs in Education." *Agricultural History* 15 (Apr. 1941): 68–71.

Chin, Carol. "Beneficent Imperialists: American Women Missionaries in China at the Turn of the Century." *Diplomatic History* 27 (June 2003): 327–52.

Clark, John G. "Making Environmental Diplomacy an Integral Part of Diplomatic History." *Diplomatic History* 21 (Summer 1997): 453–60.

———. "Environmental Development vs. Sustainable Societies: Reflections on the Players in a Crucial Contest." *Annual Review of Ecology and Systematics* 26 (1995): 225–48.

Clark, Noble. "Hungry Poland." *Survey Graphic* 37 (Mar. 1948): 116–18.

Clayton, E. S. "Marketing Problems in Peasant Agriculture." *Span* 8 (1965): 146–49.

Cockburn, W. C. "The International Contribution to the Standardization of Biological Substances. 1. Biological Standards and the League of Nations, 1921–1946." *Biologicals* 19 (1991): 161–69.

Collard, David. "A. C. Pigou, 1877–1959." In *Pioneers of Modern Economics in Britain,* edited by D. P. O'Brien and John R. Presley, 72–75. London: Macmillan, 1981.

Conning, Jonathan. "Outreach, Sustainability and Leverage in Monitored and Peer-Monitored Lending." *Journal of Development Economics* 60 (1999): 51–77.

Cook, Robert C. "World-Wide War on Malaria: Prelude to a Greater Challenge." *Population Bulletin* 14 (Mar. 1958): 1–15.

Cooke, Jay. "The Work of the Federal Food Administration." *Annals of the American Academy of Political and Social Science* 78 (July 1918): 175–84.

Cooper, M. McG. "Change in Higher Agricultural Education." *Span* 8 (1965): 3–35.

Copeman, W. S. "The Evolution of Clinical Method in English Medical Education." *Proceedings of the Royal Society of Medicine* 58 (1965): 887–94.

Cottrell, P. L. "The Bank of England in its International Setting, 1918–1972." In *The Bank of England: Money, Power and Influence, 1694–1994,* edited by Richard Roberts and David Kynaston, 86–110. Oxford, UK: Clarendon, 1995.

Cowen, Michael, and Robert Shenton. "The Invention of Development." In *Power of Development,* edited by Jonathan Crush, 27–43. London: Routledge, 1995.

Craig, George B., Jr. "Hormones for Control of Anopheles." *Miscellaneous Publications of the Entomological Society of America* 7 (May 1970): 130–33.

Crawford, Elisabeth. "The Universe of International Science, 1880–1939." In *Solomon's House Revisited: The Organization and Institutionalization of Science,* edited by Tore Frängsmyr, 259–60. Canton, Mass.: Science History, 1990.

Creedy, John. "F. Y. Edgeworth, 1845–1926." In *Pioneers of Modern Economics in Britain,* edited by D. P. O'Brien and John R. Presley, 106–109. London: Macmillan, 1981.

Cueto, Marcos. "Sanitation from Above: Yellow Fever and Foreign Intervention in Perú, 1919–1922." *Hispanic American Historical Review* 72 (1992): 1–22.

Cuff, Robert D. "Harry Garfield, the Fuel Administration, and the Search for a Cooperative Order during World War I." *American Quarterly* 30 (Spring 1978): 39–53.

———. "Herbert Hoover, the Ideology of Voluntarism and War Organization during the Great War." *Journal of American History* 64 (Sept. 1977): 358–72.

Cullather, Nick. "Miracles of Modernization: The Green Revolution and the Apotheosis of Technology." *Diplomatic History* 28 (Apr. 2004): 227–54.

Darnell, Adrian. "A. L. Bowley, 1869–1957." In *Pioneers of Modern Economics in Britain,* edited by D. P. O'Brien and John R. Presley, 168–69. London: Macmillan, 1981.

Davidson, G., and J. B. Kitzmiller. "Application of New Procedures to Control: Genetic Controls of Anophelines." *Miscellaneous Publications of the Entomological Society of America* 7 (May 1970): 118–29.

Davis, Chester C. "The Agricultural Adjustment Act and National Recovery." *Journal of Farm Economics* 18 (1936): 229–43.

Davis, Joseph S. "New International Wheat Agreements." *Wheat Studies* 19 (Nov. 1942): 25–79.

Davis, Kenneth S. "The Deadly Dust: The Unhappy History of DDT." *American Heritage* 22 (Feb. 1971): 45–47.

de Zulueta, J., and D. A. Muir. "Malaria Eradication in the Near East." *Transactions of the Royal Society of Tropical Medicine and Hygiene* 66 (1972): 679–96.

Dickson, Maxcy R. "The Food Administration: Educator." *Agricultural History* 16 (Apr. 1942): 91–96.

Doriot, Georges F. "Food and War." *Nutrition Reviews* 1 (Aug. 1943): 289–92.

Dorsey, Kurk. "Scientists, Citizens, and Statesmen: U.S.-Canadian Wildlife Protection Treaties in the Progressive Era." *Diplomatic History* 19 (Summer 1995): 407–29.

Downing, W. "Control of Animal Parasites." *Span* 8 (1965): 39–42.

Durand, John D. "World Population: Trend and Prospect." In *Population and World Politics,* edited by P. M. Hauser. Glencoe, Ill.: Free Press, 1958.

Durrheim, D. N., and R. Speare. "Global Leprosy Elimination: Time to Change More than the Elimination Target Date: Contentious Elimination Target Requires Rethinking." *Journal of Epidemiology and Community Health* 57 (May 2003): 316–18.

"The Effect of War on Nutrition in England." *Nutrition Reviews* 1 (Apr. 1943): 173–74.

"8 Years of Public Law 480." *Foreign Agriculture* 1 (18 Feb. 1963): 6–9.

Einsiedel, Edna F., and Melissa P. Innes. "Communications and Development: Challenges of the New Information and Communication Technologies." In *Transforming Development: Foreign Aid for a Changing World,* edited by Jim Freedman, 255–67. Toronto: Univ. of Toronto Press, 2000.

Erdmann, Andrew P. N. "Mining for the Corporatist Synthesis: Gold in American Foreign Economic Policy, 1931–1936." *Diplomatic History* 17 (Spring 1993): 171–200.

"Eradication of Malaria." *British Medical Journal* (2 Apr. 1960): 1033–34.

Escobar, Arturo. "Imagining a Post-Development Era." In *Power of Development,* edited by Jonathan Crush, 211–27. London: Zed, 1997.

Esteva, G. "Development." In *The Development Dictionary: A Guide to Knowledge as Power,* edited by Wolfgang Sachs. London: Zed, 1992.

Evans, J. W. "The Facts in the Case." *Survey Graphic* 37 (Mar. 1948): 105–107, 179.

Falcon, Walter P. "Further Comment." *Quarterly Journal of Economics* 77 (May 1963): 323–26.

Farnsworth, Helen C. "Decline and Recovery of Wheat Prices in the Nineties." *Wheat Studies* 10 (June–July 1934): 289–341.

Fausold, Martin L. "President Hoover's Farm Policies, 1929–1933." *Agricultural History* 51 (Apr. 1977): 362–77.

Ferguson, Thomas. "From Normalcy to New Deal: Industrial Structure, Party Competition, and American Public Policy in the Great Depression." *International Organization* 38 (Winter 1984): 41–94.

Ferreira, Francisco H., and Louise C. Keely. "The World Bank and Structural Adjustment: Lessons from the 1980s." In *The World Bank: Structure & Policies,* edited by Christopher L. Gilbert and David Vines, 159–95. Cambridge, UK: Cambridge Univ. Press, 2000.

Fletcher, T. W. "The Great Depression of English Agriculture, 1873–1896." In *Essays in Agrarian History,* vol. 2, edited by W. E. Minchinton, 241–55. New York: Augustus M. Kelley, 1968.

Fussell, G. E. "The Collection of Agricultural Statistics in Great Britain: Its Origin and Evolution." *Agricultural History* 18 (Oct. 1944): 161–67.

Gafafer, William M. "Peter Ludwig Panum's 'Observations on the Contagium of Measles.'" *Isis* 24 (Dec. 1935): 90–101.

Galambos, Louis. "Technology, Political Economy, and Professionalization: Central Themes of the Organizational Synthesis." *Business History Review* 57 (Winter 1983): 471–93.

Galbraith, John K., and John D. Black. "The Maintenance of Agricultural Production during Depression: The Explanations Reviewed." *Journal of Political Economy* 46 (June 1938): 305–23.

Galloway, B. T. "Plant Pathology: A Review of the Development of the Science in the United States." *Agricultural History* 2 (Apr. 1928): 49–60.

Gibson, T. E. "The Cost of Animal Parasites." *Span* 7 (1964): 99–102.

Gidney, R. D., and W. P. J. Millar. "The Reorientation of Medical Education in Late Nineteenth-Century Ontario: The Proprietary Medical Schools and the Founding of the Faculty in Medicine at the University of Toronto." *Journal of the History of Medicine and Allied Sciences* 49 (1994): 52–78.

Girault, Réne. "The Impact of the Economic Situation on the Foreign Policy of France, 1936–1939." In *The Fascist Challenge and the Policy of Appeasement,* edited by Wolfgang J. Mommsen and Lothar Kettenacker, 214–23. London: Allen and Unwin, 1983.

Goetz, Anne Marie. "Feminism and the Limits of the Claim to Know: Contradictions in the Feminist Approach to Women in Development." *Millennium: Journal of International Studies* 17 (1988): 477–96.

Graham, A. B. "Boys' and Girls' Agricultural Clubs." *Agricultural History* 15 (Apr. 1941): 65–68.

Granshaw, Lindsay. "'Upon This Principle I Have Based a Practice': The Development and Reception of Antisepsis in Britain, 1867–90." In *Medical Innovations in Historical Perspective,* edited by John V. Pickstone, 17–46. New York: St. Martin's, 1992.

Graves, Harold N., Jr. "The Bank as International Mediator: Three Episodes." In *The World Bank since Bretton Woods: The Origins, Policies, Operations, and Impact of the International Bank for Reconstruction and Development and Other Members of the World Bank Group,* edited by Edward S. Mason and Robert E. Asher, 595–643. Washington, D.C.: Brookings Institution, 1973.

Griffith, Robert. "Dwight D. Eisenhower and the Corporate Commonwealth." *American Historical Review* 87 (Feb. 1982): 87–122.

Grin, Carolyn. "The Unemployment Conference of 1921: An Experiment in National Cooperative Planning." *Mid-America* 55 (Apr. 1973): 83–107.

Gunderson, Frank. "The Food and Nutrition of Industrial Workers in War Time." *Nutrition Reviews* 1 (Nov. 1942): 13–14.

Guth, James L. "The National Cooperative Council and Farm Relief, 1929–42." *Agricultural History* 51 (Apr. 1977): 441–58.

Gutteridge, Frank. "The World Health Organization: Its Scope and Achievement." *Temple Law Quarterly* 37 (Fall 1963): 1–14.

Hackett, L. "Once upon a Time." *American Journal of Tropical Medicine* (1960): 105–15.

Hardin, Charles M., ed. "Agricultural Policy, Politics, and the Public Interest." *Annals of the American Academy of Political and Social Science* 331 (Sept. 1960).

Harper, P. A., E. T. Lisansky, and B. E. Sasse. "Malaria and Other Insect-Borne Diseases in the South Pacific Campaign, 1942–1945: General Aspects and Control Measures." *American Journal of Tropical Medicine* 27: supplement to 3 (May 1947): 1–68.

Hawley, Ellis W. "Herbert Hoover, the Commerce Secretariat, and the Vision of an 'Associative State,' 1921–1928." *Journal of American History* 61 (June 1974): 116–40.

———. "Three Facets of Hooverian Associationalism: Lumber, Aviation, and Movies, 1921–1930." In *Regulation in Perspective,* edited by Thomas K. McCraw, 95–123. Cambridge, Mass.: Harvard Univ. Press, 1981.

———. "The Discovery and Study of a 'Corporate Liberalism.'" *Business History Review* 52 (Autumn 1978): 309–30.

Hays, Samuel P. "The Politics of Reform in Municipal Government in the Progressive Era." *Pacific Northwest Quarterly* 55 (Oct. 1964): 157–69.

Heiss, Mary Ann. "The United States, Great Britain, and the Creation of the Iranian Oil Consortium, 1953–1954." *International History Review* 16 (Aug. 1994): 511–35.

Hirschman, Albert O. "A Dissenter's Confession: 'The Strategy of Economic Development' Revisited." In *Pioneers in Development,* edited by Gerald M. Meier and Dudley Seers, 90–91. New York: Oxford Univ. Press, 1984.

Hoberman, John. "Toward a Theory of Olympic Internationalism." *Journal of Sport History* 22 (Spring 1995): 1–37.

Hoff, Joan. "The American Century: From Sarajevo to Sarajevo." In *The Ambiguous Legacy: U.S. Foreign Relations in the "American Century,"* edited by Michael J. Hogan, 183–231. New York: Cambridge Univ. Press, 1999.

Hogan, Michael J. "Corporatism: A Positive Appraisal." *Diplomatic History* 10 (Fall 1986): 363–72.

Holland, G. A. "The World Commonwealth: A Study of International Co-operative Politics." Pamphlet of the National Co-operative Men's Guild, Manchester, UK, 1932.

Huerkamp, Claudia. "The Making of the Modern Medical Profession, 1800–1940: Prussian Doctors in the Nineteenth Century." In *German Professions, 1800–1950,* edited by Geoffrey Cocks and Konrad H. Jarausch, 66–84. New York: Oxford Univ. Press, 1990.

Huntington, Samuel P. "Transnational Organizations in World Politics." *World Politics* 25 (1973): 333–68.

Hyde, H. van Zile. "The Nature of the WHO." *Public Health Report* 68 (June 1953): 601–605.

Ikenberry, G. John. "Creating Yesterday's New World Order: Keynesian 'New Thinking' and the Anglo-American Postwar Settlement." In *Ideas and Foreign Policy: Beliefs, Institutions, and Political Change,* edited by Judith Goldstein and Robert O. Keohane, 57–86. Ithaca, N.Y.: Cornell Univ. Press, 1993.

"Important Foods for British Infants." *Nutrition Reviews* 1 (May 1943): 223–24.

"Influenza in Europe." *Relevé Épidémiologique Hebomadaire/Weekly Epidemiological Record* 24 (12 Jan. 1949): 18.

"The Interim Commission on Food and Agriculture and the FAO." *American Journal of International Law* 38 (Oct. 1944): 708–11.

Jacyna, Stephen. "Robert Carswell and William Thomson at the Hôtel-Dieu of Lyons: Scottish Views of French Medicine." In *British Medicine in an Age of Reform,* edited by Roger French and Andrew Wear, 110–35. London: Routledge, 1991.

Jaquette, Jane S. "Women and Modernization Theory: A Decade of Feminist Critique." *World Politics* 34 (Jan. 1982): 267–84.

Jenks, C. Wilfrid. "Coordination, a New Problem of International Organization." *Recueil des Cours* 77 (1950): 157–302.

Johnson, Glenn L. "Philosophic Foundation of Agricultural Economic Thought from World War II to the mid-1970s." In *A Survey of Agricultural Economics Literature,* vol. 4: *Agriculture in Economic Development, 1940s to 1990s,* edited by Lee R. Martin, 976–81. Minneapolis: Univ. of Minnesota Press for the American Agricultural Economics Association, 1992.

Johnson, Vance. "55,000 for Breakfast." *Collier's* 125 (11 Mar. 1950): 24–25, 34.

Johnston, Bruce F. "Farm Surpluses and Foreign Policy." *World Politics* 10 (Oct. 1957): 1–23.

Jones, W. E. "Advisory Services Today and Tomorrow." *Span* 7 (1964): 6–9.

Kane, N. Stephen. "Bankers and Diplomats: The Diplomacy of the Dollar in Mexico, 1921–1924." *Business History Review* 47 (1973): 335–52.

Karl, Barry D. "Presidential Planning and Social Science Research: Mr. Hoover's Experts." *Perspectives in American History* 3 (1969): 347–409.

Kennedy, David M. "Overview: The Progressive Era." *Historian* 37 (1975): 453–68.

Khoury, Inge. "The World Bank and the Feminization of Poverty." In *50 Years Is Enough: The Case against the World Bank and the International Monetary Fund,* edited by Kevin Danaher, 121–23. Boston, Mass.: South End, 1994.

King, Clyde L., ed. "The World's Food." *Annals of the American Academy of Political and Social Science* 74 (Nov. 1917).

Koistinen, Paul A. C. "The 'Industrial-Military Complex' in Historical Perspective: World War I." *Business History Review* 41 (Winter 1967): 367–403.

Knapp, Vincent J. "The Democratization of Meat and Protein in Late Eighteenth- and Nineteenth-Century Europe." *Historian* 59 (Spring 1997): 541–51.

Koerselman, Gary H. "Secretary Hoover and National Farm Policy: Problems of Leadership." *Agricultural History* 51 (Apr. 1977): 378–95.

Kusmer, Kenneth L. "The Functions of Organized Charity in the Progressive Era: Chicago as a Case Study." *Journal of American History* 60 (Dec. 1973): 657–78.

Kust, Matthew J. "Economic Development and Agricultural Surpluses." *Foreign Affairs* 35 (Oct. 1956): 105–15.

La Berge, Ann. "Medical Microscopy in Paris, 1830–1855." In *French Medical Culture in the Nineteenth Century,* edited by Ann La Berge and Mordechai Feingold, 296–326. Amsterdam: Editions Rodopi B. V., 1994.

Leavitt, Judith Walzer. "Public Health and Preventive Medicine." In *The Education of American Physicians: Historical Essays,* edited by Ronald L. Numbers, 250–72. Berkeley: Univ. of California Press, 1980.

Leffler, Melvyn P. "Herbert Hoover, the 'New Era,' and American Foreign Policy." In *Herbert Hoover as Secretary of Commerce,* edited by Ellis W. Hawley, 149–71. Iowa City: Univ. of Iowa Press, 1981.

Lilienthal, David E. "The Road to Change: Development of People Must Be the Goal." *International Development Review* 6 (Dec. 1964): 9–14.

———. "Another 'Korea' in the Making?" *Collier's* 128 (4 Aug. 1951): 22–23, 56–58.

Louis, William Roger. "Dulles, Suez, and the British." In *John Foster Dulles and the Diplomacy of the Cold War,* edited by Richard Immerman, 133–58. Princeton, N.J.: Princeton Univ. Press, 1990.

Lytle, Mark H. "An Environmental Approach to American Diplomatic History." *Diplomatic History* 20 (Spring 1996): 279–300.

Maier, Charles S. "The Politics of Productivity: Foundations of American International Economic Policy after World War II." In *In Search of Stability: Explorations in Historical Political Economy,* edited by Charles S. Maier, 121–52. Cambridge, UK: Cambridge Univ. Press, 1987.

"Malaria and Other Insect-Borne Diseases in the South Pacific Campaign, 1942–1945." Special supplemental issue of *American Journal of Tropical Medicine* 27 (May 1947): 1–128.

Malin, James C. "The Background of the First Bill to Establish a Bureau of Markets, 1911–12." *Agricultural History* 6 (July 1932): 107–29.

Mangelsdorf, Paul C. "Hybrid Corn." *Scientific American* 185 (Aug. 1951): 39–47.

Mauer, Marc. "Mass Imprisonment and the Disappearing Voters." In *Invisible Punishment: The Collateral Consequences of Mass Imprisonment,* edited by Marc Mauer and Meda Chesney-Lind, 50–58. New York: New Press, 2002.

McCall, A. G. "The Development of Soil Science." *Agricultural History* 5 (Apr. 1931): 43–56.

McCollum, E. V. "A Decade of Progress in Nutrition." *Annals of the American Academy of Political and Social Science* 151 (Sept. 1930): 82–91.

———. "Some Essentials to a Safe Diet." *Annals of the American Academy of Political and Social Science* 74 (Nov. 1917): 95–108.

McCormick, Richard L. "The Discovery That Business Corrupts Politics: A Reappraisal of the Origins of Progressivism." *American Historical Review* 86 (Apr. 1981): 247–74.

McCormick, Thomas J. "Drift or Mastery? A Corporatist Synthesis for American Diplomatic History." *Reviews in American History* 10 (Dec. 1982): 318–30.

Miscamble, Wilson D. "Catholics and American Foreign Policy from McKinley to McCarthy: A Historiographical Survey." *Diplomatic History* 4 (Summer 1980): 223–40.

Monod, Francois. "Food for France and Its Public Control." *Annals of the American Academy of Political and Social Science* 74 (Nov. 1917): 84–91.

Moore, Frederick T. "The World Bank and Its Economic Missions." *Review of Economics and Statistics* 42 (Feb. 1960): 81–93.

Morantz, Regina Markell. "Feminism, Professionalism, and Germs." *American Quarterly* 34 (Winter 1982): 460–78.

Mudalair, Ascot. "World Health Problems." *International Conciliation* 491 (1953): 229–59.

Mullins, William H. "Self-Help in Seattle, 1931–1932: Herbert Hoover's Concept of Cooperative Individualism and the Unemployed Citizens' League." *Pacific Northwest Quarterly* 72 (1981): 11–19.

Palmby, Clarence D. "Feeding the World: The Economic Incentive." *Span* 6 (1963): 3–5.

Peréz, Louis A., Jr. "Dependency." In *Explaining the History of American Foreign Relations,* edited by Michael J. Hogan and Thomas G. Paterson, 99–110. Cambridge, UK: Cambridge Univ. Press, 1991.

Péteri, György. "Central Bank Diplomacy: Montagu Norman and Central Europe's Monetary Reconstruction after World War I." *Contemporary European History* 1 (Nov. 1992): 233–58.

Pett, L. B. "The Canadian Nutrition Program." *Nutrition Reviews* 1 (May 1943): 193–94.

Pickering, Kathleen, and David W. Mushinski. "Cultural Aspects of Credit Institutions: Transplanting the Grameen Bank Credit Group Structure to the Pine Ridge Indian Reservation." *Journal of Economic Issues* 35 (June 2001): 459–67.

Pickstone, John V. "A Profession of Discovery: Physiology in Nineteenth-Century History." *British Journal of the History of Science* 23 (1990): 207–16.

Pierce, Diana. "The Feminization of Poverty." *Journal for Peace and Justice Studies* 2 (1990): 1–20.

Pinchot, Gifford. "An Agricultural Policy for the United States in War Time." *Annals of the American Academy of Political and Social Science* 74 (Nov. 1917): 181–87.

Reagan, Patrick D. "From Depression to Depression: Hooverian National Planning, 1921–1933." *Mid-America* 70 (Jan. 1988): 35–60.

"The Resurgence and Eradication of Malaria." *Social Science and Medicine* 22 (1986).

Rich, Bruce. "World Bank/IMF: 50 Years Is Enough." In *50 Years Is Enough: The Case against the World Bank and the International Monetary Fund,* edited by Kevin Danaher, 6–13. Boston, Mass.: South End, 1994.

Roberts, Lydia J. "Status of Nutrition Work with Children." *Annals of the American Academy of Political and Social Science* 212 (Nov. 1940): 111–20.

Rosenberg, Emily S. "Revisiting Dollar Diplomacy: Narratives of Money and Manliness." *Diplomatic History* 22 (Spring 1998): 165–71.

———. "Foundations of United States International Financial Power: Gold Standard Diplomacy, 1900–1905." *Business History Review* 59 (Summer 1985): 169–202.

Rosenberg, Emily S., and Norman L. Rosenberg. "From Colonialism to Professionalism: The Public/Private Dynamic in United States Foreign Financial Advising, 1898–1929." *Journal of American History* 74 (June 1987): 59–82.

Ross, Earle D. "The Land-Grant College: A Democratic Adaptation." *Agricultural History* 15 (Jan. 1941): 26–36.

———. "The 'Father' of the Land-Grant College." *Agricultural History* 12 (Apr. 1938): 151–86.

Rostow, W. W. "Four Needs of Developing Agriculture." *Span* 8 (1965): 8–9.

Ruttan, Vernon W. "Positive Policy in the Fertilizer Industry." *Journal of Political Economy* 68 (Dec. 1960): 634.

———. "The Politics of U.S. Food Aid Policy: A Historical Review." In *Why Food Aid?* edited by Vernon W. Ruttan, 2–36. Baltimore, Md.: Johns Hopkins Univ. Press, 1993.

Russell, Sir E. John. "Rothamsted and Its Experiment Station." *Agricultural History* 16 (Oct. 1942): 161–83.

Rydell, Robert W. "The Trans-Mississippi and International Exposition: 'To Work Out the Problem of Universal Civilization.'" *American Quarterly* 33 (1981): 587–607.

Ryerson, Knowles A. "History and Significance of the Foreign Plant Introduction Work of the United States Department of Agriculture." *Agricultural History* 7 (July 1933): 110–28.

Schapsmeier, Edward L., and Frederick H. Schapsmeier. "Eisenhower and Ezra Taft Benson: Farm Policy in the 1950s." *Agricultural History* 44 (Oct. 1970): 369–78.

Schmidt, Louis Bernard. "The Agricultural Revolution in the Prairies and the Great Plains of the United States." *Agricultural History* 8 (Oct. 1934): 169–95.

Schofer, Evan. "Science Associations in the International Sphere, 1875–1990: The Rationalization of Science and the Scientization of Society." In *Constructing World Culture: International Nongovernmental Organizations since 1875,* edited by John Boli and George M. Thomas, 249–66. Stanford, Calif.: Stanford Univ. Press, 1999.

Shideler, James H. "The Development of the Parity Price for Agriculture, 1919–1923." *Agricultural History* 27 (July 1953): 77–84.

Singer, H. W. "An Historical Perspective." In *The U.N. and the Bretton Woods Institutions: New Challenges for the Twenty-first Century,* edited by Mahbub ul Haq, Richard Jolly, Paul Streeten, and Khadija Haq, 17–25. New York: St. Martin's, 1995.

"Sir John Orr and the U.S.A." *Grain Market Features* 18 (19 May 1948): 1.

Smith, Carroll N. "Repellants for Anopheline Mosquitos." *Miscellaneous Publications of the Entomological Society of America* 7 (May 1970): 99–117.

Smith, Shannon. "From Relief to Revolution: American Women and the Russian-American Relationship, 1890–1917." *Diplomatic History* 19 (Fall 1995): 601–16.

Solorzano, Armando. "Sowing the Seeds of Neo-Imperialism: The Rockefeller Foundation's Yellow Fever Campaign in Mexico." *International Journal of Health Services* 22 (1992): 529–54.

Spengler, Joseph J. "Economic Factors in the Development of Densely Populated Areas." *Proceedings of the American Philosophical Society* (Feb. 1951): 38–39.

Stearns, Raymond Phineas. "Agricultural Adaptation in England, 1875–1900: Part I." *Agricultural History* 6 (Apr. 1932): 84–101.

Stern, Robert M. "Agricultural Surplus Disposal and U.S. Economic Policies." *World Politics* 12 (Apr. 1960): 422–33.

"Supplementary Food and the Nutrition of Schoolchildren." *Nutrition Reviews* 1 (Sept. 1943): 343–45.

Taylor, Alonzo E. "The International Wheat Conferences during 1930–31." *Wheat Studies* 7 (Aug. 1931): 439–66.

Temkin, Owsei. "The Scientific Approach to Disease: Specific Entity and Individual Illness." In *Scientific Change: Historical Studies in the Intellectual, Social and Technical Conditions for Scientific Discovery and Technical Invention, from Antiquity to the Present,* edited by A. C. Crombie, 629–47. New York: Basic, 1963.

Thelen, David P. "Patterns of Consumer Consciousness in the Progressive Movement: Robert M. La Follette, the Antitrust Persuasion, and Labor Legislation." In *The Quest for Social Justice,* edited by Ralph M. Aderman, 19–47. Madison: Univ. of Wisconsin Press, 1983.

———. "Social Tensions and the Origins of Progressivism." *Journal of American History* 56 (Sept. 1969): 323–41.

Tontz, Robert L. "200 Years of U.S. Farm Trade Policy: Increased Interdependence, 1947–1976." *Foreign Agriculture* 14 (25 Oct. 1976): 6–8, 12.

Vogel, Morris J. "The Transformation of the American Hospital, 1850–1920." In *Health Care in America: Essays in Social History,* edited by Susan Reverby, 108–12. Philadelphia, Pa.: Temple Univ. Press, 1979.

Waite, Warren C., and John D. Black. "Nutrition and Agricultural Policy." *Annals of the American Academy of Political and Social Science* 188 (Nov. 1936): 218–29.

Ward, Ronald A., and John E. Scanlon, eds. "Conference on Anopheline Biology and Malaria Eradication: A Symposium at the Walter Reed Army Institute of Research." *Miscellaneous Publications of the Entomological Society of America* 7 (May 1970).

Weinstein, James. "Organized Business and the City Commission and Manager Movements." *Journal of Southern History* 28 (May 1962): 166–82.

Weld, L. D. H. "The After-War Fall in Meat Prices." *Annals of the American Academy of Political and Social Science* 89 (May 1920): 51–54.

Wells, O. V. "The Depression of 1873–79." *Agricultural History* 11 (July 1937): 237–49.

Whetzel, H. H. "The History of Industrial Fellowships in the Department of Plant Pathology at Cornell University." *Agricultural History* 19 (Apr. 1945): 99–104.

Wickizer, V. D. "Shipping and Freight Rates in the Overseas Grain Trade." *Wheat Studies* 15 (Oct. 1938): 49–120.

Wightman, David R. "Food Aid and Economic Development." *International Conciliation* 567 (Mar. 1968): 1–72.

Wilson, Joan Hoff. "Hoover's Agricultural Policies, 1921–1928." *Agricultural History* 51 (Apr. 1977): 335–61.

Winslow, Charles-Edward Amory. "World Health Organization." *International Conciliation* 437 (1948): 109–52.

Wittner, Lawrence S. "The Transnational Movement against Nuclear Weapons: A Preliminary Survey." In *Peace Movements and Political Cultures,* edited by Charles Chatfield and Peter van den Dungen, 264–94. Knoxville: Univ. of Tennessee Press, 1988.

"World Food Congress." *Foreign Agriculture* 1 (17 June 1963): 3–10.

"World Food Congress Tops FAO Schedule for 1963; Focus on Underdeveloped Areas." *Foreign Agriculture* 1 (28 Jan. 1963): 6–7.

Wright, Almon R. "Food Purchases of the Allies, 1917–1918." *Agricultural History* 16 (Apr. 1942): 97–102.

Yalem, Ronald J. "The Study of International Organization, 1920–1965: A Survey of the Literature." *Background* 10 (1966): 1–56.

Yunus, Muhammad. "Redefining Development." In *50 Years Is Enough: The Case against the World Bank and the International Monetary Fund,* edited by Kevin Danaher, ix–xiii. Boston, Mass.: South End, 1994.

Zieger, Robert H. "Herbert Hoover, the Wage-Earner, and the 'New Economic System,' 1919–1929." *Business History Review* 51 (Summer 1977): 161–89.

Unpublished Sources

American Association of State Colleges and Universities. "American Democracy Project." Available at www.aascu.org/programs/adp/about/default.htm. Accessed 13 July 2004.

Brown, Peter John. "Cultural Adaptations to Endemic Malaria and the Socioeconomic Effects of Malaria Eradication in Sardinia." Ph.D. diss., State Univ. of New York at Stony Brook, 1979.

Dadashi, Alieh. "Soviet Policy in the World Health Organization." M.A. thesis, Univ. of Washington, 1978.

Deccan Development Society. "Deccan Development Society." Available at www.ddsindia. com. Accessed 9 Aug. 2003.

Dorn, Glenn J. "The United States, Argentina, and the Inter-American Order, 1946–1950." Ph.D. diss., Ohio State Univ., 1997.

Druyvesteyn, Kenten. "The World's Parliament of Religions." Ph.D. diss., Univ. of Chicago, 1976.

Find 18: Faith in Democracy. "Have Faith in Democracy!" Available at www.find18.org//. Accessed 13 July 2004.

Greenston, Peter Michael. "The Food for Peace Program and Brazil: Valuation and Effects of the Commodity Inflow." Ph.D. diss., Univ. of Minnesota, 1972.

Gunderson, Gordon W. "History of the National School Lunch Program," excerpted from *National School Lunch Program: Background and Development.* Washington, D.C.: USDA Food and Nutrition Service, n.d. Available at www.cde.state.co.us/cdenutrition/ download/pdf/SEC26.pdf. Accessed 5 Jan. 2004.

Kohlmeyer, Frederick W. "The Movement toward International Cooperation in Food and Agriculture: Background of the FAO of the UN." Ph.D. diss., Univ. of Minnesota, 1954.

Lafontaine, Alain. "Environmental Aspects of Sustainable Development: The Role of the World Bank." M.A. thesis, Carleton Univ., 1990.

Lyngel, Inger Johanne. "The Oslo Breakfast–An Optimal Diet in One Meal: On the Scientification of Everyday Life as Exemplified by Food." Translated by Alan Crozier. *Ethnologia Scandinavica* 28 (1998): 62–78. Available at www.etn.lu.se/ethscand/text/1998/1998_62–76.pdf. Accessed 5 Jan. 2004.

McFadden, David Fancher. "International Cooperation and Pandemic Diseases: Regimes and the Role of Epistemic Communities in Combatting Cholera, Smallpox, and AIDS." Ph.D. diss., Claremont Graduate School, 1995.

Moazami, Zahra. "The Functional Approach to Integration: A Case Study of the World Health Organization." M.A. thesis, Tulane Univ., 1979.

MTV. "Rock the Vote." Available at www.rockthevote.org/rtv_about.php. Accessed 13 July 2004.

Paisant, Marcel Rieul. "La Commission Internationale d'Agriculture et son rôle dans l'Économie Européenne." Ph.D. diss., Université de Paris, 6 Mar. 1936.

Santos, Luiz Antonio de Castro. "Power, Ideology and Public Health in Brazil, 1889–1930." Ph.D. diss., Harvard Univ., 1987.

Save Our Cumberland Mountains. "Social Progress Committee: Voter Rights." Available at www.socm.org/racism.html#voterrights. Accessed 13 July 2004.

Schoenfeld, Frederick A. "Congressional Appropriations as an Instrument of Foreign Aid Policy Formulation: The Case of Food for Peace." M.A. thesis, Univ. of Arizona, 1967.

Weaver, David R. "Public Law 480, India, and the Objectives of United States Foreign Aid, 1954–1966." Ph.D. diss., Univ. of Cincinnati, 1963.

Wilson, Tamar Diana. "Malaria as a Political Disease: The Political Economy of Malaria Resurgence and Solutions for Malaria Eradication in Mexico and Central America." M.A. thesis, Univ. of California at Los Angeles, 1987.

Index

Council of International Organizations of Medical Sciences, 155, 269n38
Cuba, 169, 236n44
Cumming, Hugh, 135
Curran, C. H., 178
Czechoslovakia, 58; health, 140, 149; WHO, 262n9, 265n18, 267n29; World Bank, 42

Davies, J. A. C., 104
Dawes Commission, 11
DDT (dichloro-diphenyl-trichloroethane), 139–40, 160, 162–64, 172, 176–79
de Brancion, Georges, 260n1
Deccan Development Society (DDS), 187–91, 193; balwadis, 188; biodiversity, 189; Community Grain Fund, 188; Community Green Fund, 189; Community Media Trust, 190; crop insurance program, 189; food security, 187–88; food sovereignty, 188; green school, 188; jatras, 188; media sovereignty, 189–91; medicinal commons, 189; prajateerpu, 190; sanghams, 187, 191; seed bank, 188, 191
decolonization, 45
de Gaulle, Charles, 114, 118
de Lesseps, Ferdinand, 61
Demuth, Richard, 35
Denmark: agriculture, 65, 71, 117; FAO, 91; WHO Interim Commission, 140; World Bank, 26, 61
de Saeger, H., 178
Development Decade, 180–81
dichloro-diphenyl-trichloroethan. See DDT
Diouf, Jacques, 183
diphtheria, 125, 130–31, 184
Dodd, Norris E., 83, 91–92, 96–103, 106
Dominican Republic, 236n44
Dulles, John Foster, 60–61
Dunstan, E. Fleetwood, 29
Dutch Bakers' and Millers' Association, 113
dysentery, 130

economic development, 12, 92, 195n1; agricultural development, 92; as basis of democracy, 38–41; as basis of peace, 33–34, 40, 87–88, 90–91, 134, 146; barriers, 37–38; birth of development, 1, 7, 180; dependent development, 41; development banks, 120; environmental concerns, 43, 45; full employment, 91–92, 94; grassroots approach, 42, 187; human development, 100, 106, 119; indigenous peoples, 43–45; industrial development, 92, 94; Middle East, 57; river-development schemes, 12, 38, 43; significance in Cold War period, 1, 15;

sustainability, 2; women's roles, 43, 45; World Bank, 22–45
Economic Development Institute (EDI), 37–38, 42
economics (profession), 8–12, 65, 67, 74; agricultural, 67–69, 76; in Great Britain, 9–10; Keynesian, 12; laissez-faire, 9; in the United States, 9–10; welfare economics, 9
economy, global, 21, 31, 39, 46–47, 166; agricultural, 64; balance-of-payments difficulties, 95, 110; Bretton Woods system, 8, 14, 19, 22; debt crisis, 180–82; dollar gap, 33, 96–97; foreign-exchange issues, 8, 12–14, 19, 98, 108, 142; gap between rich and poor countries, 41, 181; globalization, 7; inflation, 182; interwar period, 5, 25; law of comparative advantage, 40, 109; potential of agricultural economy to catalyze global economy, 77–78, 82, 86–87, 91; structural adjustment, 180–81, 184; tariffs, 11, 13, 31, 33, 39; trade, 8; trade barriers, 39
Ecuador, 100, 236n44
Eden, Anthony, 51, 60
Edinburgh Laboratory, 66
eggs, 65, 70, 73, 75
Egypt, 111; FAO, 100, 236n44; health, 162; Sanitary, Maritime, and Quarantine Council, 128, 139, 148; WHO, 139, 145, 148, 262n9, 265n18; World Bank, 45, 56–63
Eisenhower administration, 37, 102, 109–11, 166, 170
Eisenhower, Dwight D., 106, 110, 170
El-Emary, H. E. Abdel Galeel, 56
El Salvador, 154, 165
Enlightenment, 123
epidemiology, 122, 124, 127–30, 135, 138–39
Eriksen, Erik, 91
Esperanto movement, 4
Estonia, 74
Ethiopia: FAO, 100; WHO, 140, 168, 262n9
Europe, 182; Eastern Europe, 10, 129; economy, 14, 28, 32, 40; health, 82, 122, 126, 129, 131–32, 140, 145, 154, 157, 159
European Confederation of Agriculture (ECA), 239n6
Evang, Karl, 132, 142, 148
Export-Import (Exim) Bank, 33, 36, 110
expropriation, 34–35

4-H clubs, 66
famine relief, 86, 88, 93, 110–11
farming: dry-land, 68; experimental, 65, 67; management, 67

Mossadegh, Muhammad, 47–53
Movement Internationale de la Jeunesse Agricole et Rural Catholique, 239n6
Mozambique, 169
Müller, Paul H., 162
multinational corporations, 28, 34, 41, 52

Nasser, Gamal Abdel, 56–63
National Advisory Committee on International Monetary and Financial Matters (NAC), 19–20, 25
National Association of Manufacturers, 35
National Citizens Political Action Committee, 203n27
National Farmers Union, 203n27
National Foreign Trade Council, 203n27
nationalism, 161; agricultural, 71; Iranian, 50; Third World, 46, 62
National Planning Association, 203n27
national sovereignty, 70, 77, 82, 111, 121
Nazism, 6, 114
Neguib, Mohammed, 56
Netherlands, 92; Dutch Bakers' and Millers' Association, 113–14; economy, 72; FAO, 104, 121, 183, 236n44; nutritional programs, 71; WHO, 142, 262n9, 265n18; World Bank, 41, 61
New Deal, 12, 13, 26, 28, 71, 96, 102
New Guinea, 162
New York Port Authority, 38
New York State Bankers Association, 19
New Zealand: FAO, 79, 98, 116; health, 140, 149; WHO, 262n9, 265n18
Nicaragua, 41
Nigeria, 116, 170, 184
Nile water rights, 57
non-aligned movement, 60
non-governmental organizations (NGOs), 101–3, 105–9, 112–15, 117–18, 120, 184, 186
Norman, Montagu, 10
Northern Ireland, 68
North Korea, 150
Norway: FAO, 117; health, 132–33, 140, 142; WHO, 150, 152, 262n9, 265n18; World Bank, 61
NOVIB, 114
nutrition, 64, 66, 68, 72–74, 76, 79, 81, 83, 85, 102, 106, 108, 117, 138, 192; relation to agriculture, 73; standards, 73–74, 87; WHO, 154, 269n38
nutritional programs, 117; concessionary sales, 86; during Great Depression, 71–74; for poor, 71, 73; for school children, 68–69, 71, 73, 108, 110–11, 116; for vulnerable populations, 93, 101; war-time food rationing, 75, 82, 96, 114

Office International des Epizooties, 270n38
Office International d'Hygiène Publique (OIHP), 122–23, 128–30, 133, 135, 137, 139
oil, 47–53, 182
Orr, John Boyd, 68, 71–73, 75–77, 79–81, 83–96, 103–4, 106
Oslo Agreement, 72
Oslo breakfast, 68
Ottawa agreements, 72
Outboard Marine Corporation of the United States, 116
Oxford Committee for Famine Relief (OXFAM), 115

Pakistan, 45, 46, 53–56, 62, 147, 236n44
Palestine, 95; health, 140, 148
Pampana, Emilio, 260n1
Panama, 162, 175
Pan American Sanitary Bureau (PASB), 122–23, 128, 137; malaria, 164, 166, 170–71; publications, 128; statistics, 128; technical assistance, 128; WHO relationship, 133, 135, 139, 148–49; zonal offices, 149
Pan-Arabism, 147
Panum, Peter Ludwig, 124
Paraguay, 175, 236n44
Parker, Chauncey G., 29
Parliament of Religions, 4
Parran, Thomas, 133
Pasteur, Louis, 125
peace, 33–34, 40, 87–88, 90–91, 134, 146
Peace Corps, 113
Pearson, Lester B., 79–80
Perón, Juan, 31, 41
Peru, 190; FAO, 100; PASB, 149; WHO, 169
Philippines, 166; FAO, 236n44; WHO, 141, 168; World Bank, 41
physiology, 122–23, 252n8
plague, 128, 130
plant breeding, 65–66
plant pathology, 65, 70
pneumonia, 161
Point IV program, 36, 151, 172, 195n1
Poland: FAO, 94, 114; health, 129; WHO, 149, 265n18, 267n29; World Bank, 29, 42
Pope John XXIII, 107
Portugal, 41, 127, 262n9
Progressivism, 2–4, 6–7, 9–10, 12, 22, 28, 30, 37, 46, 65–66, 82, 102, 105, 137, 160
Prud'homme, Hector, 49–52
public-private cooperation, 3–4, 6, 11, 16–17, 25, 28, 35, 67, 105, 112, 120, 159, 170